EEC COMPETITION LAW HANDBOOK
1992 EDITION

AUSTRALIA
The Law Book Company Ltd.
Sydney

CANADA
The Carswell Company Ltd.
Toronto, Ontario

INDIA
N. M. Tripathi (Private) Ltd.
Bombay

and

Eastern Law House (Private) Ltd.
Calcutta

M.P.P. House
Bangalore

ISRAEL
Steimatzky's Agency Ltd.
Tel Aviv

PAKISTAN
Pakistan Law House
Karachi

EEC COMPETITION LAW HANDBOOK 1992 EDITION

By

MARC VAN DER WOUDE

Legal Secretary at the
European Court of Justice in Luxembourg

CHRISTOPHER JONES

Cabinet of Sir Leon Brittan
Commission of European Communities

XAVIER LEWIS

Member of the Legal Service of the
Commission of European Communities

Preface to the First Edition
by GIANFRANCO ROCCA

Preface to the Second Edition
by JUDGE KAPETYN

LONDON
Sweet & Maxwell
1992

Published in 1992 by
Sweet & Maxwell Limited of
South Quay Plaza, 183 Marsh Wall, London E14 9FT
Phototypeset by LBJ Enterprises Limited, of Chilcompton and Aldermaston
and printed in Scotland by Thomson Litho

British Library Cataloguing in Publication Data

A catalogue record
for this book is available
from the British Library

ISBN 0–421–46560–3

All rights reserved.
No part of this publication may be
reproduced or transmitted, in any form
or by any means, electronic, mechanical, photocopying,
recording or otherwise, or stored in any retrieval
system of any nature, without the written permission
of the copyright holder and the publisher, application
for which shall be made to the publisher.

©
Marc van der Woude   Christopher Jones   Xavier Lewis
1992

Note: *The yellow star device is used in co-operation with
the Office of Official Publications of the
European Communities.*

*This is not an official publication of the
European Communities.*

PREFACE TO THE FIRST EDITION

Council Regulation No. 17/62 forsees, *inter alia*, the possibility for undertakings to notify to the Commission their agreements and practices in order to obtain a negative clearance or an exemption. This Regulation has equally opened to natural or legal persons the right to file complaints regarding restrictive practices.

Corresponding to these rights and obligations is the requirement that the Commission examines the compatibility of these agreements and practices with European Competition Law and also undertakes the relevant procedures with a view to the termination of illegal practices.

At present, approximately 220 agreements are notified to the Commission each year. In addition to this, an ever-increasing number of proceedings which result from complaints or which are opened on the Commission's own initiative must be taken into account.

This represents a considerable work-load when seen in the light of the fact that only 85 European civil servants work in the anti-trust section of the Commission. All this becomes even more significant if one compares the number of these "fonctionnaires" — competent for all the 12 Member States — to those in analogous national administrations, certain of which employ more than twice this number.

One of the main preoccupations of the Commission has always been to reconcile the need to take a position rapidly on notifications by undertakings with this very limited level of human resources. In this context, the Commission has striven, where possible, to make use of Regulations giving exemption by category and explanatory notices intended for the benefit of companies active on the European market. The adoption of such texts has the intention, insofar as possible, of reducing the number of agreements notified, whilst guaranteeing the legal security of undertakings participating in an agreement or concerted practice.

The work undertaken by the authors of this book, all fonctionnaires at the Directorate-General for Competition, may be interpreted as a confirmation of the wish of the Commission to facilitate as far as possible the application of European competition law, by permitting an easier access and a better comprehension of this law to those who wish to deepen their knowledge of this subject matter or must, through professional vocation, advise companies on matters being considered by Community authorities.

The effort accomplished by these fonctionnaires is all the more admirable in that it was accomplished in addition to the many daily tasks demanded of them. Their work involves the preparation of legal and administrative acts of the Commission in the sector of anti-trust.

I hope that the sense of public service that has led the authors to write this book may find its confirmation and justification in the practical usage that the reader makes of it.

Gianfranco ROCCA
Director at the Directorate-General
for Competition of the Commission of the
European Communities.

PREFACE TO THE SECOND EDITION

The editors of the EEC Competition Law Handbook should be congratulated. The first edition was published in 1990 and is already out of print. The innovative way of presenting the materials on European competition law and the fact that new editions of the book will be published annually are clearly the main reasons why the editors have found ready buyers in a highly competitive market.

The users of the Handbook have reason to be grateful it could be updated not much more than a year after its first publication, for EEC Competition law is a rapidly expanding area of law.

Apart from the continuing flow of Court judgments and Commission decisions, other important developments have taken place since the first edition of the Handbook. The Court of First Instance has rendered its first judgments in competition cases. A new regulation on merger control has been adopted by the Council and implemented by the Commission, by means of two regulations, two notices and several decisions. In the coal and steel sector we have witnessed a revival of competition policy. There is, moreover an increased tendency to adopt specific rules for differing industrial sectors (telecommunications and financial services). All these new developments have been taken into account by the editors in this second edition.

New sections on coal and steel, on free movement and intellectual property rights and on financial services have been included. A bibliography has been added. Other changes in the structure of the Handbook aim at making the users' access to the materials more practical.

In the preface to the first edition, Director Rocca expressed the hope that the sense of public service that had led the authors to write this book might find its confirmation and justification in the practical usage that the reader makes of it. This hope has now, as is evident from the publication of a second edition so quickly after the first, become a certitude.

P.J.G. KAPTEYN
Judge at the EC Court of Justice

EEC COMPETITION LAW HANDBOOK — 1992 EDITION
USER GUIDE

1. The **Handbook** is designed with the practitioner in mind. It is therefore organised so as to enable the swift identification of cases, legislation and other documents relevant to any question of EEC competition law. In many respects, it represents a hybrid — half case citator, half text manual.

2. It is recommended that the user begins by reading the table of contents carefully. This will give a good overview of the layout of the **Handbook**. The main bulk of the **Handbook** is contained in Book One, General Competition Rules, which is subdivided into ten Parts: for instance, Part V deals with Industrial and Intellectual Property Agreements and Part VI with Joint Ventures. Books Two and Three, to be found nearer to the end of the **Handbook**, deal specifically with Mergers and Acquisitions and with Coal and Steel. At the front of each Book are a series of Lists and Tables, which provide detailed references and information about the cases relevant to that Book. At the front of the whole Handbook are complete Alphabetical Lists of all decisions and judgments referred to in Books One, Two and Three combined.

3. Each Part is sub-divided into chapters covering particular types of agreement, practice or legal question, and should contain all legislation, documents and case references necessary for a practitioner's daily work. Thus, for example, Part IV, Chapter 1, on Exclusive and Non-Exclusive Distribution Agreements contains the full texts of Regulation 1983/83 and the relevant Commission explanatory Notice, as well as a case citator organised on an agreement-by-agreement and clause-by-clause basis. The most important or interesting cases are marked with an asterisk.

4. The Lists and Tables at the front of each Book are comprehensive. They will assist in researching cases relevant to a particular product sector (see for example Book One, Table 1, Commission Decisions, and 5, ECJ Judgments), and in relation to fines imposed. References are given to the Official Journal of the European Communities, the European Court Reports, the Common Market Law Reports and the Commerce Clearing House Reports. A case can be located by using either the chronological tables or the alphabetical tables.

5. Throughout the book each case or judgment is given a unique number. This enables the user to rapidly find the reference of the case or judgment in the tables at the front of the book. To differentiate between the various types of decision and judgment the following numbering system is adopted:

- Commission decisions pursuant to Articles 85/86 EEC
    Simple roman name and number, *e.g.* "Hilti 282"
- Commission decisions pursuant to the Merger Regulation
    Number preceded by letter M, *e.g.* "Volvo/Renault M1"
- Commission decisions relating to the ECSC
    Preceded by letters CS, *e.g.* "Scrap fund I CSI"
- Commission cases reported in Annual Competition Report
    Reference to Report and paragraph always given,
    e.g. "Sarabox, 8th Comp. Rep. (paras 35–37)"
- Judgments of the Court of First Instance
    Italic name; roman number preceded by letter T,
    e.g.; "Tetra Pak v. *Commission* T7"
- Judgments of the Court of Justice
    Italic name; roman number,
    e.g. "Michelin v. *Commission* 102"
- Judgments of the Court of Justice relating to the ECSC
    Italic name; number preceded by CS
    e.g. "Nold v. *Commission* CS23"

Listings always follow this order in the text.

6. A number of different methods can be used to locate the relevant section listing the case law applicable to any particular problem (each user will develop a different preference as have the authors). The following examples indicate, for example, how the case-law relevant to the assessment of a non-competition clause in a patent licence may be located:

- **Through the Table of Contents**: Book One, Part V deals with Intellectual Property Agreements, Chapter 2 thereof relates to Patent Licensing Agreements and Section A lists relevant cases.

- **Through the Index**: by consulting either competition clause, patent licences, or licensing, the relevant section can be located.

- **Through the table on the inside cover**: this gives the location of the most important Regulations. All cases relevant to a particular Block Exemption Regulation are cited immediately after the text of the Regulation. By locating the Regulation, the relevant cases can thus be identified.

7. There are the following additions and modifications to last year's **Handbook**:

- For increased ease of reference, the **1992 Handbook** has been divided into three "Books", with separate Books devoted to Mergers and Acquisitions and to Coal and Steel as well as the main Book dealing with General Competition Rules.

- The Lists and Tables relating to Mergers and Acquisitions now appear at the beginning of Book Two, while the Lists and Tables relating to Coal and Steel are located at the beginning of Book Three. Alphabetical Lists for all three Books combined appear immediately after this User Guide.

- Again in order to improve the **Handbook's** ease of use, the Annex materials and Forms which had in previous editions been contained in the Appendices are now included at the appropriate point in the main body of the **Handbook**.

— New texts reproduced in the **1992 Handbook** include Regulation 1534/91 on the Application of Article 85(3) to the Insurance Sector, Regulation 479/92 on the Application of Article 85(3) to Liner Shipping Companies (Consortia), the Telecommunications Guidelines and the Draft Joint Venture Guidelines.

— Numerous recent Commission decisions and ECJ/CFI judgments have also been added.

— The **1992 Handbook** is up to date to March 1, 1992 but also contains some more recent material where this has been available.

Note
A new edition of the **EEC Competition Law Handbook** is published every year. This is the third annual edition of the **Handbook.**

COMPLETE ALPHABETICAL LIST OF COMMISSION DECISIONS

'M' denotes Mergers and Acquisition. See Book Two for references
'CS' denotes Coal and Steel. See Book Three for references
For all other Decisions, see Book One for references

ABC Générale des Eaux/Canal & W.H. Smith	M45
ABG/Oil Companies	113
ABI	262
ACEC/Berliet	14
AEG-Telefunken	179
AG/AMEV	M2
AM & S Europe	146
AOIP/Beyrard	98
APB	314
ARD	312
ARG/Unipart	278
AROW/BNIC	190
ASBL	31
ASPA	30
Advocaat Zwarte Kip	79
Aérospatiale-Alenia/de Havilland	M48
Alba	39
Alcatel/AEG Kabel	M61
Alcatel/ANT	319
Alcatel/Telettra	M18
Alliance des Constructeurs Français	12
Aluminium	228
Amersham Buchler	184
ANSAC	333a
Apollinaris/Schweppes	M30
Arbed	CS62
Arbed/Cockerill-Sambre	CS96
Arbed/Rodange	CS71
Arbed/Unimetal	CS102
Arbed/Usinor-Sacilor	CS107
Arjomari/Wiggins Teape	M4
Arthur Bell & Sons Ltd.	135
Asko/Jacobs/Adia	M22
Asko/Omni	M13
Asphaltoid-Keller	42
Assurpol	347
ATT/NCR	M9
BBC Brown Boveri	291
BIFFEX	271
BMW	82
BMW Belgium	126
BNP/Dresdner Bank	M10
BNP/Dresdner (Czechoslovakia)	M43
BP/Bayer	284
BP/Kellogg	235
BP Kemi/DDSF	147
BP/Petromed	M39
BPCL/ICI	215
BPICA I	116
BPICA II	180
BSC/Dunlop & Ranken	CS81
BSC/Lye Trading	CS43
BSC/Walter Blume	CS57
Baccarat	338
Bank America/Security Pacific	M52
Bayer Dental	327
Bayonox	313
Baxter Nestlé/Salvia	M11
Bayer/Gist-Brocades	100
Beecham/Parke Davis	144
Belgian Banking Association	261
Belgian Wallpaper	78
Bendix/Mertens and Straet	3
Boehringer	45
Boël/Claberg	CS87
Bomée-Stichting	97
Boosey & Hawkes	273
Boussois/Interpane	264
Breeders' rights; roses	236
British Dental Trade Association	285
British Fuel	CS101
British Leyland	212
British Plasterboard	299
British steel producers	CS66
British Steel/Walker	CS105
British Sugar	286
British Telecommunications	188
Bronbemaling	95
Burroughs/Delplanque	50
Burroughs/Geha	51
CAMPSA	M63
CFA	18
CICG	36
CLIF/Marine-Firminy	CS48
COBECHAR I	CS2
COBECHAR II	CS7
COBECHAR III	CS14
COBECHAR IV	CS27
COBECHAR V	CS36
COBECHAR VI	CS55
COBECHAR VII	CS76
COIMPRE	CS69
CONAGRA/IDEA	M24
CSV	105
CSV	134
Cafeteros de Colombia	187
Campari	130
Canary Islands	268
Cane Sugar Supply Agreements	150
Carbon Gas Technologie	205
Cargill/Unilever	M6
Carlsberg	214
Cast-iron & Steel Rolls	198
Castrol	192
Cauliflowers	119
Cekacan	326
Cematex I	43

x

Complete Alphabetical List of Commission Decisions

Cematex II	193
Central Bureau voor de Rijwielhandel	118
Central Heating	60
Ceramic Tiles	35
Cereol/Continentale Italiana	M55
Chamber of Coal Traders	CS86
Chamber of Coal Traders II	CS91
Charles Jourdan	298
Chaufourniers	20
Chiquita	101
Christiani & Nielsen	21
Cimbel	66
Clima Chappée	25
Cobelaz	15
Cobelaz Cokes	16
Cobelpa/VNP	115
Cockerill/Estel	CS78
Cockerill/Klöckner	CS77
Comptoir d'Importation	167
Computerland	270
Concordato	316
Continental/Michelin	290
Continental Can	46
Convention Faience	2
Courtaulds/SNIA	M62
Creusot/Loire	CS23
Creusot-Loire/Vgine	CS73
DECA	6
DRU/Blondel	7
Danish Steel Distributors	CS39
Davidson Rubber	56
Decca	304
De Laval/Stork I	114
De Laval/Stork II	281
Delta Airlines/PanAm	M46
Delta Chemie	292
Deutsche Philips	73
D'Ieteren	329
Digital/Kienzle	M14
Digital/Philips	M44
Dillinger/Arbed I	CS32
Dillinger/Arbed II	CS54
Dillinger/Arbed III	CS60
Distillers Company, The	123
Distillers-Victuallers	157
Draeger/IBM/HMP	M33
Dupont de Nemours Germany	71
DuroDyne	83
Dutch Banking Association	310
Dutch Cement	65
Dutch Express Delivery	318
Dyestuffs	27
EATE Levy	231
ECS/AKZO	242
ECS/AKZO-Interim measures	197
EDS/SD-Scicon	M36
EGAM/Vetrocoke	CS52
EMO (I)	19
EMO (II)	140
EMO (III)	303
ENI/Montedison	256
Enichem/ICI	279
Eco System	344a
Elf/BC/CEPSA	M29
Elf/Enterprise	M38
Eirpage	344
Elf/Ertoil	M21
Elf/Occidental	M28
Ericaaon/Korlee	M72
Eridania/ISI	M40
Eschweiler/Ruhr Kohle	CS103
Euro coal	CS89
Eurocom/RSCG	M60
Eurogypsum	11
European Sugar Industry	69
Eurotunnel	293
FEDETAB	133
FN/CF	37
FRUBO	80
Fabbricca Lastre	154
Fabbrica Pisana	153
Falck/Redaelli I	CS21
Falck/Redaelli II	CS75
Fatty Acids	254
Fédération Chaussure de France	183
Fiat/Ford	M12
Fides	145
Fire Insurance	175, 220
Fireplaces	90
Fisher-Price	275
Flat Glass	300
Flat Glass (Benelux)	216
Floral	148
Ford Werke AG	199
Ford Werke-Interim Measures	182
Framtek	CS70
Franco-Japanese Ball-Bearings	81
GAFTA	260
GEC-Siemens Plessey	325
GEC/Weir Sodium Circulators	117
GISA	67
GKN/Miles Druce	CS41
GVL	166
Gambogi/Cogel	M66
Geitling I	CS9
Geitling II	CS10
Geitling III	CS12
Geitling IV	CS18
Geitling V	CS25
Gelsenberg	CS45
Gema I	38
Gema II	58
Gema Statutes	174

Complete Alphabetical List of Commission Decisions

General Motors	84
German Blacksmiths	120
German rolled steel	CS84
German Scrap Cartel	CS28
Gerofabriek	111
Goodyear Italiana/Euram	85
Gosme/Martell	340
Greek Insurance	230
Grohe Sales System	222
Grosfillex/Fillestorf	1
Grundig	232
Grundig/Consten	5
Hasselblad	173
Heaters and Boilers	72
Henkel/Colgate	52
Hennessy/Henkell	162
Hilti	282
Hoesch/Benteler	CS35
Hoesch/Rheinstahl	CS30
Hoogovens/Ijzerhandel	CS85
Hudson Bay	294
Hugin/Liptons	121
Hummel Isbecque	8
IATA Cargo	343
IATA Passengers	342
IBM PC	210
ICI	333
ICI/Tisxide	M3
ICL/Nokia Data	M35
IFTRA Aluminium	92
IFTRA Glass	77
IMA Rules	158
IPEL	255
IPTC Belgium	202
IVECO	CS50
IVECO/Ford	287
Ideal Standard Sales System	223
Ijsselcentrale	335
Inchapel/IEP	M71
Ingersoll Rand/Dresser	M59
Intergroup	91
International Dental Exhibition	274
International Energy Agency	207
Irish Bank Standing Committee	252
Irish Steel/Dunkerque	CS80
Italian Cast Glass	163
Italian Flat Glass	164
Ivoclar	234
Jaz/Peter I	26
Jaz/Peter II	128
John Deere	226
Johnson & Johnson	160
Julien/Van Katwijk	32
Junghans	109
KEWA	103

KSB	328
Kabelmetal/Luchaire	94
Kali & Salz/Kalichemie	76
Kawasaki	141
Kelt/American Express	M45
Kempense	CS20
Klöckner/Maxhütte IV	CS63
Kodak	29
Konica	277
Konsortium ECR 900	323
Krups	155
Krupp/Stahlwerke	CS49
Kyowa/Saitama	M16
Lange/Stinnes	CS79
Langenscheidt/Hachette	168
LdPE	306
London Cocoa Market	239
London Coffee Market	240
London Grain Market	257
London Meat Exchange	259
London Potato Market	258
London Rubber Market	241
London Sugar Market	238
Lucas/Eaton	M57
Lyonnaise des Eaux/Brochier	M34
MAN/SAVIEM	54
MBB/Aerospatiale	M15
Maes	41
Magill	307
Magneti–Marcell/CEAC	M23
Maier/Röchling	CS67
Maison Jallatte	9
Maize Seeds	137
Manganese	CS83
Manganese II	CS97
Mannesmann/Boge	M47
Mannesmann/VDO	M58
Marcoke	CS47
Matsushita/MCA	M8
Maxhütte/Klöckner I	CS31
Maxhütte/Klöckner II	CS53
Maxhütte/Klockner III	CS59
Mecaniver/PPG	225
Mediobanca/Generali	M65
Meldoc	253
Metaleurop	321
Metallgesellachft/Dynamit Nobel	M49
Metallgesellachft/Safic Alcan	53
Michelin	165
Milchfoerderungsfonds	221
Miller	108
Minerais Préréduits	CS51
Misal	62
Mitchell Cotts/Sofiltra	267
Mitsubishi/UCAR	M7
Moët et Chandon (London) Ltd	172
Moosehead	320

Complete Alphabetical List of Commission Decisions

Murat	200
NAVEWA-ANSEAU	178
NAVEWA-ANSEAU (Bosch)	185
NCH	53
NICIA	CS99
National Panasonic	186
National Panasonic (Belgium)	176
National Panasonic (France)	177
National Sulphuric Acid Assoc. I	156
National Sulphuric Acid Assoc. II	308
Natursteinplatten	159
Net Book Agreements	301
New Potatoes	276
Nicholas Frères Vitapro	4
Nissan/Richard Nissan	M32
Nuovo-CEGAM	209
Nutricia	206
OKB I	CS4
OKB II	CS6
OKB III	CS15
OKB IV	CS34
Odin	322
Olivetti/Canon	280
Olympic Airways	229
Omega	33
Optical Fibres	249
Otto/Grattan	M17
P & I Clubs	243
PVC	305
Pabst & Richerz/BNIA	106
Paribas/MTH	M50
Penney	127
Peroxide Products	218
Peugeot	250
Pioneer	152
Pirelli/Dunlop	28
Pittsburgh Corning	63
Polistil/Arbois	211
Polypropylene	247
Präsident I	CS8
Präsident II	CS13
Präsident III	CS19
Präsident IV	CS26
Promodes/Dirsa	M5
Pronuptia	266
Prym/Beka	74
Quinine Cartel	24
RAI/Unitel	131
RVI/VBC/HEULIEZ	M25
Rank/SOPELEM	86
Raymond-Nagoya	57
Redoute/Empire Stores	M19
Renault/Volvo	M1
Rennet	149
Reuter/BASF	107
Rich Products	203
Rieckerman	17
Röchling-Posser I	CS98
Rockwell/IVECO	196
Rodenstock	61
Rogesa	CS88
Roofing Felt	248
Rötzel/Krupp	CS61
Ruhrkohle	CS37
Ruhrkohle	CS46
Ruhrkohle	CS104
Ruhrkohle/Brennstoff handel	CS72
Röchling-Biobach	CS68
SABA I	99
SABA II	208
SABENA	295
SAFCO	48
SCPA/Kali & Salz	70
SEIFA	23
SHV/Chevron	87
SIAE	44
SMM & T	201
SNPE-LEL	132
SOPELEM/Langen	49
SOPELEM/Vickers I	125
SOPELEM/Vickers II	171
SOREMA	CS11
SSI	181
Saab/Ericsson Spacem	M68
Saarlor I	CS24
Saarlor II	CS42
Saarlor III	CS56
Saarlor IV	CS64
Saarlor V	CS82
Saarlor VI	CS100
Sandoz	272
Sanofi/Sterling Drugs	M27
Schlegel/CPIO	204
Schweizer Rück/ELVIA	M70
Scottish Nuclear	339
Scrap Fund I	CS1
Scrap Fund II	CS3
Screensport/EBU	337
Secrétama	329a
ServiceMaster	296
Siemens/Fanuc	246
Sippa	336
Sirdar Phildar	89
Socemans	13
Solvay	332
Solvay/CFK	331
Solvay/ICI	330
Spanish Courier Services	324
Sperry New Holland	245
Spices	124

Complete Alphabetical List of Commission Decisions

Stahlring I	CS17
Stahlring II	CS33
Stahlring III	CS65
Stahlring IV	CS93
Stainless Steel Cartel	CS106
Steelmaking Supplies	CS40
Steelmaking Supplies II	CS96
Sugar Beet	315
Sunrise	M67
Supexie	34
Synthetic Fibres	213
TNT/Canada Post	M56
Teacher & Sons	136
Teko	317
Telos	170
Tetra Pak I	289
Tetra Pak II	348
Tetra Pak/Alfa-Laval	M37
Theal/Watts	110
Thin Paper	59
Thomson/Pilkington	M51
Thyssen/Krupp/Wuppermann	CS29
Thyssen/Rheinstahl	CS38
Thyssen/Solmer	CS44
Tinned Mushrooms	88
Tipp-Ex	269
Toltecs/Dorcet	191
Transocean Marine Paint Assoc. I	10
Transocean Marine Paint Assoc. II	75
Transocean Marine Paint Assoc. III	96
Transocean Marine Paint Assoc. IV	151
Transocean Marine Paint Assoc. V	297
UAP/Transatlantic/Sunlife	M54
UIP	309
UK Tractors	347
UNICO	CS94
UNIDI I	93
UNIDI II	219
Uniform Eurochèques	224
Uniform Eurochèques Manufacturing	302
Union Brasserie	40
Union Charbonnière	CS5
United Reprocessors	102
Usinor/ASD	M20
Usinor/Sacilor/Normandie	CS92
VBA	288
VBBB/VBVB	169
VCH	47
VCRO	CS74
VIAG/Brühl	M64
VIAG/Continental Can	M26
VIFKA	251
VVVF	22
VW/MAN	203
Vacuum Interrupters I	112
Vacuum Interrupters II	161
Vaessen/Moris	143
Varta/Bosch	M41
Vegetable Parchment	129
Velcro/Aplix	233
Vichy	334
Video Cassette Recorders	122
Viho/Toshiba	341
Villeroy & Boch	244
Vimpoltu	195
Vitamins	104
Volvo/Atlas	M69
WANO	138
WEA/Filipacchi Music S.A.	68
Walker/Champion	CS58
Walzstahlkontor I	CS16
Walzstahlkontor II	CS22
Welded Steel Mesh	311
Whisky and Gin	237
White Lead	142
Wild/Leitz	55
Windsurfing International	194
Woodpulp	227
X/Open Group	263
Yves Rocher	265
Yves Saint Laurent	345
Zanussi	139
Zentralkokerei	CS90
Zinc	189
Zinc Producer Group	217
Zoja/CSC-ICI	64

COMPLETE ALPHABETICAL LIST OF COURT OF FIRST INSTANCE JUDGMENTS

See Book One for references

Atochem v. Commission	T20	Norsk Hydro v. Commission	T4
Automec v. Commission	T6	Petrofina v. Commission	T19
BASF v. Commission	T23	Peugeot v. Commission	T3
BBC v. Commission	T15	Peugeot v. Commission	T17
Bayer v. Commission	T13	Prodifarma v. Commission	T11
Cement Industries v. Commission	T39	PTT v. Commission	T13b
Cosimex v. Commission	T1	PVC	T28
DSM v. Commission	T26	Rhône Poulenc v. Commission	T18
Enichem v. Commission	T24	RTE v. Commission	T14
Hilti v. Commission	T21	SEP v. Commission	T8
Filtrona v. Commission	T5	SEP v. Commission	T22
Flat Glass	T30	Shell v. Commission	T33
Hoechst v. Commission	T32	Sofacar v. Commission	T38
Hüls v. Commission	T31	Solomon v. Commission	T2
ICI v. Commission	T35	Solvay v. Commission	T34
ITV v. Commission	T16	Tetra Pak v. Commission	T7
La Cinq v. Commission	T27	Vichy v. Commission	T13a
Linz v. Commission	T37	Vichy v. Commission	T29
Montedipe v. Commission	T36	VNZ v. Commission	T10
Nefarma v. Commission	T9		

COMPLETE ALPHABETICAL LIST OF EUROPEAN COURT JUDGMENTS

'CS' denotes Coal and Steel cases. See Book Three for references
For all other cases, see Book One for references

ACF Chemiefarma v. Commission	14
ACNA v. Commission	31
AEG v. Commission	100
AKZO v. Commission I	132
AKZO v. Commission II	133
AKZO v. Commission III	186
AMP v. Binon	119
AM&S v. Commission	92
ANCIDES v. Commission	143
ANTIB v. Commission	142
Ahlsthom v. Sulzer	180
Ahmed Saeed v. Zentrale	162
Allen & Hanburys v. Generics	148
Alsatel v. Nordsam	160
Anne Marty v. Estée Lauder	77
Asia Motors v. Commission	176
BASF v. Commission	24
BAT v. Commission & Philip Morris	116
BAT v. Commission	146
BMW Belgium v. Commission	69
BNIC v. Clair	115
BNIC/Aubert	147
BRT v. SABAM I	36
BRT v. SABAM II	38
Basset v. SACEM	141
Batista Morais	193
Bayer v. Commission	25
Bayer v. Süllhöfer	158
Bayern v. Eurim-Pharm	183
Béguelin v. GL	22
Belasco v. Commission	166
Benzine & Petroleum BV v. Commission	65
Bilger v. Jehle	12
Bodson v. Pompes Funèbres	150
Bond van Adverteerders	149a
Boehringer v. Commission	16
Boehringer v. Commission	33
Boekhandels v. Eldi Records	73
BoschDe Geus	1
Bosman v. Commission	187
British Leyland	136
Buchler & Co. v. Commission	15
CICCE v. Commission	118
Cadillon v. Höss	18
Camera Care v. Commission	72
Cassella v. Commission	29
Cement Dealers v. Commission	32
Centrafarm v. AHP	66
Centrafarm & De Peijper v. Sterling Drug	41
Centrafarm & De Peijper v. Winthrop	42

Ceratel v. Le Campion	137
Centre-Midi v. HA	CS7
Cholay	178
Ciba-Geigy v. Commission	26
Cimenteries v. Commission	6
Ciments et Bétons v. Kerpen	104
Cinéthèque	122a
CNL-Sucal v. Hag	177
Coditel v. Cine-Vog	96
Commission v. Germany	42a
Commission v. Germany	137a
Commission v. Greece	153
Commission v. Ireland	73a
Commission v. Italy	141a
Commission v. Italy	191
Commission v. UK	192
Consten & Grundig v. Commission	4
Continental Can v. Commission	35
Costa v. ENEL	2
Cullet v. LeClerc	114
Dansk Supermarket v. Imerco	83
Dassonville	40a
Debauve	72b
De Bloos v. Boyer	60
De Haecht v. Wilkin I	7
De Haecht v. Wilkin II	34
Delimitis v. Henninger Bräu	181
Demo Schmidt v. Commission	99
De Norre v. Concordia	54
Deutsche Grammaphon v. Metro	19
Distillers v. Commission	75
Dow v. Commission	145
Dow Benelux v. Commission	170
Dow Iberica v. Commission	171
Duphar	106
EMI-CBS	50
EMI-CBS	51
EMI-CBS	52
EMI v. Patricia	161a
ERT v. DEP	185
ETA v. DKI	126
Eisen und Stahlindustrie v. HA	CS6
FEDETAB v. Commission	80
Fire Insurance v. Commission	139
Fonderies Roubaix v. Fonderies Roux	49
Ford v. Commission	108
Ford v. Commission	123
France v. Commission	95
France v. Commission	182
France v. HA	CS1
Francolor v. Commission	28
Frubo v. Commission	44

Complete Alphabetical List of European Court Judgments

GAARM v. Commission	112
GB-INNO v. ATAB	59
GVL v. Commission	97
Geitling v. HA	CS4
Geitling v. HA	CS10
Geitling v. HA	CS15
Gema v. Commission	70
Générale Sucrière v. Commission	55
General Motors v. Commission	46
Greenwich v. SACEM	71
Hasselblad v. Commission	107
Hoechst v. Commission I	30
Hoechst v. Commission II	140
Hoechst v. Commission III	169
Hoffmann-La Roche v. Centrafarm	56
Hoffmann-La Roche v. Centrafarm	63
Hoffmann-La Roche v. Commission	67
Höfner v. Macrotron	184
Hugin v. Commission	68
Hydrotherm v. Andreoli	111
IBM v. Commission	88
ICI v. Commission	23
ICI & CSC v. Commission	37
IDG v. Beele	91
Inter-Huiles	97a
Italy v. Commission	117
Italy v. Council and Commission	5
Italy v. HA	CS2
Kali & Salz v. Commission	43
Keurkoop v. Nancy Kean Gifts	95a
Kohl v. Ringelhahn	111a
Komponistenverband v. Commission	20
LTM v. MBU	3
Lancôme v. Etos	78
Le Campion	137
LeClerc	113
Louis Erauw v. La Hesbignonne	00
Lord Bethell v. Commission	93
L'Oréal v. De Nieuwe AMCK	81
Lucazeau v. SACEM	168
Marchandise	181a
Maxicar v. Renault	161
Membran/K-Tel v. Gema	82
Merci v. Siderurgica	188
Merck & Co. v. Stephar	87
Metro v. Commission I	58
Metro v. Commission II	134
Michelin v. Commission	102
Miles Druce v. Commission I	CS21
Miles Druce v. Commission II	CS22
Miller v. Commission	61
Ministère Public v. Tournier	167
Miro	122b
Muller	21
NAVEWA v. Commission	101

NSO v. Commission	128
National Panasonic v. Commission	74
Netherlands v. Commission	190
Netherlands v. HA	CS3
Netherlands v. HA	CS19
Nold v. HA	CS5
Nold v. HA	CS9
Nold v. Commission	CS23
Nouvelles Frontières	131
Nungesser v. Commission	94
Opinion: Amendment to Article 65	CS14
Orkem v. Commission	172
Ottung v. Klee	164
Pall v. Dahlhausen	179
Papiers Peints v. Commission	47
Parfums Rochas v. Bitsch	13
Parke, Davis v. Centrafarm	8
Pfizer v. Eurim-Pharm	89
Pharmon v. Hoechst	120
Philip Morris v. Commission	79
Pioneer v. Commission	98
Polydor v. Harlequin Record Shops	90
Portelange v. Smith Corona	11
Prantl	107a
Präsident v. HA	CS13
Procureur v. Cognet	135
Procureur v. Commission	76
PTT v. Commission	184a
Publishers Association v. Commission	165
Pronuptia v. Schillgalis	129
RTE & BBC v. Commission	163
Remia v. Commission	121
Roussel v. Netherlands	103
Royal Pharmaceutical Society	169a
RTT v. G.B. Inno	189
SOREMA v. HA	CS18
SOREMA v. HA	CS20
Sacchi	39
SSI v. Commission	127
St. Herblain v. Syndicat des Libraires	122
Salonia v. Poidomani & Baglieri	85
Sandoz v. Commission	27
Sandoz v. Commission	174
Schlieker v. HA	CS17
Sirena v. Eda	17
Solvay v. Commission	173
Stanley Adams v. Commission	125
Stork v. HA	CS8
Stremsel v. Commission	84
Suiker Unie v. Commission	48
Syndicat v. Leclerc Aigle	154
Télémarketing v. CLT	124
Tepea v. Commission	64
Terrapin v. Terranova	53
Thetford Corp. v. Fiamma	152

xvii

Complete Alphabetical List of European Court Judgments

Tipp-Ex v. Commission 175
Transocean Marine Paint Association 40b

UNILEC v. Larroche 156
United Brands v. Commission 62

VAG v. Magne 138
VBVB & VBBB v. Commission 105
Van Ameyde v. UCI 57
Vander Haar v. Kaveka 110
Van Eycke v. Aspa 155
Van Vliet v. Dalle Crode 45

Van Zuylen v. Hag 40
Vlaamse Reisbureaus 144
Völk v. Vervaecke 10
Volvo v. Veng 159

Walt Wilhelm 9
Warner Brothers v. Christiansen 151
Windsurfing v. Commission 130
Woodpulp 157
Worms v. HA CS16

Zinc Producers v. Commission 109
Zuechner v. Bayerishe Vereinshank .. 86

TABLE OF CONTENTS

	page
List of Commonly Used Regulations	inside front cover
Preface to the First Edition	v
Preface to the Second Edition	vi
User Guide	vii
Complete Alphabetical List of Commission Decisions	x
Complete Alphabetical List of Court of First Instance Judgments	xv
Complete Alphabetical List of European Court Judgments	xvi

BOOK ONE: GENERAL COMPETITION RULES

Lists and Tables

1. Chronological List of Commission Decisions (EEC)—References 5
2. Chronological List of Commission Decisions (EEC)—Contents 15
3. Chronological List of Court of First Instance Judgments (EEC)—References 27
4. Chronological List of Court of First Instance Judgments (EEC)—Contents 29
5. Chronological List of European Court Judgments (EEC)—References 31
6. Chronological List of European Court Judgments (EEC)—Contents 38
7. Alphabetical List of Commission Decisions 44
8. Alphabetical List of Court of First Instance Judgments 48
9. Alphabetical List of European Court Judgments 49
10. Fines 52
11. List of Legislation and Documents 62

Table of Contents

PART I

CONDITIONS FOR THE APPLICATION OF BOTH ARTICLES 85 AND 86

1. Undertakings

1.	Natural persons	71
2.	Change of corporate structure	71
3.	Collective responsibility of the group	71
4.	Intra-enterprise conspiracy doctrine	71
5.	Difference between undertaking and public bodies	71

2. Effect on Trade between Member States

A.	Delimitation of Community competence	71
B.	The assessment of the effect on trade	72
1.	Direct, indirect, actual or potential effect	72
2.	Structural arguments	72
2.1	Agreement may affect the structure of competition in the Common Market	72
2.2	Elimination of a competitor	72
2.3	Involvement of a transnational company	72
3.	Cumulative effect of parallel agreements	72
3.1	Similar agreements concluded by the same and other companies	72
3.2	Similar agreements concluded by the same company	72
4.	Consideration of the agreement as a whole	72
5.	Contractual export bans, a *per se* rule?	72
6.	Use of raw material for a product/service that is exported	73
C.	Types of agreement that do not necessarily affect trade between Member States	73
1.	Minor importance: appreciability	73
2.	Trade with third states	73
2.1.	Export to third states	73
2.2	Import from third states	73
3.	Export boosters: increasing trade	73
4.	National cartels	73

3. Within the Common Market: Extra Territoriality

A.	Cases	74
B.	Text of Notice on imports from Japan 1972	74

xx

Table of Contents

PART II

ARTICLE 85(1),(2) and (3)

1. Agreements

A.	Definition of agreement	75
1.1.	Understanding	75
1.2.	Understanding may be tacit or express	75
2.	Irrelevance of the form of the agreement	75
2.1.	Written or oral	75
2.2.	Gentleman's agreement	75
2.3.	Meetings	75
2.4.	Unilateral conduct of a company in a contractual context	75
2.4.1.	Sales conditions	75
2.4.2.	Circular/recommendation	75
2.4.3.	Refusal to sell in the framework of selective distribution agreements	75
2.5.	Court settlement	76
3.	Relation between restriction of competition and agreement	76
3.1.	Causation	76
3.2.	Agreement continues to produce its effects after termination of agreement	76
4.	Distinction between agreement and public authority decision	76
B.	Concerted practice	76
1.	Concept	76
1.1.	Definition	76
1.2.	Difference between concerted practice and agreement	76
2.	Evidence of a concerted practice	77
2.1.	Similarity of behaviour	77
2.2.	Exchange of information	77
2.3.	Meetings	77
2.4.	Difference between concerted practice and market behaviour resulting from the structure of the relevant market	77
C.	Decisions of associations of undertakings	77
1.	Association of undertakings	77
2.	Decision	77
2.1.	Definition of decision	77
2.2.	Agreements with associations of undertakings	77
2.3.	Agreements between associations of undertakings	77
D.	The prevention, restriction or distortion of competition	78
1.	Concept	78
1.1.	Interbrand or intrabrand competition	78
1.2.	Competition between the parties and competition with third parties	78

1.3.	Actual and potential competition	78
1.4.	Price or non-price competition	78
1.5.	State interference and competition	78
2.	Object and effect	78
2.1.	Object of restriction alone suffices	78
2.2.	Definition of the relevant market in Article 85	78
3.	Restriction must be appreciable	78
3.1.	Text of Commission Notice on agreements of minor importance	78
3.2.	Cases regarding appreciability	81
4.	Rule of reason/ancillary restraints: assessing the restriction in the context of the relevant market	81

2. Article 85(2)

1.	Concept of nullity	81
2.	Retroactive effect	81
3.	Severability of offending clauses	81
4.	Effect of a Commission Decision	82

3. Article 85(3)

A.	Conditions for the grant of an individual exemption	82
1.	Contribution to the improvement, or the production or distribution of goods promoting technical progress	82
2.	Allowing consumers a fair share of the resulting benefit	82
3.	No Imposition on the undertakings concerned of restrictions which are dispensable to the attainment of these objectives	82
4.	Not affording such undertakings the possibility of eliminating competition in respect of a substantial part of the products in question	82
B.	Elements relevant to the assessment of Article 85(3)	82
1.	Balancing the pros and cons	82
2.	Social considerations	82
3.	Environmental considerations	82
4.	Burden of proof	82
5.	Unilateral behaviour extraneous to contractual terms	82
6.	Advantage must be objective	82
7.	Conditions are cumulative	83
8.	Discretion of the Commission	83
9.	Can an Article 86 abuse be exempted?	83
10.	Contribution to other EC policies	83
C.	Exemption by category	83
1.	Delegation of the authority to adopt regulations to the Commission	83
1.1.	Text of Regulation 19/65	83
1.2.	Text of Regulation 2821/71	86
1.3.	Other Regulations	88
2.	List of Commission Regulations providing for exemption by category	88
3.	Opposition procedures in Commission block exemptions	88
4.	Effect of a group exemption regulation	88
5.	Withdrawal of the benefit of a group exemption regulation	88
6.	Letter of Commission	88

PART III

HORIZONTAL AGREEMENTS

1. Cartels

A.	List of cartel cases	89
B.	Specific clauses or agreements typically arising under cartel schemes	90
1.	Production related schemes or clauses	90
1.1.	Production quotas for existing capacity	90
1.2.	Provisions regulating capacity	90
1.2.1.	Prohibition of new capacity	90
1.2.2.	Prohibition on sale of capacity outside cartel	90
1.3.	Clauses relating to the nature of the product	90
1.3.1.	Common product range	90
1.3.2.	Sharing of product ranges between competitors	90
1.4.	Supply agreements	90
1.4.1.	Emergency supply agreements	90
1.4.2.	Reciprocal supply arrangements	90
1.5.	Production information exchange schemes	90
1.6.	Compensation schemes	90
2.	Market sharing schemes, agreements or clauses	90
2.1.	Dividing territories between competitors	90
2.1.1.	Between Member States	90
2.1.2.	Third country markets	91
2.2.	Quotas	91
2.3.	Dividing customers between competitors	91
2.4.	Market and/or sales information exchange	91
2.5.	Compensation schemes	91
3.	Price agreements between competitors	91
3.1.	Agreed minimum prices	91
3.2.	Agreed common prices	91
3.3	Agreed recommended prices	92
3.4.	Agreed price increase	92
3.5.	Collective R.P.M.	92
3.6.	Common rebate/discount policy	92
3.7.	Bidding agreements	92
3.8.	Aligning prices in another territory	92
3.9.	Price information exchange agreements	93
4.	Sales agreements	93
4.1.	Common or joint sales	93
4.2.	Common exports	93
4.3.	Common sales policy	93
4.4.	Common purchasing policy	93
4.5.	Common sales conditions	93
4.6.	Information exchange on sales conditions	93
4.7.	Mutual respect for distribution channels	93
5.	Exclusionary practices	93
5.1.	Collective exclusive dealing	93

5.2.	Agreements intended to control the supply of a product	94
5.3.	Predatory price cutting agreements	94
5.4.	Joint production with exclusive purchasing	94
5.5.	Collective refusal to supply	94
5.6.	Agregate rebates	94
5.7.	Patent pooling	94
6.	Practices used by cartels to enforce agreements	94
6.1.	Boycotting non-members	94
6.2.	Fines on cartel members for breach of rules	94
7.	Crisis cartels	94

2. Co-operation Agreements

A.	List of cases on co-operation agreements	95
B.	Text of relevant Notices	95
1.	Co-operation agreements	95
1.1.	Text of Notice of 29 July, 1968	95
1.2.	Cases on the interpretation of the Notice	99
2.	Text of Notice on subcontracting agreements	99
3.	Reference to connected legislation	101
C.	Types/categories of co-operation agreements	101
1.	Sharing of R&D costs	101
2.	Patent pools	101
3.	Sharing of production capacity	101
4.	Building consortia	101
5.	Uniform manufacturing standards	101
6.	Uniform sales conditions	101
7.	Joint or common advertising	101
8.	Adoption of common trademarks or quality marks	101
9.	Joint sales	101
10.	Inter-bank agreements	101
11.	Buying groups	101

3. Specialisation Agreements

A.	List of cases on specialisation agreements	101
B.	Text of Regulation 417/85	101
C.	Cases on the interpretation of the Regulation	105
D.	Categories of specialisation agreements	105
1.	Agreements to expand the range of goods produced/sold by the parties	105
2.	Agreements to share R&D costs	105
3.	Joint distribution agreements	105
4.	Restructuring agreements	105
E.	Clauses typical of specialisation agreements	105
1.	Exchange of information/licences	105
2.	Reciprocal distribution rights	105

Table of Contents

3.	Obligation to supply or purchase from the other party	105
3.1.	Exclusive purchasing obligation	105
3.2.	Obligation to supply the other party	105
3.3.	Right of first refusal to sell new products	105
3.4.	Most favoured customer clause	105
4.	Non-competitive clause	105
5.	Territorial restriction	106
6.	Trademark related clauses	106

4. Research and Development Agreements

A.	List of cases on R&D agreements	106
B.	The text of Regulation 418/85	106
C.	Cases on the interpretation of the Regulation	113
D.	Categories of R&D agreements	113
1.	Joint R&D without production	113
2.	Joint R&D with subsequent joint production	113
E.	Clauses comonly figuring in R&D agreements	113
1.	Territorial provisions	113
1.1.	Division of the EEC into exclusive territories between the contracting parties regarding exploitation of results	114
1.2.	Prohibition of active sales outside exclusive territory	114
1.3.	Prohibition of passive sales policy outside exclusive territory	114
1.4.	Export prohibition into the Common Market	114
2.	Supply and purchase obligations	114
2.1.	Exclusive purchasing obligations	114
2.2.	Mutual supply obligations	114
2.3.	Most favoured customer clause	114
3.	Non-competition clauses	114
3.1.	Prohibition from engaging in competing R&D	114
3.2.	Prohibition from engaging into R&D in unconnected fields	114
4.	Customer limitation clause	114
5.	Clauses relating to the fruits of the R&D	114
5.1.	Minimum quality norms	114
5.2.	Restrictions on the quantities that the parties may sell	114
5.3.	Field of use restrictions	114
6.	Clauses relating to intellectual property and related rights	114
6.1.	Exchange of technical information	114
6.2.	Field of use restrictions	114
6.3.	Obligation to maintain confidentiality of know-how	114
6.4.	Grant of licences to third-parties/sub-licensing	114
6.5.	Patent pooling	115
6.6.	Post-term use ban of jointly developed technology	115
6.7.	Patent no-challenge clause	115
6.8.	Obligation to inform the other party of patent infringment	115
7.	Duration of the agreement	115
7.1.	Between competitors	115
7.2.	Between non-competitors	115
8.	Royalty provisions	115
8.1.	Obligation to pay royalties to other party if contribution to R&D is unequal	115

8.2.	Obligation to share royalties received from third parties	115
8.3.	Profit-sharing through royalty payments	115

5. Trade Associations

A.	Cases on trade associations	115
1.	General list	115
2.	List of cases where a trade association was acting as a cartel	115
B.	Stipulation common to trade association agreements	116
1.	Rules regarding membership of association	116
1.1.	Objective criteria for membership	116
1.2.	Limit on numbers of members	116
1.3.	Provisions limiting withdrawal from association	116
2.	Pricing obligations	116
3.	Agreement to purchase minimum percentages from domestic producers	116
4.	Discriminatory conditions against non-members	116
5.	Industry organised distribution schemes	116
6.	Collective exclusive dealing	116

6. Trade Fair and Exhibition Agreements

A.	Cases on trade fair and exhibition agreements	116
B.	Stipulations common to exhibition agreements	116
1.	Agreement not to exhibit at other exhibitions	116
2.	Objective criteria for admittance	117
3.	Discrimination against foreign exhibitors	117

PART IV

VERTICAL AGREEMENTS

1. Exclusive and Non-Exclusive Distribution Agreements

A.	List of cases on exclusive distribution	119
B.	List of cases on non-exclusive distribution	119
C.	Text of Regulation 1983/83	119
D.	Cases on the interpretation of the Regulation	123
E.	Text of the Notice on the interpretation of the Regulation	123
F.	Clauses commonly figuring within distribution agreements	132

1.	Territorial restrictions	132
1.1.	Grant of an exclusive territory to the distributor	132
1.2.	No active sales policy outside agreed territory	132
1.3.	Profit pass over clause	133
1.4.	Export ban on direct sales by distributor	133
1.4.1.	Between Members States	133
1.4.2.	Into the EEC	133
1.4.3.	Outside the EEC	133
1.5.	Export ban on indirect sales, *i.e.* export ban reimposed upon its customers	133
2.	Clauses relating to the product that the distributor may sell	133
2.1.	Non-competition clause	133
2.2.	Minimum purchasing obligations	133
2.3.	Exclusive purchasing requirements	133
2.4.	Guarantee/after sales service	133
2.5.	Assembly and manufacture by distributor	134
2.6.	Stocking requirement	134
3.	Clauses related to the price of the product	134
3.1.	Resale price maintenance	134
3.2.	Discriminatory pricing between different territories	134
3.3.	Obligation to transmit recommended prices	134
4.	Clauses relating to the costumers to which the distributor may sell	134
5.	Distribution agreement between competing manufacturers	134
5.1.	Reciprocal	134
5.2.	Non-reciprocal	134

2. Exclusive Purchasing Agreements

A.	Cases on exclusive purchasing agreements	134
B.	Text of Regulation 1984/83	134
C.	Cases on the interpretation of the Regulation	142
D.	Notice on the interpretation of the Regulation	142
E.	Clauses commonly figuring within exclusive purchasing agreements	142
1.	Exclusivity	142
2.	Non-competition clause	142
3.	English clause	142
4.	Purchasing or supply obligations	142
5.	Resale price maintenance	142

3. Selective Distribution Agreements

A.	Cases on selective distribution agreements	142
B.	Text of Regulation 123/85	142
C.	Cases on the interpretation of the Regulation	151
D.	Text of the Notice on the interpretation of the Regulation	151
E.	The assessment of selective distribution agreements	154

1.	Nature of the product which justifies selective distribution	154
2.	Selection of the dealer	154
2.1.	Qualitative criteria (experience, professional qualifications, after sales service)	154
2.2.	Quantitative criteria	154
2.2.1.	Related to population in alloted territory	154
2.2.2.	Related to the turnover of the distributor	154
2.2.3.	Stocking requirements	154
3.	Procedure for the authorisation of the dealer	154
3.1.	Objective	154
3.2.	Not related to prices	154
3.2.1.	Non-discriminatory application of the criteria	154
3.2.2.	Refusal to supply	154
3.2.3.	Impeding parallel trade in the framework of a selective distribution	155
F.	Features and clauses common in selective distribution agreements	155
1.	Territorial restrictions	155
1.1.	Exclusivity	155
1.2.	No active sales policy outside agreed territory	155
1.3.	Export bans	155
1.4.	Control of sales by principal	155
2.	Clauses relating to the customer to which the dealer may sell	155
2.1.	Inherent restriction (horizontal sales only to other authorised dealers)	155
2.2.	Separation of wholesale and retail level	155
2.3.	Sales to specific types of customers	155
3.	Clauses relating to the product which is authorised to sell	155
3.1.	Exclusive purchasing obligations imposed on the dealer	156
3.2.	Non-competition clause	156
3.3.	Guarantee and after sales service	156
3.4.	Obligation to sell product in specified packaging	156
3.5.	Obligation not to sell incompatible products	156
4.	Clauses relating to the prices of the contract products	156
4.1.	Effect on prices resulting from selective distribution	156
4.2.	Resale price maintenance	156

4. Agency Agreements

A.	Cases on agency agreements	156
B.	Text of the Commission Notice on agency agreements	156
C.	Cases on the interpretation of the Notice	158

5. Franchising Agreements

A.	Cases on franchising agreements	158
B.	Text of Regulation 4087/88	158
C.	Cases on the interpretation of the Regulation	165
D.	Clauses commonly stipulated in franchising agreements	165

Table of Contents

1.	Clauses relating to the franchise	165
1.1.	Selection of the franchisee	165
1.2.	Non-competition clauses	165
1.2.1.	Obligation not to engage in competing activities during agreement	165
1.2.2.	Post-term non-competition clause	165
1.3.	Best endeavours clause	165
2.	Licences of the know-how or trademarks	165
2.1.	Grant of license	165
2.2.	Royalties	165
2.3.	Field of use restrictions	165
2.4.	Grant back of improvements	165
2.5.	Post-term use ban	165
2.6.	No-challenge clause	165
3.	Clauses promoting the uniformity of the franchise network	165
3.1.	Regarding the decoration of the shop	165
3.2.	Collective advertising provisions	165
3.3.	Business methods	165
3.4.	Guarantees	166
4.	Territorial restrictions	166
4.1.	Fixed location of retail outlet	166
4.2.	Exclusivity in the contract territory	166
4.3.	Obligation not to open a new outlet outside agreed territory	166
5.	Clauses related to the product the franchisee is authorised to sell	166
5.1.	Obligation not to sell competing products in authorised outlet	166
5.2.	Purchase obligations on the franchisee	166
5.2.1.	General	166
5.2.2.	Obligation to purchase goods of defined quality	166
5.2.3.	Exclusive purchasing	166
6.	Clauses relating to the customers the franchisee may serve	166
6.1.	Obligation not to sell outside the network	166
6.2.	Restrictions on the franchisee regarding the customers to which it may sell	166
7.	Recommended prices	166

6. Agreements Preventing Parallel Trade

A.	Cases on agreements preventing parallel trade	166
B.	Clauses or practices which may have the object/effect of preventing parallel trade	167
1.	General sales conditions	167
2.	Circular sent by principal to distributors	167
3.	Pressure exercised by principal distributor	167
4.	Discriminatory trading conditions	167
4.1.	Quality marks	167
4.2.	On grounds of nationality	167
4.3.	State of the product	167

Table of Contents

PART V

INDUSTRIAL AND INTELLECTUAL PROPERTY AGREEMENTS

1. **Articles 30, 36, 59 Free Movement**

A.	Cases	169

2. **Patent Licensing Agreements**

A.	Cases on patent licensing	169
B.	Text of Regulation 2349/84	169
C.	Cases on the interpretation of the Regulation	178
D.	Clauses commonly stipulated in patent licensing agreements	178
1.	Territorial provisions	178
1.1.	Right to use the patent exclusively within an agreed territory	178
1.1.1.	To manufacture the product	178
1.1.2.	To exploit the product	178
1.2.	Obligation not to pursue an active sales policy outside agreed territory	179
1.3.	Obligation not to export outside agreed territory (passive sales)	179
1.3.1.	Between Member States	179
1.3.2.	To third countries	179
1.3.3.	Into the Common Market	179
1.4.	Limitation on site of manufacture	179
2.	Clauses relating to the product that the licensee may sell	179
2.1.	Non-competition clause	179
2.2.	Obligation on licensee to restrict production to fixed maximums	179
2.3.	Quality norms	179
2.4.	Purchase or supply obligations	179
2.4.1.	Exclusive purchasing	179
2.4.2.	Tying	179
2.5.	Trademark related clauses	179
3.	Pricing restrictions on the licensee	179
4.	Restrictions upon the customers which the licensee may serve	179
5.	Clauses relating to the protection afforded to or by the patents	179
5.1.	Field of use restrictions	179
5.2.	Patent no-challenge clause	179
5.3.	Guaranteed rights to any subsequent improvements	180
5.4.	Restrictions on sub-licensing	180
6.	Royalties	180
6.1.	Obligations to pay minimum royalties/produce minimum quantities	180
6.2.	Obligation to pay royalties after expiration or invalidity of the patent	180
6.3.	Most favoured licensee clause	180
6.4.	Obligation to pay royalty even if patent not used	180

Table of Contents

7.	Clauses relating to the duration of the agreement, post-term provisions	180
7.1.	Automatic extension of agreement if additional patents granted	180
7.2.	Post-term use restrictions	180
8.	Patent dispute settlements	180
9.	Patent pooling	180

3. Know-How Licensing Agreements

A.	Cases on know-how Agreements	180
B.	Text of Regulation 556/89	181
C.	Cases on the interpretation of the Regulation	193
D.	Clauses commonly stipulated in know-how agreements	193
1.	Territorial provisions	193
1.1.	Right to use the know-how exclusively within an agreed territory	193
1.1.1.	To manufacture the product	193
1.1.2.	To exploit the know-how	193
1.2.	Obligation not to pursue an active sales policy outside agreed territory	193
1.3.	Obligation not to export outside agreed territory (passive sales)	193
1.3.1.	Between Members States	193
1.3.2	To third countries	193
1.3.3.	Into the EEC	193
1.4.	Grant of an non-exclusive licence outside the exclusive territory	193
2.	Clauses relating to the product which the licensee may sell	194
2.1.	Non-competition clause	194
2.2.	Maximum limits set upon the quantities that the licensee may sell or produce	194
2.3.	Obligation to purchase materials exclusively from the licensor	194
2.4.	Trademark related obligations	194
2.5.	Obligations on the licensee to respect quality norms	194
3.	Pricing restrictions imposed on the licensee	194
4.	Restrictions upon the customers which the licensee may serve	194
5.	Clauses relating to the substance of the licensed know-how	194
5.1.	Requirement that the substantial know-how be fully specified in the agreement	194
5.2.	Field of use restrictions	194
5.3.	Obligation not to contest the secrecy of the know-how/accompanying patents	194
5.4.	Obligation to respect confidentiality	194
5.5.	Guaranteed rights to any subsequent improvements	194
5.6.	Restrictions on sub-licensing	194
5.7.	Best endeavours clause	194
5.8.	Obligation on licensee to inform licensor of any misappropriation of know-how	194
6.	Clauses relating to the royalties paid	194
6.1.	Obligation to pay minimum royalties or produce minimum quantities	195
6.2.	Obligation to pay royalties once know-how is in the public domain	195
6.3.	Most favoured licensee clause	195
7.	Clauses relating to the duration	195

7.1.	Maximum duration of the licence	195
7.2.	Automatic extension of the licence	195
7.3.	Post-term use restrictions	195

4. Trademark Licensing and Cession Agreements

A.	Cases on trademark licensing agreements	195
B.	Cases on trademark assignments	195
C.	Cases on the creation of a joint trademark	195
D.	Trademark delimitation agreements	195
E.	Clauses commonly figuring in trademark licensing or cessation/assignment agreements	195
1.	Territorial restrictions	195
1.1.	Right to use the trademark exclusively within an agreed territory	195
1.2.	Export ban	195
1.3.	Grant of exclusivity gives licensee ability to prevent parallel imports	195
2.	Trademark no-challenge clause	196
3.	Duration of the validity of the trademark	196

5. Copyright and Design Right Agreements

A.	Cases on copyright agreements	196
B.	Cases on design right agreements	196
C.	Clauses typically stipulated under copyright/design right agreements	196
1.	Territorial restrictions	196
1.1.	Exclusivity	196
1.2.	Export bans	196
2.	No-challenge clause	196
3.	Royalties	196
4.	Non-competition restraint of trade clause	196
5.	Improvements	196
6.	Tying	196

6. Breeders' Rights Licensing Agreements

A.	Cases on breeders' rights	196
B.	Clauses commonly figuring in breeders' rights agreements	197
1.	Territorial restrictions	197
1.1.	Exclusivity	197
1.2.	Export ban	197
2.	Non-competition restraint of trade clause	197
3.	Control on prices by licensor	197
4.	No-challenge clause	197
5.	Grant back of improvements	197
6.	Purchasing obligations on licensee	197
7.	Customer limitation clause	197

PART VI

JOINT VENTURES

1. List of cases on joint venture agreements

2. Types of joint venture

1.	Joint R&D	199
2.	Joint buying	199
3.	Joint production	199
4.	Joint sales	200
5.	Co-ordination centres	200

3. Purposes of the co-operation

1.	Market extension	200
2.	Technological progress/transfer of technology	200
3.	Restructuring operations	200
4.	Market sharing	200
5.	Rationalisation of production capacity	200

4. Draft Commission Notice

1.	Guidelines for the appraisal of co-operative joint ventures in the light of Article 85 of the EEC Treaty	200

5. Operations/clauses typical of joint venture agreements

1.	Restrictions of competition which may result from the creation of the joint venture	212
1.1.	Competition between the parent companies	212
1.1.1.	Actual competition	212
1.1.2.	Potential competition	212
1.1.3.	Spill-over effect	212
1.2.	Effect of the joint venture on the competitive position of third parties	212
1.3.	Restriction of future competition resulting from the joint venture agreements	212
1.3.1.	Between parents and the joint venture	212
1.3.2.	Between several joint ventures having a common parent company	212
2.	Ancillary clauses which may restrict competition	212
2.1.	Non-competition clauses	212
2.2.	Co-ordination of investment policy	213
2.3.	Post-termination provisions	213
2.4.	Licensing and exchange of technical information	213
2.5.	Joint price fixing	213
2.6.	Purchasing and supply obligations	213
2.7.	Grant of exclusive distribution rights	213
2.8.	Territorial restrictions	213
2.9.	Trademark-related clauses	213

PART VII

ARTICLE 86

1. The Establishment of a Dominant Position

A.	The relevant market	215
1.	The relevant product market	215
1.1.	Economic analysis of the relevant market	215
1.2.	Narrow definition of the relevant market	215
1.3.	Definition given by defendant	215
1.4.	Time factor and substituability	215
2.	The relevant geographic market	215
B.	A substantial part of the Common Market	215
C.	Dominance	216
1.	The definition of dominance	216
2.	Joint and collective dominance	216
3.	The establishment of dominance	216
3.1.	Statutory dominance or monopoly	216
3.2.	Ownership of intellectual/industrial property rights	216
3.3.	Market shares	216
3.4.	Size or importance of competitors	216
3.5.	Range of products	216
3.6.	Technical advantages over competitors	216
3.7.	Commercial advantages over competitors	216
3.8.	Size and resources of the group	217
3.9.	Dependence of consumers	217
3.10.	Ability to determine prices unilaterally	217
3.11.	Barriers to entry	217
3.11.1.	Statutory	217
3.11.2.	Large capital requirement or technical barriers to entry	217
3.11.3.	Mature/saturated nature of the market	217
3.12.	Circular argument	217

2. Abuse of a Dominant Position

A.	Concept of an abuse of a dominant position	217
B.	Examples of abuses	217
1.	Unfair terms imposed on clients	217
2.	Unfair or excessive prices	217
3.	Exclusive purchasing	218
4.	Exclusive distribution systems	218
5.	Discriminatory pricing	218
6.	Discriminatory conditions between different customers	218
7.	Discrimination on grounds of nationality	218
8.	Discriminatory allocation of products during supply shortages	218

Table of Contents

9.	Predatory pricing	218
10.	Refusal to supply	218
11.	Tying	218
12.	Rebates and discounts	219
13.	Using dominance to move into ancillary markets	219
14.	Actions preventing parallel trade	219
15.	Refusal to disclose technical details of products	219
16.	Abusive registration of a trademark	219
17.	Restricting intra-brand competition	219
18.	Abusive use of intellectual/industrial property rights	219
C.	Objective justification	219

PART VIII

STATE INTERFERENCE

1. Article 90

A.	Text of Article 90	221
B.	Consideration of Article 90	221
1.	Cases on the interpretation of Article 90(1)	221
2.	Article 90(2)	221
2.1.	Direct effect	221
2.2.	Cases on the interpretation of Article 90(2)	221
3.	Article 90(3)	221
4.	Directives applying Article 90	222
4.1.	Text of Directive 88/301	222
4.2.	Cases on Directive 88/301	226
4.3.	Text of Directive 90/388	226
4.4.	Text of Telecommunications Guidelines	234
4.5.	Cases on telecommunications	259
4.6.	References to connected legislation	259

2. State Responsibility

A.	State responsibility under Articles 3f and 5 of the Treaty for facilitating or encouraging behaviour contrary to Articles 85 and 86	260
B.	Governmental silence or approval is no excuse for infringing Articles 85 and 86	260

PART IX

SECTORIAL APPLICATION OF EEC COMPETITION RULES

1. Agriculture

A.	Text of Regulation 26/62	261
B.	Cases regarding agriculture and competition	263
1.	General cases	263
2.	Cases in which Regulation 26/62 was applicable	263
3.	Cases in which Regulation 26/62 was not applicable	263

2. Transport: general

A.	Text of Council Regulation 141/62	263
B.	Cases on the interpretation of the Regulation	264

3. Inland Waterways, Rail and Road Transport

A.	Legislation	264
1.	Text of Council Regulation 1017/68	264
2.	Text of Commission Regulation 1629/69	276
3.	Annex to Commission Regulation 1629/69	277
4.	Text of Commission Regulations 1630/69	289
B.	Cases on the interpretation and application of the Regulations	291

4. Maritime Transport

A.	Legislation	291
1.	Text of Council Regulation 4056/86	291
2.	Text of Commission Regulation 4260/88	302
3.	Annexes to Commission Regulation 4260/88	307
4.	Text of Council Regulation 479/92	312
B.	Cases	314

5. Air Transport

A.	Legislation	315
1.	Text of Council Regulation 3975/87	315
2.	Text of Council Regulation 3976/87	322
3.	Text of Commission Regulation 82/91	325
4.	Text of Commission Regulation 83/91	327
5.	Text of Commission Regulation 84/91	331
6.	Text of Commission Regulation 4261/88	336

Table of Contents

7.	Annexes to Commission Regulation 4261/88	340
8.	References to connected legislation	354
8.1.	Computer reservation systems	354
8.1.1.	Regulation 2299/89	354
8.1.2.	Explanatory note C184/2	354
8.2.	Air fares	354
8.2.1.	Regulation 2342/90	354
8.2.2.	Commission Decision 27th November 1991 L5/26	354
8.3.	Regulation 2343/90	354
9.	Notices	354
9.1.	Notice Article 4 and 5 of Regulation 2671/88	354
9.2.	Notice Article 4(1)(a) of Regulation 2671/88	354
B.	Cases	355

6. Financial Services

A.	Legislation	356
1.	Text of Regulation 1534/91	356
B.	Cases	358
1.	Banking	358
2.	Insurance	359

PART X

PROCEDURE AND REMEDIES

1. Procedural Legislation

A.	Relevant provisions of the Treaty	361
1.	Article 87	361
2.	Cases on the interpretation of Article 87	361
3.	Articles 88–89	361
4.	Cases on the interpretation of Articles 88–89	361
B.	Relevant Legislative Procedures	361
1.	Text of Regulation 17/62	361
2.	Text of Regulation 27/62	369
3.	Annex to Commission Regulation 27/62	371
4.	Text of Regulation 99/63	384
5.	Text of Regulation 2988/74	386

2. The Handling of a Case

A.	The opening of a file	388
1.	Method of notification: what constitutes a valid notification	388
1.1.	When is notification necessary	388

1.2.	Effect of notification	389
1.2.1.	Possibility of the grant of an exemption	389
1.2.2.	Immunity from fines	389
1.2.3.	Provisional validity for old agreements	389
1.3.	Opposition procedures	389
2.	Complaints	389
2.1.	Method of lodging a complaint *locus standi*	389
2.2.	Rights and obligations of complainant	389
3.	Ex-officio investigation	389
B.	The investigation of a case	389
1.	By letter	389
1.1.	Potential addressees of a letter pursuant to Article 11 Regulation 17/62	389
1.2.	Simple request for information	389
1.2.1.	Text of a typical example of a letter sent pursuant to Article 11	389
1.2.2.	Cases	390
1.3.	Request for information by decision	390
2.	By inspection	390
2.1.	Inspectors	390
2.1.1.	National inspectors	390
2.1.2.	Commission inspectors	390
2.2.	Powers of inspectors	390
2.3.	Inspection without decision	390
2.3.1.	Text of typical authorisation to investigate	390
2.3.2.	Text of annex to authorisation to investigate under Article 14(2)	392
2.3.3.	Cases on the interpretation of Article 14(2)	393
2.4.	Inspection with decision	393
2.4.1.	Text of explanatory document accompanying Article 14(3) decision	393
2.4.2.	Cases on the interpretation of Article 14(3)	394
3.	Sectorial investigation	394
4.	Co-operation with national authorities	394
C.	Procedural steps and safeguards	394
1.	In relation to an infringement decision	394
1.1.	Initiation of proceedings	394
1.2.	Statement of objections	394
1.3.	Grant of access to all documents upon which the Commission relies	394
1.4.	Reply to the statement of objections by the parties	395
1.4.1.	In writing	395
1.4.2.	Oral hearing	395
1.4.3.	Text of Commission Decision on the powers of the hearing officer	395
1.4.4.	Role of the Hearing Officer	397
1.4.5.	General considerations on the right to be heard	397
1.5.	Advisory committee	397
2.	Relating to a positive decision	397
2.1.	Publication of Notice	397
2.2.	Advisory committee	397
3.	Relating to a rejection of a complaint	397
4.	General procedural safeguards	397
4.1.	Legal professional privilege	397

4.2.	Obligation of the Commission as to confidentiality	397
4.2.1.	General obligation	397
4.2.2.	Business secrets	397
4.2.3.	Result of disclosure of business secrets or confidential information	397
D.	Informal steps often taken by the Commission	397
1.	Negotiations and modifications of agreements	397
2.	Informal settlement	398
2.1.	Undertakings	398
3.	Comfort letter	398
3.1.	Text of Commission Notices	398
3.1.1.	Text of Notice concerning applications for negative clearance pursuant to Article 2 Regulation 17/62	398
3.1.2.	Text of Notice concerning notification pursuant to Article 4 Regulation 17/62	399
3.2.	Text of a typical comfort letter	400
3.3.	Cases on comfort letters	400
E.	Commission decisions	400
1.	Administrative decisions	400
2.	Provisions decisions	400
2.1.	Removal of immunity from fines	400
2.2.	Interim measures	400
3.	Recommendation	400
4.	Final decisions	400
4.1.	Negative clearance	400
4.2.	Exemption (Article 85(3))	401
4.2.1.	Duration of exemption	401
4.2.2.	Conditions or obligations for exemption	401
4.2.3.	Renewal of exemption	401
4.2.4.	Revocation of exemption	401
4.2.5.	Effect of an exemption	401
4.3.	Prohibition	401
4.3.1.	Order to cease	401
4.3.2.	Order to act	401
4.3.3.	Neutral: obligation of parties to suggest remedy	401
4.3.4.	Date of commencement of prohibition	401
4.3.5.	Effects in time	401
4.4.	Rejection of complaint	401
5.	Formal requirements regarding the form/content of decisions	401
5.1.	Decisions must be reasoned	401
5.2.	Burden of proof	402
5.3.	Must contain only that which figured in the statement of objections	402
5.4.	Obligation to take account of the defendant's views in the decision	402
5.5.	Obligation to respect internal procedural rules	402
F.	Fines and periodic penalty payments	402
1.	Periodic penalty payments	402
2.	Fines for infringement of procedural rules	402
3.	Fines for substantive infringements	402

3.1.	Requirements for the imposition of a fine	402
3.1.1.	Intentional infringement	402
3.1.2.	Negligence	402
4.	Factors taken into account in assessing the level of the fine for substantive infringements	402
4.1.	Gravity of the infringement	402
4.2.	Length of the infringement	403
4.3.	Effect of the infringement	403
4.4.	Extent of culpability	403
4.5.	Non-enforcement of infringement	403
4.6.	Difficult market conditions	403
4.7.	Size and profitability of the undertaking	403
4.8.	Co-operative attitude of the undertaking	403
4.8.1.	Undertakings and modification of agreements at Commission's request	403
4.8.2.	Introduction of a compliance programme	403
4.9.	State of the law	404
4.9.1.	State of legal development	404
4.9.2.	Well-documented infringement	404
4.9.3.	Ignorance of the law, obtaining wrong legal opinion	404
4.9.4.	Repeated infringement	404
4.9.5.	Continuation of infringement following clarification of the law	404
4.10.	Governmental pressure	404
4.11.	Additional profit from infringement	404
4.12.	*Ne bis in idem* (double jeopardy)	404
4.13.	Unco-operative attitude	404
5.	Limitation periods	404

3. Judicial Review

A.	Jurisdiction	405
1.	Text of Article 164	405
2.	Text of Article 172	405
3.	Article 17, Regulation 17/62	405
4.	Competence of the Court of First Instance	405
B.	Types of procedure	405
1.	Article 169	405
1.1.	Text of Article 169	405
1.2.	Cases on the interpretation of Article 169	405
2.	Article 173	405
2.1.	Text of Article 173	405
2.2.	Direct and individual concern	405
2.3.	Challengeable acts	406
2.3.1.	Procedural steps	406
2.3.2.	Interim decisions	406
2.3.3.	Disclosure of confidential information	406
2.3.4.	Rejection of a complaint	406
2.3.5.	Absence of legal effect	406
2.4.	Limitation periods	406
2.5.	Estoppel	406
2.6.	Scope of judicial review	406
3.	Article 175	406
3.1.	Text of Article 175	406

3.2.	Cases on the interpretation of Article 175	406
4.	Article 177	406
4.1.	Text of Article 177	406
4.2.	Cases on the interpretation of Article 177	406
5.	Articles 178, 215	407
5.1.	Text of Articles 178, 215	407
5.2.	Cases on the interpretation of Article 178, 215	407
6.	Interim measures	407
6.1.	Text of Articles 185 and 186	407
6.2.	Cases on the interpretation of Article 186	407
7.	Request of interpretation of court judgment	407

4. National Jurisdication and Authorities

A.	National authorities	407
1.	What is a national authority?	407
2.	Competence	407
3.	Co-operation between the national authorities and the Commission	407
B.	National jurisdictions	407
1.	Direct effect of Articles 85 and 86	407
2.	Conflict rules	408
2.1.	General	408
2.2.	Provisional validity for old agreements	408
3.	Commission desire to encourage national enforcement of Articles 85 and 86	408
4.	Suspension of Commission decision by national court	408
5.	Damages for breach of competition rules	408

5. Conflict Rules

A.	National law	408
1.	Supremacy of EEC competition law over national law in general	408
2.	Supremacy of EEC law over national competition rules	408
3.	National property law	408
4.	National defence interests	408
B.	International law, including European Convention on Human Rights	408

6. International Law

1.	General	408
2.	European Convention on Human Rights	409
2.1.	Selected Articles	409
2.2.	Cases	410
2.2.1.	Community cases	410
2.2.2.	Strasbourg cases	410
3.	Agreements concluded by the Community	410
3.1.	Text of Competition Laws Co-operation Agreement 1991 (EEC-USA)	410

Table of Contents

BOOK TWO: MERGERS AND ACQUISITIONS

Lists and Tables

1. Table Chronological List of Merger Decisions (EEC)—References	421
2. Table Chronological List of Merger Decisions (EEC)—Contents	424
3. Table Chronological List of Relevant Commission Decisions (Articles 85 and 86) (EEC)—References	427
4. Table Chronological List of Relevant Court of First Instance Judgments (Articles 85 and 86) (EEC)—References	429
5. Table Chronological List of European Court Judgments (Articles 85 and 86) (EEC)—References	430
6. Table Alphabetical List of Merger Decisions	431

1. Legislation 433

1.	Text of Council Regulation 4064/89	433
2.	Text of Commission Regulation 2367/90	446
3.	Form CO, Annex to Commission Regulation No. 2367/90	451
4.	Text of Commission Notice regarding concentrative and co-operative operations	469
5.	Text of Commission Notice regarding restrictions ancillary to concentration	475
6.	Text of Notes on the Council and Commission on Council Regulation (EEC) No. 4064/89	480

2. Jurisdiction: cases and references

A.	Concentration	483
1.	Definition of the term "concentration" (control)	483
2.	Specific types of concentrations	483
2.1.	Acquisition of sole control	483
2.2.	Acquisition/creation of joint control	483
2.3.	Purchase of option	483
2.4.	Passage from joint to sole control	483
2.5.	Break-up of a company	483
B.	Community Dimension	483
1.	Calculation of turnover	483
2.	Companies taken into account in calculation: definition of "control" for purposes of turnover calculation	483
3.	Specific cases	483
3.1.	Joint ventures	483
3.2.	Acquisition of part of an undertaking	483

xlii

3.3.	Banks and other financial institutions		483
3.4.	Insurance companies		483
3.5.	Airlines		483
C.	Concentration *v.* Co-operation: partial mergers		483
1.	List of relevant cases		483
2.	Autonomous economic entity		484
2.1.	Full function JV		484
2.2.	Own commercial policy		484
2.3.	Permanent structural change		484
3.	No co-ordination of competitive behaviour		484
3.1.	Actual competition		484
3.2.	Potential competition between parents		484
3.3.	Neighbouring market spill-over		484
3.4.	Upstream/downstream market spill-over		484
3.5.	Competition between parents and the JV		484
D.	Residual applicability of Articles 85 and 86		484
1.	Do Articles 85 and 86 still apply to concentrations?		484
2.	List of cases relevant to Article 85(1)		484
3.	List of cases relevant to Article 86		485
E.	Article 9: Referral to a Member State		485
1.	Concept		485
2.	Accepted requests		485
3.	Rejected requests		485
4.	Cases in which request received and proceedings opened		485
F.	Article 22(3): referral to the Commission		485
G.	Legitimate interests		485

3. Substantive Issues: cases and references

A.	Relevant market		485
1.	Relevant product market		485
1.1.	Definition of the term "relevant product market"		485
1.2.	Relevant factors		485
1.2.1.	Physical characteristics/end use		485
1.2.2.	Price		485
1.2.3.	Consumer preference		486
1.2.4.	Supply-side substitutability/potential competition		486
1.2.5.	Industry product classifications		486
1.2.6.	Relevant evidence		486
1.2.6.1.	Consumer surveys		486
1.2.6.2.	"Conditions of competition"		486
1.2.6.3.	Historical evidence on cross-elasticity		486
2.	Relevant geographic market		486
2.1.	Definition of the term "relevant geographic market"		486
2.2.	Relevant factors		486
2.2.1.	Regulatory trade barriers		486
2.2.2.	Local specification requirements		486

Table of Contents

2.2.3.	National procurement policies	486
2.2.4.	Adequate distribution facilities	486
2.2.5.	Transport costs	486
2.2.6.	Language	486
2.2.7.	Consumer preferences	486
2.3.	Relevant evidence	486
2.3.1.	Price difference between neighbouring areas	486
2.3.2.	Market shared differences between neighbouring areas	486
2.3.3.	Homogeneous conditions of competition	486
2.4.	Examples of local markets	487
2.5.	Examples of regional markets	487
2.6.	Examples of national markets	487
2.7.	Examples of Community markets	487
2.8.	Examples of world markets	487
B.	Dominance	487
1.	Definition of the term "dominance"	487
2.	Relevant factors	487
2.1.	Market share	487
2.2.	Size and importance of competitors	487
2.3.	Commercial advantages over competitors (product range)	487
2.4.	Technical advantages over competitors	487
2.5.	Statutory dominance or monopoly	487
2.6.	Supply-side substitutability: entry barriers	487
2.6.1.	Basic concept	488
2.6.2.	Regulatory barriers	488
2.6.3.	Risk	488
2.7.	Imperfect substitutes	488
2.8.	Buying power	488
2.9.	Stage of market development	488
2.10.	Capitals requirements	488
3.	Vertical Mergers	488
4.	Conglomerate mergers	488
C.	Significant impediment of competition	488
D.	Efficiency defence	488
E.	Failing-form defence	488
F.	Oligopolistic or joint dominance	488
G.	Ancillary Restraints	488
1.	Trademark licences	488
2.	Patent/know-how licences	488
3.	Product/service supply agreement	488
4.	Non-competition clause	488

Table of Contents

4. Procedural aspects

1.	Pre-notification guidance	489
2.	Notification	489
3.	Suspension	489
4.	Fact finding	489
5.	Opening of proceedings	489
6.	Rights of defense and complainants	489
7.	Role of the Member States	489
8.	Time limits	489
9.	Types of decisions available to the Commission	489
10.	Amendments to concentration to get clearance/undertakings	489
10.1.	1st stage	489
10.2.	2nd stage	489

Table of Contents

BOOK THREE: COAL AND STEEL

Lists and Tables

1. Chronological List of ECSC Legislation	495
2. Chronological List of Commission Decisions (ECSC)—References	496
3. Chronological List of Commission Decisions (ECSC)—Contents	500
4. Chronological List of European Court Judgments (ECSC)—References	504
5. Chronological List of European Court Judgments (ECSC)—Contents ..	505
6. Alphabetical List of Commission Decisions (ECSC)	506
7. Alphabetical List of European Court Judgments (ECSC)	507

1. Restrictive Practices

A.		Text of Article 65 ECSC	509
B.		Form of practice within the ambit of the Treaty	510
	1.	Binding agreements	510
	2.	Recommendations	510
	3.	Concerted practices	510
	4.	Declarations of intent	510
	5.	Associations of undertakings	510
C.		Prohibited practices	510
	1.	Text of Communication on co-operation (French text)	510
	1.1.	Agreements fixing or determining prices	514
	1.2.	Uniform pricing method/joint prices	514
	1.3.	Circulation of price lists	514
	1.4.	Uniform discounts	515
	1.5.	Setting maximum prices	515
	1.6.	Most favoured customer clause	515
	1.7.	Mutually co-ordinated prices	515
	1.8.	Common point based transport tariff	515
	1.9.	Purchase quotas	515
	1.10.	Information on producer prices	515
	1.11.	Price equalisation system	515
	1.12.	Equalisation system in event of market change	515
	2.	Restricting or controlling production, technical development or investment	515
	2.1.	Agreement to stop/prohibit production	515
	2.2.	Co-ordination of production	515
	2.3.	Co-ordination of investment	515
	2.4.	Purchase of shareholding	515
	3.	Sharing markets, products, customers or sources of supply	515
	3.1.	Joint buying agreements	515
	3.2.	Agreements to refrain from buying	516

3.3.	Joint selling agreements	516
3.4.	Agreements to refrain from selling/market partitioning	516
3.5.	Exclusive purchasing/selling agreements	516
3.6.	Product/know-how exchange agreements	516
3.7.	Direct sales obligation	516
3.8.	Joint production	516
3.9.	Allocation system in times of shortage	516
3.10.	Co-ordination of transport	516
3.11.	New undertaking joining cartel	516
D.	Void agreements	516
E.	Authorisation of agreements	516
1.	Specialisation agreements	516
2.	Joint buying agreements	516
3.	Joint selling agreements	517
4.	Formation of a jointly held undertaking	517
5.	Factors considered in assessing these agreements	517
5.1.	Improvement in production or distribution	517
5.1.1.	Efficient allocation of production	517
5.1.2.	Avoid duplication of investment	517
5.1.3.	Reduce overcapacity	517
5.1.4.	Adjustment to structural decline	517
5.1.5.	Injection of capital	517
5.1.6.	Reduce overheads	517
5.1.7.	Ensure continuity of supply	517
5.1.8.	Existence of Community crisis measures	517
5.1.9.	Non-exclusive agreement	518
5.2.	Agreements essential and no more restrictive than necessary	518
5.3.	Power to determine prices, or control or restrict production or marketing	518
5.3.1.	Relevant market: whole Community	518
5.3.2.	Relevant market: whole or part of Member State	518
5.3.3.	Competition from outside Community	518
5.3.4.	Competition from alternative products	518
5.3.5.	*De minimis*/small market share	518
5.3.6.	Group effect	518
5.3.7.	Cumulative effect of agreements with other undertakings	518
5.3.8.	Independence of the parties maintained	518

2. Concentrations

A.	Text of Article 66 ECSC	519
B.	Concentrations subject to prior authorisation	521
1.	Decisions applying Decision No. 24–25	521
1.1.	Acquisitions of under 25 per cent. of share capital	521
1.2.	Acquisitions of over 25 per cent. but under 50 per cent. share capital	521
1.3.	Acquisitions of over 50 per cent. of share capital	521
1.4.	Creation of jointly held undertaking	521
1.5.	Contested or hostile bids	521
1.6.	Acquisition by the State	521
C.	Conditions for authorisation	521

Table of Contents

1.	Power to determine prices	521
2.	Power to control or restrict production or distribution	522
3.	Power to hinder effective competition	522
4.	Establishing an artificially privileged position	522
D.	Analysis of the market	522
1.	Relevant geographical market: whole of Common Market	522
2.	Relevant geographical market: Member State	522
3.	Competition from third countries	522
4.	Competition from substitute products	522
5.	Small market share	522
6.	Compatibility with EEC rules on competition	522
E.	Exemption by category	522
1.	Text of Article 66(3)	522
1.1.	Text of Decision No. 25–67	522
F.	Dominant position	527

3. State Behaviour

1.	Article 67	527

4. Procedure

A.	Control by Commission	527
1.	Exclusive control of Article 65	527
2.	Exclusive power in concentrations	527
B.	Obtaining information	527
1.	In general	527
2.	For the purpose of Article 65	528
3.	For the purpose of Article 66	528
C.	Rights of the defence	528
D.	Secrecy	528
E.	Notification	528
1.	Notification of agreements under Article 65	528
2.	Notification of concentrations	528
2.1.	Obligatory notification	528
2.2.	Failure to notify	528
2.2.1.	Authorisation withheld	528
2.2.2.	Authorisation with fine for failure to notify	528
2.3.	Effects of notification	528
F.	Decisions taken by the Commission	528
1.	Decisions pursuant to Article 65	528
1.1.	Authorisation	528
1.1.1.	Conditional authorisation	528

Table of Contents

1.1.2.	Conditions aiming to prevent discrimination between trading partners	528
1.1.3.	Conditions preventing cross directorships or management	528
1.1.4.	Other conditions to safeguard competition	528
1.1.5.	Authorisation conditional upon existence of crisis measures	529
1.1.6.	Conditions requiring submission of information	529
1.1.7.	Temporary authorisation	529
1.1.8.	Revocation of authorisation	529
1.2.	Prohibition	529
1.3.	Fines	529
1.4.	Limitation periods	529
2.	Decisions pursuant to Article 66	529
2.1.	Authorisation	529
2.1.1.	Conditional authorisation	529
2.1.2.	Conditions aiming to prevent discrimination between trading partners	529
2.1.3.	Conditions preventing cross directorships or management	529
2.1.4.	Other conditions to safeguard competition	529
2.1.5.	Conditions requiring submission of information	529
2.1.6.	Authorisation with fines for failure to notify	529
2.2.	Prohibition	529
2.2.1.	Interim order	529
2.2.2.	Divestiture order	529
2.2.3.	Exccutory measures	530
2.3.	Periodic penalty payments	530
2.4.	Fines	530
G.	Challenging decisions before the Court of Justice	530
1.	Exercise of control by the Court	530
1.1.	In general	530
1.2.	In cases of concentrations	530
2.	Time limits	530
3.	Interim measures	530
4.	Suspensory effect	530
4.1.	In general	530
4.2.	In cases of interim measures	530
EEC Treaty Articles		533
List of Staff at DG IV		539
Glossary		541
Bibliography		547
Index		581

BOOK ONE

GENERAL COMPETITION RULES

(*see* Book Two for Mergers and Acquisitions
and Book Three for Coal and Steel)

BOOK ONE—CONTENTS

Lists and Tables

Table 1:	Chronological List of Commission Decisions (EEC)—References	5
Table 2:	Chronological List of Commission Decisions (EEC)—Contents	15
Table 3:	Chronological List of Court of First Instance Judgments (EEC)—References	27
Table 4:	Chronological List of Court of First Instance Judgments (EEC)—Contents	29
Table 5:	Chronological List of European Court Judgments (EEC)—References	31
Table 6:	Chronological List of European Court Judgments (EEC)—Contents	38
Table 7:	Alphabetical List of Commission Decisions	44
Table 8:	Alphabetical List of Court of First Instance Judgments	48
Table 9:	Alphabetical List of European Court Judgments	49
Table 10:	Fines	52
Table 11:	List of Legislation and Documents	62
Part I:	Conditions for the application of both Articles 85 and 86	71
Part II:	Article 85(1), (2) and (3)	75
Part III:	Horizontal Agreements	89
Part IV:	Vertical Agreements	119
Part V:	Industrial and Intellectual Property Agreements	169
Part VI:	Joint Ventures	199
Part VII:	Article 86	215
Part VIII:	State Interference	221
Part IX:	Sectorial Application of EEC Competition Rules	261
Part X:	Procedure and Remedies	361

TABLE 1
CHRONOLOGICAL LIST OF COMMISSION DECISIONS (EEC)—REFERENCES

No.	NAME	DATE	O.J.[1]	C.M.L.R.[2]	C.C.H.[3]
1.	Grosfillex/Fillestorf	11.3.64	J.O. 915/64	[1964] 237	—
2.	Convention Faience	13.5.64	J.O. 1167/64	—	—
3.	Bendix/Mertens and Straet	1.6.64	J.O. 1426/64	[1964] 416	—
4.	Nicholas Frères Vitapro	30.7.64	J.O. 2287/64	[1964] 505	—
5.	Grundig/Consten	23.9.64	J.O. 2545/64	[1964] 489	—
6.	DECA	22.10.64	J.O. 2761/64	[1965] 50	—
7.	DRU/Blondel	8.7.65	J.O. 2194/65	[1965] 182	—
8.	Hummel/Isbecque	17.9.65	J.O. 2581/65	[1965] 242	—
9.	Maison Jallatte	17.12.65	J.O. 37/66	[1966] D1	—
10.	Transocean Marine Paint Association I	27.6.67	J.O. 10/67	[1967] D9	—
11.	Eurogypsum	26.2.68	[1968] L57/9	[1968] D1	—
12.	Alliance des Constructeurs Français	17.7.68	[1968] L201/1	[1968] D23	—
13.	Socemas	17.7.68	[1968] L201/4	[1968] D28	—
14.	ACEC/Berliet	17.7.68	[1968] L201/7	[1968] D35	—
15.	Cobelaz	6.11.68	[1968] L276/13	[1968] D45	—
16.	Cobelaz Cokes	6.11.68	[1968] L276/19	[1968] D68	—
17.	Rieckerman	6.11.68	[1968] L276/25	[1968] D78	—
18.	CFA	6.11.68	[1968] L276/29	[1968] D57	—
19.	EMO I	13.3.69	[1969] L69/13	[1969] D1	—
20.	Chaufourniers	5.5.69	[1969] L122/8	[1969] D15	—
21.	Christiani & Nielsen	18.6.69	[1969] L165/12	[1969] D36	—
22.	VVVF	25.6.69	[1969] L168/22	[1969] D1	—
23.	SEIFA	30.6.69	[1969] L173/8	—	—

[1] Official Journal of the European Communities.
[2] Common Market Law Reports.
[3] Commerce Clearing House.

Book One—Table 1

No.	NAME	DATE	O.J.		C.M.L.R.		C.C.H.
24.	Quinine Cartel	16.7.69	[1969]	L192/5	[1969]	D41	—
25.	Clima Chappée	22.7.69	[1969]	L195/1	[1970]	D7	—
26.	Jaz/Peter I	22.7.69	[1969]	L195/5	[1970]	D129	—
27.	Dyestuffs	24.7.69	[1969]	L195/11	[1969]	D23	—
28.	Pirelli/Dunlop	5.12.69	[1969]	L242/41			9336
29.	Kodak	30.6.70	[1970]	L147/24	[1970]	D19	9378
30.	ASPA	30.6.70	[1970]	L148/9	[1970]	D25	9379
31.	ASBL	29.6.70	[1970]	L153/14	[1970]	D31	9380
32.	Julien/Van Katwijk	28.10.70	[1970]	L242/18	[1970]	D43	9395
33.	Omega	28.10.70	[1970]	L242/22	[1970]	D49	9396
34.	Supexie	23.12.70	[1970]	L10/12	[1971]	D1	9408
35.	Ceramic Tiles	29.12.70	[1970]	L10/15	[1971]	D6	9409
36.	CICG	1.2.71	[1971]	L34/13	[1971]	D23	9416
37.	FN/CF	28.5.71	[1971]	L134/6			9439
38.	Gema I	2.6.71	[1971]	L134/15	[1971]	D35	9438
39.	Alba	18.6.71	[1971]	L161/2			9444
40.	Union des Brasseries	18.6.71	[1971]	L161/6			9444
41.	Maes	18.6.71	[1971]	L161/10			9445
42.	Asphaltoïd/Keller	2.7.71	[1971]	L161/32			9460
43.	Cematex I	24.9.71	[1971]	L227/26	[1973]	D135	9474
44.	SIAE	9.11.71	[1971]	L254/15	[1972]	D112	9484
45.	Boehringer	25.11.71	[1971]	L282/46	[1972]	D121	9481
46.	Continental Can	9.12.71	[1971]	L7/25	[1972]	D11	9492
47.	VCH	16.12.71	[1971]	L13/34			9487
48.	SAFCO	16.12.71	[1971]	L13/44	[1972]	D83	9488
49.	SOPELEM/Langen	20.12.71	[1971]	L13/47	[1972]	D77	9485
50.	Burroughs/Delplanque	22.12.71	[1971]	L13/50	[1972]	D67	9484
51.	Burroughs/Geha	22.12.71	[1971]	L13/53	[1972]	D72	9486
52.	Henkel/Colgate	23.12.71	[1971]	L14/14			9491
53.	NCH	23.12.71	[1971]	L22/16	[1973]	D257	9493
54.	MAN/SAVIEM	17.1.72	[1972]	L31/29	[1974]	2D123	9494
55.	Wild/Leitz	23.2.72	[1972]	L61/27	[1972]	D36	9496
56.	Davidson Rubber	9.6.72	[1972]	L143/31	[1972]	D52	9512
57.	Raymond/Nagoya	9.6.72	[1972]	L143/39	[1972]	D45	9513
58.	Gema II	6.7.72	[1972]	L166/22	[1972]	D94	9521
59.	Thin Paper	26.7.72	[1972]	L182/24	[1972]	D94	9523
60.	Central Heating	20.10.72	[1972]	L264/22	[1972]	D130	9535

Chronological List of Commission Decisions (EEC)—References

No.	NAME	DATE	O.J.	C.M.L.R.			C.C.H.
61.	Rodenstock	28.9.72	L267/17		[1973]	D40	9536
62.	Misal	28.9.72	L267/20		[1973]	D37	9536
63.	Pittsburgh Corning	23.11.72	L272/35		[1973]	D2	9539
64.	Zoja/CSC-ICI	14.12.72	L299/51		[1973]	D50	9543
65.	Dutch Cement	18.12.72	L303/7		[1973]	D149	9543A
66.	Cimbel	22.12.72	L303/24		[1973]	D167	9544
67.	GISA	22.12.72	L303/45		[1973]	D125	9545
68.	WEA/Filipacchi Music S.A.	22.12.72	L303/52		[1973]	D43	9545A
69.	European Sugar Industry	2.1.73	L140/17		[1973]	D65	9570
70.	SCPA/Kali & Salz	11.5.73	L217/3		[1973]	D219	9569
71.	Dupont de Nemours Germany	14.6.73	L194/27		[1973]	D226	9578
72.	Heaters and Boilers	3.7.73	L217/34		[1973]	D231	9587
73.	Deutsche Philips	5.10.73	L293/40		[1973]	D241	9606
74.	Prym/Beka	8.10.73	L296/24		[1973]	D250	9609
75.	Transocean Marine Paint Association II	21.12.73	L19/18	1	[1974]	D11	9628
76.	Kali & Salz/Kalichemie	21.12.73	L19/22	1	[1974]	D1	9627
77.	IFTRA Glass	15.5.74	L160/1	2	[1974]	D50	9658
78.	Belgian Wallpaper	23.7.74	L237/3	2	[1974]	D102	9668
79.	Advocaat Zwarte Kip	24.7.74	L237/12	2	[1974]	D79	9672
80.	FRUBO	25.7.74	L237/16	2	[1974]	D89	9673
81.	Franco Japanese Ball Bearings	29.11.74	L343/19	1	[1974]	D8	9697
82.	BMW	13.12.74	L29/1	1	[1974]	D44	9701
83.	DuroDyne	19.12.74	L29/11	1	[1975]	D62	9708A
84.	General Motors	19.12.74	L29/14	1	[1975]	D20	9705
85.	Goodyear Italiana/Euram	19.12.74	L38/10	1	[1975]	D31	9708
86.	Rank/SOPELEM	20.12.74	L29/20	1	[1975]	D72	9707
87.	SHV/Chevron	20.12.74	L38/14	1	[1975]	D68	9709
88.	Tinned Mushrooms	8.1.75	L29/27	1	[1975]	D83	9710
89.	Sirdar/Phildar	5.3.75	L125/27	1	[1975]	D93	9741
90.	Fireplaces	3.6.75	L159/17	2	[1975]	D1	9753
91.	Intergroup	14.7.75	L212/23	2	[1975]	D14	9759
92.	IFTRA Aluminium	15.7.75	L228/32	2	[1975]	D20	9769
93.	UNIDI I	17.7.75	L228/17	2	[1975]	D51	9760
94.	Kabelmetal/Luchaire	18.7.75	L222/34	2	[1975]	D40	9761
95.	Bronbemaling	25.7.75	L249/27	2	[1975]	D67	9776
96.	Transocean Marine Paint Association III	23.10.75	L286/27	2	[1975]	D75	9783
97.	Bomée-Stichting	21.11.75	L329/30	1	[1976]	D1	9792

Book One—Table 1

No.	NAME	DATE	O.J.	C.M.L.R.	C.C.H.
98.	AOIP/Beyrard	2.12.75	[1975] L6/8	1 [1976] D14	9801
99.	SABA I	15.12.75	[1975] L28/19	1 [1976] D61	9802
100.	Bayer/Gist-Brocades	15.12.75	[1976] L30/13	1 [1976] D98	9808
101.	Chiquita	17.12.75	[1975] L95/1	1 [1976] D28	9800
102.	United Reprocessors	23.12.75	[1975] L51/7	2 [1976] D1	9807
103.	KEWA	23.12.75	[1975] L51/15	2 [1976] D15	9807
104.	Vitamins	9.6.76	[1976] L223/27	2 [1976] D25	9853
105.	CSV	25.6.76	[1976] L192/27	—	9859
106.	Pabst & Richarz/BNIA	26.7.76	[1976] L231/24	2 [1976] D63	9863
107.	Reuter/BASF	26.7.76	[1976] L254/40	2 [1976] D44	9862
108.	Miller	1.12.76	[1976] L357/40	1 [1977] D61	9901
109.	Junghans	21.12.76	[1976] L30/10	1 [1977] D82	9912
110.	Theal/Watts	21.12.76	[1976] L39/19	1 [1977] D44	9913
111.	Gerofabriek	22.12.76	[1976] L16/1618	1 [1977] D35	9914
112.	Vacuum Interrupters I	20.1.77	[1977] L48/32	2 [1977] D67	9926
113.	ABG/Oil Companies	19.4.77	[1977] L117/1	1 [1977] D1	9944
114.	DeLaval/Stork I	25.7.77	[1977] L215/11	2 [1977] D69	9972
115.	Cobelpa/VNP	8.9.77	[1977] L242/10	2 [1977] D28	9980
116.	BPICA I	7.11.77	[1977] L299/18	2 [1977] D43	9995
117.	GEC/Weir Sodium Circulators	23.11.77	[1977] L327/26	2 [1978] D42	10 000
118.	Centraal Bureau voor de Rijwielhandel	2.12.77	[1977] L20/18	1 [1978] 198	10 009
119.	Cauliflowers	2.12.77	[1977] L21/23	2 [1978] D66	10 005
120.	German Blacksmiths	8.12.77	[1977] L10/32	1 [1978] 126	10 004
121.	Hugin/Liptons	8.12.77	[1977] L22/23	1 [1978] D63	10 007
122.	Video Cassette Recorders	20.12.77	[1977] L47/42	2 [1978] D19	10 015
123.	The Distillers Company	20.12.77	[1977] L50/16	1 [1978] 160	10 011
124.	Spices	21.12.77	[1977] L53/20	2 [1978] 400	10 017
125.	SOPELEM/Vickers I	21.12.77	[1977] L70/47	2 [1978] 116	10 014
126.	BMW Belgium	23.12.77	[1977] L46/33	2 [1978] 146	10 008
127.	Penney	23.12.77	[1977] L60/19	2 [1978] 100	10 032
128.	Jaz/Peter II	23.12.77	[1977] L61/67	2 [1978] 186	10 013
129.	Vegetable Parchment	23.12.77	[1977] L70/54	1 [1978] 534	10 016
130.	Campari	23.12.77	[1977] L70/69	2 [1978] 397	10 035
131.	RAI/Unitel	26.5.78	[1978] L157/39	3 [1978] 306	10 009
132.	SNPE/LEL	12.6.78	[1978] L191/41	2 [1978] 758	10 064
133.	FEDETAB	20.7.78	[1978] L224/29	3 [1978] 524	10 070
134.	CSV	20.7.78	[1978] L242/15	1 [1978] 11	10 076

Chronological List of Commission Decisions (EEC)—References

No.	NAME	DATE	O.J.	C.M.L.R.	C.C.H.
135.	Arthur Bell & Sons Ltd	28.7.78	[1978] L235/15	3 [1978] 298	10 074
136.	Teacher & Sons	28.7.78	[1978] L235/20	3 [1978] 298	10 075
137.	Maize Seeds	21.9.78	[1978] L286/23	3 [1978] 434	10 083
138.	WANO	20.10.78	[1978] L322/26	1 [1979] 403	10 089
139.	Zanussi	23.10.78	[1978] L322/36	1 [1979] 81	10 090
140.	EMO II	12.12.78	[1978] L11/16	1 [1979] 419	10 098
141.	Kawasaki	12.12.78	[1978] L16/9	1 [1979] 448	10 097
142.	White Lead	12.12.78	[1978] L21/16	1 [1979] 464	10 111
143.	Vaessen/Moris	10.01.79	[1979] L19/32	1 [1979] 511	10 107
144.	Beecham/Parke Davis	17.1.79	[1979] L70/11	2 [1979] 157	10 121
145.	Fides	31.1.79	[1979] L57/33	1 [1979] 650	10 119
146.	AM & S Europe	6.7.79	[1979] L199/31	3 [1979] 376	10 153
147.	BP Kemi/DDSF	5.9.79	[1979] L286/32	3 [1979] 684	10 165
148.	Floral	28.11.79	[1979] L39/51	2 [1980] 285	10 184
149.	Rennet	5.12.79	[1979] L51/19	2 [1980] 402	10 188
150.	Cane sugar Supply Agreements	7.12.79	[1979] L39/64	2 [1980] 559	10 183
151.	Transocean Marine Paint Association IV	12.12.79	[1979] L39/73	1 [1980] 694	10 186
152.	Pioneer	14.12.79	[1979] L60/21	1 [1980] 457	10 185
153.	Fabbrica Pisana	20.12.79	[1979] L75/30	2 [1980] 354	10 209
154.	Fabbrica Lastre	20.12.79	[1979] L75/35	2 [1980] 362	10 209
155.	Krups	17.4.80	[1980] L120/26	3 [1980] 374	10 223
156.	National Sulphuric Acid Association I	9.7.80	[1980] L260/24	3 [1980] 429	10 246
157.	Distillers-Victuallers	22.7.80	[1980] L233/43	3 [1980] 244	10 253
158.	IMA Rules	18.9.80	[1980] L318/1	2 [1981] 498	10 264
159.	Natursteinplatten	16.10.80	[1980] L318/32	2 [1981] 308	10 268
160.	Johnson & Johnson	25.11.80	[1980] L377/16	2 [1981] 287	10 277
161.	Vacuum Interrupters II	11.12.80	[1980] L383/1	2 [1981] 217	10 296
162.	Hennessy/Henkell	11.12.80	[1980] L383/11	1 [1981] 601	10 283
163.	Italian Cast Glass	17.12.80	[1980] L383/19	2 [1982] 61	10 285
164.	Italian Flat Glass	28.9.81	[1981] L326/32	3 [1982] 366	10 338
165.	Michelin	7.10.81	[1981] L353/33	1 [1982] 643	10 340
166.	GVL	29.10.81	[1981] L370/49	1 [1982] 223	10 345
167.	Comptoir d'Importation	17.11.81	[1981] L27/31	1 [1982] 440	10 348
168.	Langenscheidt/Hachette	17.11.81	[1981] L39/25	1 [1982] 181	10 350
169.	VBBB/VBVB	25.11.81	[1981] L54/36	2 [1982] 344	10 351
170.	Telos	25.11.81	[1981] L58/19	1 [1982] 267	10 356
171.	SOPELEM/Vickers II	26.11.81	[1981] L391/1	3 [1982] 443	10 393

Book One—Table 1

No.	NAME	DATE	O.J.	C.M.L.R.	C.C.H.
172.	Moët et Chandon (London) Ltd.	27.11.81	[1981] L94/7	2 [1982] 66	10 352
173.	Hasselblad	2.12.81	[1981] L161/18	2 [1982] 233	10 356
174.	Gema Statutes	4.12.81	[1981] L94/22	2 [1982] 482	10 357
175.	Fire Insurance	9.12.81	[1981] L80/36	2 [1982] 159	10 381
176.	National Panasonic (Belgium)	11.12.81	[1981] L113/3	2 [1982] 410	10 365
177.	National Panasonic (France)	11.12.81	[1981] L211/32	3 [1982] 623	10 409
178.	NAVEWA-ANSEAU	17.12.81	[1981] L167/17	2 [1982] 193	10 368
179.	AEG-Telefunken	6.1.82	[1982] L117/15	2 [1982] 386	10 366
180.	BPICA II	30.4.82	[1982] L156/16	2 [1983] 40	10 402
181.	SSI	15.7.82	[1982] L232/1	2 [1982] 702	10 408
182.	Ford Werke-Interim Measures	18.8.82	[1982] L256/20	3 [1982] 267	10 419
183.	Fédération Chaussure de France	27.10.82	[1982] L319/12	1 [1983] 575	10 435
184.	Amersham Buchler	29.10.82	[1982] L314/34	1 [1983] 619	10 431
185.	NAVEWA-ANSEAU (Bosch)	4.11.82	[1982] L325/20	1 [1983] 470	10 564
186.	National Panasonic	7.12.82	[1982] L354/28	1 [1983] 497	10 441
187.	Cafeteros de Colombia	10.12.82	[1982] L360/31	1 [1983] 703	10 448
188.	British Telecommunications	10.12.82	[1982] L360/36	1 [1983] 457	10 443
189.	Zinc	14.12.82	[1982] L362/40	2 [1983] 285	10 447
190.	AROW/BNIC	15.12.82	[1982] L379/1	2 [1983] 240	10 458
191.	Toltecs/Dorcet	15.12.82	[1982] L379/19	1 [1983] 412	10 459
192.	Castrol	10.1.83	[1983] L114/26	3 [1983] 165	10 484
193.	Cematex II	24.5.83	[1983] L140/27	1 [1983] 234	10 491
194.	Windsurfing International	11.7.83	[1983] L229/1	1 [1984] 1	10 515
195.	Vimpoltu	13.7.83	[1983] L200/44	3 [1983] 619	10 504
196.	Rockwell/IVECO	13.7.83	[1983] L224/19	3 [1983] 709	10 509
197.	ECS/AKZO-Interim Measures	29.7.83	[1983] L252/13	3 [1983] 694	10 517
198.	Cast-iron & Steel Rolls	17.10.83	[1983] L317/1	1 [1984] 694	10 543
199.	Ford Werke AG	16.11.83	[1983] L327/31	1 [1984] 596	10 539
200.	Murat	5.12.83	[1983] L348/20	1 [1984] 219	10 544
201.	SMM&T	5.12.83	[1983] L376/1	1 [1984] 611	10 552
202.	IPTC Belgium	5.12.83	[1983] L376/7	2 [1984] 131	10 564
203.	VW/MAN	5.12.83	[1983] L376/11	1 [1984] 621	10 551
204.	Schlegel/CPIO	6.12.83	[1983] L351/20	2 [1984] 179	10 545
205.	Carbon Gas Technologie	8.12.83	[1983] L376/17	2 [1985] 275	10 562
206.	Nutricia	12.12.83	[1983] L376/22	2 [1984] 165	10 567
207.	International Energy Agency	12.12.83	[1983] L376/30	2 [1984] 186	10 563
208.	SABA II	21.12.83	[1983] L376/41	2 [1984] 676	10 568

Chronological List of Commission Decisions (EEC)—References

No.	NAME	DATE	O.J.	C.M.L.R.	C.C.H.
209.	Nuovo-CEGAM	30.3.84	L99/29	2 [1984] 484	10 584
210.	IBM PC	18.4.84	L118/24	2 [1984] 342	10 585
211.	Polistil/Arbois	16.5.84	L136/9	2 [1984] 594	10 587
212.	British Leyland	2.7.84	L207/11	3 [1984] 92	10 601
213.	Synthetic Fibres	4.7.84	L207/17	1 [1985] 787	10 606
214.	Carlsberg	12.7.84	L207/26	1 [1985] 735	10 607
215.	BPCL/ICI	19.7.84	L212/1	1 [1985] 330	10 611
216.	Flat Glass (Benelux)	23.7.84	L212/13	2 [1985] 350	10 612
217.	Zinc Producer Group	6.8.84	L220/27	2 [1985] 108	10 617
218.	Peroxide Products	23.11.84	L35/1	1 [1985] 481	10 645
219.	UNIDI II	23.11.84	L322/10	2 [1985] 38	10 642
220.	Fire Insurance	5.12.84	L35/20	3 [1985] 246	10 653
221.	Milchfoerderungsfonds	7.12.84	L35/35	3 [1985] 101	10 649
222.	Grohe Sales System	10.12.84	L19/17	4 [1988] 612	10 661
223.	Ideal Standard Sales System	10.12.84	L20/38	4 [1988] 627	10 662
224.	Uniform Eurochèques	10.12.84	L35/43	3 [1985] 434	10 651
225.	Mecaniver/PPG	12.12.84	L35/54	3 [1985] 359	10 650
226.	John Deere	14.12.84	L35/58	2 [1985] 554	10 652
227.	Woodpulp	19.12.84	L85/1	3 [1985] 474	10 654
228.	Aluminium	19.12.84	L92/1	3 [1987] 813	10 658
229.	Olympic Airways	23.1.85	L46/51	1 [1985] 730	10 668
230.	Greek Insurance	24.4.85	L152/25	—	
231.	EATE Levy	10.7.85	L219/35	4 [1988] 677	10 713
232.	Grundig	10.7.85	L233/1	4 [1988] 865	10 701
233.	Velcro/Aplix	12.7.85	L233/22	4 [1989] 157	10 719
234.	Ivoclar	27.11.85	L369/1	4 [1988] 781	10 751
235.	BP/Kellogg	2.12.85	L369/6	2 [1986] 619	10 747
236.	Breeders' rights; roses	13.12.85	L369/9	4 [1988] 193	10 757
237.	Whisky and Gin	13.12.85	L369/19	2 [1986] 664	10 750
238.	London Sugar Market	13.12.85	L369/25	4 [1988] 138	10 759
239.	London Cocoa Market	13.12.85	L369/28	4 [1988] 143	10 759
240.	London Coffee Market	13.12.85	L369/31	4 [1988] 155	10 759
241.	London Rubber Market	13.12.85	L369/34	4 [1988] 149	10 759
242.	ECS/AKZO	14.12.85	L374/1	3 [1986] 273	10 748
243.	P&I Clubs	16.12.85	L376/2	4 [1989] 178	10 752
244.	Villeroy & Boch	16.12.85	L376/15	4 [1988] 461	10 758
245.	Sperry New Holland	16.12.85	L376/21	4 [1988] 306	10 749

Book One—Table 1

No.	NAME	DATE	O.J.	C.M.L.R.	C.C.H.
246.	Siemens/Fanuc	18.12.85	[1985] L376/29	4 [1988] 945	10 765
247.	Polypropylene	23.4.86	[1986] L230/1	4 [1988] 347	10 782
248.	Roofing Felt	10.7.86	[1986] L232/15	4 [1991] 130	10 805
249.	Optical Fibres	14.7.86	[1986] L236/30		10 813
250.	Peugeot	25.9.86	[1986] L295/19	4 [1989] 371	10 820
251.	VIFKA	30.9.86	[1986] L291/46	—	10 828
252.	Irish Banks Standing Committee	30.9.86	[1986] L295/28	2 [1987] 601	10 829
253.	Meldoc	26.11.86	[1986] L348/50	4 [1989] 853	10 853
254.	Fatty Acids	2.12.86	[1986] L3/17	4 [1989] 445	10 855
255.	IPEL	4.12.86	[1986] L3/27	4 [1989] 280	10 848
256.	ENI/Montedison	4.12.86	[1986] L5/13	4 [1989] 444	10 860
257.	London Grain Market	10.12.86	[1986] L19/18-30	4 [1989] 294	10 850
258.	London Potato Market	10.12.86	[1986] L19/18-30	4 [1989] 301	10 850
259.	London Meat Exchange	10.12.86	[1986] L19/18-30	4 [1989] 308	10 850
260.	GAFTA	10.12.86	[1986] L19/18-30	4 [1989] 287	10 850
261.	Belgian Banking Association	11.12.86	[1986] L7/27	4 [1989] 141	10 847
262.	ABI	12.12.86	[1986] L43/51	4 [1989] 238	10 846
263.	X/Open Group	15.12.86	[1986] L35/36	4 [1989] 542	10 865
264.	Boussois/Interpane	15.12.86	[1986] L50/30	4 [1988] 124	10 859
265.	Yves Rocher	17.12.86	[1986] L8/49	4 [1988] 592	10 855
266.	Pronuptia	17.12.86	[1986] L13/39	4 [1989] 355	10 854
267.	Mitchell Cotts/Sofiltra	17.12.86	[1986] L41/31	4 [1988] 111	10 852
268.	Canary Islands	22.6.87	[1987] L194/28	1 [1988] 331	—
269.	Tipp-Ex	10.7.87	[1987] L222/1	4 [1989] 425	10 899
270.	Computerland	13.7.87	[1987] L222/12	4 [1989] 259	10 906
271.	BIFFEX	13.7.87	[1987] L222/24	4 [1989] 314	10 908
272.	Sandoz	13.7.87	[1987] L222/28	4 [1989] 628	10 907
273.	Boosey & Hawkes	29.7.87	[1987] L286/36	4 [1988] 67	10 920
274.	International Dental Exhibition	18.9.87	[1987] L293/58	—	10 992
275.	Fisher-Price	18.12.87	[1987] L49/19	4 [1989] 553	10 955
276.	New Potatoes	18.12.87	[1987] L59/25	4 [1988] 790	10 978
277.	Konica	18.12.87	[1987] L78/34	4 [1988] 848	10 977
278.	ARG/Unipart	22.12.87	[1987] L45/34	4 [1988] 513	10 968
279.	Enichem/ICI	22.12.87	[1987] L50/18	4 [1989] 54	10 962
280.	Olivetti/Canon	22.12.87	[1987] L52/51	4 [1989] 940	10 961
281.	De Laval-Stork II	22.12.87	[1987] L59/32	4 [1988] 714	10 954
282.	Hilti	22.12.87	[1987] L65/19	4 [1989] 677	10 976

Chronological List of Commission Decisions (EEC)—References

No.	NAME	DATE	O.J.		C.M.L.R.		C.C.H.
283.	Rich Products	22.12.87	[1987]	L69/21	4 [1988]	527	10 956
284.	BP/Bayer	5.5.88	[1988]	L150/35	4 [1989]	24	10 995
285.	British Dental Trade Association	11.7.88	[1988]	L233/15	4 [1989]	1021	11 014
286.	British Sugar	18.7.88	[1988]	L284/41	4 [1990]	196	11 012
287.	IVECO/Ford	20.7.88	[1988]	L230/39	4 [1989]	40	11 013
288.	VBA	26.7.88	[1988]	L262/27	4 [1989]	500	11 024
289.	Tetra Pak I	26.7.88	[1988]	L272/27	4 [1990]	47	11 015
290.	Continental/Michelin	11.10.88	[1988]	L305/33	4 [1989]	920	11 034
291.	BBC Brown Boveri	11.10.88	[1988]	L301/68	4 [1989]	610	11 035
292.	Delta Chemie	13.10.88	[1988]	L309/34	4 [1989]	535	2 254
293.	Eurotunnel	24.10.88	[1988]	L311/36	4 [1989]	419	11 037
294.	Hudson Bay	28.10.88	[1988]	L316/43	4 [1989]	340	11 042
295.	SABENA	4.11.88	[1988]	L317/47	4 [1989]	662	11 043
296.	Service Master	14.11.88	[1988]	L332/38	4 [1989]	581	2 287
297.	Transocean Marine Paint Association V	2.12.88	[1988]	L351/40	4 [1989]	621	2 003
298.	Charles Jourdan	2.12.88	[1988]	L35/31	4 [1989]	591	2 119
299.	British Plasterboard	5.12.88	[1988]	L10/50	4 [1990]	464	2 008
300.	Flat Glass	7.12.88	[1988]	L33/44	4 [1990]	535	2 077
301.	Net Book Agreements	12.12.88	[1988]	L22/12	4 [1989]	825	2 035
302.	Uniform Eurochèques Manufacturing	19.12.88	[1988]	L36/16	4 [1989]	907	2 111
303.	EMO III	20.12.88	[1988]	L37/11	4 [1990]	231	2 130
304.	Decca	21.12.88	[1988]	L43/24	4 [1990]	627	2 137
305.	PVC	21.12.88	[1988]	L74/1	4 [1990]	345	2 167
306.	LdPE	21.12.88	[1988]	L74/21	4 [1990]	382	2 193
307.	Magill	21.12.88	[1988]	L78/43	4 [1989]	749	2 223
308.	National Sulphuric Acid Association II	9.6.89	[1989]	L190/22	4 [1990]	612	2 006
309.	UIP	12.7.89	[1989]	L226/25	4 [1990]	749	2 019
310.	Dutch Banking Association	19.7.89	[1989]	L253/1	4 [1990]	768	2 032
311.	Welded Steel Mesh	2.8.89	[1989]	L260/1	4 [1991]	13	2 051
312.	ARD	15.9.89	[1989]	L284/36	4 [1990]	841	2 109
313.	Bayonox	13.12.89	[1989]	L21/71	4 [1990]	930	2 066
314.	APB	14.12.89	[1989]	L18/35	4 [1990]	619	2 060
315.	Sugar Beet	19.12.89	[1989]	L31/35	4 [1991]	629	2 077

* In 1989, the full citation of the C.C.H. Common Market Reporter became [YEAR](Volume No.)CEC(Page No.). In this Handbook, the volume numbers are shown before the year, for ease of reference.

Book One—Table 1

No.	NAME	DATE	O.J.		C.M.L.R.		C.C.H.	
316.	Concordato	20.12.89	[1989]	L15/27	4 [1991]	199	1 [1990]	2 053
317.	TEKO	20.12.89	[1989]	L13/34	4 [1990]	957	1 [1990]	2 045
318.	Dutch express delivery	20.12.89	[1989]	L10/47	4 [1990]	947	1 [1990]	2 038
319.	Alcatel/ANT	12.1.90	[1990]	L32/19	4 [1991]	208	1 [1990]	2 096
320.	Moosehead	23.3.90	[1990]	L100/32	4 [1991]	391	1 [1990]	2 127
321.	Metaleurop	12.7.90	[1990]	L179/41	4 [1991]	222	2 [1990]	2 033
322.	Odin	13.7.90	[1990]	L209/15	4 [1991]	832	2 [1990]	2 066
323.	Konsortium ECR 900	27.7.90	[1990]	L228/31	4 [1992]	54	2 [1990]	2 082
324.	Spanish courier services	1.8.90	[1990]	L223/19	4 [1991]	560	2 [1990]	2 087
325.	GEC-Siemens/Plessey	1.9.90	[1990]	C239/2	—		—	
326.	Cekacan	30.10.90	[1990]	L299/64	—		2 [1990]	2 056
327.	Bayer Dental	28.11.90	[1990]	L351/46	4 [1992]	61	1 [1991]	2 003
328.	KSB	12.12.90	[1990]	L19/25	—		1 [1991]	2 009
329.	D'Ieteren	19.12.90	[1990]	L20/42	4 [1992]	339	1 [1991]	2 025
329a.	Secrétama	19.12.90	[1990]	L35/23	—		1 [1991]	2 048
330.	Solvay/ICI	19.12.90	[1990]	L152/1	—		2 [1991]	2 003
331.	Solvay/CFK	19.12.90	[1990]	L152/16	—		2 [1991]	2 022
332.	Solvay	19.12.90	[1990]	L152/21	—		2 [1991]	2 029
333.	ICI	19.12.90	[1990]	L152/40	—		2 [1991]	2 053
333a.	ANSAC	19.12.90	[1990]	L152/54	—		2 [1991]	2 071
334.	Vichy	11.1.91	[1991]	L75/57	—		1 [1991]	2 062
335.	IJsselcentrale	16.1.91	[1991]	L28/32	—		2 [1991]	2 029
336.	Sippa	15.2.91	[1991]	L60/19	—		1 [1991]	2 055
337.	Screensport/EBU	19.2.91	[1991]	L63/32	—		1 [1991]	2 093
338.	Baccarat	15.3.91	[1991]	L97/16	—		1 [1991]	2 109
339.	Scottish Nuclear	30.4.91	[1991]	L178/31	—		2 [1991]	2 103
340.	Gosme/Martell	10.5.91	[1991]	L185/23	—		2 [1991]	2 110
341.	Viho/Toshiba	5.6.91	[1991]	L287/39	—		2 [1991]	2 196
342.	IATA Passengers	30.7.91	[1991]	L258/18	—		2 [1991]	2 160
343.	IATA Cargo	30.7.91	[1991]	L258/29	—		2 [1991]	2 175
344.	Eirpage	18.10.91	[1991]	L306/22	—		1 [1992]	2 057
344a.	Eco System	4.12.91	[1992]	L66/1	—		—	
345.	Yves Saint Laurent	16.12.91	[1992]	L12/24	—		1 [1992]	2 071
346.	Assurpol	14.1.92	[1992]	L37/16	—		1 [1992]	2 096
347.	U.K. Tractors	17.2.92	[1992]	L68/19	—		—	
348.	Tetra Pak II	24.7.91	[1992]	L72/1	—		—	

TABLE 2
CHRONOLOGICAL LIST OF COMMISSION DECISIONS (EEC)—CONTENTS

No.	NAME	TYPE OF DECISION	PRODUCT	SUBJECT	FINE[4]	No. of ECJ and/or CFI* Ruling
1.	Grosfillex/Fillestorf	Clearance	Plastics	Exclusive Distribution	—	—
2.	Convention Faience	Recommendation	China	Collective Exclusive Dealing	—	—
3.	Bendix/Mertens and Straet	Clearance	Brakes	Non-exclusive Distribution	—	—
4.	Nicholas Frères Vitapro	Clearance	Cosmetics	Non-Competition	—	—
5.	Grundig/Consten	Infringement 85	Consumer Electronics	Exclusive Distribution	—	4
6.	DECA	Clearance	Construction	Bidding Agreement	—	—
7.	DRU/Blondel	Exemption	Household Products	Exclusive Distribution	—	—
8.	Hummel/Isbecque	Exemption	Agricultural Machines	Exclusive Distribution	—	—
9.	Maison Jallatte	Exemption	Shoes	Exclusive Distribution	—	—
10.	Transocean Marine Paint Association I	Exemption	Paint	Co-operation Agreement	—	—
11.	Eurogypsum	Clearance	Plaster	R&D Agreement	—	—
12.	Alliance des Constructeurs Francais	Clearance	Machine Tools	Common Export Agency	—	—
13.	Socemas	Clearance	Foodstuffs	Buying Group	—	—
14.	ACEC/Berliet	Exemption	Heavy Vehicles	R&D Agreement	—	—
15.	Cobelaz	Clearance	Fertilisers	Sales Agency	—	—
16.	Cobelaz Cokes	Clearance	Fertilisers	Sales Agency	—	—
17.	Rieckerman	Clearance	Heating Equipment	Exclusive Distribution	—	—
18.	CFA	Exemption	Fertilisers	Sales Agency	—	—
19.	EMO I	Clearance	Machine Tools	Exhibition Agreements	—	—
20.	Chaufourniers	Clearance	Cement	Production Cartel	—	—
21.	Christiani & Nielsen	Clearance	Construction	Intra-enterprise Co-operation	—	—
22.	VVVF	Clearance	Paint	Common Quality Standards	—	—

[4] Represents total fine in millions of ECU. For breakdown, see Table 10 (fines), p.52.
* CFI = Court of First Instance of the European Communities.

No.	NAME	TYPE OF DECISION	PRODUCT	SUBJECT	FINE	No. of ECJ and/or CFI Ruling
23.	SEIFA	Clearance	Fertilisers	Sales Agency	—	—
24.	Quinine Cartel	Infringement 85	Quinine	Cartel	0.50	14-16
25.	Clima Chappée	Exemption	Air-Conditioning	Specialisation	—	—
26.	Jaz/Peter I	Exemption	Clocks	Specialisation	—	—
27.	Dyestuffs	Infringement 85	Dyes	Cartel	0.49	23-31
28.	Pirelli/Dunlop	Clearance	Tyres	Production Capacity Swap	—	—
29.	Kodak	Clearance	Photographic Equipment	Sales Conditions	—	—
30.	ASPA	Clearance	Toiletries	Collective Exclusive Dealing	—	—
31.	ASBL	Clearance	Welded Steel Tubes	Joint Promotion	—	—
32.	Julien/Van Katwijk	Infringement 85	Cardboard Tubes	Cartel	—	—
33.	Omega	Exemption	Watches	Selective Distribution	—	—
34.	Supexie	Clearance	Fertilisers	Sales Agency	—	—
35.	Ceramic Tiles	Infringement 85	Ceramic Tiles	Aggregate Rebates	—	—
36.	CICG	Article 11(5)	Tape Recorders	Royalty Collecting Agreement	—	—
37.	FN/CF	Exemption	Shotgun Cartridges	Specialisation	—	—
38.	Gema I	Infringement 86	Copyright Royalties	Performing Rights Society	—	—
39.	Alba	Article 11(5)	Beer	—	—	—
40.	Union des Brasseries	Article 11(5)	Beer	—	—	—
41.	Maes	Article 11(5)	Beer	—	—	—
42.	Asphaltoïd/Keller	Exemption	Bitumen	—	—	—
43.	Cematex I	Article 11(5)	Textile Machinery	Exhibition Agreement	—	—
44.	SIAE	Rejection of request	Copyright Royalties	Performing Rights Society	—	—
45.	Boehringer	Infringement 86	Quinine	Cartel	—	33
46.	Continental Can	Infringement 85	Containers	Acquisition	—	35
47.	VCH	Clearance	Cement	Cartel	—	32
48.	SAFCO	Exemption	Foodstuffs	Export Agency	—	—
49.	SOPELEM/Langen	Clearance	Optical Systems	Specialisation Agreement	—	—
50.	Burroughs/Delplanque	Clearance	Carbon Paper	Patent Licence	—	—
51.	Burroughs/Geha	Exemption	Carbon Paper	Patent Licence	—	—
52.	Henkel/Colgate	Infringement 85	Detergents	R&D Agreement	—	—
53.	NCH	Exemption	Cement	Sales Agency	—	—
54.	MAN/SAVIEM	Exemption	Heavy Vehicles	Specialisation	—	—
55.	Wild/Leitz	Clearance	Microscopes	Specialisation	—	—

Chronological List of Commission Decisions (EEC)—Contents

No.	NAME	TYPE OF DECISION	PRODUCT	SUBJECT	FINE	No. of ECJ and/or CFI Ruling
56.	Davidson Rubber	Exemption	Car Seats	Patent Licence	—	—
57.	Raymond/Nagoya	Clearance	Car Components	Patent Licence	—	—
58.	Gema II	Addendum	Copyright Royalties	Performing Rights Society	—	—
59.	Thin Paper	Exemption	Thin Paper	Specialisation	—	—
60.	Central Heating	Infringement 85	Heating Equipment	Collective Exclusive Dealing	—	—
61.	Rodenstock	Article 11(5)	Glasses	Exclusive Distribution	—	—
62.	Misal	Article 11(5)	Various Products	Exclusive Distribution	—	—
63.	Pittsburgh Corning	Infringement 85	Glass	Preventing Parallel Trade	0.10	—
64.	Zoja/CSC-ICI	Infringement 86	Pharmaceuticals	Refusal to Supply	0.20, PP0.001[5]	37
65.	Dutch Cement	Infringement 85	Cement	Cartel	—	—
66.	Cimbel	Infringement 85	Cement	Cartel	—	—
67.	GISA	Infringement 85	Sanitary Equipment	Collective Exclusive Dealing	—	—
68.	WEA/Filipacchi Music S.A.	Infringement 85	Records	Preventing Parallel Trade	0.06	—
69.	European Sugar Industry	Infringement 85/86	Sugar	Cartel	9.0	48&55
70.	SCPA/Kali & Salz	Infringement 85	Fertilisers	Cartel	—	—
71.	Dupont de Nemours Germany	Clearance	Photographic Materials	Sales Conditions	—	—
72.	Heaters and Boilers	Infringement 85	Heating Equipment	Cartel	—	—
73.	Deutsche Philips	Infringement 85	Consumer Electronics	Preventing Parallel Trade	0.06	—
74.	Prym/Beka	Exemption	Needles	Exclusive Purchasing	—	—
75.	Transocean Marine Paint Association II	Exemption	Paint	Co-operation Agreement	—	42
76.	Kali & Salz/Kalichemie	Infringement 85	Fertilisers	Exclusive Distribution	—	43
77.	IFTRA Glass	Infringement 85	Glass Containers	Cartel	—	—
78.	Belgian Wallpaper	Infringement 85	Wallpaper	Cartel	—	47
79.	Advocaat Zwarte Kip	Infringement 85	Alcoholic Drinks	Trade Mark Assignment	0.358	—
80.	FRUBO	Infringement 85	Fruit	Exclusionary Practice	—	44
81.	Franco Japanese Ball Bearings	Infringement 85	Ball bearings	Cartel	—	—
82.	BMW	Exemption	Cars	Selective Distribution	—	—
83.	DuroDyne	Exemption	Heating/Air-conditioning	Exclusive Distribution	—	—
84.	General Motors	Infringement 86	Cars	Excessive Pricing	0.10	46

[5] Penalty Payments.

Book One—Table 2

No.	NAME	TYPE OF DECISION	PRODUCT	SUBJECT	FINE	No. of ECJ and/or CFI Ruling
85.	Goodyear Italiana/Euram	Exemption	Packaging Material	Exclusive Distribution	—	—
86.	Rank/SOPELEM	Exemption	Optical Equipment	Specialisation	—	—
87.	SHV/Chevron	Clearance	Petroleum	Joint Venture	—	—
88.	Tinned Mushrooms	Infringement 85	Mushrooms	Cartel	0.10	—
89.	Sirdar/Phildar	Article 15(6)	Wool	Trademark Delimitation	—	—
90.	Fireplaces	Infringement 85	Heating Equipment	Collective Exclusive Dealing	—	—
91.	Intergroup	Clearance	Foodstuffs	Buying Group	—	—
92.	IFTRA Aluminium	Infringement 85	Aluminium	Cartel	—	—
93.	UNIDI I	Exemption	Dental Equipment	Exhibition Agreement	—	—
94.	Kabelmetal/Luchaire	Exemption	Steel Components	Know-how/Patent Licence	—	—
95.	Bronbemaling	Article 15(6)	Drainage Equipment	Patent Pooling	—	—
96.	Transocean Marine Paint Association III	Exemption	Paint	Co-operation Agreement	—	—
97.	Bomée-Stichting	Infringement 85	Toiletries	Collective Exclusive Dealing	—	—
98.	AOIP/Beyrard	Infringement 85	Variable Resistors	Patent Licence	—	—
99.	SABA I	Exemption	Consumer Electronics	Selective Distribution	—	58
100.	Bayer/Gist-Brocades	Exemption	Pharmaceuticals	Specialisation	—	—
101.	Chiquita	Infringement 86	Bananas	Refusal to Supply	1.0. PP.001	62
102.	United Reprocessors	Exemption	Nuclear Waste	Joint Venture	—	—
103.	KEWA	Exemption	Nuclear Waste	Joint Venture	—	67
104.	Vitamins	Infringement 86	Vitamins	Exclusionary Practices	0.3	—
105.	CSV	Article 11(5)	Fertilisers	Sales Agency	—	—
106.	Pabst & Richarz/BNIA	Infringement 85	Alcoholic Drinks	Preventing Parallel Trade	—	—
107.	Reuter/BASF	Infringement 85	Base Chemicals	Non-Competition	—	—
108.	Miller	Infringement 85	Records	Preventing Parallel Trade	.07	61
109.	Junghans	Exemption	Clocks	Selective Distribution	—	—
110.	Theal/Watts	Infringement 85	Record Cleaners	Preventing Parallel Trade	.025	64
111.	Gerofabriek	Infringement 85	Cutlery	Resale Price Maintenance	—	—
112.	Vacuum Interrupters I	Exemption	Electrical Equipment	Joint Venture	—	—
113.	ABG/Oil Companies	Infringement 86	Petroleum	Refusal to Supply	—	65
114.	De Laval/Stork I	Exemption	Heavy Machinery	Joint Venture	—	—
115.	Cobelpa/VNP	Infringement 85	Paper	Information Exchange	—	—

Chronological List of Commission Decisions (EEC)—Contents

No.	NAME	TYPE OF DECISION	PRODUCT	SUBJECT	FINE	No. of ECJ and/or CFI Ruling
116.	BPICA I	Exemption	Cars	Exhibition Agreement	—	—
117.	GEC/Weir Sodium Circulators	Exemption	Electrical Equipment	Joint Venture	—	—
118.	Centraal Bureau voor de Rijwielhandel	Infringement 85	Bicycles	Collective Exclusive Dealing	—	—
119.	Cauliflowers	Infringement 85	Foodstuffs	—	—	—
120.	German Blacksmiths	Article 14(3)	Forges	Exclusionary Practice	—	68
121.	Hugin/Liptons	Infringement 86	Cash Registers	Refusal to Supply	0.05	—
122.	Video Cassette Recorders	Infringement 85	Consumers Electronics	Patent Licence	—	75
123.	The Distillers Company	Infringement 85	Alcoholic Drinks	Preventing Parallel Trade	—	—
124.	Spices	Infringement 85	Foodstuffs	Exclusive Purchasing	—	—
125.	SOPELEM/Vickers I	Exemption	Microscopes	Specialisation	—	—
126.	BMW Belgium	Infringement 85	Cars	Selective Distribution	0.2035	69
127.	Penney	Clearance	Textiles	Trademark Delimitation	—	—
128.	Jaz/Peter II	Exemption	Clocks	Specialisation	—	—
129.	Vegetable Parchment	Infringement 85	Paper	Information Exchange	0.115	—
130.	Campari	Exemption	Alcoholic Drinks	Trademark Licence	—	—
131.	RAI/Unitel	Article 11(5)	Performing Rights	Exclusive Licence	—	—
132.	SNPE/LEL	Article 15(6)	Explosive Engineering	Cartel	—	—
133.	FEDETAB	Infringement 85	Tobacco	Cartel	—	80
134.	CSV	Infringement 85	Fertilisers	Sales Agency	—	—
135.	Arthur Bell & Sons Ltd	Infringement 85	Alcoholic Drinks	Preventing Parallel Trade	—	—
136.	Teacher & Sons	Infringement 85	Alcoholic Drinks	Preventing Parallel Trade	—	—
137.	Maize Seeds	Infringement 85	Seeds	Breeders' rights Licence	—	94
138.	WANO	Clearance	Explosives	Joint Venture	—	—
139.	Zanussi	Exemption	Consumer Electronics	Guarantee	—	—
140.	EMO II	Infringement 85	Machine Tools	Exhibition Agreement	—	—
141.	Kawasaki	Infringement 85	Motor Cycles	Preventing Parallel Trade	0.1	—
142.	White Lead	Infringement 85	White Lead	Cartel	—	—
143.	Vaessen/Moris	Exemption	Machinery	Patent Licence	—	—
144.	Beecham/Parke Davis	Article 14(3)	Pharmaceuticals	Research & Development	—	—
145.	Fides	Article 14(3)	Glass	Cartel	—	—
146.	AM & S Europe	Infringement 85	Zinc	Cartel	—	92
147.	BP Kemi/DDSF	Infringement 85	Chemicals	Exclusive Purchasing	—	—
148.	Floral	Infringement 85	Fertilisers	Sales Agency	0.08	—
149.	Rennet	Infringement 85	Foodstuffs	Exclusive Purchasing	—	84

19

Book One—Table 2

No.	NAME	TYPE OF DECISION	PRODUCT	SUBJECT	FINE	No. of ECJ and/or CFI Ruling
150.	Cane sugar Supply Agreements	Clearance	Sugar	Exclusive Purchasing	—	—
151.	Transocean Marine Paint Association IV	Exemption	Paint	Co-operation Agreement	—	—
152.	Pioneer	Infringement 85	Consumer Electronics	Preventing Parallel Trade	6.95	98
153.	Fabbrica Pisana	Article 15(1)	Glass	Incorrect Infomation	0.005	—
154.	Fabbrica Lastre	Article 15(1)	Glass	Incorrect Information	0.005	—
155.	Krups	Clearance	Consumer Electronics	Selective Distribution	—	—
156.	National Sulphuric Acid Association I	Exemption	Base Chemical	Buying Group	—	—
157.	Distillers-Victuallers	Clearance	Alcoholic Drinks	Sales Conditions	—	—
158.	IMA Rules	Infringement 85	Plywood	Exclusionary Practice	PP0.001	—
159.	Natursteinplatten	Clearance	Stones	Co-operation Agreement	—	—
160.	Johnson & Johnson	Infringement 85	Para-pharmaceuticals	Preventing Parallel Trade	0.2	—
161.	Vacuum Interrupters II	Exemption	Electrical Machinery	Joint Venture	—	—
162.	Hennessy/Henkell	Infringement 85	Alcoholic Drinks	Exclusive Distribution	—	—
163.	Italian Cast Glass	Infringement 85	Glass	Cartel	—	—
164.	Italian Flat Glass	Infringement 85	Glass	Cartel	—	102
165.	Michelin	Infringement 86	Tyres	Rebate Scheme	0.68	97
166.	GVL	Infringement 86	Copyright	Performing Rights Society	—	—
167.	Comptoir d'Importation	Article 15(1)	Consumer Electronics	Incorrect Information	0.005	—
168.	Langenscheidt/Hachette	Exemption	Books	Joint Venture	—	—
169.	VBBB/VBVB	Infringement 85	Books	Collective Resale Price Maintenance	—	105
170.	Telos	Article 15(1)	Cameras	Incorrect Information	0.005	—
171.	SOPELEM/Vickers II	Exemption	Microscopes	Specialisation	—	—
172.	Moët et Chandon (London) Ltd.	Infringement 85	Alcoholic Drinks	Preventing Parallel Trade	1.1	—
173.	Hasselblad	Infringement 85	Cameras	Preventing Parallel Trade	0.755	107
174.	Gema Statutes	Clearance	Copyright	Performing Rights Society	—	—
175.	Fire Insurance	Article 11(5)	Insurance	Request for Information	—	—
176.	National Panasonic (Belgium)	Article 15(1)	Consumer Electronics	Incorrect Information	0.005	—
177.	National Panasonic (France)	Article 15(1)	Consumer Electronics	Incorrect Information	0.005	—
178.	NAVEWA-ANSEAU	Infringement 85	Domestic Appliances	Preventing Parallel Trade	0.939	101
179.	AEG-Telefunken	Infringement 85	Consumer Electronics	Selective Distribution	1.0	100
180.	BPICA II	Exemption	Cars	Exhibition Agreement	—	—
181.	SSI	Infringement 85	Tobacco	Cartel	1.475	127,128

Chronological List of Commission Decisions (EEC)—Contents

No.	NAME	TYPE OF DECISION	PRODUCT	SUBJECT	FINE	No. of ECJ and/or CFI Ruling
182.	Ford Werke-Interim Measures	Interim measures	Cars	Selective Distribution	—	108
183.	Fédération Chaussure de France	Article 15(1)	Shoes	Incorrect Information	0.005	—
184.	Amersham Buchler	Exemption	Nuclear Materials	Joint Venture	—	—
185.	NAVEWA-ANSEAU (Bosch)	Withdrawal of fine	Domestic Appliances	Preventing Parallel Trade	—	—
186.	National Panasonic	Infringement 85	Consumer Electronics	Preventing Parallel Trade	0.45	—
187.	Cafeteros de Colombia	Infringement 86	Coffee	Preventing Parallel Trade	—	—
188.	British Telecommunications	Infringement 85	Telecommunications	Exclusionary Practices	—	117
189.	Zinc	Infringement 85	Zinc	Cartel	0.90	109
190.	AROW/BNIC	Infringement 85	Alcoholic Drinks	Cartel	0.16	—
191.	Toltecs/Dorcet	Infringement 85	Tobacco	Trademark Delimitation	0.05	116
192.	Castrol	Article 11(5)	Petroleum Products	—	—	—
193.	Cematex II	Exemption	Textile Machinery	Exhibition Agreement	—	—
194.	Windsurfing International	Infringement 85	Leisure Articles	Patent Licence	0.095	130
195.	Vimpoltu	Infringement 85	Agricultural Machines	Cartel	—	—
196.	Rockwell/IVECO	Exemption	Vehicle Components	Joint Venture	—	—
197.	ECS/AKZO-Interim Measures	Interim measures 86	Chemicals	Predatory Pricing	—	—
198.	Cast iron & Steel Rolls	Infringement 85	Steel Products	Cartel	1.250	—
199.	Ford Werke AG	Infringement 85	Cars	Preventing Parallel Trade	—	123
200.	Murat	Clearance	Jewellery	Selective Distribution	—	—
201.	SMM&T	Exemption	Cars	Exhibition Agreement	—	—
202.	IPTC Belgium	Infringement 85	Domestic Appliances	Preventing Parallel Trade	0.005	—
203.	VW/MAN	Exemption	Heavy Vehicles	Specialisation	—	—
204.	Schlegel/CPIO	Exemption & Clearance	Vehicle Components	Exclusive Purchasing	—	—
205.	Carbon Gas Technologie	Exemption	Chemical Processes	R&D Agreement	—	—
206.	Nutricia	Infringement 85	Foodstuffs	Acquisition	—	121
207.	International Energy Agency	Exemption	Petroleum	Co-operation Agreement	—	—
208.	SABA II	Exemption	Consumer Electronics	Selective Distribution	—	134
209.	Nuovo-CEGAM	Exemption	Insurance	Co-operation Agreement	—	—
210.	IBM PC	Clearance	Computers	Selective Distribution	—	—
211.	Polistil/Arbois	Infringement 85	Toys	Preventing Parallel Trade	0.06	—
212.	British Leyland	Infringement 86	Cars	Preventing Parallel Trade	0.35	136
213.	Synthetic Fibres	Exemption	Textiles	Restructuring Agreement	—	—
214.	Carlsberg	Exemption	Beer	Distribution Agreement	—	—
215.	BPCL/ICI	Exemption	Base Chemicals	Restructuring Agreement	—	—
216.	Flat Glass (Benelux)	Infringement 85	Glass	Cartel	4.0	—

Book One—Table 2

No.	NAME	TYPE OF DECISION	PRODUCT	SUBJECT	FINE	No. of ECJ and/or CFI Ruling
217.	Zinc Producer Group	Infringement 85	Zinc	Cartel	3.3	—
218.	Peroxide Products	Infringement 85	Chemicals	Cartel	9.0	—
219.	UNIDI II	Exemption	Dental Equipment	Exhibition Agreement	—	143
220.	Fire Insurance	Infringement 85	Insurance	Cartel	—	139
221.	Milchfoerderungsfonds	Infringement 85	Milk	Export Subsidies	—	—
222.	Grohe Sales System	Infringement 85	Sanitary Equipment	Selective Distribution	—	—
223.	Ideal Standard Sales System	Infringement 85	Sanitary Equipment	Selective Distribution	—	—
224.	Uniform Eurochèques	Exemption	Banking	Co-operation Agreement	—	—
225.	Mecaniver/PPG	Clearance	Glass	Acquisition	—	—
226.	John Deere	Infringement 85	Agricultural Machines	Preventing Parallel Trade	2.0	—
227.	Woodpulp	Infringement 85	Woodpulp	Cartel	4.125	157
228.	Aluminium	Infringement 85	Aluminium	Cartel	—	—
229.	Olympic Airways	Article 11(5)	Airline Services	—	—	—
230.	Greek Insurance	Infringement 90	Insurance	Discrimination	—	153
231.	EATE Levy	Infringement Reg. 1017/68	Waterway Transport	Cartel	—	142
232.	Grundig	Exemption	Consumer Electronics	Selective Distribution	—	—
233.	Velcro/Aplix	Infringement 85	Fasteners	Patent Licence	—	—
234.	Ivoclar	Exemption	Dental Equipment	Selective Distribution	—	—
235.	BP/Kellogg	Exemption	Chemicals	R&D Agreement	—	—
236.	Breeders' rights; roses	Infringement 85	Flowers	Breeders' Rights Licence	—	—
237.	Whisky and Gin	Exemption	Alcoholic Drinks	Exclusive Distribution	—	—
238.	London Sugar Market	Clearance	Sugar	Futures Market	—	—
239.	London Cocoa Market	Clearance	Cocoa	Futures Market	—	—
240.	London Coffee Market	Clearance	Coffee	Futures Market	—	—
241.	London Rubber Market	Clearance	Rubber	Futures Market	—	—
242.	ECS/AKZO	Infringement 86	Chemicals	Predatory Pricing	10.0	186
243.	P&I Clubs	Exemption	Insurance	Co-operation Agreement	—	—
244.	Villeroy & Boch	Clearance	China	Selective Distribution	—	—
245.	Sperry New Holland	Infringement 85	Agricultural Machinery	Preventing Parallel Trade	0.75	—
246.	Siemens/Fanuc	Infringement 85	Electronic Machinery	Exclusive Distribution	2.0	—
247.	Polypropylene	Infringement 85	Base Chemicals	Cartel	57.85	T18–20, T23–26, T31-37
248.	Roofing Felt	Infringement 85	Construction Materials	Cartel	0.985	166

Chronological List of Commission Decisions (EEC)—Contents

No.	NAME	TYPE OF DECISION	PRODUCT	SUBJECT	FINE	No. of ECJ and/or CFI Ruling
249.	Optical Fibres	Exemption	Optical Fibres	Joint Venture	—	—
250.	Peugeot	Infringement 85	Cars	Preventing Parallel Trade	—	—
251.	VIFKA	Exemption	Office Equipment	Exhibition Agreement	—	—
252.	Irish Banks Standing Committee	Clearance	Banking	Co-operation Agreement	—	—
253.	Meldoc	Infringement 85	Milk	Cartel	6.550	—
254.	Fatty Acids	Infringement 85	Chemicals	Cartel	0.15	—
255.	IPEL	Clearance	Petroleum	Futures Market	—	—
256.	ENI/Montedison	Exemption	Base Chemicals	Restructuring Agreement	—	—
257.	London Grain Market	Clearance	Cereals	Futures Market	—	—
258.	London Potato Market	Clearance	Potatoes	Futures Market	—	—
259.	London Meat Exchange	Clearance	Meat	Futures Market	—	—
260.	GAFTA	Clearance	Soya Beans	Futures Market	—	—
261.	Belgian Banking Association	Exemption	Banking	Co-operation Agreement	—	—
262.	ABI	Exemption	Banking	Co-operation Agreement	—	—
263.	X/Open Group	Exemption	Computer Systems	Co-operation Agreement	—	—
264.	Boussois/Interpane	Exemption	Glass	Know-how Licence	—	—
265.	Yves Rocher	Exemption	Cosmetics	Franchising	—	—
266.	Pronuptia	Exemption	Textiles	Franchising	—	—
267.	Mitchell Cotts/Sofiltra	Exemption	Air Filters	Joint Venture	—	—
268.	Canary Islands	Infringement 90	Transport	Discrimination	—	—
269.	Tipp-Ex	Infringement 85	Stationary	Preventing Parallel Trade	0.41	75
270.	Computerland	Exemption	Computers	Franchising	—	—
271.	BIFFEX	Clearance	Maritime Transport	Futures Market	—	—
272.	Sandoz	Infringement 85	Pharmaceuticals	Preventing Parallel Trade	0.8	74
273.	Boosey & Hawkes	Interim-Measures 86	Musical Instruments	Refusal to Supply	—	—
274.	International Dental Exhibition	Exemption	Dental Equipment	Exhibition Agreement	—	—
275.	Fisher-Price	Infringement 85	Toys	Preventing Parallel Trade	0.3	—
276.	New Potatoes	Regulation 26/62	Potatoes	National Market Organisation	—	—
277.	Konica	Infringement 85	Photographic Material	Preventing Parallel Trade	0.15	—
278.	ARG/Unipart	Exemption	Car Components	Exclusive Distribution	—	—
279.	Enichem/ICI	Exemption	Base Chemicals	Restructuring Agreement	—	—
280.	Olivetti/Canon	Exemption	Office Equipment	Joint Venture	—	—
281.	De Laval-Stork II	Exemption	Heavy Machinery	Joint Venture	—	—
282.	Hilti	Infringement 85	Tools	Tying	6.0	T21

Book One—Table 2

No.	NAME	TYPE OF DECISION	PRODUCT	SUBJECT	FINE	No. of ECJ and/or CFI Ruling
283.	Rich Products	Exemption	Foodstuffs	Know-how Licence	—	—
284.	BP/Bayer	Exemption	Base Chemicals	Restructuring Agreement	—	—
285.	British Dental Trade Association	Infringement 85	Dental equipment	Exhibition Agreement	0.1	—
286.	British Sugar	Infringement 86	Sugar	Predation	3.0	—
287.	IVECO/Ford	Exemption	Heavy Vehicles	Joint Venture	—	—
288.	VBA	Infringement 85	Flowers	Exclusionary Practice	—	—
289.	Tetra Pak I	Infringement 86	Packaging Machinery	Acquisition	—	T7
290.	Continental/Michelin	Exemption	Tyres	R&D Agreement	—	—
291.	BBC Brown Boveri	Exemption	Batteries	Joint Venture	—	—
292.	Delta Chemie	Exemption	Household Products	Know-how Licence	—	—
293.	Eurotunnel	Clearance	Construction	Building Consortium	—	—
294.	Hudson Bay	Infringement 85	Furs	Exclusionary Practices	0.50	—
295.	SABENA	Infringement 86	Computer Reservations	Exclusionary Practices	0.10	—
296.	Service Master	Exemption	Cleaning Services	Franchising	—	—
297.	Transocean Marine Paint Association V	Exemption	Paint	Co-operation Agreement	—	—
298.	Charles Jourdan	Exemption	Luxury Products	Franchising	—	*
299.	British Plasterboard	Infringement 86	Building Materials	Exclusionary Practice	3.15	T30
300.	Flat Glass	Infringement 85/86	Glass	Cartel	13.4	165
301.	Net Book Agreements	Infringement 85	Books	Collective RPM	—	—
302.	Uniform Eurochèques Manufacturing	Exemption	Manufacturing	Common Standards	—	—
303.	EMO III	Exemption	Machine Tools	Exhibition Agreement	—	—
304.	Decca	Infringement 85/86	Radar	Patent Licence	—	T28
305.	PVC	Infringement 85	Base Chemicals	Cartel	23.5	*
306.	LdPE	Infringement 85	Base Chemicals	Cartel	37	T14, T15, T16
307.	Magill	Infringement 86	TV Guides	Intellectual Property Rights	—	—
308.	National Sulphuric Acid Assoc. II	Exemption	Base Chemicals	Buying Group	—	—
309.	UIP	Exemption	Cinema	Joint Venture	—	*
310.	Dutch Banking Association	Infringement 85	Banking	Co-operation Agreement	—	*
311.	Welded Steel Mesh	Exemption	Construction Materials	Cartel	9.50	*
312.	ARD	Exemption	Cinema	Purchasing Agreement	—	—
313.	Bayonox	Infringement 85	Animal-feed	Preventing Parallel Trade	0.5	T13

* Appeal pending.

Chronological List of Commission Decisions (EEC)—Contents

No.	NAME	TYPE OF DECISION	PRODUCT	SUBJECT	FINE	No. of ECJ and/or CFI Ruling
314.	APB	Clearance	Para-pharmaceuticals	Co-operation Agreement	—	—
315.	Sugar Beet	Infringement 85	Sugar Beet	Exclusionary practice	—	—
316.	Concordato	Exemption	Insurance	Co-operation Agreement	—	—
317.	TEKO	Exemption	Insurance	Co-operation Agreement	—	—
318.	Dutch express delivery	Article 90	Mail delivery	Monopolisation	—	190
319.	Alcatel/ANT	Exemption	Satelites	R&D Agreement	—	—
320.	Moosehead	Exemption	Beer	Trademark Licence	—	—
321.	Metaleurop	Clearance	Metal	Merger	—	—
322.	Odin	Clearance	Packaging Material	Joint Venture	—	—
323.	Konsortium ECR 900	Clearance	Telecommunications	R&D Agreement	—	—
324.	Spanish courier services	Article 90	Mail delivery	Monopolisation	—	—
325.	GEC-Siemens/Plessey	Article 6 Reg. 99/63	Electronics	Joint Take Over	—	—
326.	Cekakan	Exemption	Packaging Material	Joint Venture	—	—
327.	Bayer Dental	Infringement 85	Dental Equipment	Preventing Parallel Trade	—	—
328.	KSB	Exemption	Machinery	R&D Agreements	—	—
329.	D'Ieteren	Clearance	Motoroil	Selective Distribution	—	—
329a.	Secrétama	Article 16 Reg. 4056/86	Maritime Transport	Incorrect Information	0.05	—
330.	Solvay/ICI	Infringement 85	Soda Ash	Cartel	14	*
331.	Solvay/CFK	Infringement 85	Soda Ash	Cartel	4	*
332.	Solvay	Infringement 86	Soda Ash	Tying	20	*
333.	ICI	Infringement 86	Soda Ash	Tying	10	*
333a.	ANSAC	Infringement 85	Soda Ash	Joint Sales	—	—
334.	Vichy	Article 15(6)	Cosmetics	Selective Distribution	—	T29
335.	Ijssel-centrale	Infringement 85	Electricity	Collective Exclusive Dealing	—	*
336.	Sippa	Exemption	Paper	Exhibition Agreement	—	—
337.	Screensport/EBU	Infringement 85	Television	Joint Venture	—	—
338.	Baccarat	Article 16	Luxury Products	Penalty Payments	0.01	—
339.	Scottish nuclear	Exemption	Energy	Exclusive Purchasing	—	—
340.	Gosme/Martell	Prohibition	Alcoholic Drinks	Preventing Parallel Trade	0.35	—
341.	Viho/Toshiba	Prohibition	Photocopiers	Preventing Parallel Trade	2	—
342.	IATA Passengers	Exemption	Agency-Services	Similar Distribution systems	—	—
343.	IATA Cargo	Exemption	Agency-Services	Similar Distribution systems	—	—

Book One—Table 2

No.	NAME	TYPE OF DECISION	PRODUCT	SUBJECT	FINE	No. of ECJ and/or CFI Ruling
344.	Eirpage	Exemption	Paging Services	Joint Venture	—	—
344a.	Eco System	Prohibition	Cars	Selective Distribution	—	—
345.	Yves Saint Laurent	Exemption	Cosmetics	Selective Distribution	—	*
346.	Assurpol	Exemption	Insurance	Co-operation Agreement	—	—
347.	U.K. Tractors	Prohibition	Tractors	Information Exchange	—	—
348.	Tetra Pak II	Infringement 86	Packing Materials	Exclusionary Practices	75	*

TABLE 3

CHRONOLOGICAL LIST OF COURT OF FIRST INSTANCE JUDGMENTS (EEC)—REFERENCES

No.	NAME	CASE No.	DATE	E.C.R.	C.M.L.R.	C.C.H.	APPEAL
T1	Cosimex v. Commission	T-131/89R	6.12.89	II [1990] 1	—	—	—
T2	Solomon v. Commission	T-55/89	9.2.90	not published	—	—	—
T3	Peugeot v. Commission	T-23/90R	21.5.90	II [1990] 195	4 [1990] 674	—	—
T4	Norsk Hydro v. Commission	T-106/89	19.6.90	not published	—	—	—
T5	Filtrona v. Commission	T-125/89	10.7.90	II [1990] 393	4 [1990] 832	—	—
T6	Automec v. Commission	T-64/89	10.7.90	II [1990] 367	4 [1991] 177	—	—
T7	Tetra Pak v. Commission	T-51/89	10.7.90	II [1990] 309	4 [1991] 334	2 [1990] 409	—
T8	SEP v. Commission	T-39/90	21.11.90	II [1990] 649	—	—	—
T9	Nefarma v. Commission	T-113/89	13.12.90	II [1990] 797	—	—	—
T10	VNZ v. Commission	T-114/89	13.12.90	II [1990] 827	—	—	—
T11	Prodifarma v. Commission	T-116/89	13.12.90	II [1990] 843	—	—	—
T12	Prodifarma v. Commission II	T-3/90	23.1.91	II [1991] 1	—	—	—
T13	Bayer v. Commission	T-12/90	29.5.91	—	—	—	—
T13a	Vichy v. Commission	T-19/91R	7.6.91	—	—	—	—
T13b	PTT v. Commission	T-42/91	21.6.91	—	—	—	—
T14	RTE v. Commission	T-69/89	10.7.91	—	4 [1991] 586	2 [1991] 114	*
T15	BBC v. Commission	T-70/89	10.7.91	—	4 [1991] 669	2 [1991] 147	*
T16	ITV v. Commission	T-76/89	10.7.91	—	4 [1991] 745	2 [1991] 174	*
T17	Peugeot v. Commission	T-23/90	12.7.91	—	—	—	—
T18	Rhône Poulenc v. Commission	T-1/89	24.10.91	—	—	—	—

* Appeal pending

Book One—Table 3

No.	NAME	CASE No.	DATE	E.C.R.	C.M.L.R.	C.C.H.	APPEAL
T19	Petrofina v. Commission	T-2/89	24.10.91	—	—	—	—
T20	Atochem v. Commission	T-3/89	24.10.91	—	—	—	—
T21	Hilti v. Commission	T-30/89	12.12.91	—	4 [1992] 16	1 [1992] 155	*
T22	SEP v. Commission	T-39/89	12.12.91	—	—	—	—
T23	BASF v. Commission	T-4/89	17.12.91	—	—	—	—
T24	Enichem v. Commission	T-6/89	17.12.91	—	—	—	—
T25	Hercules v. Commission	T-7/89	17.12.91	—	4 [1992] 84	1 [1992] 207	—
T26	DSM v. Commission	T-8/89	17.12.91	—	—	—	—
T27	La Cinq v. Commission	T-44/90	24.1.92	—	—	—	—
T28	PVC	T-79, 84–86, 89, 91, 92, 94, 96, 98, 102, 104/89	27.2.92	—	4 [1992] 449	—	*
T29	Vichy v. Commission	T-19/91	27.2.92	—	—	—	—
T30	Flat Glass	T-68, 77, 78/89	10.3.92	—	—	—	—
T31	Hüls v. Commission	T-9/89	10.3.92	—	—	—	—
T32	Hoechst v. Commission	T-10/89	10.3.92	—	—	—	—
T33	Shell v. Commission	T-11/89	10.3.92	—	—	—	—
T34	Solvay v. Commission	T-12/89	10.3.92	—	—	—	—
T35	ICI v. Commission	T-13/89	10.3.92	—	—	—	—
T36	Montedipe v. Commission	T-14/89	10.3.92	—	—	—	—
T37	Linz v. Commission	T-15/89	10.3.92	—	—	—	—
T38	Sofacar v. Commission	T-27/91	21.2.92	—	—	—	—
T39	Cement Industries v. Commission	T-10–15/92R	23.3.92	—	—	—	—

Chronological List of Court of First Instance Judgments (EEC)—Contents

TABLE 4

CHRONOLOGICAL LIST OF COURT OF FIRST INSTANCE JUDGMENTS (EEC)—CONTENTS

No.	NAME	ARTICLE	SUBJECT	RESULT	PRODUCT/SERVICE
T1	Cosimex v. Commission	185	Interim Measures	Refused	Cosmetics
T2	Solomon v. Commission	175	—	Refused	Records
T3	Peugeot v. Commission	185	Interim Measures	Refused	Cars
T4	Norsk Hydro v. Commission	173	Cartel	Inadmissible	Base Chemicals
T5	Filtrona v. Commission	173	Rejection complaint	Inadmissible	Cigarette Filters
T6	Automec v. Commission	173	Letter DGIV	Inadmissible	Cars
T7	Tetra Pak v. Commission	173	Article 86	Upheld	Packaging Material
T8	SEP v. Commission	185	Article 11, Regulation 17	Refused	Electricity
T9	Nefarma v. Commission	173	Commission Letter	Inadmissible	Pharmaceuticals
T10	VNZ v. Commission	173	Commission Letter	Inadmissible	Pharmaceuticals
T11	Prodifarma v. Commission	173	Commission Letter	Inadmissible	Pharmaceuticals
T12	Prodifarma v. Commission II	175	Commission Letter	Refused	Pharmaceuticals
T13	Bayer v. Commission	173	Limitation periods	Inadmissible	Animal-feed
T13a	Vichy v. Commission	185	Interim Measures	Refused	Cosmetics
T13b	PTT v. Commission	173	Competence CFI	Transfer	Courier Services
T14	RTE v. Commission	173	Article 86	Upheld	TV Guides
T15	BBC v. Commission	173	Article 86	Upheld	TV Guides
T16	ITV v. Commission	173	Article 86	Upheld	TV Guides
T17	Peugeot v. Commission	173	Interim Measures	Upheld	Cars
T18	Rhône Poulenc v. Commission	173	Cartel	Fine Reduced	Base Chemicals
T19	Petrofina v. Commission	173	Cartel	Upheld	Base Chemicals
T20	Atochem v. Commission	173	Cartel	Upheld	Base Chemicals
T21	Hilti v. Commission	173	Article 86	Upheld	Tools
T22	SEP v. Commission	173	Article 11, Regulation 17	Upheld	Electricity

29

Book One—Table 4

No.	NAME	ARTICLE	SUBJECT	RESULT	PRODUCT/SERVICE
T23	BASF v. Commission	173	Cartel	Fine Reduced	Base Chemicals
T24	Enichem v. Commission	173	Cartel	Fine Reduced	Base Chemicals
T25	Hercules v. Commission	173	Cartel	Upheld	Base Chemicals
T26	DSM v. Commission	173	Cartel	Upheld	Base Chemicals
T27	La Cinq v. Commission	173	Interim Measures	Annulled	Television
T28	PVC	173	Cartel	Inadmissible/ Non-existence	Base Chemicals
T29	Vichy v. Commission	173	Article 15, paragraph 6, Regulation 17	Upheld	Cosmetics
T30	Flat Glass	173	Cartel	Fine Reduced	Flat Glass
T31	Hüls v. Commission	173	Cartel	Fine Reduced	Base Chemicals
T32	Hoechst v. Commission	173	Cartel	Upheld	Base Chemicals
T33	Shell v. Commission	173	Cartel	Fine Reduced	Base Chemicals
T34	Solvay v. Commission	173	Cartel	Upheld	Base Chemicals
T35	ICI v. Commission	173	Cartel	Fine Reduced	Base Chemicals
T36	Montedipe v. Commission	173	Cartel	Upheld	Base Chemicals
T37	Linz v. Commission	173	Cartel	Upheld	Base Chemicals
T38	Sofacar v. Commission	175	Competence CFI	No transfer	Cars
T39	Cement Industries v. Commission	185	Interim Measures	Refused	Cement

TABLE 5
CHRONOLOGICAL LIST OF EUROPEAN COURT JUDGMENTS (EEC)—REFERENCES

No.	NAME	CASE No.	DATE	E.C.R.[1]		C.M.L.R.[2]		C.C.H.[3]
1.	Bosch v. De Geus	13/61	6.4.62	[1962]	45	[1962]	1	8003
2.	Costa v. ENEL	6/64	15.7.64	[1964]	545	[1964]	425	8023
3.	LTM v. MBU	56/65	30.6.66	[1966]	337	[1966]	357	8047
4.	Consten & Grundig v. Commission	56 & 58/64	13.7.66	[1966]	299	[1966]	418	8046
5.	Italy v. Council and Commission	32/65	13.7.66	[1966]	389	[1966]	39	8048
6.	Cimenteries v. Commission	8-11/66	15.3.67	[1967]	75	[1967]	77	8052
7.	De Haecht v. Wilkin I	23/67	12.12.67	[1967]	407	[1968]	407	8053
8.	Parke, Davis v. Centrafarm	24/67	29.2.68	[1968]	55	[1968]	47	8054
9.	Walt Wilhelm	14/68	13.2.69	[1969]	1	[1969]	100	8056
10.	Völk v. Vervaecke	5/69	9.7.69	[1969]	295	[1969]	273	8074
11.	Portelange v. Smith Corona	10/69	9.7.69	[1969]	309	1[1969]	397	8075
12.	Bilger v. Jehle	43/69	18.3.70	[1970]	127	1[1974]	382	8076
13.	Parfums Rochas v. Bitsch	1/70	30.6.70	[1970]	515	[1971]	104	8102
14.	ACF Chemiefarma v. Commission	41/69	15.7.70	[1970]	661			8083
15.	Buchler & Co. v. Commission	44/69	15.7.70	[1970]	733	—		8084
16.	Boehringer v. Commission	45/69	15.7.70	[1970]	769	[1972]	121	8085
17.	Sirena v. Eda	40/70	18.1.71	[1971]	69	[1971]	260	8101
18.	Cadillon v. Höss	1/71	6.5.71	[1971]	351	[1971]	420	8135
19.	Deutsche Grammophon v. Metro	78/70	8.6.71	[1971]	487	[1971]	631	8106
20.	Komponistenverband v. Commission	8/71	13.7.71	[1971]	705	[1973]	902	8143
21.	Muller	10/71	14.7.71	[1971]	821	—		8140
22.	Béguelin v. GL	22/71	25.11.71	[1971]	949	[1972]	81	8149
23.	ICI v. Commission	48/69	14.7.72	[1972]	619	[1972]	557	8161
24.	BASF v. Commission	49/69	14.7.72	[1972]	713	[1972]	557	8162
25.	Bayer v. Commission	51/69	14.7.72	[1972]	745	[1972]	557	8163

[1] European Court Reports.
[2] Common Market Law Reports.
[3] Commerce Clearing House.

Book One—Table 5

No.	NAME	CASE No.	DATE	E.C.R.[1]	C.M.L.R.[2]	C.C.H.[3]
26.	Ciba-Geigy v. Commission	52/69	14.7.72	[1972] 787	[1972] 557	8164
27.	Sandoz v. Commission	53/69	14.7.72	[1972] 845	[1972] 557	8165
28.	Francolor v. Commission	54/69	14.7.72	[1972] 851	[1972] 557	8166
29.	Cassella v. Commission	55/69	14.7.72	[1972] 887	[1972] 557	8167
30.	Hoechst v. Commission I	56/69	14.7.72	[1972] 927	[1972] 557	8168
31.	ACNA v. Commission	57/69	14.7.72	[1972] 933	[1972] 557	8169
32.	Cement Dealers v. Commission	8/72	17.10.72	[1972] 977	[1973] 7	8179
33.	Boehringer v. Commission	7/72	14.12.72	[1972] 1218	[1973] 864	8191
34.	De Haecht v. Wilkin II	48/72	6.2.73	[1973] 77	[1973] 287	8170
35.	Continental Can v. Commission	6/72	21.2.73	[1973] 215	[1973] 199	8171
36.	BRT v. SABAM I	127/73	30.1.74	[1974] 51	2[1974] 238	8268
37.	ICI & CSC v. Commission	6 & 7/73	6.3.74	[1974] 223	1[1974] 309	8209
38.	BRT v. SABAM II	127/73	27.3.74	[1974] 313	2[1974] 238	8269
39.	Sacchi	155/73	30.4.74	[1974] 409	2[1974] 177	8267
40.	Van Zuylen v. Hag	192/73	3.7.74	[1974] 731	2[1979] 127	8230
40a.	Dassonville	8/74	11.7.74	[1974] 837	2[1979] 436	8276
40b.	Transocean Marine Paint Association	17/74	23.10.74	[1974] 1063	2[1974] 459	8241
41.	Centrafarm & De Peijper v. Sterling Drug	15/74	31.10.74	[1974] 1147	2[1974] 480	8246
42.	Centrafarm & De Peijper v. Winthrop	16/74	31.10.74	[1974] 1183	1[1974] 1	8247
42a.	Commission v. Germany	12/74	20.2.75	[1975] 181	1[1975] 340	8293
43.	Kali & Salz v. Commission	19 & 20/74	14.5.75	[1975] 499	2[1975] 154	8284
44.	Frubo v. Commission	71/74	15.5.75	[1975] 563	2[1975] 123	8285
45.	Van Vliet v. Dalle Crode	25/75	1.10.75	[1975] 1103	2[1975] 549	8314
46.	General Motors v. Commission	26/75	13.11.75	[1975] 1367	1[1976] 95	8320
47.	Papiers Peints v. Commission	73/74	26.11.75	[1975] 1491	1[1976] 589	8335
48.	Suiker Unie v. Commission	40-48, 50, 54-56, 111, 113 & 114/75	16.12.75	[1975] 1663	1[1976] 295	8334
49.	Fonderies Roubaix v. Fonderies Roux	63/75	3.2.76	[1976] 111	1[1976] 538	8341
50.	EMI-CBS	51/75	15.6.76	[1976] 811	2[1976] 235	8350
51.	EMI-CBS	86/75	15.6.76	[1976] 871	2[1976] 235	8351
52.	EMI-CBS	96/75	15.6.76	[1976] 913	2[1976] 235	8352
53.	Terrapin v. Terranova	119/75	22.6.76	[1976] 1039	2[1976] 482	8362
54.	De Norre v. Concordia	47/76	1.2.77	[1977] 65	1[1977] 378	8386
55.	Générale Sucrière v. Commission	41, 43 & 44/73	9.3.77	[1977] 445	—	8395
56.	Hoffmann-La Roche v. Centrafarm	107/76	24.5.77	[1977] 975	3[1978] 217	8414

Chronological List of European Court Judgments (EEC)—References

No.	NAME	CASE No.	DATE	E.C.R.[1]	C.M.L.R.[2]	C.C.H.[3]
57.	Van Ameyde v. UCI	90/76	9.6.77	[1977] 1091	2[1977] 478	8425
58.	Metro v. Commission I	26/76	25.10.77	[1977] 1875	2[1978] 1	8435
59.	GB-INNO v. ATAB	13/77	16.11.77	[1977] 2115	1[1978] 283	8442
60.	De Bloos v. Boyer	59/77	14.12.77	[1977] 2359	1[1978] 511	8444
61.	Miller v. Commission	19/77	1.2.78	[1978] 131	2[1978] 334	8439
62.	United Brands v. Commission	27/76	14.2.78	[1978] 207	1[1978] 429	8429
63.	Hoffmann-La Roche v. Centrafarm	102/77	23.5.78	[1978] 1139	3[1978] 217	8466
64.	Tepea v. Commission	28/77	20.6.78	[1978] 1391	3[1978] 392	8467
65.	Benzine & Petroleum BV v. Commission	77/77	29.6.78	[1978] 1513	3[1978] 174	8465
66.	Centrafarm v. AHP	3/78	10.10.78	[1978] 1823	1[1979] 326	8475
67.	Hoffmann-La Roche v. Commission	85/76	13.2.79	[1979] 461	3[1979] 211	8527
68.	Hugin v. Commission	22/78	31.5.79	[1979] 1869	3[1979] 345	8524
69.	BMW Belgium v. Commission	32, 36-82/78	12.7.79	[1979] 2435	1[1980] 370	8548
70.	GEMA v. Commission	125/78	18.10.79	[1979] 3173	2[1980] 177	3568
71.	Greenwich v. SACEM	22/79	25.10.79	[1979] 3275	1[1980] 629	8567
72.	Camera Care v. Commission	792/79R	17.1.80	[1980] 119	1[1980] 334	8645
72a.	Coditel v. Ciné Vog	62/79	18.3.80	[1980] 881	2[1981] 362	8662
72b.	Debauve	52/79	18.3.80	[1980] 833	2[1981] 362	8661
73.	Boekhandels v. Eldi Records	106/79	20.3.80	[1980] 1137	3[1980] 719	8646
73a.	Commission v. Ireland	113/80	17.6.80	[1980] 1625	1[1982] 706	8762
74.	National Panasonic v. Commission	136/79	26.6.80	[1980] 2033	3[1980] 169	8682
75.	Distillers v. Commission	30/78	10.7.80	[1980] 2229	3[1980] 121	8613
76.	Procureur v. Guerlain	253/78, 1-3/79	10.7.80	[1980] 2327	2[1981] 99	8712
77.	Anne Marty v. Estée Lauder	37/79	10.7.80	[1980] 2481	2[1981] 143	8713
78.	Lancôme v. Etos	99/79	10.7.80	[1980] 2511	2[1981] 164	8714
79.	Philip Morris v. Commission	730/79	17.9.80	[1980] 2671	2[1981] 321	8615
80.	FEDETAB v. Commission	209-215, 218/78	29.10.80	[1980] 3125	3[1981] 134	8687
81.	L'Oréal v. De Nieuwe AMCK	31/80	11.12.80	[1980] 3775	2[1981] 235	8715
82.	Membran/K-Tel v. GEMA	55 & 57/80	20.1.81	[1981] 147	2[1981] 44	8670
83.	Dansk Supermarked v. Imerco	58/80	22.1.81	[1981] 181	3[1981] 590	8729
84.	Stremsel v. Commission	61/80	25.3.81	[1981] 851	1[1982] 240	8709
85.	Salonia v. Poidomani & Baglieri	126/80	16.6.81	[1981] 1563	1[1982] 64	8758
86.	Zuechner v. Bayerische Vereinsbank	172/80	14.7.81	[1981] 2021	1[1982] 313	8706
87.	Merck & Co v. Stephar	187/80	14.7.81	[1981] 2063	3[1981] 463	8707
88.	IBM v. Commission	60/81	11.11.81	[1981] 2639	3[1981] 635	8708
89.	Pfizer v. Eurim-Pharm	1/81	3.12.81	[1981] 2913	1[1982] 406	8737

No.	NAME	CASE No.	DATE	E.C.R.[1]		C.M.L.R.[2]		C.C.H.[3]
90.	Polydor v. Harlequin Record Shops	270/80	9.2.82	[1982]	329	1[1982]	677	8806
91.	IDG v. Beele	6/81	2.3.82	[1982]	717	3[1983]	102	8817
92.	AM & S v. Commission	155/79	18.5.82	[1982]	1575	2[1982]	264	8757
93.	Lord Bethell v. Commission	246/81	10.5.82	[1982]	2277	3[1982]	300	8858
94.	Nungesser v. Commission	258/78	8.6.82	[1982]	2015	1[1983]	278	8805
95.	France v. Commission	188-190/80	6.7.82	[1982]	2545	3[1982]	144	8852
95a.	Keurkoop v. Nancy Kean Gifts	144/81	14.9.82	[1982]	2853	2[1983]	47	8861
96.	Coditel v. Cine-Vog	262/81	6.10.82	[1982]	3381	3[1982]	328	8662
97.	GVL v. Commission	7/82	2.3.83	[1982]	483	3[1983]	645	8636
97a.	Inter-Huiles	172/82	10.3.83	[1983]	555	3[1983]	485	—
98.	Pioneer v. Commission	100-103/80	7.6.83	[1983]	1825	3[1983]	221	8880
99.	Demo Schmidt v. Commission	210/81	11.10.83	[1983]	3045	1[1984]	63	14 009
100.	AEG v. Commission	107/82	25.10.83	[1983]	3151	3[1984]	413	14 018
101.	NAVEWA v. Commission	96-102, 104, 105, 108 & 110/82	8.11.83	[1983]	3369	3[1984]	276	14 023
102.	Michelin v. Commission	322/81	9.11.83	[1983]	3461	1[1985]	282	14 031
103.	Roussel v. Netherlands	181/82	29.11.83	[1983]	3489	1[1985]	348	14 044
104.	Ciments et Bétons v. Kerpen	319/82	14.12.83	[1983]	4173	1[1985]	511	14 043
105.	VBVB & VBBB v. Commission	43 & 63/82	17.1.84	[1984]	19	1[1985]	27	14 042
106.	Duphar	238/82	7.2.84	[1984]	523	1[1985]	256	14 052
107.	Hasselblad v. Commission	86/82	21.2.84	[1984]	883	1[1984]	559	14 014
107a.	Prantl	16/83	13.3.84	[1984]	1299	2[1985]	238	14 089
108.	Ford v. Commission	228 & 229/82	28.2.84	[1984]	1129	1[1984]	649	14 025
109.	Zinc Producers v. Commission	29 & 30/83	28.3.84	[1984]	1679	2[1984]	108	14 085
110.	Van der Haar v. Kaveka	177 & 178/82	5.4.84	[1984]	1797	2[1985]	566	14 094
111.	Hydrotherm v. Andreoli	170/83	12.7.84	[1984]	2999	3[1985]	224	14 112
111a.	Kohl v. Ringelhahn	177/83	6.11.84	[1984]	3651	3[1985]	340	14 123
112.	GAARM v. Commission	289/83	13.12.84	[1984]	4295	1[1986]	15	14 158
113.	Leclerc	229/83	10.1.85	[1985]	1	2[1985]	286	14 111
114.	Cullet v. Leclerc	231/83	29.1.85	[1985]	305	2[1985]	524	14 139
115.	BNIC v. Clair	123/83	30.1.85	[1985]	391	2[1985]	430	14 160
116.	BAT v. Commission	35/83	30.1.85	[1985]	363	2[1985]	470	14 166
117.	Italy v. Commission	41/83	20.3.85	[1985]	873	3[1985]	368	14 168
118.	CICCE v. Commission	298/83	28.3.85	[1985]	1105	1[1986]	486	14 157
119.	AMP v. Binon	243/83	3.7.85	[1985]	2015	3[1985]	800	14 218
120.	Pharmon v. Hoechst	19/84	9.7.85	[1985]	2281	3[1985]	775	14 206

Chronological List of European Court Judgments (EEC)—References

No.	NAME	CASE No.	DATE	E.C.R.[1]	C.M.L.R.[2]	C.C.H.[3]
121.	Remia v. Commission	42/84	11.7.85	[1985] 2545	1[1987] 1	14 217
122.	St. Herblain v. Syndicat des Libraires	299/83	11.7.85	[1985] 2515	—	14 219
122a.	Cinéthèque	60 & 61/84	11.7.85	[1985] 2605	1[1986] 365	14 220
122b.	Miro	182/84	26.11.85	[1985] 3731	3[1986] 545	14 263
123.	Ford v. Commission	25 & 26/84	17.9.85	[1985] 2725	3[1985] 528	14 144
124.	Télémarketing v. CLT	311/84	3.10.85	[1985] 3261	2[1986] 558	14 246
125.	Stanley Adams v. Commission	145/83	7.11.85	[1985] 3539	2[1986] 506	14 260
126.	ETA v. DKI	31/85	10.12.85	[1985] 3933	2[1986] 674	14 276
127.	SSI v. Commission	240-242, 261, 262, 268 & 269/82	10.12.85	[1985] 3831	3[1987] 661	14 265
128.	NSO v. Commission	260/82	10.12.85	[1985] 3801	4[1988] 755	14 266
129.	Pronuptia v. Schillgalis	161/84	28.1.86	[1986] 353	1[1986] 414	14 245
130.	Windsurfing v. Commission	193/83	25.2.86	[1986] 611	3[1986] 489	14 271
131.	Nouvelles Frontières	209-213/84	30.4.86	[1986] 1425	3[1986] 173	14 287
132.	AKZO v. Commission I	53/85	24.6.86	[1986] 1965	1[1987] 231	14 318
133.	AKZO v. Commission II	5/85	23.9.86	[1986] 2585	3[1987] 716	14 366
134.	Metro v. Commission II	75/84	22.10.86	[1986] 3021	1[1987] 118	14 326
135.	Procureur v. Cognet	355/85	23.10.86	[1986] 3231	3[1987] 942	14 388
136.	British Leyland	226/84	11.11.86	[1986] 3263	1[1987] 184	14 336
137.	Cerafel v. Le Campion	218/85	25.11.86	[1986] 3513	1[1988] 83	14 379
137a.	Commission v. Germany	179/85	4.12.86	[1986] 3879	1[1988] 135	14 384
138.	VAG v. Magne	10/86	18.12.86	[1986] 4071	4[1988] 98	14 390
139.	Fire Insurance v. Commission	45/85	27.1.87	[1987] 405	4[1988] 264	—
140.	Hoechst v. Commission II	46/87R	26.3.87	[1987] 1549	4[1988] 430	—
141.	Basset v. SACEM	402/85	9.4.87	[1987] 1747	3[1987] 173	14 422
141a.	Commission v. Italy	118/85	16.6.87	[1987] 2599	3[1988] 255	—
142.	ANTIB v. Commission	272/85	20.5.87	[1987] 2201	4[1988] 677	14 458
143.	ANCIDES v. Commission	43/85	9.7.87	[1987] 3131	4[1988] 821	14 467
144.	Vlaamse Reisbureaus	311/85	1.10.87	[1987] 3801	4[1989] 213	14 499
145.	Dow v. Commission	85/87R	28.10.87	[1987] 4367	4[1989] 439	—
146.	BAT v. Commission & Philip Morris	142 & 156/84	17.11.87	[1987] 4487	4[1988] 24	14 405
147.	BNIC/Aubert	136/86	3.12.87	[1987] 4789	4[1988] 331	1 [1989] 363*

* In 1989, the full citation of the C.C.H. Common Market Reporter became [YEAR](Volume No.)CEC(Page No.) In this Handbook, the volume numbers are shown before the year, for ease of reference.

No.	NAME	CASE No.	DATE	E.C.R.[1]	C.M.L.R.[2]	C.C.H.[3]
148.	Allen & Hanburys v. Generics	434/85	3.3.88	[1988] 1245	1[1988] 701	14 446
149.	Louis Erauw v. La Hesbignonne	27/87	19.4.88	[1988] 1919	4[1988] 576	2 [1989] 637
149a.	Bond van Adverteerders	352/85	26.4.88	[1988] 2085	3[1989] 113	2 [1989] 697
150.	Bodson v. Pompes Funèbres	30/87	4.5.88	[1988] 2479	4[1989] 984	1 [1990] 3
151.	Warner Brothers v. Christiansen	158/86	17.5.88	[1988] 2605	3[1990] 684	1 [1990] 33
152.	Thetford Corp. v. Fiamma	35/87	30.6.88	[1988] 3585	3[1988] 549	14 497
153.	Commission v. Greece	226/87	30.6.88	[1988] 3611	3[1989] 569	
154.	Syndicat v. Leclerc Aigle	254/87	14.7.88	[1988] 4457	4[1990] 37	1 [1990] 94
155.	Van Eycke v. Aspa	267/86	21.9.88	[1988] 4769	4[1990] 330	1 [1990] 293
156.	UNILEC v. Larroche	212/87	22.9.88	[1988] 5075	1[1990] 592	1 [1990] 439
157.	Woodpulp	89, 104, 114 116, 117, 125–129/85	27.9.88	[1988] 5193	4[1988] 901	14 491
158.	Bayer v. Süllhöfer	65/86	27.9.88	[1988] 5249	4[1990] 182	1 [1990] 220
159.	Volvo v. Veng	238/87	5.10.88	[1988] 6211	4[1989] 122	14 498
160.	Alsatel v. Novosam	247/86	5.10.88	[1988] 5987	4[1990] 434	1 [1990] 248
161.	Maxicar v. Renault	53/87	5.10.88	[1988] 6039	4[1990] 265	1 [1990] 59
161a.	EMI v. Patricia	341/87	24.1.89	[1989] 79	2[1989] 413	1 [1990] 322
162.	Ahmeed Saeed v. Zentrale	66/86	11.4.89	[1989] 803	4[1990] 102	2 [1989] 654
163.	RTE & BBC v. Commission	76,77 & 91/89R	11.5.89	[1989] 1141	4[1989] 749	
164.	Ottung v. Klee	320/87	12.5.89	[1989] 1194	4[1990] 915	2 [1990] 674
164a.	Royal Pharmaceutical Society	266 & 267/86	18.5.89	[1989] 1295	2[1989] 751	1 [1990] 415
165.	Publishers Association v. Commission	56/89R	13.6.89	[1989] 1693	4[1989] 816	
166.	Belasco v. Commission	246/86	11.7.89	[1989] 2181	4[1991] 96	2 [1990] 912
167.	Ministère Public v. Tournier	395/87	13.7.89	[1989] 2521	4[1991] 248	2 [1990] 815
168.	Lucazeau v. SACEM	110, 241 & 242/88	13.7.89	[1989] 2811	4[1991] 248	2 [1990] 856
169.	Hoechst v. Commission III	46/87, 227/88	21.9.89	[1989] 2859	4[1991] 410	1 [1991] 280
170.	Dow Benelux v. Commission	85/87	17.10.89	[1989] 3137	4[1991] 410	2 [1991] 3
171.	Dow Iberica v. Commission	97–99/87	17.10.89	[1989] 3165	4[1991] 410	
172.	Orkem v. Commission	374/87	18.10.89	[1989] 3283	4[1991] 502	2 [1991] 19
173.	Solvay v. Commission	27/88	18.10.89	[1989] 3355	4[1991] 502	
174.	Sandoz v. Commission	C-277/87	11.1.90	1 [1990] 47		
175.	Tipp-Ex v. Commission	C-279/87	8.2.90	1 [1990] 263		
176.	Asia Motors v. Commission	C-72/90	23.5.90	1 [1990] 2182		
177.	CNL-Sucal v. Hag	C-10/89	17.10.90	1 [1990] 3711	3[1990] 571	2 [1991] 457
178.	Cholay	C-270/86	12.12.90	1 [1990] 4687		

Chronological List of European Court Judgments (EEC)—References

No.	NAME	CASE No.	DATE	E.C.R.[1]	C.M.L.R.[2]	C.C.H.[3]
179.	Pall v. Dahlhausen	C-238/89	13.12.90	[1990] 4824	—	—
180.	Ahlsthom v. Sulzer	C-339/89	24.1.91	[1991] 107	—	—
181.	Delimitis v. Henninger Bräu	C-234/89	28.2.91	[1991] 935	—	—
181a.	Marchandise	C-332/89	28.2.91	[1991] 1627	—	—
182.	France v. Commission	C-202/88	19.3.91	[1991] 1223	—	—
183.	Bayern v. Eurim-Pharm	C-347/89	16.4.91	[1991] 1747	—	—
184.	Höfner v. Macrotron	C-41/90	23.4.91	[1991] 1979	—	—
184a.	PTT v. Commission	C-66/90	4.6.91	—	—	—
185.	ERT v. DEP	C-269/89	18.6.91	—	—	—
186.	AKZO v. Commission III	C-62/86	3.7.91	—	—	—
187.	Bosman v. Commission	C-117/91	4.10.91	—	—	—
188.	Merci v. Siderurgica	C-179/90	10.12.91	—	—	—
189.	RTT v. GB-Inno	C-18/88	13.12.91	—	—	—
190.	Netherlands v. Commission	C-48 & 66/90	12.2.92	—	—	—
191.	Commission v. Italy	C-235/89	18.2.92	—	—	—
192.	Commission v. U.K.	C-30/90	18.2.92	—	—	—
193.	Batista Morais	C-60/91	19.3.92	—	—	—

Book One—Table 6

TABLE 6
CHRONOLOGICAL LIST OF EUROPEAN COURT JUDGMENTS (EEC)—CONTENTS

No.	NAME	ARTICLE	SUBJECT	RESULT	PRODUCT/SERVICE
1.	Bosch v. De Geus	177	Provisional Validity	—	Domestic Appliances
2.	Costa v. ENEL	177	Supremacy EEC Treaty	—	Electricity
3.	LTM v. MBU	177	Exclusive Distribution	—	Machinery
4.	Consten & Grundig v. Commission	173	Exclusive Distribution	Upheld	Consumer Electronics
5.	Italy v. Council and Commission	173	Regulation 19/65	Upheld	Distribution
6.	Cimenteries v. Commission	173	Article 15(6) letter	Annulled	Cement
7.	De Haecht v. Wilkin I	177	Exclusive Purchase	—	Brewery Contracts
8.	Parke, Davis v. Centrafarm	177	Patent rights	—	Pharmaceuticals
9.	Walt Wilhelm	177	Supremacy EEC Treaty	—	Dyestuffs
10.	Völk v. Vervaecke	177	De Minimis	—	Domestic Appliances
11.	Portelange v. Smith Corona	177	Provisional validity	—	Typewriters
12.	Bilger v. Jehle	177	Article 4 Regulation 17/62	—	Beer
13.	Parfums Rochas v. Bitsch	177	Provisional validity	—	Cosmetics
14.	ACF Chemiefarma v. Commission	173	Cartel	Fine reduced	Quinine
15.	Buchler & Co. v. Commission	173	Cartel	Fine reduced	Quinine
16.	Boehringer v. Commission	173	Cartel	Fine reduced	Quinine
17.	Sirena v. Eda	177	Trade marks	—	Cosmetics
18.	Cadillon v. Höss	177	Exclusive Distribution	—	Building Tools
19.	Deutsche Grammophon v. Metro	177	Copyright	—	Records
20.	Komponistenverband v. Commission	175	Right to be heard	Upheld	Performing Rights
21.	Muller	177	Article 90(2)	—	Dredging
22.	Béguelin v. GL	177	Exclusive Distribution	—	Lighters
23.	ICI v. Commission	173	Cartel(price)	Upheld	Dyestuffs
24.	BASF v. Commission	173	Cartel(price)	Upheld	Dyestuffs
25.	Bayer v. Commission	173	Cartel(price)	Upheld	Dyestuffs
26.	Ciba-Geigy v. Commission	173	Cartel(price)	Upheld	Dyestuffs
27.	Sandoz v. Commission	173	Cartel(price)	Upheld	Dyestuffs
28.	Francolor v. Commission	173	Cartel(price)	Upheld	Dyestuffs
29.	Cassella v. Commission	173	Cartel(price)	Upheld	Dyestuffs
30.	Hoechst v. Commission I	173	Cartel(price)	Upheld	Dyestuffs
31.	ACNA v. Commission	173	Cartel(price)	Fine reduced	Dyestuffs

Chronological List of European Court Judgments (EEC)—Contents

No.	NAME	ARTICLE	SUBJECT	RESULT	PRODUCT/SERVICE
32.	Cement Dealers v. Commission	173	Cartel(national)	Upheld	Cement
33.	Boehringer v. Commission	173	Non bis in idem	Upheld	Quinine
34.	De Haecht v. Wilkin II	177	Conflict Rules	—	Brewery contract
35.	Continental Can v. Commission	173	Merger 86	Annulled	Cans
36.	BRT v. SABAM I	177	Conflict rules	—	Performing Rights
37.	ICI & CSC v. Commission	173	Refusal to deal	Fine reduced	Pharmaceuticals
38.	BRT v. SABAM II	177	Copyright 86	—	Performing Rights
39.	Sacchi	177	Public Monopoly	—	TV Advertising
40.	Van Zuylen v. Hag	177	Trade Marks	—	Coffee
40a.	Dassonville	177	Exclusive Distribution	—	Whisky
40b.	Transocean Marine Paint Association	173	Hearing	Annulled	Marine Paints
41.	Centrafarm v. Sterling Drug	177	Patent rights	—	Pharmaceuticals
42.	Centrafarm v. Winthrop	177	Trade Marks	—	Pharmaceuticals
42a.	Commission v. Germany	169	Origin Specification	—	Sekt
43.	Kali & Salz v. Commission	173	Cartel (distribution)	Annulled	Fertilisers
44.	Frubo v. Commission	173	Exclusionary Practices	Upheld	Fruit
45.	Van Vliet v. Dalle Crode	177	Exclusive Distribution	—	Paint Brushes
46.	General Motors v. Commission	173	Excessive Pricing 86	Annulled	Cars
47.	Papiers Peints v. Commission	173	Cartel (price)	Annulled	Wallpaper
48.	Suiker Unie v. Commission	173	Market Sharing	Fines reduced	Sugar
49.	Fonderies Roubaix v. Fonderies Roux	177	Exclusive Distribution	—	Foundries
50.	EMI-CBS	177	Trade Mark Rights	—	Records
51.	EMI-CBS	177	Trade Mark Rights	—	Records
52.	EMI-CBS	177	Trade Mark Rights	—	Records
53.	Terrapin v. Terranova	177	Trade Mark Rights	—	Building Materials
54.	De Norre v. Concordia	177	Exclusive Purchasing	—	Brewery Contracts
55.	Générale Sucrière v. Commission	173	Currency of Fine	Upheld	Sugar
56.	Hoffmann-La Roche v. Centrafarm	177	Trade Mark Rights	—	Pharmaceuticals
57.	Van Ameyde v. UCI	177	Article 90(1)	—	Insurance
58.	Metro v. Commission I	173	Selective Distribution	Upheld	Consumer Electronics
59.	GB-INNO v. ATAB	177	State Responsibility	—	Tobacco
60.	De Bloos v. Boyer	177	Provisional Validity	—	Agricultural Machines
61.	Miller v. Commission	173	Export Ban	Upheld	Records
62.	United Brands v. Commission	173	Excessive Pricing 86	Fine reduced	Bananas
63.	Hoffmann-La Roche v. Centrafarm	177	Trade Mark Rights	—	Pharmaceuticals
64.	Tepea v. Commission	177	Trade Mark Licence	Upheld	Record Cleaners
65.	Benzine & Petroleum BV v. Commission	173	Refusal to Deal 86	Annulled	Petrol

Book One—Table 6

No.	NAME	ARTICLE	SUBJECT	RESULT	PRODUCT/SERVICE
66.	Centrafarm v. AHP	177	Trade Mark Rights	—	Pharmaceuticals
67.	Hoffmann-La Roche v. Commission	173	Exclusionary Practices 86	Upheld (in part)	Vitamins
68.	Hugin v. Commission	173	Refusal to Deal 86	Annulled	Cash Registers
69.	BMW Belgium v. Commission	173	Export Ban	Upheld	Cars
70.	Gema v. Commission	175	Copyright	Dismissed	Performing Rights
71.	Greenwich v. SACEM	177	Copyright 86	—	Performing Rights
72.	Camera Care v. Commission	173	Interim Measures	Upheld	Cameras
72a.	Coditel v. Ciné-Vog	177	Copyright	—	Cable TV
72b.	Debauve	177	Monopoly	—	Cable TV
73.	Boekhandels v. Eldi Records	177	Notification	—	Records
73a.	Commission v. Ireland	169	Origin Specification	—	Souvenirs
74.	National Panasonic v. Commission	173	Inspection	Upheld	Consumer Electronics
75.	Distillers v. Commission	173	Notification	Upheld	Alcoholic Drinks
76.	Procureur v. Guerlain	177	Comfort Letter	—	Perfumes
77.	Anne Marty v. Estée Lauder	177	Comfort Letter	—	Perfumes
78.	Lancôme v. Etos	177	Selective Distribution	—	Cosmetics
79.	Philip Morris v. Commission	173	State Aids	Upheld	Tobacco
80.	FEDETAB v. Commission	177	Cartel	Upheld	Tobacco
81.	L'Oréal v. De Nieuwe AMCK	177	Selective Distribution	—	Cosmetics
82.	Membran/K-Tel v. Gema	177	Copyright	—	Records
83.	Dansk Supermarked v. Imerco	177	Copyright & Trade Mark	—	China
84.	Stremsel v. Commission	173	Exclusive Purchasing	Upheld	Rennet
85.	Salonia v. Poidomani & Baglieri	177	Selective Distribution	—	Newspapers
86.	Zuechner v. Bayerische Vereinsbank	177	Concerted Practice	—	Banking
87.	Merck & Co v. Stephar	177	Patent Rights	—	Pharmaceuticals
88.	IBM v. Commission	173	Statement of Objections	Upheld	Computers
89.	Pfizer v. Eurim-Pharm	177	Trade Mark Rights	—	Pharmaceuticals
90.	Polydor v. Harlequin Record Shops	177	Copyright	—	Records
91.	IDG v. Beele	177	Counterfeit	—	Building Materials
92.	AM & S v. Commission	173	Legal Professional privilege	Annulled (part)	Zinc
93.	Lord Bethell v. Commission	175	Locus Standi	Dismissed	Transport
94.	Nungesser v. Commission	173	Breeders' rights	Annulled (part)	Maize Seeds
95.	France v. Commission	173	Article 90(3)	Upheld	Public Undertakings
95a.	Keurkoop v. Nancy Kean Gifts	177	Design rights	—	Leatherwear
96.	Coditel v. Cine-Vog	177	Copyright	—	Cable TV
97.	GVL v. Commission	173	Copyright 86	Upheld	Performing Rights
97a.	Inter-Huiles	177	Article 90	—	Waste Collection

Chronological List of European Court Judgments (EEC)—Contents

No.	NAME	ARTICLE	SUBJECT	RESULT	PRODUCT/SERVICE
98.	Pioneer v. Commission	173	Export Ban	Fine reduced	Consumer Electronics
99.	Demo Schmidt v. Commission	173	Complaint/Select Distribution	Upheld	Consumer Electronics
100.	AEG v. Commission	173	Selective Distribution	Upheld	Electrical Goods
101.	NAVEWA v. Commission	173	Preventing Parallel Trade	Upheld	Domestic Appliances
102.	Michelin v. Commission	173	Discounts 86	Fine reduced	Tyres
103.	Roussel v. Netherlands	177	Pricing Legislation	—	Pharmaceuticals
104.	Ciments et Bétons v. Kerpen	177	Resale Prohibition	—	Cement
105.	VBVB & VBBB v. Commission	173	Collective RPM	Upheld	Books
106.	Duphar	177	Drug Re-imbursement Scheme	—	Pharmaceuticals
107.	Hasselblad v. Commission	173	Preventing Parallel Trade	Fine reduced	Cameras
107a.	Prantl	177	Design rights	—	Bottles
108.	Ford v. Commission	173	Interim Measures	Annulled	Cars
109.	Zinc Producers v. Commission	173	Cartel	Fine cancelled	Zinc
110.	Van der Haar v. Kaveka	177	Pricing Legislation	—	Tobacco
111.	Hydrotherm v. Andreoli	177	Regulation 67/67	—	Heating Equipment
111a.	Kohl v. Ringelhahn	177	Logo	—	Pharmaceutical Equipment
112.	GAARM v. Commission	215	Failure to Act	Dismissed	New Potatoes
113.	Leclerc	177	State Responsibility	—	Books
114.	Cullet v. Leclerc	177	State Responsibility	—	Petroleum Products
115.	BNIC v. Clair	177	Price Fixing	—	Alcoholic Drinks
116.	BAT v. Commission	173	Trade Marks	Fine cancelled	Cigarettes
117.	Italy v. Commission	173	Refusal to Supply 86	Upheld	Telecommunications
118.	CICCE v. Commission	173	Duties of a Complainant	Upheld	Cinema
119.	AMP v. Binon	177	Selective Distribution	—	Newspapers
120.	Pharmon v. Hoechst	177	Patent Rights	—	Pharmaceuticals
121.	Remia v. Commission	173	Acquisition	Upheld	Foodstuffs
122.	St. Herblain v. Syndicat des Libraires	177	State Responsibility	—	Books
122a.	Cinéthèque	177	Copyright	—	Video cassettes
122b.	Miro	177	Product denomination	—	Cinema
123.	Ford v. Commission	173	Preventing Parallel Trade	Upheld	Cars
124.	Télémarketing v. CLT	177	Tying 86	—	TV Advertising
125.	Stanley Adams v. Commission	215	Confidentiality	Damages awarded	—
126.	ETA v. DKI	177	Guarantee	—	Watches
127.	SSI v. Commission	173	Cartel	Upheld	Tobacco
128.	NSO v. Commission	173	Cartel	Upheld	Tobacco
129.	Pronuptia v. Schillgalis	177	Franchising	—	Wedding Dresses

Book One—Table 6

No.	NAME	ARTICLE	SUBJECT	RESULT	PRODUCT/SERVICE
130.	Windsurfing v. Commission	173	Patent Licences	Fine reduced	Leisure Products
131.	Nouvelles Frontières	177	State Responsibility	—	Air Transport
132.	AKZO v. Commission I	173	Business Secrets	Annulled	Chemicals
133.	AKZO v. Commission II	173	Investigations	Upheld	Chemicals
134.	Metro v. Commission II	173	Selective Distribution	Upheld	Radios
135.	Procureur v. Cognet	177	State Responsibility	—	—
136.	British Leyland	173	Preventing Parallel Trade 86	Upheld	Cars
137.	Cerafel v. Le Campion	177	National Market Organisation	—	Vegetables
137a.	Commission v. Germany	169	Product Specification	—	Bottles
138.	VAG v. Magne	177	Regulation 123/85	—	Cars
139.	Fire Insurance v. Commission	173	Cartel	Upheld	Fire Insurance
140.	Hoechst v. Commission II	186	Investigation	Dismissed	Chemicals
141.	Basset v. SACEM	177	Copyright 86	—	Performing Rights
141a.	Commission v. Italy	169	Article 90	—	State aids
142.	ANTIB v. Commission	173	Cartel	Upheld	River Transport
143.	ANCIDES v. Commission	173	Exhibition Agreement	Upheld	Dental Equipment
144.	Vlaamse Reisbureaus	177	State Responsibility	—	Travel Agents
145.	Dow v. Commission	186	Investigation	Dismissed	Chemicals
146.	BAT v. Commission & Philip Morris	173	Minority Share Acquisition	Upheld	Cigarettes
147.	BNIC/Aubert	177	Production Quotas	—	Spirits
148.	Allen & Hanburys v. Generics	177	Licence of Right	—	Pharmaceuticals
149.	Louis Erauw v. La Hesbignonne	177	Breeders' rights	—	Seeds
149a.	Bond van Adverteerders	177	Monopoly	—	Cable TV
150.	Bodson v. Pompes Funèbres	177	Articles 90 and 86	—	Undertakers
151.	Warner Brothers v. Christiansen	177	Copyright	—	Performing Rights
152.	Thetford Corp. v. Fiamma	177	Patent Rights	—	Toilets
153.	Commission v. Greece	169	Article 90	—	Insurance
154.	Syndicat v. Leclerc Aigle	177	State Responsibility	—	Books
155.	Van Eycke v. Aspa	177	State Responsibility	—	Banking
156.	UNILEC v. Larroche	177	National Market Organisation	—	Fruit & Vegetables
157.	Woodpulp	173	Extraterritoriality	Upheld	Woodpulp
158.	Bayer v. Süllhöfer	177	Patent licence	—	Chemicals
159.	Volvo v. Veng	177	Patent Rights 86	—	Car Parts
160.	Alsatel v. Novosam	177	Article 86	—	Telephones
161.	Maxicar v. Renault	177	Patent Rights 86	—	Car Parts
161a.	EMI v. Patricia	177	Copyright	—	Records
162.	Ahmed Saeed v. Zentrale	177	Price-fixing	—	Air Transport

Chronological List of European Court Judgments (EEC)—Contents

No.	NAME	ARTICLE	SUBJECT	RESULT	PRODUCT/SERVICE
163.	*RTE & BBC v. Commission*	186	Copyright 86	Suspended	TV Guide
164.	*Ottung v. Klee*	177	—	Patent Licensing	Brewery Machines
164a.	*Royal Pharmaceutical Society*	177	Drug Prescription Rules	—	Drugs
165.	*Publishers Association v. Commission*	186	Cartel	Suspended	Books
166.	*Belasco v. Commission*	173	Cartel	Upheld	Construction Machines
167.	*Ministère Public v. Tourner*	177	Excessive Pricing	—	Copyright
168.	*Lucazeau v. SACEM*	177	Excessive Pricing 86	—	Copyright
169.	*Hoechst v. Commission III*	173	Investigation	Upheld	Base Chemicals
170.	*Dow Benelux v. Commission*	173	Investigation	Upheld	Base Chemicals
171.	*Dow Iberica v. Commission*	173	Investigation	Upheld	Base Chemicals
172.	*Orkem v. Commission*	173	Information	Partial Annulment	Base Chemicals
173.	*Solvay v. Commission*	173	Information	Partial Annulment	Pharmaceuticals
174.	*Sandoz v. Commission*	173	Preventing Parallel Trade	Fine reduced	Stationary
175.	*Tipp-Ex v. Commission*	173	Preventing Parallel Trade	Upheld	Cars
176.	*Asia Motors v. Commission*	175/178	Competence of the Court	Transfer to Court of First Instance	
177.	*CNL-Sucal v. Hag*	177	Trade Marks	—	Coffee
178.	*Cholay*	177	Copyright	—	Performing Rights
179.	*Pall v. Dahlhausen*	177	Trade Mark law	—	Filters
180.	*Ahlsthom v. Sulzer*	177	Product-Liability	—	Ship engines
181.	*Delimitis v. Henninger Bräu*	177	Exclusive Purchasing	—	Beer
181a.	*Marchandise*	177	Opening hours	—	Retail business
182.	*France v. Commission*	173	Article 90	—	Telecommunications
183.	*Bayern v. Eurim-Pharm*	177	Drug Registration	—	Pharmaceuticals
184.	*Höfner v. Macrotron*	177	Article 90	—	Recruitment Services
184a.	*PTT v. Commission*	173	Competence CFI	Transfer	Courier Services
185.	*ERT v. DEP*	177	Article 90	—	Television
186.	*AKZO v. Commission III*	173	Predatory Pricing	Fine reduced	Chemicals
187.	*Bosman v. Commission*	173/178	Rejection of Complaint	Inadmissible	Football
188.	*Merci v. Siderurgica*	177	Article 90	—	Portactivities
189.	*RTT v. GB-Inno*	177	Article 90	—	Telecommunication
190.	*Netherlands v. Commission*	173	Article 90	Annuled	Courier Services
191.	*Commission v. Italy*	169	Compulsory Licensing	—	Patents
192.	*Commission v. U.K.*	169	Compulsory Licensing	—	Patents
193.	*Batista Morais*	177	State Interference	—	Drivers Licence

43

TABLE 7

ALPHABETICAL LIST OF COMMISSION DECISIONS

(Note: Lists of Commission Decisions relating to Mergers and the ECSC are set out at the beginning of Books 2 and 3 respectively; a combined list for all three Books appears at page x)

ABG/Oil Companies	113	Burroughs/Delplanque	50
ABI	262	Burroughs/Geha	51
ACEC/Berliet	14		
AEG-Telefunken	179		
AM & S Europe	146	CFA	18
ANSAC	333a	CICG	36
AOIP/Beyrard	98	CSV	105
APB	314	CSV	134
ARD	312	Cafeteros de Colombia	187
ARG/Unipart	278	Campari	130
AROW/BNIC	190	Canary Islands	268
ASBL	31	Cane Sugar Supply Agreements	150
ASPA	30	Carbon Gas Technologie	205
Advocaat Zwarte Kip	79	Carlsberg	214
Alba	39	Cast-iron & Steel Rolls	198
Alcatel/ANT	319	Castrol	192
Alliance des Constructeurs Français	12	Cauliflowers	119
Aluminium	228	Cekacan	326
Amersham Buchler	184	Cematex I	43
Arthur Bell & Sons Ltd.	135	Cematex II	193
Asphaltoid-Keller	42	Central Bureau voor de Rijwielhandel	118
Assurpol	347	Central Heating	60
		Ceramic Tiles	35
BBC Brown Boveri	291	Charles Jourdan	298
BIFFEX	271	Chaufourniers	20
BMW	82	Chiquita	101
BMW Belgium	126	Christiani & Nielsen	21
BP/Bayer	284	Cimbel	66
BP/Kellogg	235	Clima Chappée	25
BP Kemi/DDSF	147	Cobelaz	15
BPCL/ICI	215	Cobelaz Cokes	16
BPICA I	116	Cobelpa/VNP	115
BPICA II	180	Comptoir d'Importation	167
Baccarat	338	Computerland	270
Bayer Dental	327	Concordato	316
Bayonox	313	Continental/Michelin	290
Bayer/Gist-Brocades	100	Continental Can	46
Beecham/Parke Davis	144	Convention Faience	2
Belgian Banking Association	261		
Belgian Wallpaper	78		
Bendix/Mertens and Straet	3	DECA	6
Boehringer	45	DRU/Blondel	7
Bomée-Stichting	97	Davidson Rubber	56
Boosey & Hawkes	273	Decca	304
Boussois/Interpane	264	De Laval/Stork I	114
Breeders' rights; roses	236	De Laval/Stork II	281
British Dental Trade Association	285	Delta Chemie	292
British Leyland	212	Deutsche Philips	73
British Plasterboard	299	D'Ieteren	329
British Sugar	286	Distillers Company, The	123
British Telecommunications	188	Distillers-Victuallers	157
Bronbemaling	95	Dupont de Nemours Germany	71

Alphabetical List of Commission Decisions

DuroDyne	83
Dutch Banking Association	310
Dutch Cement	65
Dutch Express Delivery	318
Dyestuffs	27
EATE Levy	231
ECS/AKZO	242
ECS/AKZO-Interim measures	197
EMO (I)	19
EMO (II)	140
EMO (III)	303
ENI/Montedison	256
Enichem/ICI	279
Eco System	344a
Eirpage	344
Eurogypsum	11
European Sugar Industry	69
Eurotunnel	293
FEDETAB	133
FN/CF	37
FRUBO	80
Fabbricca Lastre	154
Fabbrica Pisana	153
Fatty Acids	254
Fédération Chaussure de France	183
Fides	145
Fire Insurance	175, 220
Fireplaces	90
Fisher-Price	275
Flat Glass	300
Flat Glass (Benelux)	216
Floral	148
Ford Werke AG	199
Ford Werke-Interim Measures	182
Franco-Japanese Ball-Bearings	81
GAFTA	260
GEC-Siemens Plessey	325
GEC/Weir Sodium Circulators	117
GISA	67
GVL	166
Gema I	38
Gema II	58
Gema Statutes	174
General Motors	84
German Blacksmiths	120
Gerofabriek	111
Goodyear Italiana/Euram	85
Gosme/Martell	340
Greek Insurance	230
Grohe Sales System	222
Grosfillex/Fillestorf	1
Grundig	232
Grundig/Consten	5
Hasselblad	173
Heaters and Boilers	72
Henkel/Colgate	52
Hennessy/Henkel	162
Hilti	282
Hudson Bay	294
Hugin/Liptons	121
Hummel Isbecque	8
IATA Cargo	343
IATA Passengers	342
IBM PC	210
ICI	333
IFTRA Aluminium	92
IFTRA Glass	77
IMA Rules	158
IPEL	255
IPTC Belgium	202
IVECO/Ford	287
Ideal Standard Sales System	223
Ijsselcentrale	335
Intergroup	91
International Dental Exhibition	274
International Energy Agency	207
Irish Bank Standing Committee	252
Italian Cast Glass	163
Italian Flat Glass	164
Ivoclar	234
Jaz/Peter I	26
Jaz/Peter II	128
John Deere	226
Johnson & Johnson	160
Julien/Van Katwijk	32
Junghans	109
KEWA	103
KSB	328
Kabelmetal/Luchaire	94
Kali & Salz/Kalichemie	76
Kawasaki	141
Kodak	29
Konica	277
Konsortium ECR 900	323
Krups	155
Langenscheidt/Hachette	168
LdPE	306
London Cocoa Market	239
London Coffee Market	240
London Grain Market	257
London Meat Exchange	259
London Potato Market	258
London Rubber Market	241
London Sugar Market	238
MAN/SAVIEM	54

Book One—Table 7

Maes	41
Magill	307
Maison Jallatte	9
Maize Seeds	137
Mecaniver/PPG	225
Meldoc	253
Metaleurop	321
Metallgesellachft/Safic Alcan	53
Michelin	165
Milchfoerderungsfonds	221
Miller	108
Misal	62
Mitchell Cotts/Sofiltra	267
Moët et Chandon (London) Ltd	172
Moosehead	320
Murat	200
NAVEWA-ANSEAU	178
NAVEWA-ANSEAU (Bosch)	185
NCH	53
National Panasonic	186
National Panasonic (Belgium)	176
National Panasonic (France)	177
National Sulphuric Acid Assoc. I	156
National Sulphuric Acid Assoc. II	308
Natursteinplatten	159
Net Book Agreements	301
New Potatoes	276
Nicholas Frères Vitapro	4
Nuovo-CEGAM	209
Nutricia	206
Odin	322
Olivetti/Canon	280
Olympic Airways	229
Omega	33
Optical Fibres	249
P & I Clubs	243
PVC	305
Pabst & Richerz/BNIA	106
Penney	127
Peroxide Products	218
Peugeot	250
Pioneer	152
Pirelli/Dunlop	28
Pittsburgh Corning	63
Polistil/Arbois	211
Polypropylene	247
Pronuptia	266
Prym/Beka	74
Quinine Cartel	24
RAI/Unitel	131
Rank/SOPELEM	86
Raymond-Nagoya	57
Rennet	149
Reuter/BASF	107
Rich Products	203
Rieckerman	17
Rockwell/IVECO	196
Rodenstock	61
Roofing Felt	248
SABA I	99
SABA II	208
SABENA	295
SAFCO	48
SCPA/Kali & Salz	70
SEIFA	23
SHV/Chevron	87
SIAE	44
SMM & T	201
SNPE-LEL	132
SOPELEM/Langen	49
SOPELEM/Vickers I	125
SOPELEM/Vickers II	171
SSI	181
Sandoz	272
Schlegel/CPIO	204
Scottish Nuclear	339
Screensport/EBU	337
Secrétama	329a
ServiceMaster	296
Siemens/Fanuc	246
Sippa	336
Sirdar Phildar	89
Socemans	13
Solvay	332
Solvay/CFK	331
Solvay/ICI	330
Spanish Courier Services	324
Sperry New Holland	245
Spices	124
Sugar Beet	315
Supexie	34
Synthetic Fibres	213
Teacher & Sons	136
Teko	317
Telos	170
Tetra Pak I	289
Tetra Pak II	348
Theal/Watts	110
Thin Paper	59
Tinned Mushrooms	88
Tipp-Ex	269
Toltecs/Dorcet	191
Transocean Marine Paint Assoc. I	10
Transocean Marine Paint Assoc. II	75
Transocean Marine Paint Assoc. III	96
Transocean Marine Paint Assoc. IV	151
Transocean Marine Paint Assoc. V	297
UIP	309

Alphabetical List of Commission Decisions

UK Tractors	347
UNIDI I	93
UNIDI II	219
Uniform Eurochèques	224
Uniform Eurochèques Manufacturing	302
Union Brasserie	40
United Reprocessors	102
VBA	288
VBBB/VBVB	169
VCH	47
VIFKA	251
VVVF	22
VW/MAN	203
Vacuum Interrupters I	112
Vacuum Interrupters II	161
Vaessen/Moris	143
Vegetable Parchment	129
Velcro/Aplix	233
Vichy	334
Video Cassette Recorders	122
Viho/Toshiba	341
Villeroy & Boch	244
Vimpoltu	195
Vitamins	104
WANO	138
WEA/Filipacchi Music S.A.	68
Welded Steel Mesh	311
Whisky and Gin	237
White Lead	142
Wild/Leitz	55
Windsurfing International	194
Woodpulp	227
X/Open Group	263
Yves Rocher	265
Yves Saint Laurent	345
Zanussi	139
Zinc	189
Zinc Producer Group	217
Zoja/CSC-ICI	64

TABLE 8

ALPHABETICAL LIST OF COURT OF FIRST INSTANCE JUDGMENTS

Atochem v. Commission	T20	Norsk Hydro v. Commission	T4
Automec v. Commission	T6	Petrofina v. Commission	T19
BASF v. Commission	T23	Peugeot v. Commission	T3
BBC v. Commission	T15	Peugeot v. Commission	T17
Bayer v. Commission	T13	Prodifarma v. Commission	T11
Cement Industries v. Commission	T39	PTT v. Commission	T13b
Cosimex v. Commission	T1	PVC	T28
DSM v. Commission	T26	Rhône Poulenc v. Commission	T18
Enichem v. Commission	T24	RTE v. Commission	T14
Hilti v. Commission	T21	SEP v. Commission	T8
Filtrona v. Commission	T5	SEP v. Commission	T22
Flat Glass	T30	Shell v. Commission	T33
Hoechst v. Commission	T32	Sofacar v. Commission	T38
Hüls v. Commission	T31	Solomon v. Commission	T2
ICI v. Commission	T35	Solvay v. Commission	T34
ITV v. Commission	T16	Tetra Pak v. Commission	T7
La Cinq v. Commission	T27	Vichy v. Commission	T13a
Linz v. Commission	T37	Vichy v. Commission	T29
Montedipe v. Commission	T36	VNZ v. Commission	T10
Nefarma v. Commission	T9		

TABLE 9
ALPHABETICAL LIST OF EUROPEAN COURT JUDGMENTS

Case	No.
ACF Chemiefarma v. Commission	14
ACNA v. Commission	31
AEG v. Commission	100
AKZO v. Commission I	132
AKZO v. Commission II	133
AKZO v. Commission III	186
AMP v. Binon	119
AM&S v. Commission	92
ANCIDES v. Commission	143
ANTIB v. Commission	142
Ahlsthom v. Sulzer	180
Ahmed Saeed v. Zentrale	162
Allen & Hanburys v. Generics	148
Alsatel v. Nordsam	160
Anne Marty v. Estée Lauder	77
Asia Motors v. Commission	176
BASF v. Commission	24
BAT v. Commission & Philip Morris	116
BAT v. Commission	146
BMW Belgium v. Commission	69
BNIC v. Clair	115
BNIC/Aubert	147
BRT v. SABAM I	36
BRT v. SABAM II	38
Basset v. SACEM	141
Batista Morais	193
Bayer v. Commission	25
Bayer v. Süllhöfer	158
Bayern v. Eurim-Pharm	183
Béguelin v. GL	22
Belasco v. Commission	166
Benzine & Petroleum BV v. Commission	65
Bilger v. Jehle	12
Bodson v. Pompes Funèbres	150
Bond van Adverteerders	149a
Boehringer v. Commission	16
Boehringer v. Commission	33
Boekhandels v. Eldi Records	73
BoschDe Geus	1
Bosman v. Commission	187
British Leyland	136
Buchler & Co. v. Commission	15
CICCE v. Commission	118
Cadillon v. Höss	18
Camera Care v. Commission	72
Cassella v. Commission	29
Cement Dealers v. Commission	32
Centrafarm v. AHP	66
Centrafarm & De Peijper v. Sterling Drug	41
Centrafarm & De Peijper v. Winthrop	42
Cerafel v. Le Campion	137
Cholay	178
Ciba-Geigy v. Commission	26
Cimenteries v. Commission	6
Ciments et Bétons v. Kerpen	104
Cinéthèque	122a
CNL-Sucal v. Hag	177
Coditel v. Cine-Vog	96
Commission v. Germany	42a
Commission v. Germany	137a
Commission v. Greece	153
Commission v. Ireland	73a
Commission v. Italy	141a
Commission v. Italy	191
Commission v. U.K.	192
Consten & Grundig v. Commission	4
Continental Can v. Commission	35
Costa v. ENEL	2
Cullet v. LeClerc	114
Dansk Supermarket v. Imerco	83
Dassonville	40a
Debauve	72b
De Bloos v. Boyer	60
De Haecht v. Wilkin I	7
De Haecht v. Wilkin II	34
Delimitis v. Henninger Bräu	181
Demo Schmidt v. Commission	99
De Norre v. Concordia	54
Deutsche Grammaphon v. Metro	19
Distillers v. Commission	75
Dow v. Commission	145
Dow Benelux v. Commission	170
Dow Iberica v. Commission	171
Duphar	106
EMI-CBS	50
EMI-CBS	51
EMI-CBS	52
EMI v. Patricia	161a
ERT v. DEP	185
ETA v. DKI	126
FEDETAB v. Commission	80
Fire Insurance v. Commission	139
Fonderies Roubaix v. Fonderies Roux	49
Ford v. Commission	108
Ford v. Commission	123
France v. Commission	95
France v. Commission	182
Francolor v. Commission	28
Frubo v. Commission	44
GAARM v. Commission	112

GB-INNO v. ATAB	59
GVL v. Commission	97
Gema v. Commission	70
Générale Sucrière v. Commission	55
General Motors v. Commission	46
Greenwich v. SACEM	71
Hasselblad v. Commission	107
Hoechst v. Commission I	30
Hoechst v. Commission II	140
Hoechst v. Commission III	169
Hoffmann-La Roche v. Centrafarm	56
Hoffmann-La Roche v. Centrafarm	63
Hoffmann-La Roche v. Commission	67
Höfner v. Macrotron	184
Hugin v. Commission	68
Hydrotherm v. Andreoli	111
IBM v. Commission	88
ICI v. Commission	23
ICI & CSC v. Commission	37
IDG v. Beele	91
Inter-Huiles	97a
Italy v. Commission	117
Italy v. Council and Commission	5
Kali & Salz v. Commission	43
Keurkoop v. Nancy Kean Gifts	95a
Kohl v. Ringelhahn	111a
Komponistenverband v. Commission	20
LTM v. MBU	3
Lancôme v. Etos	78
Le Campion	137
LeClerc	113
Louis Erauw v. La Hesbignonne	00
Lord Bethell v. Commission	93
L'Oréal v. De Nieuwe AMCK	81
Lucazeau v. SACEM	168
Marchandise	181a
Maxicar v. Renault	161
Membran/K-Tel v. Gema	82
Merci v. Siderurgica	188
Merck & Co. v. Stephar	87
Metro v. Commission I	58
Metro v. Commission II	134
Michelin v. Commission	102
Miller v. Commission	61
Ministère Public v. Tournier	167
Miro	122b
Muller	21
NAVEWA v. Commission	101
NSO v. Commission	128
National Panasonic v. Commission	74
Netherlands v. Commission	190
Nouvelles Frontières	131
Nungesser v. Commission	94
Orkem v. Commission	172
Ottung v. Klee	164
PTT v. Commission	184a
Pall v. Dahlhausen	179
Papiers Peints v. Commission	47
Parfums Rochas v. Bitsch	13
Parke, Davis v. Centrafarm	8
Pfizer v. Eurim-Pharm	89
Pharmon v. Hoechst	120
Philip Morris v. Commission	79
Pioneer v. Commission	98
Polydor v. Harlequin Record Shops	90
Portelange v. Smith Corona	11
Prantl	107a
Procureur v. Cognet	135
Procureur v. Commission	76
Publishers Association v. Commission	165
Pronuptia v. Schillgalis	129
RTE & BBC v. Commission	163
RTT v. G.B. Inno	189
Remia v. Commission	121
Roussel v. Netherlands	103
Royal Pharmaceutical Society	169a
SSI v. Commission	127
Sacchi	39
St. Herblain v. Syndicat des Libraires	122
Salonia v. Poidomani & Baglieri	85
Sandoz v. Commission	27
Sandoz v. Commission	174
Sirena v. Eda	17
Solvay v. Commission	173
Stanley Adams v. Commission	125
Stremsel v. Commission	84
Suiker Unie v. Commission	48
Syndicat v. Leclerc Aigle	154
Télémarketing v. CLT	124
Tepea v. Commission	64
Terrapin v. Terranova	53
Thetford Corp. v. Fiamma	152
Tipp-Ex v. Commission	175
Transocean Marine Paint Association	40b

Alphabetical List of European Court Judgments

UNILEC v. Larroche 156
United Brands v. Commission 62

VAG v. Magne 138
VBVB & VBBB v. Commission 105
Van Ameyde v. UCI 57
Vander Haar v. Kaveka 110
Van Eycke v. Aspa 155
Van Vliet v. Dalle Crode 45
Van Zuylen v. Hag 40
Vlaamse Reisbureaus 144

Völk v. Vervaecke 10
Volvo v. Veng 159

Walt Wilhelm 9
Warner Brothers v. Christiansen 151
Windsurfing v. Commission 130
Woodpulp 157

Zinc Producers v. Commission 109
Zuechner v. Bayerishe Vereinshank .. 86

TABLE 10

FINES

All fines are denominated in ECUs

1. PROCEDURAL FINES

	COMMISSION		COURT OF JUSTICE
A. Article 11 Regulation 17: supplying incorrect information			
111. Theal/Watts	5 000		
168. Comptoir d'Importation	5 000		
171. Telos	5 000		
175. National Panasonic Belgium	5 000		
180. National Panasonic France	5 000		
251. Peugeot	4 000		
329a. Secrétama (maritime transport)	5 000		
B. Article 14 Regulation 17 : Production of incomplete documents			
153. Fabbrica Pisana	5 000		
154. Fabbrica Lastre	5 000		
183. Fédération Chaussure de France	5 000		
C. Article 16 Regulation 17 : Periodic penalty clauses			
64. Zoju IKSC–ICI	1 000		
101. Chiquita	1 000		
105. CSV	1 000		
121. Hugin/Liptons	1 000		
158. IMA Rules	100-300		
173. Hasselblad	500-1 000		
182. Ford Werke-Interim Measures	1 000	Annulled:	123. *Ford* v. *Commission*
197. ECS/AKZO	1 000		
273. Boosey & Hawkes	1 000		

2. FINES FOR SUBSTANTIVE INFRINGEMENTS

COMMISSION		COURT OF JUSTICE	
24. Quinine		14. *ACF Chemiefarma* v. *Commission*	
ACF Chemiefarma	210 000		200 000
Boehringer	190 000	16. *Boehringer* v. *Commission*	180 000
Buchler	65 000	15. *Buchler & Co.* v. *Commission*	55 000
Pointet	12 500	No Appeal	
Nogentaise	12 500	No Appeal	
Pharmacie Centrale	10 000	No Appeal	
Total	500 000	Total	435 000

Fines

COMMISSION		COURT OF JUSTICE	
27. Dyestuffs			
ICI	50 000	23. *ICI* v. *Commission*	50 000
BASF	50 000	24. *BASF* v. *Commission*	50 000
Bayer	50 000	25. *Bayer* v. *Commission*	50 000
Geigy	50 000	26. *Geigy* v. *Commission*	50 000
Sandoz	50 000	27. *Sandoz* v. *Commission*	50 000
Francolor	50 000	28. *Francolor* v. *Commission*	50 000
Cassella	50 000	29. *Cassella* v. *Commission*	50 000
Hoechst	50 000	30. *Hoechst* v. *Commission*	50 000
ACNA	40 000	31. *ACNA* v. *Commission*	30 000
Ciba	50 000	No Appeal	
Total	490 000	Total	430 000
63. Pittsburgh Corning	100 000	No Appeal	
64. Zoja/CSC-ICI	200 000	37. *ICI & CSC* v. *Commission*	100 000
68. WEA/Filipacchi Music S.A.	60 000	No Appeal	
69. European Sugar Industry		48. *Suiker Unie* v. *Commission*	
Tirlemontoise	1 500 000	Tirlmemointoise	600 000
SAY	500 000	SAY	80 000
Bégin	700 000	Bégin	100 000
Générale Sucrière	400 000	Générale Sucrière	80 000
Eridania	1 000 000	Eridania	Quashed
Societa Generale	300 000	Societa Generale	Quashed
Cavarzere	200 000	Cavarzere	Quashed
AIE	100 000	AIE	Quashed
Volano	100 000	Volano	Quashed
SADAM	100 000	SADAM	Quashed
CVS	800 000	Suiker Unie	200 000
CSM	600 000	CSM	150 000
Pfeifer	800 000	Pfeifer	240 000
Süd Deutsche	700 000	Süd Deutsche	Quashed
Süd Zucker	200 000	Süd Zucker	40 000
Total	9 000 000	Total	1 590 000
73. Deutsche Philips	60 000	No Appeal	
78. Belgian Wallpaper		47. *Papiers peints* v. *Commission*	
Brepols	67 500	Brepols	Quashed
Genval	120 000	Genval	Quashed
Peters	135 000	Peters	Quashed
Van der Borght	36 000	Van der Borght	Quashed
Total	358 500		
84. General Motors	100 000	46. *General Motors* v. *Commission*	Quashed

Book One—Table 10

COMMISSION		COURT OF JUSTICE	
88. Tinned Mushrooms		No Appeal	
Blanchoud	32 000		
Champex	8 000		
Champifrance	26 000		
Euroconserves	32 000		
Faval	2 000		
Total	100 000		
101. Chiquita	1 000 000	62. *United Brands* v. *Commission*	850 000
104. Hoffmann-La Roche	300 000	67. *Hoffmann-La Roche* v. *Commission*	200 000
108. Miller International	70 000	61. *Miller* v. *Commission*	70 000
110. Theal Watts		64. *Tepea* v. *Commission*	
Tepea	10 000	Tepea	10 000
Watts	10 000	Watts	10 000
121. Hugin Liptons	50 000	68. *Hugin* v. *Commission*	50 000
126. BMW Belgium		69. *BMW Belgium* v. *Commission*	
BMW Belgium	150 000		Fines Upheld
5 Dealers	each 2 000		
3 Dealers	each 1 500		
39 Dealers	each 1 000		
Total	203 500		
129. Vegetable Parchment		No Appeal	
Dalle	25 000		
Feldmuehle	15 000		
Nicolaus	25 000		
Rube	10 000		
Schbeipen	25 000		
Serlachius	15 000		
Total	115 000		
141. Kawasaki	100 000	No Appeal	
148. Floral	85 000	No Appeal	
152. Pioneer		98. *Pioneer* v. *Commission*	
MDF	850 000	MDF	600 000
Pioneer Europe BV	4 350 000	Pioneer Europe BV	2 000 000
C.Melchers & Co.	1 450 000	C.Melchers & Co.	400 000
Pioneer High Fidelity	300 000	Pioneer High Fidelity	200 000
Total	6 950 000	Total	3 200 000

Fines

COMMISSION		**COURT OF JUSTICE**	
160. Johnson & Johnson	200 000	No Appeal	
165. Michelin	680 000	102. *Michelin* v. *Commission*	300 000
172. Moët et Chandon (London) Ltd	1 100 000	No Appeal	
173. Hasselblad		107. *Hasselblad* v. *Commission*	
Victor Hasselblad Sweden	560 000	Victor Hasselblad Sweden	560 000
Hasselblad U.K.	165 000	Hasselblad U.K.	80 000
Ilford	10 000	Ilford	10 000
Telos	10 000	Telos	10 000
Prolux	10 000	Prolux	10 000
Total	755 000	Total	670 000
178. NAVEWA-ANSEAU		101. *Navewa* v. *Commission* Fines Upheld	
7 machine producers	each 76 500		
9 machine producers	each 38 500		
6 machine producers	each 9 500		
Total	939 000		
179. AEG Telefunken	1 000 000	100. *AEG* v. *Commission*	1 000 000
181. SSI		127. *SSI* v. *Commission*	
		128. *NSO* v. *Commission*	
Lourens	425 000	Lourens	425 000
BAT	350 000	BAT	350 000
Turmac	325 000	Turmac	325 000
Reynolds	150 000	Reynolds	100 000
Philip Morris	125 000	Philip Morris	125 000
Niemeyer	100 000	Niemeyer	100 000
Total	1 475 000	Total	1 425 000
186. National Panasonic	450 000	No Appeal	
189. Zinc		109. *Zinc Producers* v. *Commission*	
CRAM	400 000	CRAM	Quashed
RZ	500 000	RZ	Quashed
Total	900 000		
190. AROW/BNIC	160 000	No Appeal	
191. Toltecs/Dorcet	50 000	116. *BAT* v. *Commission*	Quashed

Book One—Table 10

COMMISSION		COURT OF JUSTICE	
194. Windsurfing International		130. *Windsurfing* v. *Commission*	
Windsurfing International	50 000	Windsurfing International	25 000
Ostermann	15 000	No Appeal	
Akutec	10 000	No Appeal	
Klepper	10 000	No Appeal	
Shark	5 000	No Appeal	
VWSC	5 000	No Appeal	
Total	95 000		
198. Cast-iron & steel rolls		No Appeal	
Griffin	45 000		
Marichal	80 000		
SAFAK	75 000		
Achenbach	27 000		
E.Breitenbach	16 000		
L.Breitenbach	17 000		
Buch	65 000		
Gontermann	26 000		
Walzen	72 000		
Krupp	9 000		
Roland	21 000		
Thyssen	42 000		
Chambre Syndicale	29 000		
Chavanne	40 000 +25 000		
Berlaimont	86 000 +25 000		
Gorcy	13 000 +12 500		
Usinor	24 000 +12 500		
Innocenti	111 000		
Agostino	14 000		
Gregorio	10 000		
Zeno	8 000		
Davy Roll	85 000		
Midlang	63 000		
Tennent	26 000		
Sulzau	71 000		
Bofors	100 000		
Total	1 175 000 +75 000		
202. IPTC Belgium	5 000	No Appeal	
211. Polistil/Arbois	30 000	No Appeal	
212. British Leyland	350 000	136. *British Leyland* v. *Commission*	350 000

Fines

COMMISSION		**COURT OF JUSTICE**	
216. Flat Glass (Benelux)		No Appeal	
BSN	935 000		
Glaverbel	850 000		
St. Gobain	1 450 000		
St. Roch	765 000		
Total	4 000 000		
217. Zinc Producer Group		No Appeal	
Billiton	350 000		
Metallgeselleschaft	500 000		
Penarroya	500 000		
Preussag	500 000		
RTZ	500 000		
Union Minière	950 000		
Total	3 300 000		
218. Peroxide Products		No Appeal	
Solvay	3 000 000		
Laporte	2 000 000		
Dagussa	3 000 000		
Air Liquide	500 000		
Atochem	500 000		
Total	9 000 000		
226. John Deere	2 000 000	No Appeal	
227. Woodpulp		153. *Woodpulp*	
Bowater	500 000		
International Pulp	250 000		
St.Anne & 2 others	200 000 each	Appeal pending	
McMillan & 8 others	150 000 each		
British Colombia & 6 others	100 000 each		
Weldwood & 14 others	50 000 each		
Total	4 150 000		
242. ECS/AKZO	10 000 000	186. *AKZO v. Commission III*	7 500 000
245. Sperry New Holland	750 000	No Appeal	
246. Siemens/Fanuc		No Appeal	
Siemens	1 000 000		
Fanuc	1 000 000		
Total	2 000 000		

Book One—Table 10

COMMISSION | COURT OF JUSTICE

COMMISSION		COURT OF JUSTICE	
247. Polypropylene			
Anic	750 000	T24 *Enichem* v. *Commission*	450 000
Atochem	1 750 000	T20 *Atochem* v. *Commission*	Fine Upheld
BASF	2 500 000	T23 *BASF* v. *Commission*	2 125 000
DSM	2 750 000	T26 *DSM* v. *Commission*	Fine Upheld
Hercules	2 750 000	T25 *Hercules* v. *Commission*	Fine Upheld
Hoechst	9 000 000	T32 *Hoechst* v. *Commission*	9 000 000
Hüls	2 750 000	T31 *Hüls* v. *Commission*	2 337 000
ICI	10 000 000	T35 *ICI* v. *Commission*	9 000 000
Linz	1 000 000	T37 *Linz* v. *Commission*	1 000 000
Montedipe	11 000 000	T36 *Montedipe* v. *Commission*	11 000 000
Petrofina	600 000	T19 *Petrofina* v. *Commission*	300 000
Rhône Poulenc	500 000	T18 *Rhône Poulenc* v. *Commission*	500 000
Shell	9 000 000	T33 *Shell* v. *Commission*	8 100 000
Solvay	2 500 000	T34 *Solvay* v. *Commission*	2 500 000
Statoil	1 000 000	No appeal	1 000 000
Total	57 850 000	Total	54 562 500
248. Roofing Felt		166. *Belasco* v. *Commission* Fines Upheld	
Antwerps Teer	420 000		
Compagnie Générale	150 000		
Lummerzheim	200 000		
Limburgse Asfalt	30 000		
Kempische Asfalt	75 000		
De Boer	75 000		
Vlaams Asfalt	50 000		
Belgisch Asfalt	15 000		
Total	985 000		
250. Peugeot	50 000	No Appeal	
253. Meldoc		No Appeal	
Coberco	1 360 000		
Campina	1 020 000		
Menken	425 000		
Melk Unie	3 150 000		
DOMO	600 000		
Total	6 550 000		
254. Fatty Acids		No Appeal	
Unilever	50 000		
Henkel	50 000		
Oliofina	50 000		
Total	150 000		

Fines

COMMISSION		COURT OF JUSTICE	
269. Tipp-Ex		175. *Tipp-Ex v. Commission*	
Gott	400 000	Fines Upheld	
Beiersdorf	10 000		
Total	410 000		
272. Sandoz	800 000	174. *Sandoz v. Commission*	500 000
275. Fisher Price	300 000		
277. Konica	150 000		
282. Hilti	6 000 000	T21 *Hilti v. Commission*	
			Fine Upheld
285. British Dental Trade Association	100 000	No Appeal	
286. British Sugar	3 000 000	No Appeal	
294. Hudson Bay	500 000	Appeal Pending	
295. Sabena	100 000	No Appeal	
299. British Plaster Board		Appeal Pending	
British Gypsum	3 000 000		
British Plasterboard	150 000		
Total	3 150 000		
300. Flat Glass		T30 *Flat Glass*	1 000 000
Fabrica Pisana	7 000 000		671 428
Societa Italiana	4 700 000		Quashed
Vernante	1 700 000		
Total	13 400 000	Total	1 671 428
305. PVC		T28 *PVC*	
Atochem	3 200 000	*Non-existence of Decision*	
Basf	1 500 000		
DSM	600 000		
Enichem	2 500 000		
Hoechst	1 500 000		
Huels	2 000 000		
ICI	2 500 000		
LVM	750 000		
Montedison	1 750 000		
Norsk Hydro	750 000		
Shell	850 000		
SAV	400 000		
Solvay	3 500 000		
Wacker	1 500 000		
Total	23 500 000	Total	0 000 000

Book One—Table 10

COMMISSION		COURT OF JUSTICE	
306. LdPE		Appeal Pending	
Atochem	3 600 000		
BASF	5 500 000		
Bayer	2 500 000		
BP	750 000		
CdF	5 000 000		
DOW	2 250 000		
DSM	3 300 000		
Enichem	4 000 000		
Hoechst	1 000 000		
ICI	3 500 000		
Linz	500 000		
Monsanto	150 000		
Montedison	2 500 000		
Neste Oy	1 000 000		
Repsol	100 000		
Shell	850 000		
Statoil	500 000		
Total	37 000 000		
311. Welded Steel Mesh		Appeal Pending	
Tréfil Union	1 375 000		
SMN	50 000		
STPS	150 000		
Sotralentz	228 000		
Tréfilarbed	1 143 000		
Steelinter	315 000		
Usines bustave Boël	550 000		
Thibo Bouwstaal	420 000		
Van Merksteijn Bouwstaal	375 000		
2nd Bouwstaal	42 000		
Baustahlgewebe	4 500 000		
ILRO	13 000		
Ferriere Nord	320 000		
Martinelli	20 000		
Total	9 501 000		
313. Bayonox	500 000	T13 *Bayer* v. *Commission*	Inadmissible
330. Solvay/ICI		Appeal Pending	
Solvay	7 000 000		
ICI	7 000 000		
Total	14 000 000		
331. Solvay/CFK		Appeal Pending	
Solvay	3 000 000		
CFK	1 000 000		
Total	4 000 000		
332. Solvay	20 000 000	Appeal Pending	
333. ICI	10 000 000	Appeal Pending	

Fines

COMMISSION | **COURT OF JUSTICE**

340. Gosme/Martell
  Martell 300 000
  DMP 50 000

  Total 350 000

341. Viho/Toshiba
  Toshiba 2 000 000

348. Tetra Pak II 75 000 000

TABLE 11

LIST OF LEGISLATION AND DOCUMENTS

(The page references given opposite the items listed below indicate the places in the Handbook where the relevant legislation and documents are reproduced.)

A. COUNCIL REGULATIONS

			Page
1. **Regulation 17/62**	J.O. 204/62;	[1962] O.J. Spec. Ed. 87	361

First Regulation implementing Articles 85 and 86 of the Treaty

2. **Regulation 26/62**	J.O. 62/62;	[1962] O.J. Spec. Ed. 129	261

Applying certain rules on competition to production of and trade in agricultural products

3. **Regulation 141/62**	J.O. 2753/62;	[1962] O.J. Spec. Ed. 291	263

Exempting transport from the application of Council Regulation No. 17

4. **Regulation 19/65**	J.O. 533/65;	[1965] O.J. Spec. Ed. 35	83

On application of Article 85(3) of the Treaty to certain categories of agreements and concerted practices

5. **Regulation 1017/68**	[1968] O.J. L175/1;	[1968] O.J. Spec. Ed. 302	264

Applying rules of competition to transport by rail, road and inland waterway

6. **Regulation 2821/71**	[1971] O.J. L285/46;	[1971] O.J. Spec. Ed. 1032	86

On the application of Article 85(3) of the Treaty to categories of agreements, decisions and concerted practices (modified by Regulation 2743/72 of 19 December 1972—O.J. L 291, 28.12.1972, p.144—Special Edition 1972, 28–30 Dec., p.60)

7. **Regulation 2988/74**	[1974] O.J. L319/1	386

Concerning limitation periods in proceedings and the enforcement of sanctions under the rules of the European Economic Community relating to transport and competition

8. **Regulation 4056/86**	[1986] O.J. L378/4	291

Laying down detailed rules for the application of Articles 85 and 86 of the Treaty to maritime transport

9. **Regulation 3975/87**	[1987] O.J. L374/1	315

Laying down the procedure for the application of the rules on competition to undertakings in the air transport sector

10. **Regulation 3976/87**	[1987] O.J. L374/9	323

On the application of Article 85(3) of the Treaty to certain categories of agreements and concerted practices in the air transport sector as amended by Regulation 2344/90 O.J. L217,11.8.1990, p.15

List of Legislation and Documents

11. Regulation 4064/89 [1990] O.J. L257/14 433

On the control of concentrations between undertakings.

12. Regulation 1534/91 [1991] O.J. L143/1 356

On the application of Article 85(3) of the Treaty to certain agreements, decisions, and concerted practices in the insurance sector.

13. Regulation 479/92 [1992] O.J. L55/3 312

On the application of Article 85(3) of the Treaty to certain categories of agreements, decisions and concerted practices between liner shipping companies (consortia).

Book One—List of Legislation and Documents

B. COMMISSION REGULATIONS AND DIRECTIVES Page

1. **Regulation 27/62**   J.O. 1118/62; [1962] O.J. Spec. Ed. 132   370
   Regulation 2526/85   Last amendment [1985] O.J. L240/1

   Form, content and other details concerning applications and notifications (with annex and complementary note).

2. **Regulation 99/63**   J.O. 2263/63; [1963] O.J. Spec. Ed. 47   384

   On the hearings provided for in Article 19(1) and (2) of Council Regulation No. 17.

3. **Regulation 67/67**   [1967] O.J. L57/849; [1967] O.J. Spec. Ed. 10

   On the application of Article 85(3) of the Treaty to certain categories of exclusive dealing agreements **(not included)**.

4. **Regulation 1629/69**   [1969] O.J. L209/1; [1969] O.J. Spec. Ed. II 371   276

   On the form, content and other details of complaints pursuant to Article 10, applications pursuant to Article 12 and notifications pursuant to Article 14(1) of Council Regulation 1017/68.

5. **Regulation 1630/69**   [1969] O.J. L209/11; [1969] O.J. Spec. Ed. 381   289

   Concerning hearings pursuant to Article 26 paragraphs 1 and 2 of Council Regulation 1017/68

6. **Regulation 2779/72**   [1972] O.J. L292/23. **(Not included)**.

7. **Regulation 3604/82**   [1982] O.J. L376/33. **(Not included)**.

8. **Regulation 1983/83**   [1983] O.J. L173/1, Corrigendum in [1983] O.J. L281/24   119

   On the application of Article 85(3) of the Treaty to categories of exclusive distribution agreements.

9. **Regulation 1984/83**   [1983] O.J. L173/5, Corrigendum in [1983] O.J. L281/24   134

   On the application of Article 85(3) of the Treaty to categories of Exclusive purchasing agreements.

10. **Regulation 2349/84**   [1984] O.J. L219/15, Corrigendum in [1985] O.J. L113/34   169

    On the application of Article 85(3) of the Treaty to certain categories of patent licensing agreements.

11. **Regulation 123/85**   [1985] O.J. L15/16   142

    On the application of Article 85(3) of the Treaty to certain categories of motor vehicle distribution and servicing agreements.

List of Legislation and Documents

12. Regulation 417/85   [1985] O.J. L53/1   102

On the application of Article 85(3) of the Treaty to categories of specialization agreements.

13. Regulation 418/85   [1985] O.J. L53/5   106

On the application of Article 85(3) of the Treaty to categories of research and development agreement.

14. Directive 88/301   [1988] O.J. L131/73   222

On competition in the markets in telecommunications terminal equipment.

15. Regulation 2671/88   [1988] O.J. L239/9

On the application of Article 85(3) of the Treaty to certain categories of agreements between undertakings, decisions of associations of undertakings and concerted practices concerning joint planning and co-ordination of capacity, sharing of revenue and consultations on tariffs on scheduled air services and slot allocation at airports. **(Not included)**.

16. Regulation 2672/88   [1988] O.J. L239/13

On the application of Article 85(3) of the Treaty to certain categories of agreements between undertakings relating to computer reservation systems for air transport services. **(Not included)**.

17. Regulation 2673/88   [1988] O.J. L239/17

On the application of Article 85(3) of the Treaty to certain categories of agreements between undertakings decisions of associations of undertakings and concerted practices concerning ground handling services. **(Not included)**.

18. Regulation 4087/88   [1988] O.J. L359/46   158

On the application of Article 85(3) of the Treaty to categories of franchise agreements.

19. Regulation 4260/88   [1988] O.J. L376/1   302

On the communications, complaints and the hearings provided for in Regulation 4056/86 laying down detailed rules for the application of Articles 85 and 86 of the Treaty to maritime transport.

20. Regulation 4261/88   [1988] O.J. L376/10   336

On the complaints, applications and hearings provided for in Regulation 3975/87 laying down the procedure for the application of the rules on competition to undertakings in the air transport sector.

21. Regulation 556/89   [1989] O.J. L61/1   181

On the application of Article 85(3) of the Treaty to certain categories of know-how licensing agreements.

Book One—List of Legislation and Documents

22. Directive 90/388 [1988] O.J. L192/10 226

On competition in the market for telecommunications services.

23. Regulation 2367/90 [1990] O.J. L219/5 446

On the notification time-limits and hearings provided for in Council Regulation 4064/89.

24. Regulation 82/91 [1991] O.J. L10/7 325

On the Application of Article 85(3) of the Treaty to certain categories of agreements and concerted practices concerning ground handling services.

25. Regulation 83/91 [1991] O.J. L10/9 327

On the Application to Article 85(3) of the treaty to certain categories of agreements, decisions and concerted practices concerning joint planning and coordination of capacity, consultations on passenger and cargo tariff rates on scheduled air services and slot allocation at airports.

26. Regulation 84/91 [1991] O.J. L10/14 331

On the Application of Article 85(3) of the Treaty to certain categories of agreements, decision and concerted practices concerning joint planning and conciliation of capacity consultations on passenger and cargo tariff rates on scheduled air services and slot allocation at airports.

List of Legislation and Documents

C. ANNEXES TO REGULATIONS

Annex to Commission Regulation 1629/69	277
Form I to Commission Regulation 1629/69	277
Form II to Commission Regulation 1629/69	281
Form III to Commission Regulation 1629/69	285
Annexes to Commission Regulation 4260/88	307
Form MAR to Commission Regulation 4260/88	307
Annexes to Commission Regulation 4261/88	341
Form AER to Commission Regulation 4261/88	341
Annex to Commission Regulation 27/62	371
Form A/B Commission Regulation 27/62	372
Annex to authorisation to investigate under Article 14(2) of Regulation 17/62	392
Annex to Commission Regulation 2367/90	452
Form CO to Commission Regulation 2367/90	452

D. NOTICES

1. Notice on exclusive dealing contracts with commercial agents.................. 156
   [1962] J.O. 139/62.

2. Notice on patent licenses of 24.12.1962. **(Not included)**.
   Withdrawn by [1984] O.J. L220/14; [1962] O.J. 139/2922.

3. Notice on co-operation between enterprises................................. 95
   [1968] O.J. C75/3; [1968] O.J. C84/14.

4. Notice on imports into the Community of Japanese goods..................... 74
   [1972] O.J. C111/13.

5. Notice on subcontracting agreements.. 99
   [1979] O.J. C1/2.

6. Terms of reference of the hearing officer..................................... 395
   [1982] O.J. C251/2; 13th Competition Report pp.273–274.

7. Notice concerning applications for negative clearance pursuant to Article 2 Regulation 17/62.. 398
   [1982] O.J. C343/4.

8. Notice concerning notifications pursuant to Article 4 Regulation 17/62......... 398
   [1983] O.J. C295/7.

9. Notice concerning Regulations 1983/83 and 1984/83......................... 123
   [1985] O.J. C101/2.

10. Notice concerning Regulation 123/85 151
    [1985] O.J. C17/4.

11. Notice on agreements of minor importance 79
    [1986] O.J. C231/2.

12. Notice concerning procedures for communications to the Commission pursuant to Articles 4 and 5 of Commission Regulation 2671/88 (mutatis mutandis Regulation 84/91).. 354
    [1988] O.J. C257/4.

13. Notice concerning the application of Article 4(1)(a) of Commission Regulation 2671/88 (mutatis mutandis Regulation 89/91)................................ 354
    [1989] O.J. C119/4.

14. Notice on the concentrative and co-operative operations under Council Regulation 4069/89.. 469
    [1990] O.J. C203/10.

15. Notice on restrictions ancillary to concentration 475
    [1990] O.J. C203/5.

16. Notice clarifying the application of Community competition rules to the market participants in the telecommunications sector 235
    [1991] O.J. C233/2.

List of Legislation and Documents

E. OTHER DOCUMENTS

Competition Laws Co-operation Agreement, EEC-USA, of September 23, 1991.	410
Draft Notice on Guidelines for Joint Ventures.	200

PART I

CONDITIONS FOR THE APPLICATION OF BOTH ARTICLE 85 AND 86

CHAPTER 1

UNDERTAKINGS

1. Natural persons

AOIP/Beyrard 98*
RAI/Unitel 131
Reuter/BASF 107
Hydrotherm v. *Andreoli* 111 (ground 11)

2. Change of corporate structure

Zinc Producer Group 217 (para. 83)
Polypropylene 247 (paras. 99–101)*
ARG/Unipart 278 (para. 25)
PVC 305 (paras. 41–42)
LdPE 306 (para. 49)
Welded Steel Mesh 311. (para. 194)
ARD 312 (para. 38)
Enichem v. *Commission* T24 (grounds 235–242)*
Zinc Producers v. *Commission* 109 (grounds 7, 9)

3. Collective responsibility of the group

Dyestuffs 27
Continental Can 46 (para. 2)
Zoja/CSC-ICI 64
Moët et Chandon (London) Ltd. 172 (para. 21)*
Zinc Producers Group 217 (para. 83)
Peroxide 218 (para. 49)
Aluminium 228 (para. 9)
British Plasterboard 299 (Articles 3–4)
Decca 304 (para. 82)
PVC 305 (paras. 45–46)
LdPE 306 (paras. 49, 55)
Shell v. *Commission* T33 (grounds 311–312)*
ICI v. *Commission* 23 (grounds 131–146)*
Geigy v. *Commission* 26 (grounds 43–45)
Sandoz v. *Commission* 27 (grounds 43–45)
Continental Can v. *Commission* 35 (grounds 15–16)
ICI & CSC v. *Commission* 37 (grounds 36–41)
AEG v. *Commission* 100 (grounds 49, 53)
Orkem v. *Commission* 172 (grounds 5–7)

4. Intra-enterprise conspiracy doctrine

Christiani & Nielsen 21
Kodak 29*
BMW Belgium 126 (para. 21)
Moët et Chandon (London) Ltd. 172
Ijsselcentrale 335 (para. 22–24)
Gosme/Martell 340 (para. 30)
Zip fasteners. 7th Comp. Rep. (paras. 29–32)
Consten & Grundig v. *Commission* 4
Italy v. *Council and Commission* 5
Beguélin v. *GL* 22 (grounds 7–9)
Centrafarm v. *Sterling Drug* 41 (para. 41)*
Centrafarm v. *Winthrop* 42 (paras. 31–32)
BMW Belgium v. *Commission* 69 (paras. 36–37)
Bodson v. *Pompes Funèbres* 150 (grounds 19–21)
Ahmed Saeed v. *Zentrale* 162 (grounds 35–36)

5. Difference between undertakings and public bodies

Cane Sugar Supply Agreements 150 (paras. 2, 20)
Aluminium 228 (para. 9)
Magill 307 (para. 19)
Spanish Courier Services 324
ARD 312
Ijsselcentrale (para. 21)
Sacchi 39
Italy v. *Commission* 117 (grounds 18–20)*
Bodson v. *Pompes Funèbres* 150 (ground 18)
Höfner v. *Macrotron* 184 (grounds 21–23)*

CHAPTER 2

EFFECT ON TRADE BETWEEN MEMBER STATES

A. DELIMITATION OF COMMUNITY COMPETENCE

Grundig/Consten 5*

---

* Indicates Most Important Cases

Book One: Part I—Conditions for the Application of both Article 85 and 86

De Laval/Stork I 114 (para. 3)
Woodpulp 227 (para. 136)
LTM v. *MBU* 3
Consten & Grundig v. *Commission* 4*
Walt Wilhelm 9 (para. 3)
Völk v. *Vervaecke* 10 (grounds 5–7)
Bilger v. *Jehle* 12 (grounds 5–6)
Hugin v. *Commission* 68 (ground 17)
Alsatel v. *Novosam* 160 (ground 11)

B. THE ASSESSMENT OF THE EFFECT ON TRADE

1. Direct, indirect, actual or potential effect

ServiceMaster 296 (para. 23)
Scottish Nuclear 339 (para. 31)
RTE v. *Commission* T14 (grounds 76–78)
BBC v. *Commission* T15 (grounds 64–67)
LTM v. *MBU* 3*
Völk v. *Vervaecke* 10 (grounds 5–7)
Bilger v. *Jehle* 12 (grounds 5–6)
Cadillon v. *Höss* 18 (ground 6)
Béguelin v. *GL* 22 (ground 18)
Suiker Unie v. *Commission* 48 (grounds 305–310, 530–553, 578–602)
Miller v. *Commission* 61 (grounds 8–10)
Hugin v. *Commission* 68 (ground 17)
Pioneer v. *Commission* 98 (ground 84)
AEG v. *Commission* 100 (ground 60)
Michelin v. *Commission* 102 (ground 104)
Höfner v. *Macrotron* 184 (grounds 32–33)
Delimitis v. *Henninger Braü* 181*

2. Structural arguments

2.1. Agreement may affect the structure of competition in the Common Market

Centraal Bureau voor de Rijwielhandel 118 (para. 30)
Aluminium 228 (para. 13)
ENI/Montedison 256*
Continental Can 46 (para. 32)
ABG/Oil Companies 113
Michelin 165 (paras. 51–52)
ECS/AKZO 242 (para. 88)
Tetra Pak I 289 (para. 48)
British Sugar/Napier Brown 286 (para. 79)
ICI & CSC v. *Commission* 37 (ground 33)*
Stremsel v. *Commission* 84 (grounds 14–15)
United Brands v. *Commission* 62 (grounds 197–203)
Hoffmann-La Roche v. *Commission* 67 (grounds 124–127)
Greenwich v. *SACEM* 71 (grounds 11–13)
GVL v. *Commission* 97 (grounds 37–38)
Bodson v. *Pompes Funèbres* 150 (grounds 22–25)

2.2. Elimination of a competitor

ABG/Oil Companies 113

ECS/AKZO 242 (para. 88)*
British Sugar/Napier Brown 286 (para. 79)
SABENA 295 (para. 33)
United Brands v. *Commission* 62 (grounds 197–203)

2.3. Involvement of a transnational company

De Laval/Stork I 114 (para. 8)
Flat Glass 216 (para. 47)
Fire Insurance 220 (paras. 30–32)
Fatty Acids 254 (para. 48)*
Belgian Banking Association 261 (paras. 38–43)
ABI 262 (paras. 46, 52)
Yves Rocher 265 (para. 55)
Continental/Michelin 290 (paras. 19–20)
Flat Glass 300
Eirpage 344 (para. 13)
Assukpol 346 (para 34)
Fire Insurance v. *Commission* 139 (grounds 48–49)*
Bodson v. *Pompes Funèbres* 150 (grounds 22–25)

3. Cumulative effect of parallel agreements

3.1. Similar agreements concluded by the same and other companies

Breeders' rights; roses 236 (para. 24)
Vichy v. *Commission* T29 (ground 80)
De Haecht v. *Wilkin I* 7*
Bilger v. *Jehle* 12 (ground 5)
De Norre v. *Concordia* 54 (grounds 6–7)
Lancôme v. *Etos* 78

3.2. Similar agreements concluded by the same company

Nutrasweet (18th Comp. Rep. Para. 50)
Béguelin v. *GL* 22 (grounds 13–18)
Dassonville 41 (ground 13)
Louis Erauw v. *La Hesbigonne* 149 (ground 18)*

4. Consideration of the agreement as a whole

Aluminium Import 228 (para. 13)
Windsurfing v. *Commission* 130 (grounds 96–97)*
Louis Erauw v. *La Hesbigonne* 149 (ground 16)

5. Contractual export bans, a *per se* rule?

WEA/Fillipacci Music S.A. 68 (para. 8)
Zwarte Kip 79
Miller 108 (paras. 5–6, 10–17)
Gerofabriek 111
BMW Belgium 126 (para. 23)*

Part I—1 Undertakings

Arthur Bell & Sons Ltd. 135
Teacher & Sons 136
Johnson & Johnson 160 (paras. 35–36)
Moët et Chandon (London) Ltd. 172 (para. 13)
National Panasonic 186 (paras. 55–56)
Polistil/Arbois 211 (40–43, 50–51)
Bayer/Dental 327
Gosme/Martell 340 (para. 36)
Miller v. *Commission* 61 (grounds 7–15)*

6. Use of raw material for a product/service that is exported

Aluminium 228 (para. 13)
ABI 262 (para. 48)
BNIC v. *Clair* 115 (grounds 28–30)*
Vlaamse Reisbureaus 144
BNIC/Aubert 147 (ground 18)

C. TYPES OF AGREEMENT THAT DO NOT NECESSARILY AFFECT TRADE BETWEEN MEMBER STATES

1. Minor importance: appreciability

See Notice on agreements of minor importance on page 79
SAFCO 48
Zwarte Kip 79
Miller 108 (paras. 12–15)
BMW Belgium 126 (para. 23)
Natursteinplatten 159
Polistil/Arbois 211 (para. 51)
Fire Insurance 220 (paras. 33–36)
Breeders' rights: roses 236
ABI 262 (paras. 37–41)*
Charles Jourdan 298 (para. 35)
Vichy 334 (para. 19)
Eco System 344a (para 23)*
Völk v. *Vervaecke* 10 (ground 7)*
Cadillon v. *Hoss* 18 (grounds 8–9)
Papiers Peints v. *Commission* 47 (grounds 27–29)
Miller v. *Commission* 61 (grounds 10, 15)*
Hugin v. *Commission* 68 (grounds 15–26)
Salonia v. *Poidomani & Baglieri* 85 (ground 17)
AEG v. *Commission* 100 (ground 58)
Ciments et Bétons v. *Kerpen* 104 (ground 8)
Van Der Haar v. *Kaveka* 110 (grounds 13–14)
Louis Erauw v. *La Hesbignonne* 149

2. Trade with third states

2.1 Export to third states

DECA 6
Cobelaz 15–16
CFA 18
VVVF 22*
SEIFA 23
Omega 33 (para. 5)
Supexi 34
The Distillers Company 123 (paras. I.2.1, III.1.1(b))*
Zinc 189
Greenwich v. *SACEM* 71 (grounds 11–13)*
Zinc Producers v. *Commission* 109

2.2 Import from third states

Grosfillex/Fillestorf
Bendix/Merstens and Straat 3
Rieckerman 17
Kodak 29 (para. 20)
Raymond/Nagoya 57
Frubo 80
Franco Japanese Ball Bearings 81
Aluminium 228 (para. 13)
Siemens-FANUC 246
BBC Brown Boveri 291 (para. 22)
EMI-CBS 50 (grounds 25–29)*
Frubo v. *Commission* 44 (grounds 33–39)*
Tepea v. *Commission* 64 (grounds 47–48)

3. Export boosters: increasing trade

Convention Faïence 2
Grundig 5
Ceramic Tiles 35
Floral 148 (para. II.3)*
Milchfoerderungfonds 221 (para. 31)
Consten & Grundig v. *Commission* 4*
ANTIB v. *Commission* 142 (ground 30)

4. National cartels

Cobelaz 15, 16 (para. 6)
CFA 18
SEIFA 23
Supexie 34
Ceramic Tiles 35
VCH 47 (para. 17)
Central Heating 60
Heaters and Boilers 72
Belgian Wallpaper 78
Fireplaces 90
Bronbemaling 95
Bomée Stichting 97
Centraal Bureau voor de Rijwielhandel 118 (para. 30)
CSV 134 (paras. 73–80)
Fire Insurance 220 (paras. 29–36)
Roofing Felt 248 (paras. 87–93)*
Meldoc 253 (paras. 70–73)
Flat Glass 300 (para. 71)
Dutch Banking Association 310 (paras. 58–60)
Eirpage 344 (para. 13)
Assurpol 346 (para. 33)
U.K. Tractors 347 (paras. 57–58)
Cement Dealers v. *Commission* 32 (grounds 28–32)*
Papiers Peints v. *Commission* 47 (grounds 25–27)*

Book One: Part I—Conditions for the Application of both Article 85 and 86

FEDETAB v. Commission 80 (grounds 165–172)
Salonia v. Poidomani & Baglieri 85 (grounds 11–17)
Remia v. Commission 121 (grounds 22–24)
SSI v. Commission 127 (ground 46)
NSO v. Commission 128 (ground 58)
Belasco v. Commission 166 (grounds 33–37)

CHAPTER 3

WITHIN THE COMMON MARKET: EXTRA TERRITORALITY

A. CASES

Grosfillex/Fillestorf 1
Bendix/Mertens and Straet 3
Rieckermann 17
VVVF 22
Dyestuffs 27
Raymond/Nagoya 57
Franco Japanese Ball Bearings 81
White Lead 142 (para. 32)
Campari 130
Cast-iron & Steel Rolls 198 (para. 66)

Woodpulp 227 (paras. 78–79)*
Aluminium 228 (para. 14)
Polypropylene 247 (para. 95)
PVC 305 (para. 40)
ANSAC 333a
LdPE 306 (paras. 47–48)
1st Comp. Rep. (para. 131)
2nd Comp. Rep. (paras. 4–6, 17)
The Tripoli & Teheran Oil Agreements 2nd Comp. Rep. (para. 61)
6th Comp. Rep. (paras. 37–39)
11th Comp. Rep. (paras. 34–42)
Béguelin v. GVL 22 (ground 11)
ICI v. Commission 23 (grounds 125–130)
Geigy v. Commission 26 (grounds 10–12, 41–52)
Sandoz v. Commission 27 (grounds 10–12, 41–52)
Contintental Can v. Commission 35 (ground 16)
Greenwich v. SACEM 71
Zinc Producers v. Commission 109
Woodpulp 157*

B. TEXT OF NOTICE ON IMPORTS FROM JAPAN 1972
(reproduced below)

Notice of October 21, 1972 on Imports of Japanese Products

([1972] O.J. C111/13)

(PUBLISHERS' TRANSLATION)

Recently and with increasing frequency, there have been cases of Japanese industries preparing measures, in part independently, in part after consultation with the corresponding European industries, which are intended to restrict imports of Japanese products into the Community or to control them in another way from the point of view of quantity, price, quality or any other respect.

The Commission deems it necessary to draw the attention of those concerned to the fact that, by virtue of Article 85, para. 1, of the Treaty establishing the European Economic Community, all agreements between undertakings, all decisions on associations of undertakings and all concerted practices liable to affect trade between Member States and aimed at having the effect of preventing, restricting or distorting competition within the common market are incompatible with the common market and are forbidden. The fact that the head offices of several or all the participant undertakings are outside the Community does not prevent this provision from being applied, as long as the results of the agreements, decisions or concerted practices spread to the territory of the common market.

The Commission recommends those concerned to notify in good time such agreements, decisions and practices, as provided for by Regulation 17 of the Council on the application of Articles 85 and 86 of the Treaty. The Commission will examine these agreements, decisions and practices in order to determine whether they can be deemed compatible with the Community provisions on competition. At the same time the Commission will closely follow the development of the sectors concerned, and if need be will propose the appropriate measures of commercial policy with a view to remedying the problems in question.

PART II

ARTICLE 85(1), (2) and (3)

CHAPTER 1

AGREEMENTS

A. DEFINITION OF AGREEMENT

1.1. Understanding

Kodak 29 (paras. 11–13)
Franco-Japanese Ball-bearing 81
Polypropylene 247 (paras. 81–82)*
Fisher Price 275 (para. 19)
PVC 305 (paras. 29–31)
LdPE 306 (paras. 37–38)
Rhône Poulenc v. *Commission* T18 (ground 120)
Petrofina v. *Commission* T19 (ground 211)
BASF v. *Commission* T23 (ground 238)
Enichem v. *Commission* T24 (ground 198)
Hercules v. *Commission* T25 (ground 256)
DSM v. *Commission* T26 (ground 227)
Hüls v. *Commission* T31 (ground 291)
Hoechst v. *Commission* T32 (ground 287)
Solvay v. *Commission* T34 (ground 252)
ICI v. *Commission* T35 (ground 253)
Montedipe v. *Commission* T36 (ground 230)
Linz v. *Commission* T37 (ground 301)
Tepea v. *Commission* 64 (grounds 17–41)

1.2. Understanding may be tacit or express

FEDETAB 133 (para. 78)
Belgian Banking Association 261 (para. 36)
Bayer Dental 327 (para. 9)
Solvay/CFK 331 (para. 11)
Gosme/Martell 340 (para. 43)
AEG v. *Commission* 100 (ground 38)*
Sandoz v. *Commission* 174 (grounds 6–12)

2. Irrelevance of the form of the agreement

2.1. Written or oral

NCH 53 (para. 7)
SCPA/Kali & Salz 70
Theal/Watts 110
National Panasonic 186 (paras. 5, 43–47)
Tipp-Ex 269 (para. 48)
Flat Glass 300 (para. 62)

Solvay/CFK 331 (para. 11)
Tepea v. *Commission* 64 (grounds 17–41)*
Tipp-Ex v. *Commission* 175 (ground 19)

2.2. Gentleman's agreement

Quinine Cartel 24 (para. 19)*
ACF Chemiefarma v. *Commission* 14 (grounds 110–114)
Boehringer v. *Commission* 16 (grounds 27–29)

2.3. Meetings

Polypropylene 247 (paras. 81–86)

2.4. Unilateral conduct of a company in a contractual context

2.4.1. Sales conditions

Kodak 29 (para. 14)*
Du Pont de Nemours 71
Deutsche Philips 73
Gerofabriek 111 (para. II.a)
Arthur Bell & Sons Ltd. 135
Teacher & Sons 136
Johnson & Johnson 160 (para. 28)*
Moët et Chandon (London) Ltd. 172 (para. 10)
Sandoz 272 (para. 49)
Fisher Price 275 (para. 49)
Bayer Dental 327

2.4.2. Circular/recommendation

WEA/Fillipachi Music S.A. 68
BMW Belgium 126 (paras. 3–5, 19–21)
FEDETAB 133 (paras. 58–61, 94)
Ford Werke AG 199 (paras. 21, 36)
Konica 277 (para. 36)*
Eco System 344 (para. 23)
FEDETAB v. *Commission* 80 (grounds 85–89, 102)
Ford v. *Commission* 123 (grounds 20–21)

2.4.3. Refusal to sell in the framework of selective distribution agreements

Ford Werke-Interim Measures 182 (paras. 11–15, 35–37)
Ford Werke AG 199 (paras. 21–25, 36)
Peugot 250 (paras. 38, 40)

75

Tipp-Ex 269 (para. 49)
Peugeot v. *Commission* T17
AEG v. *Commission* 100 (ground 38)*
Ford v. *Commission* 123 (grounds 20–21)
Tipp-Ex v. *Commission* 175 (grounds 18–24)

2.5. Court settlement

Nungesser v. *Commission* 94 (grounds 82–89)
Bayer v. *Süllhöffer* 158 (ground 15)

3. Relation between restriction of competition and agreement

3.1. Causation

IFTRA Aluminium 92
Flat Glass (Benelux) 216 (paras. 40–42)
EATE Levy 231 (para. 43)
VBA 288 (para. 108)*

3.2. Agreement continues to produce its effects after termination of agreement

Quinine Cartel 24 (para. 20)
Zwarte Kip 79
Hercules v. *Commission* T25 (ground 257)
Sirena v. *Eda* 17 (ground 12)
EMI-CBS I 50 (ground 30)*
AMP v. *Binon* 119 (ground 17)

4. Distinction between agreement and public authority decision

Pabst Richarz 106 (paras. II.1, IV)
Arow/BNIC 190 (paras. 2–5, 48–57)
Aluminium Import 228 (para. 10)
Duphar 106 (ground 30)
BNIC v. *Clair* 115 (grounds 17–22)*
BNIC v. *Aubert* 147 (ground 11)
Bodson v. *Pompes Funèbres* 150 (ground 18)

B. CONCERTED PRACTICE

1. Concept

1.1. Definition

Peroxide Products 218 (para. 45)
Polypropylene 247 (paras. 86–88)
Flat Glass 300 (para. 63)
PVC 305 (para. 33)
LdPE 306 (para. 40)
Solvay/ICI 330 (paras 54–56)
Rhône Poulenc v. *Commission* T18 (grounds 121–124)
Petrofina v. *Commission* T19 (grounds 213–216)
BASF v. *Commission* T23 (grounds 240–242)
Enichem v. *Commission* T24 (grounds 199–262)
Hercules v. *Commission* T25 (grounds 250–261)
DSM v. *Commission* T26 (grounds 229–231)
Hüls v. *Commission* T31 (ground 293)
Hoechst v. *Commission* T32 (grounds 289–291)
Solvay v. *Commission* T34 (grounds 254–256)
ICI v. *Commission* T35 (grounds 255–257)
Montedipe v. *Commission* T36 (grounds 232–235)
Linz v. *Commission* T37 (grounds 303–306)
ICI v. *Commission* 23 (ground 64)*
BASF v. *Commission* 24 (ground 22)
Bayer v. *Commission* 25 (ground 25)
Geigy v. *Commission* 26 (ground 26)
Sandoz v. *Commission* 27 (ground 26)
Francolor v. *Commission* 28 (ground 51)
Cassella v. *Commission* 29 (ground 30)
Hoechst v. *Commission* 30 (ground 30)
ACNA v. *Commission* 31 (ground 49)
Suiker Unie v. *Commission* 48 (grounds 26–28, 148–155, 172–174)*
Züchner v. *Bayerische Vereinsbank* 86 (paras. 12–17, 21)
Zinc Producers v. *Commission* 109 (grounds 14–20)

1.2. Difference between concerted practice and agreement

Quinine Cartel 24 (para. 20)
Pittsburgh Corning 63
Polypropylene 247 (paras. 86–87)*
Flat Glass 300 (para. 63)
PVC 305 (para. 34)
LdPE 306 (para. 41)
Rhône Poulenc v. *Commission* T18 (grounds 118–128)
Petrofina v. *Commission* T19 (grounds 209–219)
BASF v. *Commission* T23 (grounds 236–246)
Enichem v. *Commission* T24 (grounds 196–206)
Hercules v. *Commission* T25 (grounds 254–269)
DSM v. *Commission* T26 (grounds 225–235)
Hüls v. *Commission* T31 (grounds 297–299)
Hoechst v. *Commission* T32 (grounds 293–295)
Solvay v. *Commission* T34 (grounds 258–260)
ICI v. *Commission* T35 (grounds 259–261)
Montedipe v. *Commission* T36 (grounds 236–238)
Linz v. *Commission* T37 (grounds 307–309)

Part II—1 Agreements

Flat Glass T30 (ground 330)

2. Evidence of a concerted practice

2.1. Similarity of behaviour

Dyestuffs 27
SCPA/Kali & Salz 70
Vegetable Parchment 129 (paras. 55–59)
BP Kemi/DDSF 147 (paras. 54–55)
Hasselblad 173 (paras. 42–48)
SSI 181 (para. 123)
Zinc 189
Woodpulp 227 (paras. 82–83)
Flat Glass 300 (paras. 63–64)
ICI v. *Commission* 23 (ground 66)*
BASF v. *Commission* 24
Bayer v. *Commission* 25
Geigy v. *Commission* 26
Sandoz v. *Commission* 27
Francolor v. *Commission* 28
Cassella v. *Commission* 29
Hoechst v. *Commission* 30
ACNA v. *Commission* 31

2.2. Exchange of information

Cobelpa/VNP 115 (para. 27)
Vegetable Parchment 129 (paras. 63–69)*
White Lead 142 (paras. 21–23)
BP Kemi/DDSF 147 (para. 55)
Hasselblad 173 (paras. 49–51)
Woodpulp 227 (paras. 106–113)

2.3. Meetings

Vegetable parchment 129 (para. 71)
Pioneer 152 (paras. 51–57)
Zinc Producer Group 217 (para. 80)*
Polypropylene 247 (grounds 81–86)
Solvay/ICI 330 (paras. 30–33)

2.4. Difference between concerted practice and market behaviour resulting from the structure of the relevant market

Dyestuffs 27*
SSI 181 (para. 123)
Zinc Producer Group 217 (paras. 75–76)
Woodpulp 227 (paras. 83–165)
Solvay/ICI 330 (para. 44)
ICI v. *Commission* 23 (grounds 68–119)*
BASF v. *Commission* 24
Bayer v. *Commission* 25
Geigy v. *Commission* 26
Sandoz v. *Commission* 27
Francolor v. *Commission* 28
Cassella v. *Commission* 29
Hoechst v. *Commission* 30
ACNA v. *Commission* 31
Zinc Producers v. *Commission* 109 (ground 20)*

C. DECISIONS OF ASSOCIATIONS OF UNDERTAKINGS

1. Association of undertakings

Ceramic tiles 35
VCH 47 (para. 15)
Fireplaces 90
BPICA 116 (para. II.1)
AROW/BNIC 190 (para. 52)
Milchfoerderungsfonds 221 (para. 27)
Roofing Felt 248 (para. 75)*
ABI 262 (para. 32)
Hudson Bay 294 (para. 8)
Assurpol 346 (para. 26)
FEDETAB v. *Commission* 80 (grounds 87–89)

2. Decision

2.1. Definition of decision

EMO I 19
VVVF 22
ASPA 30 (para. 14)
ASBL 31
Ceramic Tiles 35
VCH 47 (para. 15)
GISA 67
Belgian Wallpaper 78
Bomée-Stichting 97
Pabst & Richarz/BNIA 106 (para. II.1)
Centraal Bureau voor de Rijwielhandel 118 (para. 18)
FEDETAB 133 (paras. 77–79)
AROW/BNIC 190 (para. 49)
Nuovo/CEGAM 209 (para. 13)
Fire Insurance 220 (para. 23)*
Belgian Banking Association 261 (para. 36)
Net Book Agreements 301 (paras. 47–49)
Papiers Peints v. *Commission* 47 (grounds 15–21)
FEDETAB v. *Commission* 80 (grounds 85–89)
NAVEWA v. *Commission* 101 (grounds 19–21)
Fire Insurance v. *Commission* 139 (grounds 29–32)*

2.2. Agreements with associations of undertakings

SOCEMAS 13
NAVEWA-ANSEAU 178 (paras. 37–41)
SMM&T 201 (para. 14)
VIFKA 250 (para. 12)
Roofing Felt 251 (para. 71)
International Dental Exhibition 274 (para. 12)
APB 314 (para. 33)
NAVEWA v. *Commission* 101 (grounds 19–21)*

2.3. Agreements between associations of undertakings

Central Heating 60

Book One: Part II—Article 85(1), (2) and (3)

FRUBO 80
VBBB/VBVB 169 (paras. 35–37)*
NAVEWA-ANSEAU 178 (para. 38)
EATE Levy 231 (para. 40)
Frubo v. *Commission* 44 (grounds 28–32)
BNIC v. *Clair* 115 (ground 20)
BNIC/Aubert 147 (grounds 1, 7, 13)

D. THE PREVENTION, RESTRICTION, OR DISTORTION OF COMPETITION

1. Concept

1.1. Interbrand or intrabrand competition

Grundig/Consten 5
DRU/Blondel 7
Hummel/Isbecque 8
Delta Chemie 292 (para. 27)
Eco System 344a (paras. 26,27)
Consten & Grundig v. *Commission* 4*

1.2. Competition between the parties and competition with third parties

Transocean Marine Paint Association I 10
SAFCO 48
De Laval/Stork I 114 (para. 6)*
EATE Levy 231 (para. 47)

1.3. Actual and potential competition

Chaufourniers 20
Clima Chappée 25
SOPELEM/Langen 49
Wild/Leitz 55
Vacuum Interrupters 112 (para. 16)*
SOPELEM/Vickers 125 (para. III.1)
Distillers-Victuallers 157 (paras. 12–17)
U.K. Tractors 347 (para. 51)

1.4. Price or non-price competition

Dyestuffs 27
Henkel/Colgate 52
Fatty acids 254 (paras. 34–41)
U.K. Tractors 347 (para. 52)
Metro v. *Commission* I 58 (grounds 20–22)*
VBVB & VBBB v. *Commission* 105 (grounds 41–46)

1.5. State interference and competition

See also page 221
FEDETAB 133 (para. 83)
Cane Sugar Supply Agreements 150 110–133)
SSI 181 (paras. 88–96)
Suiker Unie v. *Commission* 48 (grounds 65–73)*
FEDETAB v. *Commission* 80
SSI v. *Commission* 127 (grounds 12–45)

NSO v. *Commission* 128 (grounds 18–27)

2. Object and effect

2.1. Object of restriction alone suffices

WEA/Filipacchi Music S.A. 68
IFTRA Aluminium 92
BMW Belgium 126 (para. 22)
Flat Glass (Benelux) 216 (para. 42)
Zinc Producer Group 217 (para. 71)
John Deere 226 (para. 26)
Polypropylene 247 (para. 90)
Roofing Felt 248 (para. 78)
PVC 305 (para. 37)
LdPE 306 (para. 44)
Rhône Poulenc v. *Commission* T18 (grounds 210–211)
Enichem v. *Commission* T24 (grounds 215–216)
Hercules v. *Commission* T25 (grounds 271–272)
DSM v. *Commission* T26 (grounds 242)
Hüls v. *Commission* T31 (ground 305)
Hoechst v. *Commission* T32 (ground 301)
Solvay v. *Commission* T34 (ground 271)
ICI v. *Commission* T35 (grounds 290–293)
Montedipe v. *Commission* T36 (ground 247)
Linz v. *Commission* T37 (ground 315)
LTM v. *MBU* 3
Consten & Grundig v. *Commission* 4*
Zinc Producers v. *Commission* 109 (ground 26)
BNIC v. *Clair* 116 (ground 22)
Sandoz v. *Commission* 174 (paras. 14–18)

2.2. Definition of the relevant market in Article 85

WEA/Fillipacchi Music S.A. 68
KEWA 103
Miller 108 (para. 12)
Vaessen/Moris 143 (para. 16)
Natursteinplatten 159 (para. 30)
Whisky and Gin 237
Olivetti/Canon 280
Vichy v. *Commission* T29 (grounds 61–64)
Flat Glass T30 (grounds 158–171)
LTM v. *MBU* 3*
Miller v. *Commission* 61 (ground 10)
Hoffmann-La Roche v. *Commission* 67 (grounds 122–123)
Hasselblad v. *Commission* 107 (grounds 19–22)
Windsurfing v. *Commission* 130 (grounds 12–19)
Delimitis v. *Henninger Bräu* 181 (grounds 10–27)*

3. Restriction must be appreciable

3.1. Text of Commission Notice on agreements of minor importance (reproduced below)

Part II—1 Agreements

Commission Notice of September 3, 1986

On agreements of minor importance which do not fall under Article 85(1) of the Treaty establishing the European Economic Community

([1986] O.J. C231/2)

I

1. The Commission considers it important to facilitate co-operation between undertakings where such co-operation is economically desirable without presenting difficulties from the point of view of competition policy, which is particularly true of co-operation between small and medium-sized undertakings. To this end it published the "Notice concerning agreements, decisions and concerted practices in the field of co-operation between undertakings" listing a number of agreements that by their nature cannot be regarded as restraints of competition. Furthermore, in the Notice concerning its assessment of certain subcontracting agreements the Commission considered that this type of contract which offers opportunities for development, in particular, to small and medium-sized undertakings is not in itself caught by the prohibition in Article 85(1). By issuing the present Notice, the Commission is taking a further step towards defining the field of application of Article 85(1), in order to facilitate co-operation between small and medium-sized undertakings.

2. In the Commission's opinion, agreements whose effects on trade between Member States or on competition are negligible do not fall under the ban on restrictive agreements contained in Article 85(1). Only those agreements are prohibited which have an appreciable impact on market conditions, in that they appreciably alter the market position, in other words the sales or supply possibilities, of third undertakings and of users.

3. In the present Notice the Commission, by setting quantitative criteria and by explaining their application, has given a sufficiently concrete meaning to the concept "appreciable" for undertakings to be able to judge for themselves whether the agreements they have concluded with other undertakings, being of minor importance, do not fall under Article 85(1). The quantitative definition of "appreciable" given by the Commission is, however, no absolute yardstick; in fact, in individual cases even agreements between undertakings which exceed these limits may still have only a negligible effect on trade between Member States or on competition, and are therefore not caught by Article 85(1).

4. As a result of this Notice, there should no longer be any point in undertakings obtaining negative clearance, as defined by Article 2 of Council Regulation No. 17, for the agreements covered, nor should it be necessary to have the legal position established through Commission decisions in individual cases; notification with this end in view will no longer be necessary for such agreements. However, if it is doubtful whether in an individual case an agreement appreciably effects trade between Member States or competition, the undertakings are free to apply for negative clearance or to notify the agreement.

5. In cases covered by the present Notice the Commission, as a general rule, will not open proceedings under Regulation No. 17, either upon application or upon its own initiative. Where, due to exceptional circumstances, an agreement which is covered by the present Notice nevertheless falls under Article 85(1), the Commission will not impose fines. Where undertakings have failed to notify an agreement falling under Article 85(1) because they wrongly assumed, owing to a mistake in calculating their market share or aggregate turnover, that the agreement was covered by the present Notice, the Commission will not consider imposing fines unless the mistake was due to negligence.

6. This Notice is without prejudice to the competence of national courts to apply Article 85(1) on the basis of their own jurisdiction, although it constitutes a factor which such courts may take into account when deciding a pending case. It is also without prejudice to any interpretation which may be given by the Court of Justice of the European Communities.

II

7. The Commission holds the view that

agreements between undertakings engaged in the production or distribution of goods or in the provision of services generally do not fall under the prohibition of Article 85(1) if:
— the goods or services which are the subject of the agreement (hereinafter referred to as "the contract goods") together with the participating undertakings' other goods or services which are considered by users to be equivalent in view of their characteristics, price and intended use, do not represent more than five per cent. of the total market for such goods or services (hereinafter referred to as "products") in the area of the common market affected by the agreement and
— the aggregate annual turnover of the participating undertakings does not exceed 200 million ECU.

8. The Commission also holds the view that the said agreements do not fall under the prohibition of Article 85(1) if the abovementioned market share or turnover is exceeded by not more than one-tenth during two successive financial years.

9. For the purposes of this Notice, participating undertakings are:
(a) undertakings party to the agreement;
(b) undertakings in which a party to the agreement, directly or indirectly,
— owns more than half the capital or business assets or
— has the power to exercise more than half the voting rights, or
— has the power to appoint more than half the members of the supervisory board, board of management or bodies legally representing the undertakings, or
— has the right to manage the affairs;
(c) undertakings which directly or indirectly have in or over a party to the agreement the rights or powers listed in (b);
(d) undertakings in or over which an undertaking referred to in (c) directly or indirectly has the rights or powers listed in (b).
Undertakings in which several undertakings as referred to in (a) to (d) jointly have, directly or indirectly, the rights or powers set out in (b) shall also be considered to be participating undertakings.

10. In order to calculate the market share, it is necessary to determine the relevant market. This implies the definition of the relevant product market and the relevant geographical market.

11. The relevant product market includes besides the contract products any other products which are identical or equivalent to them. This rule applies to the products of the participating undertakings as well as to the market for such products. The products in question must be interchangeable. Whether or not this is the case must be judged from the vantage point of the user, normally taking the characteristics, price and intended use of the goods together. In certain cases, however, products can form a separate market on the basis of their characteristics, their price or their intended use alone. This is true especially where consumer preferences have developed.

12. Where the contract products are components which are incorporated into another product by the participating undertakings, reference should be made to the market for the latter product, provided that the components represent a significant part of it. Where the contract products are components which are sold to third undertakings, reference should be made to the market for the components. In cases where both conditions apply, both markets should be considered separately.

13. The relevant geographical market is the area within the Community in which the agreement produces its effects. This area will be the whole common market where the contract products are regularly bought and sold in all Member States. Where the contract products cannot be bought and sold in a part of the common market, or are bought and sold only in limited quantities or at irregular intervals in such a part, that part should be disregarded.

14. The relevant geographical market will be narrower than the whole common market in particular where:
— the nature and characteristics of the contract product, e.g. high transport costs in relation to the value of the product, restrict its mobility; or
— movement of the contract product within the common market is hindered by barriers to entry to national markets resulting from State intervention, such as quantitative restrictions, severe taxation differentials and non-tariff barriers, e.g. type approvals or safety standard certifications. In such cases the national territory may have to be considered as the relevant geographical market. However, this will only be justified if the existing barriers to entry cannot be overcome by reasonable effort and at an acceptable cost.

Part II—1 Agreements

15. Aggregate turnover includes the turnover in all goods and services, excluding tax, achieved during the last financial year by the participating undertaking. In cases where an undertaking has concluded similar agreements with various other undertakings in the relevant market, the turnover of all participating undertakings should be taken together. The aggregate turnover shall not include dealings between participating undertakings.

16. The present Notice shall not apply where in a relevant market competition is restricted by the cumulative effects of parallel networks of similar agreements established by several manufacturers or dealers.

17. The present Notice is likewise applicable to decisions by associations of undertakings and to concerted practices.

3.2. Cases regarding appreciability

SOCEMAS 13
Chaufourniers 20
Burroughs/Delplanque 50
Burroughs/Geha 51
WEA/Filipacchi Music S.A. 68 (See also 2nd Comp. Rep. para. 40)
INTERGROUP 91
Penney 127 (para. II.4)*
Vaessen/Moris 143 (paras. 8, 16–17)
Floral 148 (para. II.4)*
Distillers-Victuallers 157 (paras. 12–17)
Natursteinplatten 159 (paras. 30, 40–41)
Villeroy & Boch 244 (paras. 29, 30)
Peugot 250 (para. 35)
Fatty Acids 254 (paras. 45, 47)*
ServiceMaster 296 (para. 10)
Charles Jourdan 298 (para. 35)
ARD 312 (para. 43)
APB 314 (paras. 33–42)
GEC-Siemens/Plessey 325 (para 19, 26, 35, 36)*
Moosehead 320 (para. 15)
Alcatel/ANT 329 (paras 12–18)
Odin 322 (paras. 22–28)
Vichy 334 (para. 19)
PME 7th Comp. Rep. (paras. 21–26)
13th Comp. Rep. (paras. 23, 24)
Völk v. Vervaecke 10 (grounds 5–7)
Cadillon v. Höss 18
Tepea v. Commission 64 (ground 50)
Hoffmann-La Roche v. Commission 67 (grounds 122–123)
Distillers v. Commission 75 (grounds 27–28)
NSO v. Commission 128 (grounds 46–49)

4. Rule of reason/ancillary restraints: assessing the restriction in the context of the relevant market

Nicholas Frères Vitapro 4
Alliance de Constructeurs Français 12
SOCEMAS 13
Chaufourniers 20
Pirelli/Dunlop 28
SAFCO 48
Reuter/BASF 107
AEG/Telefunken 179 (para. 54)
Amersham Buchler 184 (para. 13)
Nutricia 206 (paras. 26, 27)
Mecaniver/PPG 225 (para. 15)
Villeroy & Boch 244 (paras. 29, 31–33)
Tetra Pak I 289 (paras. 54–57)
Moosehead 320 (para. 15)
Konsortium ECR 900 323
Odin 322 (paras. 29–35)
U.K. Tractors 347 (para. 37–48)
Flat Glass T30 (grounds 158–171)
Montedipe v. Commission T36 (grounds 264–265)
LTM v. MBU 3*
Consten & Grundig v. Commission 4 (pp. 342–343)
De Haecht v. Wilkin I 7
Kali & Salz v. Commission 43 (grounds 1–7)
Metro v. Commission (I) 58 (ground 43)*
Nungesser v. Commission 94 (grounds 44–58)*
Coditel v. Ciné-Vog 96 (grounds 7, 15–19)
Remia v. Commission 121 (grounds 18–20)
Pronuptia v. Schillgallis 129
Metro v. Commission (II) 134 (grounds 40–47)
Delimitis v. Henninger Bräu 181 (grounds 10–27)*

CHAPTER 2

ARTICLE 85(2)

1. Concept of nullity

Bosch v. Van Rijn 1
LTM v. MBU 3*
Béguelin v. GL 22 (grounds 25–29)
Ciments et Bétons v. Kerpen 104 (grounds 11–12)
VAG v. Magne 137 (grounds 14–15)
Ahmed Saeed v. Zentrale 162 (grounds 20, 26–29)

2. Retroactive effect

Bosch v. Van Rijn 1
Bilger v. Jehle 12 (grounds 10–11)
De Haecht v. Wilkin II 34 (ground 27)*

3. Severability of offending clauses

LTM v. MBU 3*
Consten & Grundig v. Commission 4
Ciments et Bétons v. Kerpen 104 (ground 11)

VAG v. *Magne* 137 (grounds 14–15)

4. Effect of a Commission Decision

Velcro/Aplix 233
VBA 288 (para. 168)*
Ciments et Bétons v. *Kerpen* 104 (grounds 11–12)

CHAPTER 3

ARTICLE 85(3)

A. CONDITIONS FOR THE GRANT OF AN INDIVIDUAL EXEMPTION

1. Contribution to the improvement, production or distribution of goods, or promoting technical progress

Bayer/Gist Brocades 100 (p. 14, para. 1)
United Reprocessors 102
Cobelpa/VNP 115 (para. 41)
FEDETAB 133 (para. 93)
WANO 138
Carlsberg 214 (para. 8)
Optical Fibres 249 (para. 59)
ENI/Montedison 256 (paras. 30–31)
BBC Brown Boveri 291 (para. 23)
GEC-Siemens/Plessey 325 (paras. 20–25)
Screensport/EBU 337 (para. 71)*
Metro v. *Commission* I 58 (grounds 43–44)
FEDETAB v. *Commission* 80 (grounds 174–186)
Remia v. *Commission* 121 (grounds 42)
NSO v. *Commission* 128 (grounds 61)

2. Allowing consumers a fair share of the resulting benefit

Synthetic Fibres 213 (paras. 39–42)*
P&I Clubs 243 (para. 41)
Scottish Nuclear 339 (para. 37)
Metro v. *Commission* I 58 (grounds 44–45)

3. No imposition on the undertakings concerned of restrictions which are not indispensable to the attainment of these objectives

Convention Faïence 2
Bayer/Gist Brocades 100
SOPELEM/Vickers 125
Grundig 232
Optical Fibres 249 (paras. 62–63)*
Net Book Agreements 301 (paras. 73–75)
Metro v. *Commission* I 58 (grounds 40–48)

4. Not affording such undertakings the possibility of eliminating competition in respect of a substantial part of the products in question

Bayer/Gist-Brocades 100

United Reprocessors 102
IVECO/Ford 287 (paras. 37–40)
PRB/Shell. 17th Comp. Rep. (para. 74)
Metro v. *Commission* 58 (grounds 49–59)
FEDETAB v. *Commission* 80 (grounds 187–189)
ANCIDES v. *Commission* 143 (ground 13)

B. ELEMENTS RELEVANT TO THE ASSESSMENT OF ARTICLE 85(3)

1. Balancing the pros and cons

NCH 53 (para. 9)
MAN/SAVIEM 54 (para. 28)
FEDETAB 133 (para. 129)
Natursteinplatten 159 (paras. 31–32)
VBBB/VBVB 169 (para. 53)
Ford Werke AG 199 (paras. 35, 43)
SABA II 208
Ivoclar 234 (para. 21)
X/Open Group 263 (para. 42)
GEC-Siemens/Plessey 325 (para. 43)
FEDETAB v. *Commission* 80 (ground 185)*

2. Social considerations

Synthetic Fibres 213 (para. 37)*
Metro v. *Commission* I 58 (ground 29)*
FEDETAB v. *Commission* I 80 (ground 182)
Remia v. *Commission* 121 (ground 42)
Metro v. *Commission* II 134 (ground 65)

3. Environmental considerations

Carbon Gas Technologie 205
KSB 328
Assurpol 346 (para. 38)

4. Burden of proof

FEDETAB 133 (para. 93)
Consten & Grundig v. *Commission* 4
VBVB & VBBB v. *Commission* 105 (ground 52)*
Remia v. *Commission* 121 (ground 45)
Metro v. *Commission* II 134
Fire Insurance v. *Commission* 139 (grounds 58–59)

5. Unilateral behaviour extraneous to contractual terms

Ford Werke-Interim measures 182 (paras. 21–25, 36)
Ford Werke AG 199 (para. 36)
Peugeot 250 (para. 40)
Ford v. *Commission* 123*

6. Advantage must be objective

Convention Faïence 2
Fire Insurance 220 (para. 41)
ANSAC 333A (para. 29)

Consten & Grundig v. *Commission* 4*

7. Conditions are cumulative

FRUBO 80
Consten & Grundig v. *Commission* 4

8. Discretion of the Commission

Ford Werke AG 199 (para. 35)
Metro v. *Commission* I 58 (ground 45)*

9. Can an Article 86 abuse be exempted?

Decca 304 (para. 122)
Tetra Pak v. *Commission* T7*
Ahmed Saeed v. *Zentale* 162 (ground 32)

10. Contribution to other EC policies

IATA Passengers 342 (paras. 68–71)
IATA Cargo 343 (paras. 58–61)

C. EXEMPTION BY CATEGORY

1. Delegation of the authority to adopt Regulations to the Commission

1.1. Text of Regulation 19/65 (reproduced below)

Council Regulation 19/65 of March 2, 1965

On application of Article 85(3) of the Treaty to certain categories of agreements and concerted practices

(J.O. 533/65; [1965] O.J. Spec. Ed. 35)

THE COUNCIL OF THE EUROPEAN ECONOMIC COMMUNITY,

Having regard to the Treaty establishing the European Economic Community, and in particular Article 87 thereof;

Having regard to the proposal from the Commission;

Having regard to the Opinion of the European Parliament;

Having regard to the Opinion of the Economic and Social Committee;

(1) Whereas Article 85(1) of the Treaty may in accordance with Article 85(3) be declared inapplicable to certain categories of agreements, decisions and concerted practices which fulfil the conditions contained in Article 85(3);

(2) Whereas the provisions for implementation of Article 85(3) must be adopted by way of regulation pursuant to Article 87;

(3) Whereas in view of the large number of notifications submitted in pursuance of Regulation 17 it is desirable that in order to facilitate the task of the Commission it should be enabled to declare by way of regulation that the provisions of Article 85(1) do not apply to certain categories of agreements and concerted practices;

(4) Whereas it should be laid down under what conditions the Commission, in close and constant liaison with the competent authorities of the Member States, may exercise such powers after sufficient experience has been gained in the light of individual decisions and it becomes possible to define categories of agreements and concerted practices in respect of which the conditions of Article 85(3) may be considered as being fulfilled;

(5) Whereas the Commission has indicated by the action it has taken, in particular by Regulation 153, that there can be no easing of the procedures prescribed by Regulation 17 in respect of certain types of agreements and concerted practices that are particularly liable to distort competition in the common market;

(6) Whereas under Article 6 of Regulation 17 the Commission may provide that a decision taken pursuant to Article 85(3) of the Treaty shall apply with retroactive effect; whereas it is desirable that the Commission be also empowered to adopt, by regulation, provisions to the like effect;

(7) Whereas under Article 7 of Regulation 17 agreements, decisions and concerted practices may, by decision of the Commission, be exempted from prohibition in particular if they are modified in such manner that they satisfy the requirements of Arti-

cle 85(3); whereas it is desirable that the Commission be enabled to grant like exemption by regulation to such agreements and concerted practices if they are modified in such manner as to fall within a category defined in an exempting regulation;

(8) Whereas since there can be no exemption if the conditions set out in Article 85(3) are not satisfied, the Commission must have power to lay down by decision the conditions that must be satisfied by an agreement or concerted practice which owing to special circumstances has certain effects incompatible with Article 85(3).

HAS ADOPTED THIS REGULATION:

Article 1

1. Without prejudice to the application of Regulation 17 and in accordance with Article 85(3) of the Treaty the Commission may by regulation declare that Article 85(2) shall not apply to categories of agreements to which only two undertakings are party and:
(a)— whereby one party agrees with the other to supply only to that other certain goods for resale within a defined area of the common market; or
— whereby one party agrees with the other to purchase only from that other certain goods for resale; or
— whereby the two undertakings have entered into obligations, as in the two preceding sub-paragraphs, with each other in respect of exclusive supply and purchase for resale;
(b) which include restrictions imposed in relation to the acquisition or use of industrial property rights—in particular of patents, utility models, designs or trade marks—or to the rights arising out of contracts for assignment of, or the right to use, a method of manufacture or knowledge relating to the use or to the application of industrial processes.

2. The regulation shall define the categories of agreements to which it applies and shall specify in particular:
(a) the restrictions or clauses which must not be contained in the agreements;
(b) the clauses which must be contained in the agreements, or the other conditions which must be satisfied.

3. Paragraphs (1) and (2) shall apply by analogy to categories of concerted practices to which only two undertakings are party.

Article 2

1. A regulation pursuant to Article 1 shall be made for a specified period.

2. It may be repealed or amended where circumstances have changed with respect to any factor which was basic to its being made; in such case, a period shall be fixed for modification of the agreements and concerted practices to which the earlier regulation applies.

Article 3

A regulation pursuant to Article 1 may stipulate that it shall apply with retroactive effect to agreements and concerted practices to which, at the date of entry into force of that regulation, a decision issued with retroactive effect in pursuance of Article 6 of Regulation 17 would have applied.

Article 4

1. A regulation pursuant to Article 1 may stipulate that the prohibition contained in Article 85(1) of the Treaty shall not apply, for such period as shall be fixed by that regulation, to agreements and concerted practices already in existence on 13 March 1962 which do not satisfy the conditions of Article 85(3), ; or
A regulation pursuant to Article 1 may stipulate that the prohibition contained in Article 85(1) of the Treaty shall not apply, for such period as shall be fixed by that regulation, to agreements and concerted practices already in existence at the date of accession to which Article 85 applies by virtue of accession and which do not satisfy the conditions of Article 85(3), where;
— within three months from the entry into force of the regulation, they are so modified as to satisfy the said conditions in accordance with the provisions of the regulation; and
— the modifications are brought to the notice of the Commission within the time limit fixed by the regulation.
The provisions of the preceding subparagraph shall apply in the same way in the case of the accession of the Hellenic Republic, the Kingdom of Spain and of the Portuguese Republic.

2. Paragraph (1) shall apply to agreements and concerted practices which had to be

notified before 1 February 1963, in accordance with Article 5 of Regulation 17, only where they have been so notified before that date.

Paragraph (1) shall not apply to agreements and concerted practices to which Article 85(1) of the Treaty applies by virtue of accession and which must be notified before 1 July 1973, in accordance with Articles 5 and 25 of Regulation 17, unless they have been so modified before that date.

Paragraph (1) shall not apply to agreements and concerted practices to which Article 85(1) of the Treaty applies by virtue of the accession of the Hellenic Republic and which must be notified before 1 July 1981, in accordance with Articles 5 and 25 of Regulation 17, unless they have been so notified before that date.

Paragraph 2 shall not apply to agreements and concerted practices to which Article 85(1) of the Treaty applies by virtue of the accession of the Kingdom of Spain and of the Portuguese Republic and which must be notified before 1 July 1986, in accordance with Articles 5 and 26 of Regulation 17, unless they have been so notified before that date.

3. The benefit of the provisions laid down pursuant to paragraph (1) may not be claimed in actions pending at the date of entry into force of a regulation adopted pursuant to Article 1; neither may it be relied on as grounds for claims for damages against third parties.

Article 5

Before adopting a regulation, the Commission shall publish a draft thereof and invite all persons concerned to submit their comments within such time limit, being not less than one month, as the Commission shall fix.

Article 6

1. The Commission shall consult the Advisory Committee on Restrictive Practices and Monopolies;

(a) before publishing a draft regulation;
(b) before adopting a regulation.

2. Article 10(5) and (6) of Regulation 17, relating to consultation with the Advisory Committee, shall apply by analogy, it being understood that joint meetings with the Commission shall take place not earlier than one month after dispatch of the notice convening them.

Article 7

Where the Commission, either on its own initiative or at the request of a Member State or of natural or legal persons claiming a legitimate interest, finds that in any particular case agreements or concerted practices to which a regulation adopted pursuant to Article 1 of this regulation applies have nevertheless certain effects which are incompatible with the conditions laid down in Article 85(3) of the Treaty, it may withdraw the benefit of application of that regulation and issue a decision in accordance with Articles 6 and 8 of Regulation 17, without any notification under Article 4(1) of Regulation 17 being required.

Article 8

The Commission shall, before 1 January 1970, submit to the Council a proposal for a regulation for such amendment of this regulation as may prove necessary in the light of experience.

This regulation shall be binding in its entirety and directly applicable in all Member States.

Done at Brussels, 2 March 1965.

1.2. Text of Council Regulation 2821/71 (reproduced over)

Council Regulation 2821/71 of December 20, 1971

On Application of Article 85(3) of the Treaty to categories of agreements, decisions and concerted practices

(J.O. 46/71; [1971] O.J. Spec. Ed. 1032)

THE COUNCIL OF THE EUROPEAN COMMUNITIES,

Having regard to the Treaty establishing the European Economic Community, and in particular Article 87 thereof;

Having regard to the proposal from the Commission;

Having regard to the Opinion of the European Parliament;

Having regard to the Opinion of the Economic and Social Committee;

(1) Whereas Article 85(1) of the Treaty may in accordance with Article 85(3) be declared inapplicable to categories of agreements, decisions and concerted practices which fulfil the conditions contained in Article 85(3);

(2) Whereas the provisions for implementation of Article 85(3) must be adopted by way of regulation pursuant to Article 87;

(3) Whereas the creation of a common market requires that undertakings be adopted to the conditions of the enlarged market and whereas co-operation between undertakings can be a suitable means of achieving this;

(4) Whereas agreements, decisions and concerted practices for co-operation between undertakings which enable the undertakings to work more rationally and adapt their productivity and competitiveness to the enlarged market may, in so far as they fall within the prohibition contained in Article 85(1), be exempted therefrom under certain conditions; whereas this measure is necessary in particular as regards agreements, decisions and concerted practices relating to the application of standards and types, research and development of products or processes up to the stage of industrial application, exploitation of the results thereof and specialisation;

(5) Whereas it is desirable that the Commission be enabled to declare by way of regulation that the provisions of Article 85(1) do not apply to those categories of agreements, decisions and concerted practices, in order to make it easier for undertakings to co-operate in ways which are economically desirable and without adverse effect from the point of view of competition policy;

(6) Whereas it should be laid down under what conditions the Commission, in close and constant liaison with the competent authorities of the Member States, may exercise such powers;

(7) Whereas under Article 6 of Regulation 17 the Commission may provide that a decision taken in accordance with Article 85(3) of the Treaty shall apply with retroactive effect; whereas it is desirable that the Commission be empowered to issue regulations whose provisions are to the like effect;

(8) Whereas under Article 7 of Regulation 17 agreements, decisions and concerted practices may by decision of the Commission be exempted from prohibition, in particular if they are modified in such manner that Article 85(3) applies to them; whereas it is desirable that the Commission be enabled to grant by regulation like exemption to such agreements, decisions and concerted practices if they are modified in such manner as to fall within a category defined in an exempting regulation;

(9) Whereas the possibility cannot be excluded that, in a specific case, the conditions set out in Article 85(3) may not be fulfilled; whereas the Commission must have power to regulate such a case in pursuance of Regulation 17 by way of decision having effect for the future;

HAS ADOPTED THIS REGULATION:

Article 1

1. Without prejudice to the application of Regulation 17 the Commission may, by regulation and in accordance with Article 85(3) of the Treaty, declare that Article 85(1) shall not apply to categories of agreements between undertakings, decisions of associations of undertakings and concerted practices which have as their object:

(a) the application of standards or types;
(b) the research and development of products or processes up to the stage of industrial application, and exploitation of the results, including provisions regarding industrial property rights and confidential technical knowledge;
(c) specialisation, including agreements necessary for achieving it.

2. Such regulation shall define the categories of agreements, decisions and concerted practices to which it applies and shall specify in particular:
(a) the restrictions or clauses which may, or may not, appear in the agreements, decisions and concerted practices;
(b) the clauses which must be contained in the agreements, decisions and concerted practices or the other conditions which must be satisfied.

Article 2

1. Any regulation pursuant to Article 1 shall be made for a specified period.

2. It may be repealed or amended where circumstances have changed with respect to any of the facts which were basic to its being made; in such case, a period shall be fixed for modification of the agreements, decisions and concerted practices to which the earlier regulation applies.

Article 3

A regulation pursuant to Article 1 may provide that it shall apply with retroactive effect to agreements, decisions and concerted practices to which, at the date of entry into force of that regulation, a decision issued with retroactive effect in pursuance of Article 6 of Regulation 17 would have applied.

Article 4

1. A regulation pursuant to Article 1 may provide that the prohibition contained in Article 85(1) of the Treaty shall not apply, for such period as shall be fixed by that regulation, to agreements, decisions and concerted practices already in existence on 13 March 1962 which do not satisfy the conditions of Article 85(3), where:
— within six months from the entry into force of the regulation, they are so modified as to satisfy the said conditions in accordance with the provisions of the regulation; and
— the modifications are brought to the notice of the Commission within the time limit fixed by the regulation.

A regulation adopted pursuant to Article 1 may lay down that the prohibition referred to in Article 85(1) of the Treaty shall not apply, for the period fixed in the same regulation, to agreements and concerted practices which existed at the date of accession and which, by virtue of accession, come within the scope of Article 85 and do not fulfil the conditions set out in Article 85(3).

The provisions of the preceding subparagraph shall apply in the same way in the case of the accession of the Hellenic Republic, the Kingdom of Spain and of the Portuguese Republic.

2. Paragraph 1 shall apply to agreements, decisions and concerted practices which had to be notified before 1 February 1963, in accordance with Article 5 of Regulation 17, only where they have been so notified before that date.

Paragraph (1) shall be applicable to those agreements and concerted practices which, by virtue of the accession, come within the scope of Article 85(1) of the Treaty and for which notification before 1 July 1973 is mandatory, in accordance with Articles 5 and 25 of Regulation 17, only if notification was given before that date.

Paragraph (1) shall not apply to agreements and concerted practices to which Article 85(1) of the Treaty applies by virtue of the accession of the Hellenic Republic and which must be notified before 1 July 1981, in accordance with Articles 5 and 25 of Regulation 17, unless they had been so notified before that date.

Paragraph 1 shall not apply to agreements and concerted practices to which Article 85(1) of the Treaty applied by virtue of the accession of the Kingdom of Spain and of the Portuguese Republic and which must be notified before 1 July 1986, in accordance with Articles 5 and 25 of Regulation 17, unless they have been so notified before that date.

3. The benefit of the provisions laid down pursuant to paragraph (1) may not be claimed in actions pending at the date of entry into force of a regulation adopted pursuant to Article 1; neither may it be relied on as grounds for claims for damages against third parties.

Book One: Part II—Article 85(1), (2) and (3)

Article 5

Before making a regulation, the Commission shall publish a draft thereof to enable all persons and organisations concerned to submit their comments within such time limit, being not less than one month, as the Commission shall fix.

Article 6

1. The Commission shall consult the Advisory Committee on Restrictive Practices and Monopolies:
(a) before publishing a draft regulation;
(b) before making a regulation.

2. Paragraphs (5) and (6) of Article 10 of Regulation 17, relating to consultation with the Advisory Committee, shall apply by analogy, it being understood that joint meetings with the Commission shall take place not earlier than one month after dispatch of the notice convening them.

Article 7

Where the Commission, either on its own initiative or at the request of a Member State or of natural or legal persons claiming a legitimate interest, finds that in any particular case agreements, decisions or concerted practices to which a regulation made pursuant to Article 1 of this regulation applies have nevertheless certain effects which are incompatible with the conditions laid down in Articles 85(3) of the Treaty, it may withdraw the benefit of application of that regulation and take a decision in accordance with Articles 6 and 8 of Regulation 17, without any notification under Article 4(1) of Regulation 17 being required.

This regulation shall be binding in its entirety and directly applicable in all Member States.

Done at Brussels, 20 December 1971.

1.3. Other Regulations

The Council Regulations authorising the Commission to adopt Block Exemption regulation in the transport sector may be found under Part IX, page 264.

2. List of Commission Regulations providing for exemption by category

1983/83
Exclusive Distribution	[1983] O.J. L173
Corrigendum	[1983] O.J. L281
Commission Notice	[1984] O.J. C101

1984/83
Exclusive purchasing	[1983] O.J. L173
Corrigendum	[1983] O.J. L281
Commission Notice	[1984] O.J. C101

2349/84
Patent Licensing	[1984] O.J. L219
Corrigendum	[1985] O.J. L113

123/85
Motor Vehicle Licensing	[1985] O.J. L15
Commission Notice	[1985] O.J. C17

417/85
Specialisation	[1985] O.J. L53

418/85
Research & Development	[1985] O.J. L53

4087/88
Franchising	[1985] O.J. L359

556/89
Know-how Licensing	[1989] O.J. L61

3. Opposition procedures in Commission block exemptions

Patent Licensing, Article 4 of Regulation 2349/84
Specialisation, Article 4 of Regulation 417/85
Research & Development, Article 4 of Regulation 418/85
Franchising, Article 6 of Regulation 4087/88
Know-How, Article 4 of Regulation 556/89
13th Comp. Rep. para. 73.

4. Effect of a group exemption Regulation

Fonderies Roubaix v. *Fonderier Roux* 49 (grounds 10–11)
VAG v. *Magne* 138 (grounds 10–11)
Delimitis v. *Henninger Bräu* 181 (ground 46)

5. Withdrawal of the benefit of a group exemption regulation

13th Comp. Rep., (para. 73)
Tetra Pak I 289 (paras. 53, 58–59)
Tetra Pak v. *Commission* T7

6. Letter of Commission

De Bloos v. *Boyer* 60 (grounds 17–18)

PART III

HORIZONTAL AGREEMENTS

CHAPTER 1

CARTELS

A. LIST OF CARTEL CASES

Convention Faience 2
Cobelaz 15, 16
CFA 18
Chaufourniers 20
VVVF 22
SEIFA 23
Quinine Cartel 24
Dyestuffs 27
ASPA 30
Supexie 34
Ceramic Tiles 35
VCH 47
SAFCO 48
NCH 53
Central Heating 60
Dutch Cement 65
Cimbel 66
GISA 67
European Sugar Industry 69
SCPA/Kali & Salz 70
Heaters and Boilers 72
Kali & Salz/Kalichemie 76
IFTRA Glass 77
Belgian Wallpaper 78
FRUBO 80
Franco-Japanese Ball Bearings 81
Tinned Mushrooms 88
Fireplaces 90
IFTRA Aluminium 92
Bomée-Stichting 97
Pabst & Richarz/BNIA 106
Cobelpa/VNP 115
Centraal Bureau voor de Rijwielhandel 118
Cauliflowers 119
Vegetable Parchment 129
SNPE/LEL 132 (paras. 4–7, 13–15)
FEDETAB 133
CSV 134
White Lead 142
BP Kemi/DDSF 147
Floral 148
Rennet 149
IMA Rules 158
Natursteinplatten 159
Italian Cast Glass 163
Italian Flat Glass 164
VBBB/VBVB 169
SSI 181
Zinc 189
AROW/BNIC 190
Vimpoltu 195
Cast-iron & Steel Rolls 198
International Energy Agency 207
Synthetic Fibres 213
Flat Glass (Benelux) 216
Zinc Producer Group 217
Peroxide Products 218
Fire Insurance 220
Milchfoerderungsfonds 221
Woodpulp 227
Aluminium 228
Siemens/Fanuc 246
Polypropylene 247
Roofing Felt 248
Meldoc 253
Fatty Acids 254
VBA 288
Hudson Bay 294
Net Book Agreements 301
Flat Glass II 300
PVC 305
LdPE 306
Welded Steel Mesh 311
Sugar Beet 315
Solvay/ICI 330
Solvay/CFK 331
ANSAC 333a
U.K. Tractors 344
Lino Cartel 5th Comp. Rep. (para. 35)
Rhône Poulenc v. *Commission* T18
Petrofina v. *Commission* T19
BASF v. *Commission* T23
Enichem v. *Commission* T24
Hercules v. *Commission* T25
DSM v. *Commission* T26
Hüls v. *Commission* T31
Hoechst v. *Commission* T32
Shell v. *Commission* T33
Solvay v. *Commission* T34
ICI v. *Commission* T35
Montedipe v. *Commission* T36
Linz v. *Commission* T37
PVC T28
Flat Glass T30
ACF Chemiefarma v. *Commission* 14
Boehringer v. *Commission* 16
ICI v. *Commission* 23
BASF v. *Commission* 24
Bayer v. *Commission* 25
Geigy v. *Commission* 26

Book One: Part III—Horizontal Agreements

Sandoz v. *Commission* 27
Francolor v. *Commission* 28
Cassella v. *Commission* 29
Hoechst v. *Commission* 30
ACNA v. *Commission* 31
Cement Dealers v. *Commission* 32
Boehringer v. *Commission* 33
Kali & Salz v. *Commission* 43
Frubo v. *Commission* 44
Papiers Peints v. *Commission* 47
Suiker Unie v. *Commission* 48
FEDETAB v. *Commission* 80
Stremsel v. *Commission* 84
Züchner v. *Bayerische Vereinsbank* 86
VBVB & VBBB v. *Commission* 105
Zinc Producers v. *Commission* 109
BNIC v. *Clair* 115
SSI v. *Commission* 127
NSO v. *Commission* 128
Fire Insurance v. *Commission* 139
BNIC/Aubert 147
Ahmed Saeed v. *Zentrale* 162
Belasco v. *Commission* 166.

B. SPECIFIC CLAUSES OR AGREEMENTS TYPICAL OF CARTEL SCHEMES

1. Production related schemes or clauses

1.1. Production quotas for existing capacity

Chaufourniers 20
Quinine Cartel 24 (para. 30)*
Vegetable Parchment 129 (paras. 17–23)
Italian Cast Glass 163
Synthetic Fibres 213
Zinc Producer Group 217 (para. 67)
Fruit Agreements. 5th Comp. Rep. (para. 38)
Air-Forge 12th Comp. Rep. (para. 85)

1.2. Provisions regulating capacity

1.2.1. Prohibition of new capacity

Chaufourniers 20

1.2.2. Prohibition on sale of capacity outside cartel

Cimbel 66 (paras. 13–14)
Roofing Felt 248 (para. 73)*

1.3. Clauses relating to the nature of the product

1.3.1. Common product range

Roofing Felt 248
Belasco v. *Commission* 166 (ground 30)

1.3.2. Sharing of product ranges between competitors

Italian Cast Glass 163

1.4. Supply agreements

1.4.1. Emergency supply agreements

Zinc 189
Zinc Producers v. *Commission* 109 (grounds 132–137)

1.4.2. Reciprocal supply arrangements

Flat Glass 300 (para. 70)
Solvay/ICI 330 (paras. 36–39)
Sand Producers 6th Comp. Rep. (paras. 123–125)
Nitrogenous Fertilisers 6th Comp. Rep. (paras. 126–127)
Flat Glass T30 (grounds 338–339)

1.5. Production information exchange schemes

Cimbel 66
Tinned Mushrooms 88
Cobelpa/VNP 115 (paras. 5, 9, 24–28)
Italian Cast Glass 163*
Zinc Producer Group 217 (para. 68)
2nd Comp. Rep. (para. 18)

1.6. Compensation schemes

Chaufourniers 20

2. Market sharing schemes, agreements or clauses

2.1. Dividing territories between competitors

2.1.1. Between Member States

Quinine Cartel 24 (para. 28)
Cimbel 66 (para. 13)
European Sugar Industry 69*
SCPA/Kali & Salz 70
Tinned Mushrooms 88
Vegetable Parchment 129 (paras. 17–33, 55–62)
SNPE/LEL 132
White Lead 142 (paras. 12–17, 27–29)*
Italian Flat Glass 164
Cast-iron & Steel Rolls 198 (paras. 3, 5, 53–54)
Flat glass (Benelux) 216
Zinc Producer Group 217 (para. 77)
Peroxide 218
Woodpulp 227
Aluminium 228
Meldoc 253 (para. 21)
Welded Steel mesh 311
Solvay/ICI 330
Sheet Glass 1st Comp. Rep. (paras. 4, 6)
International Cable Development Corp. 1st Comp. Rep. (para. 4)
Cleaning Products 1st Comp. Rep. (para. 4)

Part III—1 Cartels

Sand Producers 6th Comp. Rep. (para. 122)
Nitrogenous Fertilisers 6th Comp. Rep. (paras. 126–128)

2.1.2. Third country markets
DECA 6
Cobelaz 15, 16
CFA 18
VVVF 22
SEIFA 23
Quinine Cartel 24 (para. 28)
Supexie 34
CSV 134 (paras. 18, 20–62, 77)*

2.2. Quotas
Quinine Cartel 24 (para. 28)*
NCH 53
Thin Paper 59
Dutch Cement 65
Cimbel 66 (para. 13)
European Sugar Industry 69
Tinned Mushrooms 88
CSV 134 (paras. 18, 20, 62, 72)
White Lead 142 (paras. 12, 15–17, 27–29)
BP Kemi/DDSF 147 (paras. 28a, 38, 82)
Italian Cast Glass 163
Italian Flat Glass 164
Cast-iron & Steel Rolls 198 (paras. 3, 5, 53c–d, 54)
Flat glass (Benelux) 216 (para. 44)
Peroxide Products 218*
Aluminium 228 (para. 11)*
Polypropylene 247 (paras. 52–53, 80, 89, Article 89)
Roofing Felt 248 (paras. 73–74)
Meldoc 253 (paras. 21, 60)
Flat Glass 300 (para. 67)
PVC 305 (para. 10)
Welded Steel Mesh 311
Solvay/CFK 331
Sheet Glass 1st Comp. Rep. (paras. 4, 6) 2nd Comp. Rep. (para. 19)
Air-Forge 12th Comp. Rep. (para. 85)
Solvay/CFK 331
ACF Chemiefarma v. *Commission* 14 (grounds 126–129)
Boehringer v. *Commission* 16 (grounds 41–44)
BNIC/Aubert 147 (grounds 1, 7)

2.3. Dividing customers between competitors
FEDETAB 133
BP Kemi/DDSF 147 (paras. 28e, 38, 80)
Peroxide Products 218
Roofing Felt 248 (para. 74)
Woodpulp 227 (paras. 71–76, 133–134)*

2.4. Market and/or sales information exchange
Tinned Mushrooms 88
Cobelpa/VNP 115 (paras. 5, 9, 24–28)
Vegetable Parchment 129 (paras. 34–39, 63–70)
SNPE/LEL 132 (paras. 7, 13)
CSV 134 (para. 25)
BP Kemi/DDSF 147 (paras. 28c, 38, 51, 78–79)
Italian Cast Glass 163
Italian Flat Glass 164
White Lead 142 (paras. 12–16, 25–27)
Flat Glass (Benelux) 216 (para. 45)
Peroxide 218
Polypropylene 247 (paras. 66, 80)
Fatty Acids 254*
Solvay/ICI 330 (paras. 30–33)
U.K. Tractors 347*
Non Ferrous Metals 5th Comp. Rep. (para. 39)
Paper Machine Wire Manu 6th Comp. Rep. (para. 134)
7th Comp. Rep. (paras. 5–8)
EWIS 18th Comp. Rep. (paras. 63)

2.5. Compensation schemes
Transocean Marine Paint Association 10
Quinine Cartel 24 (para. 28)
Cimbel 66 (para. 13)
CSV 134 (paras. 18e, 62, 72)*
White Lead 142 (para. 12)
BP Kemi/DDSF 147 (paras. 28b, 41, 82)
Roofing Felt 248 (para. 73)
Meldoc 253 (paras. 21–60)*
PVC 305 (para. 11)
BNIC/Aubert 147 (grounds 1, 7)
Solvay/CFK 331

3. Price agreements between competitors

3.1. Agreed minimum prices
VVVF 22
VCH 47 (para. 16)
GISA 67
IFTRA Glass 77 (para. 35)
Centraal Bureau voor de Rijwielhandel 118 (paras. 10, 25)*
FEDETAB 133 (paras. 19–21, 81, 96–97)
AROW/BNIC 190 (paras. 11–47, 58–65, 67–71)
Cast-iron & Steel Rolls 198 (paras. 3, 5–6, 10, 53a, 54)
Aluminium 228 (para. 11)
Polypropylene 247 (paras. 16, 22–23, 80, 89)
Herbage Seed 6th Comp. Rep. (para. 119)
BNIC v. *Clair* 115

3.2. Agreed common prices
Quinine Cartel 24 (paras. 22–24)*
VCH 47
NSH 53

Book One: Part III—Horizontal Agreements

Cimbel 66
Belgian Wallpaper 78
IFTRA Aluminium 92
Cobelpa/VNP 115 (paras. 5, 21)
Vegetable Parchment 129 (paras. 28, 40–52, 71–73)
CSV 134 (paras. 18, 20, 62, 72)
BP Kemi/DDSF 147 (paras. 28d, 40, 52–54, 81–82)
Natursteinplatten 159 (paras. 7–12, 22, 27, 40–41)
Italian Flat Glass 164
SSI 181 (paras. 107, 110d, 116d, 123, 127)
Flat Glass (Benelux) 216 (paras. 40–43)
Zinc Producer Group 217 (para. 66)
Woodpulp 227 (paras. 17–27)*
Roofing Felt 248
Flat Glass 300 (para. 61)
Welded Steel Mesh 311
Sheet Glass 1st Comp. Rep. (para. 6)
Lino Cartel 5th Comp. Rep. (para. 35)
EBU 16th Comp. Rep. (para. 62)
Papiers Peints v. Commission 47 (grounds 6–12)
Züchner v. Bayerische Vereinsbank 86 (ground 17)
Ahmed Saeed v. Zentrale 162 (ground 19)
Belasco v. Commission 166 (grounds 12–15)

3.3. Agreed recommended prices

VCH 47 (para. 16)
IFTRA Aluminium 92
Vimpoltu 195 (paras. 25–27, 39–40)
Fire Insurance 220 (para. 23)
Ship Chains 5th Comp. Rep. (para. 40)
Cement Dealers v. Commission 32 (grounds 21–25)*

3.4. Agreed price increase

Dyestuffs 27*
European Sugar Industry 69
Franco Japanese Ball-Bearings 81
SSI 181 (para. 110a)
Cast-iron & Steel Rolls 198 (paras. 6, 8, 10, 20, 53a, 54)
Zinc Producer Group 217 (paras. 75–76)
Fire Insurance 222
PVC 305 (paras. 17–22, 35)
LdPE 306 (paras. 26–27, 42)
Woollen Fabrics 12th Comp. Rep. (para. 71)
ICI v. Commission 23 (grounds 83–103)*

3.5. Collective R.P.M.

ASPA 30
Belgian Wallpaper 78
Fireplaces 90
Centraal Bureau voor de Rijwielhandel 118 (paras. 10, 25)

FEDETAB 133 (paras. 28–39, 82)
VBBB/VBVB 169 (paras. 9, 41–42, 48–63)*
Net Book Agreements 301
Dutch Cartridges 3rd Comp. Rep. (paras. 55–56)
SARABEX 8th Comp. Rep. (paras. 35–37)
Dutch Pharmaceuticals 8th Comp. Rep. (paras. 81–82)
VEB/Shell 16th Comp. Rep. (para. 55)
Papiers Peints v. Commission 47 (grounds 6–12)
FEDETAB v. Commission 80 (grounds 96, 157–162)
VBBB/VBVB v. Commission 105

3.6. Common rebate/discount policy

Quinine Cartel 24 (paras. 22–24)
Ceramic Tiles 35
VCH 47 (para. 16)
Cimbel 66 (para. 15)
Heaters and Boilers 72
Belgian Wallpaper 78
Fireplaces 90
IFTRA Aluminium 92
Centraal Bureau voor de Rijwielhandel 118 (paras. 11–12, 27)
FEDETAB 133 (paras. 35, 74–75, 86, 90, 98)*
BP Kemi/DDSF 147 (paras. 28, 81)
Natursteinplatten 159 (paras. 8, 15, 27–28)
Italian Flat Glass 164
SSI 181 (paras. 98–99, 114a–b, 133)
Vimpoltu 195 (paras. 16–17, 35)
Roofing Felt 248 (paras. 73–74)
Flat Glass 300 (para. 61)
Net Book Agreements 301
Gosme/Martell 340 (para. 30–32)
1st Comp. Rep. (para. 24)
Dutch Liquorice 2nd Comp. Rep. (para. 34)
Belgian & Dutch Electrodes 4th Comp. Rep. (para. 78)
Glass Industry 4th Comp. Rep. (para. 79)
Lino Cartel 5th Comp. Rep. (para. 35)
FEDETAB v. Commission 80 (grounds 103, 142–146)*
Vlaamse Reisebureas 144

3.7. Bidding agreements

DECA 6
European Sugar Industry 69
Cast-iron & Steel Rolls 198 (paras. 3, 5, 8, 10, 53a, 54)*
Irish Distillers (18th Comp. Rep. Para. 80)

3.8. Aligning prices in another's territory

IFTRA Glass 77
IFTRA Aluminium 92*
Italian Flat Glass 164
Herbage Seed 6th Comp. Rep. (para. 119)

3.9. Price information exchange agreements

IFTRA Glass 77 (paras. 40–47)
Belgian Wallpaper 78
Vegetable Parchment 129 (paras. 34–39, 63–70)
IFTRA Aluminium 92
Cobelpa/VNP 115 (paras. 5, 15, 29–30, 42)*
Vimpoltu 195 (paras. 23–27, 38)
Polypropylene 247 (para. 80)
Dutch Cartridges 3th Comp. Rep. (paras. 55–56)
Paper Machine Wire Manu. 6th Comp. Rep. (para. 134)
7th Comp. Rep. (paras. 5–8)
EWIS 18th. Comp. Rep. (para. 63)
Ahmed Saeed v. *Zentrale* 162 (ground 27)

4. Sales agreements

4.1. Common or joint sales

Cobelaz 15, 16
CFA 18
SEIFA 23
Supexie 34
SAFCO 48
NCH 53
SCPA-Kali & Salz 71
Kali & Salz/KaliChemie 76
CSV 134 (paras. 18–19, 62, 72)*
Floral 148
Siemens/Fanuc 246
Meldoc 253 (paras. 38–44, 65–67)
Hudson Bay 294 (paras. 9–10)
ANSAC 333a (para. 19)
1st Comp. Rep. (para. 11)
CIM 1st Comp. Rep. (para. 14)
3rd Comp. Rep. (paras. 50–52)
Safety Glass 5th Comp. Rep. (para. 34)

4.2. Common exports

Alliance de Constructeurs Français 12
Cobelaz 15, 16 (para. 6)
CFA 18
SEIFA 23
Supexie 34
SAFCO 48
Milchfoerderungsfonds 221*

4.3. Common sales policy

Tinned Mushrooms 88
Meldoc 253 (paras. 21, 60)
Feldmühle/Stora 12th Comp. Rep. (para. 73)

4.4. Common purchasing policy

Quinine Cartel 24 (para. 30)
Italian Flat Glass 164*

Aluminium 228 (para. 11)
Belgian Wood Cartel. 5th Comp. Rep. (para. 37)

4.5. Common sales conditions

Cobelaz 15, 16 (paras. 7)
CFA 18
SEIFA 23
Supexie 34
NCH 53
VCH 47 (para. 16)
Cimbel 66 (para. 13)
GISA 67
Heaters and Boilers 72
IFTRA Glass 77 (paras. 36–37, 48–50)
Belgian Wallpaper 78
Pabst & Richarz/BNIA 106
Cobelpa/VNP 115 (paras. 5, 21)
Centraal Bureau voor de Rijwielhandel 118 (paras. 11–12, 25–26)
FEDETAB 133 (paras. 51–52, 63–73, 76, 86, 99–104)*
BP Kemi/DDSF 147 (paras. 28, 81)
Natursteinplatten 159 (paras. 8–12, 27–28)
Vimpoltu 195 (paras. 18–20, 28–30, 35–36, 39)
Zinc Producer Group 217 (para. 67)
Roofing Felt 248 (paras. 73–74)
Net Book Agreements 301*
Lino Cartel 5th Comp. Rep. (para. 35)
Finpap 19th Comp. Rep. (para. 44)
FEDETAB v. *Commission* 80 (grounds 99, 103, 147–156)*

4.6. Information exchange on sales conditions

Cobelpa VNP 115 (paras. 5, 29–30, 42)
Vegetable Parchment 129 (paras. 34–39, 63–70)*
CSV 134 (para. 25)
PVC 305 (paras. 12, 15, 35)
LdPE 306 (paras. 10, 18–19, 42)
EWIS 18th Comp. Rep. (para. 63)

4.7. Mutual respect for distribution channels

Cobelpa/VNP 115 (paras. 7–8, 16, 31–32, 43)
Centraal Bureau voor de Rijwielhandel 118 (paras. 2–7, 21–22)*
IATA Passenger 342 (para. 48–99)
IATA Cargo 343 (para. 43–44)
FEDETAB v. *Commission* 80 (grounds 95–141)

5. Exclusionary practices

5.1. Collective exclusive dealing

Convention Faience 1

Book One: Part III—Horizontal Agreements

ASPA 30
VCH 47
Central Heating 60
GISA 67
Heaters and Boilers 72
FRUBO 80
Fireplaces 90
Bomée-Stichting 97
Centraal Bureau voor de Rijwielhandel 118 (paras. 5–9, 21–22)*
Cauliflowers 119
FEDETAB 133
Rennet 149 (paras. 5–7, 22–23, 31)*
IMA Rules 158 (paras. 19–20, 43–47, 57–66, 68–73)
Natursteinplatten 159 (para. 14)
VBBB/VBVB 169 (paras. 9, 39–40, 48)
Sugar Beet 315 (paras. 21–41, 73–87)
Ijsselcentrale 335
1st Comp. Rep. (paras. 19–23)
Hibin 2nd Comp. Rep. (para. 32)
Dutch Cartridges. 3rd Comp. Rep. (para. 55)
Dutch Record Agreement. 4th Comp. Rep. (para. 76)
Dutch Transport Insurers. 6th Comp. Rep. (para. 120)
SARABEX 8th Comp. Rep. (paras. 35–37)
Dutch Pharmaceuticals. 8th Comp. Rep. (paras. 81–82)
Irish Timber Importers, 20th Comp. Rep. (para. 98)
Frubo v. *Commission* 44 (grounds 33–39)
FEDETAB v. *Commission* 80 (grounds 95–141)
Stremsel v. *Commission* 84

5.2. Agreements intended to control the supply of a product

FRUBO 80
Pabst & Richarz/BNIA 106 (Prohibition of bulk sales)
Zinc Producers Group 217 (para. 67)
Aluminium 228 (para. 11)*
VBA 288
Hudson Bay 294 (paras. 8–10)
Ijsselcentrale 335

5.3. Predatory price cutting agreements

Meldoc 253 (paras. 27–49, 65 69)

5.4. Joint production with exclusive purchasing

Rennet 149 (paras. 5–7, 22–23, 31)
Ijsselcentrale 335

5.5. Collective refusal to supply

Belgian Wallpaper 78
Bronbemaling 95

FEDETAB 133 (para. 87)
Ministère public v. *Tournier* 167 (grounds 23–26)
Lucazeau v. *SACEM* 168 (ground 15–19)

5.6. Aggregate rebates

Ceramic Tiles 35*
Belgian Wallpaper 78
FEDETAB 133 (paras. 35, 74–75, 86, 90, 98)*
Natursteinplatten 159 (paras. 15, 28)
Dutch Liquorice 2nd Comp. Rep. (para. 34)
FEDETAB v. *Commission* 80 (grounds 103, 142–146)*

5.7. Patent pooling

Bronbemoaling 95
Concast/Mannesmann 11th Comp. Rep. (paras. 92–93)
IGR Stereo TV 11th Comp. Rep. (para. 94)
IGR 14th Comp. Rep. (para. 92)

6. Practices used by cartels to enforce agreements

6.1. Boycotting non-members

Belgian Wallpaper 78
FEDETAB 133 (para. 87)

6.2. Fines on cartel members for breach of rules

IFTRA Glass 77 (para. 39)
Fire Places 90
Centraal Bureau voor de Rijwielhandel 118 (para. 13)
Rennet 149 (paras. 9, 22, 24, 31)
IMA Rules 158 (paras. 20, 32–33)
Vimpoltu 195 (paras. 21–22, 37)*
Synthetic Fibres 213

7. Crisis cartels

Chaufourniers 20
Zinc 189
International Energy Agency 207
Synthetic Fibres 213*
Polyester fibres 2nd Comp. Rep. (para. 31)
Zinc Producers 13th Comp. Rep. (paras. 56–61)
Man-made fibres 8th Comp. Rep. (para. 42)
Man-made fibres 11th Comp. Rep. (paras. 46–48)
12th Comp. Rep. (paras. 38–41)
ACF Chemiefarma v. *Commission* 14 (grounds 126–131)
Boehringer v. *Commission* 16 (grounds 41–44)

Part IV—2 Co-operation Agreements

CHAPTER 2

CO-OPERATION AGREEMENTS

A. LIST OF CASES ON CO-OPERATION AGREEMENTS

Transocean Marine Paint Association 10
Eurogypsum 11
Alliance de Constructeurs Française 12
VVVF 22
Pirelli/Dunlop 28
ASBL 31
SAFCO 48
Video Cassette Recorders 122
SOPELEM/Vickers I 125
SNPE/LEL 132
SOPELEM/Vickers II 171
NAVEWA-ANSEAU 178
VW/MAN 203
International Energy Agency 207
Nuovo-CEGAM 209
Uniform Eurochèques 224
Irish Bank Standing Committee 252
Belgian Banking Association 261
ABI 262
X/Open Group 263
Eurotunnel 293
Uniform Eurochèque Manufacturing 302
Dutch Banking Association 310
APB 314
TEXO 317
Concordato 316
IATA Passengers 342
IATA Cargo 343
BP-Ruhrgas 9th Comp. Rep. (para. 94)
ICL/Fujitsu 16th Comp. Rep. (para. 72)
FIEC-CFETB 18th Comp. Rep. (para. 62)
EWIS 18th Comp. Rep. (para. 63)

B. TEXT OF RELEVANT NOTICES

1. Co-operation agreements

1.1. Notice of July 29, 1968
(reproduced below)

Notice of July 29, 1968

On co-operation between enterprises

([1968] O.J. C75/3)
(Amended by corrigendum, [1968] O.J. C84/14)

Questions are frequently put to the Commission of the European Communities on the attitude it intends to take up, within the framework of the implementation of the competition rules contained in the Treaties of Rome and Paris, with regard to co-operation between enterprises. In this Notice, it endeavours to provide guidance which, though not exhaustive, could prove useful to enterprises in the correct interpretation of Article 85(1) of the EEC Treaty and Article 65(1) of the ECSC Treaty.

I. The Commission welcomes co-operation among small- and medium-sized enterprises where such co-operation enables them to work more rationally and increase their productivity and competitiveness on a larger market. The Commission considers that it is its task to facilitate co-operation among small- and medium-sized enterprises in particular. However, co-operation among large enterprises, too, can be economically justifiable without presenting difficulties from the angle of competition.

Article 85(1) of the Treaty establishing the European Economic Community (EEC Treaty) and Article 65(1) of the Treaty establishing the European Coal and Steel Community (ECSC Treaty) provide that all agreements, decisions and concerted practices (hereafter referred to as "agreements") which have as their object or result the prevention, restriction or distortion of competition (hereafter referred to as "restraints of competition") in the common market are incompatible with the common market and are forbidden; under Article 85(1) of the EEC Treaty this applies, however, only if these agreements are liable to impair trade between the Member States.

The Commission feels that in the interests of the small- and medium-sized enterprises in particular it should make known the considerations by which it will be guided when interpreting Article 85(1) of the EEC Treaty and Article 65(1) of the ECSC Treaty and applying them to certain co-operation arrangements between enterprises, and indicate which of these arrangements in its opinion do not come under these provisions. This notice applies to all enterprises, irrespective of their size.

There may also be forms of co-operation between enterprises other than the forms of co-operation listed below which are not prohibited by Article 85(1) of the EEC Treaty or Article 65(1) of the ECSC Treaty. This applies in particular if the market position of the enterprises co-operating with each other is in the aggregate too weak as to lead, through the agreement between them, to an appreciable restraint of competition in the common market and—for Article 85 of the EEC Treaty—to impair trade between the Member States.

It is also pointed out, in respect of other forms of co-operation between enterprises or agreements containing additional clauses, that where the rules of competition of the Treaties apply, such forms of co-operation or agreements can be exempted by virtue of Article 85(3) of the EEC Treaty or be authorised by virtue of Article 65(2) of the ECSC Treaty.

The Commission intends to clarify rapidly, by means of suitable decisions in individual cases or by general notices, the status of the various forms of co-operation in relation with the provisions of the Treaties.

No general statement can be made at this stage on the application of Article 86 of the EEC Treaty on the abuse of dominant positions within the common market or within a part of it. The same applies to Article 66(7) of the ECSC Treaty.

As a result of this notice, as a general rule, it will no longer be useful for enterprise to obtain negative clearance, as defined by Article 2 of Regulation 17, for the agreements listed, nor should it be necessary for the legal situation to be clarified through a Commission decision on an individual case; this also means that notification will no longer be necessary for agreements of this type. However, if it is doubtful whether in an individual case an agreement between enterprises restricts competition or if other forms of co-operation between enterprises which in the view of the enterprises do not restrict competition are not listed here, the enterprises are free to apply, where the matter comes under Article 85(1) of the EEC Treaty, for negative clearance, or to file as a precautionary measure, where Article 65(1) of the ECSC Treaty is the relevant clause, an application on the basis of Article 65(2) of the ECSC Treaty.

This Notice does not prejudice interpretation by the Court of Justice of the European Communities.

II. The Commission takes the view that the following agreements do not restrict competition.

1. Agreements having as their sole object:
   (a) An exchange of opinion or experience;
   (b) Joint market research,
   (c) The joint carrying out of comparative studies of enterprises or industries,
   (d) The joint preparation of statistics and calculation models.

Agreements whose sole purpose is the joint procurement of information which the various enterprises need to determine their future market behaviour freely and independently, or the use by each of the enterprises of a joint advisory body, do not have as their object or result the restriction of competition. But if the scope of action of the enterprises is limited or if the market behaviour is co-ordinated either expressly or through concerted practices, there may be restraint of competition. This is in particular the case where concrete recommendations are made or where conclusions are given such a form that they induce at least some of the participating enterprises to behave in an identical manner on the market.

The exchange of information can take place between the enterprises themselves or through a body acting as an intermediary. It is, however, particularly difficult to distinguish between information which has no bearing on competition on the one hand and behaviour in restraint of competition on the other, if there are special bodies which have to register orders, turnover figures, investment figures, and prices, so that it can as a rule not be automatically assumed that Article 85(1) of the EEC Treaty or Article 65(1) of the ECSC Treaty do not apply to them. A restraint of competition may occur in particular on an oligopolist market for homogenous products.

In the absence of more far-reaching co-operation between the participating enterprises, joint market research and comparative studies of different enterprises and industries to collect information and ascertain facts and market conditions do not in themselves impair competition.

Part III—2 Co-operation Agreements

Other arrangements of this type, as for instance the joint establishment of economic and structural analyses, are so obviously not impairing competition that there is no need to mention them specifically.

Calculation models containing specified rates of calculations are to be regarded as recommendations that may lead to restraints of competition.

2. Agreements having as their sole object:
   (a) Co-operation in accounting matters,
   (b) Joint provision of credit guarantees,
   (c) Joint debt-collecting associations,
   (d) Joint business or tax consultant agencies.

These are cases of co-operation relating to fields that do not concern the supply of goods and services and the economic decisions of the enterprises involved, so that they cannot lead to restraints of competition.

Co-operating in accounting matters is neutral from the point of view of competition as it only serves for the technical handling of the accounting work. Nor is the creation of credit guarantee associations affected by the competition rules, since it does not modify the relationship between supply and demand.

Debt-collecting associations whose work is not confined to the collection of outstanding payments in line with the intentions and conditions of the participating enterprises, or which fix prices or exert in any other way an influence on price formation, may restrict competition. Application of uniform conditions by all participating firms may constitute a case of concerted practices, as may joint comparison of prices. In this connection, no objection can be raised against the use of standardised printed forms; their use must, however, not be combined with an understanding or tacit agreement on uniform prices, rebates or conditions of sale.

3. Agreements having as their sole object:
   (a) The joint implementation of research and development projects,
   (b) The joint placing of research and development contracts,
   (c) The sharing out of research and development projects among participating enterprises.

In the field of research, too, the mere exchange of experience and results serves for information only and does not restrict competition. It therefore need not be mentioned expressly.

Agreements on the joint execution of research work or the joint development of the results of research up to the stage of industrial application do not affect the competitive position of the parties. This also applies to the sharing of research fields and development work if the results are available to all participating enterprises. However, if the enterprises enter into commitments which restrict their own research and development activity or the utilisation of the results of joint work so that they do not have a free hand with regard to their own research and development outside the joint projects, this can constitute an infringement of the rules of competition of the Treaties. Where firms do not carry out joint research work, contractual obligations or concerted practices binding them to refrain from research work of their own either completely or in certain sectors may result in a restraint of competition. The sharing out of sectors of research without an understanding providing for mutual access to the results is to be regarded as a case of specialisation that may restrict competition.

There may also be a restraint of competition if agreements are concluded or corresponding concerted practices applied with regard to the practical exploitation of the results of research and development work carried out jointly, particularly if the participating enterprises undertake or agree to manufacture only products or the types of products developed jointly or to share out future production among themselves.

It is of the essence of joint research that the results should be exploited by the participating enterprises in proportion to their participation. If the participation of certain enterprises is confined to a specific sector of the common research project or to the provision of only limited financial assistance, there is no restraint of competition so far as there has been any joint research at all—if the results of research are made available to these enterprises only in relation with the degree of their participation. There may, however, be a restraint of competition if certain participating enterprises are excluded from the exploitation of the results, either entirely or to an extent not commensurate with their participation.

If the granting of licences to third parties is expressly or tacitly excluded, there may be a restraint of competition; the fact that research is carried out jointly warrants, however, arrangements binding the enterprises to grant licences to third parties only by common agreement or by majority decision.

For the assessment of the compatibility of the agreement with the rules of competition, it does not matter what legal form the common research and development work takes.

4. Agreements which have as their only object the joint use of production facilities and storing and transport equipment.

These forms of co-operation do not restrict competition because they are confined to organisational and technical arrangements for the use of the facilities. There may be a restraint of competition if the enterprises involved do not bear the cost of utilisation of the installation or equipment themselves or if agreements are concluded or concerted practices applied regarding joint production or the sharing out of production or the establishment or running of a joint enterprise.

5. Agreements having as their sole object the setting up of working partnerships for the common execution of orders, where the participating enterprises do not compete with each other as regards the work to be done or where each of them by itself is unable to execute the orders.

Where enterprises do not compete with each other they cannot restrict competition by setting up associations. This applies in particular to enterprises belonging to different industries but also to firms of the same industry to the extent that their contribution under the working partnership consist only of goods or services which cannot be supplied by the other participating enterprises. It is not a question of whether the enterprises compete with each other in other industries so much as whether in the light of the concrete circumstances of a particular case there is a possibility that in the foreseeable future they may compete with each other with regard to the products or services involved. If the absence of competition between the enterprises and the maintenance of this situation is based on agreements or concerted practices, there may be a restraint of competition.

But even in the case of working partnerships formed by enterprises which compete with each other there is no restraint of competition if the participating enterprises cannot execute the specific order by themselves. This applies in particular if, for lack of experience, specialised knowledge, capacity of financial resources these enterprises, when working alone, have no chance of success or cannot finish the work within the required time-limit or cannot bear the financial risk. Nor is there a restraint of competition if it is only by the setting up of an association that the enterprises are put in a position to make a promising offer. There may, however, be a restraint of competition if the enterprises undertake to work solely in the framework of an association.

6. Agreements having as their sole object:
  (a) Joint selling arrangements,
  (b) Joint after-sales and repair service, provided the participating enterprises are not competitors with regard to the products or services covered by the agreement.

As already explained in detail under Section 5, co-operation between enterprises cannot restrict competition if the firms do not compete with each other.

Very often joint selling by small- or medium-sized enterprises—even if they are competing with each other—does not entail an appreciable restraint of competition; it is, however, impossible to establish in this Notice any general criteria or to specify what enterprises may be deemed "small- or medium-sized."

There is no joint after-sales and repair service if several manufacturers, without acting in concert with each other, arrange for an after-sales and repair service for their product to be provided by an enterprise which is independent. In such a case there is no restraint of competition, even if the manufacturers are competitors.

7. Agreements having as their sole object joint advertising.

Joint advertising is designed to draw the buyers' attention to the products of an industry or to a common brand; as such it does not restrict competition between the participating enterprises. However, if the participating enterprises are partly or wholly prevented, by agreements or concerted practices, from themselves advertising or if they are subjected to other restrictions, there may be a restraint of competition.

8. Agreements having as their sole object the use of a common label to designate a certain quality, where the label is available to all competitors on the same conditions.

Such associations for the joint use of a quality label do not restrict competition if other competitors, whose products objectively meet the stipulated quality requirements, can use the label on the same conditions as the members. Nor do the obligations to accept quality control of the products provided with the label, to issue uniform instructions for use, or to use the label for the products meeting the quality standards constitute restraints of competition. But there may be restraint of competition if the right to use the label is linked to obligations regarding production, marketing, price formations or obligations of any other type, as is for instance the case when the participating enterprises are obliged to manufacture or sell only products of guaranteed quality.

1.2. Cases on the interpretation of the Notice

IFTRA Glass 77
IFTRA Aluminium 93
Cobelpa 115 (para. 27)
Vegetable Parchment 129 (para. 65)
Beecham/Parke Davis 144 (para. 33)
Roofing Felt 248 (para. 73)
Siemens/Fanuc 256 (para. 30)
Eurotunnel 293*
ANSAC 333a (para. 30)

2. Text of Notice on subcontracting Agreements (reproduced below)

Commission Notice of December 18, 1978

Concerning its assessment of certain subcontracting agreements in relation to Article 85(1) of the EEC Treaty

([1979] O.J. C1/2)

1. In this Notice the Commission of the European Communities gives its view as to subcontracting agreements in relation to Article 85(1) of the Treaty establishing the European Economic Community. This class of agreement is at the present time a form of work distribution which concerns firms of all sizes, but which offers opportunities for development in particular to small and medium-sized firms.

The Commission considers that agreements under which one firm, called 'the contractor', whether or not in consequence of a prior order from a third party, entrusts to another, called 'the subcontractor', the manufacture of goods, the supply of services or the performance of work under the contractor's instructions, to be provided to the contractor or performed on his behalf, are not of themselves caught by the prohibition in Article 85(1).

To carry out certain subcontracting agreements in accordance with the contractor's instructions, the subcontractor may have to make use of particular technology or equipment which the contractor will have to provide. In order to protect the economic value of such technology or equipment, the contractor may wish to restrict their use by the subcontractor to whatever is necessary for the purpose of the agreement. The question arises whether such restrictions are caught by Article 85(1). They are assessed in this Notice with due regard to the purpose of such agreements, which distinguishes them from ordinary patent and knowhow licensing agreements.

2. In the Commission's view, Article 85(1) does not apply to clauses whereby:
— technology or equipment provided by the contractor may not be used except for the purposes of the subcontracting agreement,
— technology or equipment provided by the contractor may not be made available to third parties,
— the goods, services or work resulting from the use of such technology or equipment may be supplied only to the contractor or performed on his behalf

provided that and in so far as this technology or equipment is necessary to enable the subcontractor, under reasonable conditions to manufacture the goods, to supply the services or to carry out the work in accordance with the contractor's instructions. To that extent the subcontractor is providing goods, services or work in respect of which he is not an independent supplier in the market.

The above proviso is satisfied where performance of the subcontracting agreement makes necessary the use by the subcontractor of:

- industrial property rights of the contractor or at his disposal, in the form of patents, utility models, designs protected by copyright, registered designs or other rights, or
- secret knowledge or manufacturing processes (know-how) of the contractor or at his disposal, or of
- studies, plans or documents accompanying the information given which have been prepared by or for the contractor, or
- dies, patterns or tools, and accessory equipment that are distinctively the contractor's,

which, even though not covered by industrial property rights nor containing any element of secrecy, permit the manufacture of goods which differ in form, function or composition from other goods manufactured or supplied on the market.

However, the restrictions mentioned above are not justifiable where the subcontractor has at his disposal or could under reasonable conditions obtain access to the technology and equipment needed to produce the goods, provide the services or carry out the work. Generally, this is the case when the contractor provides not more than general information which merely describes the work to be done. In such circumstances the restrictions could deprive the subcontractor of the possibility of developing his own business in the fields covered by the agreement.

3. The following restrictions in connection with the provision of technology by the contractor may in the Commission's view also be imposed by subcontracting agreements without giving grounds for objection under Article 85(1):

- an undertaking by either of the parties not to reveal manufacturing processes or other know-how of a secret character, or confidential information given by the other party during the negotiation and performance of the agreement, as long as the know-how or information in question has not become public knowledge,
- an undertaking by the subcontractor not to make use, even after expiry of the agreement, of manufacturing processes or other know-how of a secret character received by him during the currency of the agreement, as long as they have not become public knowledge,
- an undertaking by the subcontractor to pass on to the contractor on a non-exclusive basis any technical improvements which he has made during the currency of the agreement, or, where a patentable invention has been discovered by the subcontractor, to grant non-exclusive licences in respect of inventions relating to improvements and new applications of the original invention to the contrctor for the term of the patent held by the latter.

This undertaking by the subcontractor may be exclusive in favour of the contractor in so far as improvements and intentions made by the subcontractor during the currency of the agreement are incapable of being used independently of the contractor's secret know-how or patent, since this does not constitute an apprecialbe restriction of competition.

However, any undertaking by the subcontractor regarding the right to dispose of the results of his own research and development work may restrain competition, where such results are capable of being used independently. In such circumstances, the subcontracting relationship is not sufficient to displace the ordinary competition rules on the disposal of industrial property rights or secret know-how.

4. Where the subcontractor is authorised by a subcontracting agreement to use a specified trade mark, trade name or get-up, the contractor may at the same time forbid such use by the subcontractor in the case of goods, services or work which are not to be supplied to the contractor.

5. Although this Notice should in general obviate the need for firms to obtain a ruling on the legal position by an individual Commission Decision, it does not affect the right of the firms concerned to apply for negative clearance as defined by Article 2 of Regulation No 17 or to notify the agreement to the Commission under Article 4(1) of that Regulation.

The 1968 notice on co-operation between enterprises, which lists a number of agreements that by their nature are not to be regarded as anti-competitive, is thus supplemented in the subcontracting field. The Commission also reminds firms that, in order to promote co-operation between small and medium-sized businesses, it has published a Notice concerning agreements of minor importance which do not fall under Article 85(1) of the Treaty establishing the European Economic Community.

This Notice is without prejudice to the view that may be taken of subcontracting agreements by the Court of justice of the European Communities.

3. Reference to connected legislation

Regulation 2137/85 On the European Economic Interest grouping O.J. L199/1.

C. TYPES/CATEGORIES OF CO-OPERATION AGREEMENTS

1. Sharing of research and development (R&D) Costs

See R&D agreements, Chapter 4, p.106

2. Patent pools

Video Cassette Recorders 122 (paras. 12, 15, 24)
Continental/Michelin 290*
Concast/Mannesmann 11th Comp. Rep. (paras. 92–93)
IGR Stereo TV 11th Comp. Rep. (para. 94)

3. Sharing of production capacity

Dunlop/Pirelli 28

4. Building consortia

Eurotunnel 293

5. Uniform manufacturing standards

VVVF 22
Video Cassette Recorders 122
SOPELEM/Vickers 125
X/Open Group 263*
Uniform Eurocheques Manufacturing 302

6. Uniform sales conditions

Nuovo-CEGAM 209*
Uniform Eurocheque 224
Irish Bank Standing Committee 252
Belgian Banking Association 261
ABI 262 (para. 41)

7. Joint or common advertising

ASBL 31

8. Adoption of common trademarks or quality marks

Transocean Marine Paint Association I 10*
ASBL 31

Belgian Wallpaper 78
Intergroup 91
NAVEWA-ANSEAU 178*
APB 314
1st Comp. Rep. (para. 39)
Poroton. 10th Comp. Rep. (paras. 130–132)

9. Joint sales

Alliance de Constructeurs Français 12
SAFCO 48*
SOPELEM/Vickers 125

10. Inter-bank agreements

See Part IX, Chapter 6, p. 358

11. Buying groups

SOCEMAS 13
Intergroup 91*
Rennet 149
National Sulphuric Acid Assoc. 156, 308
IMA Rules 158
Fisher Price 275 (para. 18)
1st Comp. Rep. (paras. 40–41)
Orptie 20th Comp. Rep. (para. 120)
Stremsel v. *Commission* 84

CHAPTER 3

SPECIALISATION AGREEMENTS

A. LIST OF CASES ON SPECIALISATION AGREEMENTS

ACEC/Berliet 14
Clima Chappée 25
Jaz/Peter 26, 128
FN-CF 37
SOPELEM/Langen 49
MAN/SAVIEM 54
Wild/Leitz 55
Thin Paper 59
Prym/Beka 74
Kali & Salz/Kalichemie 76
Rank/SOPELEM 86
Bayer/Gist Brocades 100
SOPELEM/Vickers 125, 171
Italian Cast Glass 163
Zinc 189
VW/MAN 203
BPCL/ICI 215
ENI-Montedison 256
Alcatel/ANT 319
1st Comp. Rep. (paras. 26–29)
2nd Comp. Rep. (paras. 8–11, 35)
7th Comp. Rep. (paras. 35, 36)
VFA/SAVER 15th Comp. Rep. (para. 78)

B. TEXT OF REGULATION 417/85 (reproduced over)

Book One: Part III—Horizontal Agreements

Commission Regulation 417/85 of December 19, 1984

On the application of Article 85(3) of the Treaty to categories of specialisation agreements

([1985] O.J. L53/1)

THE COMMISSION OF THE EUROPEAN COMMUNITIES,

Having regard to the Treaty establishing the European Economic Community,

Having regard to Council Regulation 2821/71 of 20 December 1971 on the application of Article 85(3) of the Treaty to categories of agreements, decisions and concerted practices, as last amended by the Act of Accession of Greece, and in particular Article 1 thereof,

Having published a draft of this Regulation,

Having consulted the Advisory Committee on Restrictive Practices and Dominant Positions,

Whereas:

(1) Regulation 2821/71 empowers the Commission to apply Article 85(3) of the Treaty by Regulation to certain categories of agreements, decisions and concerted practices falling within the scope of Article 85(1) which relate to specialisation, including agreements necessary for achieving it.

(2) Agreements on specialisation in present or future production may fall within the scope of Article 85(1).

(3) Agreements on specialisation in production generally contribute to improving the production or distribution of goods, because undertakings concerned can concentrate on the manufacture of certain products and thus operate more efficiently and supply the products more cheaply. It is likely that, giving effective competition, consumers will receive a fair share of the resulting benefit.

(4) Such advantages can arise equally from agreements whereby each participant gives up the manufacture of certain products in favour of another participant and from agreements whereby the participants undertake to manufacture certain products or have them manufactured only jointly.

(5) The Regulation must specify what restrictions of competition may be included in specialisation agreements. The restrictions of competition that are permitted in the Regulation in addition to reciprocal obligations to give up manufacture are normally essential for the making and implementation of such agreements. These restrictions are therefore, in general, indispensable for the attainment of the desired advantages for the participating undertakings and consumers. It may be left to the parties to decide which of these provisions they include in their agreements.

(6) The exemption must be limited to agreements which do not give rise to the possibility of eliminating competition in respect of a substantial part of the products in question. The Regulation must therefore apply only as long as the market share and turnover of the participating undertakings do not exceed a certain limit.

(7) It is, however, appropriate to offer undertakings which exceed the turnover limit set in the Regulation a simplified means of obtaining the legal certainty provided by the block exemption. This must allow the Commission to exercise effective supervision as well as simplifying its administration of such agreements.

(8) In order to facilitate the conclusion of long-term specialisation agreements, which can have a bearing on the structure of the participating undertakings, it is appropriate to fix the period of validity of the Regulation at 13 years. If the circumstances on the basis of which the Regulation was adopted should change significantly within this period, the Commission will make the necessary amendments.

(9) Agreements, decisions and concerted practices which are automatically exempted pursuant to this Regulation need not be notified. Undertakings may none the less in an individual case request a decision pursuant to Council Regulation No. 17, as last amended by the Act of Accession of Greece.

HAS ADOPTED THIS REGULATION:

Part III—3 Specialisation Agreements

Article 1

Pursuant to Article 85(3) of the Treaty and subject to the provisions of this Regulation, it is hereby declared that Article 85(1) of the Treaty shall not apply to agreements on specialisation whereby, for the duration of the agreement, undertakings accept reciprocal obligations:
(a) not to manufacture certain products or to have them manufactured, but to leave it to other parties to manufacture the products or have them manufactured; or
(b) to manufacture certain products or have them manufactured only jointly.

Article 2

1. Apart from the obligations referred to in Article 1, no restrictions of competition may be imposed on the parties other than:
(a) an obligation not to conclude with third parties specialisation agreements relating to identical products or to products considered by users to be equivalent in view of their characteristics, price and intended use;
(b) an obligation to procure products which are the subject of the specialisation exclusively from another party, a joint undertaking or an undertaking jointly charged with their manufacture, except where they are obtainable on more favourable terms elsewhere and the other party, the joint undertaking or the undertaking charged with manufacture is not prepared to offer the same terms;
(c) an obligation to grant other parties the exclusive right to distribute products which are the subject of the specialisation provided that intermediaries and users can also obtain the products from other suppliers and the parties do not render it difficult for intermediaries or users thus to obtain the products.

2. Article 1 shall also apply where the parties undertake obligations of the types referred to in paragraph 1 but with a more limited scope than is permitted by that paragraph.

3. Article 1 shall apply notwithstanding that any of the following obligations, in particular, are imposed:
(a) an obligation to supply other parties with products which are the subject of the specialisation and in so doing to observe minimum standards or quality;
(b) an obligation to maintain minimum stocks of products which are the subject of the specialisation and of replacement parts for them;
(c) an obligation to provide customer and guarantee services for products which are the subject of the specialisation.

Article 3

1. Article 1 shall apply only if:
(a) the products which are the subject of the specialisation together with the participating undertakings' other products which are considered by users to be equivalent in view of their characteristics, price and intended use do not represent more than 20 per cent. of the market for such products in the common market or a substantial part thereof;
(b) the aggregate annual turnover of all the participating undertakings does not exceed 500 million ECU.

2. Article 1 shall continue to apply if the market share referred to in paragraph 1(a) or the turnover referred to in paragraph 1(b) is exceeded during any period of two consecutive financial years by not more than one-tenth.

3. Where one of the limits laid down in paragraphs 1 and 2 is exceeded, Article 1 shall continue to apply for a period of six months following the end of the financial year during which it was exceeded.

Article 4

1. The exemption provided for in Article 1 shall also apply to agreements involving participating undertakings whose aggregate turnover exceeds the limits laid down in Article 3(1)(b) and (2), on condition that the agreements in question are notified to the Commission in accordance with the provisions of Commission Regulation No. 27, and that the Commission does not oppose such exemption within a period of six months.

2. The period of six months shall run from the date on which the notification is received by the Commission. Where, however, the notification is made by registered post, the period shall run from the date shown on the postmark of the place of posting.

3. Paragraph 1 shall apply only if:
(a) express reference is made to this Article in the notification or in a communication accompanying it; and
(b) the information furnished with the notification is complete and in accordance with the facts.

4. The benefit of paragraph 1 may be claimed for agreements notified before the entry into force of this Regulation by submitting a communication to the Commission referring expressly to this Article and to the notification. Paragraphs 2 and 3(b) shall apply *mutatis mutandis*.

5. The Commission may oppose the exemption. It shall oppose exemption if it receives a request to do so from a Member State within three months of the forwarding to the Member State of the notification referred to in paragraph 1 of the communication referred to in paragraph 4. This request must be justified on the basis of considerations relating to the competition rules of the Treaty.

6. The Commission may withdraw the opposition to the exemption at any time. However, where the opposition was raised at the request of a Member State and this request is maintained, it may be withdrawn only after consultation of the Advisory Committee on Restrictive Practices and Dominant Positions.

7. If the opposition is withdrawn because the undertakings concerned have shown that the conditions of Article 85(3) are fulfilled, the exemption shall apply from the date of notification.

8. If the opposition is withdrawn because the undertakings concerned have amended the agreement so that the conditions of Article 85(3) are fulfilled, the exemption shall apply from the date on which the amendments take effect.

9. If the Commission opposes exemption and the opposition is not withdrawn, the effects of the notification shall be governed by the provisions of Regulation No. 17.

Article 5

1. Information acquired pursuant to Article 4 shall be used only for the purposes of this Regulation.

2. The Commission and the authorities of the Member States, their officials and other servants shall not disclose information acquired by them pursuant to this Regulation of a kind that is covered by the obligation of professional secrecy.

3. Paragraphs 1 and 2 shall not prevent publication of general information or surveys which do not contain information relating to particular undertakings or associations of undertakings.

Article 6

For the purpose of calculating total annual turnover within the meaning of Article 3(1)(b), the turnovers achieved during the last financial year by the participating undertakings in respect of all goods and services excluding tax shall be added together. For this purpose, no account shall be taken of dealings between the participating undertakings or between those undertakings and a third undertaking jointly charged with manufacture.

Article 7

1. For the purposes of Article 3(1)(a) and (b) and Article 6, participating undertakings are:
(a) undertakings party to the agreement;
(b) undertakings in which a party to the agreement, directly or indirectly:
— owns more than half the capital or business assets,
— has the power to exercise more than half the voting rights,
— has the power to appoint at least half the members of the supervisory board, board of management or bodies legally representing the undertakings, or
— has the right to manage the affairs;
(c) undertakings which directly or indirectly have in or over a party to the agreement the rights or powers listed in (b);
(d) undertakings in or over which an undertaking referred to in (c) directly or indirectly has the rights or powers listed in (b).

2. Undertakings in which the undertakings referred to in paragraph 1(a) to (d) directly or indirectly jointly have the rights or powers set out in paragraph 1(b) shall also be considered to be participating undertakings.

Article 8

The Commission may withdraw the benefit of this Regulation, pursuant to Article 7 of Regulation 2821/71, where it finds in a particular case that an agreement exempted by this regulation nevertheless has effects which are incompatible with the conditions set out in Article 85(3) of the Treaty, and in particular where:
(a) the agreement is not yielding significant results in terms of rationalisation or consumers are not receiving a fair share of the resulting benefit; or

(b) the products which are not the subject of the specialisation are not subject in the common market or a substantial part thereof to effective competition from identical products or products considered by users to be equivalent in view of their characteristics, price and intended use.

Article 9

This Regulation shall apply *mutatis mutandis* to decisions of associations of undertakings and concerted practices.

Article 10

1. This Regulation shall enter into force on 1 March 1985. It shall apply until 31 December 1997.
2. Commission Regulation 3604/82 is hereby repealed.
This Regulation shall be binding in its entirety and directly applicable in all Member States.

Done at Brussels, 19 December 1984.

C. CASES ON THE INTERPRETATION OF THE REGULATION

Italian Cast Glass 163

D. CATEGORIES OF SPECIALISATION AGREEMENTS

1. Agreements to expand the range of goods produced/sold by the parties

Clima-Chappée 25
Jaz/Peter I 26*
FN/CF 37
SOPELEM/Langen 49
MAN/SAVIEM 54
Wild/Leitz 55
Rank/SOPELEM 86
SOPELEM/Vickers 125, 171
VW/MAN 203

2. Agreements to share R&D costs

ACEC/Berliet 14*
Rank/SOPELEM 86
Bayer/Gist Brocades 100
Alcatel/ANT 319 (para. 6c)

3. Joint distribution agreements

SOPELEM/Vickers 125
VW/MAN 203 (paras. 8–9, 20, 28)*

4. Restructuring agreements

Thin Paper 59
Prym/Beca 74
Cast-iron & Steel Rolls 198
BPCL/ICI 215
ENI/Montedison 256*

E. CLAUSES TYPICAL OF SPECIALISATION AGREEMENTS

1. Exchange of information/licenses

ACEC/Berliet 14
MAN/SAVIEM 54. (para. 27)*
Bayer/Gist-Brocades 100
SOPELEM/Vickers 125
Alcatel/ANT 319 (paras. 6d and 6f)

2. Reciprocal distribution rights

Article 2(1)(c)
Clima Chappée 25
Jaz Peter I 26. (paras. 5–6), 126
FN-CF 37
SOPELEM/Langen 49
MAN/SAVIEM 54
Wild/Leitz 55
Rank/SOPELEM 86
SOPELEM/Vickers 125

3. Obligation to supply or purchase from the other party

3.1. Exclusive purchasing obligation

Article 2(1)(b)
ACEC/Berliet 14*
Clima Chappée 25
SOPELEM/Langen 49
Prym/Beca 74
Zinc 189
VW/MAN 203
Alcatel/ANT (para. 6c)
Perlite 19th Comp. Rep. (para. 39)

3.2. Obligation to supply the other party

Article 2(3)
ACEC/Berliet 14*
Bayer/Gist Brocades 100
Zinc 189
Alcatel/ANT 319 (paras. 6c and 6h)
VFA/SAVER 15th Comp. Rep. (para. 78)

3.3. Right of first refusal to sell new products

Jaz/Peter I 26 (paras. 5–6, 126)

3.4. Most favoured customer clause

ACEC/Berliet 14

4. Non-competitive clause

Article 2(1)(a)

Book One: Part III—Horizontal Agreements

Jaz/Peter I 26 (paras. 5–6, 126)
FN/CF 37
SOPELEM/LANGEN 49
MAN/SAVIEM 54 (paras. 15–22)*
Prym/Beca 74
Bayer/Gist Brocades 100 (para. II.3)
SOPELEM/Vickers 125
Zinc 189
VW/MAN 203 (paras. 10, 17, 19, 26, 31)

5. Territorial restriction

MAN/SAVIEM 54
Rank/SOPELEM 86*

6. Trademark related clauses

Jaz/Peter I 26 (paras. 5–6)
Rank/SOPELEM 86

CHAPTER 4

RESEARCH AND DEVELOPMENT AGREEMENTS

A. LIST OF CASES ON R&D AGREEMENTS

Eurogypsum 11

ACEC/Berliet 14
Henkel/Colgate 52
MAN/SAVIEM 54
Rank/SOPELEM 86
De Laval/Stork 114, 281
GEC/Weir Sodium Circulators 117
Beecham/Parke Davis 144
Vacuum Interrupters 112, 161
VW/MAN 203
Carbon Gas Technologie 205
BP/Kellogg 235
Canon/Olivetti 280
Continental/Michelin 290
BBC/Brown Boveri 291
Alcatel/ANT 319
Odin 322
Konsortium ECR 900 323
KSB 328
1st Comp. Rep. (paras. 31–35)
NCB 15th Comp. Rep. (para. 71)
Bayer/Hoechst 20th Comp. Rep. (para. 99)

B. TEXT OF REGULATION 418/85
(reproduced below)

Commission Regulation 418/85 of December 19, 1984

([1985] O.J. L53/5)

On the application of Article 85(3) of the Treaty to categories of research and development agreements

THE COMMISSION OF THE EUROPEAN COMMUNITIES,
   Having regard to the Treaty establishing the European Economic Community,
   Having regard to Council Regulation 2821/71 of 20 December 1971, on the application of Article 85(3) of the Treaty to categories of agreements, decisions and concerted practices, as last amended by the Act of Accession of Greece, and in particular Article 1 thereof,
   Having published a draft of this Regulation,
   Having consulted the Advisory Committee on Restrictive Practices and Dominant Positions,

Whereas:
(1) Regulation 2821/71 empowers the Commission to apply Article 85(3) of the Treaty by Regulation to certain categories of agreements, decisions and concerted practices falling within the scope of Article 85(1) which have as their object the research and development of products or processes up to the stage of industrial application, and exploitation of the results, including provisions regarding industrial property rights and confidential technical knowledge.

(2) As stated in the Commission's 1968 notice concerning agreements, decisions and concerted practices in the field of

cooperation between enterprises, agreements on the joint execution of research work or the joint development of the results of the research, up to but not including the stage of industrial application, generally do not fall within the scope of Article 85(1) of the Treaty. In certain circumstances, however, such as where the parties agree not to carry out other research and development in the same field, thereby foregoing the opportunity of gaining competitive advantages over the other parties, such agreements may fall within Article 85(1) and should therefore not be excluded from this Regulation.

(3) Agreements providing for both joint research and development and joint exploitation of the results may fall within Article 85(1) because the parties jointly determine how the products developed are manufactured or the processes developed are applied or how related intellectual property rights of know-how are exploited.

(4) Cooperation in research and development and in the exploitation of the results generally promotes technical and economic progress by increasing the dissemination of technical knowledge between the parties and avoiding duplication of research and development work, by stimulating new advances through the exchange of complementary technical knowledge, and by rationalising the manufacture of the products or application of the processes arising out of the research and development. These aims can be achieved only where the research and development programme and its objectives are clearly defined and each of the parties is given the opportunity of exploiting any of the results of the programme that interest it; where universities or research institutes participate and are not interested in the industrial exploitation of the results, however, it may be agreed that they may use the said results solely for the purpose of further research.

(5) Consumers can generally be expected to benefit from the increased volume and effectiveness of research and development through the introduction of new or improved products or services or the reduction of prices brought about by new or improved processes.

(6) This Regulation must specify the restrictions of competition which may be included in the exempted agreements. The purpose of the permitted restrictions is to concentrate the research activities of the parties in order to improve their chances of success, and to facilitate the introduction of new products and services onto the market. These restrictions are generally necessary to secure the desired benefits for the parties and consumers.

(7) The joint exploitation of results can be considered as the natural consequence of joint research and development. It can take different forms ranging from manufacture to the exploitation of intellectual property rights or know-how that substantially contributes to technical or economic progress. In order to attain the benefits and objectives described above and to justify the restrictions of competition which are exempted, the joint exploitation must relate to products or processes for which the use of the results of the research and development is decisive. Joint exploitation is not therefore justified where it relates to improvements which were not made within the framework of a joint research and development programme but under an agreement having some other principal objective, such as the licensing of intellectual property rights, joint manufacture or specialisation, and merely containing ancillary provisions on joint research and development.

(8) The exemption granted under the Regulation must be limited to agreements which do not afford the undertakings the possibility of eliminating competition in respect of a substantial part of the products in question. In order to guarantee that several independent poles of research can exist in the common market in any economic sector, it is necessary to exclude from the block exemption agreements between competitors whose combined share of the market for products capable of being improved or replaced by the results of the research and development exceeds a certain level at the time the agreement is entered into.

(9) In order to guarantee the maintenance of effective competition during joint exploitation of the results, it is necessary to provide that the block exemption will cease to apply if the parties' combined shares of the market for the products arising out of the joint research and development become too great. However, it should be provided that the exemption will continue to apply, irrespective of the parties' market shares, for a certain period after the commencement of joint exploitation, so as to await stabilisation of their

market shares, particularly after the introduction of an entirely new product, and to guarantee a minimum period of return on the generally substantial investments involved.

(10) Agreements between undertakings which do not fulfil the market share conditions laid down in the Regulation may, in appropriate cases, be granted an exemption by individual decision, which will in particular take account of world competition and the particular circumstances prevailing in the manufacture of high technology products.

(11) It is desirable to list in the Regulation a number of obligations that are commonly found in research and development agreements but that are normally not restrictive of competition and to provide that, in the event that, because of the particular economic or legal circumstances, they should fall within Article 85(1), they also would be covered by the exemption. This list is not exhaustive.

(12) The Regulation must specify what provisions may not be included in agreements if these are to benefit from the block exemption by virtue of the fact that such provisions are restrictions falling within Article 85(1) for which there can be no general presumption that they will lead to the positive effects required by Article 85(3).

(13) Agreements which are not automatically covered by the exemption because they include provisions that are not expressly exempted by the Regulation and are not expressly excluded from exemption are none the less capable of benefiting from the general presumption of compatibility with Article 85(3) on which the block exemption is based. It will be possible for the Commission rapidly to establish whether this is the case for a particular agreement. Such an agreement should therefore be deemed to be covered by the exemption provided for in this Regulation where it is notified to the Commission and the Commission does not oppose the application of the exemption within a specified period of time.

(14) Agreements covered by this Regulation may also take advantage of provisions contained in other block exemption Regulations of the Commission, and in particular Regulation 417/85 on specialisation agreements, Regulation 1983/83 on exclusive distribution agreements, Regulation 1984/83, on exclusive purchasing agreements and Regulation 2349/84 on patent licensing agreements, if they fulfil the conditions set out in these Regulations. The provisions of the aforementioned Regulations are, however, not applicable in so far as this Regulation contains specific rules.

(15) If individual agreements exempted by this Regulation nevertheless have effects which are incompatible with Article 85(3), the Commission may withdraw the benefit of the block exemption.

(16) The Regulation should apply with retroactive effect to agreements in existence when the Regulation comes into force where such agreements already fulfil its conditions or are modified to do so. The benefit of these provisions may not be claimed in actions pending at the date of entry into force of this Regulation, nor may it be relied on as grounds for claims for damages against third parties.

(17) Since research and development cooperation agreements are often of a long-term nature, especially where the cooperation extends to the exploitation of the results, it is appropriate to fix the period of validity of the Regulation at 13 years. If the circumstances on the basis of which the Regulation was adopted should change significantly within this period, the Commission will make the necessary amendments.

(18) Agreements which are automatically exempted pursuant to this Regulation need not be notified. Undertakings may nevertheless in a particular case request a decision pursuant to Council Regulation No. 17, as last amended by the Act of Accession of Greece,

HAS ADOPTED THIS REGULATION:

Article 1

1. Pursuant to Article 85(3) of the Treaty and subject to the provisions of this Regulation, it is hereby declared that Article 85(1) of the Treaty shall not apply to agreements entered into between undertakings for the purpose of:
(a) joint research and development of products or processes and joint exploitation of the results of that research and development;
(b) joint exploitation of the results of research and development of products or processes jointly carried out pursuant to a

prior agreement between the same undertakings; or

(c) joint research and development of products or processes excluding joint exploitation of the results, in so far as such agreements fall within the scope of Article 85(1).

2. For the purposes of this Regulation:

(a) *research and development of products or processes* means the acquisition of technical knowledge and the carrying out of theoretical analysis, systematic study or experimentation, including experimental production, technical testing of products or processes, the establishment of the necessary facilities and the obtaining of intellectual property rights for the results;

(b) *contract processes* means processes arising out of the research and development;

(c) *contract products* means products or services arising out of the research and development or manufactured or provided applying the contract processes;

(d) *exploitation of the results* means the manufacture of the contract products or the application of the contract processes or the assignment or licensing of intellectual property rights or the communication of know-how required for such manufacture or application;

(e) *technical knowledge* means technical knowledge which is either protected by an intellectual property right or is secret (know-how).

3. Research and development of the exploitation of the results are carried out *jointly* where:

(a) the work involved is:
— carried out by a joint team, organisation or undertaking,
— jointly entrusted to a third party, or
— allocated between the parties by way of specialisation in research, development or production;

(b) the parties collaborate in any way in the assignment or the licensing of intellectual property rights or the communication of know-how, within the meaning of paragraph 2(d), to third parties.

Article 2

The exemption provided for in Article 1 shall apply on condition that:

(a) the joint research and development work is carried out within the framework of a programme defining the objectives of the work and the field in which it is to be carried out;

(b) all the parties have access to the results of the work;

(c) where the agreement provides only for joint research and development, each party is free to exploit the results of the joint research and development and any pre-existing technical knowledge necessary therefor independently;

(d) the joint exploitation relates only to results which are protected by intellectual property rights or constitute know-how which substantially contributes to technical or economic progress and that the results are decisive for the manufacture of the contract products or the application of the contract processes;

(e) any joint undertaking or third party charged with manufacture of the contract products is required to supply them only to the parties;

(f) undertakings charged with manufacture by way of specialisation in production are required to fulfil orders for supplies from all the parties.

Article 3

1. Where the parties are not competing manufacturers of products capable of being improved or replaced by the contract products, the exemption provided for in Article 1 shall apply for the duration of the research and development programme and, where the results are jointly exploited, for five years from the time the contract products are first put on the market within the common market.

2. Where two or more of the parties are competing manufacturers within the meaning of paragraph 1, the exemption provided for in Article 1 shall apply for the period specified in paragraph 1 only if, at the time the agreement is entered into, the parties' combined production of the products capable of being improved or replaced by the contract products does not exceed 20 per cent. of the market for such products in the common market or a substantial part thereof.

3. After the end of the period referred to in paragraph 1, the exemption provided for in Article 1 shall continue to apply as long as the production of the contract products together with the parties' combined production of other products which are considered by users to be equivalent in view of their characteristics, price and intended use does not exceed 20 per cent. of the total market for such products in the com-

mon market or a substantial part thereof. Where contract products are components used by the parties for the manufacture of other products, reference shall be made to the markets for such of those latter products for which the components represent a significant part.

4. The exemption provided for in Article 1 shall continue to apply where the market share referred to in paragraph 3 is exceeded during any period of two consecutive financial years by not more than one-tenth.

5. Where market shares referred to in paragraphs 3 and 4 are exceeded, the exemption provided for in Article 1 shall continue to apply for a period of six months following the end of the financial year during which it was exceeded.

Article 4

1. The exemption provided for in Article 1 shall also apply to the following restrictions of competition imposed on the parties:

(a) an obligation not to carry out independently research and development in the field to which the programme relates or in a closely connected field during the execution of the programme;

(b) an obligation not to enter into agreements with third parties on research and development in the field to which the programme relates or in a closely connected field during the execution of the programme;

(c) an obligation to procure the contract products exclusively from parties, joint organisations or undertakings or third parties, jointly charged with their manufacture;

(d) an obligation not to manufacture the contract products or apply the contract processes in territories reserved for other parties;

(e) an obligation to restrict the manufacture of the contract products or application of the contract processes to one or more technical fields of application, except where two or more of the parties are competitors within the meaning of Article 3 at the time the agreement is entered into;

(f) an obligation not to pursue, for a period of five years from the time the contract products are first put on the market within the common market, an active policy of putting the products on the market in territories reserved for other parties, and in particular not to engage in advertising specifically aimed at such territories or to establish any branch or maintain any distribution depot there for the distribution of the products, provided that users and intermediaries can obtain the contract products from other suppliers and the parties do not render it difficult for intermediaries and users to thus obtain the products;

(g) an obligation on the parties to communicate to each other any experience they may gain in exploiting the results and to grant each other non-exclusive licences for inventions relating to improvements or new applications.

2. The exemption provided for in Article 1 shall also apply where in a particular agreement the parties undertake obligations of the types referred to in paragraph 1 but with a more limited scope than is permitted by that paragraph.

Article 5

1. Article 1 shall apply notwithstanding that any of the following obligations, in particular, are imposed on the parties during the currency of the agreement:

(a) an obligation to communicate patented or non-patented technical knowledge necessary for the carrying out of the research and development programme for the exploitation of its results;

(b) an obligation not to use any know-how received from another party for purposes other than carrying out the research and development programme and the exploitation of its results;

(c) an obligation to obtain and maintain in force intellectual property rights for the contract products or processes;

(d) an obligation to preserve the confidentiality of any know-how received or jointly developed under the research and development programme; this obligation may be imposed even after the expiry of the agreement;

(e) an obligation:
   (i) to inform other parties of infringements of their intellectual property rights,
   (ii) to take legal action against infringers, and
   (iii) to assist in any such legal action or share with the other parties in the cost thereof;

(f) an obligation to pay royalties or render services to other parties to compensate for

unequal contributions to the joint research and development or unequal exploitation of its results;
(g) an obligation to share royalties received from third parties with other parties;
(h) an obligation to supply other parties with minimum quantities of contract products and to observe minimum standards of quality.

2. In the event that, because of particular circumstances, the obligations referred to in paragraph 1 fall within the scope of Article 85(1), they also shall be covered by the exemption. The exemption provided for in this paragraph shall also apply where in particular by agreement the parties undertake obligations of the types referred to in paragraph 1 but with a more limited scope than is permitted by that paragraph.

Article 6

The exemption provided for in Article 1 shall not apply where the parties, by agreement, decision or concerted practice:
(a) are restricted in their freedom to carry out research and development independently or in cooperation with third parties in a field unconnected with that to which the programme relates or, after its completion, in the field to which the programme relates or in a connected field;
(b) are prohibited after completion of the research and development programme from challenging the validity of intellectual property rights which the parties hold in the common market and which are relevant to the programme or, after the expiry of the agreement, from challenging the validity of intellectual property rights which the parties hold in the common market and which protect the results of the research and development;
(c) are restricted as to the quantity of the contract products they may manufacture or sell or as to the number of operations employing the contract process they may carry out;
(d) are restricted in their determination of prices, components of prices or discounts when selling the contract products to third parties;
(e) are restricted as to the customers they may serve, without prejudice to Article 4(1)(e);
(f) are prohibited from putting the contract products on the market or pursuing an active sales policy for them in territories within the common market that are reserved for other parties after the end of the period referred to in Article 4(1)(f);
(g) are prohibited from allowing third parties to manufacture the contract products or apply the contract processes in the absence of joint manufacture;
(h) are required:
— to refuse without any objectively justified reason to meet demand from users or dealers established in their respective territories who would market the contract products in other territories within the common market, or
— to make it difficult for users or dealers to obtain the contract products from other dealers within the common market, and in particular to exercise intellectual property rights to take measures so as to prevent users or dealers from obtaining, or from putting on the market within the common market, products which have been lawfully put on the market within the common market by another party or with its consent.

Article 7

1. The exemption provided for in this Regulation shall also apply to agreements of the kinds described in Article 1 which fulfil the conditions laid down in Articles 2 and 3 and which contain obligations restrictive of competition which are not covered by Articles 4 and 5 and do not fall within the scope of Article 6, on condition that the agreements in question are notified to the Commission in accordance with the provisions of Commission Regulation No. 27, and that the Commission does not oppose such exemption within a period of six months.

2. The period of six months shall run from the date on which the notification is received by the Commission. Where, however, the notification is made by registered post, the period shall run from the date shown on the postmark of the place of posting.

3. Paragraph 1 shall apply only if:
(a) express reference is made to this Article in the notification or in a communication accompanying it, and
(b) the information furnished with the notification is complete and in accordance with the facts.

4. The benefit of paragraph 1 may be claimed for agreements notified before the

entry into force of this Regulation by submitting a communication to the Commission referring expressly to this Article and to the notification. Paragraphs 2 and 3(b) shall apply *mutatis mutandis*.

5. The Commission may oppose the exemption. It shall oppose exemption if it receives a request to do so from a Member State within three months of the forwarding to the Member State of the notification referred to in paragraph 1 or of the communication referred to in paragraph 4. This request must be justified on the basis of considerations relating to the competition rules of the Treaty.

6. The Commission may withdraw the opposition to the exemption at any time. However, where the opposition was raised at the request of a Member State and this request is maintained, it may be withdrawn only after consultation of the Advisory Committee on Restrictive Practices and Dominant Positions.

7. If the opposition is withdrawn because the undertakings concerned have shown that the conditions of Article 85(3) are fulfilled, the exemption shall apply from the date of notification.

8. If the opposition is withdrawn because the undertakings concerned have amended the agreement so that the conditions of Article 85(3) are fulfilled, the exemption shall apply from the date on which the amendments take effect.

9. If the Commission opposes exemption and the opposition is not withdrawn, the effects of the notification shall be governed by the provisions of Regulation No. 17.

Article 8

1. Information acquired pursuant to Article 7 shall be used only for the purposes of this Regulation.

2. The Commission and the authorities of the Member States, their officials and other servants shall not disclose information acquired by them pursuant to this Regulation of a kind that is covered by the obligation of professional secrecy.

3. Paragraphs 1 and 2 shall not prevent publication of general information or surveys which do not contain information relating to particular undertakings or associations of undertakings.

Article 9

1. The provisions of this Regulation shall also apply to rights and obligations which the parties create for undertakings connected with them. The market shares held and the actions and measures taken by connected undertakings shall be treated as those of the parties themselves.

2. Connected undertakings for the purposes of this Regulation are:
(a) undertakings in which a party to the agreement, directly or indirectly:
— owns more than half the capital or business assets,
— has the power to exercise more than half the voting rights,
— has the power to appoint more than half the members of the supervisory board, board of directors or bodies legally representing the undertakings, or
— has the right to manage the affairs;
(b) undertakings which directly have in or over a party to the agreement the rights or powers listed in (a);
(c) undertakings in or over which an undertaking referred to in (b) directly or indirectly has the rights or powers listed in (a);

3. Undertakings in which the parties to the agreement or undertakings connected with them jointly have, directly or indirectly, the rights or powers set out in paragraph 2(a) shall be considered to be connected with each of the parties to the agreement.

Article 10

The Commission may withdraw the benefit of this Regulation, pursuant to Article 7 of Regulation 2821/71, where it finds in a particular case that an agreement exempted by this Regulation nevertheless has certain effects which are incompatible with the conditions laid down in Article 85(3) of the Treaty, and in particular where:
(a) the existence of the agreement substantially restricts the scope for third parties to carry out research and development in the relevant field because of the limited research capacity available elsewhere;
(b) because of the particular structure of supply, the existence of the agreement substantially restricts the access of third parties to the market for the contract products;
(c) without any objectively valid reason, the parties do not exploit the results of the joint research and development;

Part III—4 R&D Agreements

(d) the contract products are not subject in the whole or a substantial part of the common market to effective competition from identical products or products considered by users as equivalent in view of their characteristics, price and intended use.

Article 11

1. In the case of agreements notified to the Commission before 1 March 1985, the exemption provided for in Article 1 shall have retroactive effect from the time at which the conditions for application of this Regulation were fulfilled or, where the agreement does not fall within Article 4(2)(3)(b) of Regulation No. 17, not earlier than the date of notification.

2. In the case of agreements existing on 13 March 1962 and notified to the Commission before 1 February 1963, the exemption shall have retroactive effect from the time at which the conditions for application of this Regulation were fulfilled.

3. Where agreements which were in existence on 13 March 1962 and which were notified to the Commission before 1 February 1963, or which are covered by Article 4(2)(3)(b) of Regulation No. 17 and were notified to the Commission before 1 January 1967, are amended before 1 September 1985 so as to fulfil the conditions for application of this Regulation, such amendment being communicated to the Commission before 1 October 1985, the prohibition laid down in Article 85(1) of the Treaty shall not apply in respect of the period prior to the amendment. The communication of amendments shall take effect from the date of their receipt by the Commission. Where the communication is sent by registered post, it shall take effect from the date shown on the postmark of the place of posting.

4. In the case of agreements to which Article 85 of the Treaty applies as a result of the accession of the United Kingdom, Ireland and Denmark, paragraphs 1 to 3 shall apply except that the relevant dates shall be 1 January 1973 instead of 13 March 1962 and 1 July 1973 instead of 1 February 1963 and 1 January 1967.

5. In the case of agreements to which Article 85 of the Treaty applies as a result of the accession of Greece, paragraphs 1 to 3 shall apply except that the relevant dates shall be 1 January 1981 instead of 13 March 1962 and 1 July 1981 instead of 1 February 1963 and 1 January 1967.

Article 12

This Regulation shall apply *mutatis mutandis* to decisions of associations of undertakings.

Article 13

This Regulation shall enter into force on 1 March 1985.
It shall apply until 31 December 1997.
This Regulation shall be binding in its entirely and directly applicable in all Member States.

Done at Brussels, 19 December 1984.

C. CASES ON THE INTERPRETATION OF THE REGULATION

BP/Kellogg 235
Continental/Michelin 290 (para. 21)
BBC Brown Boveri 291 (paras. 16, 21)
Welded Steel Mesh 311 (paras. 190–191)
Alcatel/ANT 319 (para. 17)
KSB 328*
17th Comp. Rep. (para. 31)

D. CATEGORIES OF R&D AGREEMENTS

1. Joint R&D without production

ACEC/Berliet 14
Henkel/Colgate 52*
MAN/SAVIEM 54
Rank/SOPELEM 86
Beecham/Parke Davis 144
Continental/Michelin 290
BBC/Brown Boveri 291
Alcatel/ANT 319

2. Joint R&D with subsequent joint production

Vacuum Interrupters 112, 161
De Laval/Stork 114, 281
GEC-Weir Sodium Circulators 117
Carbon Gas Technologie 205
BP/Kellogg 235
Canon/Olivetti 280*
Odin 322
Konsortium ECR 900 323
KSB 328*

E. CLAUSES COMMONLY FIGURING IN R&D AGREEMENTS

1. Territorial provisions

Book One: Part III—Horizontal Agreements

1.1. Division of the EEC into exclusive territories between the contracting parties for exploitation of results
Article 4(1)(d)
ACEC/Berliet 14*
MAN/SAVIEM 54 (para. 17)
Rank/SOPELEM 86
Beecham/Parke Davis 144 (paras. 20, 43)

1.2. Prohibition of active sales outside exclusive territory
Articles 4(1)(f), 6(f)
Rank/SOPELEM 86

1.3. Prohibition of passive sales outside exclusive territory
Article 6(h)
MAN/SAVIEM 54 (para. 17)

1.4. Export prohibition to the Common Market
BBC/Brown Boveri 291 (paras. 18, 22)

2. Supply and purchase obligations

2.1. Exclusive purchasing obligations
Article 4(1)(c)
ACEC/Berliet 14
Vacuum Interrupters 112, 161
Alcatel/ANT 319 (para. 6c)
KSB 328 (para. 22)*

2.2. Mutual supply obligations
Article 5(1)(h)
ACEC/Berliet 14
MAN/SAVIEM 54
Alcatel/ANT 319 (para. 6h)

2.3. Most favoured customer clause
ACEC/Berliet 14

3. Non-competition clauses

3.1. Prohibition from engaging in competing R&D
Articles 4(1)(a)–(b), 6(a)
MAN/SAVIEM 54 (paras. 15, 22)
GEC/Weir Sodium Circulators 117*
Beecham/Parke Davis 144 (paras. 14, 29)
Carbon Gas Technologie 205
BP/Kellogg 235 (para. 9)*
Continental/Michelin 290 (para. 13)
BBC/Brown Boveri 291 (para. 16)
Alcatel/ANT 319 (para. 6c)
Konsortium ECR 900 323

3.2 Prohibition from engaging in R&D in unconnected fields
Article 6(a)

MAN/SAVIEM 54 (paras. 15–16)
Vacuum Interrupters (II) 161
GEC/Weir Sodium Circulators 117
Carbon Gas Technologie 205
BP/Kellogg 235 (paras. 8–9)*

4. Customer limitation clause
Article 6(e)
MAN/SAVIEM 54 (paras. 20–21)

5. Clauses relating to the fruits of the R&D

5.1. Minimum quality norms
Article 5(1)(h)

5.2. Restrictions on the quantities that the parties may sell
Article 6(c)

5.3. Field of use restrictions
Article 4(1)(e)

6. Clauses relating to intellectual property and related rights

6.1. Exchange of technical information
Articles 4(1)(g), 5(1)(a)
ACEC/Berliet 14
Henkel/Colgate 52
GEC/Weir Sodium Circulators 117
Beecham/Parke Davis 144 (paras. 9–11, 16–21, 33, 39–41)*
Vacuum Interrupters 112, 161
Carbon Gas Technologie 205
BP/Kellogg 235
Continental/Michelin 290 (paras. 7, 17)
BBC/Brown Boveri 291 (para. 19)
Alcatel/ANT 319 (paras. 6d & 6f)
Odin 322 (para. 6–9)
Konsortium ECR 900 323

6.2. Field of use restrictions
Odin 322 (paras. 6–9)
Article 5(1)(b)
ACEC/Berliet 14
Alcatel/ANT 319 (para. 6d)
Odin 322 (paras. 6–9)

6.3. Obligation to maintain confidentiality of know-how
Article 5(1)(d)
MAN/SAVIEM 54 (para. 27)
Carbon Gas Technologie 205
Alcatel/ANT 319 (para 6e)
Odin 322 (para. 19)
KSB 328 (para. 18)

6.4. Grant of licences to third parties/sub-licensing
Article 6(g)

Henkel/Colgate 52
Beecham/Parke Davis 144 (paras. 9–11, 16–21, 33, 39–41)
BP/Kellogg 235
KSB 328 (para. 18)*

6.5. Patent pooling

Video Cassette Recorders 122 (paras. 12, 15, 24)
Continental/Michelin 290 (para. 15)
Alcatel/ANT 319 (para. 6d)
See also Part IV, Chapter 1, page 89

6.6. Post-term use ban of jointly developed technology

Carbon Gas Technologie 205

6.7. Patent no-challenge Clause

Article 6(b)

6.8. Obligation to inform the other party of patent infringement

Article 5(1)(e)

7. Duration of the agreement

7.1. Between competitors

Article 3(2)–(5)
Henkel/Colgate 52
KSB 328*

7.2. Between non-competitors

Article 3(1),(3),(5)

8. Royalty provisions

8.1. Obligation to pay royalties to the other party if contribution to R&D is unequal

Article 5(1)(f)
Beecham/Parke Davis 144 (paras. 18, 43c)

8.2. Obligation to share royalties received from third parties

Article 5(1)(g)
Continental/Michelin 290 (para. 15)

8.3. Profit-sharing through royalty payments

Beecham/Parke Davis 140 (para. 18, 43c)

CHAPTER 5

TRADE ASSOCIATIONS

A. CASES ON TRADE ASSOCIATIONS

1. General list

Eurogypsum 11
ASBL 31
London Sugar Market 238
London Cocoa Market 239
London Coffee Market 240
London Rubber Market 241
P&I Clubs 243
IPEL 254
GAFTA 260
London Grain Market 261
London Potato Market 262
London Meat Exchange 263
BIFFEX 270
Sarabex 8th Comp. Rep. (paras. 35–37)
Department Stores 9th Comp. Rep. (para. 89)

2. List of cases where a trade association was acting as a cartel

VVVF 22
ASPA 30
Ceramic Tiles 35
Cimbel 66
GISA 67
Heaters and Boilers 77
Belgian Wallpaper 78
FRUBO 80
Bomée Stichting 97
Pabst & Richarz/BNIA 106
Centraal Bureau voor de Rijwielhandel 118
Cauliflowers 119
FEDETAB 133
Rennet 151
National Sulphuric Acid Association 157, 308
IMA Rules 158
Natursteinplatten 159
Italian Flat Glass 164
VBBB/VBVB 170
SSI 181
Vimpoltu 194
Fire Insurance 222
Roofing Felt 248
VBA 287
Hudson Bay 292
Sugar Beet 315
U.K. Tractors 347
Herbage Seed 6th Comp. Rep. (para. 119)
Dutch Transport Insurers 6th Comp. Rep. (para. 120)
Dutch Pharmaceuticals 8th Comp. Rep. (paras. 81–82)
Frubo v. *Commission* 44 (grounds 33–39)

FEDETAB v. *Commission* 80
Stremsel v. *Commission* 84 (grounds 12–13)

B. STIPULATIONS COMMON TO TRADE ASSOCIATION AGREEMENTS

1. Rules regarding membership of associations

1.1. Objective criteria for membership

Centraal Bureau voor de Rijwielhandel 118 (paras. 3, 19–20)
Cauliflowers 119
FEDETAB 133 (paras. 6, 40–43, 84)*
IMA Rules 158 (paras. 12–18, 42–45)
Natursteinplatten 159 (paras. 36–38)
Nuovo-CEGAM 209 (para. 16)
London Sugar Market 238
London Cocoa Market 239
London Coffee Market 240
London Rubber Market 241
IPEL 254
GAFTA 260
London Grain Market 261
X/Open Group 264*

1.2. Limit on numbers of members

FEDETAB 133 (paras. 40–43, 84)
IMA Rules 158 (para. 45)
SSI 181 (paras. 99d, 116a, 134–137)
Dept. Stores. 9th Comp. Rep. (para. 89)
FEDETAB v. *Commission* 80 (ground 97)*

1.3. Provisions limiting withdrawal from association

Rennet 151 (paras. 9, 22–24, 31)
P&I Clubs 243*

2. Pricing obligations

FEDETAB 133
Natursteinplatten 159
London Sugar Market 238
London Cocoa Market 239
London Coffee Market 240
London Rubber Market 241
P&I Clubs 243
IPEL 254
GAFTA 260
London Grain Market 261
London Potato Market 262
London Meat Exchange 263
BIFFEX 271
Sarabex. 8th Comp. Rep. (paras. 35–37)
Dutch Pharmaceuticals. 8th Comp. Rep. (paras. 81–82)
FEDETAB v. *Commission* 80 (grounds 96, 157–162)

3. Agreement to purchase minimum percentages from domestic producers

GISA 67*
Rennet 151 (paras. 5–7, 22–23, 31)

4. Discriminatory conditions against non-members

Ceramic Tiles 35 (para. 2c)
Belgian Wallpaper 78
SSI 181 (paras. 99b, 111, 116c)
EATE levy 231 (para. 47)*
Sugar Beet 315

5. Industry organised distribution schemes

FEDETAB 133 (paras. 19–27, 81, 96–97)
Rennet 151
National Sulphuric Acid Association 157
IMA Rules 158

6. Collective exclusive dealing

See Cartels, page 89.

CHAPTER 6

TRADE FAIR AND EXHIBITION AGREEMENTS

A. CASES ON TRADE FAIR AND EXHIBITION AGREEMENTS

EMO 19, 140, 303
Cematex 43, 193
UNIDI 93 & 219
BPICA 116, 180
SMM&T 201
VIFKA 251
International Dental Exhibition 274
British Dental Trade Association 285
Sippa 336
1st Comp. Rep. (paras. 42–43)
Ancides v. *Commission* 143

B. STIPULATIONS COMMON TO EXHIBITION AGREEMENTS

1. Agreement not to exhibit at other exhibitions

EMO 19, 140, 303
Cematex 43, 193
UNIDI 93, 219
BPICA 116, 180
SMM&T 201
VIFKA 251*
International Dental Exhibition 274
British Dental Trade Association 285

2. Objective criteria for admittance

BPICA I 116 (para. 9)
International Dental Exhibition 274*
Sippa 336

3. Discrimination against foreign exhibitors

British Dental Trade Association 285*
EUMAPRINT Exhibition 3rd Comp. Rep. (para. 57)

PART IV

VERTICAL AGREEMENTS

CHAPTER 1

EXCLUSIVE AND NON-EXCLUSIVE DISTRIBUTION AGREEMENTS

A. LIST OF CASES ON EXCLUSIVE DISTRIBUTION

Grosfillex/Fillestorf 1
Grundig/Consten 5*
DRU/Blondel 7
Hummel/Isbecque 8
Maison Jallatte 9
Rieckerman 17
Omega 33
Pittsburgh Corning 63
DuroDyne 83
Goodyear Italiana/Euram 85
SABA I 99
Miller 108
Junghans 109
Theal/Watts 110
Pioneer 152
Hennessy/Henkel 162
Moët et Chandon (London) Ltd. 172
Hasselblad 173
National Panasonic 186
SABA II 208
Polistil/Arbois 211
Carlsberg 214
John Deere 226
Whisky and Gin 237
Sperry New Holland 245
Siemens/Fanuc 246
Tipp-Ex 269
ARG/Unipart 278

Gosme/Martell 340
Viho/Toshiba 341
Eco System 344a
1st Comp. Rep. (paras. 45–57)
2nd Comp. Rep. (para. 40)
Beecham Pharma. 6th Comp. Rep. (para. 129)
Seita 10th Comp. Rep. (para. 124)
18th Comp. Rep. (paras. 21 and 50–56)
Consten & Grundig v. *Commission* 4
Italy v. *Council and Commission* 5
Völk v. *Vervaecke* 10
Cadillon v. *Höss* 18
Béguelin v. *GL* 22
Dassonville 41 (grounds 12–15)
Ciments et Bétons v. *Kerpen* 104
ETA v. *DKI* 126

B. LIST OF CASES ON NON-EXCLUSIVE DISTRIBUTION

Bendix/Mertens and Straet 3
Dupont de Nemours Germany 71
Deutsche Philips 73
Kali & Salz/Kalichemie 76
Gerofabriek 111
The Distillers Company 123
Spices 124
Arthur Bell & Sons Ltd. 135
Teacher & Sons 136
Zanussi 139
Distillers-Victuallers 157
Johnson & Johnson 160
Moët et Chandon (London) Ltd. 172
Cafeteros de Colombia 187

C. TEXT OF REGULATION 1983/83
(reproduced below)

Book One: Part IV—Vertical Agreements

Commission Regulation 1983/83 of June 22, 1983

On the application of Article 85(3) of the Treaty to categories of exclusive distribution agreements

([1983] O.J. L173/1)

(Amended by [1983] O.J. L281/24)

THE COMMISSION OF THE EUROPEAN COMMUNITIES,

Having regard to the Treaty establishing the European Economic Community.

Having regard to Council Regulation 19/65 of 2 March 1965 on the application of Article 85(3) of the Treaty to certain categories of agreements and concerted practices, as last amended by the Act of Accession of Greece, and in particular Article 1 thereof,

Having published a draft of this Regulation,

Having consulted the Advisory Committee on Restrictive Practices and Dominant Positions,

(1) Whereas Regulation 19/65 empowers the Commission to apply Article 85(3) of the Treaty by regulation to certain categories of bilateral exclusive distribution agreements and analogous concerted practices falling within Article 85(1);

(2) Whereas experience to date makes it possible to define a category of agreements and concerted practices which can be regarded as normally satisfying the conditions laid down in Article 85(3);

(3) Whereas exclusive distribution agreements of the category defined in Article 1 of this Regulation may fall within the prohibition contained in Article 85(1) of the Treaty; whereas this will apply only in exceptional cases to exclusive agreements of this kind to which only undertakings from one Member State are party and which concern the resale of goods within that Member State; whereas, however, to the extent that such agreements may affect trade between Member States and also satisfy the requirements set out in this Regulation there is no reason to withhold from them the benefit of the exemption by category;

(4) Whereas it is not necessary expressly to exclude from the defined category those agreements which do not fulfil the conditions of Article 85(1) of the Treaty;

(5) Whereas exclusive distribution agreements lead in general to an improvement in distribution because the undertaking is able to concentrate its sales activities, does not need to maintain numerous business relations with a larger number of dealers and is able, by dealing with only one dealer, to overcome more easily distribution difficulties in international trade resulting from linguistic, legal and other differences;

(6) Whereas exclusive distribution agreements facilitate the promotion of sales of a product and lead to intensive marketing and to continuity of supplies while at the same time rationalising distribution; whereas they stimulate competition between the products of different manufacturers; whereas the appointment of an exclusive distributor who will take over sales promotion, customer services and carrying of stocks is often the most effective way, and sometimes indeed the only way, for the manufacturer to enter a market and compete with other manufacturers already present; whereas this is particularly so in the case of small and medium-sized undertakings; whereas it must be left to the contracting parties to decide whether and to what extent they consider it desirable to incorporate in the agreements terms providing for the promotion of sales;

(7) Whereas, as a rule, such exclusive distribution agreements also allow consumers a fair share of the resulting benefit as they gain directly from the improvement in distribution, and their economic and supply position is improved as they can obtain products manufactured in particular in other countries more quickly and more easily;

(8) Whereas this Regulation must define the obligations restricting competition which may be included in exclusive distribution agreements; whereas the other restrictions on competition allowed under this Regulation in addition to the exclusive supply obligation produce a clear division of functions between the parties and compel the exclusive distributor to concentrate his sales efforts on the contract goods and

the contract territory; whereas they are, where they are agreed only for the duration of the agreement, generally necessary in order to attain the improvement in the distribution of goods sought through exclusive distribution; whereas it may be left to the contracting parties to decide which of these obligations they include in their agreements; whereas further restrictive obligations and in particular those which limit the exclusive distributor's choice of customers or his freedom to determine his prices and conditions of sale cannot be exempted under this Regulation;

(9) Whereas the exemption by category should be reserved for agreements for which it can be assumed with sufficient certainty that they satisfy the conditions of Article 85(3) of the Treaty;

(10) Whereas it is not possible, in the absence of a case-by-case examination, to consider that adequate improvements in distribution occur where a manufacturer entrusts the distribution of his goods to another manufacturer with whom he is in competition; whereas such agreements should, therefore, be excluded from the exemption by category; whereas certain derogations from this rule in favour of small and medium-sized undertakings can be allowed;

(11) Whereas consumers will be assured of a fair share of the benefits resulting from exclusive distribution only if parallel imports remain possible; whereas agreements relating to goods which the user can obtain only from the exclusive distributor should therefore be excluded from the exemption by category; whereas the parties cannot be allowed to abuse industrial property rights or other rights in order to create absolute territorial protection; whereas this does not prejudice the relationship between competition law and industrial property rights, since the sole object here is to determine the conditions for exemption by category;

(12) Whereas, since competition at the distribution stage is ensured by the possibility of parallel imports, the exclusive distribution agreements covered by this Regulation will not normally afford any possibility of eliminating competition in respect of a substantial part of the products in question; whereas this is also true of agreements that allot to the exclusive distributor a contract territory covering the whole of the common market;

(13) Whereas, in particular cases in which agreements or concerted practices satisfying the requirements of this Regulation nevertheless have effects incompatible with Article 85(3) of the Treaty, the Commission may withdraw the benefit of the exemption by category from the undertakings party to them;

(14) Whereas agreements and concerted practices which satisfy the conditions set out in this Regulation need not be notified; whereas an undertaking may nonetheless in a particular case where real doubt exists, request the Commission to declare whether its agreements comply with this Regulation;

(15) Whereas this Regulation does not affect the applicability of Commission Regulation 3604/82 of 23 December 1982 on the application of Article 85(3) of the Treaty to categories of specialization agreements; whereas it does not exclude the application of Article 86 of the Treaty.

HAS ADOPTED THIS REGULATION:

Article 1

Pursuant to Article 85(3) of the Treaty and subject to the provisions of this Regulation, it is hereby declared that Article 85(1) of the Treaty shall not apply to agreements to which only two undertakings are party and whereby one party agrees with the other to supply certain goods for resale within the whole or a defined area of the common market only to that other.

Article 2

1. Apart from the obligation referred to in Article 1 no restriction on competition shall be imposed on the supplier other than the obligation not to supply the contract goods to users in the contract territory.

2. No restriction on competition shall be imposed on the exclusive distributor other than:
(a) the obligation not to manufacture or distribute goods which compete with the contract goods;
(b) the obligation to obtain the contract goods for resale only from the other party;
(c) the obligation to refrain, outside the contract territory and in relation to the contract goods, from seeking customers,

from establishing any branch and from maintaining any distribution depot.

3. Article 1 shall apply notwithstanding that the exclusive distributor undertakes all or any of the following obligations:
(a) to purchase complete ranges of goods or minimum quantities;
(b) to sell the contract goods under trade marks or packed and presented as specified by the other party;
(c) to take measures for promotion of sales, in particular:
— to advertise,
— to maintain a sales network or stock of goods,
— to provide customer and guarantee services,
— to employ staff having specialized or technical training.

Article 3

Article 1 shall not apply where:
(a) manufacturers of identical goods or of goods which are considered by users as equivalent in view of their characteristics, price and intended use enter into reciprocal exclusive distribution agreements between themselves in respect of such goods;
(b) manufacturers of identical goods or of goods which are considered by users as equivalent in view of their characteristics, price and intended use enter into a non-reciprocal exclusive distribution agreement between themselves in respect of such goods unless at least one of them has a total annual turnover of no more than 100 million ECU;
(c) users can obtain the contract goods in the contract territory only from the exclusive distributor and have no alternative source of supply outside the contract territory;
(d) one or both of the parties makes it difficult for intermediaries or users to obtain the contract goods from other dealers inside the common market or, in so far as no alternative source of supply is available there, from outside the common market, in particular where one or both of them:
  (i) exercises industrial property rights so as to prevent dealers or users from obtaining outside, or from selling in, the contract territory properly marked or otherwise properly marketed contract goods;
  (ii) exercises other rights or takes other measures so as to prevent dealers or users from obtaining outside, or from selling in, the contract territory contract goods.

Article 4

1. Article 3(a) and (b) shall also apply where the goods there referred to are manufactured by an undertaking connected with a party to the agreement.

2. Connected undertakings are:
(a) undertakings in which a party to the agreement, directly or indirectly:
— owns more than half the capital or business assets, or
— has the power to exercise more than half the voting rights, or
— has the power to appoint more than half the members of the supervisory board, board of directors or bodies legally representing the undertaking, or
— has the right to manage the affairs;
(b) undertakings which directly or indirectly have in or over a party to the agreement the rights or powers listed in (a);
(c) undertakings in which an undertaking referred to in (b) directly or indirectly has the rights or powers listed in (a).

3. Undertakings in which the parties to the agreement or undertakings connected with them jointly have the rights or powers set out in paragraph 2(a) shall be considered to be connected with each of the parties to the agreement.

Article 5

1. For the purpose of Article 3(b), the ECU is the unit of account used for drawing up the budget of the Community pursuant to Articles 207 and 209 of the Treaty.

2. Article 1 shall remain applicable where during any period of two consecutive financial years the total turnover referred to in Article 3(b) is exceeded by no more than 10 per cent.

3. For the purpose of calculating total turnover within the meaning of Article 3(b), the turnovers achieved during the last financial year by the party to the agreement and connected undertakings in respect of all goods and services, excluding all taxes and other duties, shall be added together. For this purpose no account shall be taken of dealings between the party to the agreement and its undertakings or between the connected undertakings.

Part IV—1 Exclusive/Non-Exclusive Distribution Agreements

Article 6

The Commission may withdraw the benefits of this Regulation, pursuant to Article 7 of Regulation 19/65, when it finds in a particular case that an agreement which is exempted by this Regulation nevertheless has certain effects which are incompatible with the conditions set out in Article 85(3) of the Treaty, and in particular where:

(a) the contract goods are not subject, in the contract territory, to effective competition from identical goods considered by users as equivalent in view of their characteristics, price and intended use;
(b) access by other suppliers to the different stages of distribution within the contract territory is made difficult to a significant extent;
(c) for reasons other than those referred to in Article 3(c) and (d) it is not possible for intermediaries or users to obtain supplies of the contract goods from dealers outside the contract territory on the terms there customary;
(d) the exclusive distributor:
  (i) without any objectively justified reasons refuses to supply in the contract territory categories of purchasers who cannot obtain contract goods elsewhere on suitable terms or applies to them differing prices or conditions of sale;
  (ii) sells the contract goods at excessively high prices.

Article 7

In the period 1 July 1983 to 31 December 1986, the prohibition in Article 85(1) of the Treaty shall not apply to agreements which were in force on 1 July 1983 or entered into force between 1 July and 31 December 1983 and which satisfy the exemption conditions of Regulation 67/67.

Article 8

This Regulation shall not apply to agreements entered into for the resale of drinks in premises used for the sale and consumption of drinks or for the resale of petroleum products in service stations.

Article 9

This Regulation shall apply *mutatis mutandis* to concerted practices of the type defined in Article 1.

Article 10

This Regulation shall enter into force on 1 July 1983.
It shall expire on 31 December 1997.
This Regulation shall be binding in its entirety and directly applicable in all Member States.

Done at Brussels, 22 June 1983.

D. CASES ON THE INTERPRETATION OF THE REGULATION

Ivoclar 234
Whisky and Gin 237
Siemens/Fanuc 246 (para. 24)
Yves Rocher 265 (para. 57)
Computerland 270 (para. 29)
ARG/Unipart 278
Delta Chemie 292
Charles Jourdan 298 (para. 36)
Welded Steel Mesh 309 (paras. 188, 189)
13th Comp. Rep. (paras. 26–32)
17th Comp. Rep. (paras. 27–28)
Béguelin v. *GL* 22 (ground 23)
Van Vliet v. *Dalle Crode* 45
Fonderies Roubaix v. *Fonderies Roux* 49 (grounds 12–19)
Salonia v. *Poidomani & Baglieri* 85
Hydrotherm v. *Andreoli* 111 (ground 20)
Pronuptia v. *Schillgalis* 129

E. TEXT OF THE NOTICE ON THE INTERPRETATION OF THE REGULATION (reproduced over)

Book One: Part IV—Vertical Agreements

Commission Notice concerning Commission Regulations 1983/83 and 1984/83 of June 22, 1983

On the application of Article 85(3) of the Treaty to categories of exclusive distribution and exclusive purchasing agreements

([1984] O.J. C/101/02)

I. Introduction

1. Commission Regulation 67/67 of 22 March 1967 on the application of Article 85(3) of the Treaty to certain categories of exclusive dealing agreements expired on 30 June 1983 after being in force for over 15 years. With Regulations 1983/83 and 1984/83, the Commission has adapted the block exemption of exclusive distribution agreements and exclusive purchasing agreements to the intervening developments in the common market and in Community law. Several of the provisions in the new Regulations are new. A certain amount of interpretative guidance is therefore called for. This will assist undertakings in bringing their agreements into line with the new legal requirements and will also help ensure that the Regulations are applied uniformly in all the Member States.

2. In determining how a given provision is to be applied, one must take into account, in addition to the ordinary meaning of the words used, the intention of the provision as this emerges from the preamble. For further guidance, reference should be made to the principles that have been evolved in the case law of the Court of Justice of the European Communities and in the Commission's decisions on individual cases.

3. This notice sets out the main consideration which will determine the Commission's view of whether or not an exclusive distribution or purchasing agreement is covered by the block exemption. The notice is without prejudice to the jurisdiction of national courts to apply the Regulations, although it may well be of persuasive authority in proceedings before such courts. Nor does the notice necessarily indicate the interpretation which might be given to the provisions by the Court of Justice.

II. Exclusive distribution and exclusive purchasing agreements (Regulations (EEC) 1983/83 and (EEC) 1984/83)

1. Similarities and differences

4. Regulations 1983/83 and 1984/83 are both concerned with exclusive agreements between two undertakings for the purpose of the resale of goods. Each deals with a particular type of such agreements. Regulation 1983/83 applies to exclusive distribution agreements, Regulation 1984/83 to exclusive purchasing agreements. The distinguishing feature of exclusive distribution agreements is that one party, the supplier, allots to the other, the reseller, a defined territory (the contract territory) in which the reseller has to concentrate his sales effort, and in return undertakes not to supply any other reseller in that territory. In exclusive purchasing agreements, the reseller agrees to purchase the contract goods only from the other party and not from any other supplier. The supplier is entitled to supply other resellers in the same sales area and at the same level of distribution. Unlike an exclusive distributor, the tied reseller is not protected against competition from other resellers who, like himself, receive the contract goods direct from the supplier. On the other hand, he is free of restrictions as to the area over which he may make his sales effort.

5. In keeping with their common starting point, the Regulations have many provisions that are the same or similar in both Regulations. This is true of the basic provision in Article 1, in which the respective subject-matters of the block exemption, the exclusive supply or purchasing obligation, are defined, and of the exhaustive list of restrictions of competition which may be agreed in addition to the exclusive supply or purchasing obligation (Article 2(1) and (2)), the nonexhaustive enumera-

Part IV—1 Exclusive/Non-Exclusive Distribution Agreements

tion of other obligations which do not prejudice the block exemption (Article 2(3)), the inapplicability of the block exemption in principle to exclusive agreements between competing manufacturers (Article 3(a) and (b), 4 and 5), the withdrawal of the block exemption in individual cases (Article 6 of Regulation 1983/83 and Article 14 of Regulation 1984/83), the transitional provisions (Article 7 of Regulation 1983/83 and Article 15(1) of Regulation 1984/83), and the inclusion of concerted practices within the scope of the Regulations (Article 9 of Regulation 1983/83 and Article 18 of Regulation 1984/83). In so far as their wording permits, these parallel provisions are to be interpreted in the same way.

6. Different rules are laid down in the Regulations wherever they need to take account of matters which are peculiar to the exclusive distribution agreements or exclusive purchasing agreements respectively. This applies in Regulation 1983/83, to the provisions regarding the obligation on the exclusive distributor not actively to promote sales outside the contract territory (Article 2(2)(c)) and the inapplicability of the block exemption to agreements which give the exclusive distributor absolute territorial protection (Article 3(c) and (d)) and, in Regulation 1984/83, to the provisions limiting the scope and duration of the block exemption for exclusive purchasing agreements in general (Article 3(c) and (d)) and for beer-supply and service-station agreements in particular (Titles II and III).

7. The scope of the two Regulations has been defined so as to avoid any overlap (Article 16 of Regulation 1984/83).

2. Basic provision

(Article 1)

8. Both Regulations apply only to agreements entered into for the purpose of the resale of goods to which not more than two undertakings are party.

(a) "For resale"

9. The notion of resale requires that the goods concerned be disposed of by the purchasing party to others in return for consideration. Agreements on the supply or purchase of goods which the purchasing party transforms or processes into other goods or uses or consumes in manufacturing other goods are not agreements for resale. The same applies to the supply of components which are combined with other components into a different product. The criterion is that the goods distributed by the reseller are the same as those the other party has supplied to him for that purpose. The economic identity of the goods is not affected if the reseller merely breaks up and packages the goods in smaller quantities, or repackages them, before resale.

10. Where the reseller performs additional operations to improve the quality, durability, appearance or taste of the goods (such as rust-proofing of metals, sterilisation of food or the addition of colouring matter or flavourings to drugs), the position will mainly depend on how much value the operation adds to the goods. Only a slight addition in value can be taken not to change the economic identity of the goods. In determining the precise dividing line in individual cases, trade usage in particular must be considered. The Commission applies the same principles to agreements under which the reseller is supplied with concentrated extract for a drink which he has to dilute with water, pure alcohol or another liquid and to bottle before reselling.

(b) "Goods"

11. Exclusive agreements for the supply of services rather than the resale of goods are not covered by the Regulations. The block exemption still applies, however, where the reseller provides customer or after-sales services incidental to the resale of the goods. Nevertheless, a case where the charge for the service is higher than the price of the goods would fall outside the scope of the Regulations.

12. The hiring out of goods in return for payment comes closer, economically speaking, to a resale of goods than to provision of services. The Commission therefore regards exclusive agreements under which the purchasing party hires out or leases to others the goods supplied to him as covered by the Regulations.

(c) "Only two undertakings party"

13. To be covered by the block exemption, the exclusive distribution or purchasing agreement must be between only one supplier and one reseller in each case. Several undertakings forming one economic unit count as one undertaking.

14. This limitation on the number of undertakings that may be party relates solely to the individual agreement. A sup-

plier does not lose the benefit of the block exemption if he enters into exclusive distribution or purchasing agreements covering the same goods with several resellers.

15. The supplier may delegate the performance of his contractual obligations to a connected or independent undertaking which he has entrusted with the distribution of his goods, so that the reseller has to purchase the contract goods from the latter undertaking. This principle is expressly mentioned only in Regulation 1984/83 (Article 1, 6 and 10), because the question of delegation arises mainly in connection with exclusive purchasing agreements. It also applies, however, to exclusive distribution agreements under Regulation 1983/83.

16. The involvement of undertakings other than the contracting parties must be confined to the execution of deliveries. The parties may accept exclusive supply or purchase obligations only for themselves, and not impose them on third parties, since otherwise more than two undertakings would be party to the agreement. The obligation of the parties to ensure that the obligations they have accepted are respected by connected undertakings is, however, covered by the block exemption.

3. Other restrictions on competition that are exempted

(Article 2(1) and (2))

17. Apart from the exclusive supply obligation (Regulation 1983/83) or exclusive purchase obligation (Regulation 1984/83), obligations defined in Article 1 which must be present if the block exemption is to apply, the only other restrictions of competition that may be agreed by the parties are those set out in Article 2(1) and (2). If they agree on further obligations restrictive of competition, the agreement as a whole is no longer covered by the block exemption and requires individual exemption. For example, an agreement will exceed the bounds of the Regulations if the parties relinquish the possibility of independently determining their prices or conditions of business or undertake to refrain from, or even prevent, cross-border trade, which the Regulations expressly state must not be impeded. Among other clauses which in general are not permissible under the Regulations are those which impede the reseller in his free choice of customers.

18. The obligations restrictive of competition that are exempted may be agreed only for the duration of the agreement. This also applies to restrictions accepted by the supplier or reseller on competing with the other party.

4. Obligations upon the reseller which do not prejudice the block exemption

(Article 2(3))

19. The obligations cited in this provision are examples of clauses which generally do not restrict competition. Undertakings are therefore free to include one, several or all of these obligations in their agreements. However, the obligations may not be formulated or applied in such a way as to take on the character of restrictions of competition that are not permitted. To forestall this danger, Article 2(3)(*b*) of Regulation 1984/83 expressly allows minimum purchase obligations only for goods that are subject to an exclusive purchasing obligation.

20. As part of the obligation to take measures for promotion of sales and in particular to maintain a distribution network (Article 2(3)(*c*) of Regulation 1983/83 and Article 2(3)(*d*) of Regulation 1984/83), the reseller may be forbidden to supply the contract goods to unsuitable dealers. Such clauses are unobjectionable if admission to the distribution network is based on objective criteria of a qualitative nature relating to the professional qualifications of the owner of the business or his staff or the suitability of his business premises, if the criteria are the same for all potential dealers, and if the criteria are actually applied in a nondiscriminatory manner. Distribution systems which do not fulfil these conditions are not covered by the block exemption.

5. Inapplicability of the block exemption to exclusive agreements between competing manufacturers

(Articles 3(*a*) and (*b*), 4 and 5)

21. The block exemption does not apply if either the parties themselves or undertakings connected with them are manufacturers, manufacture goods belonging to the same product market, and enter into exclusive distribution or purchasing agreements with one another in respect of those goods. Only identical or equivalent goods are regarded as belonging to the same product market. The goods in question must be interchangeable. Whether or not this is the case must be judged from the vantage point of the user, normally

Part IV—1 Exclusive/Non-Exclusive Distribution Agreements

taking the characteristics, price and intended use of the goods together. In certain cases, however, goods can form a separate market on the basis of their characteristics, their price or their intended use alone. This is true especially where consumer preferences have developed. The above provisions are applicable regardless of whether or not the parties or the undertakings connected with them are based in the Community and whether or not they are already actually in competition with one another in the relevant goods inside or outside the Community.

22. In principle, both reciprocal and non-reciprocal exclusive agreements between competing manufacturers are not covered by the block exemption and are therefore subject to individual scrutiny of their compatibility with Article 85 of the Treaty, but there is an exception for non-reciprocal agreements of the abovementioned kind where one or both of the parties are undertakings with a total annual turnover of no more than 100 million ECU (Article 3(*b*)). Annual turnover is used as a measure of the economic strength of the undertakings involved. Therefore, the aggregate turnover from goods and services of all types, and not only from the contract goods, is to be taken. Turnover taxes and other turnover-related levies are not included in turnover. Where a party belongs to a group of connected undertakings, the world-wide turnover of the group, excluding intra-group sales (Article 5(3)), is to be used.

23. The total turnover limit can be exceeded during any period of two successive financial years by up to 10 per cent. without loss of the block exemption. The block exemption is lost if, at the end of the second financial year, the total turnover over the preceding two years has been over 220 million ECU (Article 5(2)).

6. Withdrawal of the block exemption in individual cases

(Article 6 of Regulation 1983/83 and Article 14 of Regulation 1984/83)

24. The situations described are meant as illustrations of the sort of situations in which the Commission can exercise its powers under Article 7 of Council Regulation 19/65 to withdraw a block exemption. The benefit of the block exemption can only be withdrawn by a decision in an individual case following proceedings under Regulation No. 17. Such a decision cannot have retroactive effect. It may be coupled with an individual exemption subject to conditions or obligations or, in an extreme case, with the finding of an infringement and an order to bring it to an end.

7. Transitional provisions

(Article 7 of Regulation 1983/83 and Article 15(1) of Regulation 1984/83)

25. Exclusive distribution or exclusive purchasing agreements which were concluded and entered into force before 1 January 1984 continue to be exempted under the provisions of Regulation 67/67 until 31 December 1986. Should the parties wish to apply such agreements beyond 1 January 1987, they will either have to bring them into line with the provisions of the new Regulations or to notify them to the Commission. Special rules apply in the case of beer-supply and service-station agreements (see paragraphs 64 and 65 below).

8. Concerted practices

(Article 9 of Regulation 1983/83 and Article 18 of Regulation 1984/83)

26. These provisions bring within the scope of the Regulations exclusive distribution and purchasing arrangements which are operated by undertakings but are not the subject of a legally binding agreement.

III. Exclusive distribution agreements (Regulation 1983/83)

1. Exclusive supply obligation

(Article 1)

27. The exclusive supply obligation does not prevent the supplier from providing the contract goods to other resellers who afterwards sell them in the exclusive distributor's territory. It makes no difference whether the other dealers concerned are established outside or inside the territory. The supplier is not in breach of his obligation to the exclusive distributor provided that he supplies the resellers who wish to sell the contract goods in the territory only at their request and that the goods are handed over outside the territory. It does not matter whether the reseller takes delivery of the goods himself or through an intermediary, such as a freight for-

warder. However, supplies of this nature are only permissible if the reseller and not the supplier pays the transport costs of the goods into the contract territory.

28. The goods supplied to the exclusive distributor must be intended for resale in the contract territory. The basic requirement does not, however, mean that the exclusive distributor cannot sell the contract goods to customers outside his contract territory should he receive orders from them. Under Article 2(2)(c), the supplier can prohibit him only from seeking customers in other areas, but not from supplying them.

29. It would also be incompatible with the Regulation for the exclusive distributor to be restricted to supplying only certain categories of customers (*e.g.* specialist retailers) in his contract territory and prohibited from supplying other categories (*e.g.* department stores), which are supplied by other resellers appointed by the supplier for that purpose.

2. Restriction on competition by the supplier

(Article 2(1))

30. The restriction on the supplier himself supplying the contract goods to final users in the exclusive distributor's contract territory need not be absolute. Clauses permitting the supplier to supply certain customers in the territory—with or without payment of compensation to the exclusive distributor—are compatible with the block exemption provided the customers in question are not resellers. The supplier remains free to supply the contract goods outside the contract territory to final users based in the territory. In this case the position is the same as for dealers (see para. 27 above).

3. Inapplicability of the block exemption in cases of absolute territorial protection

(Articles 3(c) and (d))

31. The block exemption cannot be claimed for agreements that give the exclusive distributor absolute territorial protection. If the situation described in Article 3(c) obtains, the parties must ensure either that the contract goods can be sold in the contract territory by parallel importers or that users have a real possibility of obtaining them from undertakings outside the contract territory, if necessary outside the Community, at the prices and on the terms there prevailing. The supplier can represent an alternative source of supply for the purposes of this provision if he is prepared to supply the contract goods on request to final users located in the contract territory.

32. Article 3(*d*) is chiefly intended to safeguard the freedom of dealers and users to obtain the contract goods in other Member States. Action to impede imports into the Community from third countries will only lead to loss of the block exemption if there are no alternative sources of supply in the Community. This situation can arise especially where the exclusive distributor's contract territory covers the whole or the major part of the Community.

33. The block exemption ceases to apply as from the moment that either of the parties takes measures to impede parallel imports into the contract territory. Agreements in which the supplier undertakes with the exclusive distributor to prevent his other customers from supplying into the contract territory are ineligible for the block exemption from the outset. This is true even if the parties agree only to prevent imports into the Community from third countries. In this case it is immaterial whether or not there are alternative sources of supply in the Community. The inapplicability of the block exemption follows from the mere fact that the agreement contains restrictions on competition which are not covered by Article 2(1).

IV. Exclusive purchasing agreements (Regulation (EEC) 1984/83)

1. Structure of the Regulation

34. Title I of the Regulation contains general provisions for exclusive purchasing agreements and Titles II and III special provisions for beer-supply and service-station agreements. The latter types of agreement are governed exclusively by the special provisions, some of which (Articles 9 and 13), however, refer to some of the general provisions, Article 17 also excludes the combination of agreements of the kind referred to in Title I with those of the kind referred to in Titles II or III to which the same undertakings or undertakings connected with them are party. To prevent any avoidance of the special provisions for beer-supply and service-station agreements, it is also made clear that the provisions governing the exclusive distribution of goods do not apply to agree-

Part IV—1 Exclusive/Non-Exclusive Distribution Agreements

ments entered into for the resale of drinks on premises used for the sale or consumption of beer or for the resale of petroleum products in service stations (Article 8 of Regulation 1983/83).

2. Exclusive purchasing obligation

(Article 1)

35. The Regulation only covers agreements whereby the reseller agrees to purchase all his requirements for the contract goods from the other party. If the purchasing obligation relates to only part of such requirements, the block exemption does not apply. Clauses which allow the reseller to obtain the contract goods from other suppliers, should these sell them more cheaply or on more favourable terms than the other party are still covered by the block exemption. The same applies to clauses releasing the reseller from his exclusive purchasing obligation should the other party be unable to supply.

36. The contract goods must be specified by brand or denomination in the agreement. Only if this is done will it be possible to determine the precise scope of the reseller's exclusive purchasing obligation (Article 1) and of the ban on dealing in competing products (Article 2(2)).

3. Restriction on competition by the supplier

(Article 2(1))

37. This provision allows the reseller to protect himself against direct competition from the supplier in his principal sales area. The reseller's principle sales area is determined by his normal business activity. It may be more closely defined in the agreement. However, the supplier cannot be forbidden to supply dealers who obtain the contract goods outside this area and afterwards resell them to customers inside it or to appoint other resellers in the area.

4. Limits of the block exemption

(Article 3(c) and (d))

38. Article 3(c) provides that the exclusive purchasing obligation can be agreed for one or more products, but in the latter case the products must be so related as to be thought of as belonging to the same range of goods. The relationship can be founded on technical (e.g. a machine, accessories and spare parts for it) or commercial grounds (e.g. several products used for the same purpose) or on usage in the trade (different goods that are customarily offered for sale together). In the latter case, regard must be had to the usual practice at the reseller's level of distribution on the relevant market, taking into account all relevant dealers and not only particular forms of distribution. Exclusive purchasing agreements covering goods which do not belong together can only be exempted from the competition rules by an individual decision.

39. Under Article 3(d), exclusion purchasing agreements concluded for an indefinite period are not covered by the block exemption. Agreements which specify a fixed term but are automatically renewable unless one of the parties gives notice to terminate are to be considered to have been concluded for an indefinite period.

V. Beer-supply agreements (Title II of Regulation (EEC) No. 1984/83)

1. Exclusive purchasing obligation

(Article 6)

40. The beers and other drinks covered by the exclusive purchasing obligation must be specified by brand or denomination in the agreement. An exclusive purchasing obligation can only be imposed on the reseller for drinks which the supplier carries at the time the contract takes effect and provided that they are supplied in the quantities required, at sufficiently regular intervals and at prices and on conditions allowing normal sales to the consumer. Any extension of the exclusive purchasing obligation to drinks not specified in the agreement requires an additional agreement, which must likewise satisfy the requirements of Title II of the Regulation. A change in the brand or denomination of a drink which in other respects remains unchanged does not constitute such an extension of the exclusive purchasing obligation.

41. The exclusive purchasing obligation can be agreed in respect of one or more premises used for the sale and consumption of drinks which the reseller runs at the time the contract takes effect. The name and location of the premises must be stated in the agreement. Any extension of the exclusive purchasing obligation to other such premises requires an additional agreement, which must likewise satisfy the provisions of Title II of the Regulation.

42. The concept of "premises used for the sale and consumption of drinks" covers any licensed premises used for this purpose. Private clubs are also included. Exclusive purchasing agreements between the supplier and the operator of an off-licence shop are governed by the provisions of Title I of the Regulation.

43. Special commercial or financial advantages are those going beyond what the reseller could normally expect under an agreement. The explanations given in the 13th recital are illustrations. Whether or not the supplier is affording the reseller special advantage depends on the nature, extent and duration of the obligation undertaken by the parties. In doubtful cases usage in the trade is the decisive element.

44. The reseller can enter into exclusive purchasing obligations both with a brewery in respect of beers of a certain type and with a drinks wholesaler in respect of beers of another type and/or other drinks. The two agreements can be combined into one document. Article 6 also covers cases where the drinks wholesaler performs several functions at once, signing the first agreement on the brewery's and the second on his own behalf and also undertaking delivery of all the drinks. The provisions of Title II do not apply to the contractual relations between the brewery and the drinks wholesaler.

45. Article 6(2) makes the block exemption also applicable to cases in which the supplier affords the owner of premises financial or other help in equipping them as a public house, restaurant, etc., and in return the owner imposes on the buyer or tenant of the premises an exclusive purchasing obligation in favour of the supplier. A similar situation, economically speaking, is the transmission of an exclusive purchasing obligation from the owner of a public house to his successor. Under Article 8(1)(e) this is also, in principle, permissible.

2. Other restrictions of competition that are exempted

(Article 7)

46. The list of permitted obligations given in Article 7 is exhaustive. If any further obligations restricting competition are imposed on the reseller, the exclusive purchasing agreement as a whole is no longer covered by the block exemption.

47. The obligation referred to in paragraph 1(a) applies only so long as the supplier is able to supply the beers or other drinks specified in the agreement and subject to the exclusive purchasing obligation in sufficient quantities to cover the demand the reseller anticipates for the products from his customers.

48. Under paragraph 1(b), the reseller is entitled to sell beer of other types in draught form if the other party has tolerated this in the past. If this is not the case, the reseller must indicate that there is sufficient demand from his customers to warrant the sale of other draught beers. The demand must be deemed sufficient if it can be satisfied without a simultaneous drop in sales of the beers specified in the exclusive purchasing agreement. It is definitely not sufficient if sales of the additional draught beer turn out to be so slow that there is a danger of its quality deteriorating. It is for the reseller to assess the potential demand of his customers for other types of beer; after all, he bears the risk if his forecasts are wrong.

49. The provision in paragraph 1(c) is not only intended to ensure the possibility of advertising products supplied by other undertakings to the minimum extent necessary in any given circumstances. The advertising of such products should also reflect their relative importance *vis-à-vis* the competing products of the supplier who is party to the exclusive purchasing agreement. Advertising for products which the public house has just begun to sell may not be excluded or unduly impeded.

50. The Commission believes that the designations of types customary in inter-State trade and within the individual Member States may afford useful pointers to the interpretation of Article 7(2). Nevertheless the alternative criteria stated in the provision itself are decisive. In doubtful cases, whether or not two beers are clearly distinguishable by their composition, appearance or taste depends on custom at the place where the public house is situated. The parties may, if they wish, jointly appoint an expert to decide the matter.

3. Agreements excluded from the block exemption

(Article 8)

51. The reseller's right to purchase drinks from third parties may be restricted only to the extent allowed by Articles 6 and 7. In his purchases of goods other than drinks and in his procurement of services

which are not directly connected with the supply of drinks by the other party, the reseller must remain free to choose his supplier. Under Article 8(1)(a) and (b), any action by the other party or by an undertaking connected with or appointed by him or acting at his instigation or with his agreement to prevent the reseller exercising his rights in this regard will entail the loss of the block exemption. For the purposes of these provisions it makes no difference whether the reseller's freedom is restricted by contract, informal understanding, economic pressures or other practical measures.

52. The installation of amusement machines in tenanted public houses may by agreement be made subject to the owner's permission. The owner may refuse permission on the ground that this would impair the character of the premises or he may restrict the tenant to particular types of machines. However, the practice of some owners of tenanted public houses to allow the tenant to conclude contracts for the installation of such machines only with certain undertakings which the owner recommends is, as a rule, incompatible with this Regulation, unless the undertakings are selected on the basis of objective criteria of a qualitative nature that are the same for all potential providers of such equipment and are applied in a non-discriminatory manner. Such criteria may refer to the reliability of the undertaking and its staff and the quality of the services it provides. The supplier may not prevent a public house tenant from purchasing amusement machines rather than renting them.

53. The limitation of the duration of the agreement in Article 8(1)(c) and (d) does not affect the parties' right to renew their agreement in accordance with the provisions of Title II of the Regulation.

54. Article 8(2)(b) must be interpreted in the light both of the aims of the Community competition rules and of the general legal principle whereby contracting parties must exercise their rights in good faith.

55. Whether or not a third undertaking offers certain drinks covered by the exclusive purchasing obligation on more favourable terms than the other party for the purposes of the first indent of Article 8(2)(b) is to be judged in the first instance on the basis of a comparison of prices. This should take into account the various factors that go to determine the prices. If a more favourable offer is available and the tenant wishes to accept it, he must inform the other party of his intentions without delay so that the other party has an opportunity of matching the terms offered by the third undertaking. If the other party refuses to do so or fails to let the tenant have his decision within a short period, the tenant is entitled to purchase the drinks from the other undertaking. The Commission will ensure that exercise of the brewery's or drinks wholesaler's right to match the prices quoted by another supplier does not make it significantly harder for other suppliers to enter the market.

56. The tenant's right provided for in the second indent of Article 8(2)(b) to purchase drinks of another brand or denomination from third undertakings obtains in cases where the other party does not offer them. Here the tenant is not under a duty to inform the other party of his intentions.

57. The tenant's rights arising from Article 8(2)(b) override any obligation to purchase minimum quantities imposed upon him under Article 9 in conjunction with Article 2(3)(b) to the extent that this is necessary to allow the tenant full exercise of those rights.

VI. Service station agreements (Title III of Regulation 1984/83)

1. Exclusive purchasing obligation

(Article 10)

58. The exclusive purchasing obligation can cover either motor vehicle fuels (e.g. petrol, diesel fuel, LPG, kerosene) alone or motor vehicle fuels and other fuels (e.g. heating oil, bottled gas, paraffin). All the goods concerned must be petroleum-based products.

59. The motor vehicle fuels covered by the exclusive purchasing obligations must be for use in motor-powered land or water vehicles or aircraft. The term "service station" is to be interpreted in a correspondingly wide sense.

60. The Regulation applies to petrol stations adjoining public roads and fuelling installations on private property not open to public traffic.

Book One: Part IV—Vertical Agreements

2. Other restrictions on competition that are exempted

(Article 11)

61. Under Article 11(b) only the use of lubricants and related petroleum-based products supplied by other undertakings can be prohibited. This provision refers to the servicing and maintenance of motor vehicles, i.e. to the reseller's activity in the field of provision of services. It does not affect the reseller's freedom to purchase the said products from other undertakings for resale in the service station. The petroleum-based products related to lubricants referred to in paragraph (b) are additives and brake fluids.

62. For the interpretation of Article 11(c), the considerations stated in paragraph 49 above apply by analogy.

3. Agreements excluded from the block exemption

(Article 12)

63. These provisions are analogous to those of Article 8(1)(a), (b), (d) and (e) and 8(2)(a). Reference is therefore made to paragraphs 51 and 53 above.

VII. Transitional provisions for beer-supply and service station agreements (Article 15(2) and (3))

64. Under Article 15(2), all beer-supply and service-station agreements which were concluded and entered into force before 1 January 1984 remain covered by the provision of Regulation 67/67 until 31 December 1988. From 1 January 1989 they must comply with the provisions of Titles II and III of Regulation 1984/83. Under Article 15(3), in the case of agreements which were in force on 1 July 1983, the same principle applies except that the 10-year maximum duration for such agreements laid down in Article 8(1)(d) and Article 12(1)(c) may be exceeded.

65. The sole requirement for the eligible beer-supply and service station agreements to continue to enjoy the block exemption beyond 1 January 1989 is that they be brought into line with the new provisions. It is left to the undertakings concerned how they do so. One way is for the parties to agree to amend the original agreement, another for the supplier unilaterally to release the reseller from all obligations that would prevent the application of the block exemption after 1 January 1989. The latter method is only mentioned in Article 15(3) in relation to agreements in force on 1 July 1983. However, there is no reason why this possibility should not also be open to parties to agreements entered into between 1 July 1983 and 1 January 1984.

66. Parties lose the benefit of application of the transitional provisions if they extend the scope of their agreement as regards persons, places or subject-matter, or incorporate into it additional obligations restrictive of competition. The agreement then counts as a new agreement. The same applies if the parties substantially change the nature or extent of their obligations to one another. A substantial change in this sense includes a revision of the purchase price of the goods supplied to the reseller or of the rent for a public house or service station which goes beyond mere adjustment to the changing economic environment.

F. CLAUSES COMMONLY STIPULATED IN DISTRIBUTION AGREEMENTS

1. Territorial restrictions

1.1. Grant of an exclusive territory to the distributor

Articles 1, 2(1)
Grundig/Consten 5
DRU/Blondel 7
Hummel/Isbecque 8
Maison Jallatte 9
Omega 33 (paras. 2, 5, 7)
DuroDyne 83
Goodyear Italiana/Euram 85
SABA I 99 (paras. 13, 32, 46)
Junghans 109 (paras. 28, 31)
Theal/Watts 110
Hennessy/Henkell 162
Hasselblad 173
Polistil/Arbois 211 (para. 22)
Whisky and Gin 237
Sperry New Holland 245
Tipp-Ex 269
1st Comp. Rep. (paras. 45–52)
2nd Comp. Rep. (para. 42)
7th Comp. Rep. (paras. 9–16)
SEITA 10th Comp. Rep. (para. 124)
Consten & Grundig v. *Commission* 4*
Italy v. *Council and Commission* 5

1.2. No active sales policy outside agreed territory

Articles 2(1), 2(2)(c)

Part IV—1 Exclusive/Non-Exclusive Distribution Agreements

Goodyear Italiana/Euram 87
SABA I 99 (paras. 13, 32, 46)*
Junghans 109 (paras. 9, 29, 31)
Whisky and Gin 237
Sperry New Holland 245 (paras. 54–55)*
Tipp-Ex 269 (para. 13)
Maison des Bibliothèques 14th Comp. Rep. (para. 68)

1.3. Profit pass over clause

Polistil/Arbois 211 (para. 22)
Ivoclar 234

1.4. Export ban on direct sales by distributor

1.4.1 Between Member States

Articles 2(1), 2(2)(c), 3(a)
Grundig/Consten 5
Omega 33 (para. 9)
Miller 108 (paras. 5–6, 11–15)
Gerofabriek 111
The Distillers Company 123
Arthur Bell & Sons Ltd. 135
Teacher & Sons 136
Moët et Chandon (London) Ltd. 172
John Deere 226 (paras. 16, 24)
Sperry New Holland 245 (paras. 24, 26, 53)
Viho/Toshiba 341
1st Comp. Rep. (para. 54)
Beecham Pharma. 6th Comp. Rep. (para. 129)
Consten & Grundig v. *Commission* 4*
Völk v. *Vervaecke* 10
Parfums Rochas v. *Bitsch* 13 (grounds 2, 5, 7)
Cadillon v. *Höss* 18 (grounds 9–10)
ETA v. *DKI* 126 (ground 10)

1.4.2. Into the EEC

Grosfillex/Fillertorf 1
Rieckermann 17*

1.4.3. Outside the EEC

Deutsche Philips 73
Omega 33 (para. 5)*
Goodyear Italian/Euram 87 (para. 8)
Junghans 109 (paras. 10, 24)
The Distillers Company 123
Arthur Bell & Sons Ltd. 135
Teacher & Sons 136

1.5. Export ban on indirect sales, *i.e.* **export ban reimposed upon its customers**

Articles 2(1), 2(2)(c), 3(a)

Grundig/Consten 5
Du Pont de Nemours Germany 71
Deutsche Philips 73
Miller 108 (paras. 5–6, 11–15)
Theal/Watts 110
The Distillers Company 123
Johnson & Johnson 160 (paras. 13–23, 29–34)
Hasselblad 178 (paras. 10–29, 52–55)
Polistil/Arbois 211 (paras. 26, 40–43)
Tipp-Ex 269 (paras. 13, 51–52, 60–62)
Gosme/Martell 340 (para. 35)
Consten & Grundig v. *Commission* 4*
Miller v. *Commission* 61 (ground 7)
Tepea v. *Commission* 64 (grounds 33–45, 53–57)

2. Clauses relating to the product that the distributor may sell

2.1. Non-competition clause

Article 2(2)(a)
Maison Jallatte 9*
Goodyear Italian/Euram 87 (para. 2)
SABA I 99 (paras. 13, 32, 46)
Junghans 109 (paras. 14, 28, 31)
Gerofabriek 111
Spices 124 (paras. 12, 17, 19–20)
Hennessy/Henkell 162 (paras. 5, 18–19)
Whisky and Gin 237

2.2. Minimum purchasing obligations

Article 2(3)(a)
Goodyear Italian/Euram 87 (para. 1)
Carlsberg 214 (para. 3.1)

2.3. Exclusive purchasing requirements

Article 2(2)(b)
Rieckerman 17
Hennessy/Henkell 162 (paras. 5, 19)

2.4. Guaranteed after sales service

See also Part IV, Chapter 3, page 142
Article 2(3)(c)
Grundig/Consten 5
Omega 33 (paras. 2, 5)
Zanussi 139 (paras. 10–13)*
Hasselblad 173 (paras. 30–32, 52–55)*
Ideal Standard Sales System 223 (para. 16)
Constructa 4th Comp. Rep. (para. 109)
7th Comp. Rep. (paras. 17–20)
Moulinex 10th Comp. Rep. (para. 122)
Matsushita 12th Comp. Rep. (para. 77)
Ford Germany 13th Comp. Rep. (paras. 104–106)
Fiat 14th Comp. Rep. (para. 70–71)
16th Comp. Rep. (para. 56)

Sony 17th Comp. Rep. (para. 67)
AKZO 19th Comp. Rep. (para. 45)
ETA v. *DKI* 126 (grounds 12–14)*
Hasselblad v. *Commission* 107 (grounds 33–34)*

2.5. Assembly and manufacture by distributor

Omega 33 (paras. 2, 5)

2.6. Stocking requirement

Article 2(3)(*c*)
Omega 33 (paras. 2, 5)
Spices 124 (para. 12)*

3. Clauses related to the price of the product

3.1. Resale price maintenance

Omega 33 (para. 3)
Dupont de Nemours Germany 71
Deutsche Philips 73*
Junghans 109 (paras. 17–8)
Gerofabriek 111*
Spices 124 (paras. 12, 17)
Hennessy/Henkell 162 (paras. 5, 11–15, 20, 28–29, 32–33)
1st Comp. Rep. (para. 55)
VEB/Shell 16th Comp. Rep. (para. 54)
AMP v. *Binon* 119 (grounds 44–46)*
Louis Erauw v. *La Hesbignonne* 149 (ground 15)

3.2. Discriminatory pricing between different territories

Pittsburgh Corning 63*
The Distillers Company 123
Polistil/Arbois 211 (para. 43–51)
Sperry New Holland 245 (paras. 28, 54)
Gosme/Martell 340 (para. 31)
1st Comp. Rep. (para. 48)
Maison des Bibliothèques. 14th Comp. Rep. (para. 69)
Distillers 17th Comp. Rep. (para. 65)

3.3. Obligation to transmit recommended prices

ARG/Unipart 278 (para. 32)

4. Clauses relating to the customers to which the distributor may sell

Omega 33 (para. 9)
Du Pont Germany 71
Deutsche Phillips 73*
Gerofabriek 111
Junghans 109 (para. 21)

Distillers-Victuallers 157 (paras. 12–17)
Cafeteros de Colombia 187
Brazilian Coffee 5th Comp. Rep. (para. 33)
Beecham Pharma 6th Comp. Rep. (para. 129)
Brazilian Coffee 6th Comp. Rep. (para. 54)
IBC 16th Comp. Rep. (para. 54)
Ciments et Bétons v. *Kerpen* 104 (ground 6)*

5. Distribution agreements between competing manufacturers

5.1. Reciprocal

Article 3(*a*)
SNPE/LEL 132 (paras. 4, 13)
Siemens/Fanuc 246*
Fluke/Phillips 19th Comp. Rep. (para. 47)

5.2. Non-reciprocal

Article 3(*b*)
European Sugar Industry 69
Kali & Salz-Kalichemie 76
Carlsberg 214 (paras. 3, 11)
Whisky and Gin 237*

CHAPTER 2

EXCLUSIVE PURCHASING AGREEMENTS

A. CASES ON EXCLUSIVE PURCHASING AGREEMENTS

Spices 124
BP Kemi/DDSF 147 (paras. 26, 33–37, 57–71, 93–97)
Cane Sugar Supply Agreements 150 (paras. 11, 1219–24)
Rennet 151
National Sulphuric Acid Association 156, 308
IMA Rules 158
Schlegel/CPIO 204 (paras. 4–5, 14–21)
Ijsselcentrale 335 (para. 28)
Scottish Nuclear 339
Sand Producers. 6th Comp. Rep. (paras. 123–125)
7th Comp. Rep. (paras. 9–16)
Soda Ash. 11th Comp. Rep. (paras. 73–76)
Nutrasweet 18th Comp. Rep. (para. 53)
De Haecht v. *Wilkin I* 7
De Norre v. *Concordia* 54
Stremsel v. *Commission* 84
Delimitis v. *Henninger Bräu* 181

B. TEXT OF REGULATION 1984/83 (reproduced over)

Part IV—2 Exclusive Purchasing Agreements

Commission Regulation 1984/83 of June 22, 1983

On the application of Article 85(3) of the Treaty to categories of exclusive purchasing agreements

([1983] O.J. L173/5)

(Amended by [1983] O.J. L281/24)

THE COMMISSION OF THE EUROPEAN COMMUNITIES,

Having regard to the Treaty establishing the European Economic Community,

Having regard to Council Regulation 19/65 of 2 March 1965 on the application of Article 85(3) of the Treaty to certain categories of agreements and concerted practices, as last amended by the Act of Accession of Greece, and in particular Article 1 thereof,

Having published a draft of this Regulation,

Having consulted the Advisory Committee on Restrictive Practices and Dominant Positions,

(1) Whereas Regulation 19/65 empowers the Commission to apply Article 85(3) of the Treaty by regulation to certain categories of bilateral exclusive purchasing agreements entered into for the purpose of the resale of goods and corresponding concerted practices falling within Article 85(1),

(2) Whereas experience to date makes it possible to define three categories of agreements and concerted practices which can be regarded as normally satisfying the conditions laid down in Article 85(3); whereas the first category comprises exclusive purchasing agreements of short and medium duration in all sectors of the economy; whereas the other two categories comprise long-term exclusive purchasing agreements entered into for the resale of beer in premises used for the sale and consumption of drinks (beer supply agreements) and of petroleum products in filling stations (service-station agreements);

(3) Whereas exclusive agreements of the categories defined in this Regulation may fall within the prohibition contained in Article 85(1) of the Treaty; whereas this will often be the case with agreements concluded between undertakings from different Member States; whereas an exclusive purchasing agreement to which undertakings from only one Member State are party and which concerns the resale of goods within that Member State may also be caught by the prohibition whereas this is in particular the case where it is one of a number of similar agreements which together may affect trade between Member States;

(4) Whereas it is not necessary expressly to exclude from the defined categories those agreements which do not fulfil the conditions of Article 85(1) of the Treaty;

(5) Whereas the exclusive purchasing agreements defined in this Regulation lead in general to an improvement in distribution; whereas they enable the supplier to plan the sales of his goods with greater precision and for a longer period and ensure that the reseller's requirements will be met on a regular basis for the duration of the agreement; whereas this allows the parties to limit the risk to them of variations in market conditions and to lower distribution costs;

(6) Whereas such agreements also facilitate the promotion of the sales of a product and lead to intensive marketing because the supplier, in consideration of the exclusive purchasing obligation, is as a rule under an obligation to contribute to the improvement of the structure of the distribution network, the quality of the promotional effort or the sales success; whereas, at the same time, they stimulate competition between the products of different manufacturers; whereas the appointment of several resellers, who are bound to purchase exclusively from the manufacturer and who take over sales promotion, customer services and carrying of stock, is often the most effective way, and sometimes the only way, for the manufacturer to penetrate a market and compete with other manufacturers already present; whereas this is particularly so in the case of small and medium-size undertakings; whereas it must be left to the contracting parties to decide whether and

Book One: Part IV—Vertical Agreements

to what extent they consider it desirable to incorporate in their agreements terms concerning the promotion of sales;

(7) Whereas, as a rule, exclusive purchasing agreements between suppliers and resellers also allow consumers a fair share of the resulting benefit as they gain the advantages of regular supply and are able to obtain the contract goods more quickly and more easily;

(8) Whereas this Regulation must define the obligations restricting competition which may be included in an exclusive purchasing agreement; whereas the other restrictions of competition allowed under this Regulation in addition to the exclusive purchasing obligation lead to a clear division of functions between the parties and compel the reseller to concentrate his sales efforts on the contract goods; whereas they are, where they are agreed only for the duration of the agreement, generally necessary in order to attain the improvement in the distribution of goods sought through exclusive purchasing; whereas further restrictive obligations and in particular those which limit the reseller's choice of customers or his freedom to determine his prices and conditions of sale cannot be exempted under this Regulation;

(9) Whereas the exemption by categories should be reserved for agreements for which it can be assumed with sufficient certainty that they satisfy the conditions of Article 85(3) of the Treaty;

(10) Whereas it is not possible, in the absence of a case-by-case examination, to consider that adequate improvements in distribution occur where a manufacturer imposes an exclusive purchasing obligation with respect to his goods on a manufacturer with whom he is in competition; whereas such agreements should, therefore, be excluded from the exemption by categories; whereas certain derogations from this rule in favour of small and medium-sized undertakings can be allowed;

(11) Whereas certain conditions must be attached to the exemption by categories so that access by other undertakings to the different stages of distribution can be ensured; whereas, to this end, limits must be set to the scope and to the duration of the exclusive purchasing obligation; whereas it appears appropriate as a general rule to grant the benefit of a general exemption from the prohibition on restrictive agreements only to exclusive purchasing agreements which are concluded for a specified product or range of products and for not more than five years;

(12) Whereas, in the case of beer supply agreements and service station agreements, different rules should be laid down which take account of the particularities of the markets in question;

(13) Whereas these agreements are generally distinguished by the fact that, on the one hand, the supplier confers on the reseller special commercial or financial advantages by contributing to his financing, granting him or obtaining for him a loan on favourable terms, equipping him with a site or premises for conducting his business, providing him with equipment or fittings, or undertaking other investments for his benefit and that, on the other hand the reseller enters into a long-term exclusive purchasing obligation which in most cases is accompanied by a ban on dealing in competing products;

(14) Whereas beer supply and service-station agreements, like the other exclusive purchasing agreements dealt with in this Regulation, normally produce an appreciable improvement in distribution in which consumers are allowed a fair share of the resulting benefit;

(15) Whereas the commercial and financial advantages conferred by the supplier on the reseller make it significantly easier to establish, modernise, maintain and operate premises used for the sale and consumption of drinks and service stations; whereas the exclusive purchasing obligation and the ban on dealing in competing products imposed on the reseller incite the reseller to devote all the resources at his disposal to the sale of the contract goods; whereas such agreements lead to durable cooperation between the parties allowing them to improve or maintain the quality of the contract goods and of the services to the customer and sales efforts of the reseller; whereas they allow long-term planning of sales and consequently a cost effective organisation of production and distribution; whereas the pressure of competition between products of different makes obliges the undertakings involved to determine the number and character of premises used for the sale and consumption of drinks and service stations, in accordance with the wishes of customers;

(16) Whereas consumers benefit from the improvements described, in particular

because they are ensured supplies of goods of satisfactory quality at fair prices and conditions while being able to choose between the products of different manufacturers;

(17) Whereas the advantages produced by beer supply agreements and service station agreements cannot otherwise be secured to the same extent and with the same degree of certainty; whereas the exclusive purchasing obligation on the reseller and the non-competition clause imposed on him are essential components of such agreements and thus usually indispensable for the attainment of these advantages; whereas, however, this is true only as long as the reseller's obligation to purchase from the supplier is confined in the case of premises used for the sale and consumption of drinks to beers and other drinks of the types offered by the supplier, and in the case of service stations to petroleum-based fuel for motor vehicles and other petroleum-based fuels; whereas the exclusive purchasing obligation for lubricants and related petroleum-based products can be accepted only on condition that the supplier provides for the reseller or finances the procurement of specific equipment for the carrying out of lubrication work; whereas this obligation should only relate to products intended for use within the service station;

(18) Whereas, in order to maintain the reseller's commercial freedom and to ensure access to the retail level of distribution on the part of other suppliers, not only the scope but also the duration of the exclusive purchasing obligation must be limited; whereas it appears appropriate to allow drinks suppliers a choice between a medium-term exclusive purchasing agreement covering a range of drinks and a long-term exclusive purchasing agreement for beer; whereas it is necessary to provide special rules for those premises used for the sale and consumption of drinks which the supplier lets to the reseller; whereas, in this case the reseller must have the right to obtain from other undertakings, under the conditions specified in this Regulation, other drinks, except beer, supplied under the agreement or of the same type but bearing a different trade mark; whereas a uniform maximum duration should be provided for service-station agreements, with the exception of tenancy agreements between the supplier and the reseller, which takes account of the long-term character of the relationship between the parties;

(19) Whereas to the extent that Member States provide, by law or administrative measures, for the same upper limit of duration for the exclusive purchasing obligation upon the reseller in service-station agreements as laid down in this Regulation but provide for a permissible duration which varies in proportion to the consideration provided by the supplier or generally provide for a shorter duration than that permitted by this Regulation, such laws or measures are not contrary to the objectives of this Regulation which, in this respect, merely sets an upper limit to the duration of service-station agreements; whereas the application and enforcement of such national laws or measures must therefore be regarded as compatible with the provisions of this Regulation;

(20) Whereas the limitations and conditions provided for in this Regulation are such as to guarantee effective competition on the markets in question; whereas, therefore, the agreements to which the exemption by category applies do not normally enable the participating undertakings to eliminate competition for a substantial part of the products in question;

(21) Whereas, in particular cases in which agreements or concerted practices satisfying the conditions of this Regulation nevertheless have effects incompatible with Article 85(3) of the Treaty, the Commission may withdraw the benefit of the exemption by category from the undertakings party thereto;

(22) Whereas agreements and concerted practices which satisfy the conditions set out in this Regulation need not be notified; whereas an undertaking may nonetheless, in a particular case where real doubt exists, request the Commission to declare whether its agreements comply with this Regulation;

(23) Whereas this Regulation does not affect the applicability of Commission Regulation 3604/82 of 23 December 1982 on the application of Article 85(3) of the Treaty to categories of specialisation agreements; whereas it does not exclude the application of Article 86 of the Treaty,

HAS ADOPTED THIS REGULATION:

TITLE I—GENERAL PROVISIONS

Article 1

Pursuant to Article 85(3) of the Treaty, and subject to the conditions set out in Articles 2 to 5 of this Regulation, it is hereby declared that Article 85(1) of the Treaty shall not apply to agreements to which only two undertakings are party and whereby one party, the reseller, agrees with the other, the supplier, to purchase certain goods specified in the agreement for resale only from the supplier or from a connected undertaking or from another undertaking which the supplier has entrusted with the sale of his goods.

Article 2

1. No other restriction of competition shall be imposed on the supplier than the obligation not to distribute the contract goods or goods which compete with the contract goods in the reseller's principal sales area and at the reseller's level of distribution.

2. Apart from the obligation described in Article 1, no other restriction of competition shall be imposed on the reseller than the obligation not to manufacture or distribute goods which compete with the contract goods.

3. Article 1 shall apply notwithstanding that the reseller undertakes any or all of the following obligations;
(a) to purchase complete ranges of goods;
(b) to purchase minimum quantities of goods which are subject to the exclusive purchasing obligation;
(c) to sell the contract goods under trademarks, or packed and presented as specified by the supplier;
(d) to take measures for the promotion of sales, in particular:
— to advertise,
— to maintain a sales network or stock of goods,
— to provide customer and guarantee services,
— to employ staff having specialised or technical training.

Article 3

Article 1 shall not apply where:
(a) manufacturers of identical goods or of goods which are considered by users as equivalent in view of their characteristics, price and intended use enter into reciprocal exclusive purchasing agreements between themselves in respect of such goods;
(b) manufacturers of identical goods or of goods which are considered by users as equivalent in view of their characteristics, price and intended use enter into a non-reciprocal exclusive purchasing agreement between themselves in respect of such goods, unless at least one of them has a total annual turnover of no more than 100 million ECU;
(c) the exclusive purchasing obligation is agreed for more than one type of goods where these are neither by their nature nor according to commercial usage connected to each other;
(d) the agreement is concluded for an indefinite duration or for a period of more than five years.

Article 4

1. Article 3(a) and (b) shall also apply where the goods there referred to are manufactured by an undertaking connected with a party to the agreement.

2. Connected undertakings are:
(a) undertakings in which a party to the agreement, directly or indirectly:
— owns more than half the capital or business assets, or
— has the power to exercise more than half the voting rights, or
— has the power to appoint more than half the members of the supervisory board, board of directors or bodies legally representing the undertaking, or
— has the right to manage the affairs;
(b) undertakings which directly or indirectly have in or over a party to the agreement the rights or powers listed in (a);
(c) undertakings in which an undertaking referred to in (b) directly or indirectly has the rights or powers listed in (a).

3. Undertakings in which the parties to the agreement or undertakings connected with them jointly have the rights or powers set out in paragraph 2(a) shall be considered to be connected with each of the parties to the agreement.

Article 5

1. For the purpose of Article 3(b), the ECU is the unit of account used for drawing up

the budget of the Community pursuant to Articles 207 and 209 of the Treaty.

2. Article 1 shall remain applicable where during any period of two consecutive financial years the total turnover referred to in Article 3(b) is exceeded by no more than 10 per cent.

3. For the purpose of calculating total turnover within the meaning of Article 3(b), the turnovers achieved during the last financial year by the party to the agreement and connected undertakings in respect of all goods and services, excluding all taxes and other duties, shall be added together. For this purpose no account shall be taken of dealings between the party to the agreement and its connected undertakings or between its connected undertakings.

TITLE II—SPECIAL PROVISIONS FOR BEER SUPPLY AGREEMENTS

Article 6

1. Pursuant to Article 85(3) of the Treaty, and subject to Articles 7 to 9 of this Regulation, it is hereby declared that Article 85(1) of the Treaty shall not apply to agreements to which only two undertakings are party and whereby one party, the reseller, agrees with the other, the supplier, in consideration for the according special commercial or financial advantages, to purchase only from the supplier, an undertaking connected with the supplier or another undertaking entrusted by the supplier with the distribution of his goods, certain beers, or certain beers and certain other drinks, specified in the agreement for resale in premises used for the sale and consumption of drinks and designated in the agreement.

2. The declaration in paragraph 1 shall also apply where exclusive purchasing obligations of the kind described in paragraph 1 are imposed on the reseller in favour of the supplier by another undertaking which is itself not a supplier.

Article 7

1. Apart from the obligation referred to in Article 6, no restriction on competition shall be imposed on the reseller other than:
(a) the obligation not to sell beers and other drinks which are supplied by other undertakings and which are of the same type as the beers or other drinks supplied under the agreement in the premises designated in the agreement;
(b) the obligation, in the event that the reseller sells in the premises designated in the agreement beers which are supplied by other undertakings and which are of a different type from the beers supplied under the agreement, to sell such beers only in bottles, cans or other small packages, unless the sale of such beers in draught form is customary or is necessary to satisfy a sufficient demand from consumers;
(c) the obligation to advertise goods supplied by other undertakings within or outside the premises designated in the agreement only in proportion to the share of these goods in the total turnover realized in the premises.

2. Beers or other drinks are of different types where they are clearly distinguishable by their composition, appearance and taste.

Article 8

1. Article 6 shall not apply where:
(a) the supplier or a connected undertaking imposes on the reseller exclusive purchasing obligations for goods other than drinks or for services;
(b) the supplier restricts the freedom of the reseller to obtain from an undertaking of his choice either services or goods for which neither an exclusive purchasing obligation nor a ban on dealing in competing products may be imposed;
(c) the agreement is concluded for an indefinite duration or for a period of more than five years and the exclusive purchasing obligation relates to specified beers and other drinks;
(d) the agreement is concluded for an indefinite duration or for a period of more than 10 years and the exclusive purchasing obligation relates only to specified beers;
(e) the supplier obliges the reseller to impose the exclusive purchasing obligation on his successor for a longer period than the reseller would himself remain tied to the supplier.

2. Where the agreement relates to premises which the supplier lets to the reseller or allows the reseller to occupy on some other basis in law or in fact, the following provisions shall also apply:

(a) notwithstanding paragraphs (1)(c) and (d), the exclusive purchasing obligations and bans on dealing in competing products specified in this Title may be imposed on the reseller for the whole period for which the reseller in fact operates the premises;
(b) the agreement must provide for the reseller to have the right to obtain:
— drinks, except beer, supplied under the agreement from other undertakings where these undertakings offer them on more favourable conditions which the supplier does not meet,
— drinks, except beer, which are of the same type as those supplied under the agreement but which bear different trade marks, from other undertakings where the suppliers does not offer them.

Article 9

Articles 2(1) and (3), 3(a) and (b), 4 and 5 shall apply *mutatis mutandis*.

TITLE III—SPECIAL PROVISIONS FOR SERVICE-STATION AGREEMENTS

Article 10

Pursuant to Article 85(3) of the Treaty and subject to Articles 11 to 13 of this Regulation, it is hereby declared that Article 85(1) of the Treaty shall not apply to agreements to which only two undertakings are party and whereby one party, the reseller, agrees with the other, the supplier, in consideration for the according of special commercial or financial advantages, to purchase only from the supplier, an undertaking connected with the supplier or another undertaking entrusted by the supplier with the distribution of his goods, certain petroleum-based motor-vehicle fuels or certain petroleum-based motor-vehicle and other fuels specified in the agreement for resale in a service station designated in the agreement.

Article 11

Apart from the obligation referred to in Article 10, no restriction on competition shall be imposed on the reseller other than:
(a) the obligation not to sell motor-vehicle fuel and other fuels which are supplied by other undertakings in the service station designated in the agreement;
(b) the obligation not to use lubricants or related petroleum-based products which are supplied by other undertakings within the service station designated in the agreement where the supplier or a connected undertaking has made available to the reseller, or financed, a lubrication bay or other motor-vehicle lubrication equipment;
(c) the obligation to advertise goods supplied by other undertakings within or outside the service station designated in the agreement only in proportion to the share of these goods in the total turnover realized in the service station;
(d) the obligation to have equipment owned by the supplier or a connected undertaking or financed by the supplier or a connected undertaking serviced by the supplier of an undertaking designated by him.

Article 12

1. Article 10 shall not apply where:
(a) the supplier or a connected undertaking imposes on the reseller exclusive purchasing obligations for goods other than motor-vehicle and other fuels or for services, except in the case of the obligations referred to in Article 11(b) and (d);
(b) the supplier restricts the freedom of the reseller to obtain from an undertaking of his choice goods or services for which under the provisions of this Title neither an exclusive purchasing obligation nor a ban on dealing in competing products may be imposed;
(c) the agreement is concluded for an indefinite duration or for a period of more than 10 years;
(d) the supplier obliges the reseller to impose the exclusive purchasing obligation on his successor for a longer period than the reseller would himself remain tied to the supplier.

2. Where the agreement relates to a service station which the supplier lets to the reseller, or allows the reseller to occupy on some other basis, in law or in fact, exclusive purchasing obligations or bans on dealing in competing products specified in this title may, notwithstanding paragraph 1(c), be imposed on the reseller for the whole period for which the reseller in fact operates the premises.

Article 13

Articles 2(1) and (3), 3(a) and (b), 4 and 5 of this Regulation shall apply *mutatis mutandis*.

TITLE IV—MISCELLANEOUS PROVISIONS

Article 14

The Commission may withdraw the benefit of this Regulation, pursuant to Article 7 of Regulation No. 19/65/EEC, when it finds in a particular case that an agreement which is exempted by this Regulation nevertheless has certain effects which are incompatible with the conditions set out in Article 85(3) of the Treaty, and in particular where:
(a) the contract goods are not subject, in a substantial part of the common market, to effective competition from identical goods or goods considered by users as equivalent in view of their characteristics, price and intended use;
(b) access by other suppliers to the different stages of distribution in a substantial part of the common market is made difficult to a significant extent;
(c) the supplier without any objectively justified reason:
  (i) refuses to supply categories of resellers who cannot obtain the contract goods elsewhere on suitable terms or applies to them differing prices or conditions of sale;
  (ii) applies less favourable prices or conditions of sale to resellers bound by an exclusive purchasing obligation as compared with other resellers at the same level of distribution.

Article 15

1. In the period 1 July 1983 to 31 December 1986, the prohibition in Article 85(1) of the Treaty shall not apply to agreements of the kind described in Article 1 which either were in force on 1 July 1983 or entered into force between 1 July and 31 December 1983 and which satisfy the exemption conditions of Regulation 67/67 EEC(¹).

2. In the period 1 July 1983 to 31 December 1988, the prohibition in Article 85(1) of the Treaty shall not apply to agreements of the kinds described in Articles 6 and 10 which either were in force on 1 July 1983 or entered into force between 1 July and 31 December 1983 and which satisfy the exemption conditions of Regulation 67/67.

3. In the case of agreements of the kinds described in Articles 6 and 10, which were in force on 1 July 1983 and which expire after 31 December 1988, the prohibition in Article 85(1) of the Treaty shall not apply in the period from 1 January 1989 to the expiry of the agreement but at the latest to the expiry of this Regulation to the extent that the supplier releases the reseller, before 1 January 1989, from all obligations which would prevent the application of the exemption under Titles II and III.

Article 16

This Regulation shall not apply to agreements by which the supplier undertakes with the reseller to supply only to the reseller certain goods for resale, in the whole or in a defined part of the Community, and the reseller undertakes with the supplier to purchase these goods from the supplier.

Article 17

This Regulation shall not apply where the parties or connected undertakings, for the purpose of resale in one and the same premises used for the sale and consumption of drinks or service station, enter into agreements both of the kind referred to in Title I and of a kind referred to in Title II or III.

Article 18

This Regulation shall apply *mutatis mutandis* to the categories of concerted practices defined in Articles 1, 6 and 10.

Article 19

This Regulation shall enter into force on 1 July 1983.
It shall expire on December 31, 1997.
This Regulation shall be binding in its entirety and directly applicable in all Member States.

Done at Brussels, June 22, 1983.

Book One: Part IV—Vertical Agreements

C. CASES ON THE INTERPRETATION OF THE REGULATION

BP Kemi/DDSF 147 (paras. 91–95)
ARG/Unipart 278 (para. 35)
VBA 288
13th Comp. Rep. (paras. 26–32)
17th Comp. Rep. (para. 29)
20th Comp Rep. (para. 84–88)
Delimitis v. *Henninger Bräu* (grounds 34–42)

D. NOTICE ON THE INTERPRETATION OF THE REGULATION

See text on page 124.

E. CLAUSES COMMONLY FIGURING IN EXCLUSIVE PURCHASING AGREEMENTS

1. Exclusivity

Articles 1, 2(1)
BP Kemi/DDSF 147 (paras. 26, 57–61, 67–71)
Natrium Carbonate 11th Comp. Rep. (paras. 73–76)
Nutrasweet 18th Comp. Rep. (para. 53)
Industrial Gases 19th Comp. Rep. (para. 62)
Delimitis v. *Henninger Bräu* 181*

2. Non-competition clause

Spices 124 (paras. 12, 17, 19–20)*
Rennet 149
Stremsel v. *Commission* 84 (grounds 12–13)

3. English clause

Article 8(2)(*b*)
BP Kemi-DDSF 147 (paras. 63–66)
Industrial Gases 19th Comp. Rep. (para. 62)

4. Purchasing or supply obligations

Article 2(3)(*a*),(*b*)
BP Kemi/DDSF 147 (para. 26)
Scottish Nuclear 339 (para. 29)
Shotton Paper 20th Comp. Rep. (para. 93)

5. Resale price maintenance

Spices 124 (paras. 12, 17)

CHAPTER 3
SELECTIVE DISTRIBUTION AGREEMENTS

A. CASES ON SELECTIVE DISTRIBUTION AGREEMENTS

Omega 3
BMW 82
SABA I 99
Junghans 109
BMW Belgium 126
Kawasaki 141
Krups 155
Hasselblad 173
AEG/Telefunken 179
Ford Werke–Interim Measures 182
National Panasonic 186
Ford-Werke AG 199
Murat 200
SABA II 208
IBM PC 210
Grohe Sales System 222
Ideal Standard Sales System 223
Grundig 232
Ivoclar 234
Villeroy & Boch 244
Peugeot 250
Charles Jourdan 298
D'Ieteren 329
Vichy 334
Eco System 344a
Yves Saint Laurent 345
1st Comp. Rep. (paras. 56–57)
3rd Comp. Rep. (paras. 7–12)
4th Comp. Rep. (paras. 33–36)
Dior & Lancôme Sales. 4th Comp. Rep. (paras. 93–95)
5th Comp. Rep. (paras. 12–13, 54, 57–61)
9th Comp. Rep. (paras. 5, 6)
13th Comp. Rep. (paras. 33–39)
Interlübcke 15th Comp. Rep. (para. 15)
Memrad 15th Comp. Rep. (para. 64)
Rodenstock 15th Comp. Rep. (para. 65)
16th Comp. Rep. (paras. 97–106)
Vichy v. *Commission* T29
Metro v. *Commission* I 58
BMW Belgium v. *Commission* 69 (grounds 20–34)
FEDETAB v. *Commission* 80 (grounds 135–141)
L'Oréal v. *De Nieuwe AMCK* 81 (grounds 14–17)
Salonia v. *Poidomani & Baglieri* 85
Demo Schmidt v. *Commission* 99 (grounds 17–22)
AEG v. *Commission* 100
AMP v. *Binon* 119
Ford v. *Commission* 123
Metro v. *Commission* II 134

B. TEXT OF REGULATION 123/85 (reproduced below)

Part IV—3 Selective Distribution Agreements

Commission Regulation 123/85 of December 12, 1984

On the application of Article 85(3) of the Treaty to certain categories of motor vehicle distribution and servicing agreements

([1985] O.J. L15/16)

THE COMMISSION OF THE EUROPEAN COMMUNITIES,

Having regard to the Treaty establishing the European Economic Community,

Having regard to Council Regulation 19/65 of 2 March 1965 on the application of Article 85(3) of the Treaty to certain categories of agreements and concerted practices, as last amended by the Act of Accession of Greece,

Having published a draft of this Regulation,

Having consulted the Advisory Committee on Restrictive Practices and Dominant Positions,

Whereas:

(1) Under Article 1(1)(a) of Regulation 19/65 the Commission is empowered to declare by means of a Regulation that Article 85(3) of the Treaty applies to certain categories of agreements falling within Article 85(1) to which only two undertakings are party and by which one party agrees with the other to supply only to that undertaking other certain goods for resale within a defined territory of the common market. In the light of experience since Commission Decision 75/73 and of the many motor vehicle distribution and servicing agreements which have been notified to the Commission pursuant to Articles 4 and 5 of the Council Regulation 17, as last amended by Regulation 2821/71, a category of agreements can be defined as satisfying the conditions laid down in Regulation 19/65. They are agreements, for a definite or an indefinite period, by which the supplying party entrusts to the reselling party the task of promoting the distribution and servicing of certain products of the motor vehicle industry in a defined area and by which the supplier undertakes to supply contract goods for resale only to the dealer, or only to a limited number of undertakings within the distribution network besides the dealer, within the contract territory.

A list of definitions for the purpose of this Regulation is set out in Article 13.

(2) Notwithstanding that the obligations imposed by distribution and servicing agreements which are listed in Articles 1, 2 and 3 of this Regulation normally have as their object or effect the prevention, restriction or distortion of competition within the common market and are normally apt to affect trade between Member States, the prohibition in Article 85(1) of the Treaty may nevertheless be declared inapplicable to these agreements by virtue of Article 85(3), albeit only under certain restrictive conditions.

(3) The applicability of Article 85(1) of the Treaty to distribution and servicing agreements in the motor vehicle industry stems in particular from the fact that restrictions on competition and the obligations connected with the distribution system listed in Articles 1 to 4 of this Regulation are regularly imposed in the same or similar form throughout the common market for the products supplied within the distribution system of a particular manufacturer. The motor vehicle manufacturers cover the whole common market or substantial parts of it by means of a cluster of agreements involving similar restrictions on competition and affect in this way not only distribution and servicing within Member States but also trade between them.

(4) The exclusive and selective distribution clauses can be regarded as indispensable measures of rationalization in the motor vehicle industry because motor vehicles are consumer durables which at both regular and irregular intervals require expert maintenance and repair, not always in the same place. Motor vehicle manufacturers cooperate with the selected dealers and repairers in order to provide specialized servicing for the product. On grounds of capacity and efficiency alone, such a form of cooperation cannot be extended to an unlimited number of dealers and repairers. The linking of servicing and distribution must be regarded as more efficient than a separation between a distribution organization for new vehicles on the one hand and a servicing organization which would also distribute spare parts on the other, particularly as, before a new vehicle is

delivered to the final consumer, the undertaking within the distribution system must give it a technical inspection according to the manufacturer's specification.

(5) However, obligatory recourse to the authorized network is not in all respects indispensable for efficient distribution. The exceptions to the block exemption provide that the supply of contract goods to resellers may not be prohibited where they:
— belong to the same distribution system (Article 3, point 10(a)), or
— purchase spare parts for their own use in effecting repairs or maintenance (Article 3, point 10(b)).

Measures taken by a manufacturer or by undertakings within the distribution system with the object of protecting the selective distribution system are compatible with the exemption under this Regulation. This applies in particular to a dealer's obligation to sell vehicles to a final consumer using the services of an intermediary only where that consumer has authorized that intermediary to act as his agent (Article 3, point 11).

(6) It should be possible to bar wholesalers not belonging to the distribution system from reselling parts originating from motor vehicle manufacturers. It may be supposed that the system of rapid availability of spare parts across the whole contract programme, including those with a low turnover, which is beneficial to the consumer, could not be maintained without obligatory recourse to the authorized network.

(7) The ban on dealing in competing products and that on dealing in other vehicles at stated premises may in principle be exempted, because they contribute to concentration by the undertakings in the distribution network of their efforts on the products supplied by the manufacturer or with his consent, and thus ensure distribution and servicing appropriate for the vehicles (Article 3, point 3). Such obligations provide an incentive for the dealer to develop sales and servicing of contract goods and thus promote competition in the supply of those products as well as between those products and competing products.

(8) However, bans on dealing in competing products cannot be regarded as indispensable in all circumstances to efficient distribution. Dealers must be free to obtain from third parties supplies of parts which match the quality of those offered by the manufacturer, for example where the parts are produced by a sub-contract manufacturer who also supplies the motor vehicle manufacturer, and to use and sell them. They must also keep their freedom to choose parts which are usable in motor vehicles within the contract programme and which not only match but exceed the quality standard. Such a limit on the ban on dealing in competing products takes account of the importance of vehicle safety and of the maintenance of effective competition (Article 3, point 4 and Article 4(1), points 6 and 7).

(9) The restrictions imposed on the dealer's activities outside the allotted area lead to more intensive distribution and servicing efforts in an easily supervised contract territory, to knowledge of the market based on closer contact with consumers, and to more demand-orientated supply (Article 3, points 8 and 9). However, demand for contract goods must remain flexible and should not be limited on a regional basis. Dealers must not be confined to satisfying the demand for contract goods within their contract territories, but must also be able to meet demand from persons and undertakings in other areas of the common market. Dealers' advertising in a medium which is directed to customers in the contract territory but also covers a wider area should not be prevented, because it does not run counter to the obligation to promote sales within the contract territory.

(10) The obligations listed in Article 4(1) are directly related to the obligations in Article 1, 2 and 3, and influence their restrictive effect. These obligations, which might in individual cases be caught by the prohibition in Article 85(1) of the Treaty, may also be exempted because of their direct relationship with one or more of the obligations exempted by Articles 1, 2 and 3 (Article 4(2)).

(11) According to Article 1(2)(b) of Regulation 19/65, conditions which must be satisfied if the declaration of inapplicability is to take effect must be specified.

(12) Under Article 5(1), points 1(a) and (b) it is a condition of exemption that the undertaking should honour the minimum guarantee and provide the minimum free servicing and vehicle recall work laid down by the manufacturer, irrespective of where in the common market the vehicle was purchased. These provisions are

Part IV—3 Selective Distribution Agreements

intended to prevent the consumer's freedom to buy anywhere in the common market from being limited.

(13) Article 5(1), point 2(a) is intended to allow the manufacturer to build up a coordinated distribution system, but without hindering the relationship of confidence between dealers and sub-dealers. Accordingly, if the supplier reserves the right to approve appointments of sub-dealers by the dealer, he must not be allowed to withhold approval arbitrarily.

(14) Article 5(1), point 2(b) obliges the supplier not to impose on a dealer within the distribution system requirements, as defined in Article 4(1), which are discriminatory or inequitable.

(15) Article 5(1), point 2(c) is intended to counter the concentration of the dealer's demand on the supplier which might follow from cumulation of discounts. The purpose of this provision is to allow spare-parts suppliers which do not offer as wide a range of goods as the manufacturer to compete on equal terms.

(16) Article 5(1), point 2(d) makes exemption subject to the conditions that the dealer must be able to purchase for customers in the common market volume-produced passenger cars with the specifications appropriate for their place of residence or where the vehicle is to be registered, in so far as the corresponding model is also supplied by the manufacturer through undertakings within the distribution system in that place (Article 13, point 10). This provision obviates the danger that the manufacturer and undertakings within the distribution network might make use of product differentiation as between parts of the common market to partition the market.

(17) Article 5(2) makes the exemption of the no-competition clause and of the ban on dealing in other makes of vehicle subject to further threshold conditions. This is to prevent the dealer from becoming economically over-dependent on the supplier because of such obligations, and abandoning the competitive activity which is nominally open to him, because to pursue it would be against the interests of the manufacturer or other undertakings within the distribution network.

(18) Under Article 5(2), point 1(a), the dealer may, where there are exceptional reasons, oppose application of excessive obligations covered by Article 3, point 3 or 5.

(19) The supplier may reserve the right to appoint further distribution and servicing undertakings in the contract territory or to alter the territory, but only if he can show that there are exceptional reasons for doing so (Article 5(2), point 1(b) and Article 5(3)). This is, for example, the case where there would otherwise be reason to apprehend a serious deterioration in the distribution or servicing of contract goods.

(20) Article 5(2), points 2 and 3 lay down minimum requirements for exemption which concern the duration and termination of the distribution and servicing agreement; the combined effect of a no-competition clause or a ban on dealing in other makes of vehicle, the investments the dealer makes in order to improve the distribution and servicing of contract goods and a short-term agreement or one terminable at short notice is greatly to increase the dealer's dependence on the supplier.

(21) In accordance with Article 1(2)(a) of Regulation 19/65, restrictions or provisions which must not be contained in the agreements, if the declaration of inapplicability of Article 85(1) by this Regulation is to take effect, are to be specified.

(22) Agreements under which one motor vehicle manufacturer entrusts the distribution of its products to another must be excluded from the block exemption under this Regulation because of their far-reaching impact on competition (Article 6, point 1).

(23) An obligation to apply minimum resale prices or maximum trade discounts precludes exemption under this Regulation (Article 6, point 2).

(24) The exemption does not apply where the parties agree between themselves obligations concerning goods covered by this Regulation which would be acceptable in the combination of obligations which is exempted by Commission Regulations 1983/83 or 1984/83 on the application of Article 85(3) of the Treaty to categories of exclusive distribution agreements and exclusive purchasing agreements respectively, but which go beyond the scope of the obligations exempted by this Regulation (Article 6, point 3).

(25) Distribution and servicing agreements can be exempted, subject to the conditions laid down in Articles 5 and 6, so long as the application of obligations covered by Articles 1 to 4 of this Regulation brings

about an improvement in distribution and servicing to the benefit of the consumer and effective competition exists, not only between manufacturers' distribution systems but also to a certain extent within each system within the common market. As regards the categories of products set out in Article 1 of this Regulation, the conditions necessary for effective competition, including competition in trade between Member States, may be taken to exist at present, so that European consumers may be considered in general to take an equitable share in the benefit from the operation of such competition.

(26) Articles 7, 8 and 9, concerning the retroactive effect of the exemption, are based on Articles 3 and 4 of Regulation 19/65 and Articles 4 to 7 of Regulation No. 17. Article 10 embodies the Commission's powers under Article 7 of Regulation 19/65 to withdraw the benefit of its exemption or to alter its scope in individual cases, and lists several important examples of such cases.

(27) In view of the extensive effect of this Regulation on the persons it concerns, it is appropriate that it should not enter into force until 1 July 1985. In accordance with Article 2(1) of Regulation 19/65, the exemption may be made applicable for a definite period. A period extending until 30 June 1995 is appropriate, because overall distribution schemes in the motor vehicle sector must be planned several years in advance.

(28) Agreements which fulfil the conditions set out in this Regulation need not be notified.

(29) This Regulation does not affect the application of Regulations 1983/83 or 1984/83 or of Commission Regulation 3604/82 of 23 December 1982 on the application of Article 85(3) of the Treaty to categories of specialization agreements, or the right to request a Commission decision in an individual case pursuant to Council Regulation No. 17. It is without prejudice to laws and administrative measures of the Member States by which the latter, having regard to particular circumstances, prohibit or declare unenforceable particular restrictive obligations contained in an agreement exempted under this Regulation; the foregoing cannot, however, affect the primacy of Community law,

HAS ADOPTED THIS REGULATION:

Article 1

Pursuant to Article 85(3) of the Treaty it is hereby declared that subject to the conditions laid down in this Regulation Article 85(1) shall not apply to agreements to which only two undertakings are party and in which one contracting party agrees to supply within a defined territory of the common market
— only to the other party, or
— only to the other party and to a specified number of other undertakings within the distribution system,
for the purpose of resale certain motor vehicles intended for use on public roads and having three or more road wheels, together with spare parts therefor.

Article 2

The exemption under Article 85(3) of the Treaty shall also apply where the obligation referred to in Article 1 is combined with an obligation on the supplier neither to sell contract goods to final consumers nor to provide them with servicing for contract goods in the contract territory.

Article 3

The exemption under Article 85(3) of the Treaty shall also apply where the obligation referred to in Article 1 is combined with an obligation on the dealer:
1. not, without the supplier's consent, to modify contract goods or corresponding goods, unless such modification is the subject of a contract with a final consumer and concerns a particular motor vehicle within the contract programme purchased by that final consumer;
2. not to manufacture products which compete with contract goods;
3. neither to sell new motor vehicles which compete with contract goods nor to sell, at the premises used for the distribution of contract goods, new motor vehicles other than those offered for supply by the manufacturer;
4. neither to sell spare parts which compete with contract goods and do not match the quality of contract goods nor to use them for repair or maintenance of contract goods or corresponding goods;
5. not to conclude with third parties distribution or servicing agreements for

goods which compete with contract goods;

6. without the supplier's consent, neither to conclude distribution or servicing agreements with undertakings operating in the contract territory for contract goods or corresponding goods nor to alter or terminate such agreements;

7. to impose upon undertakings with which the dealer has concluded agreements in accordance with point 6 obligations corresponding to those which the dealer has accepted in relation to the supplier and which are covered by Articles 1 to 4 and are in conformity with Articles 5 and 6;

8. outside the contract territory;
(a) not to maintain branches or depots for the distribution of contract goods or corresponding goods,
(b) not to seek customers for contract goods or corresponding goods;

9. Not to entrust third parties with the distribution or servicing of contract goods or corresponding goods outside the contract territory;

10. to supply to a reseller:
(a) contract goods or corresponding goods only where the reseller is an undertaking within the distribution system, or
(b) spare parts within the contract programme only where they are for the purposes of repair or maintenance of a motor vehicle by the reseller;

11. to sell motor vehicles within the contract programme or corresponding goods to final consumers using the services of an intermediary only if that intermediary has prior written authority to purchase a specified motor vehicle and, as the case may be, to accept delivery thereof on their behalf;

12. to observe the obligations referred to in points 1 and 6 to 11 for a maximum period of one year after termination or expiry of the agreement.

Article 4

1. Articles 1, 2 and 3 shall apply notwithstanding any obligation imposed on the dealer to:
(1) observe, for distribution and servicing, minimum standards which relate in particular to:
  (a) the equipment of the business premises and of the technical facilities for servicing;
  (b) the specialized and technical training of staff;
  (c) advertising;
  (d) the collection, storage and delivery to customers of contract goods or corresponding goods and servicing relating to them;
  (e) the repair and maintenance of contract goods and corresponding goods, particularly as concerns the safe and reliable functioning of motor vehicles;

(2) order contract goods from the supplier only at certain times or within certain periods, provided that the interval between ordering dates does not exceed three months;

(3) endeavour to sell, within the contract territory and within a specified period, such minimum quantity of contract goods as may be determined by agreement between the parties or, in the absence of such agreement, by the supplier on the basis of estimates of the dealer's potential sales;

(4) keep in stock such quantity of contract goods as may be determined by agreement between the parties or, in the absence of such agreement, by the supplier on the basis of estimates of the dealer's potential sales of contract goods within the contract territory and within a specified period;

(5) keep such demonstration vehicles within the contract programme, or such number thereof, as may be determined by agreement between the parties or, in the absence of such agreement, by the supplier on the basis of estimates of the dealer's potential sales of motor vehicles within the contract programme;

(6) perform guarantee work, free servicing and vehicle recall work for contract goods and corresponding goods;

(7) use only spare parts within the contract programme or corresponding goods for guarantee work, free servicing and vehicle recall work in respect of contract goods or corresponding goods;

(8) inform customers, in a general manner, of the extent to which spare parts from other sources might be used for the repair or maintenance of contract goods or corresponding goods;

(9) inform customers whenever spare parts from other sources have been used for the repair or maintenance of contract goods or corresponding goods for which spare parts within the contract programme or corresponding goods, bearing a mark of the manufacturer, were also available.

2. The exemption under Article 85(3) of the Treaty shall also apply where the obligation referred to in Article 1 is combined with obligations referred to in paragraph 1 above and such obligations fall in individual cases under the prohibition contained in Article 85(1).

Article 5

1. Articles 1, 2 and 3 and Article 4(2) shall apply provided that:
(1) the dealer undertakes
   (a) in respect of motor vehicles within the contract programme or corresponding thereto which have been supplied in the common market by another undertaking within the distribution network, to honour guarantees and to perform free servicing and vehicle recall work to an extent which corresponds to the dealer's obligation covered by point 6 of Article 4(1) but which need not exceed that imposed upon the undertaking within the distribution system or accepted by the manufacturer when supplying such motor vehicles;
   (b) to impose upon the undertakings operating within the contract territory with which the dealer has concluded distribution and servicing agreements as provided for in point 6 of Article 3 an obligation to honour guarantees and to perform free servicing and vehicle recall work at least to the extent to which the dealer himself is so obliged;
(2) the supplier
   (a) shall not without objectively valid reasons withhold consent to conclude, alter or terminate sub-agreements referred to in Article 3, point 6;
   (b) shall not apply, in relation to the dealer's obligations referred to in Article 4(1), minimum requirements or criteria for estimates such that the dealer is subject to discrimination without objectively valid reasons or is treated inequitably;
   (c) shall, in any scheme for aggregating quantities or values of goods obtained by the dealer from the supplier and from connected undertakings within a specified period for the purpose of calculating discounts, at least distinguish between supplies of
   — motor vehicles within the contract programme
   — spare parts within the contract programme, for supplies of which the dealer is dependent on undertakings within the distribution network, and
   — other goods;
   (d) shall also apply to the dealer, for the purpose of performance of a contract of sale concluded between the dealer and a final customer in the common market, any passenger car which corresponds to a model within the contract programme and which is marketed by the manufacturer or with the manufacturer's consent in the Member State in which the vehicle is to be registered.

2. In so far as the dealer has, in accordance with Article 5(1), assumed obligations for the improvement of distribution and servicing structures, the exemption referred to in Article 3, points 3 and 5 shall apply to the obligation not to sell new motor vehicles other than those within the contract programme or not to make such vehicles the subject of a distribution and servicing agreement, provided that
(1) the parties
   (a) agree that the supplier shall release the dealer from the obligations referred to in Article 3, points 3 and 5 where the dealer shows that there are objectively valid reasons for doing so;
   (b) agree that the supplier reserves the right to conclude distribution and servicing agreements for contract goods with specified further undertakings operating within the contract territory or to alter the contract territory only where the supplier shows that there are objectively valid reasons for doing so;
(2) the agreement is for a period of at least four years or, if for an indefinite period, the period of notice for regular termination of the agreement is at least one year for both parties, unless
   — the supplier is obliged by law or by special agreement to pay appropriate compensation on termination of the agreement, or
   — the dealer is a new entrant to the distribution system and the period of the agreement, or the period of notice for regular termination of the agreement, is the first agreed by that dealer.
(3) each party undertakes to give the other at least six months' prior notice of inten-

tion not to renew an agreement concluded for a definite period.

3. A party may only invoke particular objectively valid grounds within the meaning of this Article which have been exemplified in the agreement if such grounds are applied without discrimination to undertakings within the distribution system in comparable cases.

4. The conditions for exemption laid down in this Article shall not affect the right of a party to terminate the agreement for cause.

Article 6

Articles 1, 2 and 3 and Article 4(2) shall not apply where:

1. both parties to the agreement or their connected undertakings are motor vehicle manufacturers; or

2. the manufacturer, the supplier or another undertaking within the distribution system obliges the dealer not to resell contract goods or corresponding goods below stated prices or not to exceed stated rates of trade discount; or

3. the parties make agreements or engage in concerted practices concerning motor vehicles having three or more road wheels or spare parts therefor which are exempted from the prohibition in Article 85(1) of the Treaty under Regulations 1983/83, or 1984/83 to an extent exceeding the scope of this Regulation.

Article 7

1. As regards agreements existing on 13 March 1962 and notified before 1 February 1963 and agreements, whether notified or not, falling under Article 4(2), point 1 of Regulation No. 17, the declaration of inapplicability of Article 85(1) of the Treaty contained in this Regulation shall apply with retroactive effect from the time at which the conditions of this Regulation were fulfilled.

2. As regards all other agreements notified before this Regulation entered into force, the declaration of inapplicability of Article 85(1) of the Treaty contained in this Regulation shall apply from the time at which the conditions of this Regulation were fulfilled, or from the date of notification, whichever is the later.

Article 8

If agreements existing on 13 March 1962 and notified before 1 February 1963 or agreements to which Article 4(2), point 1 of Regulation No. 17 applies and which were notified before 1 January 1967 are amended before 1 October 1985 so as to fulfil the conditions for application of this Regulation, and if the amendment is communicated to the Commission before 31 December 1985, the prohibition in Article 85(1) of the Treaty shall not apply in respect of the period prior to the amendment. The communication shall take effect from the time of its receipt by the Commission. Where the communication is sent by registered post, it shall take effect from the date shown on the postmark of the place of posting.

Article 9

1. As regards agreements to which Article 85 of the Treaty applies as a result of the accession of the United Kingdom, Ireland and Denmark, Articles 7 and 8 shall apply except that the relevant dates shall be 1 January 1973 instead of 13 March 1962 and 1 July 1973, instead of 1 February 1963 and 1 January 1967.

2. As regards agreements to which Article 85 of the Treaty applies as a result of the accession of Greece, Articles 7 and 8 shall apply except that the relevant dates shall be 1 January 1981 instead of 13 March 1962 and 1 July 1981 instead of 1 February 1963 and 1 January 1967.

Article 10

The Commission may withdraw the benefit of the application of this Regulation, pursuant to Article 7 of Regulation 19/65, where it finds that in an individual case an agreement which falls within the scope of this Regulation nevertheless has effects which are incompatible with the provisions of Article 85(3) of the Treaty, and in particular:

1. where, in the common market or a substantial part thereof, contract goods or corresponding goods are not subject to competition from products considered by consumers as similar by reason of their characteristics, price and intended use;

2. where the manufacturer or an undertaking within the distribution system continu-

ously or systematically, and by means not exempted by this Regulation, makes it difficult for final consumers or other undertakings within the distribution system to obtain contract goods or corresponding goods, or to obtain servicing for such goods, within the common market;

3. where, over a considerable period, prices or conditions of supply for contract goods or for corresponding goods are applied which differ substantially as between Member States, and such substantial differences are chiefly due to obligations exempted by this Regulation;

4. where, in agreements concerning the supply to the dealer of passenger cars which correspond to a model within the contract programme, prices or conditions which are not objectively justifiable are applied, with the object or the effect of partitioning the common market.

Article 11

The provisions of this Regulation shall also apply in so far as the obligations referred to in Articles 1 to 4 apply to undertakings which are connected with a party to an agreement.

Article 12

This Regulation shall apply *mutatis mutandis* to concerted practices of the types defined in Articles 1 to 4.

Article 13

For the purposes of this Regulation the following terms shall have the following meanings.

1. "Distribution and servicing agreements" are framework agreements between two undertakings, for a definite or indefinite period, whereby the party supplying goods entrusts to the other the distribution and servicing of those goods.

2. "Parties" are the undertakings which are party to an agreement within the meaning of Article 1: "the supplier" being the undertaking which supplies the contract goods, and the "the dealer," the undertaking entrusted by the supplier with the distribution and servicing of contract goods.

3. The "contract territory" is the defined territory of the common market to which the obligation of exclusive supply in the meaning of Article 1 applies.

4. "Contract goods" are motor vehicles intended for use on public roads and having three or more road wheels, and spare parts therefor, which are the subject of an agreement within the meaning of Article 1.

5. The "contract programme" refers to the totality of the contract goods.

6. "Spare parts" are parts which are to be installed in or upon a motor vehicle so as to replace components of that vehicle. They are to be distinguished from other parts and accessories according to customary usage in the trade.

7. The "manufacturer" is the undertaking.
(a) which manufactures or procures the manufacture of the motor vehicles in the contract programme, or
(b) which is connected with an undertaking described at (a).

8. "Connected undertakings" are:
(a) undertakings one of which directly or indirectly
— holds more than half of the capital or business assets of the other, or
— has the power to exercise more than half the voting rights in the other, or
— has the power to appoint more than half the members of the supervisory board, board of directors or bodies legally representing the other, or
— has the right to manage the affairs of the other;
(b) undertakings in relation to which a third undertaking is able directly or indirectly to exercise such rights or powers as are mentioned in (a) above.

9. "Undertakings within the distribution system" are, besides the parties to the agreement, the manufacturer and undertakings which are entrusted by the manufacturer or with the manufacturer's consent with the distribution or servicing of contract goods or corresponding goods.

10. A "passenger car which corresponds to a model within the contract programme" is a passenger car
— manufactured or assembled in volume by the manufacturer, and
— identical as to body style, drive-line, chassis, and type of motor with a passenger car within the contract programme.

11. "Corresponding goods," "corresponding motor vehicles" and "corresponding parts" are those which are similar in kind to those in the contract programme, are

Part IV—3 Selective Distribution Agreements

distributed by the manufacturer or with the manufacturer's consent, and are the subject of a distribution or servicing agreement with an undertaking within the distribution system.

12. "Distribute" and "sell" include other forms of supply such as leasing.

Article 14

This Regulation shall enter into force on 1 July 1985.

It shall remain in force until 30 June 1995.

This Regulation shall be binding in its entirety and directly applicable in all Member States.

Done at Brussels, 12 December 1984.

C. CASES ON THE INTERPRETATION OF THE REGULATION

Peugeot 250 (para. 38)
ARG/Unipart 278 (para. 35)
D'Ieteren 329
Eco System 344a
Citroën 18th Comp. Rep. (para. 56)
20th Comp. Rep. (para. 42)
VAG v. *Magne* 137
Peugeot v. *Commission* T3 (grounds 19–22)
Peugeot v. *Commission* T17

D. TEXT OF THE NOTICE ON THE INTERPRETATION OF THE REGULATION (reproduced below)

Commission Notice concerning Regulation 123/85 of December 12, 1984

On the application of Article 85(3) of the Treaty to certain categories of motor vehicle distribution and servicing agreements

([1985] O.J. C17/3)

In Regulation 123/85 on the block exemption of motor vehicle distribution agreements the Commission recognises that exclusive and selective distribution in this industry is in principle compatible with Article 85(3) of the Treaty. This assessment is subject to a number of conditions. At the request of some of the commercial sectors involved, this notice sets out some of those conditions and lays down certain administrative principles for the procedures which the Commission might initiate under Article 7 of Council Regulation 19/65 in combination with Article 10, points 3 and 4 of Regulation 123/85, taking account of the present stage of integration of the European Community.

I

1. Freedom of movement of European consumers and limited availability of vehicle models

The Commission starts from the position that the common market affords advantages to European consumers, and that this is especially so where there is effective competition. Accordingly, Regulation 123/85 presupposes that in the motor vehicles sector effective competition exists between manufacturers and between their distribution networks. The European consumer must derive a fair share of the benefits which flow from the distribution and servicing agreements. Admittedly, the consumer may benefit from the fact that servicing is carried out by specialists (Article 3, points 3 and 5) and that such service can be obtained throughout the network from dealers and repairers who are obliged to observe minimum requirements (Article 4(1)).

However, the European consumer's basic rights include above all the right to buy a motor vehicle and to have it maintained or repaired wherever prices and quality are most advantageous to him.

(a) This right to buy relates to new vehicles from a manufacturer each of whose dealers offers them in a form and specification mainly required by final consumers in the dealer's contract territory (contract goods).

(b) In the interests of competition at the various stages of distribution in the common market and in those of European consumers, a certain limited availability of other vehicles within the distribution system is also considered indispensable. Any dealer within the distribution system must be able to order from a supplier within the distribution system any volume-produced passenger car which a final consumer has ordered from him and intends to register in another Member State, in the form and specification marketed by the manufacturer or with his consent in that Member State (passenger cars corresponding to those in the contract programme, Article 5(1), point 2(d) and Article 13, point 10 of Regulation 123/85).

This provision does not oblige the manufacturer to produce vehicles which he would not otherwise offer within the common market. Nor does it oblige the manufacturer to sell particular vehicle models in any particular part of the common market where he does not, or does not yet, wish to market them. He is only obliged to supply to a dealer within his distribution system a new passenger car required by that dealer to fulfil a contract with a final consumer and intended for another Member State where that dealer's contract programme includes cars of a corresponding kind.

2. Abusive hindrance

The European consumer must not be subject to abusive hindrance either in the exporting country, where he wishes to buy a vehicle, or in the country of destination, where he seeks to register it. The restrictions inherent in an exempted exclusive and selective distribution system do not represent abuses. However, further agreements or concerted practices between undertakings in the distribution system that limit the European consumer's final freedom to purchase do jeopardize the exemption given by the Regulation, as do unilateral measures on the part of a manufacturer or his importers or dealers which have a widespread effect against consumers' interests (Article 10, point 2). Examples are: dealers refuse to perform guarantee work on vehicles which they have not sold and which have been imported from other Member States; manufacturers or their importers withhold their cooperation in the registration of vehicles which European consumers have imported from other Member States; abnormally long delivery periods.

3. Intermediaries

The European consumer must be able to make use of the services of individuals or undertakings to assist in purchasing a new vehicle in another Member State (Article 3, points 10 and 11). However, except as regards contracts between dealers within the distribution system for the sale of contract goods, undertakings within the distribution system can be obliged not to supply new motor vehicles within the contract programme or corresponding vehicles to or through a third party who represents himself as an authorised reseller of new vehicles within the contract programme or corresponding vehicles or carries on an activity equivalent to that of a reseller. It is for the intermediary or the consumer to give the dealer within the distribution system documentary evidence that the intermediary, in buying and accepting delivery of a vehicle, is acting on behalf and for account of the consumer.

II

The Commission may withdraw the benefit of the application of Regulation 123/85, pursuant to Article 7 of Regulation 19/65, where it finds that in an individual case an agreement which falls within the scope of Regulation 123/85 nevertheless has effects which are incompatible with the provisions of Article 85(3) of the Treaty, and in particular
— where, over a considerable period, prices or conditions of supply for contract goods or for corresponding goods are applied which differ substantially as between Member States, and such substantial differences are chiefly due to obligations exempted by Regulation 123/85 (Article 10, point 3);
— where, in agreements concerning the supply to the dealer of passenger cars which correspond to a model within the contract programme, prices or conditions which are not objectively justifiable are applied, with the object or effect of partitioning the common market (Article 10, point 4).

The Commission may pursue such proceedings in individual cases, upon application (particularly on the basis of complaints from consumers) or on its own initiative, in accordance with the procedural rules laid down in Council Regulation No. 17 and Commission Regulation No. 99/63 EEC, under which the parties concerned must be informed of the objections raised and given an opportunity to respond to them before the Commission

Part IV—3 Selective Distribution Agreements

adopts a decision. Whether the Commission initiates such proceedings depends chiefly on the results of preliminary inquiries, the circumstances of the case and the degree of prejudice to the public interest.

Price differentials for motor vehicles as between Member States are to a certain extent a reflection of the particular play of supply and demand in the areas concerned. Substantial price differences generally give reason to suspect that national measures or private restrictive practices are behind them.

In view of the present stage of integration of the common market, for the time being certain circumstances will not of themselves justify an investigation of whether an agreement exempted by Regulation 123/85 is incompatible with the conditions of Article 85(3) of the Treaty. For the time being, the Commission does not propose to carry out investigations into private practices under Article 10, point 3 or 4 of Regulation 123/85 where the following circumstances obtain (this does not include intervention by the Commission in particular cases):

1. Price differentials between Member States (Article 10, point 3 in association with Article 13, point 11)

Recommended net prices for resale to final consumers (list prices) of a motor vehicle within the contract programme in one Member State and of the same or a corresponding motor vehicle in another Member State differ, and

(a) the difference expressed in ECU does not exceed 12 per cent. of the lower price, or, over a period of less than one year, exceeds that percentage either
— by not more than a further 6 per cent. of the list price, or
— only in respect of an insignificant portion of the motor vehicles within the contract programme, or

(b) the difference is to be attributed, following analysis of the objective datas, to the fact that
— the purchaser of the vehicle in one of those Member States must pay taxes, charges or fees amounting in total to more than 100 per cent. of the net price, or
— the freedom to set the price or margin for the resale of the vehicle is directly or indirectly subject in one of those Member States to restriction by national measures lasting longer than one year;

and that such measures do not represent infringements of the Treaty.

Insofar as they are public knowledge, prices net of discounts shall replace recommended net prices. Particular account will be taken, for an appropriate period, or alterations of the parities within the European Monetary System or fluctuations in exchange rates in a Member State.

2. Price differentials between passenger cars within the contract programme and corresponding cars (Article 10, point 4 in association with Article 5(1), point 2(d) and Article 13, point 10)

When selling to a dealer a passenger car corresponding to a model within the contract programme, the supplier charges an objectively justifiable supplement on account of special distribution costs and any differences in equipment and specification.

In a Member State where pricing is affected in the manner described at II1(b) above, the supplier charges a further supplement; however, he does not exceed the price which would be charged in similar cases in that Member State not subject to such effects in which the lowest price net of tax is recommended for the sale to a final consumer of that vehicle within the contract programme (or, as the case may be, of a corresponding vehicle).

3. Where the limits indicated above are exceeded, the Commission may open a procedure on its own initiative under Article 10, points 3 and 4 of Regulation 123/85; whether it does so or not will depend mainly on the results of investigations that may be made as to whether the exempted agreement is in fact the principal cause of actual price differences in the meaning of Article 10, point 3 or 4, as the case may be, has led to a partitioning of the common market or is, in the light of experience, liable to do so. Price comparisons made in this connection will take account of differences in equipment and specification and in ancillary items such as the extent of the guarantee, delivery services or registration formalities.

III

1. The rights of Member States, persons and associations of persons to make applications to the Commission under Article 3 of Council Regulation No. 17 (i.e. complaints) are unaffected. The Commission will examine such complaints with all due diligence.

Book One: Part IV—Vertical Agreements

2. This notice is without prejudice to any finding of the Court of Justice of the European Communities or of courts of the Member States.

3. Any withdrawal of or amendment to this notice will be effected by publication in the *Official Journal of the European Communities.*

E. THE ASSESSMENT OF SELECTIVE DISTRIBUTION AGREEMENTS

1. Nature of the product which justifies selective distribution

IBM PC 210 (para. 14)
Grohe Sales System 222 (para. 15)
Ideal Standard Sales System 223
Villeroy & Boch 244 (paras. 21–24)*
Vichy 334 (para. 6–7)
Yves Saint Laurent 345 (para. 5)
Vichy v. *Commission* T29 (ground 69–70)
FEDETAB v. *Commission* 80 (ground 138)
L'Oréal v. *De Nieuwe AMCK* 81 (ground 16)
AMP v. *Binon* 119 (ground 32)*
ETA v. *DKI* 126 (ground 16)
Metro v. *Commission II* 134 (grounds 53–56)*

2. Selection of the dealer

2.1. Qualitative criteria (experience, professional qualifications, specialisation, after sales service)

Omega 33 (paras. 2, 5)
BMW 82 (paras. 13, 20–22)
SABA I 99 (paras. 27–28)
Junghans 109 (paras. 22–23)
Krups 155
Murat 200 (paras. 6–7, 13–15)
SABA II 208
IBM PC 210 (para. 16)
Grundig 232 (para. 2)
D'Ieteren 329
Villeroy & Boch 244 (paras. 24–28)
Vichy 334 (para. 18)
Yves Saint Laurent 345 (page 25, para. 5)
Metro v. *Commission I* 58 (grounds 20, 34–37)*
L'Oréal v. *De Nieuwe AMCK* 81 (grounds 15–16)
Salonia v. *Poidomani & Baglieri* 85 (grounds 21–27)
AMP v. *Binon* 119 (grounds 31–34)
Metro v. *Commission II* 134 (grounds 40–47)

2.2. Quantitative criteria

2.2.1. Related to population in allotted territory

Omega 33 (paras. 2, 5)*
BMW 82 (paras. 13–15, 24, 30)
Hasselblad 173 (paras. 35, 63–66)*
AEG/Telefunken 179 (paras. 61, 64)
Ivoclar 234 (paras. 29–30)
Vichy 334 (para. 18)
Vichy v. *Commission* T29 (grounds 67–68)
L'Oréal v. *De Nieuwe AMCK* 81 (ground 17)

2.2.2 Related to the turnover of the distributor

SABA I 99 (paras. 29, 40)
SABA II 208
Ivoclar 234
Yves Saint Laurent 345 (para. 6B)
Metro v. *Commission I* 58 (grounds 37, 39–50)*
L'Oréal v. *De Nieuwe AMCK* 81 (ground 16)

2.2.3. Stocking requirements

BMW 82 (para. 13)
SABA I 99 (paras. 29, 40)
Krups 155
Murat 200 (para. 7)
SABA II 208
Grundig 232 (para. 3)*
Villeroy & Boch 244 (paras. 29, 31–33)*
Yves Saint Laurent 345 (para. 6C)
L'Oréal v. *De Nieuwe AMCK* 81 (ground 16)

3. Procedure for the authorisation of the dealer

3.1. Objective

AEG/Telefunken 179 (paras. 56, 61–64)
SABA II 208*
Grundig 232 (para. 29)
Yves Saint Laurent (para. 6A)

3.2. Not related to prices

AEG/Telefunken 179 (paras. 57–58)

3.2.1. Non-discriminatory application of the criteria

AEG/Telefunken 179 (para. 54)
AEG v. *Commission* 100 (grounds 36–39)
AMP v. *Binon* 119 (ground 37)*
Metro v. *Commission II* 134 (grounds 72–74)

3.2.2. Refusal to supply

Ford Werke–Interim measures 182 (paras. 11–15, 35–37)

Part IV—3 Selective Distribution Agreements

Ford Werke AG 199 (paras. 21–25, 36–46)*
Peugeot 250 (paras. 38–41)
Ford v. Commission 123*

3.2.3. Impeding parallel trade in the framework of a selective distribution

Kawasaki 141 (paras. 4–25, 43–46)*
Ford Werke–Interim Measures 182 (paras. 11–15, 35–37)
National Panasonic 186 (paras. 23–39, 48–54)
Ford Werke AG 199 (paras. 21–25, 36–46)
Peugeot 250 (para. 38)*
Eco System 344a
Fiat 14th Comp. Rep. (paras. 70–71)
VW 19th Comp. Rep. (para. 48)
Dior & Lancôme. 4th Comp. Rep. (para. 74)
Peugeot v. Commission T3
Peugeot v. Commission T17

F. FEATURES AND CLAUSES COMMON IN SELECTIVE DISTRIBUTION AGREEMENTS

1. Territorial restrictions

1.1. Exclusivity

BMW 82 (paras. 15–16, 26–27, 30)
Ford Werke AG 199 (paras. 14, 30–34)
Ivoclar 234
Peugeot 250 (paras. 12, 34)*
Charles Jourdan 298 (paras. 34–35)

1.2. No active sales policy outside agreed territory

BMW 82 (paras. 17, 27, 30)
Junghans 109 (paras. 29, 33)
Kawasaki 141 (paras. 4–25, 43–46)
Ivoclar 234
Peugeot 250 (paras. 12, 34)*
Yves Saint Laurent 345 (para. 6D)

1.3. Export bans

1.3.1. Between Member States

Dupont de Nemours 71 (para. III)
Deutsche Philips 73
Junghans 109
BMW Belgium 126 (paras. 3–5, 19–21)
Kawasaki 141 (paras. 4–25, 43–46)*
Hasselblad 173 (paras. 35, 59, 61, 69)
Ford Werke–Interim measures 182 (paras. 11–15, 35–37)*
National Panasonic 186 (paras. 23–29, 48–54)
Ford Werke AG 199 (paras. 21, 23–25, 36–46)
ADOX. 2nd Comp. Rep. (para. 43)

BMW Belgium v. Commission 69 (grounds 20–34)*
Ford v. Commission 123

1.3.2. Outside the EEC

SABA I 99 (para. 35)
Junghans 109 (para. 24)

1.4 Control of sales by principal
Yves Saint Laurent 345 (para. 7)*

2. Clauses relating to the customer to which the dealer may sell

2.1. Inherent restriction (horizontal sales only to other authorised dealers)

Omega 33 (para. 9)*
BMW 82 (para. 14)
SABA I 99 (paras. 23, 31, 34, 49)
Junghans 109 (paras. 7, 21)
BMW Belgium 126 (paras. 7–11)
Hasselblad 173 (paras. 33, 59)
Ford Werke AG 199 (paras. 31–33)
Murat 200 (para. 10)
SABA II 208
Grundig 232 (para. 3)
Villeroy & Boch 244 (para. 34)
Bayonox 313 (para. 93)
Vichy 334 (para. 10)
Metro v. Commission I 58 (grounds 26–27)
Hasselblad v. Commission 107 (ground 46)

2.2. Separation of wholesale and retail level

Dupont de Nemours 71 (para. III)
Deutsche Philips 73
SABA I 99 (para. 34)
Grundig 232 (para. 2.f)
Villeroy & Boch 244 (para. 36)
Yves Saint Laurent 345 (para. 5)
Metro v. Commission I 58 (grounds 26–30)*

2.3. Sales to specific types of customers

Omega 33 (para. 9)
SABA 99 (paras. 15, 34)
Distillers-Victuallers 156 (paras. 12–17)
Grohe Sales System 222 (paras. 16, 20–22)
Ideal Standard Sales System 223*
Villeroy & Boch 244 (paras. 37–38)
Peugeot 250 (paras. 13, 35)
Yves Saint Laurent 345 (para. 5)
Metro v. Commission (I) 58 (grounds 31–33)*

3. Clauses relating to the product which the dealer is authorised to sell

3.1. Exclusive purchase obligations imposed on the dealer

Omega 33 (para. 9)
Olio-Fiat 17th Comp. Rep. (para. 84)

3.2. Non-competition clause

BMW 82 (paras. 18, 28, 30)
Ford Werke AG 199 (paras. 13, 31–34)
Peugeot 250 (paras. 12, 35)*
Charles Jourdan 298 (paras. 15, 31)

3.3. Guarantee and after-sales service

Omega 33 (paras. 2, 5)
Zanussi 139 (paras. 10–13)*
Hasselblad 173 (paras. 30–32, 52–55)*
Ideal Standard Sales System 223 (para. 16)
D'leteren 329 (para. 11)
Constructa 4th Comp. Rep. (para. 109)
7th Comp. Rep. (paras. 17–20)
Moulinex 10th Comp. Rep. (para. 122)
Matsushita 12th Comp. Rep. (para. 77)
Ford Germany 13th Comp. Rep. (paras. 104–106)
16th Comp. Rep. (para. 56)
Hasselblad v. *Commission* 107 (grounds 33–34)
ETA v. *DKI* 126 (grounds 12–14)*

3.4. Obligation to sell product in specified packaging

Du Pont de Nemours Germany 71

3.5 Obligation not to sell incompatible products

Yves Saint Laurent 345 (pages 25, 26, para. 5)

4. Clauses relating to the prices of the contract products

4.1. Effect on prices resulting from selective distribution

Grohe Sales System 222 (paras. 26, 27)
Ideal Standard Sales System 223
AEG v. *Commission* 100 (grounds 42–43)*

4.2. Resale price maintenance

Omega 33 (para. 8)
Junghans 109 (para. 17)
Hasselblad 173 (paras. 36–41, 65–66, 69–70)*
Interlübcke 15th Comp. Rep. (para. 61)
Italian Specs 15th Comp. Rep. (paras. 66–67)
Vlaamse Reisbureaus 144 (ground 17)*
Louis Erauw v. *La Hesbignonne* 149 (ground 15)

CHAPTER 4

AGENCY AGREEMENTS

A. CASES ON AGENCY AGREEMENTS

Pittsburgh Corning 63
European Sugar Industry 69
IMA Rules 158 (paras. 61–63, 71–72)
Fisher Price 275 (para. 18)
ARG/Unipart 278
Eco System 344a (paras. 26–32)
Suiker Unie v. *Commission* 48 (grounds 473–498)*
Vlaamse Reisbureaus 144 (grounds 19–20)*

B. TEXT OF NOTICE ON AGENCY AGREEMENTS
(reproduced opposite)

Part IV—4   Agency Agreements

Notice of December 24, 1962,

On exclusive agency contracts made with commercial agents

(J.O. 139/62)

I. The Commission considers that contracts made with commercial agents, in which those agents undertake, for a specified part of the territory of the Common Market:
— to negotiate transactions on behalf of an enterprise, or
— to conclude transactions in the name and on behalf of an enterprise, or
— to conclude transactions in their own name and on behalf of this enterprise,
are not covered by the prohibition laid down in Article 85, paragraph (1) of the Treaty.

It is essential in this case that the contracting party, described as a commercial agent, should, in fact, be such, by the nature of his functions and that he should neither undertake nor engage in activities proper to an independent trader in the course of commercial operations. The Commission regards as the decisive criterion, which distinguishes the commercial agent from the independent trader, the agreement—express or implied—which deals with responsibility for the financial risks bound up with the sale or with the performance of the contract. Thus the Commission's assessment is not governed by the way the "representative" is described. Except for the usual *del credere* guarantee, a commercial agent must not, by the nature of his functions, assume any risk resulting from the transaction. If he does assume such risks his function becomes economically akin to that of an independent trader and he must therefore be treated as such for the purposes of the rules of competition. In such circumstances exclusive agency contracts must be regarded as agreements made with independent traders.

The Commission considers that an "independent trader" is most likely to be involved where the contracting party described as a commercial agent:
— is required to keep or does in fact keep, as his own property, a considerable stock of the products covered by the contract, or
— is required to organise, maintain or ensure at his own expense a substantial service to customers free of charge, or does in fact organise, maintain or ensure such a service, or
— can determine or does in fact determine prices or terms of business.

II. In contrast to what is envisaged in this announcement about contracts made with commercial agents, the possibility that Article 85, paragraph (1), may be applicable to exclusive agency contracts with independent traders cannot be ruled out. In the case of such exclusive contracts the restriction of competition lies either in the limitation of supply, when the vendor undertakes to supply a given product only to one purchaser, or in the limitation of demand, when the purchaser undertakes to obtain a given product only from one vendor. In the case of reciprocal undertakings there will be such restrictions of competition on both sides. The question whether a restriction of competition of this nature is liable to affect trade between Member States depends on the circumstances of the case.

On the other hand, in the Commission's opinion, the conditions for the prohibition laid down in Article 85, paragraph (1), are not fulfilled by exclusive agency contracts made with commercial agents, since they have neither the object nor the effect of preventing, restricting or distorting competition within the common market. The commercial agent only performs an auxiliary function in the commodity market. In that market he acts on the instructions and in the interest of the enterprise on whose behalf he is operating. Unlike the independent trader, he himself is neither a purchaser nor a vendor, but seeks purchasers or vendors in the interest of the other party to the contract, who is the person doing the buying or selling. In this type of exclusive representation contract, the selling or buying enterprise does not cease to be a competitor; it merely uses an auxiliary, *i.e.* the commercial agent, to dispose of or acquire products on the market.

The legal status of commercial agents is determined, more or less uniformly, by statute in most of the member countries and by case law in others. The characteristic feature which all commercial agents have in common is their function as auxiliaries in the negotiation of business deals. The powers of commercial agents are subject to the rules laid down in civil law on "mandate" and "procuration." Within the limits of those provisions the other party to the contract—who is the person selling or buying—is free to decide the product and the territory in respect of which he is willing to assign those functions to his agent.

Apart from the competitive situation on those markets where the commercial agent functions as an auxiliary to the other party to the contract, one has to consider the particular market on which commercial agents offer their services for the negotiation or conclusion of transactions. The obligation assumed by the agent—to work exclusively for one principal for a certain period of time—entails a limitation of supply on that market; the obligation assumed by the other party to the contract—to appoint him sole agent for a given territory—involves a limitation of demand on the market. Nevertheless, the Commission views these restrictions as a result of the special obligation between the commercial agent and his principal to protect each other's interests and therefore considers that they involve no restriction of competition.

The object of this Notice is to give enterprises some indication of the consideration by which the Commission will be guided when interpreting Article 85(1) of the Treaty and applying it to exclusive dealing contracts with commercial agents. The situation having thus been clarified, it will as a general rule no longer be useful for enterprises to obtain negative clearance for the agreements mentioned, nor will it be necessary to have the legal position established through a Commission decision on an individual case; this also means that notification will no longer be necessary for agreements of this type. This Notice is without prejudice to any interpretation that may be given by other competent authorities and in particular by the courts.

C. CASES ON THE INTERPRETATION OF THE NOTICE

Pittsburgh Corning 63
European Sugar Industry 69
IMA Rules 158 (para. 62)
Fisher Price 275 (para. 18)
ARG/Unipart 278 (para. 26)

CHAPTER 5

FRANCHISING AGREEMENTS

A. CASES ON FRANCHISING AGREEMENTS

Yves Rocher 265
Pronuptia 266
Computerland 270
ServiceMaster 296
Charles Jourdan 298
16th Comp. Rep. (paras. 107–111)
19th Comp.Rep. (para. 20)
Pronuptia v. *Schillgallis* 129

B. TEXT OF REGULATION 4087/88 (reproduced below)

Commission Regulation 4087/88 of November 30, 1988

On the application of Article 85(3) of the Treaty to categories of franchise agreements

([1988] O.J. L359/46)

THE COMMISSION OF THE EUROPEAN COMMUNITIES,

Having regard to the Treaty establishing the European Economic Community,

Having regard to Council Regulation 19/65 of 2 March 1965 on the application of Article 85(3) of the Treaty to certain categories of agreements and concerted practices, as last amended by the Act of Accession of Spain and Portugal, and in particular Article 1 thereof,

Part IV—5 Franchising Agreements

Having published a draft of this Regulation,

Having consulted the Advisory Committee on Restrictive Practices and Dominant Positions,

Whereas:

(1) Regulation 19/65 empowers the Commission to apply Article 85(3) of the Treaty by Regulation to certain categories of bilateral exclusive agreements falling within the scope of Article 85(1) which either have as their object the exclusive distribution or exclusive purchase of goods, or include restrictions imposed in relation to the assignment or use of industrial property rights.

(2) Franchise agreements consist essentially of licences of industrial or intellectual property rights relating to trade marks or signs and know-how, which can be combined with restrictions relating to supply or purchase of goods.

(3) Several types of franchise can be distinguished according to their object: industrial franchise concerns the manufacturing of goods, distribution franchise concerns the sale of goods, and service franchise concerns the supply of services.

(4) It is possible on the basis of the experience of the Commission to define categories of franchise agreements which fall under Article 85(1) but can normally be regarded as satisfying the conditions laid down in Article 85(3). This is the case for franchise agreements whereby one of the parties supplies goods or provides services to end users. On the other hand, industrial franchise agreements should not be covered by this Regulation. Such agreements, which usually govern relationships between producers, present different characteristics than the other types of franchise. They consist of manufacturing licences based on patents and/or technical know-how, combined with trademark licences. Some of them may benefit from other block exemptions if they fulfil the necessary conditions.

(5) This Regulation covers franchise agreements between two undertakings, the franchisor and the franchisee, for the retailing of goods or the provision of services to end users, or a combination of these activities, such as the processing or adaptation of goods to fit specific needs of their customers. It also covers cases where the relationship between franchisor and franchisees is made through a third undertaking, the master franchisee. It does not cover wholesale franchise agreements because of the lack of experience of the Commission in that field.

(6) Franchise agreements as defined in this Regulation can fall under Article 85(1). They may in particular affect intra-Community trade where they are concluded between undertakings from different Member States or where they form the basis of a network which extends beyond the boundaries of a single Member State.

(7) Franchise agreements as defined in this Regulation normally improve the distribution of goods and/or the provision of services as they give franchisors the possibility of establishing a uniform network with limited investments, which may assist the entry of new competitors on the market, particularly in the case of small and medium-sized undertakings, thus increasing interbrand competition. They also allow independent traders to set up outlets more rapidly and with higher chance of success than if they had to do so without the franchisor's experience and assistance. They have therefore the possibility of competing more efficiently with large distribution undertakings.

(8) As a rule, franchise agreements also allow consumers and other end users a fair share of the resulting benefit, as they combine the advantage of a uniform network with the existence of traders personally interested in the efficient operation of their business. The homogeneity of the network and the constant cooperation between the franchisor and the franchisees ensures a constant quality of the products and services. The favourable effect of franchising on interbrand competition and the fact that consumers are free to deal with any franchisee in the network guarantees that a reasonable part of the resulting benefits will be passed on to the consumers.

(9) This Regulation must define the obligations restrictive of competition which may be included in franchise agreements. This is the case in particular for the granting of an exclusive territory to the franchisees combined with the prohibition on actively seeking customers outside that territory, which allows them to concentrate their efforts on their allotted territory. The same applies to the granting of an exclusive territory to a master franchisee combined with the obligation not to conclude franchise agreements with third parties outside that territory. Where the franchisees

sell or use in the process of providing services, goods manufactured by the franchisor or according to its instructions and or bearing its trade mark, an obligation on the franchisees not to sell, or use in the process of the provision of services, competing goods, makes it possible to establish a coherent network which is identified with the franchised goods. However, this obligation should only be accepted with respect to the goods which form the essential subject-matter of the franchise. It should notably not relate to accessories or spare parts for these goods.

(10) The obligations referred to above thus do not impose restrictions which are not necessary for the attainment of the above-mentioned objectives. In particular, the limited territorial protection granted to the franchisees is indispensable to protect their investment.

(11) It is desirable to list in the Regulation a number of obligations that are commonly found in franchise agreements and are normally not restrictive of competition and to provide that if, because of the particular economic or legal circumstances, they fall under Article 85(1), they are also covered by the exemption. This list, which is not exhaustive, includes in particular clauses which are essential either to preserve the common identity and reputation of the network or to prevent the know-how made available and the assistance given by the franchisor from benefiting competitors.

(12) The Regulation must specify the conditions which must be satisfied for the exemption to apply. To guarantee that competition is not eliminated for a substantial part of the goods which are the subject of the franchise, it is necessary that parallel imports remain possible. Therefore, cross deliveries between franchisees should always be possible. Furthermore, where a franchise network is combined with another distribution system, franchisees should be free to obtain supplies from authorized distributors. To better inform consumers, thereby helping to ensure that they receive a fair share of the resulting benefits, it must be provided that the franchisee shall be obliged to indicate its status as an independent undertaking, by any appropriate means which does not jeopardize the common identity of the franchised network. Furthermore, where the franchisees have to honour guarantees for the franchisor's goods, this obligation should also apply to goods supplied by the franchisor, other franchisees or other agreed dealers.

(13) The Regulation must also specify restrictions which may not be included in franchise agreements if these are to benefit from the exemption granted by the Regulation, by virtue of the fact that such provisions are restrictions falling under Article 85(1) for which there is no general presumption that they will lead to the positive effects required by Article 85(3). This applies in particular to market sharing between competing manufacturers, to clauses unduly limiting the franchisee's choice of suppliers or customers, and to cases where the franchisee is restricted in determining its prices. However, the franchisor should be free to recommend prices to the franchisees, where it is not prohibited by national laws and to the extent that it does not lead to concerted practices for the effective application of these prices.

(14) Agreements which are not automatically covered by the exemption because they contain provisions that are not expressly exempted by the Regulation and not expressly excluded from exemption may nonetheless generally be presumed to be eligible for application of Article 85(3). It will be possible for the Commission rapidly to establish whether this is the case for a particular agreement. Such agreements should therefore be deemed to be covered by the exemption provided for in this Regulation where they are notified to the Commission and the Commission does not oppose the application of the exemption within a specified period of time.

(15) If individual agreements exempted by this Regulation nevertheless have effects which are incompatible with Article 85(3), in particular as interpreted by the administrative practice of the Commission and the case law of the Court of Justice, the Commission may withdraw the benefit of the block exemption. This applies in particular where competition is significantly restricted because of the structure of the relevant market.

(16) Agreements which are automatically exempted pursuant to this Regulation need not be notified. Undertakings may nevertheless in a particular case request a decision pursuant to Council Regulation No 17 as last amended by the Act of Accession of Spain and Portugal.

(17) Agreements may benefit from the provisions either of this Regulation or of

Part IV—5 Franchising Agreements

another Regulation, according to their particular nature and provided that they fulfil the necessary conditions of application. They may not benefit from a combination of the provisions of this Regulation with those of another block exemption Regulation,

HAS ADOPTED THIS REGULATION:

Article 1

1. Pursuant to Article 85(3) of the Treaty and subject to the provisions of this Regulation, it is hereby declared that Article 85(1) of the Treaty shall not apply to franchise agreements to which two undertakings are party, which include one or more of the restrictions listed in Article 2.

2. The exemption provided for in paragraph 1 shall also apply to master franchise agreements to which two undertakings are party. Where applicable, the provisions of this Regulation concerning the relationship between franchisor and franchisee shall apply *mutatis mutandis* to the relationship between franchisor and master franchisee and between master franchisee and franchisee.

3. For the purposes of this Regulation:
(a) 'franchise' means a package of industrial or intellectual property rights relating to trade marks, trade names, shop signs, utility models, designs, copyrights, know-how or patents, to be exploited for the resale of goods or the provision of services to end users;
(b) "franchise agreement" means an agreement whereby one undertaking, the franchisor, grants the other, the franchisee, in exchange for direct or indirect financial consideration, the right to exploit a franchise for the purposes of marketing specified types of goods and/or services; it includes at least obligations relating to:
— the use of a common name or shop sign and a uniform presentation of contract premises and/or means of transport,
— the communication by the franchisor to the franchisee of know-how,
— the continuing provision by the franchisor to the franchisee of commercial or technical assistance during the life of the agreement;
(c) "master franchise agreement" means an agreement whereby one undertaking, the franchisor, grants the other, the master franchisee, in exchange of direct or indirect financial consideration, the right to exploit a franchise for the purposes of concluding franchise agreements with third parties, the franchisees;
(d) "franchisor's goods" means goods produced by the franchisor or according to its instructions, and/or bearing the franchisor's name or trade mark;
(e) "contract premises" means the premises used for the exploitation of the franchise or, when the franchise is exploited outside those premises, the base from which the franchise operates the means of transport used for the exploitation of the franchise (contract means of transport);
(f) "know-how" means a package of non-patented practical information, resulting from experience and testing by the franchisor, which is secret, substantial and identified;
(g) "secret" means that the know-how, as a body or in the precise configuration and assembly of its components, is not generally known or easily accessible; it is not limited in the narrow sense that each individual component of the know-how should be totally unknown or unobtainable outside the franchisor's business;
(h) "substantial" means that the know-how includes information which is of importance for the sale of goods or the provision of services to end users, and in particular for the presentation of goods for sale, the processing of goods in connection with the provision of services, methods of dealing with customers, and administration and financial management; the know-how must be useful for the franchisee by being capable, at the date of conclusion of the agreement, of improving the competitive position of the franchisee, in particular by improving the franchisee's performance or helping it to enter a new market;
(i) "identified" means that the know-how must be described in a sufficiently comprehensive manner so as to make it possible to verify that it fulfils the criteria of secrecy and substantiality; the description of the know-how can either be set out in the franchise agreement or in a separate document or recorded in any other appropriate form.

Article 2

The exemption provided for in Article 1 shall apply to the following restrictions of competition:
(a) an obligation on the franchisor, in a defined area of the common market, the contract territory, not to:

— grant the right to exploit all or part of the franchise to third parties,
— itself exploit the franchise, or itself market the goods or services which are the subject-matter of the franchise under a similar formula.
— itself supply the franchisor's goods to third parties;
(b) an obligation on the master franchisee not to conclude franchise agreement with third parties outside its contract territory;
(c) an obligation on the franchisee to exploit the franchise only from the contract premises;
(d) an obligation on the franchisee to refrain, outside the contract territory, from seeking customers for the goods or the services which are the subject-matter of the franchise;
(e) an obligation on the franchisee not to manufacture, sell or use in the course of the provision of services, goods competing with the franchisor's goods which are the subject-matter of the franchise; where the subject-matter of the franchise is the sale or use in the course of the provision of services both certain types of goods and spare parts or accessories therefor, that obligation may not be imposed in respect of these spare parts or accessories.

Article 3

1. Article 1 shall apply notwithstanding the presence of any of the following obligations on the franchisee, in so far as they are necessary to protect the franchisor's industrial or intellectual property rights or to maintain the common identity and reputation of the franchised network:
(a) to sell, or use in the course of the provision of services, exclusively goods matching minimum objective quality specifications laid down by the franchisor;
(b) to sell, or use in the course of the provision of services, goods which are manufactured only by the franchisor or by third parties designed by it, where it is impracticable, owing to the nature of the goods which are the subject-matter of the franchise, to apply objective quality specifications;
(c) not to engage, directly or indirectly, in any similar business in a territory where it would compete with a member of the franchised network, including the franchisor; the franchisee may be held to this obligation after termination of the agreement, for a reasonable period which may not exceed one year, in the territory where it has exploited the franchise;
(d) not to acquire financial interests in the capital of a competing undertaking, which would give the franchisee the power to influence the economic conduct of such undertaking;
(e) to sell the goods which are the subject-matter of the franchise only to end users, to other franchisees and to resellers within other channels of distribution supplied by the manufacturer of these goods or with its consent;
(f) to use its best endeavours to sell the goods or provide the services that are the subject-matter of the franchise; to offer for sale a minimum range of goods, achieve a minimum turnover, plan its orders in advance, keep minimum stocks and provide customer and warranty services;
(g) to pay to the franchisor a specified proportion of its revenue for advertising and itself carry out advertising for the nature of which it shall obtain the franchisor's approval.

2. Article 1 shall apply notwithstanding the presence of any of the following obligations on the franchisee:
(a) not to disclose to third parties the know-how provided by the franchisor; the franchisee may be held to this obligation after termination of the agreement;
(b) to communicate to the franchisor any experience gained in exploiting the franchise and to grant it, and other franchisees, a non-exclusive licence for the know-how resulting from that experience;
(c) to inform the franchisor of infringements of licensed industrial or intellectual property rights, to take legal action against infringers or to assist the franchisor in any legal actions against infringers:
(d) not to use know-how licensed by the franchisor for purposes other than the exploitation of the franchise; the franchisee may be held to this obligation after termination of the agreement;
(e) to attend or have its staff attend training courses arranged by the franchisor;
(f) to apply the commercial methods devised by the franchisor, including any subsequent modification thereof, and use the licensed industrial or intellectual property rights;
(g) to comply with the franchisor's standards for the equipment and presentation of the contract premises and/or means of transport;
(h) to allow the franchisor to carry out checks of the contract premises and/or means of transport, including the goods

sold and the services provided, and the inventory and accounts of the franchisee;
(i) not without the franchisor's consent to change the location of the contract premises;
(j) not without the franchisor's consent to assign the rights and obligations under the franchise agreement.

3. In the event that, because of particular circumstances, obligations referred to in paragraph 2 fall within the scope of Article 85(1), they shall also be exempted even if they are not accompanied by any of the obligations exempted by Article 1.

Article 4

The exemption provided for in Article 1 shall apply on condition that:
(a) the franchisee is free to obtain the goods that are the subject-matter of the franchise from other franchisees; where such goods are also distributed through another network of authorized distributors, the franchisee must be free to obtain the goods from the latter;
(b) where the franchisor obliges the franchisee to honour guarantees for the franchisor's goods, that obligation shall apply in respect of such goods supplied by any member of the franchised network or other distributors which give a similar guarantee, in the common market;
(c) the franchisee is obliged to indicate its status as an independent undertaking; this indication shall however not interfere with the common identity of the franchised network resulting in particular from the common name or shop sign and uniform appearance of the contract premises and/or means of transport.

Article 5

The exemption granted by Article 1 shall not apply where:
(a) undertakings producing goods or providing services which are identical or are considered by users as equivalent in view of their characteristics, price and intended use, enter into franchise agreements in respect of such goods or services;
(b) without prejudice to Article 2(e) and Article 3(1)(b), the franchisee is prevented from obtaining supplies of goods of a quality equivalent to those offered by the franchisor;
(c) without prejudice to Article 2(e), the franchisee is obliged to sell, or use in the process of providing services, goods manufactured by the franchisor or third parties designated by the franchisor and the franchisor refuses, for reasons other than protecting the franchisor's industrial or intellectual property rights, or maintaining the common identity and reputation of the franchised network to designate as authorized manufacturers third parties proposed by the franchisee;
(d) the franchisee is prevented from continuing to use the licensed know-how after termination of the agreement where the know-how has become generally known or easily accessible, other than by breach of an obligation by the franchisee;
(e) the franchisee is restricted by the franchisor, directly or indirectly, in the determination of sale prices for the goods or services which are the subject-matter of the franchise, without prejudice to the possibility for the franchisor of recommending sale prices;
(f) the franchisor prohibits the franchisee from challenging the validity of the industrial or intellectual property rights which form part of the franchise, without prejudice to the possibility for the franchisor of terminating the agreement in such a case;
(g) franchisees are obliged not to supply within the common market the goods or services which are the subject-matter of the franchise to end users because of their place of residence.

Article 6

1. The exemption provided for in Article 1 shall also apply to franchise agreements which fulfil the conditions laid down in Article 4 and include obligations restrictive of competition which are not covered by Articles 2 and 3(3) and do not fall within the scope of Article 5, on condition that the agreements in question are notified to the Commission in accordance with the provisions of Commission Regulation No 27 and that the Commission does not oppose such exemption within a period of six months.

2. The period of six months shall run from the date on which the notification is received by the Commission. Where, however, the notification is made by registered post, the period shall run from the date shown on the postmark of the place of posting.

3. Paragraph 1 shall apply only if:
(a) express reference is made to this Article in the notification or in a communication accompanying it; and

(b) the information furnished with the notification is complete and in accordance with the facts.

4. The benefit of paragraph 1 can be claimed for agreements notified before the entry into force of this Regulation by submitting a communication to the Commission referring expressly to this Article and to the notification. Paragraphs 2 and 3 (b) shall apply *mutatis mutandis*.

5. The Commission may oppose exemption. It shall oppose exemption if it receives a request to do so from a Member State within three months of the forwarding to the Member State of the notification referred to in paragraph 1 or the communication referred to in paragraph 4. This request must be justified on the basis of considerations relating to the competition rules of the Treaty.

6. The Commission may withdraw its opposition to the exemption at any time. However, where that opposition was raised at the request of a Member State, it may be withdrawn only after consideration of the advisory Committee on Restrictive Practices and Dominant Positions.

7. If the opposition is withdrawn because the undertakings concerned have shown that the conditions of Article 85(3) are fulfilled, the exemption shall apply from the date of the notification.

8. If the opposition is withdrawn because the undertakings concerned have amended the agreement so that the conditions of Article 85(3) are fulfilled, the exemption shall apply from the date on which the amendments take effect.

9. If the Commission opposes exemption and its opposition is not withdrawn, the effects of the notification shall be governed by the provisions of Regulation No 17.

Article 7

1. Information acquired pursuant to Article 6 shall be used only for the purposes of this Regulation.

2. The Commission and the authorities of the Member States, their officials and other servants shall not disclose information acquired by them pursuant to this Regulation of a kind that is covered by the obligation of professional secrecy.

3. Paragraphs 1 and 2 shall not prevent publication of general information or surveys which do not contain information relating to particular undertakings or associations of undertakings.

Article 8

The Commission may withdraw the benefit of this Regulation, pursuant to Article 7 of Regulation No 19/65/EEC, where it finds in a particular case that an agreement exempted by this Regulation nevertheless has certain effects which are incompatible with the conditions laid down in Article 85(3) of the EEC Treaty, and in particular where territorial protection is awarded to the franchisee and:

(a) access to the relevant market or competition therein is significantly restricted by the cumulative effect of parallel networks of similar agreements established by competing manufacturers or distributors;

(b) the goods or services which are the subject-matter of the franchise do not face, in a substantial part of the common market, effective competition from goods or services which are identical or considered by users as equivalent in view of their characteristics, price and intended use;

(c) the parties, or one of them, prevent end users, because of their place of residence, from obtaining, directly or through intermediaries, the goods or services which are the subject-matter of the franchise within the common market, or use differences in specifications concerning those goods or services in different Member States, to isolate markets;

(d) franchisees engage in concerted practices relating to the sale prices of the goods or services which are the subject-matter of the franchise;

(e) the franchisor uses its right to check the contract premises and means of transport, or refuses its agreement to requests by the franchisee to move the contract premises or assign its rights and obligations under the franchise agreement, for reasons other than protecting the franchisor's industrial or intellectual property rights, maintaining the common identity and reputation of the franchised network or verifying that the franchisee abides by its obligations under the agreement.

Article 9

This Regulation shall enter into force on 1 February 1989.

It shall remain in force until 31 December 1999.
This Regulation shall be binding in its entirety and directly applicable in all Member States.
Done at Brussels, 30 November 1988.

C. CASES ON THE INTERPRETATION OF THE REGULATION

17th Comp. Rep. (paras. 35–37)
18th Comp. Rep. (para. 27)
19th Comp. Rep. (para. 20)

D. CLAUSES COMMONLY STIPULATED IN FRANCHISING AGREEMENTS

1. Clauses relating to the franchisee

1.1. Selection of the franchisee

Yves Rocher 265 (paras. 16, 41)
Pronuptia 266 (paras. 11, 25)
Computerland 270 (paras. 4, 9, 23)
ServiceMaster 296 (para. 21)
Charles Jourdan 298 (paras. 8, 27, 30)
Pronuptia v. Schillgallis 129 (ground 16)*

1.2. Non-competition restraint of trade clauses

1.2.1. Obligation not to engage in competing activities during agreement

Articles 2(e), 3(1)(c),(d)
Yves Rocher 265 (para. 47)
Pronuptia 266 (para. 27)
Computerland 270 (paras. 12, 22)
ServiceMaster 296 (para. 10)
Charles Jourdan 298 (paras. 15, 27)
Pronuptia v. Schillgallis 129 (ground 16)*

1.2.2. Post-term non-competition clause

Articles 3(1)(c), 5(d)
Yves Rocher 265 (paras. 27, 48)
Pronuptia 266 (para. 25)
Computerland 270 (paras. 12, 22)*
Service Master 296 (para. 11)

1.3. Best endeavours clause

Article 3(1)(f)
ServiceMaster 296 (para. 16)

2. Licensing of know-how or trademarks

2.1. Grant of licence

Article 3(2)

Yves Rocher 265 (paras. 22, 39–40)
Pronuptia 266 (paras. 11, 25)
Computerland 270 (paras. 5, 23)
Service Master 296 (paras. 13, 22)
Charles Jourdan 298 (paras. 11-12, 23, 27)
Pronuptia v. Schillgallis 129 (ground 16)*

2.2. Royalties

Yves Rocher 265 (para. 24)
Pronuptia 266 (paras. 11, 26)*
Computerland 270 (paras. 11, 24)
Charles Jourdan 298 (paras. 14)

2.3. Field of use restrictions

Article 3(2)(d)
Yves Rocher 265 (paras. 21, 40)
Pronuptia 266 (para. 26)*
ServiceMaster 296 (para. 8)

2.4. Grant back of improvements

Article 3(2)(b)
Computerland 270 (paras. 5, 23)
ServiceMaster 296 (para. 14)*

2.5. Post-term use ban

Article 5(d)
Computerland 270 (paras. 5, 23)
ServiceMaster 296 (para. 9)*
Charles Jourdan 298 (paras. 21, 27)

2.6. No-challenge clause

Article 5(f)

3. Clauses promoting the uniformity of the franchise network

3.1. Regarding the decoration of the shop

Yves Rocher 265 (paras. 43, 44, 49)
Pronuptia 266 (paras. 11, 25–26)*
Computerland 270 (paras. 8, 23)
ServiceMaster 296 (para. 18)
Charles Jourdan 298 (para. 28)

3.2. Collective advertising provisions

Article 3(1)(g)
Yves Rocher 265 (paras. 43, 44, 49)
Pronuptia 266 (paras. 25, 26)*
Computerland 270 (paras. 8, 23)
ServiceMaster 296 (para. 18)
Pronuptia v. Schillgallis 129 (ground 22)*

3.3. Business methods

Article 3(1)(f), 3(2)(e),(f),(g)

Yves Rocher 265 (paras. 43, 49)
Pronuptia 266 (paras. 11, 25)
Computerland 270 (para. 23)
Pronuptia v. *Schillgallis* 129 (ground 16)*

3.4. Guarantees

Article 4(*b*)

4. Territorial restrictions

4.1. Fixed location of retail outlet

Article 2(*c*), 3(2)(*i*)
Yves Rocher 265 (paras. 18, 42)
Pronuptia 266 (para. 25)
ServiceMaster 296 (paras. 15, 22)
Charles Jourdan 298 (paras. 10, 32)
Pronuptia v. *Schillgallis* 129 (ground 17, 24)*

4.2. Exclusivity in the contract territory

Articles 2(*a*),(*b*), 5(*g*)
Yves Rocher 265 (paras. 19, 54, 63)
Pronuptia 266 (paras. 28, 36)
Computerland 270 (paras. 7, 25)
ServiceMaster 296 (para. 22)
Charles Jourdan 298 (paras. 10, 32)
Pronuptia v. *Schillgallis* 129 (ground 24)*

4.3. Obligation not to open a new outlet outside agreed territory

Article 2(*c*)
Yves Rocher 265 (para. 54)
Pronuptia 266 (para. 28)
Computerland 270 (para. 25)
ServiceMaster 296 (para. 22)
Pronuptia v. *Schillgallis* 129 (ground 24)*

5. Clauses related to the product the franchisee is authorised to sell

5.1. Obligation not to sell competing products in authorised outlet

Article 2(*e*)
Yves Rocher 265 (para. 47)
Computerland 270 (para. 23)*

5.2. Purchase obligations on the franchisee

5.2.1. General

Articles 3(1)(*a*),(*b*), (4)(*a*), (5)(*b*)
Pronuptia 266 (para. 25)
Charles Jourdan 298 (paras. 16, 28)

5.2.2. Obligation to purchase goods of defined quality

Articles 3(1)(*a*), 5(*b*)

Computerland 270 (para. 23)*
ServiceMaster 296 (para. 17)

5.2.3. Exclusive purchasing

Articles 3(1)(*b*), (4)(*a*)
Pronuptia 266 (paras. 11, 25)
Pronuptia v. *Schillgallis* 129 (ground 21)

6. Clauses relating to the customers the franchisee may serve

6.1. Obligation not to sell outside the network

Article 3(1)(*e*)
Yves Rocher 265 (para. 46)
Pronuptia 266 (para. 25)*
Computerland 270 (paras. 26, 34)
Charles Jourdan 298 (paras. 6, 28)

6.2. Restrictions on the franchisee regarding the customers to which it may sell

Article 3(1)(*e*)
Yves Rocher 265 (para. 46)
Pronuptia 266 (paras. 11, 25)
Computerland 270 (paras. 26, 34)*

7. Recommended prices

Article 5(*e*)
Yves Rocher 265 (paras. 30, 51)
Pronuptia 266 (paras. 11, 26)*
Charles Jourdan 298 (paras. 18, 29)

CHAPTER 6

AGREEMENTS PREVENTING PARALLEL TRADE

A. CASES ON AGREEMENTS PREVENTING PARALLEL TRADE

Kodak 29
Pittsburgh Corning 63
GISA 67
WEA/Fillipacchi Music S.A. 68
Dupont de Nemours Germany 71
Deutsche Philips 73
Pabst & Richarz 106
Gerofabrik 111
The Distillers Company 123
BMW Belgium 126
Arthur Bell & Sons 135
Teacher & Sons 136
Zanussi 139
Kawasaki 141
Pioneer 152

Part V—6   Agreements Preventing Parallel Trade

Johnson & Johnson 160
Moët et Chandon (London) Ltd. 172
Hasselblad 173
NAVEWA/ANSEAU 178
Ford Werke–Interim Measures 182
National Panasonic 186
Cafeteros de Colombia 187
Cast-iron & Steel Rolls 198
Ford Werke AG 199
John Deere 226
Sperry New Holland 245
Tipp-Ex 269
Sandoz 272
Fisher Price 275
Konica 277
Bayonox 313
Gosme & Martell 340
Eco System 344a
2nd Comp. Rep. (para. 43)
Ford Germany. 13th Comp. Rep. (paras. 104–106)
Euglucon 13th Comp. Rep. (paras. 107–109)
BIEM-IFPI 13th Comp. Rep. (paras. 147–150)
Citroën 18th Comp. Rep. (para. 56)
AKZO Coatings 19th Comp. Rep. (para. 45)
Dassonville 41
BMW Belgium v. *Commission* 69
Peugeot v. *Commission* T3
Sandoz v. *Commission* 174
Tipp-Ex v. *Commission* 175

B. CLAUSES OR PRACTICES WHICH MAY HAVE THE OBJECT/EFFECT OF PREVENTING PARALLEL TRADE

1. General sales conditions

Kodak 29*
Dupont de Nemours Germany 71
Deutsche Philips 73
The Distillers Company 123
Kawasaki 141 (paras. 2–6, 43–46)*
Johnson & Johnson 160 (paras. 13–23, 29–34)
Moët et Chandon (London) Ltd. 172
Cafeteros de Colombia 187
Zinc 189
Sandoz 272
Bayer/Dental 327
Citroën 18th Comp. Rep. (para. 56)
Sandoz v. *Commission* 174 (grounds 6–12)

2. Circular sent by principal to distributors

WEA/Fillipacchi Music S.A. 68
BMW Belgium 126
Kawasaki 141 (paras. 7–13, 43–46)
Konica 277*
Bayonox 313 (paras. 17–22, 36–38)
Eco System 344a
BMW Belgium v. *Commission* 69 (grounds 20–34)*

3. Pressure exercised by principal on distributor

Pittsburg Corning 63
BMW Belgium 126
Kawasaki 141 (paras. 7–13, 43–46)
Pioneer 152 (paras. 48–49)
Johnson & Johnson 160 (paras. 15–23)
Hasselblad 173
National Panasonic 186
John Deere 226*
Tipp-Ex 269*
Fisher Price 275
Philips Lightbulbs. 1st Comp. Rep. (para. 54)
Euglucon 13th Comp. Rep. (para. 109)
Tipp-Ex v. *Commission* 175 (grounds. 18–24)

4. Discriminatory trading conditions

4.1. Quality marks

NAVEWA/ANSEAU 178

4.2. On grounds of nationality

GISA 67
Luxembourg Car Insurance 15th Comp. Rep. (para. 71)

4.3. State of the product

Pabst & Richarz/BNIA 106*
The Distillers Company 123
Arthur Bell & Sons 135
Teacher & Sons 136
Cafeteros de Colombia 187
IBC 5th Comp. Rep. (para. 33)
12th Comp. Rep. (para. 76)
16th Comp. Rep. (para. 54)
Bayer/Dental 327 (paras. 10–12)

PART V

INDUSTRIAL AND INTELLECTUAL PROPERTY AGREEMENTS

CHAPTER 1

ARTICLES 30, 36, 59
FREE MOVEMENT

A. CASES

Consten & Grundig v. Commission 4
Parke, Davis v. Centrafarm 8
Sirena v. Eda 17
Deutsche Grammophon v. Metro 19
Van Zuylen v. Hag 40
Centrafarm v. Sterling Drug 41
Centrafarm v. Winthrop 42
Commission v. Germany 42a
EMI v. CBS 50
EMI v. CBS 51
EMI v. CBS 52
Terrapin v. Terranova 53
Hoffmann-La Roche v. Centrafarm 63
Centrafarm v. AHP 66
Coditel v. Ciné-Vog 72a
Debauve 72b
Commission v. Ireland 73a
Membran/K-Tel v. Gema 82
Dansk Supermarked v. Imerco 83
Merck v. Stephar, 87
Pfizer v. Eurim-Pharma 89
Polydor v. Harlequin Record Shops 90
IDG v. Beele 91
Keurkoop v. Nancy Kean Gifts 95a
Coditel v. Ciné-Vog 96
Prantl 107a
Kohl v. Ringelhahn 111a
BAT v. Commission 116
Pharmon v. Hoechst 120
Cinéthèque 122a
Miro 122B
Commission v. Germany 137a
Basset v. SACEM 141
Allan & Hanburys v. Generics 148
Bond van Adverteerders 149a
Warner Brothers v. Christiansen 151
Thetford v. Fiamma 152
Bayer v. Sülhöffer 158
Volvo v. Veng 159
Maxicar v. Renault 161
EMI v. Patricia 161a
Royal Pharmaceutical Society 164a

Ministère Public v. Tournier 168
Lucazeau v. SACEM 169
CNL-Sucal v. Hag 177
Cholay 178
Pall v. Dahlhausen 179
Bayern v. Eurim-Pharm 183
Commission v. Italy 191
Commission v. U.K. 192

CHAPTER 2

PATENT LICENSING AGREEMENTS

A. CASES ON PATENT LICENSING

Burroughs/Delplanque 50
Burroughs/Geha 51
Davidson Rubber 56
Raymond/Nagoya 57
Kabelmetal/Luchaire 94
Bronbemaling 95
AOIP/Beyrard 98
Vaessen/Moris 143
Windsurfing International 194
Velcro/Aplix 233
Tetra Pak (I) 289
1st Comp. Rep. (paras. 66, 69–80)
4th Comp. Rep. (paras. 19–32)
5th Comp. Rep. (paras. 10–11, 63)
Peugeot/Zimmern. 6th Comp. Rep. (para. 159)
Pentacon 8th Comp. Rep. (paras. 118–120)
Clutch-type disc brakes 8th Comp. Rep. (para. 121)
Spitzer/Van Hool 12th Comp. Rep. (para. 86)
16th Comp. Rep. (paras. 112–116)
Pilkington/Covina 19th Comp. Rep. (para. 60)
Parke, Davis v. Centrafarm 8
Pharmon v. Hoechst 120
Windsurfing v. Commission 130
Bayer v. Süllhöfer 158
Ottung v. Klee 164

B. TEXT OF REGULATION 2349/84
(reproduced over)

Book One: Part V—Industrial and Intellectual Property Agreements

Commission Regulation 2349/84 of July 23, 1984

On the application of Article 85(3) of the Treaty to certain categories of patent licensing agreements

([1984] O.J. L219/15)

(Amended by [1985] O.J. L113/34)

THE COMMISSION OF THE EUROPEAN COMMUNITIES,

Having regard to the Treaty establishing the European Economic Community,

Having regard to Council Regulation 19/65 of 2 March 1965 on the application of Article 85(3) of the Treaty to certain categories of agreements and concerted practices, as last amended by the Act of Accession of Greece, and in particular Article 1 thereof,

Having published a draft of this Regulation,

After consulting the Advisory Committee on Restrictive Practices and Dominant Positions,

Whereas:

(1) Regulation 19/65 empowers the Commission to apply Article 85(3) of the Treaty by Regulation to certain categories of agreements and concerted practices falling within the scope of Article 85(1) to which only two undertakings are party and which include restrictions imposed in relation to the acquisition or use of industrial property rights, in particular patents, utility models, designs or trade marks, or to the rights arising out of contracts for assignment of, or the right to use, a method of manufacture or knowledge relating to the use or application of industrial processes.

(2) Patent licensing agreements are agreements whereby one undertaking, the holder of a patent (the licensor), permits another undertaking (the licensee) to exploit the patented invention by one or more of the means of exploitation afforded by patent law, in particular manufacture, use or putting on the market.

(3) In the light of experience acquired so far, it is possible to define a category of patent licensing agreements which are capable of falling within the scope of Article 85(1), but which can normally be regarded as satisfying the conditions laid down in Article 85(3). To the extent that patent licensing agreements to which undertakings in only one Member State are party and which concern only one or more patents for that Member State are capable of affecting trade between Member States, it is appropriate to include them in the exempted category.

(4) The present Regulation applies to licences issued in respect of national patents of the Member States, Community patents, or European patents granted for Member States, licenses in respect of utility models or "certificats d'utilité" issued in the Member States, and licences in respect of inventions for which a patent application is made within one year. Where such patent licensing agreements contain obligations relating not only to territories within the common market but also obligations relating to non-member countries, the presence of the latter does not prevent the present Regulation from applying to the obligations relating to territories within the common market.

(5) However, where licensing agreements for non-member countries or for territories which extend beyond the frontiers of the Community have effects within the common market which may fall within the scope of Article 85(1), such agreements should be covered by the Regulation to the same extent as would agreements for territories within the common market.

(6) The Regulation should also apply to agreements concerning the assignment and acquisition of the rights referred to in point 4 above where the risk associated with exploitation remains with the assignor, patent licensing agreements in which the licensor is not the patentee but is authorized by the patentee to grant the licence (as in the case of sub-licences) and patent licensing agreements in which the parties' rights or obligations are assumed by connected undertakings.

(7) The Regulation does not apply to agreements concerning sales alone, which are governed by the provisions of Com-

mission Regulation 1983/83 of 22 June 1983 concerning the application of Article 85(3) of the Treaty to categories of exclusive distribution agreements.

(8) Since the experience so far acquired is inadequate, it is not appropriate to include within the scope of the Regulation patent pools, licensing agreements entered into in connection with joint ventures, reciprocal licensing or licensing agreements in respect of plant breeder's rights. Reciprocal agreements which do not involve any territorial restrictions within the common market should, however, be so included.

(9) On the other hand, it is apropriate to extend the scope of the Regulation to patent licensing agreements which also contain provisions assigning, or granting the right to use, non-patented technical knowledge, since such mixed agreements are commonly concluded in order to allow the transfer of a complex technology containing both patented and non-patented elements. Such agreements can only be regarded as fulfilling the conditions of Article 85(3) for the purposes of this Regulation where the communicated technical knowledge is secret and permits a better exploitation of the licensed patents (know-how). Provisions concerning know-how are covered by the Regulation only in so far as the licensed patents are necessary for achieving the objects of the licensed technology and as long as at least one of the licensed patents remains in force.

(10) It is also appropriate to extend the scope of the Regulation to patent licensing agreements containing ancillary provisions relating to trade marks, subject to ensuring that the trade-mark licence is not used to extend the effects of the patent licence beyond the life of the patents. For this purpose it is necessary to allow the licensee to identify himself within the "licensed territory," *i.e.* the territory covering all or part of the common market where the licensor holds patents which the licensee is authorized to exploit, as the manufacturer of the "licensed product," *i.e.* the product which is the subject-matter of the licensed patent, to avoid his having to enter into a new trade-mark agreement with the licensor when the licensed patents expire in order not to lose the goodwill attaching to the licensed product.

(11) Exclusive licensing agreements, *i.e.* agreements in which the licensor undertakes not to exploit the "licensed invention," *i.e.* the licensed patented invention and any know-how communicated to the licensee, in the licensed territory himself and not to grant any further licences there, are not in themselves incompatible with Article 85(1) where they are concerned with the introduction and protection of a new technology in the licensed territory, by reason of the scale of the research which has been undertaken and of the risk that is involved in manufacturing and marketing a product which is unfamiliar to users in the licensed territory at the time the agreement is made. This may also be the case where the agreements are concerned with the introduction and protection of a new process for manufacturing a product which is already known. In so far as in other cases agreements of this kind may fall within the scope of Article 85(1), it is useful for the purposes of legal certainty to include them in Article 1, in order that they may also benefit from the exemption. However, the exemption of exclusive licensing agreements and certain export bans imposed on the licensor and his licensees is without prejudice to subsequent developments in the case law of the Court of Justice regarding the status of such agreements under Article 85(1).

(12) The obligations listed in Article 1 generally contribute to improving the production of goods and to promoting technical progress; they make patentees more willing to grant licences and licensees more inclined to undertake the investment required to manufacture, use and put on the market a new product or to use a new process, so that undertakings other than the patentee acquire the possibility of manufacturing their products with the aid of the latest techniques and of developing those techniques further. The result is that the number of production facilities and the quantity and quality of goods produced in the common market are increased. This is true, in particular, of obligations on the licensor and on the licensee not to exploit the licensed invention in, and in particular not to export the licensed product into, the licensed territory in the case of the licensor and the "territories reserved for the licensor," that is to say, territories within the common market in which the licensor has patent protection and has not granted any licences, in the case of the licensee. This is also true both of the obligation of the licensee not to conduct an active policy of putting the product on the market (*i.e.* a prohibition of active competition as defined in Article 1(1)(5)) in the territories of other licensees for a period which may

equal the duration of the licence and also the obligation of the licensee not to put the licensed product on the market in the territories of other licensees for a limited period of a few years (*i.e.* a prohibition not only of active competition but also of "passive competition" whereby the licensee of a territory simply responds to requests which he has not solicited from users or resellers established in the territories of other licensees—Article 1(1)(6)). However, such obligations may be permitted under the Regulation only in respect of territories in which the licensed product is protected by "parallel patents," that is to say, patents covering the same invention, within the meaning of the case law of the Court of Justice, and as long as the patents remain in force.

(13) Consumers will as a rule be allowed a fair share of the benefit resulting from this improvement in the supply of goods on the market. To safeguard this effect, however, it is right to exclude from the application of Article 1 cases where the parties agree to refuse to meet demand from users or resellers within their respective territories who would resell for export, or to take other steps to impede parallel imports, or where the licensee is obliged to refuse to meet unsolicited demand from the territory of other licensees (passive sales). The same applies where such action is the result of a concerted practice between the licensor and the licensee.

(14) The obligations referred to above thus do not impose restrictions which are not indispensable to the attainment of the abovementioned objectives.

(15) Competition at the distribution stage is safeguarded by the possibility of parallel imports and passive sales. The exclusivity obligations covered by the Regulation thus do not normally entail the possibility of eliminating competition in respect of a substantial part of the products in question. This is so even in the case of agreements which grant exclusive licences for a territory covering the whole of the common market.

(16) To the extent that in their agreements the parties undertake obligations of the type referred to in Articles 1 and 2 but which are of more limited scope and thus less restrictive of competition than is permitted by those Articles, it is appropriate that these obligations should also benefit under the exemptions provided for in the Regulation.

(17) If in a particular case an agreement covered by this Regulation is found to have effects which are incompatible with the provisions of Article 85(3) of the Treaty, the Commission may withdraw the benefit of the block exemption from the undertakings concerned, in accordance with Article 7 of Regulation 19/65.

(18) It is not necessary expressly to exclude from the category defined in the Regulation agreements which do not fulfil the conditions of Article 85(1). Nevertheless it is advisable, in the interests of legal certainty for the undertakings concerned, to list in Article 2 a number of obligations which are not normally restrictive of competition, so that these also may benefit from the exemption in the event that, because of particular economic or legal circumstances, they should exceptionally fall within the scope of Article 85(1). The list of such obligations given in Article 2 is not exhaustive.

(19) The Regulation must also specify what restrictions or provisions may not be included in patent licensing agreements if these are to benefit from the block exemption. The restrictions listed in Article 3 may fall under the prohibition of Article 85(1); in these cases there can be no general presumption that they will lead to the positive effects required by Article 85(3), as would be necessary for the granting of a block exemption.

(20) Such restrictions include those which deny the licensee the right enjoyed by any third party to challenge the validity of the patent or which automatically prolong the agreement by the life of any new patent granted during the life of the licensed patents which are in existence at the time the agreement is entered into. Nevertheless, the parties are free to extend their contractual relationship by entering into new agreements concerning such new patents, or to agree the payment of royalties for as long as the licensee continues to use know-how communicated by the licensor which has not entered into the public domain, regardless of the duration of the original patents and of any new patents that are licensed.

(21) They also include restrictions on the freedom of one party to compete with the other and in particular to involve himself in techniques other than those licensed, since such restrictions impede technical and economic progress. The prohibition of such restrictions should however be

reconciled with the legitimate interest of the licensor in having his patented invention exploited to the full and to this end to require the licensee to use his best endeavours to manufacture and market the licensed product.

(22) Such restrictions include, further, an obligation on the licensee to continue to pay royalties after all the licensed patents ceased to be in force and the communicated know-how has entered into the public domain, since such an obligation would place the licensee at a disadvantage by comparison with his competitors, unless it is established that this obligation results from arrangements for spreading payments in respect of previous use of the licensed invention.

(23) They also include restrictions imposed on the parties regarding prices, customers or marketing of the licensed products or regarding the quantities to be manufactured or sold, especially since restrictions of the latter type may have the same effect as export bans.

(24) Finally, they include restrictions to which the licensee submits at the time the agreement is made because he wishes to obtain the licence, but which give the licensor an unjustified competitive advantage, such as an obligation to assign to the licensor any improvements the licensee may make to the invention, or to accept other licenses or goods and services that the licensee does not want from the licensor.

(25) It is appropriate to offer to parties to patent licensing agreements containing obligations which do not come within the terms of Articles 1 and 2 and yet do not entail any of the effects restrictive of competition referred to in Article 3 a simplified means of benefiting, upon notification, from the legal certainty provided by the block exemption (Article 4). This procedure should at the same time allow the Commission to ensure effective supervision as well as simplifying the administrative control of agreements.

(26) The Regulation should apply with retroactive effect to patent licensing agreements in existence when the Regulation comes into force where such agreements already fulfil the conditions for application of the Regulations or are modified to do so (Articles 6 to 8). Under Article 4(3) of Regulation 19/65, the benefit of these provisions may not be claimed in actions pending at the date of entry into force of this Regulation, nor may it be relied on as grounds for claims for damages against third parties.

(27) Agreements which come within the terms of Articles 1 and 2 and which have neither the object nor the effect of restricting competition in any other way need no longer be notified. Nevertheless, undertakings will still have the right to apply in individual cases for negative clearance under Article 2 of Council Regulation No 17 or for exemption under Article 85(3).

HAS ADOPTED THIS REGULATION:

Article 1

1. Pursuant to Article 85(3) of the Treaty and subject to the provisions of this Regulation, it is hereby declared that Article 85(1) of the Treaty shall not apply to patent licensing agreements, and agreements combining the licensing of patents and the communication of know-how, to which only two undertakings are party and which include one or more of the following obligations:
(1) an obligation on the licensor not to licence other undertakings to exploit the licensed invention in the licensed territory, covering all or part of the common market, in so far and as long as one of the licensed patents remains in force;
(2) an obligation on the licensor not to exploit the licensed invention in the licensed territory himself in so far and as long as one of the licensed patents remains in force;
(3) an obligation on the licensee not to exploit the licensed invention in territories within the common market which are reserved for the licensor, in so far and as long as the patented product is protected in those territories by parallel patents;
(4) an obligation on the licensee not to manufacture or use the licensed product, or use the patented process or the communicated know-how, in territories within the common market which are licensed to other licensees, in so far and as long as the licensed product is protected in those territories by parallel patents;
(5) an obligation on the licensee not to pursue an active policy of putting the licensed product on the market in the territories within the common market which are licensed to other licensees, and in particular not to engage in advertising

specifically aimed at those territories or to establish any branch or maintain any distribution depot there, in so far and as long as the licensed product is protected in those territories by parallel patents;
(6) an obligation on the licensee not to put the licensed product on the market in the territories licensed to other licensees within the common market for a period not exceeding five years from the date when the product is first put on the market within the common market by the licensor or one of his licensees, in so far as and for as long as the product is protected in these territories by parallel patents;
(7) an obligation on the licensee to use only the licensor's trade mark or the get-up determined by the licensor to distinguish the licensed product, provided that the licensee is not prevented from identifying himself as the manufacturer of the licensed product.

2. The exemption of restrictions on putting the licensed product on the market resulting from the obligations referred to in paragraph 1(2), (3), (5) and (6) shall apply only if the licensee manufactures the licensed product himself or has it manufactured by a connected undertaking or by a subcontractor.

3. The exemption provided for in paragraph 1 shall also apply where in a particular agreement the parties undertake obligations of the types referred to in that paragraph but with a more limited scope than is permitted by the paragraph.

Article 2

1. Article 1 shall apply notwithstanding the presence in particular of any of the following obligations, which are generally not restrictive of competition:
(1) an obligation on the licensee to procure goods or services from the licensor or from an undertaking designated by the licensor, in so far as such products or services are necessary for a technically satisfactory exploitation of the licensed invention;
(2) an obligation on the licensee to pay a minimum royalty or to produce a minimum quantity of the licensed product or to carry out a minimum number of operations exploiting the licensed invention;
(3) an obligation on the licensee to restrict his exploitation of the licensed invention to one or more technical fields of application covered by the licensed patent;
(4) an obligation on the licensee not to exploit the patent after termination of the agreement in so far as the patent is still in force;
(5) an obligation on the licensee not to grant sub-licences or assign the licence;
(6) an obligation on the licensee to mark the licensed product with an indication of the patentee's name, the licensed patent or the patent licensing agreement;
(7) an obligation on the licensee not to divulge know-how communicated by the licensor; the licensee may be held to this obligation even after the agreement has expired;
(8) obligations:
  (a) to inform the licensor of infringements of the patent,
  (b) to take legal action against an infringer,
  (c) to assist the licensor in any legal action against an infringer,
provided that these obligations are without prejudice to the licensee's right to challenge the validity of the licensed patent;
(9) an obligation on the licensee to observe specifications concerning the minimum quality of the licensed product, provided that such specifications are necessary for a technically satisfactory exploitation of the licensed invention, and to allow the licensor to carry out related checks;
(10) an obligation on the parties to communicate to one another any experience gained in exploiting the licensed invention and to grant one another a licence in respect of inventions relating to improvements and new applications, provided that such communication or licence is non-exclusive;
(11) an obligation on the licensor to grant the licensee any more favourable terms than the licensor may grant to another undertaking after the agreement is entered into.

2. In the event that, because of particular circumstances, the obligations referred to in paragraph 1 fall within the scope of Article 85(1), they shall also be exempted even if they are not accompanied by any of the obligations exempted by Article 1.

The exemption provided for in this paragraph shall also apply where in an agreement the parties undertake obligations of the types referred to in paragraph 1 but with a more limited scope than is permitted by that paragraph.

Article 3

Articles 1 and 2(2) shall not apply where:

Part V—2 Patent Licensing Agreements

1. the licensee is prohibited from challenging the validity of licensed patents or other industrial or commercial property rights within the common market belonging to the licensor or undertakings connected with him, without prejudice to the right of the licensor to terminate the licensing agreement in the event of such a challenge;

2. the duration of the licensing agreement is automatically prolonged beyond the expiry of the licensed patents existing at the time the agreement was entered into by the inclusion in it of any new patent obtained by the licensor, unless the agreement provides each party with the right to terminate the agreement at least annually after the expiry of the licensed patents existing at the time the agreement was entered into, without prejudice to the right of the licensor to charge royalties for the full period during which the licensee continues to use know-how communicated by the licensor which has not entered into the public domain, even if that period exceeds the life of the patents;

3. one party is restricted from competing with the other party, with undertakings connected with the other party or with other undertakings within the common market in respect of research and development, manufacture, use or sales, save as provided in Article 1 and without prejudice to an obligation on the licensee to use his best endeavours to exploit the licensed invention;

4. the licensee is charged royalties on products which are not entirely or partially patented or manufactured by means of a patented process, or for the use of know-how which has entered into the public domain otherwise than by the fault of the licensee or an undertaking connected with him, without prejudice to arrangements whereby in order to facilitate payment the royalty payments for the use of a licensed invention are spread over a period extending beyond the life of the licensed patents or the entry of the know-how into the public domain;

5. the quantity of licensed products one party may manufacture or sell or the number of operations exploiting the licensed invention he may carry out are subject to limitations;

6. one party is restricted in the determination of prices, components of prices or discounts for the licensed products;

7. one party is restricted as to the customers he may serve, in particular by being prohibited from supplying certain classes of user, employing certain forms of distribution or, with the aim of sharing customers, using certain types of packaging for the products, save as provided in Article 1(1)(7) and Article 2(1)(3);

8. the licensee is obliged to assign wholly or in part to the licensor rights in or to patents for improvements or for new applications of the licensed patents;

9. the licensee is induced at the time the agreement is entered into to accept further licences which he does not want or to agree to use patents, goods or services which he does not want, unless such patents, products or services are necessary for a technically satisfactory exploitation of the licensed invention;

10. without prejudice to Article 1(1)(5), the licensee is required, for a period exceeding that permitted under Article 1(1)(6), not to put the licensed product on the market in territories licensed to other licensees within the common market or does not do so as a result of a concerted practice between the parties;

11. one or both of the parties are required:
(a) to refuse without any objectively justified reason to meet demand from users or resellers in their respective territories who would market products in other territories within the common market;
(b) to make it difficult for users or resellers to obtain the products from other resellers within the common market, and in particular to exercise industrial or commercial property rights or take measures so as to prevent users or resellers from obtaining outside, or from putting on the market in, the licensed territory products which have been lawfully put on the market within the common market by the patentee or with his consent;
or do so as a result of a concerted practice between them.

Article 4

1. The exemption provided for in Articles 1 and 2 shall also apply to agreements containing obligations restrictive of competition which are not covered by those Articles and do not fall within the scope of Article 3, on condition that the agreements in question are notified to the Commission in accordance with the provisions of Com-

mission Regulation 27, as last amended by Regulation 1699/75, and that the Commission does not oppose such exemption within a period of six months.

2. The period of six months shall run from the date on which the notification is received by the Commission. Where, however, the notification is made by registered post, the period shall run from the date shown on the postmark of the place of posting.

3. Paragraph 1 shall apply only if:
(a) express reference is made to this Article in the notification or in a communication accompanying it; and
(b) the information furnished with the notification is complete and in accordance with the facts.

4. The benefit of paragraph 1 may be claimed for agreements notified before the entry into force of this Regulation by submitting a communication to the Commission referring expressly to this Article and to the notification. Paragraphs 2 and 3(b) shall apply *mutatis mutandis*.

5. The Commission may oppose the exemption. It shall oppose exemption if it receives a request to do so from a Member State within three months of the transmission to the Member State of the notification referred to in paragraph 1 or of the communication referred to in paragraph 4. This request must be justified on the basis of considerations relating to the competition rules of the Treaty.

6. The Commission may withdraw the opposition to the exemption at any time. However, where the opposition was raised at the request of a Member State and this request is maintained, it may be withdrawn only after consultation of the Advisory Committee on Restrictive Practices and Dominant Positions.

7. If the opposition is withdrawn because the undertakings concerned have shown that the conditions of Article 85(3) are fulfilled, the exemption shall apply from the date of notification.

8. If the opposition is withdrawn because the undertakings concerned have amended the agreement so that the conditions of Article 85(3) are fulfilled, the exemption shall apply from the date on which the amendments take effect.

9. If the Commission opposes exemption and the opposition is not withdrawn, the effects of the notification shall be governed by the provisions of Regulation No 17.

Article 5

1. This Regulation shall not apply:
(a) to agreements between members of a patent pool which relate to the pooled patents;
(b) to patent licensing agreements between competitors who hold interests in a joint venture or between one of them and the joint venture, if the licensing agreements relate to the activities of the joint venture;
(c) to agreements under which the parties, albeit in separate agreements or through connected undertakings, grant each other reciprocal patent or trade-mark licences or reciprocal sales rights for unprotected products or exchange know-how, where the parties are competitors in relation to the products covered by those agreements;
(d) to licensing agreements in respect of plant breeder's rights.

2. However, this Regulation shall apply to reciprocal licences of the types referred to in paragraph 1(3) where the parties are not subject to any territorial restrictions within the common market on the manufacture, use or putting on the market of the products covered by these agreements or on the use of licensed processes.

3. To agreements under which one party grants to the other party a patent licence and that other party, albeit in separate agreements or through connected undertakings, grants to the first party a licence under patents or trade-marks or reciprocal sales rights for unprotected products or communicates to him know-how, where the parties are competitors in relation to the produce covered by those agreements.

Article 6

1. As regards agreements existing on 13 March 1962 and notified before 1 February 1963 and agreements, whether notified or not, to which Article 4(2)(2)(b) of Regulation No 17 applies, the declaration of inapplicability of Article 85(1) of the Treaty contained in this Regulation shall have retroactive effect from the time at which the conditions for application of this Regulation were fulfilled.

2. As regards all other agreements notified before this Regulation entered into force,

Part V—2 Patent Licensing Agreements

the declaration of inapplicability of Article 85(1) of the Treaty contained in this Regulation shall have retroactive effect from the time at which the conditions for application of this Regulation were fulfilled, or from the date of notification, whichever is the later.

Article 7

If agreements existing on 13 March 1962 and notified before 1 February 1963 or agreements to which Article 4(2)(2)(b) of Regulation No 17 applies and notified before 1 January 1967 are amended before 1 April 1985 so as to fulfil the conditions for application of this Regulation, and if the amendment is communicated to the Commission before 1 July 1985 the prohibition in Article 85(1) of the Treaty shall not apply in respect of the period prior to the amendment. The communication shall take effect from the time of its receipt by the Commission. Where the communication is sent by registered post, it shall take effect from the date shown on the postmark of the place of posting.

Article 8

1. As regards agreements to which Article 85 of the Treaty applies as a result of the accession of the United Kingdom, Ireland and Denmark, Articles 6 and 7 shall apply except that the relevant dates shall be 1 January 1973 instead of 13 March 1962 and 1 July 1973 instead of 1 February 1963 and 1 January 1967.

2. As regards agreements to which Article 85 of the Treaty applies as a result of the accession of Greece, Articles 6 and 7 shall apply except that the relevant dates shall be 1 January 1981 instead of 13 March 1962 and 1 July 1981 instead of 1 February 1963 and 1 January 1967.

Article 9

The Commission may withdraw the benefit of this Regulation, pursuant to Article 7 of Regulation 19/65, where it finds in a particular case that an agreement exempted by this Regulation nevertheless has certain effects which are incompatible with the conditions laid down in Article 85(3) of the Treaty, and in particular where:

1. such effects arise from an arbitration award;

2. the licensed products or the services provided using a licensed process are not exposed to effective competition in the licensed territory from identical products or services or products or services considered by users as equivalent in view of their characteristics, price and intended use;

3. the licensor does not have the right to terminate the exclusivity granted to the licensee at the latest five years from the date the agreement was entered into and at least annually thereafter if, without legitimate reason, the licensee fails to exploit the patent or to do so adequately;

4. without prejudice to Article 1(1)(6), the licensee refuses, without objectively valid reason, to meet unsolicited demand from users or resellers in the territory of other licensees;

5. one or both of the parties:
(a) without any objectively justified reason, refuse to meet demand from users or resellers in their respective territories who would market the products in other territories within the common market; or
(b) make it difficult for users or resellers to obtain the products from other resellers within the common market, and in particular where they exercise industrial or commercial property rights or take measures so as to prevent resellers or users from obtaining outside, or from putting on the market in, the licensed territory products which have been lawfully put on the market within the common market by the patentee or with his consent.

Article 10

1. This Regulation shall apply to:
(a) patent applications;
(b) utility models;
(c) applications for registration of utility models;
(d) "certificats d'utilité" and "certificats d'addition" under French law; and
(e) applications for "certificats d'utilité" and "certificats d'addition" under French law;
equally as it applies to patents.

2. This Regulation shall also apply to agreements relating to the exploitation of an invention if an application within the meaning of paragraph 1 is made in

respect of the invention for the licensed territory within one year from the date when the agreement was entered into.

Article 11

This Regulation shall also apply to:
1. patent licensing agreements where the licensor is not the patentee but is authorized by the patentee to grant a licence or a sub-licence;
2. assignments of a patent or of a right to a patent where the sum payable in consideration of the assignment is dependent upon the turnover attained by the assignee in respect of the patented products, the quantity of such products manufactured or the number of operations carried out employing the patented invention;
3. patent licensing agreements in which rights or obligations of the licensor or the licensee are assumed by undertakings connected with them.

Article 12

1. "Connected undertakings" for the purposes of this Regulation means:
(a) undertakings in which a party to the agreement, directly or indirectly:
— owns more than half the capital or business assets, or
— has the power to exercise more than half the voting rights, or
— has the power to appoint more than half the members of the supervisory board, board of directors or bodies legally representing the undertaking, or
— has the right to manage the affairs of the undertaking;
(b) undertakings which directly or indirectly have in or over a party to the agreement the rights or powers listed in (a);
(c) undertakings in which an undertaking referred to in (b) directly or indirectly has the rights or powers listed in (a).

2. Undertakings in which the parties to the agreement or undertakings connected with them jointly have, directly or indirectly the rights or powers set out in paragraph 1(a) shall be considered to be connected with each of the parties to the agreement.

Article 13

1. Information acquired pursuant to Article 4 shall be used only for the purposes of this Regulation.

2. The Commission and the authorities of the Member States, their officials and other servants shall not disclose information acquired by them pursuant to this Regulation of the kind covered by the obligation of professional secrecy.

3. The provisions of paragraphs 1 and 2 shall not prevent publication of general information or surveys which do not contain information relating to particular undertakings or associations of undertakings.

Article 14

This Regulation shall enter into force on 1 January 1985.

It shall apply until 31 December 1994.

This Regulation shall be binding in its entirety and directly applicable in all Member States.

Done at Brussels, 23 July 1984.

C. CASES ON THE INTERPRETATION OF THE REGULATION

Boussois/Interpane 264 (para. 20)
Tetra Pak I 289 (paras. 53, 58–59)
17th Comp. Rep. (paras. 32–33)
18th Comp. Rep. (para. 35)
Pilkington-Covina 19th Comp. Rep. (para. 60)
Tetra Pak v. Commission T7 (grounds 29–30)

D. CLAUSES COMMONLY STIPULATED IN PATENT LICENSING AGREEMENTS

1. Territorial provisions

1.1. Right to use the patent exclusively within an agreed territory

1.1.1. To manufacture the product

Article 1(1)(1)–(4)
Burroughs/Delplanque 50*
Burroughs/Geha 51
Kabelmetal/Luchaire 94
Tetra Pak I 289 (paras. 53, 58–59)

1.1.2. To exploit the product

Articles 1(1)(1)–(4), 3(11)

Part V—2 Patent Licensing Agreements

Burroughs/Geha 51
Davidson Rubber 56*
Raymond/Nagoya 57 (para. 1)
AOIP/Beyrard 98
Velcro/Aplix 233
Tetra Pak I 289 (paras. 53, 58–59)
Clutch-type disc brakes 8th Comp. Rep. (para. 121)

1.2. Obligation not to pursue an active sales policy outside agreed territory

Articles 1(1)(5), 3(10)–(11)

1.3. Obligation not to export outside agreed territory (passive sales)

1.3.1. Between Member States

Articles 1(1)(5)–(6), 3(10)–(11)
Davidson Rubber 56*
AOIP/Beyrard 98
Velcro/Aplix 233
Fondasol 9th Comp. Rep. (paras. 112–113)
Pilkington-Covina 19th Comp. Rep. (para. 60)

1.3.2. To third countries

Kabelmetal/Luchaire 94

1.3.3. Into the Common Market

Raymond/Nagoya 57 (para. 2)

1.4. Limitation on site of manufacture

Windsurfing International 194
Windsurfing v. *Commission* 130 (grounds 85–88)*

2. Clauses relating to the product that the licensee may sell

2.1. Non-competition clause

Article 3(3)
AOIP/Beyrard 98*
Velcro/Aplix 233
Spitzer/Van Hool. 12th Comp. Rep. (para. 86)

2.2. Obligation on licensee to restrict production to fixed maximums

Article 3(5)

2.3. Quality norms

Article 2(9)

Burroughs/Geha 50
Burroughs/Delplanque 51
Raymond/Nagoya 57
Windsurfing v. *Commission* 130 (ground 45–53)*

2.4. Purchase or supply obligations

2.4.1. Exclusive purchasing

Article 2(1)
Vaessen/Moris 143 (paras. 1–2, 5–6, 15, 23)*
Velcro/Aplix 233
Bramley/Gilbert 10th Comp. Rep. (para. 128)

2.4.2. Tying

Article 3(9)
Video Cassette Recorders 122
Vaessen/Moris 143
Windsurfing International 194
Windsurfing v. *Commission* 130*

2.5. Trademark clauses

Articles 1(1)(7), 2(6)
Burroughs/Geha 50
Burroughs/Delplanque 51
Windsurfing International 196
Velcro/Aplix 233*
Windsurfing v. *Commission* 130 (ground 81)

3. Pricing restrictions on the licensee

Article 3(6)
Plastic Omnium. (Bulletin 6–1988 pt 2.1.107)

4. Restrictions upon the customers which the licensee may serve

Article 3(7)
Bramley/Gilbert. 10th Comp. Rep. (para. 128)

5. Clauses relating to the protection afforded to or by the patents

5.1. Field of use restrictions

Article 2(1)(3)
Windsurfing International 194
France/Suralmo 9th Comp. Rep. (paras. 114–115)
Windsurfing v. *Commission* 130*

5.2. Patent no-challenge clause

Article 3(1)

Book One: Part V—Industrial and Intellectual Property Agreements

Burroughs/Geha 51
Davidson Rubber 56 (para. 16)
Raymond/Nagoya 57 (para. 3)
Bronbemaling 95
AOIP/Beyrard 98*
Bayer/Gist-Brocades 100
Vaessen/Moris 143 (paras. 4–6, 14, 17, 23)
Windsurfing International 194
Pentacon-Dresden. 8th Comp. Rep. (paras. 118–120)
ACC/Fabry 9th Comp. Rep. (paras. 107–108)
Spitzer/Van Hool. 12th Comp. Rep. (para. 86)
Windsurfing v. *Commission* 130 (ground 92–93)*
Bayer v. Süllhöfer 158*

5.3. Guaranteed rights to any subsequent improvements

Articles 2(10), 3(8)
Burroughs/Delplanque 50
Burroughs/Geha 51
Davidson Rubber 56 (para. 9)*
Raymond/Nagoya 57 (paras. 5–6)
Kabelmetal—Luchaire 92
Velcro/Aplix 233*
Nodet/Gougis. 10th Comp. Rep. (para. 127)
Spitzer/Van Hool. 12th Comp. Rep. (para. 86)

5.4. Restrictions on sub-licensing

Article 2(1)(5)
Burroughs/Geha 50
Burroughs/Delplanque 51
Davidson Rubber 56 (para. 9)*
AOIP/Beyrard 98
France/Suralmo. 9th Comp. Rep. (paras. 114, 115)

6. Royalties

6.1. Obligation to pay minimum royalties/ produce minimum quantities

Article 2(1)(2)
AOIP Beyrard 98
Windsurfing v. *Commission* 130 (ground 65–66)

6.2. Obligation to pay royalties after expiration or invalidity of the patent

Kabelmetal/Luchaire 94
AOIP 98
Windsurfing International 194*
Preflex/Lipski. 10th Comp. Rep. (para. 126)

UNARCO. 14th Comp. Rep. (para. 93)
Ottung v. Klee 164*

6.3. Most favoured licensee clause

Article 2(1)(11)
Kabelmetal/Luchaire 94

6.4. Obligation to pay royalty even if patent not used

AOIP/Beyrard 98
Spitzer/Van Hool. 12th Comp. Rep. (para. 86)

7. Clauses relating to the duration of the agreement, post-term provisions

7.1. Automatic extension of agreement if additional patents granted

Article 3(2)
AOIP/Beyrard 98
Velcro/Aplix 233*

7.2. Post-term use restrictions

Article 2(1)(4)
Burroughs/Geha 50
Burroughs/Delplanque 51*
Ottung v. Klee 164

8. Patent dispute settlements

Article 9(1)
Bronbemaling 95
Vaessen/Moris 143 (paras. 4–6)
Zoller & Frölich. 9th Comp. Rep. (paras. 109–111)
Bayer v. Sülhöffer 158*

9. Patent pooling
See pages 94 and 115
Article 5(1)(a)

CHAPTER 3

KNOW-HOW LICENSING AGREEMENTS

A. CASES ON KNOW-HOW AGREEMENTS

Julien/Van Katwijk 32
Davidson Rubber 56
Raymond/Nagoya 57
Kabelmetal/Luchaire 92
Video Cassette Recorders 122
Campari 130
Schlegel/CPIO 204

Part VI—3 Know-how Licensing Agreements

Boussois/Interpane 264
Mitchell Cotts/Sofiltra 267 (Joint Venture)
Rich Products 283
Tetra Pak I 289
Delta Chemie 292
Moosehead 320

1st Comp. Rep. (paras. 73–80)
Spitzer/Van Hool. 12th Comp. Rep. (para. 86)
ICL/Fujitsu 16th Comp. Rep. (para. 72)

B. TEXT OF REGULATION 556/89
(reproduced below)

Commission Regulation 556/89 of November 30, 1988

On the application of Article 85(3) of the Treaty to certain categories of know-how licensing agreements

([1989] O.J. L61/1)

THE COMMISSION OF THE EUROPEAN COMMUNITIES,

Having regard to the Treaty establishing the European Economic Community,

Having regard to Council Regulation 19/65 of 2 March 1965 on the application of Article 85(3) of the Treaty to certain categories of agreements and concerted practices ([1965] O.J. 533/65), as last amended by the Act of Accession of Spain and Portugal, and in particular to Article 1 thereof,

Having published a draft of this Regulation ([1987] O.J. C214/2),

After consulting the Advisory Committee on Restrictive Practices and Dominant Positions,

Whereas:

(1) Regulation 19/65 empowers the Commission to apply Article 85(3) of the Treaty by Regulation to certain categories of bilateral agreements and concerted practices falling within the scope of Article 85(1) which include restrictions imposed in relation to the acquisition or use of industrial property rights, in particular patents, utility models, designs or trade marks, or to the rights arising out of contracts for assignment of, or the right to use, a method of manufacture or knowledge relating to the use or application of industrial processes.

The increasing economic importance of non-patented technical information (e.g. descriptions of manufacturing processes, recipes, formulae, designs or drawings), commonly termed "know-how," the large number of agreements currently being concluded by undertakings including public research facilities solely for the exploitation of such information (so-called "pure" know-how licensing agreements) and the fact that the transfer of know-how is, in practice, frequently irreversible make it necessary to provide greater legal certainty with regard to the status of such agreements under the competition rules, thus encouraging the dissemination of technical knowledge in the Community. In the light of experience acquired so far, it is possible to define a category of such know-how licensing agreements covering all or part of the common market which are capable of falling within the scope of Article 85(1) but which can normally be regarded as satisfying the conditions laid down in Article 85(3), where the licensed know-how is secret, substantial and identified in any appropriate form ("the know-how"). These definitional requirements are only intended to ensure that the communication of the know-how provides a valid justification for the application of the present Regulation and in particular for the exemption of obligations which are restrictive of competition.

A list of definitions for the purposes of this Regulation is set out in Article 1.

(2) As well as pure know-how agreements, mixed know-how and patent licensing agreements play an increasingly important role in the transfer of technology. It is therefore appropriate to include within the scope of this Regulation mixed agreements which are not exempted by Commission Regulation 2349/84 (Article 1, 2 or 4) ([1984] O.J. L219/15) and in particular the following:

— mixed agreements in which the licensed patents are not necessary for the achievement of the objects of the licensed technology containing both patented and non-patented elements; this may be the case where such pat-

ents do not afford effective protection against the exploitation of the technology by third parties;
— mixed agreements which, regardless of whether or not the licensed patents are necessary, for the achievement of the objects of the licensed technology, contain obligations which restrict the exploitation of the relevant technology by the licensor or the licensee in Member States without patent protection, in so far and as long as such obligations are based in whole or in part on the exploitation of the licensed know-how and fulfil the other conditions set out in this Regulation.

It is also appropriate to extend the scope of this Regulation to pure or mixed agreements containing ancillary provisions relating to trade marks and other intellectual property rights where there are no obligations restrictive of competition other than those also attached to the know-how and exempted under the present Regulation.

However, such agreements, too, can only be regarded as fulfilling the conditions of Article 85(3) for the purposes of this Regulation where the licensed technical knowledge is secret, substantial and identified.

(3) The provisions of the present Regulation are not applicable to agreements covered by Regulation 2349/84 on patent licensing agreements.

(4) Where such pure or mixed know-how licensing agreements contain not only obligations relating to territories within the common market but also obligations relating to non-member countries, the presence of the latter does not prevent the present Regulation from applying to the obligations relating to territories within the common market.

However, where know-how licensing agreements for non-member countries or for territories which extend beyond the frontiers of the Community have effects within the common market which may fall within the scope of Article 85(1), such agreements should be covered by the Regulation to the same extent as would agreements for territories within the common market.

(5) It is not appropriate to include within the scope of the Regulation agreements solely for the purpose of sale, except where the licensor undertakes for a preliminary period before the licensee himself commences production using the licensed technology to supply the contract products for sale by the licensee. Also excluded from the scope of the Regulation are agreements relating to marketing know-how communicated in the context of franchising arrangements [Commission Regulation (EEC) No. 4087/88 of 30 November 1988 on the application of Article 85(3) of the Treaty to categories of franchising agreements ([1988] O.J. L359/46) or to know-how agreements entered into in connection with arrangements such as joint ventures or patent pools and other arrangements in which the licensing of the know-how occurs in exchange for other licences not related to improvements to or new applications of that know-how, as such agreements pose different problems which cannot at present be dealt with in one Regulation (Article 5).

(6) Exclusive licensing agreements, *i.e.* agreements in which the licensor undertakes not to exploit the licensed technology in the licensed territory himself or to grant further licences there, may not be in themselves incompatible with Article 85(1) where they are concerned with the introduction and protection of a new technology in the licensed territory, by reason of the scale of the research which has been undertaken and of the increase in the level of competition, in particular interbrand competition, and in the competitiveness of the undertakings concerned resulting from the dissemination of innovation within the Community.

In so far as agreements of this kind fall in other circumstances within the scope of Article 85(1), it is appropriate to include them in Article 1, in order that they may also benefit from the exemption.

(7) Both these and the other obligations listed in Article 1 encourage the transfer of technology and thus generally contribute to improving the production of goods and to promoting technical progress, by increasing the number of production facilities and the quality of goods produced in the common market and expanding the possibilities of further development of the licensed technology. This is true, in particular, of an obligation on the licensee to use the licensed product only in the manufacture of its own products, since it gives the licensor an incentive to disseminate the technology in various applications while reserving the separate sale of the licensed product to himself or other licensees. It is also true of obligations on the licensor and on the licensee to refrain

not only from active but also from passive competition, in the licensed territory, in the case of the licensor, and in the territories reserved for the licensor or other licensees in the case of the licensee. The users of technologically new or improved products requiring major investment are often not final consumers but intermediate industries which are well informed about prices and alternative sources of supply of the products within the Community. Hence, protection against active competition only would not afford the parties and other licensees the security they needed, especially during the initial period of exploitation of the licensed technology when they would be investing in tooling up and developing a market for the product and in effect increasing demand.

In view of the difficulty of determining the point at which know-how can be said to be no longer secret, and the frequent licensing of a continuous stream of know-how, especially where technology in the industry is rapidly evolving, it is appropriate to limit to a fixed number of years the periods of territorial protection, of the licensor and the licensee from one another and as between licensees, which are automatically covered by the exemption. Since, as distinguished from patent licences, know-how licences are frequently negotiated after the goods or services incorporating the licensed technology have proved successful on the market, it is appropriate to take for each licensed territory the date of signature of the first licence agreement entered into for that territory by the licensor in respect of the same technology as the starting point for the permitted periods of territorial protection of the licensor and licensee from one another. As to the protection of a licensee from manufacture, use, active or passive sales by other licensees the starting point should be the date of signature of the first licence agreement entered into by the licensor within the EEC. The exemption of the territorial protection shall apply for the whole duration of such allowed periods as long as the know-how remains secret and substantial, irrespective of when the Member States in question joined the Community and provided that each of the licensees, the restricted as well as the protected one, manufactures the licensed product himself or has it manufactured.

Exemption under Article 85(3) of longer periods of territorial protection, in particular to protect expensive and risky investment or where the parties were not already competitors before the grant of the licence, can only be granted by individual decision. On the other hand, parties are free to extend the term of their agreement to exploit any subsequent improvements and to provide for the payment of additional royalties. However, in such cases, further periods of territorial protection, starting from the date of licensing of the improvements in the EEC, may be allowed only by individual decision, in particular where the improvements to or new applications of the licensed technology are substantial and secret and not of significantly less importance than the technology initially granted or require new expensive and risky investment.

(8) However, it is appropriate in cases where the same technology is protected in some Member States by necessary patents within the meaning of recital 9 of Regulation 2349/84 to provide with respect to those Member States an exemption under this Regulation for the territorial protection of the licensor and licensee from one another and as between licensees against manufacture, use and active sales in each other's territory for the full life of the patents existing in such Member States.

(9) The obligations listed in Article 1 also generally fulfil the other conditions for the application of Article 85(3). Consumers will as a rule be allowed a fair share of the benefit resulting from the improvement in the supply of goods on the market. Nor do the obligations impose restrictions which are not indispensable to the attainment of the abovementioned objectives. Finally, competition at the distribution stage is safeguarded by the possibility of parallel imports, which may not be hindered by the parties in any circumstances. The exclusivity obligations covered by the Regulation thus do not normally entail the possibility of eliminating competition in respect of a substantial part of the products in question. This also applies in the case of agreements which grant exclusive licences for a territory covering the whole of the common market where there is the possibility of parallel imports from third countries, or where there are other competing technologies on the market, since then the territorial exclusivity may lead to greater market integration and stimulate Community-wide interbrand competition.

(10) It is desirable to list in the Regulation a number of obligations that are commonly found in know-how licensing agree-

ments but are normally not restrictive of competition and to provide that in the event that because of the particular economic or legal circumstances they should fall within Article 85(1), they also would be covered by the exemption. This list, in Article 2, is not exhaustive.

(11) The Regulation must also specify what restrictions or provisions may not be included in know-how licensing agreements if these are to benefit from the block exemption. The restrictions, which are listed in Article 3, may fall under the prohibition of Article 85(1), but in their case there can be no general presumption that they will lead to the positive effects required by Article 85(3), as would be necessary for the granting of a block exemption, and consequently an exemption can be granted only on an individual basis.

(12) Agreements which are not automatically covered by the exemption because they contain provisions that are not expressly exempted by the Regulation and not expressly excluded from exemption, including those listed in Article 4(2) of the Regulation, may nonetheless generally be presumed to be eligible for application of the block exemption. It will be possible for the Commission rapidly to establish whether this is the case for a particular agreement. Such agreements should therefore be deemed to be covered by the exemption provided for in this Regulation where they are notified to the Commission and the Commission does not oppose the application of the exemption within a specified period of time.

(13) If individual agreements exempted by this Regulation nevertheless have effects which are incompatible with Article 85(3), the Commission may withdraw the benefit of the block exemption (Article 7).

(14) The list in Article 2 includes among others obligations on the licensee to cease using the licensed know-how after the termination of the agreement ("post-term use ban") (Article 2(1)(3)) and to make improvements available to the licensor (grant-back clause) (Article 2(1)(4)). A post-term use ban may be regarded as a normal feature of the licensing of know-how as otherwise the licensor would be forced to transfer his know-how in perpetuity and this would inhibit the transfer of technology. Moreover, undertakings by the licensee to grant back to the licensor a licence for improvements to the licensed know-how and/or patents are generally not restrictive of competition if the licensee is entitled by the contract to share in future experience and inventions made by the licensor and the licensee retains the right to disclose experience acquired or grant licences to third parties where to do so would not disclose the licensor's know-how.

On the other hand, a restrictive effect on competition arises where the agreement contains both a post-term use ban and an obligation on the licensee to make his improvements to the know-how available to the licensor, even on a non-exclusive and reciprocal basis, and to allow the licensor to continue using them even after the expiry of the agreement. This is so because in such a case the licensee has no possibility of inducing the licensor to authorize him to continue exploiting the originally licensed know-how, and hence the licensee's own improvements as well, after the expiry of the agreement.

(15) The list in Article 2 also includes an obligation on the licensee to keep paying royalties until the end of the agreement independently of whether or not the licensed know-how has entered into the public domain through the action of third parties (Article 2(1)(7)). As a rule, parties do not need to be protected against the foreseeable financial consequences of an agreement freely entered into and should therefore not be restricted in their choice of the appropriate means of financing the technology transfer. This applies especially where know-how is concerned since here there can be no question of an abuse of a legal monopoly and, under the legal systems of the Member States, the licensee may have a remedy in an action under the applicable national law. Furthermore, provisions for the payment of royalties in return for the grant of a whole package of technology throughout an agreed reasonable period independently of whether or not the know-how has entered into the public domain, are generally in the interest of the licensee in that they prevent the licensor demanding a high initial payment up front with a view to diminishing his financial exposure in the event of premature disclosure. Parties should be free, in order to facilitate payment by the licensee, to spread the royalty payments for the use of the licensed technology over a period extending beyond the entry of the know-how into the public domain. Moreover, continuous payments should be allowed throughout the term of

the agreement in cases where both parties are fully aware that the first sale of the product will necessarily disclose the know-how. Nevertheless, the Commission may, where it was clear from the circumstances that the licensee would have been able and willing to develop the know-how himself in a short period of time, in comparison with which the period of continuing payments is excessively long, withdraw the benefit of the exemption under Article 7 of this Regulation.

Finally, the use of methods of royalties calculation which are unrelated to the exploitation of the licensed technology or the charging of royalties on products whose manufacture at no stage includes the use of any of the licensed patents or secret techniques would render the agreement ineligible for the block exemption (Article 3(5)). The licensee should also be freed from his obligation to pay royalties, where the know-how becomes publicly known through the action of the licensor. However, the mere sale of the product by the licensor or an undertaking connected with him does not constitute such an action (Article 2(1)(7) and Article 3(5)).

(16) An obligation on the licensee to restrict his exploitation of the licensed technology to one or more technical fields of application ("fields of use") or to one or more product markets is also not caught by Article 85(1) (Article 2(1)(8)). This obligation is not restrictive of competition since the licensor can be regarded as having the right to transfer the know-how only for a limited purpose. Such a restriction must however not constitute a disguised means of customer sharing.

(17) Restrictions which give the licensor an unjustified competitive advantage, such as an obligation on the licensee to accept quality specifications, other licences or goods and services that the licensee does not want from the licensor, prevent the block exemption from being applicable. However, this does not apply where it can be shown that the licensee wanted such specifications, licences, goods or services for reasons of his own convenience (Article 3(3)).

(18) Restrictions whereby the parties share customers within the same technological field of use or the same product market, either by an actual prohibition on supplying certain classes of customer or an obligation with an equivalent effect, would also render the agreement ineligible for the block exemption (Article 3(6)).

This does not apply to cases where the know-how licence is granted in order to provide a single customer with a second source of supply. In such a case, a prohibition on the licensee from supplying persons other than the customer concerned may be indispensable for the grant of a licence to the second supplier since the purpose of the transaction is not to create an independent supplier in the market. The same applies to limitations on the quantities the licensee may supply to the customer concerned. It is also reasonable to assume that such restrictions contribute to improving the production of goods and to promoting technical progress by furthering the dissemination of technology. However, given the present state of experience of the Commission with respect to such clauses and the risk in particular that they might deprive the second supplier of the possibility of developing his own business in the fields covered by the agreement it is appropriate to make such clauses subject to the opposition procedure (Article 4(2)).

(19) Besides the clauses already mentioned, the list of restrictions precluding application of the block exemption in Article 3 also includes restrictions regarding the selling prices of the licensed product or the quantities to be manufactured or sold, since they limit the extent to which the licensee can exploit the licensed technology and particularly since quantity restrictions may have the same effect as export bans (Article 3(7) and (8)). This does not apply where a licence is granted for use of the technology in specific production facilities and where both a specific know-how is communicated for the setting-up, operation and maintenance of these facilities and the licensee is allowed to increase the capacity of the facilities or to set up further facilities for its own use on normal commercial terms. On the other hand, the licensee may lawfully be prevented from using the licensor's specific know-how to set up facilities for third parties, since the purpose of the agreement is not to permit the licensee to give other producers access to the licensor's know-how while it remains secret (Article 2(1)(12)).

(20) To protect both the licensor and the licensee from being tied into agreements whose duration may be automatically extended beyond their initial term as freely determined by the parties, through a continuous stream of improvements

communicated by the licensor, it is appropriate to exclude agreements with such a clause from the block exemption (Article 3(10)). However, the parties are free at any time to extend their contractual relationship by entering into new agreements concerning new improvements.

(21) The Regulation should apply with retroactive effect to know-how licensing agreements in existence when the Regulation comes into force where such agreements already fulfil the conditions for application of the Regulation or are modified to do so (Articles 8 to 10). Under Article 4(3) of Regulation 19/65, the benefit of these provisions may not be claimed in actions pending at the date of entry into force of this Regulation, nor may it be relied on as grounds for claims for damages against third parties.

(22) Agreements which come within the terms of Articles 1 and 2 and which have neither the object nor the effect of restricting competition in any other way need no longer be notified. Nevertheless, undertakings will still have the right to apply in individual cases for negative clearance under Article 2 of Council Regulation No. 17 ([1962] O.J. 204/62) or for exemption under Article 85(3).

HAS ADOPTED THIS REGULATION:

Article 1

1. Pursuant to Article 85(3) of the Treaty and subject to the provisions of this Regulation, it is hereby declared that Article 85(1) of the Treaty shall not apply to pure know-how licensing agreements and to mixed know-how and patent licensing agreements not exempted by Regulation 2349/84, including those agreements containing ancillary provisions relating to trademarks or other intellectual property rights, to which only two undertakings are party and which include one or more of the following obligations:
(1) an obligation on the licensor not to license other undertakings to exploit the licensed technology in the licensed territory;
(2) an obligation on the licensor not to exploit the licensed technology in the licensed territory himself;
(3) an obligation on the licensee not to exploit the licensed technology in territories within the common market which are reserved for the licensor;
(4) an obligation on the licensee not to manufacture or use the licensed product, or use the licensed process, in territories within the common market which are licensed to other licensees;
(5) an obligation on the licensee not to pursue an active policy of putting the licensed product on the market in the territories within the common market which are licensed to other licensees, and in particular not to engage in advertising specifically aimed at those territories or to establish any branch or maintain any distribution depot there;
(6) an obligation on the licensee not to put the licensed product on the market in the territories licensed to other licensees within the common market;
(7) an obligation on the licensee to use only the licensor's trademark or the get-up determined by the licensor to distinguish the licensed product during the term of the agreement, provided that the licensee is not prevented from identifying himself as the manufacturer of the licensed products;
(8) an obligation on the licensee to limit his production of the licensed product to the quantities he requires in manufacturing his own products and to sell the licensed product only as an integral part of or a replacement part for his own products or otherwise in connection with the sale of his own products, provided that such quantities are freely determined by the licensee.

2. The exemption provided for the obligations referred to in paragraph 1(1)(2) and (3) shall extend for a period not exceeding for each licensed territory within the EEC 10 years from the date of signature of the first licence agreement entered into by the licensor for that territory in respect of the same technology.

The exemption provided for the obligations referred to in paragraph 1(4) and (5) shall extend for a period not exceeding 10 years from the date of signature of the first licence agreement entered into by the licensor within the EEC in respect of the same technology.

The exemption provided for the obligation referred to in paragraph 1(6) shall extend for a period not exceeding five yeas from the date of the signature of the first licence agreement entered into by the licensor within the EEC in respect of the same technology.

3. The exemption provided for in paragraph 1 shall apply only where the parties

Part V—3 Know-how Licensing Agreements

have identified in any appropriate form the initial know-how and any subsequent improvements to it, which become available to the parties and are communicated to the other party pursuant to the terms of the agreement and for the purpose thereof, and only for as long as the know-how remains secret and substantial.

4. In so far as the obligations referred to in paragraph 1(1) to (5) concern territories including Member States in which the same technology is protected by necessary patents, the exemption provided for in paragraph 1 shall extend for those Member States as long as the licensed product or process is protected in those Member States by such patents, where the duration of such protection exceeds the periods specified in paragraph 2.

5. The exemption of restrictions on putting the licensed product on the market resulting from the obligations referred to in paragraph 1(2), (3), (5) and (6) shall apply only if the licensee manufactures or proposes to manufacture the licensed product himself or has it manufactured by a connected undertaking or by a subcontractor.

6. The exemption provided for in paragraph 1 shall also apply where in a particular agreement the parties undertake obligations of the types referred to in that paragraph but with a more limited scope than is permitted by the paragraph.

7. For the purposes of the present Regulation the following terms shall have the following meanings:
(1) "know-how" means a body of technical information that is secret, substantial and identified in any appropriate form;
(2) the term "secret" means that the know-how package as a body or in the precise configuration and assembly of its components is not generally known or easily accessible, so that part of its value consists in the lead-time the licensee gains when it is communicated to him; it is not limited to the narrow sense that each individual component of the know-how should be totally unknown or unobtainable outside the licensor's business;
(3) the term "substantial" mean that the know-how includes information which is of importance for the whole or a significant part of (i) a manufacturing process or (ii) a product or service, or (iii) for the development thereof and excludes information which is trivial. Such know-how must thus be useful, *i.e.* can reasonably be expected at the date of conclusion of the agreement to be capable of improving the competitive position of the licensee, for example by helping him to enter a new market or giving him an advantage in competition with other manufacturers or providers of services who do not have access to the licensed secret know-how or other comparable secret know-how;
(4) the term "identified" means that the know-how is described or recorded in such a manner as to make it possible to verify that it fulfils the criteria of secrecy and substantiality and to ensure that the licensee is not unduly restricted in his exploitation of his own technology. To be identified the know-how can either be set out in the licence agreement or in a separate document or recorded in any other appropriate form at the latest when the know-how is transferred or shortly thereafter, provided that the separate document or other record can be made available if the need arises;
(5) "pure know-how licensing agreements" are agreements whereby one undertaking, the licensor, agrees to communicate the know-how, with or without an obligation to disclose any subsequent improvements, to another undertaking, the licensee, for exploitation in the licensed territory;
(6) "mixed know-how and patent licensing agreements" are agreements not exempted by Regulation (EEC) No. 2349/84 under which a technology containing both non-patented elements and elements that are patented in one or more Member States is licensed;
(7) the terms "licensed know-how" or "licensed technology" mean the initial and any subsequent know-how communicated directly or indirectly by the licensor to a licensee by means of pure or mixed know-how and patent licensing agreements; however, in the case of mixed know-how and patent licensing agreements the term "licensed technology" also includes any patents for which a licence is granted besides the communication of the know-how;
(8) the term "the same technology" means the technology as licensed to the first licensee and enhanced by any improvements made thereto subsequently, irrespective of whether and to what extent such improvements are exploited by the parties or the other licensees and irrespective of whether the technology is protected by necessary patents in any Member States;
(9) "the licensed products" are goods or services the production or provision of

which requires the use of the licensed technology;

(10) the term "exploitation" refers to any use of the licensed technology in particular in the production, active or passive sales in a territory even if not coupled with manufacture in that territory, or leasing of the licensed products;

(11) "the licensed territory" is the territory covering all or at least part of the common market where the licensee is entitled to exploit the licensed technology;

(12) "territory reserved for the licensor" means territories in which the licensor has not granted any licences and which he has expressly reserved for himself;

(13) "connected undertakings" means:
(a) undertakings in which a party to the agreement, directly or indirectly;
— owns more than half the capital or business assets, or
— has the power to exercise more than half the voting rights, or
— has the power to appoint more than half the members of the supervisory board, board of directors or bodies legally representing the undertaking, or
— has the right to manage the affairs of the undertaking;
(b) undertakings which directly or indirectly have in or over a party to the agreement the rights or powers listed in (a);
(c) undertakings in which an undertaking referred to in (b) directly or indirectly has the rights or powers listed in (a);
(d) undertakings in which the parties to the agreement or undertakings connected with them jointly have the rights or powers listed in (a): such jointly controlled undertakings are considered to be connected with each of the parties to the agreement.

Article 2

1. Article 1 shall apply notwithstanding the presence in particular of any of the following obligations, which are generally not restrictive of competition:

(1) an obligation on the licensee not to divulge the know-how communicated by the licensor; the licensee may be held to this obligation after the agreement has expired;

(2) an obligation on the licensee not to grant sublicences or assign the licence;

(3) an obligation on the licensee not to exploit the licensed know-how after termination of the agreement in so far and as long as the know-how is still secret;

(4) an obligation on the licensee to communicate to the licensor any experience gained in exploiting the licensed technology and to grant him a non-exclusive licence in respect of improvements to or new applications of that technology, provided that:

(i) the licensee is not prevented during or after the term of the agreement from freely using his own improvements, in so far as these are severable from the licensor's know-how, or licensing them to third parties where licensing to third parties does not disclose the know-how communicated by the licensor that is still secret; this is without prejudice to an obligation on the licensee to seek the licensor's prior approval to such licensing provided that approval may not be withheld unless there are objectively justifiable reasons to believe that licensing improvements to third parties will disclose the licensor's know-how, and

(ii) the licensor has accepted an obligation, whether exclusive or not, to communicate his own improvements to the licensee and his right to use the licensee's improvements which are not severable from the licensed know-how does not extend beyond the date on which the licensee's right to exploit the licensor's know-how comes to an end, except for termination of the agreement for breach by the licensee; this is without prejudice to an obligation on the licensee to give the licensor the option to continue to use the improvements after that date, if at the same time he relinquishes the post-term use ban or agrees, after having had an opportunity to examine the licensee's improvements, to pay appropriate royalties for their use;

(5) an obligation on the licensee to observe minimum quality specifications for the licensed product or to procure goods or services from the licensor or from an undertaking designated by the licensor, in so far as such quality specification, products or services are necessary for:

(i) a technically satisfactory exploitation of the licensed technology, or

(ii) for ensuring that the production of the licencee conforms to the quality standards that are respected by the licensor and other licensees,

Part V—3 Know-how Licensing Agreements

and to allow the licensor to carry out related checks;
(6) obligations:
   (a) to inform the licensor of misappropriation of the know-how or of infringements of the licensed patents, or
   (b) to take or to assist the licensor in taking legal action against such misappropriation or infringements,

provided that these obligations are without prejudice to the licensee's right to challenge the validity of the licensed patents or to contest the secrecy of the licensed know-how except where he himself has in some way contributed to its disclosure;
(7) an obligation on the licensee, in the event of the know-how becoming publicly known other than by action of the licensor, to continue paying until the end of the agreement the royalties in the amounts, for the periods and according to the methods freely determined by the parties, without prejudice to the payment of any additional damages in the event of the know-how becoming publicly known by the action of the licensee in breach of the agreement;
(8) an obligation on the licensee to restrict his exploitation of the licensed technology to one or more technical fields of application covered by the licensed technology or to one or more product markets;
(9) an obligation on the licensee to pay a minimum royalty or to produce a minimum quantity of the licensed product or to carry out a minimum number of operations exploiting the licensed technology;
(10) an obligation on the licensor to grant the licensee any more favourable terms that the licensor may grant to another undertaking after the agreement is entered into;
(11) an obligation on the licensee to mark the licensed product with the licensor's name;
(12) an obligation on the licensee not to use the licensor's know-how to construct facilities for third parties; this is without prejudice to the right of the licensee to increase the capacity of its facilities or to set up additional facilities for its own use on normal commercial terms, including the payment of additional royalties.

2. In the event that, because of particular circumstances, the obligations referred to in paragraph 1 fall within the scope of Article 85(1), they shall also be exempted even if they are not accompanied by any of the obligations exempted by Article 1.

3. The exemption provided for in paragraph 2 shall also apply where in an agreement the parties undertake obligations of the types referred to in paragraph 1 but with a more limited scope than is permitted by that paragraph.

Article 3

Articles 1 and 2(2) shall not apply where:
1. the licensee is prevented from continuing to use the licensed know-how after the termination of the agreement where the know-how has meanwhile become publicly known, other than by the action of the licensee in breach of the agreement;

2. the licensee is obliged either:
(a) to assign in whole or in part to the licensor rights to improvements to or new applications of the licensed technology;
(b) to grant the licensor an exclusive licence for improvements to or new applications of the licensed technology which would prevent the licensee during the currency of the agreement and/or thereafter from using his own improvements in so far as these are severable from the licensor's know-how, or from licensing them to third parties, where such licensing would not disclose the licensor's know-how that is still secret; or
(c) in the case of an agreement which also includes a post-term use ban, to grant back to the licensor, even on a non-exclusive and reciprocal basis, licences for improvements which are not severable from the licensor's know-how, if the licensor's right to use the improvements is of a longer duration than the licensee's right to use the licensor's know-how, except for termination of the agreement for breach by the licensee;

3. the licensee is obliged at the time the agreement is entered into to accept quality specifications or further licences or to procure goods or services which he does not want, unless such licences, quality specifications, goods or services are necessary for a technically satisfactory exploitation of the licensed technology or for ensuring that the production of the licensee conforms to the quality standards that are respected by the licensor and other licensees;

4. the licensee is prohibited from contesting the secrecy of the licensed know-how or from challenging the validity of licensed patents within the common market

belonging to the licensor or undertakings connected with him, without prejudice to the right of the licensor to terminate the licensing agreement in the event of such a challenge;

5. the licensee is charged royalties on goods or services which are not entirely or partially produced by means of the licensed technology or for the use of know-how which has become publicly known by the action of the licensor or an undertaking connected with him;

6. one party is restricted within the same technological field of use or within the same product market as to the customers he may serve, in particular by being prohibited from supplying certain classes of user, employing certain forms of distribution or, with the aim of sharing customers, using certain types of packaging for the products, save as provided in Article 1(1)(7) and Article 4(2);

7. the quantity of the licensed products one party may manufacture or sell or the number of operations exploiting the licensed technology he may carry out are subject to limitations, save as provided in Article 1(1)(8) and Article 4(2);

8. one party is restricted in the determination of prices, components of prices or discounts for the licensed products;

9. one party is restricted from competing with the other party, with undertakings connected with the other party or with other undertakings within the common market in respect of research and development, production or use of competing products and their distribution, without prejudice to an obligation on the licensee to use his best endeavours to exploit the licensed technology and without prejudice to the right of the licensor to terminate the exclusivity granted to the licensee and cease communicating improvements in the event of the licensee's engaging in any such competing activities and to require the licensee to prove that the licensed know-how is not used for the production of goods and services other than those licensed;

10. the initial duration of the licensing agreement is automatically prolonged by the inclusion in it of any new improvements communicated by the licensor, unless the licensee has the right to refuse such improvements or each party has the right to terminate the agreement at the expiry of the initial term of the agreement and at least every three years thereafter;

11. the licensor is required, albeit in separate agreements, for a period exceeding that permitted under Article 1(2) not to license other undertakings to exploit the same technology in the licensed territory, or a party is required for periods exceeding those permitted under Article 1(2) or 1(4) not to exploit the same technology in the territory of the other party or of other licensees;

12. one or both of the parties are required:
(a) to refuse without any objectively justified reason to meet demand from users or resellers in their respective territories who would market products in other territories within the common market;
(b) to make it difficult for users or resellers to obtain the products from other resellers within the common market, and in particular to exercise intellectual property rights or take measures so as to prevent users or resellers from obtaining outside, or from putting on the market in the licensed territory products which have been lawfully put on the market within the common market by the licensor or with his consent; or do so as a result of a concerted practice between them.

Article 4

1. The exemption provided for in Articles 1 and 2 shall also apply to agreements containing obligations restrictive of competition which are not covered by those Articles and do not fall within the scope of Article 3, on condition that the agreements in question are notified to the Commission in accordance with the provisions of Commission Regulation No. 27 ([1962] O.J. Spec. Ed. 132; J.O. 1118/62) and that the Commission does not oppose such exemption within a period of six months.

2. Paragraph 1 shall in particular apply to an obligation on the licensee to supply only a limited quantity of the licensed product to a particular customer, where the know-how licence is granted at the request of such a customer in order to provide him with a second source of supply within a licensed territory.
This provision shall also apply where the customer is the licensee and the licence, in order to provide a second source of supply, provides for the customer to make licensed products or have them made by a sub-contractor.

3. The period of six months shall run from the date on which the notification is

Part V—3 Know-how Licensing Agreements

received by the Commission. Where, however, the notification is made by registered post, the period shall run from the date shown on the postmark of the place of posting.

4. Paragraphs 1 and 2 shall apply only if:
(a) express reference is made to this Article in the notification or in a communication accompanying it; and
(b) the information furnished with the notification is complete and in accordance with the facts.

5. The benefit of paragraphs 1 and 2 may be claimed for agreements notified before the entry into force of this Regulation by submitting a communication to the Commission referring expressly to this Article and to the notification. Paragraphs 3 and 4(b) shall apply *mutatis mutandis*.

6. The Commission may oppose the exemption. It shall oppose exemption if it receives a request to do so from a Member State within three months of the transmission to the Member State of the notification referred to in paragraph 1 or of the communication referred to in paragraph 5. This request must be justified on the basis of considerations relating to the competition rules of the Treaty.

7. The Commission may withdraw the opposition to the exemption at any time. However, where the opposition was raised at the request of a Member State and this request is maintained, it may be withdrawn only after consultation of the Advisory Committee on Restrictive Practices and Dominant Positions.

8. If the opposition is withdrawn because the undertakings concerned have shown that the conditions of Article 85(3) are fulfilled, the exemption shall apply from the date of notification.

9. If the opposition is withdrawn because the undertakings concerned have amended the agreement so that the conditions of Article 85(3) are fulfilled, the exemption shall apply from the date on which the amendments take effect.

10. If the Commission opposes exemption and the opposition is not withdrawn, the effects of the notification shall be governed by the provisions of Regulation No 17.

Article 5

1. This Regulation shall not apply to:
(1) agreements between members of a patent or know-how pool which relate to the pooled technologies;
(2) know-how licensing agreements between competing undertakings which hold interests in a joint venture, or between one of them and the joint venture, if the licensing agreements relate to the activities of the joint venture;
(3) agreements under which one party grants the other a know-how licence and the other party, albeit in separate agreements or through connected undertakings, grants the first party a patent, trademark or know-how licence or exclusive sales rights, where the parties are competitors in relation to the products covered by those agreements;
(4) agreements including the licensing of intellectual property rights other than patents (in particular trade-marks, copyright and design rights) or the licensing of software except where these rights or the software are of assistance in achieving the object of the licensed technology and there are no obligations restrictive of competition other than those also attached to the licensed know-how and exempted under the present Regulation.

2. However, this Regulation shall apply to reciprocal licences of the types referred to in paragraph 1(3) where the parties are not subject to any territorial restriction within the common market on the manufacture, use or putting on the market of the products covered by the agreements or on the use of the licensed technologies.

Article 6

This Regulation shall also apply to:
(1) pure know-how agreements or mixed agreements where the licensor is not the developer of the know-how or the patentee but is authorised by the developer or the patentee to grant a licence or a sub-licence;
(2) assignments of know-how or of know-how and patents where the risk associated with exploitation remains with the assignor, in particular where the sum payable in consideration of the assignment is dependent upon the turnover attained by the assignee in respect of products made using the know-how or the patents, the quantity of such products manufactured or the number of operations carried out employing the know-how or the patents;
(3) pure know-how agreements or mixed agreements in which rights or obligations

of the licensor or the licensee are assumed by undertakings connected with them.

Article 7

The Commission may withdraw the benefit of this Regulation, pursuant to Article 7 of Regulation No. 19/65/EEC, where it finds in a particular case that an agreement exempted by this Regulation nevertheless has certain effects which are incompatible with the conditions laid down in Article 85(3) of the Treaty, and in particular where:

(1) such effects arise from an arbitration award;

(2) the effect of the agreement is to prevent the licensed products from being exposed to effective competition in the licensed territory from identical products or products considered by users as equivalent in view of their characteristics, price and intended use;

(3) the licensor does not have the right to terminate the exclusivity granted to the licensee at the latest five years from the date the agreement was entered into and at least annually thereafter if, without legitimate reason, the licensee fails to exploit the licensed technology or to do so adequately;

(4) without prejudice to Article 1(1)(6), the licensee refuses, without objectively valid reason, to meet unsolicited demand from users or resellers in the territory of other licencees;

(5) one or both of the parties:
(a) without objectively justified reason, refuse to meet demand from users or resellers in their respective territories who would market the products in other territories within the common market; or
(b) make it difficult for users or resellers to obtain the products from other resellers within the common market, and in particular where they exercise intellectual property rights or take measures so as to prevent resellers or users from obtaining outside, or from putting on the market in the licensed territory products which have been lawfully put on the market within the common market by the licensor or with his consent;

(6) the operation of the post-term use ban referred to in Article 2(1)(3) prevents the licensee from working an expired patent which can be worked by all other manufacturers;

(7) the period for which the licensee is obliged to continue paying royalties after the know-how has become publicly known by the action of third parties, as referred to in Article 2(1)(7), substantially exceeds the lead time acquired because of the head-start in production and marketing and this obligation is detrimental to competition in the market;

(8) the parties were already competitors before the grant of the licence and obligations on the licensee to produce a minimum quantity or to use his best endeavours as referred to in Article 2(1)(9) and Article 3(9) have the effect of preventing the licensee from using competing technologies.

Article 8

1. As regards agreements existing on 13 March 1962 and notified before 1 February 1963 and agreements, whether notified or not, to which Article 4(2)(2)(b) of Regulation No. 17 applies, the declaration of inapplicability of Article 85(1) of the Treaty contained in this Regulation shall have retroactive effect from the time at which the conditions for application of this Regulation were fulfilled.

2. As regards all other agreements notified before this Regulation entered into force, the declaration of inapplicability of Article 85(1) of the Treaty contained in this Regulation shall have retroactive effect from the time at which the conditions for application of this Regulation were fulfilled, or from the date of notification, whichever is the later.

Article 9

If agreements existing on 13 March 1962 and notified before 1 February 1963 or agreements to which Article 4(2)(2)(b) of Regulation No. 17 applies and notified before 1 January 1967 are amended before 1 July 1989 so as to fulfil the conditions for application of this Regulation, and if the amendment is communicated to the Commission before 1 October 1989 the prohibition in Article 85(1) of the Treaty shall not apply in respect of the period prior to the amendment. The communication shall take effect from the time of its receipt by the Commission. Where the communication is sent by registered post, it shall take effect from the date

Article 10

1. As regards agreements to which Article 85 of the Treaty applies as a result of the accession of the United Kingdom, Ireland and Denmark, Articles 8 and 9 shall apply except that the relevant dates shall be 1 January 1973 instead of 13 March 1962 and 1 July 1973 instead of 1 February 1963 and 1 January 1967.

2. As regards agreements to which Article 85 of the Treaty applies as a result of the accession of Greece, Articles 8 and 9 shall apply except that the relevant dates shall be 1 January 1981 instead of 13 March 1962 and 1 July 1981 instead of 1 February 1963 and 1 January 1967.

3. As regards agreements to which Article 85 of the Treaty applies as a result of the accession of Spain and Portugal, Articles 8 and 9 shall apply except that the relevant dates shall be 1 January 1986 instead of 13 March 1962 and 1 July 1986 instead of 1 February 1963 and 1 January 1967.

Article 11

1. Information acquired pursuant to Article 4 shall be used only for the purposes of the Regulation.

2. The Commission and the authorities of the Member States, their officials and other servants shall not disclose information acquired by them pursuant to this Regulation of the kind covered by the obligation of professional secrecy.

3. The provisions of paragraphs 1 and 2 shall not prevent publication of general information or surveys which do not contain information relating to particular undertakings or associations of undertakings.

Article 12

This Regulation shall enter into force on 1 April 1989.
  It shall apply until 31 December 1999.
  This Regulation shall be binding in its entirety and directly applicable in all Member States.

Done at Brussels, 30 November 1988.

C. CASES ON THE INTERPRETATION OF THE REGULATION

Moosehead 320 (para. 16.1)
17th Comp. Rep. (paras. 38–42)

D. CLAUSES COMMONLY STIPULATED IN KNOW-HOW AGREEMENTS

1. Territorial provisions

1.1. Right to use the know-how exclusively within an agreed territory

1.1.1. To manufacture the product

Articles 1(1)(1)–(4), 1(2), 1(5), 3(11),(12)
Kabelmetal/Luchaire 94
Campari 130
Boussois/Interpane 264
Rich Products 283 (paras. 28–30)*
Tetra Pak I 289 (paras. 8, 53–59)
Delta Chemie 292

1.1.2. To exploit the know-how

Articles 1(1)(1)–(4), 1(2), 1(5), 3(11),(12)
Davidson Rubber 56
Raymond/Nagoya 57
Campari 130
Boussois/Interpane 264 (paras. 4, 5, 16)
Mitchell Cotts/Sofiltra 267 (para. 23)
Delta Chemie 292 (paras. 25–26)*

1.2. Obligation not to pursue an active sales policy outside agreed territory

Articles 1(1)(5), 1(2), 1(5), 3(11),(12)
Campari 130
Boussois/Interpane 264 (para. 16)*
Mitchell Cotts/Sofiltra 267 (para. 23)

1.3. Obligation not to export outside agreed territory (passive sales)

1.3.1. Between Member States

Articles 1(1)(6), 1(2), 1(5), 3(11),(12)
Julien/Van Katwijk 32 (reimposed)
Boussois/Interpane 264 (paras. 16, 20)*

1.3.2. To third countries

Kabelmetal/Luchaire 94
Campari 130*

1.3.3. Into the EEC

Raymond/Nagoya 57

1.4. Grant of a non-exclusive licence outside the exclusive territory

Boussois/Interpane 264 (para. 5)*

Rich Products 283 (para. 31)

2. Clauses relating to the product which the licensee may sell

2.1. Non-competition clause

Article 3(9)
Campari 130
Mitchell Cotts/Sofiltra 267 (para. 22)
Spitzer/Van Hool 12th Comp. Rep. (para. 86)

2.2. Maximum limits set upon the quantities that the licensee may sell or produce

Articles 1(1)(8), 3(7)

2.3. Obligation to purchase materials exclusively from the licensor

Articles 2(1)(5), 3(3)
Schlegel/CPIO 204 (paras. 4–5, 14–21)
Rich Products 283*
Moosehead 320 (paras. 9.2, 15.3)

2.4. Trademark related obligations

Articles 1(1)(7), 2(1)(11)
Campari 130
Delta Chemie 292 (paras. 6, 16)
Moosehead 320

2.5. Obligations on the licensee to respect quality norms

Articles 2(1)(5), 3(3), 3(7)
Video Cassette Recorders 122
Campari 130
Rich Products 283 (para. 37)*
Delta Chemie 292 (para. 30)

3. Pricing restrictions imposed on the licensee

Article 3(8)

4. Restrictions upon the customers which the licensee may serve

Articles 2(1)(12), 3(6)
Campari 130

5. Clauses relating to the substance of the licensed know-how

5.1. Requirement that the substantial know-how be fully specified in the agreement

Article 1(3)

Boussois/Interpane 264 (para. 2)
Delta Chemie 292 (para. 23)*

5.2. Field of use restrictions

Articles 2(1)(8), 2(1)(12)
Rich Products 283 (para. 35)*
Delta Chemie 292 (para. 31)

5.3. Obligations not to contest the secrecy of the know-how/accompanying patents

Article 3(4)

5.4. Obligation to respect confidentiality

Article 2(1)(1)
Davidson Rubber 56 (para. 9)
Kabelmetal/Luchaire 94
Campari 130
Boussois/Interpane 264 (para. 22)
Mitchell Cotts/Sofiltra 267 (para. 21)
Rich Products 283 (para. 32)*
Delta Chemie 292 (para. 32)

5.5. Guaranteed rights to any subsequent improvements

Articles 1(3), 2(1)(4), 3(2)
Burroughs/Delplanque 51
Burroughs/Geha 50
Davidson Rubber 56 (para. 9)
Raymond/Nagoya 57
Kabelmetal/Luchaire 94
Boissois-Interpane 264 (para. 22)*
Mitchell Cotts/Sofiltra 267 (paras. 10, 21)
Rich Products 283 (para. 36)
Delta Chemie 292 (para. 33)*
Spitzer/Van Hool 12th Comp. Rep. (para. 86)

5.6. Restrictions on sub-licensing

Article 2(1)(2)
Mitchell Cotts/Sofiltra 267 (para. 21)
Rich Products 283 (para. 33)
Delta Chemie 292 (para. 36)*

5.7. Best endeavours clause

Article 3(9)
Delta Chemie 292 (para. 3)

5.8. Obligation on licensee to inform licensor of any misappropriation of know-how

Article 2(1)(6)
Delta Chemie 292 (para. 33)

6. Clauses relating to the royalties paid

6.1. Obligation to pay minimum royalties or produce minimum quantities

Article 2(1)(9)
Kabelmetal/Luchaire 94

6.2. Obligation to pay royalties once know-how is in the public domain

Article 3(1)
Boussois/Interpane 264 (paras. 7, 22)
Spitzer/Van Hool 12th Comp. Rep. (para. 86)

6.3. Most favoured licensee clause

Article 2(1)(10)
Kabelmetal/Luchaire 94

7. Clauses relating to the duration

7.1. Maximum duration of the licence

Article 1(4), 3(10)
Boussois/Interpane 264 (paras. 6, 21)
Delta Chemie 292 (paras. 19, 47, 49)*

7.2. Automatic extension of the licence

Article 3(10)

7.3. Post-term use restrictions

Articles 2(1)(3), 3(2)
Rich Products 283 (para. 34)
Delta Chemie 292 (para. 35)*
Cartoux/Terrapin 10th Comp, Rep. (para. 129)

CHAPTER 4

TRADEMARK AGREEMENTS

A. CASES ON TRADEMARK LICENSING AGREEMENTS

Jaz/Peter I 26
Burroughs/Delplanque 50
Burroughs/Geha 51
Theal/Watts 110
Campari 130
Moosehead 320
1st Comp. Rep. (paras. 61–65)
Tyler/Linde 11th Comp. Rep. (para. 96)
Campari 18th Comp. Rep. (para. 69)
Tepea v. Commission 64

B. CASES ON TRADEMARK ASSIGNMENTS

Grundig/Consten 5

Advocaat Zwarte Kip 79
Moosehead 320 (para. 16)
1st Comp. Rep. (paras. 61–65)
Remington Rand. 1st Comp. Rep. (para. 64)
Consten & Grundig v. Commission 4
Sirena v. Eda 17
EMI-CBS 50–52

C. CASES ON THE CREATION OF A JOINT TRADEMARK

Transocean Marine Paint Association 10, 75, 96, 151, 297
Proroton 10th Comp. Rep. (paras. 130–132)

D. TRADEMARK DELIMITATION AGREEMENTS

Nicholas Frères Vitapro 4
Sirdar/Phildar 89
Penney 127
Toltecs/Dorcet 191
Leopold/AFS 5th Comp. Rep. (para. 70)
Bayer/Tanabe 8th Comp. Rep. (paras. 125–127)
Winninger Domgarten. 10th Comp. Rep. (paras. 133–134)
Osram/Airam 11th Comp. Rep. (para. 97)
Syntex/Synthelabo 19th Comp. Rep. (para. 59)
Hershey/Herschi 20th Comp.Rep. (para. 111)
BAT v. Commission 116
Terrapin v. Terranova 53

E. CLAUSES COMMONLY FIGURING IN TRADEMARK LICENSING OR ASSIGNMENT AGREEMENTS

1. Territorial restrictions

1.1. Right to use the trademark exclusively within an agreed territory

Theal/Watts 110
Moosehead 320 (paras. 7, 15, 16)
Consten & Grundig v. Commission 4
Tepea v. Commission 64 (grounds 33–45, 53–57)*

1.2. Export ban

Advocaat Zwarte Kip 79

1.3. Grant of exclusivity gives licensee ability to prevent parallel imports

Theal/Watts 110
Consten & Grundig v. Commission 4

Book One: Part V—Industrial and Intellectual Property Agreements

Sirena v. *Eda* 17 (ground 11)
EMI-CBS 50 (grounds 26–29)
Terrapin v. *Terranova* 53 (grounds 5, 8)*
Tepea v. *Commission* 64 (grounds 33–45, 53–57)*

2. Trademark no-challenge clause

Goodyear Italiana/Euram 85 (para. 2)*
Penney 127 (paras. I.5, I.7, II.4.c)
Windsurfing International 194
Moosehead 320 (paras. 8, 15–4)*

3. Duration of the validity of the trademark

Velcro/Aplix 233
Tyler/Linde 11th Comp. Rep. (para. 96)

CHAPTER 5

COPYRIGHT AND DESIGN RIGHT AGREEMENTS

A. CASES ON COPYRIGHT AGREEMENTS

Decca 304 (paras. 104–107, 117–119)
ARD 312
1st Comp. Rep. (para. 67)
BBC 6th Comp. Rep. (para. 163)
The Old Man and the Sea 6th Comp. Rep. (para. 164)
English Football Assoc. 9th Comp. Rep. (paras. 116, 117)
Ernest Benn 9th Comp. Rep. (para. 118)
Nielson-Hordell 12th Comp. Rep. (paras. 88–89)
STEMRA. 11th Comp. Rep. (para. 98)
Knoll/Hille-Form. 13th Comp. Rep. (paras. 142–146)
BIEM-IFPI 13th Comp. Rep. (paras. 147–150)
GEMA 15th Comp. Rep. (para. 81)
18th Comp. Rep. (para. 42)
Coditel v. *Ciné-Vog* 96
EMI v. *Patricia* 161a
Ministère Public v. *Tournier* 167
Lucazeau v. *SACEM* 168

B. CASES ON DESIGN RIGHT AGREEMENTS

Dutch Design Institute 5th Comp. Rep. (para. 69)
ICL/Fujitsu 16th Comp. Rep. (para. 72)
Ford 20th Comp. Rep. (para. 112)

C. CLAUSES TYPICALLY STIPULATED IN COPYRIGHT/DESIGN RIGHT AGREEMENTS

1. Territorial restrictions

1.1. Exclusivity

Coditel v. *Ciné-Vog* 96 (grounds 14–19)
Ministère Public v. *Tournier* 167
Lucazeau v. *SACEM* 168

1.2. Export bans

BBC 6th Comp. Rep. (para. 163)
The Old Man and the Sea 6th Comp. Rep. (para. 164)
Ernest Benn 9th Comp. Rep. (para. 118)
STREMSA 11th Comp. Rep. (para. 98)
Nielson-Hordell 12th Comp. Rep. (paras. 88–89)
Coditel v. *Ciné-Vog* 96 (grounds 14–19)*

2. No-challenge clause

Vaessen/Moris 143
Nielson-Hordell 12th Comp. Rep. (paras. 88–89)

3. Royalties

Nielson-Hordell 12th Comp. Rep. (paras. 88–89)
GEMA 15th Comp. Rep. (para. 18)

4. Non-competition restraint of trade clause

Nielson-Hordell 12th Comp. Rep. (paras. 88–89)

5. Improvements

Nielson-Hordell 12th Comp. Rep. (paras. 88–89)

6. Tying

Ministère public v. *Tournier* 168 (ground 31–32)

CHAPTER 6

BREEDERS' RIGHTS LICENSING AGREEMENTS

A. CASES ON BREEDERS' RIGHTS

Maize Seeds 137
Breeders' rights; roses 236
Plant Royalty Bureau. 9th Comp. Rep. (para. 120)
Nungesser v. *Commission* 94 (ground 43)
Louis Erauw v. *La Hesbignonne* 149

Part V—6 Breeders' Rights Licensing Agreements

B. CLAUSES COMMONLY FIGURING IN BREEDERS' RIGHTS AGREEMENTS

1. Territorial restrictions

1.1. Exclusivity

Maize Seeds 137
Nungesser v. *Commission* 94 (grounds 49, 53–58)*

1.2. Export ban

Maize Seeds 137
Nungesser v. *Commission* 94 (grounds 53, 61, 77–78)*
Louis Erauw v. *La Hesbignonne* 149*

2. Non-competition restraint of trade clause

Maize Seeds 137

3. Control of prices by licensor

Maize Seeds 137
Louis Erauw v. *La Hesbignonne* 149 (ground 15)*

4. No-challenge clause

Breeders' rights; roses 236

5. Grant back of improvements

Breeders' rights; roses 236

6. Purchasing obligations on licensee

Maize Seeds 137

7. Customer limitation clause

Maize Seeds 137

PART VI

JOINT VENTURES

CHAPTER 1

LIST OF CASES ON JOINT VENTURE AGREEMENTS

Henkel/Colgate 52
SHV/Chevron 87
United Reprocessors 102
KEWA 103
Vacuum Interrupters 112, 161
De Laval/Stork 114, 281
GEC/Weir Sodium Circulators 117
SOPELEM/Vickers 125
SNPE/LEL 132
CSV 134
WANO 138
Floral 148
Rennet 149
National Sulphuric Acid Association of 308, 156
IMA Rules 158
Langenscheidt/Hachette 168
Amersham/Buchler 184
Rockwell/IVECO 196
Carbon Gas Technologie 205
BP/Kellogg 235
Optical Fibres 249
Mitchell Cotts/Sofiltra 267
Enichem/ICI 279
Olivetti/Canon 280
BP/Bayer 284
IVECO/Ford 287
BBC Brown Boveri 291
UIP 309
GEC-Siemens/Plessey 325
Odin 322
Cekacan 326
Screensport/EBU 337
Eirpage 344
4th Comp. Rep. (paras. 37–41)
6th Comp. Rep. (paras. 53–59)
Kaiser/Estel 9th Comp. Rep. (para. 131)
Fieldmuhle-Stora 12th Comp. Rep. (paras. 73–74)
13th Comp. Rep. (paras. 53–55)
BBC/Grenfell/Holt 14th Comp. Rep. (para. 86)
United Reprocessors 16th Comp. Rep. (para. 69)
Montedison/Hercules 17th Comp. Rep. (para. 69)
Carnaud/Sofreb 17th Comp. Rep. (para. 70)
PRB/Shell. 17th Comp. Rep. (para. 74)
EMC/DSM 18th Comp. Rep. (para. 58)
Stremsel v. *Commission* 84

CHAPTER 2

TYPES OF JOINT VENTURES

1. Joint R&D

Eurogypsum 11
Henkel/Colgate 52*
Vacuum Interrupters 112, 161
De Laval/Stork 114, 281
GEC/Weir Sodium Circulators 117
Carbon Gas Technologie 205
BP/Kellogg 235
BP/Bayer 284. (para. 22)
Olivetti/Canon 280
BBC Brown Boveri 291
Odin 322

2. Joint buying

See also Buying Groups, Part IV, page 122
Rennet 149*
National Sulphuric Acid Association 156 (paras. 20, 26–27, 32, 36, 39–54)
Enichem/ICI 279
GEC/Siemens/Plessey 325
Irish Distillers 18th Comp. Rep. (para. 80)

3. Joint production

Bayer/Gist-Brocades 100
KEWA 103
Vacuum Interrupters 112, 161
De Laval/Stork 114, 281
GEC/Weir Sodium Circulators 117
SNPE-LEL 132
WANO 138
Rennet 149
Langenscheidt/Hachette 168
Amersham/Buchler 184
Rockwell/IVECO 196
IVECO/Ford 207
Optical Fibres 249
Mitchell Cotts/Sofiltra 267
Olivetti/Canon 280*
BP/Bayer 284 (para. 21)
Odin 322
Cekacan 326
Fieldmuhle-Stora 12th Comp. Rep. (paras. 73–74)

Book One: Part VI—Joint Ventures

Shell/AKZO. 14th Comp. Rep. (para. 85)
Stremsel v. *Commission* 84
EMC/DSM 18th Comp. Rep. (para. 50)

4. Joint sales

SHV/Chevron 87
United Reprocessors 102
KEWA 103
Vacuum Interrupters 112, 161
De Laval/ Stork 114*
Sopelem/Vickers 125
CSV 134
WANO 138
Floral 148
Langenscheidt/Hachette 168
Amersham/Buchler 184
Optical Fibres 249
Mitchell Cotts/Sofiltra 267
BP/Bayer 284 (paras. 11, 20)
IVECO/Ford 287
UIP 309 (para. 41)
Odin 322
Cekacan 326
Screensport/EBU 337
Gosme/Martell 340 (para. 30)
Eirpage 344 (para. 21)
Fieldmuhle-Stora 12th Comp. Rep. (paras. 73–74)
AIR-Forge 12th Comp. Rep. (para. 85)
Finnpap 19th Comp. Rep. (para. 44)

5. Co-ordination centres

Enichem/ICI 279

CHAPTER 3

PURPOSE OF THE CO-OPERATION

1. Market extension

KEWA 103
De Laval/Stork 114, 281
Langenscheidt/Hachette 168*
Amersham/Buchler 184 (para. 11)
Mitchell Cotts/Sofiltra 267
IVECO/Ford 287

Odin 322
Cekacan 326
Screensport/EBU 337
Eirpage 344

2. Technological progress/transfer of technology

Henkel/Colgate 52
GEC/Weir Sodium Circulators 117
Vacuum Interrupters II 161
Rockwell/IVECO 196
Carbon Gas Technologie 205
Optical Fibres 249*
Olivetti/Canon 280 (para. 54)
BBC Brown Boveri 291

3. Restructuring operations

Enichem/ICI 279
BP/Bayer 284
IVECO/Ford 287
UIP 309
12th Comp. Rep. (paras. 38–41)
Shell/AKZO 14th Comp. Rep. (para. 85)

4. Market sharing

United Reprocessors 102
CSV 134
WANO 138*
Floral 148
Fieldmuhle-Stora 12th Comp. Rep. (paras. 73–74)

5. Rationalisation of production capacity

United Reprocessors 102

CHAPTER 4

DRAFT COMMISSION NOTICE

1. Draft Guidelines for the appraisal of co-operative joint ventures in the light of Article 85 of the EEC Treaty (reproduced opposite)

Part VI—4 Draft Guidelines on Co-operative Joint Ventures

Draft Guidelines for the appraisal of co-operative joint ventures in the light of Article 85 of the EEC Treaty

Discussion paper on the future treatment of co-operative joint ventures

I. Council Regulation (EEC) No. 4064/89 classes concentrative JVs (joint ventures) with concentrations and makes them subject to the same rules. Since, however, the definition given in that Regulation is very restrictive (see Article 3(2) and the interpretation given in the "Interface" Notice), the Articles 85 and 86 regime will continue to apply to the overwhelming majority of newly-created JVs.

The Commission has consistently taken the line that certain co-operative JVs — those performing all the functions of a normal firm — normally help to increase competition and therefore deserve favourable treatment.

II. Those JVs are, however, governed by legal provisions which are less favourable than those applicable to concentrative JVs:

—they tend to fall within the very broad cope of Article 85(1), which prohibits any appreciable restriction, whereas concentrative JVs can be prohibited only if they exceed the dominance threshold;

—they do not benefit from any block exemption since co-operation extending to distribution is excluded from the field of application of Regulations (EEC) No. 417/85 (specialisation) and No. 418/85 (R&D), while Regulations (EEC) No. 2349/84 (patent licences) and No. 556/89 (know-how licences) do not apply to relationships between parent companies and the JV where the parties are competitors;

—individual exemptions — unlike a decision declaring a concentration compatible with the common market or a decision not to oppose a concentration, adopted under Regulation (EEC) No. 4064/89 — may be granted only for a limited period and can be withdrawn;

—the procedure applicable to co-operative JVs under Regulation No. 17/62 is lengthy (two years on average), whereas that applicable to concentrative JVs is much quicker (one month in many cases and no more than five months in all others).

III. In order to remedy a situation which could be called discriminatory, at least in the case of fully-fledged JVs which create substantial capacity (extension of product range, production or market) by means of new investment, every avenue must be explored.

1. The annexed draft already sets out a few tentative solutions:

(a) putting greater emphasis, when dealing with potential competition, on the *"realistic economic approach"* first adopted in 1983, so as to give a reasonable field of application to the ban in Article 85(1);

(b) adopting a flexible approach to *"ancillary clauses"* so that, when the JV itself is not caught by the ban, Article 85(1) would not apply to arrangements which can reasonably be regarded as economically necessary for establishing and operating the JV, at least during the "starting-up period";

(c) accepting, subject to certain market-position limits (20 per cent. and 10 per cent. respectively, depending on whether the co-operation covers production alone or extends to marketing), *almost automatic eligibility for exemption* under Article 85(3), which in practice would mean sending a "comfort letter".

2. The partial solution outlined above could be supplemented by:

(a) *widening existing block exemptions*: this would mean adapting the "specialisation" and "R&D" Regulations so as to include joint distribution by the JV, subject to the same market-share limit of 10 per cent; relations between the parent companies and the JV should no longer be excluded from the field of application of the "patent licence" and "know-how licence" Regulations even where the parties compete with each other;

(b) *a self-imposed time-limit for the completion of the various procedures*: straightforward cases of notification of co-operative JVs should, where nothing more than the sending of a "comfort letter" — not published in the O.J. — is required, be settled within a period similar to that specified in Regulation (EEC) No. 4064/89, *i.e.* five months; present administrative constraints, in particular the time required for translation, unfortunately preclude any such commitment in cases where publication under Article 19(3) of Regulation No. 17/62 or a formal decision under that Regulation is required.

CONTENTS

I. PURPOSE

II. JOINT VENTURES
  A. Economic context
  B. The JV's effect on competition
      1. Competition between parent companies
      2. Competition between the parent companies and the JV
      3. Effects on the position of third parties
      4. Factors in the appraisal
  C. Appraising JVs in the light of Article 85(1)
      1. JVs which are not caught by the ban on restrictive agreements
          (a) JVs formed within a single group of firms
          (b) JVs whose activities are neutral in their impact on competition
              (aa) JVs which perform certain internal organisational tasks on behalf of their parent companies
              (bb) JVs which organise co-operation between their parent companies in fields removed from the markets
              (cc) JVs which, in fields which are close to the market, organise co-operation between firms which do not compete with each other
              (dd) JVs which organise co-operation between competitors in fields which are close to the market
          (c) JVs of minor economic importance
          (d) JVs which do not affect trade within the Community
      2. JVs likely to fall under the ban on restrictive agreements
          (a) JVs between non-competing firms
          (b) JVs between competing firms
              (aa) Pooling of certain specific functions
              (bb) Fully fledged JVs
          (c) Networks of JVs
  D. Exempting JVs under Article 85(3)
      1. Block exemption
          (a) "Specialisation" Regulation
          (b) "Joint research and development" Regulation
          (c) "Patent licensing" and "know-how licensing" Regulations
      2. Exemption by way of an individual decision
      3. Situations in which exemption is given sympathetic consideration
  E. Ancillary restrictions
      1. Principles of evaluation
      2. Assessment of certain additional restrictions
          (a) Restrictions on the JV
          (b) Restrictions on the parent companies

III. OTHER FORMS OF ASSOCIATION BETWEEN FIRMS
      1. Assessment in the light of Article 85(1)
      2. Assessment in the light of Article 85(3)

Part VI—4 Draft Guidelines on Co-operative Joint Ventures

I. PURPOSE

This Notice deals with the appraisal of co-operative JVs (joint ventures) in the light of Article 85 of the EEC Treaty. JVs, as defined in the Commission Notice regarding the concentrative and co-operative operations under Council Regulation (EEC) No. 4064/89 ([1990] O.J. L257/14), are undertakings that are jointly controlled by other undertakings. "Control" is taken to mean the possibility of exercising, directly or indirectly, a decisive influence on the activities of the JV. The effects on competition of other forms of association which do not involve joint control but which enable one or more firms to influence appreciably the activities of one or more other firms may, however, be similar to those of JVs. Examples include the acquisition of a minority holding, unilateral, multilateral or reciprocal, whether or not it entails representation on the various bodies of the firms concerned. Such holdings must therefore also be dealt with in this Notice.

Whether a JV or other form of association between firms can be classed as co-operative depends on whether or not it involves concentration as defined by Article 3(2) of Council Regulation (EEC) No. 4064/89 of December 21, 1989 on the control of concentration between undertakings ([1990] O.J. L257/14). Those operations should therefore be regarded as co-operative which have as their object or effect the co-ordination of the competitive behaviour of firms which remain independent. This category includes the establishment of a JV where it entails a risk of co-ordination of the competitive behaviour between the parents themselves or between the parents and the JV. This is even true where, by virtue of the agreement to establish the JV, or its existence or operation, either party, without necessarily communicating its intentions to the other, can reasonably be expected to adapt its behaviour to that of the JV in order to protect, and obtain a return on, its investment. Co-operative operations continue to fall within the scope of Article 85 and 86 of the EEC Treaty and must be considered in the light of those provisions when proceedings are conducted under Regulation No. 17 ([1962] O.J. 204/62), and Regulations (EEC) No. 1017/68 ([1968] O.J. 175), No. 4056/86 (1986] O.J. L378/4) and No. 3975/87 ([1987] O.J. L374/1).

Concurrently with the introduction of the new legal regime arising from the Regulation on the control of concentrations between undertakings the Commission intends to spell out as clearly as possible, in the interests of the legal certainty of firms, the legal and economic considerations which inform its competition policy as applied to co-operative operations under Article 85 of the Treaty.

This Notice is without prejudice to any interpretation to be given by the Court of Justice of the European Communities

II. JOINT VENTURES

A. Economic context

JVs may cover various fields of co-operation between firms: their purpose may be R&D, the purchase of basic or intermediate products, investment, production or sales planning, the fixing of prices, the sharing of markets, or joint selling.

The number of new JVs in the Community is growing steadily, mainly because enterprises:

— increasingly want to spread the risk of costly technological development;
— are tending to concentrate more on the fields of activity in which they have a great of experience, while seeking, via JVs, to remain abreast of new and promising developments in other fields;
— want to step outside what are often still the national confines of their markets and gain a foothold in other regions of the Community.

JVs can give a spur to compettition by promoting new technological developments, the creation of new products and the penetration of new markets, thus speeding up economic integration. Yet they can also act as a barrier to competition, in particular when they lead to market sharing or when they raise the barriers to entry.

In terms of its purpose, a JV may be intended by its parents as a partial and temporary instrument of co-operation, in which case it is often limited to an ancillary role such as: purchasing raw materials; acquiring know-how; carrying out certain types of research and development work and exploiting the result; financing investment; manufacturing certain products or taking over certain work or internal-management tasks such as accountancy, collection, tax or management consultancy, market research, advertising, the co-ordination of sales or the provision of certain services.

In other situations the JV performs on a lasting basis all the functions of an enterprise and in that capacity operates on the market as an independent supplier or purchaser.

B. The JV's effect on competition

The appraisal of a JV in the light of the rules on competition will focus on the relationship between the enterprises concerned and on the effects of their co-operation on third parties. In this respect the first task is to check whether the establishment or operation of the JV is likely to restrict competition between the parents or between one or more parents and the JV. This must be followed by an examination of whether the operation in question is likely to affect the competitive position of third parties. Depending on the circumstances there may be no restrictive effects at all on completion or such effects may be evident in one or more of the relationships referred to above.

1. *Competition between parent companies*

Competition between parent companies can be restricted only if those companies are already actual or potential competitors.

There is no restriction of competition if the JV operates outside the actual or potential fields of activity of the parent companies; its establishment therefore has only a positive effect, since it creates a new competitor. The same is true when the JV brings together activities of the parent companies in a field in which they cannot hold their own; this will make the JV a permanent player on the market.

If there is genuine and open competition between the parent companies and if it is intended that the JV should operate in markets identical, adjacent or related to those of its parents it is very likely that co-operation between them will entail some restriction of competition.

In order to assess in an individual case whether there is a potential-competition relationship between the parent companies (See Thirteenth Report on Competiton Policy (1983), point 55.), the approach followed must be as realistic as possible, and provide answers to the following main questions (which, while focused specifically on the production of goods, are also applicable to the provision of services):

— Contribution to the JV
  Does each parent company have sufficient financial resources to carry out the planned investment? Does each parent company have sufficiently qualified managerial capacity and the necessary knowledge to run the JV? Does each parent company have access to the necessary sources of input products?
— Production of the JV
  Is each parent company familiar with the technology being applied? Does each parent company manufacture the products upstream or downstream and have access to the necessary production facilities?
— Sales by the JV
— Is actual or potential demand such as to enable each parent company to manufacture the product on its own? Does each parent company have access to the distribution channels needed to sell the product manufactured by the JV?
— Risk factor
  Can each parent company on its own bear the technical and financial risks associated with the production operations of the JV?
— Barriers to market access
  Is each parent company on its own capable of entering the geographical market concerned? Is access to that market impeded by artificial tariff or non-tariff barriers? Can each parent company overcome those barriers without undue effort or cost?
  The parents of a JV should not be regarded as potential competitors unless, in the light of all relevant economic factors, they can reasonably be expected to enter the market individually. The relative weight given to each criterion when assessing potential competition may well vary from case to case.

2. *Competition between the parent companies and the JV*

Competition between the parent companies and the JV can be restricted only if the JV operates on the same markets as its parents, on markets upstream or downstream or on neighbouring markets. In such cases the firms concerned often divide up the geographical or product market, in particular by specialising their production, or by sharing out the customers. If, however, the parent companies and the JV remain active competitors they may well be tempted to soften competition be co-ordinating or aligning their behaviour as regards pricing or the volume of production or sales.

3. Effects on the position of third parties

The restrictive effect on third parties depends on the JV's activities in relation to those of its parents and on the combined economic strength of the firms concerned.

Where the parent companies leave it to the JV to handle their purchases or sales, the choice available to suppliers or customers is restricted. The same is true when the parent companies arrange for the JV to manufacture primary or intermediate products or to process products which they themselves have produced. The setting-up of a JV may even exclude from the market the parents' traditional suppliers and customers; that risk increases in step with the degree of oligopolisation of the market and the existence of exclusive or preferential agreements between the JV and its parents.

The existence of a JV may even be a barrier to market entry by potential competitors or impede the growth of the parents' competitors

4. Factors in the appraisal

The scale of a JV's effects on competition depends on a number of factors, the most important of which are:
— the market shares of the parent companies and the JV, the structure of the relevant market and the degree of concentration in the sector concerned;
— the economic and financial strength of the parent companies, and any technical or commercial edge which they may have;
— the market proximity of the activities carried out by the JV;
— whether the fields of activity of the parent companies and the JV are identical or interdependent;
— the scale of the JV's activities in relation to those of its parents;
— the extent to which the arrangements between the firms concerned are restrictive;
— the extent to which the operation keeps out third parties.

C. Appraising JVs in the light of Article 85(1)

The appraisal of a JV under the rules of competition does not depend on its legal structure. What matters is the restrictive nature of the clauses agreed upon by the parties, and the impact of the creation and operation of the JV on market conditions.

1. *JVs which are not caught by the ban on restrictive agreements*

Article 85(1) does not apply to the following categories of JV, since they do not have as their object or effect the prevention, restriction or distortion of competition within the common market and are not likely to have an appreciable effect on trade between Member States.

(a) *JVs formed within a single group of firms*

Where a JV is formed by firms which all belong to the same group and which are not in a position freely to decide their market behaviour, the creation of that JV is merely a matter of internal organisation and allocation of tasks within the group and is accordingly neutral in its impact on competition.

(b) *JVs whose activities are neutral in their impact on competition*

The Commission Notice of 1968 (Notice concerning agreements, decisions and concerted practices in the field of co-operation between enterprises Corrigendum [1968] O.J. C75/3; [1968] O.J. C93/14) lists forms of co-operation between firms which, by their nature, do not restrict competition.

It also deals with cases in which co-operation takes place via a JV. The definitions and delimitation criteria set out in that Notice – and apparent from the case-law of the Court of Justice and the administrative practice of the Commission - areapplicable to such JVs.

There are four types of JV in that category:

(aa) *JVs which perform certain internal organizational tasks on behalf of their parent companies*

This includes JVs which collect, analyse and process data on behalf of their parent companies, provide them with a tax or business consultancy service or perform certain internal functions on their behalf in the area of information gathering, credit guarantees or debt collection. It also includes JVs looking after the technical or organisational aspects of the joint use of existing production facilities and storage or transport equipment. In all such cases the effect on the business decisions of the parent comapnies and, hence, on competition, is nil.

(bb) *JVs which organise co-operation between their parent companies in fields removed from the markets*
JVs which deal solely with research and development do not, generally speaking, restrict competition, even where their parents compete with each other.

(cc) *JVs which, in fields which are close to the market, organize co-operation between firms which do not compete with each other*
JVs which are formed ny non-competing firms and which are designed to provide a joint selling after-sales or repair service are not caught by the ban on restrictive practices since they do not restrict competition between their parents and do not affect the position of third parties.
The same is true of JVs set up as consortia for the execution of orders where the parents do not compete with each other as regards the work to be done or where each of them by itself is unable to execute the orders.

(dd) *JVs which organise co-operation between competitors in fields which are close to the market*
Exceptionally, the ban on restrictive practices does not cover this type of JV provided that the parents' freedom to compete with each other, and the position of third parties, are unaffected. This group includes parents which pool their advertising effort or use a common quality label.

(c) *JVs of minor economic importance*
Agreements, decisions and concerted practices which form the basis of a JV also fall outside the scope of Article 85 if they do not have as their object or effect an appreciable restriction of competition. In its Notice on agreements of minor importance which do not fall under Article 85(1) of the Treaty establishing the European Economic Community ([1986] O.J. C231/2) the Commission gives concrete meaning to the concept "appreciable" by setting quantitative criteria and by explaining their application, thus enabling firms to judge for themselves whether their agreements fall under Article 85(1). The prohibition does not normally apply to such agreements if:

—the goods or services which are the subject of the agreement, together with the participating firms' other goods or services which are considered by users to be equivalent in view of their characteristics, price and intended use, do not, in the area of the common market covered by the agreement, represent more than 5 per cent. of the total market for such goods or services and

—the aggregate annual turnover of the participating firms does not exceed ECU 200 million.

(d) *JVs which do not affect trade within the Community*
Article 85(1) does not apply to JVs which are not likely to affect trade between Member States, *e.g.* when the JVs actual or foreseeable effects on competition are strictly limited to the territory of a Member State or to the territory of non-member countries.

Nor does Article 85(1) apply cases where the JV has only an insignificant effect on trade or the structure of competition within the common market. Trade between Member States is likely to be appreciably affected only when the thresholds referred to in the Notice on agreements of minor importance are exceeded.

2. *JVs likely to fall under the ban on restrictive agreements*

In the case of JVs which are likely to be caught by Article 85(1) a distinction should be made between those formed by competing firms and those formed by non-competing firms.

(a) *JVs between non-competing firms*
The appraisal of JVs between firms which do not compete with each other focuses as much on the nature of the JV's operations in relation to those of its parents (see II. B. 2) as on the effects they have on the position of third parties (see II. B. 3).

Where the JV merely markets what its parents produce the ban on restrictive agreements does not normally apply (see II. C. 1(b)(cc)).

If the JV manufactures primary or intermediate products for its parents or processes the goods produced by one or more parent companies the application of Article 85(1) cannot normally br ruled out, since there may be restrictions of competition both between the JV and its parents and *vis-à-vis* third parties. There is even a great likelihood that, where the JV is in a strong position on the markets concerned, the buying or selling possibilities of third parties will be affected

(b) *JVs between competing firms*

Depending on the functions performed by the JV on behalf of its parents there are two separate types of cases in which competition both between the firms concerned and *vis-à-vis* third parties is affected.

(aa) *Pooling of certain specific functions*

This type of case covers JVs which perform only certain functions and are not present on the market in their own right. These are JVs which are not covered by the Notice on co-operation between enterprises. Typically, they carry out certain activitites on behalf of their parents in the field of research and development, purchasing, sales or production:
— research and development JVs may, in exceptional cases, restrict competition if they exclude, individual research and development or if co-operation in the field of research and development has a direct impact on the conditions of competition on the market in the resulting product. Competition tends to be restricted when co-operation extends to activities involving exploitation of the results of research and development;
— sales JVs exclude competition between the parent companies as suppliers, thereby limiting the choice offered to buyers;
— production JVs have effects on competition which differ according to whether they take over all or part of their parents' production activities.

In the first case the parents continue to compete on the marketing side only. The room for competition is appreciably reduced, however, in that their manufacturing costs are the same; this is even true where parents sell the JV's products under different brands.

In the second case there are two separate types of situation:
— If the JV is handling the final stage of production, processing what its parents produce, competition between the parents is generally severly restricted, since their co-operation is close to the market and transfer prices tend to become uniform;
— if the JV manufacturers primary or intermediate products the likelihood of restraint of competition between the parents increases with the importance of the primary or intermediate product in the manufacture of the final product. The share of the primary or intermediate product in the cost of the final product is crucial: If it is more than 50 per cent. of total cost, competition between the parents will be heavily reduced.

(bb) *Fully-fledged JVs*

This category covers JVs which perform all the functions of a firm and are thus present on the market as suppliers or buyers. In order to determine to what extent their activities restrict competition a distinction must be made between the following subgroups:
— If the JV operates on the same market as its parents, it is very likely, not to say inevitable, that competition between the firms concerned will be restricted;
— If the JV operates on a market upstream or downstream of that of the parents with which it has supply or delivery links the effect on competition between the parents will be the same as in the case of JVs which perform only some of the functions of a firm (see (aa) above);
— if the JV operates on a market adjacent to that of its parents,

competition is restricted only if the two markets are interdependent. This is the case where a JV manufactures products which are complementary to those of its parents;
— if the JV operates on a market which is completely removed from that of its parents the JV will rarely entail any restraint of competition. Such a situation might arise where the JV's turnover becomes so important to the parent companies' profitability that their propensity to compete actively with each other is diminished.

Combinations of these types of JV are often found in everyday economic life. An overall assessment will then need to be made of the resulting restrictions of competition between the firms concerned, and of the effects which their co-operation has on third parties. Only those restrictions of competition which can be foreseen when the JV is formed and which can reasonably be expected to materialise must be taken into consideration.

(c) *Networks of JVs*

Special attention must be paid to networks of JVs in their various shapes.
— The first is where competing parent companies establish several JVs which operate on the same product market but in separate areas. On top of the restrictions of competition which can already be attributed to each JV, there will then be those which arise in the relations between JVs. At the same time, competition will be further reduced between the parent companies.

The restrictive effects on competition are also likely to be aggravated when competing parent companies set up several JVs in respect of complementary products which they themselves intend to process, or even in respect of different products which they themselves market.
— The most severe effect on competition occurs when partners competing in the same oligopolistic sector set up a multitude of JVs for related products or numerous intermediate products.
— Even where the JV is formed by non-competing firms and does not, on its own, entail any restraint of competition, it can fall under Article 85(1) if it belongs to a network of JVs set up, with different partners, by the same firm and for the same product market (optical fibres). If the said partners compete with each other there will, additionally, be restrictive effects in the relationships between them.

D. Exempting JVs under Article 85(3)

1. Block exemption

JVs falling within the scope of Article 85(1) are exempted from the ban on restrictive agreements if they satisfy the tests laid down in a block exemption regulation. Co-operation via JVs is, under the terms of two Commission Regulations, allowed in the field of research and development and production, but not in that of sales. A further two Regulations authorise certain agreements that restrict competition when technology is transferred to a JV by its parents, provied that the latter are not competitors.

(a) *"Specialisation" Regulation*

Commission Regulation (EEC) No. 417/85 on the application of Article 85(3) of the Treaty to categories of specialisation agreements ([1985] O.J. L53/1) authorises Joint manufacturing, subject to a twofold condition: the aggregate market share of the participating firms must not represent more than 20 per cent. and their aggregate annual turnover must not exceed ECU 500 million.

Where the turnover exceeds the limits specified, the participating firms may make use of an accelerated procedure in order to have the exemption under the Regulation applied to them. The exemption also covers the joint manufacture of products which were not previously made by any of the participating firms. If the JV is also handling sales it can be exempted only by way of an individual decision.

The Regulation accordingly applies only to JVs which are not fully-fledged firms. It does, however, cover the entire range of JVs which perform specific manufacturing functions. This includes the joint manufacture of primary, intermediate or finished products, provided that such products are supplied exclusively to the parent companies and that those companies are not themselves manufacturers in the same field of activity as the JV.

(b) *"Joint research and development" Regulation*

Regulation (EEC) No. 418/85 on the application of Article 85(3) of the Treaty to categories of research and development agreement ([1985] O.J. L53/5) authorises the establishment of JVs whose activities may range from research and development to the joint exploitation of the results (production and the granting of licences). The Regulation puts a ceiling of 20 per cent. on the market share but places no limit on turnover. Joint selling via a JV can, however, be exempted only by way of an individual decision.

The research and development Regulation likewise applies only to JVs which are not fully-fledged firms. It does, however, allow all forms of co-operation in the field of production, since specialisation is not made a requirement; the parent companies may therefore start or continue production in the same field as the JV. The JV's production may, however, be marketed only by its parents. On the other hand the JV may be charged with granting licences to third parties. This increased scope for co-operation is also available to large competing firms.

It is, however, limited to the exploitation of the results of Joint research and development, the exemption applying on condition that such results substantially contribute to technical or economic progress and are decisive for the manufacture of new or improved products.

(c) *"Patent licensing" and "know-how licensing" Regulations*

Regulation (EEC) No. 2349/84 on the application of Article 85(3) of the Treaty to certain categories of patent licensing agreement ([1984] O.J. L219/15) also covers agreements between the parent companies of a JV or between a parent company and the JV, provided that those agreements relate to the activities of the JV and that the parent companies are not competitors. The Regulation applies to pure patent licensing agreements and to combined patent licensing and know-how agreements.

The Regulation authorises the granting to a JV of exclusive territorial licences covering manufacture and sales; protection through a ban on exports from the respective territories of the JV and the parent companies throughout the period of validity of the contract; and protection of a JV's territory against active competition (manufacture and advertising) from other licensees throughout the period of validity of the contract and, for five years from the date on which the product is first put on the market in the Community, also against passive competition (Imports) from other licensees.

Regulation (EEC) No. 556/89 on the application of Article 85(3) of the Treaty to certain categories of know-how licensing agreements ([1989] O.J. L61/1) contains similar provisions, except that the territorial protection between the JV and its parents is limited to ten years from the signature of the first licensing agreement concluded in the Community; the signature of that agreement also marks the beginning of the period in which the JV may be protected against active competition (ten years) and passive competition (five years) from other licensees.

2. *Exemption by way of an individual decision*

An individual exemption may be granted following notification where a JV restricts competition but satisfies the four tests set out in Article 85(3).

The Commission must first check whether the JV entails objective advantages which offset the risks which its establishment and operation pose to competition.

A JV is deemed to entail objective advantages when, by improving production or distribution, in particular through the introduction of new or more advanced products and processes or through the opening-up of new markets, it helps to improve the competitiveness of the firms concerned and thus fosters dynamic competition on a market with a competitive structure. JVs which lead to major new investment usually have positive effects.

On the other hand, JVs have essentially negative effects on competition when they provide their parents with either the means to co-ordinate or align their competitive behaviour, be it in the present (in particular by fixing prices, agreeing on the quantities to be produced or sold, or sharing out markets) or in the future (in particular by joint planning of investment), or a reason for doing so.

Such JVs constitute, or operate as, a traditional cartel.

In any case the overall appraisal of the JV is bound to be negative if its establishment leads to the elimination of competition in respect of a substantial part of the products concerned. No exemption can therefore be granted in cases where, by grouping the activities of the parent companies, the JVs serve to establish, underpin or accentuate a dominant position.

That is why major cases (in terms of the economic and financial power and market share of the firms concerned) will always require a detailed individual scrutiny which enables their objective advantages to be weighed up against the resulting adverse effects on competition.

3. Situations in which exemptions is given sympathetic consideration

Some JVs must normally be given sympathetic consideration from the point of view of competition.

This applies to JVs which create substantial new capacity or which significantly increase their parents' existing capacity (whether this involves the extension of a product range, of production or of a market). They are normally granted exemption under Article 85(3), within specified limits for the aggregate market share of the firms concerned.

The said market share should not normally exceed 20 per cent. where co-operation between the parents does not extend beyond production, and 10 per cent. when it includes marketing. It is necessary to make such a distinction because the risk to competition increases as co-operation moves nearer the market.

Within those market-share limits it is fair to assume that the effects in terms of the exclusion of third parties, and the risks in terms of barriers to entry are kept within reasonable proportions and that the market structure will continue to ensure effective competition.

Networks of JVs cannot, however, be given sympathetic consideration as such and must accordingly be assessed on a case-by-case basis. Sympathetic consideration can under no circumstances be given to JVs which help further to tighten an already narrow oligopoly.

E. Ancillary restrictions

1. Principles of evaluation

A distinction must be made between restrictions of competition which are inherent in the actual creation of a JV, and additional agreements which would, on their own, constitute restrictions of competition by limiting the freedom of action in the market of the firms concerned. Those additional agreements are either directly related and necessary to the establishment and operation of the JV in so far as they cannot be dissociated from it without jeopardising its existence, or are simply concluded at the same time without having those features.

Only additional agreements which are directly related and necessary to the JV must be assessed together with the JV itself and be treated, in the light of the rules of compeition, as ancillary restrictions if they remain subordinate in importance to the main object of the JV. In particular as concerns the necessity of the restriction, it is proper not only to take account of its nature, but equally to ensure that its duration and subject-matter, and geographical field of application, do not exceed what the creation and operation of the JV reasonably requires.

If a JV does not *per se* fall within the scope of Article 85(1), then neither do any additional agreements which, while they restrict competition, are ancillary to the JV in the manner described above.

Conversely, if a JV falls within the scope of Article 85(1), then so will any ancillary restrictions. The same exemption criteria will then apply to both, and no specific justification need be given as regards the ancillary restrictions.

On the other hand, additional agreements which are not ancillary to the JV normally fall within the scope of Article 85(1), regardless of the fact that the JV itself may not. For them to be granted exemption under Article 85(3), an individual assessment must first be made based on their own merits, irrespective of the merits of the JV itself.

In view of the diversity of JVs and of the restrictions that may be linked to them, only a few examples can be given of how those principles are applied, drawing on past experience.

Part VI—4 Draft Guidelines on Co-operative Joint Ventures

2. Assessment of certain additional restrictions

When attempting to determine whether additional restrictions are ancillary a distinction must be made between those which affect the JV and those which affect the parent companies.

(a) *Restrictions on the JV*

Of the restrictions which affect the JV, those which give concrete expression to its object (*e.g.* contract clauses which specify the product range and the location of production) may be regarded as ancillary. Additional restrictions which go beyond the definition of the corporate object and which relate to quantities, prices or customers, and prohibitions of exports, may not.

Thus when a JV involves the creation of new production capacity or the transfer of technology from the parent companies, the obligation imposed on the JV not to manufacture or market products competing with the licensed products may be regarded as ancillary; the JV must seek to ensure the success of the new production unit, without depriving the parent companies of the necessary control over exploitation and dissemination of their technology (Mitchell Cotts/Sofiltra).

Depending on circumstances, other restrictions on the JV which should be seen as an inevitable consequence of the parents' wish to limit co-operation to a specific field of activity and avoid compromising the object and existence of the JV (Elopak/Metal Box–Odin), may also be regarded as ancillary.

Where the parent companies assign to the JV certain stages of production or the manufacture of certain products, obligations on the JV to purchase from or supply its parents may also be regarded as ancillary, at least during the JV's starting-up period.

(b) *Restrictions on the parent companies*

A clause which bars the parent companies from competing with the JV or from competing actively with it on its territory, at least during the starting-up period, may be regarded as ancillary. Additional restrictions relating to quantities, prices or customers, and bans on exports obviously go beyond what is required for the setting-up and proper operation of the JV.

The following in particular have been regarded as necessary during the starting-up period of a JV designed to enable a parent company to become established on a new market: territorial restrictions imposed on that parent comany, through the grant to the JV of an exclusive manufacturing licence, in respect of fields of application or product markets in which both the JV and that parent company are active (Mitchell Cotts/Sofiltra).

On the other hand the grant to the JV of an exclusive exploitation licence has been regarded as necessary (without any time-limit other than the duration of the JV itself) in cases where the parent company granting it was not active in the same field of application or on the same product market as that for which the licence was granted (Elopak/Metal Box–Odin).

This will generally be the case with JVs undertaking new activities in respect of which the parent companies are neither actual nor potential competitors.

III. OTHER FORMS OF ASSOCIATION BETWEEN FIRMS

Other forms of association between firms can produce effects on competition similar to those of JVs. This is true of minority holdings, whether unilateral, multilateral or reciprocal, whether or not they involve representation on the decision-making bodies of the firms concerned.

1. Assessment in the light of Article 85(1)

The acquisition by a firm of a non-controlling interest in a competitor is not *per se* caught by Article 85(1). It may nevertheless serve as a means of influencing the behaviour of the firms concerned in such a way as to restrict or distort competition on the market in which those firms operate. This is the case in particular where the shareholding is used to underpin co-operative links between the firms concerned or create a structure which lends itself to such co-operation (Judgment in Joined Cases 142 and 156/84 *BAT and Reynolds* v. *Commission* [1987] E.C.R. 4566).

Similar but more substantial restrictive effects on competition occur when several firms which are already competing among themselves take out a minority shareholding in a competing third party which, while it does not give them joint control over the third party, makes it possible for them to agree jointly on or align the competitive behaviour of all the firms concerned.

Cross-shareholding between competitors, especially when they are combined with representation on the decision-making bodies of the partners concerned, are likely to enable the firms to inform and influence each other. They accordingly constitute a prime means of co-ordinating their market behaviour and thus of reducing if not eliminating competition between them. In such cases the applicability of Article 85(1) is not normally in doubt.

2. Assessment in the light of Article 85(3)

The possibility of granting an exemption depends on all the circumstances surrounding the acquisition of the holdings concerned.

If it merely replaces a traditional cartel or accentuates its effects in such a way as to preserve existing market structures the conditions for granting an exemption are not deemed to be fulfilled.

If, however, the holdings are acquired as part of an effort at co-operation the positive effects of which outweigh the risks to competition, an exemption may be granted to them at the same time and on the same terms as to the co-operation itself.

CHAPTER 5

OPERATIONS/CLAUSES TYPICAL OF JOINT VENTURE AGREEMENTS

1. Restriction of competition which may result from the creation of the joint venture

1.1. Competition between the parent companies

1.1.1. Actual competition

United Reprocessors 102
GEC/Weir Sodium Circulators 117
WANO 138
Amersham/Buchler 184 (para. 7)
Enichem/ICI 279 (paras. 27, 29)
Olivetti/Canon 280 (paras. 37, 40)*

1.1.2. Potential competition

KEWA 103

De Laval/Stork I & II 114, 281*
GEC/Weir Sodium Circulators 117
WANO 138
Vacuum Interrupters II 161*
Amersham/Buchler 184 (para. 8)
Rockwell/IVECO 196
Optical Fibres 249
Olivetti/Canon 280 (para. 39)
Konsortium ECR 900 323
BP/Bayer 284 (para. 23)
Enichem/ICI 279 (para. 28)
IVECO/Ford 287 (para. 24)
UIP 309 (para. 3a)
Odin 322
Cekacan 326 (para. 30)
Screensport/EBU 337 (paras. 54–56)
Eirpage 344 (paras. 11, 12, 18)
13th Comp. Rep. (para. 55)

1.1.3. Spill-over effect

Bayer/Gist-Brocades 100
GEC/Weir Sodium Circulators 117*
CSV 134 (para. 76)
WANO 138
Odin 322 (para. 36)

1.2. Effect of the joint venture on the competitive position of third parties

Optical Fibres 249 (para. 46)
Mitchell-Cotts/Sofiltra 267 (para. 19)
Screensport/EBU 337 (para. 57–66)*
Eirpage 344 (para. 7, 20, 22, 23)

1.3. Restriction of future competition resulting from the joint venture agreements

1.3.1. Between parents and the joint venture

De Laval/Stork 114 (para. 4)
Mitchell-Cotts/Sofiltra 267 (para. 20)

1.3.2 Between several joint ventures having a common parent company

Optical Fibres 249 (para. 48)*
Mitchell-Cotts/Sofiltra 267 (para. 19)

2. Ancillary clauses which may restrict competition

2.1. Non-competition clauses

United Reprocessors 102
KEWA 103
Vacuum Interrupters 112, 161
GEC/Weir Sodium Circulators 117

Part VI—5 Operations/Clauses Typical of Joint Venture Agreements

WANO 138
Floral 148 (para. II.1)
Rennet 149
Langenscheidt/Hachette 168 (para. II.8)
Amersham/Buchler 184 (paras. 2, 13)
Rockwell/IVECO 196
BP Kellogg 235*
Mitchel-Cotts/Sofiltra 267 (para. 22)
IVECO/Ford 287 (para. 14, 15, 24–25)
BBC Brown Boveri 291 (para. 16)
Odin 322 (paras. 7 & 9)
Cekacan 326 (paras, 16, 34–35)
Eirpage 344 (para. 12)
6th Comp. Rep. (paras. 60–63)
Stremsel v. *Commission* 84

2.2. Co-ordination of investment policy

United Reprocessors 101
Enichem/ICI 279*
BP/Bayer 284 (paras. 11, 21)

2.3. Post-termination provisions

De Laval/Stork I 114 (paras. 7, 14)*
Odin 322 (para 10–13)
Eirpage 344 (para. 19)
Roquette/National Starch 14th Comp. Rep. (paras. 87–892.4)

2.4. Licensing and exchange of technical information

Henkel/Colgate 52
United Reprocessors 101
De Laval/Stork 114 (paras. 7, 14)
GEC/Weir Sodium Circulators 117
WANO 138
Langenscheidt/Hachette 168 (para. II.12)
Rockwell/IVECO 196
BP/Kellogg 235
Optical Fibres 249 (paras. 38, 49, 59)*
Mitchell-Cotts/Sofiltra 267 (paras. 9–10)
Olivetti/Canon 280 (paras. 48–50)
BP/Bayer 284 (para. 21)
BBC Brown Boveri 291 (para. 19)
Odin 322 (paras. 6–9)

2.5. Joint price fixing

United Reprocessors 101
Fieldmuhle-Stora. 12th Comp. Rep. (paras. 73–74)

2.6. Purchasing and supply obligations

WANO 138
Vacuum Interrupters 161
Rockwell/IVECO 195*
Enichem/ICI 277 (para. 26)
Olivetti/Canon 278 (para. 43)
BP/Bayer 284 (paras. 11, 20)
IVECO/Ford 287 (paras. 8, 9, 27, 28)
Cekacan 326 (paras. 17, 18, 21–22, 36, 39)
Fieldmuhle-Stora 12th Comp. Rep. (paras. 73–74)

2.7. Grant of exclusive distribution rights

De Laval/Stork I 114 (para. 7)
WANO 138
Langenscheidt/Hachette 169 (para. 9)
Amersham/Buchler 183 (paras. 3–4)
Rockwell/IVECO 195
Optical Fibres 249 (paras. 37–38)
Mitchell-Cotts/Sofiltra 266 (para. 10)*
IVECO/Ford 287 (paras. 13, 27, 28)
UIP 309 (paras. 17, 25, 26, 42, 55)
Finnpap 19th Comp. Rep. (para. 44)

2.8. Territorial restrictions

Optical Fibres 249 (paras. 37–39, 54, 67)
Mitchell-Cotts/Sofiltra 267 (paras. 11, 23)*
BBC Brown Boveri 291 (paras. 18, 30)
IVECO/Ford 287 (paras. 10, 13–15, 27–28)
Cekacan 326 (paras. 40–42)
Fieldmuhle-Stora. 12th Comp. Rep. (paras. 73–74)

2.9. Trademark-related clauses

Olivetti/Canon 280 (para. 45)
IVECO/Ford 287 (paras. 11, 26)

PART VII

ARTICLE 86

CHAPTER 1

THE ESTABLISHMENT OF A DOMINANT POSITION

A. THE RELEVANT MARKET

1. The relevant product market

1.1. Economic analysis of the relevant market

Continental Can 46 (paras. 4, 8, 15–19)
Chiquita 101 (para. II.A)
Vitamins 104 (paras. 2–5, 20)
Michelin 165 (paras. 3–7, 31–34)
ECS/AKZO 242 (para. 64)
Boosey & Hawkes 273 (para. 17)
Hilti 282
British Sugar 286 (para. 42)
Tetra Pak I 289 (paras. 29–39)
SABENA 295 (paras. 14–15)
British Plasterboard 299 (paras. 13–20, 106–109)
Decca 304 (paras. 83–87)
Magill 307 (paras. 20–21)
RTE v. Commission T14 (grounds 61–62)
BBC v. Commission T15 (grounds 48–50)
ITV v. Commission T16 (grounds 47–48)
Flat Glass T30 (ground 363)
Continental Can v. Commission 35 (grounds 31–36)*
ICI & CSC v. Commission 37 (grounds 19–22)
United Brands v. Commission 62 (grounds 12–35)
Hoffmann-La Roche v. Commission 67 (ground 28)
Michelin v. Commission 102 (ground 37)*
Alsatel v. Novosam 160 (grounds 13–17)
Ahmed Saeed v. Zentrale 162 (grounds 39–41)
AKZO v. Commission III 186 (grounds 51–54)

1.2. Narrow definition of the relevant market

General Motors 84
ABG/Oil Companies 113
Hugin/Liptons 121*
British Leyland 212
Magill 307 (paras. 14–18, 20–21)
General Motors v. Commission 46 (grounds 4–10)*
Hugin v. Commission 68 (grounds 3–8)*
Télémarketing v. CLT 124
Metro v. Commission II 134 (ground 89)
British Leyland v. Commission 136

1.3. Definition given by defendant

Hilti v. Commission T21 (ground 78)

1.4. Time factor and substituability

Tetra Pak II (paras. 94–97)*

2. The relevant geographic market

European Sugar Industry 69
Chiquita 101 (para. II.A)
Michelin 165 (paras. 8–9, 34)*
British Sugar 286 (paras. 43–48)
Tetra Pak I 289 (para. 40)
SABENA 295 (para. 16)
British Plasterboard 299 (paras. 21–24, 110–113)
Decca 304 (paras. 88–90)
Solvay 332 (paras. 42–43)
ICI 333 (para. 43–45)
Continental Can v. Commission 35
ICI & CSC v. Commission 37 (grounds 9–18)
Suiker Unie v. Commission 48 (grounds 301–317, 370–375, 441–451)
United Brands v. Commission 62 (grounds 36–57)
Alsatel v. Novosam 160 (ground 18)

B. A SUBSTANTIAL PART OF THE COMMON MARKET

Continental Can 46 (para. 21)
Michelin 165
SABENA 295 (para. 16)
Decca 304 (para. 89)
BRT v. SABAM II 38 (ground 5)
RTE v. Commission T14 (grounds 64)
Suiker Unie v. Commission 48 (grounds 370–375, 441–449)
Michelin v. Commission 102 (grounds 25–28)*

Alsatel v. *Novosam* 160 (grounds 12, 18)

C. DOMINANCE

1. The definition of dominance

Continental Can 46 (para. 3)*
Chiquita 101 (para. II.A.2)
Vitamins 104
ABG/Oil Companies 113
Boosey & Hawkes 273 (para. 19)
Hilti 282
Hilti v. *Commission* T21 (ground 90)
ICI & CSC v. *Commission* 37 (grounds 9–18)
United Brands v. *Commission* 62 (grounds 63–65)
Hoffmann-La Roche v. *Commission* 67 (grounds 38–41, 70–71)*
Michelin v. *Commission* 102 (grounds 57–59)

2. Joint & collective dominance

European Sugar Industry 69
Flat Glass 300 (paras. 78–79)*
Alsatel v. *Novosam* 160 (ground 21)
Flat Glass T30 (grounds 356–360)

3. The establishment of dominance

3.1. Statutory dominance or monopoly

Gema 38
General Motors 84*
British Telecommunications 188 (paras. 25–27)*
British Leyland 212
Magill 307 (para. 22)
SACEM & SABAM. 4th Comp. Rep. (para. 112)
Deutsche Grammophon v. *Metro* 19 (grounds 16–18)
BRT v. *SABAM II* 38 (ground 5)
Sacchi 39 (grounds 14–15)
General Motors v. *Commission* 46 (ground 4–10)*
Télémarketing v. *CLT* 124 (ground 17)
British Leyland v. *Commission* 136

3.2. Ownership of intellectual/industrial property rights

Zoja C.S.C.-I.C.I. 64
Hilti 281 (para. 71)*
Magill 307 (para. 22)
RTE v. *Commission* T14 (ground 63)
BBC v. *Commission* T15 (ground 51)
ITV v. *Commission* T16 (ground 49)
Hilti v. *Commission* T21 (ground 93)
EMI-CBS 50 (grounds 35–37)

3.3. Market shares

European Sugar Industry 69
Chiquita 101 (para. II.A.2)
Vitamins 104 (paras. 5, 21)
Michelin 165 (paras. 12, 15–17, 35)
ECS/AKZO 242 (para. 69)*
Boosey & Hawkes 273 (para. 18)
Hilti 282 (paras. 66–68)
British Sugar 286 (para. 50)
Tetra Pak I 289 (para. 44)
SABENA 295 (paras. 24–25)
British Plasterboard 299 (para. 118)
9th Comp. Rep. (para. 22)
10th Comp. Rep. (para. 150)
Gestetner v. Xerox 19th Comp. Rep. (para. 63)
Hilti v. *Commission* T21 (ground 91–92)
United Brands v. *Commission* 62 (grounds 97–108)
Hoffmann-La Roche v. *Commission* 67 (grounds 38–41, 51, 57–58, 61–63)*
Alsatel v. *Novosam* 160 (ground 19)
AKZO v. *Commission III* 186 (ground 60)

3.4. Size or importance of competitors

Chiquita 101 (para. II.A.2)
Vitamins 104 (paras. 5, 21)
Michelin 165 (paras. 15, 17, 35)
British Sugar 286 (paras. 51–54)
Tetra Pak II 348 (para 101)
United Brands v. *Commission* 62 (grounds 109–121)
Hoffmann-La Roche v. *Commission* 67 (grounds 48, 51, 58)*

3.5. Range of products

Continental Can 46 (para. 11)
Vitamins 104 (paras. 4, 21)
ECS/AKZO 242 (para. 69)
British Plasterboard 299 (paras. 42, 120)
Hoffmann-La Roche v. *Commission* 67 (grounds 45–46)*

3.6. Technical advantages over competitors

Continental Can 46 (paras. 9–10)
Chiquita 101 (para. II.A.2)
Vitamins 104 (paras. 7–8, 21)
Michelin 165 (para. 13)
Tetra Pak I 289 (para. 44)
United Brands v. *Commission* 62 (grounds 82–83)*
Hoffmann-La Roche v. *Commission* 67 (ground 48, 51)

3.7. Commercial advantages over competitors

Chiquita 101 (para. II.A.2)

Part VII—1 The Establishment of a Dominant Position

Vitamins 104 (paras. 4, 6, 8, 21)
Michelin 165 (paras. 13, 36)
British Sugar 286 (para. 56)
British Plasterboard 299 (paras. 43, 120)
United Brands v. *Commission* 62 (grounds 69–96)*
Hoffmann-La Roche v. *Commission* 67 (ground 48)
Michelin v. *Commission* 102 (grounds 57–58)

3.8. Size and resources of the group

Chiquita 101 (para. II.A.2)
Vitamins 104 (paras. 6, 21)
British Plasterboard 299 (paras. 44–47, 120)
Hoffmann-La Roche v. *Commission* 67 (ground 47)
Michelin v. *Commission* 102 (ground 55)*
Bodson v. *Pompes Funèbres* 150 (ground 29)*

3.9. Dependence of consumers

Zoja/C.S.C-I.C.I. 64
ABG/Oil Companies 113*
Hugin Liptons 121
Boosey & Hawkes 273 (para. 18)

3.10. Ability to determine prices unilaterally

ECS/AKZO 242 (para. 69)
British Sugar 286 (paras. 51–55)
Hoffmann-La Roche v. *Commission* 67 (grounds 41, 70–71, 76, 78)*

3.11. Barriers to entry

3.11.1. Statutory

British Sugar 286
Decca 300 (para. 8.92)

3.11.2 Large capital requirements or technical barriers to entry

Chiquita 101 (para. II.A.2)
Vitamins 104 (para. 21)
ECS/AKZO 242 (para. 70)
British Sugar 286 (paras. 55–59)
Tetra Pak I 289 (para. 44)
British Plasterboard 299 (paras. 45, 120)*
United Brands v. *Commission* 62 (ground 122)
Hoffmann-La Roche v. *Commission* 67 (ground 48)

3.11.3. Mature/saturated nature of the market

Hilti 282 (para. 69)

Tetra Pak 289
British Plasterboard 299
Flat Glass 300

3.12. Circular argument

Michelin 165 (para. 35)
Tetra Pak II 348 (para. 146)

CHAPTER 2

ABUSE OF A DOMINANT POSITION

A. CONCEPT OF AN ABUSE OF A DOMINANT POSITION

Continental Can 46*
Zoja C.S.C.-I.C.I. 64
ECS/AKZO 242 (para. 73)
Decca 304 (para. 96)
Hoffmann-La Roche v. *Commission* 67 (ground 91)*
Ahmed Saeed v. *Zentrale* 162 (grounds 37–38)

B. EXAMPLES OF ABUSE

1. Unfair terms imposed on clients

Gema I 38
Chiquita 101 (para. II.A.3.a)
Gema Statutes 174
British Telecommunications 188 (paras. 28–36)
Tetra Pak II 348 (paras. 108, 110, 115, 123–127)
Railway Rolling Stock 3rd Comp. Rep. (paras. 68–69)
SACEM & SABAM 4th Comp. Rep. (para. 112)
Instituto/IMC & Angus 16th Comp. Rep. (para. 76)
BRT v. *SABAM* II 38 (grounds 8–15)
Sacchi 39 (grounds 6–1)
Suiker Unie v. *Commission* 48 (grounds 383–402)
United Brands v. *Commission* 62 (paras. 130–162)*
Ahmed Saeed v. *Zentrale* 162 (grounds 42–44)

2. Unfair or excessive prices

General Motors Continental 84
Chiquita 101 (para. II.A.3.b,c)
British Leyland 212
SABENA 295 (para. 29)
Sterling Airways. 10th Comp. Rep. (paras. 136–138)
Parke, Davis v. *Centrafarm* 8
General Motors v. *Commission* 46 (grounds 11–24)*

217

Book One: Part VII—Article 86

United Brands v. Commission 62 (grounds 235–268)*
Bodson v. Pompes Funèbres 150 (grounds 31–34)
Ministère public v. Tournier 167 (ground 38–43)
Lucazeau v. SACEM 168 (ground 25–30)

3. Exclusive purchasing

Vitamins 104 (paras. 11–18, 22–27)
Solvay 332 (paras. 56–59)
ICI 333 (paras. 57–60)
Tetra Pak II 348 (paras. 116–117, 143)
Instituto/IMC & Angus 16th Comp. Rep. (para. 76)
Industrial cases 19th Comp. Rep. (para. 62)
Hoffmann-La Roche v. Commission 67 (grounds 89–120)*
AKZO v. Commission III 186 (ground 149)

4. Exclusive distribution systems

Decca 304. (paras. 97, 100–103)
Hachette. 8th Comp. Rep. (paras. 114–115)
SEITA. 10th Comp. Rep. (para. 124)

5. Discriminatory pricing

Chiquita 101 (para. II.A.3.b)
British Leyland 212
ECS/AKZO 242*
Hilti 282 (paras. 75, 80–81)
Tetra Pak II 348 (paras. 154–155, 160)
United Brands v. Commission 62 (ground 204–234)*
British Leyland v. Commission 136

6. Discriminatory conditions between different customers

Michelin 165 (paras. 25, 41)
GVL 166 (paras. 49–60)
British Telecommunications 188 (para. 30)*
British Sugar/Napier Brown 289 (paras. 33–35, 73)
British Plasterboard 299 (paras. 81–85, 142–147)*
Solvay 332 (paras. 62–64)
Tetra Pak II 348 (paras. 138, 161)

7. Discrimination on grounds of nationality

Gema 38
GVL 166 (paras. 46–47)
SACEM & SABAM. 4th Comp. Rep. (para. 112)
Boat Equipment 10th Comp. Rep. (paras. 119–120)

GVL v. Commission 97 (ground 56)*

8. Discriminatory allocation of products during supply shortages

ABG/Oil Companies 113
British Sugar 286 (paras. 20–23, 61–64)

9. Predatory pricing

ECS/AKZO 242*
Hilti 282 (paras. 80–81)
British Sugar/Napier Brown 286 (paras. 24–31, 65–68)*
Tetra Pak II 348 (paras. 147–152, 156–159)
Macron/Angus 17th Comp. Rep. (para. 81)
AKZO v. Commission III 186 (grounds 69–72)*

10. Refusal to supply

Zoja C.S.C-I.C.I. 64
European Sugar Industry 69
Chiquita 101 (para. II.A.3.d)
ABG/Oil Companies 113
Hugin/Liptons 121
British Telecommunications 188 (paras. 28–36)
British Leyland 212
Boosey & Hawkes 273 (para. 19)*
Hilti 282 (paras. 76–84)
British Sugar 286 (paras. 20–23, 61–64)
SABENA 295 (paras. 29–32)
7th Comp. Rep. (paras. 27, 28)
Boat equipment 10th Comp. Rep. (paras. 119–120)
Polaroid 13th Comp. Rep. (paras. 155–157)
Instituto/IMC & Angus. 16th Comp. Rep. (para. 76)
Volvo. 17th Comp. Rep. (para. 82)
London European/SABENA. 17th Comp. Rep. (para. 86)
ICI & CSC v. Commission 37 (ground 25)
United Brands v. Commission 62 (grounds 163–196)*
Benzine–Petroleum BV v. Commission 65 (grounds 19–34)
British Leyland v. Commission 136
Volvo v. Veng 159
Maxicar v. Renault 161
Höfner v. Macrotron 184

11. Tying

Article 86(d) EEC
Gema I 38
European Sugar Industry 69
Michelin 165 (paras. 20–24, 28, 37–50)
British Sugar/Napier Brown 286 (paras. 32, 69–72)

Hilti 292
SABENA 295 (para. 31)
Tetra Pak II 348 (paras. 116, 117, 140)
SACEM & SABAM 4th Comp. Rep. (para. 112)
IBM 14th Comp. Rep. (paras. 94–95)
IBM 16th Comp. Rep. (para. 75)
OlioFiat. 17th Comp. Rep. (para. 84)
Michelin v. *Commission* 102 (grounds 93–99)
Télémarketing v. *CLT* 124 (grounds 18–26)

12. Rebates and discounts

European Sugar Industry 69
Vitamins 104 (paras. 11–18, 22–27)
Michelin 165 (paras. 20–24, 28, 37–50)*
Hilti 282 (para. 74)
British Sugar/Napier Brown 286 (paras. 36–39, 74–76)
British Plasterboard 299 (paras. 58–59, 123–129, 86–92, 148–152)
Solvay 332 (paras. 50–64)
ICI 333 (paras. 53–62)
Tetra Pak II 348 (paras. 111–114)
Coca-Cola 19th Comp. Rep. (para. 50)
Suiker Unie v. *Commission* 48 (grounds 421, 499–528)
Hoffmann-La Roche v. *Commission* 67 (grounds 89–108)*
Michelin v. *Commission* 102 (grounds 63–99)

13. Using dominance to move into ancillary markets

Zoja C.S.C.-I.C.I.64*
Michelin 165 (para. 50)
Hilti 282 (para. 74)
Tetra Pak II 348 (para. 104)
Filtrona/Tabacalera, 19th Comp. Rep. (para. 61)
Télémarketing v. *CLT* 124 (grounds 18–26)*

14. Actions preventing parallel trade

Gema I 38
European Sugar Industry 69
General Motors Continental 84
Chiquita 101 (para. II.A.3.a)
Hilti 282 (paras. 76–77)
General Motors v. *Commission* 46 (grounds 11–24)*
Hoffmann-La Roche v. *Centrafarm* 63 (grounds 15–16)

15. Refusal to disclose technical details of products

Hilti 282 (para. 79)
Decca 304 (paras. 97, 108–110)
Tetra Pak II 348 (para. 162)
IBM 14th Comp. Rep. (paras. 94–95)*

16. Abusive registration of a trademark

Osram/Airam 11th Comp. Rep. (para. 97)

16.1. Restricting intra-band competition

Tetra Pak II 348 (paras. 162–164)

17. Abuse of intellectual/industrial property rights

Hilti 282 (para. 78)
Decca 304 (paras. 104–107)
Magill 307 (para. 23)
GEMA 15th Comp. Rep. (para. 81)
RTE v. *Commission* T14 (grounds 65–75)*
BBC v. *Commission* T15 (grounds 52–63)
ITV v. *Commission* T16 (grounds 50–61)
Hilti v. *Commission* T21 (ground 99–100)
Parke, Davis v. *Centrafarm* 8*
Sirena v. *Eda* 17 (ground 17)
Deutsche Grammophon v. *Metro* 19 (ground 19)
GVL v. *Commission* 97 (grounds 53–56)
Basset/SACEM 141
Volvo v. *Veng* 159
Maxicar v. *Renault* 161
Ministère public v. *Tournier* 167* (grounds 38–43)
Lucazeau v. *SACEM* 168* (grounds 25–30)

C. OBJECTIVE JUSTIFICATION

Hilti 282 (paras. 89–96)
Tetra Pak 289 (para. 49)
British Plasterboard 299 (paras. 70, 131–134)*
Decca 304 (paras. 111–113)
Tetra Pak II 348 (paras. 118, 119, 120, 124–127)
Hilti v. *Commission* T21 (ground 117–119)
General Motors v. *Commission* 46 (grounds 11–24)*
United Brands v. *Commission* 62 (grounds 189–190)
Ministère public v. *Tournier* 167*
Lucazeau v. *SACEM* 168*

PART VIII

STATE INTERFERENCE

CHAPTER 1

ARTICLE 90

A. TEXT OF ARTICLE 90
(reproduced below)

Article 90

1. In the case of public undertakings and undertakings to which Member States grant special or exclusive rights, Member States shall neither enact nor maintain in force any measure contrary to the rules contained in this Treaty, in particular to those rules provided for in Article 7 and Articles 85 to 94.

2. Undertakings entrusted with the operation of services of general economic interest or having the character of a revenue-producing monopoly shall be subject to the rules contained in this Treaty, in particular to the rules on competition, in so far as the application of such rules does not obstruct the performance, in law or in fact, of the particular tasks assigned to them. The development of trade must not be affected to such an extent as would be contrary to the interests of the Community.

3. The Commission shall ensure the application of the provisions of this Article and shall, where necessary, address appropriate directives or decisions to Member States.

B. CONSIDERATION OF ARTICLE 90

1. **Cases on the interpretation of Article 90(1)**

Gema I 37
Van Ameyde UCI 57 (ground 22)
GB-INNO v. *ATAB* 59 (paras. 39–51)
Commission v. *Italy* 141a
Bodson v. *Pompes Funèbres* 150 (grounds 33–34)*
Ahmed Saeed v. *Zentrale* 162 (grounds 50–52)
France v. *Commission* 182 (grounds 22, 55–57)*
ERT v. *DEP* 185 (grounds 34–38)
Höffner v. *Macrotron* 189
Merci v. *Siderurgica* 188
RTT v. *GB-Inno* 189

2. **Article 90(2)**

2.1. **Direct effect**

Mueller 21
Inter-Huiles 97a
Ahmed Zaeed v. *Zentrale* 142 (paras. 54–57)
ERT v. *DEP* 185 (grounds 33–34)*

2.2. **Cases on the interpretation of Article 90(2)**

Gema I 37
Pabst & Richarz/BNIA 106 (para. IV)
Maize Seeds 137
GVL 166 (paras. 65–68)
NAVEWA-ANSEAU 179 (paras. 64–67)
British Telecommunications 188 (paras. 41–43)
Uniform Eurochèques 224 (paras. 29–30)
Decca 304 (paras. 128–30)
Magill 307 (para. 25)
Ijsselcentrale 335 (paras. 39–52)
Screensport/EBU 337 (paras. 68–69)
RTE v. *Commission* T14 (grounds 82–84)
BRT v. *SABAM II* 38 (grounds 17–23)*
Sacchi 39 (grounds 16–18)*
Züchner v. *Bayerische Vereinsbank* 86 (paras. 6–9)
Nungesser v. *Commission* 94 (ground 9)
GVL v. *Commission* 97 (grounds 31–32)
Italy v. *Commission* 117 (grounds 33, 34)*
Télémarketing v. *CLT* 124 (ground 17)
Ahmed Saeed v. *Zentrale* 162 (grounds 54–57)
France v. *Commission* 182 (grounds 11–12)*
Höfner v. *Macrotron* 184 (grounds 24–25)
ERT v. *DEP* 185 (grounds 33–34)
Merci v. *Siderurgica* 188
RTT v. *GB-Inno* 189*

3. **Article 90(3)**

Greek Insurance 230
Canary Islands 268*
Danish PTT 20th Comp. Rep. (para. 358)
Flying German Officials 20th Comp. Rep. (para. 357)

Dutch Express Delivery 318
Spanish Courier Services 324
France v. *Commission* 95
Commission v. *Greece* 153
France v. *Commission* 182 (grounds 16–18, 21)*

Netherlands v. *Commission* 190*

4. Directives applying to Article 90

4.1. Text of Directive 88/301 (reproduced below)

Commission Directive 88/301 of May 16, 1988

On competition in the markets in telecommunications terminal equipment

([1988] O.J. L131/73)

THE COMMISSION ON THE EUROPEAN COMMUNITIES,

Having regard to the Treaty establishing the European Economic Community, and in particular Article 90(3) thereof,

Whereas:

(1) In all the Member States, telecommunications are, either wholly or partly, a State monopoly generally granted in the form of special or exclusive rights to one or more bodies responsible for providing and operating the network infrastructure and related services. Those rights, however, often go beyond the provisions of network utilisation services and extend to the supply of user terminal equipment for connection to the network. The last decades have seen considerable technical developments in networks, and the pace of development has been especially striking in the area of terminal equipment.

(2) Several Member States have, in response to technical and economic developments, reviewed their grant of special or exclusive rights in the telecommunications sector. The proliferation of types of terminal equipment and the possibility of the multiple use of terminals means that users must be allowed a free choice between the various types of equipment available if they are to benefit fully from the technological advances made in the sector.

(3) Article 30 of the Treaty prohibits quantitative restrictions on imports from other Member States and all measures having equivalent effect. The grant of special or exclusive rights to import and market goods to one organisation can, and often does, lead to restrictions on imports from other Member States.

(4) Article 37 of the Treaty states that "Member States shall progressively adjust any State monopolies of a commercial character so as to ensure that when the transitional period has ended no discrimination regarding the conditions under which goods are procured and marketed exists between nationals of Member States.

The provisions of this Article shall apply to any body through which a Member State, in law or in fact, either directly or indirectly supervises, determines or appreciably influences imports or exports between Member States. These provisions shall likewise apply to monopolies delegated by the State to others." Paragraph 2 of Article 37 prohibits Member States from introducing any new measure contrary to the principles laid down in Article 37(1).

(5) The special or exclusive rights relating to terminal equipment enjoyed by national telecommunications monopolies are exercised in such a way as, in practice, to disadvantage equipment from other Member States, notably by preventing users from freely choosing the equipment that best suits their needs in terms of price and quality, regardless of its origin. The exercise of these rights is therefore not compatible with Article 37 in all the Member States except Spain and Portugal, where the national monopolies are to be adjusted progressively before the end of the transitional period provided for by the Act of Accession.

(6) The provision of installation and maintenance services is a key factor in the purchasing or rental of terminal equipment. The retention of exclusive rights in this field would be tantamount to reten-

tion of exclusive marketing rights. Such rights must therefore also be abolished if the abolition of exclusive importing and marketing rights is to have any practical effect.

(7) Article 59 of the Treaty provides that "restrictions on freedom to provide services within the Community shall be progressively abolished during the transitional period in respect of nationals of Member States who are established in a State of the Community other than that of the person for whom the services are intended." Maintenance of terminals is a service within the meaning of Article 60 of the Treaty. As the transitional period has ended, the service in question, which cannot from a commercial point of view be dissociated from the marketing of the terminals, must be provided freely and in particular when provided by qualified operators.

(8) Article 90(1) of the Treaty provides that "in the case of public undertakings and undertakings to which Member States grant special or exclusive rights, Member States shall neither enact nor maintain in force any measure contrary to the rules contained in this Treaty, in particular to those rules provided for in Article 7 and Articles 85 to 94."

(9) The market in terminal equipment is still as a rule governed by a system which allows competition in the common market to be distorted; this situation continues to produce infringements of the competition rules laid down by the Treaty and to affect adversely the development of trade to such an extent as would be contrary to the interests of the Community. Stronger competition in the terminal equipment market requires the introduction of transparent technical specifications and type-approval procedures which meet the essential requirements mentioned in Council Directive 86/361 ([1986] O.J. L217/21) and allow the free movement of terminal equipment. In turn, such transparency necessarily entails the publication of technical specifications and type-approval procedures. To ensure that the latter are applied transparently, objectively and without discrimination, the drawing-up and application of such rules should be entrusted to bodies independent of competitors in the market in question. It is essential that the specifications and type-approval procedures are published simultaneously and in an orderly fashion. Simultaneous publication will also ensure that behaviour contrary to the Treaty is avoided. Such simultaneous, orderly publication can be achieved only by means of a legal instrument that is binding on all the Member States. The most appropriate instrument to this end is a directive.

(10) The Treaty entrusts the Commission with very clear tasks and gives it specific powers with regard to the monitoring of relations between the Member States and their public undertakings and enterprises to which they have delegated special or exclusive rights, in particular as regards the elimination of quantitative restrictions and measures having equivalent effect, discrimination between nationals of Member States, and competition. The only instrument, therefore, by which the Commission can efficiently carry out the tasks and powers assigned to it, is a Directive based on Article 90(3).

(11) Telecommunications bodies or enterprises are undertakings within the meaning of Article 90(1) because they carry on an organised business activity involving the production of goods or services. They are either public undertakings or private enterprises to which the Member States have granted special or exclusive rights for the importation, marketing, connection, bringing into service of telecommunications terminal equipment and/or maintenance of such equipment. The grant and maintenance of special and exclusive rights for terminal equipment constitute measures within the meaning of that Article. The conditions for applying the exception of Article 90(2) are not fulfilled. Even if the provision of a telecommunications network for the use of the general public is a service of general economic interest entrusted by the State to the telecommunications bodies, the abolition of their special or exclusive rights to import and market terminal equipment would not obstruct, in law or in fact, the performance of that service. This is all the more true given that Member States are entitled to subject terminal equipment to type-approval procedures to ensure that they conform to the essential requirements.

(12) Article 86 of the Treaty prohibits as incompatible with the common market any conduct by one or more undertakings that involves an abuse of a dominant position within the common market or a substantial part of it.

(13) The telecommunications bodies hold individually or jointly a monopoly on their

national telecommunications network. The national networks are markets. Therefore, the bodies each individually or jointly hold a dominant position in a substantial part of the market in question within the meaning of Article 86.

The effect of the special or exclusive rights granted to such bodies by the State to import and market terminal equipment is to:

— restrict users to renting such equipment, when it would often be cheaper for them, at least in the long term, to purchase this equipment. This effectively makes contracts for the use of networks subject to acceptance by the user of additional services which have no connection with the subject of the contracts,
— limit outlets and impede technical progress since the range of equipment offered by the telecommunications bodies is necessarily limited and will not be the best available to meet the requirements of a significant proportion of users.

Such conduct is expressly prohibited by Article 86(d) and (b), and is likely significantly to affect trade between Member States.

At all events, such special or exclusive rights in regard to the terminal equipment market give rise to a situation which is contrary to the objective of Article 3(f) of the Treaty, which provides for the institution of a system ensuring that competition in the common market is not distorted, and requires *a fortiori* that competition must not be eliminated. Member States have an obligation under Article 5 of the Treaty to abstain from any measure which could jeopardise the attainment of the objectives of the Treaty, including Article 3(f).

The exclusive rights to import and market terminal equipment must therefore be regarded as incompatible with Article 86 in conjunction with Article 3, and the grant or maintenance of such rights by a Member State is prohibited under Article 90(1).

(14) To enable users to have access to the terminal equipment of their choice, it is necessary to know and make transparent the characteristics of the termination points of the network to which the terminal equipment is to be connected. Member States must therefore ensure that the characteristics are published and that users have access to termination points.

(15) To be able to market their products, manufacturers of terminal equipment must know what technical specifications they must satisfy. Member States should therefore formalise and publish the specifications and type-approval rules, which they must notify to the Commission in draft form, in accordance with Council Directive 83/189 [O.J. 1983 L109/8]. The specifications may be extended to products imported from other Member States only insofar as they are necessary to ensure conformity with the essential requirements specified in Article 2(17) of Directive 86/361 that can legitimately be required under Community law. Member States must, in any event, comply with Articles 30 and 36 of the Treaty, under which an importing Member State must allow terminal equipment legally manufactured and marketed in another Member State to be imported on to its territory, and may only subject it to such type-approval and possibly refuse approval for reasons concerning conformity with the abovementioned essential requirements.

(16) The immediate publication of these specifications and procedures cannot be considered in view of their complexity. On the other hand, effective competition is not possible without such publication, since potential competitors of the bodies or enterprises with special or exclusive rights are unaware of the precise specifications with which their terminal equipment must comply and of the terms of the type-approval procedures and hence their cost and duration. A deadline should therefore be set for the publication of specifications and the type-approval procedures. A period of two-and-a-half years will also enable the telecommunications bodies with special or exclusive rights to adjust to the new market conditions and will enable economic operators, especially small and medium-sized enterprises, to adapt to the new competitive environment.

(17) Monitoring of type-approval specifications and rules cannot be entrusted to a competitor in the terminal equipment market in view of the obvious conflict of interest. Member States should therefore ensure that the responsibility for drawing up type-approval specifications and rules is assigned to a body independent of the operator of the network and of any other competitor in the market for terminals.

(18) The holders of special or exclusive rights in the terminal equipment in question have been able to impose on their customers long-term contracts preventing

the introduction of free competition from having a practical effect within a reasonable period. Users must therefore be given the right to obtain a revision of the duration of their contracts,

HAS ADOPTED THIS DIRECTIVE:

Article 1

For the purposes of this Directive:
— "terminal equipment" means equipment directly or indirectly connected to the termination of a public telecommunications network to send, process or receive information. A connection is indirect if equipment is placed between the terminal and the termination of the network. In either case (direct or indirect), the connection may be made by wire, optical fibre or electromagnetically. Terminal equipment also means receive-only satellite stations not reconnected to the public network of a Member State,
— "undertaking" means a public or private body, to which a Member State grants special or exclusive rights for the importation, marketing, connection, bringing into service of telecommunications terminal equipment and/or maintenance of such equipment.

Article 2

Member States which have granted special or exclusive rights within the meaning of Article 1 to undertakings shall ensure that those rights are withdrawn.

They shall, not later than three months following the notification of this Directive, inform the Commission of the measures taken or draft legislation introduced to that end.

Article 3

Member States shall ensure that economic operators have the right to import, market, connect, bring into service and maintain terminal equipment. However, Member States may:
— in the absence of technical specifications, refuse to allow terminal equipment to be connected and brought into service where such equipment does not, according to a reasoned opinion of the body referred to in Article 6, satisfy the essential requirements laid down in Article 2(17) of Directive 86/361,
— require economic operators to possess the technical qualifications needed to connect, bring into service and maintain terminal equipment on the basis of objective, non-discriminatory and publicly available criteria.

Article 4

Member States shall ensure that users have access to new public network termination points and that the physical characteristics of these points are published not later than December 31, 1988.

Access to public network termination points existing at December 31, 1988 shall be given within a reasonable period to any user who so requests.

Article 5

1. Member States shall, not later than the date mentioned in Article 2, communicate to the Commission a list of all technical specifications and type-approval procedures which are used for terminal equipment, and shall provide the publication references.

Where they have not as yet been published in a Member State, the latter shall ensure that they are published not later than the dates referred to in Article 8.

2. Member State shall ensure that all other specifications and type-approval procedures for terminal equipment are formalised and published. Member States shall communicate the technical specifications and type-approval procedures in draft form to the Commission in accordance with Directive 83/189 and according to the timetable set out in Article 8.

Article 6

Member States shall ensure that, from July 1, 1989, responsibility for drawing up the specifications referred to in Article 5, monitoring their application and granting type-approval is entrusted to a body independent of public or private undertakings offering goods and/or services in the telecommunications sector.

Article 7

Member States shall take the necessary steps to ensure that undertakings within the meaning of Article 1 make it possible for their customers to terminate, with maximum notice of one year, leasing or maintenance contracts which concern terminal equipment subject to exclusive or special

Book One: Part VIII—State Interference

rights at the time of the conclusion of the contracts.

For terminal equipment requiring type-approval, Member States shall ensure that this possibility of termination is afford by the undertakings in question no later than the dates provided for in Article 8. For terminal equipment not requiring type-approval, Member States shall introduce this possibility no later than the date provided for in Article 2.

Article 8

Member States shall inform the Commission of the draft technical specifications and type-approval procedures referred to in Article 5(2);
— not later than 31 December 1988 in respect of equipment in Category A of the list in Annex I,
— not later than 30 September 1989 in respect of equipment in category B of the list in Annex I,
— not later than 30 June 1990 in respect of other terminal equipment in category C of the list in Annex I.

Member States shall bring these specifications and type-approval procedures into force after expiry of the procedure provided for by Directive 83/189.

Article 9

Member States shall provide the Commission at the end of each year with a report allowing it to monitor compliance with the provisions of Articles 2, 3, 4, 6 and 7.

An outline of the report is attached as Annex II.

Article 10

The provisions of this Directive shall be without prejudice to the provisions of the instruments of accession of Spain and Portugal, and in particular Articles 48 and 208 of the Act of Accession.

Article 11

This Directive is addressed to the Member States.

Done at Brussels, May 16, 1988.

ANNEX I

List of terminal equipment referred to in Article 8

	Category
Additional telephone set; private automatic branch exchanges (PABXs)	A
Modems	A
Telex terminals	B
Data-transmission terminals	B
Mobile telephones	B
Receive-only satellite stations not reconnected to the public network of a Member State	B
First telephone set	C
Other terminal equipment	C

ANNEX II

Outline of the report provided for in Article 9

Implementation of Article 2
1. Terminal equipment for which legislation is being or has been modified.
By category of terminal equipment:
— date of adoption of the measure or,
— date of introduction of the bill or,
— date of entry into force of the measure.
2. Terminal equipment still subject to special or exclusive rights:
— type of terminal equipment and rights concerned.

Implementation of Article 3
— terminal equipment, the connection and/or commissioning of which has been restricted,
— technical qualifications required, giving reference of their publication.

Implementation of Article 4
— references of publications in which the physical characteristics are specified,
— number of existing network termination points,
— number of network termination points now accessible.

Implementation of Article 6
— independent body or bodies appointed.

Implementation of Article 7
— measures put into force, and
— number of terminated contracts.

4.2. Cases on Directive 88/301
France v. Commission

**4.3 Text of Directive 90/388
(reproduced opposite)**

Commission Directive 90/388 of June 28, 1990

on competition in the markets for telecommunications services

([1990] O.J. L192/10)

THE COMMISSION OF THE EUROPEAN COMMUNITIES

Having regard to the Treaty establishing the European Economic Community, and in particular Article 90(3) thereof,

Whereas:

(1) The improvement of telecommunications in the Community is an essential condition for the harmonious development of economic activities and a competitive market in the Community, from the point of view of both service providers and users. The Commission has therefore adopted a programme, set out in its Green Paper on the development of the common market for telecommunications services and equipment and in its communication on the implementation of the Green Paper by 1992, for progressively introducing competition into the telecommunications market. The programme does not concern mobile telephony and paging services, and mass communication services such as radio for television. The Council, in its resolution of June 30, 1988, [1988] O.J. C257/1, expressed broad support for the objectives of this programme, and in particular the progressive creation of an open Community market for telecommunications services. The last decades have seen considerable technological advances in the telecommunications sector. These allow an increasingly varied range of services to be provided, notably data transmission services, and also make it technically and economically possible for competition to take place between different service providers.

(2) In all the Member States the provision and operation of telecommunications networks and the provision of related services are generally vested in one or more telecommunications organisations holding exclusive or special rights. Such rights are characterised by the discretionary powers which the State exercises in various degrees with regard to access to the market for telecommunications services.

(3) The organisations entrusted with the provision and operation of the telecommunications network are undertakings within the meaning of Article 90(1) of the Treaty because they carry on an organised business activity, namely the provision of telecommunications services. They are either public undertakings or private enterprises to which the State has granted exclusive or special rights.

(4) Several Member States, while ensuring the performance of public service tasks, have already revised the system of exclusive or special rights that used to exist in the telecommunications sector in their country. In all cases, the system of exclusive or special rights has been maintained in respect of the provision and operation of the network. In some Member States, it has been maintained for all telecommunications services, while in others such rights cover only certain services. All Member States have either themselves imposed or allowed their telecommunications administrations to impose restrictions on the free provision of telecommunications services.

(5) The granting of special or exclusive rights to one or more undertakings to operate the network derives from the discretionary power of the State. The granting by a Member State of such rights inevitably restricts the provision of such services by other undertakings to or from other Member States.

(6) In prctice, restrictions on the provision of telecommunications services within the meaning of Article 59 to or from other Member States consist mainly in the prohibition on connecting leased lines by means of concentrators, multiplexers and other equipment to the switched telephone network, in imposing access charges for the connection that are out of proportion to the service provided, in prohibiting the routing of signals to or from third parties by means of leased lines or applying volume sensitive tariffs without economic justification or refusing to give service providers access to the network. The effect of the usage restrictions and the excessive charges in relation to net cost is to hinder the provision to or from other

Member States of such telecommunications services as:
— services designed to improve telecommunications functions, e.g. conversion of the protocol, code, format or speed,
— information services providing access to data bases,
— remote data-processing services,
— message storing and forwarding services, e.g. electronic mail,
— transaction services, e.g. financial transactions, electronic commercial data transfer, teleshopping and telereservations,
— teleaction services, e.g. telemetry and remote monitoring.

7. Articles 55, 56 and 66 of the Treaty allow exceptions on non-economic grounds to the freedom to provide services. The restrictions permitted are those connected, even occasionally, with the exercise of official authority, and those connected with public policy, public security or public health. Since these are exceptions, they must be interpreted restrictively. None of the telecommunications services is connected with the exercise of official authority involving the right to use undue powers compared with the ordinary law, privileges of public power or a power of coercion over the public. The supply of telecommunication services cannot in itself threaten public policy and cannot affect public health.

(8) The Court of Justice caselaw also recognises restrictions on the freedom to provide services if they fulful essential requirements in the general interest and are applied without discrimination and in proportion to the objective. Consumer protection does not make it necessary to restrict freedom to provide telecommunications services since this objective can also be attained through free competition. Nor can the protection of intellectual property be invoked in this connection. The only essential requirements derogating from Article 59 which could justify restrictions on the use of the public network are the maintenance of the integrity of the network, security of network operations and in justified cases, interoperability and data protection. The restrictions imposed, however, must be adapted to the objectives pursued by these legitimate requirements. Member States will have to make such restrictions known to the public and notify them to the Commission to enable it to assess their proportionality.

(9) In this context, the security of network operations means ensuring the availability of the public network in case of emergency. The technical integrity of the public network means ensuring its normal operation and the interconnection of public networks in the Community on the basis of common technical specifications. The concept of interoperability of services means complying with such technical specifications introduced to increase the provision of services and the choice available to users. Data protection means measures taken to warrant the confidentiality of communications and the protection of personal data.

(10) Apart from the essential requirements which can be included as conditions in the licensing or declaration procedures, Member States can include conditions regarding public-service requirements which constitute objective, non-discriminatory and transparent trade regulations regarding the conditions of performance, availability and quality of the service.

(11) When a Member State has entrusted a telecommunications organisation with the task of providing packet or circuit switched data services for the public in general and when this service may be obstructed because of competition by private providers, the Commission can allow the Member State to impose additional conditions for the provision of such a service, with respect also to geographical coverage. In assessing these measures, the Commission in the context of the achievement of the fundamental objectives of the Treaty referred to in Article 2 thereof, including that of strengthening the Community's economic and social cohesion as referred to in Article 130a, will also take into account the situation of those Member States in which the network for the provision of the packet or circuit switched service is not yet sufficiently developed and which could justify the deferment for these Member States until January 1, 1996 of the date for prohibition on the simple resale of leased line capacity.

(12) Article 59 of the treaty requires the abolition of any other restriction on the freedom of nationals of Member States who are established in a Community country to provide services to persons in other Member States. The maintenance or introduction of any exclusive or special

right which does not correspond to the abovementioned criteria is therefore a breach of Article 90 in conjunction with Article 59.

(13) Article 86 of the Treaty prohibits as incompatible with the common market any conduct by one or more undertakings that involves an abuse of a dominant position within the common market or a substantial part of it. Telecommunications organisations are also undertakings for the purposes of this Article because they carry out economic activities, in particular the service they provide by making telecommunications networks and services available to users. This provision of the network constitutes a separate services market as it is not interchangeable with other services. On each national market the competitive environment in which the network and the telecommunications services are provided is homogeneous enough for the Commission to be able to evaluate the power held by the organisations providing the services on these territories. The territories of the Member States constitute distinct geographical markets. This is essentially due to the existing difference between the rules governing conditions of access and technical operation, relating to the provision of the network and of such services. Furthermore, each Member State market forms a substantial part of the common market.

(14) In each national market the telecommunications organisations hold individually or collectively a dominant position for the creation and the exploitation of the network because they are the only ones with networks in each Member States covering the whole territory of those States and because their governments granted them the exclusive rights to provide this network either alone or in conjunction with other organisations.

(15) Where a State grants special or exclusive rights to provide telecommunications services to organisations which already have a dominant position in creating and operating the network, the effect of such rights is to strengthen the dominant position by extending it to services.

(16) Moreover, the special or exclusive rights granted to telecommunications organisations by the State to provide certain telecommunications services mean such organisations:

(a) prevent or restrict access to the market for these telecommunications services by their competitors, thus limiting consumer choice, which is liable to restrict technological progress to the detriment of consumers;

(b) compel network users to use the services subject to exclusive rights, and thus make the conclusion of network utilisation contracts dependent on acceptance of supplementary services having no connection with the subject of such contracts.

Each of these types of conduct represents a specific abuse of a dominant position which is likely to have an appreciable effect on trade between Member State, as all the services in question could in principle be supplied by providers from other Member States. The structure of competition within the common market is substantially changed by them. At all events, the special or exclusive rights for these services give rise to a situation which is contrary to the objective in Article 3(f) of the Treaty, which provides for the institution of a system ensuring that competition in the common market is not distorted, and requires *a fortiori* that competition must not be eliminated. Member States have an obligation under Article 5 of the Treaty to abstain from any measure which cold jeopardise the attainment of the objectives of the Treaty, including that of Article 3(f).

(17) The exclusive rights to telecommunications services granted to public undertakings or undertakings to which Member States have granted special or exclusive rights for the provision of the network are incompatible with Article 90(1) in conjunction with Article 86.

(18) Article 90(2) of the Treaty allows derogation from the application of Articles 59 and 86 of the Treaty where such application would obstruct the performance, in law or in fact, of the particular task assigned to the telecommunications organisations. This task consists in the provision and exploitation of a universal network, i.e. one having general geographical coverage, and being provided to any service provider or user upon request within a reasonable period of time. The financial resources for the development of the network still derive mainly from the operation of the telephone service. Consequently, the opening-up of voice telephony to competition could threaten the

financial stability of the telecommunications organisations. The voice telephony service, whether provided from the present telephone network or forming part of the ISDN service, is currently also the most important means of notifying and calling up emergency services in charge of public safety.

(19) The provision of leased lines forms an essential part of the telecommunications organisations' tasks. There is at present, in almost all Member States, a substantial difference between charges for use of the data transmission service on the switched network and for use of leased lines. balancing those tariffs without delay could jeopardise this task. Equilibrium in such charges must be achieved gradually between now and December 31, 1992. In the meantime it must be possible to require private operators not to offer to the public a service consisting merely of the resale of leased line capacity, i.e. including only such processing, switching of data, storing, or protocol conversion as is necessary for transmission in real time. The Member State may therefore establish a declaration system through which private operators would undertake not to engage in simple resale. However, no other requirement may be imposed on such operators to ensure compliance with this measure.

(20) These restrictions do not affect the development of trade to such an extent as would be contrary to the interests of the Community. Under these circumstances, these restrictions are compatible with Article 90(2) of the Treaty. This may also be the case as regards the measures adopted by Member States to ensure that the activities of private service providers do not obstruct the public switched-data services.

(21) The rules of the Treaty, including those on competition, apply to telex services; however, the use of this service is gradually declining throughout the Community owing to the emergence of competing means of telecommunications such as telefax. The abolition of current restrictions on the use of the switched telephone network and leased lines will allow telex messages to be transmitted. In view of this particular trend, an individual approach is necessary. Consequently, this Directive should not apply to telex services.

(22) The Commission will in any event reconsider in the course of 1992 the remaining special or exclusive rights on the provision of services taking account of technological development and the evolution towards a digital infrastructure.

(23) Member States may draw up fair procedures for ensuring compliance with the essential requirements without prejudice to the harmonisation of the latter at Community level within the framework of the Council Directives on open network provisions (ONP). As regards data-switching, Member States must be able, as part of such procedures, to require compliance with trade regulations from the standpoint of conditions of permanence, availability and quality of the service, and to include meaures to safeguard the task of general economic interest which they have entrusted to a telecommunications organisation. The procedures must be based on specific objective criteria should in particular be justified and proportional to the general interest objective, and be duly motivated and published. The Commission must be able to examine them in depth in the light of the rules on free competition and freedom to provide services. In any event, Member States that have not notified the Commission of their planned licensing criteria and procedures within a given time may no longer impose any restrictions on the freedomn to provide data transmission services to the public.

(24) Member States should be given more time to draw up general rules on the conditions governing the provision of packet- or circuit-switched data services for the public.

(25) Telecommunications services should not be subject to any restriction, either as regards free access by users to the services, or as regards the processing of data which may be carried out before messages are transmitted through the network or after messages have been received, except where this is warranted by an essential requirement in proportion to the objective pursued.

(26) The digitisation of the network and the technological improvement of the terminal equipment connected to it have brought about an increase in the number of functions previously carried out within the network and which can now be carried

out within the network and which can now be carried out by users themselves with increasingly sophisticated terminal equipment. It is necessary to ensure that suppliers of telecommunication services, and notably suppliers of telephone and packet or circuit-switched data transmission services enable operators to use these functions.

(27) Pending the establishing of Community standards with a view to an open network provision (ONP), the technical interfaces currently in use in the Member States should be made publicly available so that firms wishing to enter the markets for the services in question can take the necessary steps to adapt their services to the technical characteristics of the networks. If the member States have not yet established such technical interfaces, they should do so as quickly as possible. All such draft measures should be communicated to the Commission in accordance with Council Directive 83/189/EEC, [1983] O.J. L109/8., as last amended by Directive [1988] O.J. L81/75.

(28) Under national legislation, telecommunications organisations are generally given the function of regulating telecommunications services, particularly as regards licensing, control of type-approval and mandatory interface specifications, frequency allocation and monitoring of conditions of use. In some cases, the legislation lays down only general principles governing the operation of the licensed services and leaves it to the telecommunications organisations to determine the specific operating conditions.

(29) This dual regulatory and commercial function of the telecommunications organisations has a direct impact on firms offering telecommunications services in competition with the organisations in question. By this bundling of activities, the organisations determine or, at the very least, substantially influence the supply of services offered by their competitors. The delegation to an undertaking which has a dominant position for the provision and exploitation of the network, of the power to regulate access to the market for telecommunication services constitutes a strengthening of that dominant position. Because of the conflict of interests, this is likely to restrict competitors' access to the markets in telecommunications services and to limit users' freedom of choice.

Such arrangements may also limit the outlets for equipment for handling telecommunications messages and, consequently, technological progress in that field. This combination of activities therefore constitutes an abuse of the dominant position of telecommunications organisations within the meaning of Article 86. If it is the result of a State measure, the measure is also incompatible with Article 90(1) in conjunction with Article 86.

(30) To enable the Commission to carry out effectively the monitoring task assigned to it by Article 90(3), it must have available certain essential information. That information must in particular give the Commission a clear view of the measures of Membe States, so that it can ensure that access to the network and the various related services are provided by each telecommunications organisation to all its customers on non-discriminatory tariff and other terms. Such information should cover:

— measures taken to withdraw exclusive rights pursuant to this Directive,
— the conditions on which licences to provide telecommunications services are granted.

The Commission must have such information to enable it to check, in particular, that all the users of the network and services, including telecommunications organisations where they are providers of services, are treated equally and fairly.

(31) The holders of special or exclusive rights to provide telecommunications services that will in future be open to competition have been able in the past to impose long-term contracts on their customers. Such contracts would in practice limit the ability of any new competitors to offer their services to such customers and of such customers to benefit from such services. Users must therefore be given the right to terminate their contrcts within a reasonable length of time.

(32) Each Member State at present regulates the supply of telecommunications services according to its own concepts. Even the definition of certain services differs from one Member State to another. Such differences cause distortions of competition likely to make the provisions of cross-frontier telecommunications services more difficult for economic operators. This is why the Council, in its

resolution of June 30, 1988, considered that one of the objectives of a telecommunications policy was the creation of an open Community market for telecommunications services, in particular through the rapid definition, in the form of Council Directives, of technical conditions, conditions of use and principles governing charges for an open network provision (ONP). The Commission has presented a proposal to this end to the Council. Harmonisation of the conditions of access is not however the most appropriate means of removing the barriers to trade resulting from infringements of the treaty. The Commission has a duty to ensure that the provisions of the Treaty are applied effectively and comprehensively.

(33) Article 90(3) assigns clearly-defined duties and powers to the Commission to monitor relations between Member States and their public undertakings and undertakings to which they have granted special or exclusive rights, particularly as regards the removal of obstacles to freedom to provide services, discrimination between nationals of the Member States and competition. A comprehensive approach is necessary in order to end the infringements that persist in certain Member States and to give clear guidelines to those Member States that are reviewing their legislation so as to avoid further infringements. A Directive within the meaning of Article 90(3) of the Treaty is therefore the ost appropriate means of achieving that end.

HAS ADOPTED THIS DIRECTIVE:

Article 1

1. For the purpose of this Directive:
— "telecommunication organisations" means public or private bodies, and the subsidiaries they control, to which a Member State grants special or exclusive rights for the provision of a public telecommunications network and, when applicable, telecommunications services,
— "special or exclusive rights" means the rights granted by a Member State or a public authority to one or more public or private bodies through any legal, regulatory or administrative instrument reserving them the right to provide a service or undertake an activity,
— "public telecommunications network" means the public telecommunications infrastructure which permits the conveyance of signals between defined network termination points by wire, by microwave, by optical means or by other electromagnetic means,
— "telecommunications services" means services whose provision consists wholly or partly in the transmission and routing of signals on the public telecommunications network by means of telecommunications processes, with the exception of radio-broadcasting and television,
— "network termination point" means all physical connections and their technical access specifications which form part of the public telecommunications network and are necessary for access to and efficient communication through that public network,
— "essential requirements" means the non-economic reasons in the general interest which may cause a Member State to restrict access to the public telecommunications network or public telecommunications services. These reasons are security of network operations, maintenance of network integrity, and, in justified cases, interoperability of services and data protection.
Data protection may include protection of personal data, the confidentiality of information transmitted or stored as well as the protection of privacy,
— "voice telephony" means the commecial provision for the public of the direct transport and switching of speech in real-time between public switched network termination points, enabling any user to use equipment connected to such a network termination point in order to communicate with another termination point,
— "telex service" means the commercial provision for the public of direct transmission of telex messages in accordance with the relevant Comité consultatif international télégraphique et téléphonique (CCITT) recommendation between public and switched network termination points, enabling any user to use equipment connected to such a network termination point in order to communicate with another termination point,
— "packet- and circuit-switched data services" means the commercial provision for the public of direct transport of data between public and switched network termination points, enabling any user

to use equipment connected to such a network termination point in order to communicate with another termination point,
— "simple resale of capacity" means the commercial provision on leased lines for the public of data transmission as a separate service, including only such switching, processing, data storage or protocol conversion as is necessary for transmission in real time to and from the public switched network.

2. This Directive shall not apply to telex, mobile radiotelephony, paging and satellite services.

Article 2

Without prejudice to Article 1(2), Member States shall withdraw all special or exclusive rights for the supply of telecommunications services other than voice telephony and shall take the measures necessary to ensure that any operator is entitled to supply such telecommunications services.

Member States which make the supply of such services subject to a licensing or declaration procedure aimed at compliance with the esential requirements shall ensure that the conditions for the grant of licences are objective, non-discriminatory and transparent, that reasons are given for any refusal, and that there is a procedure for appealing against any such refusal.

Without prejudice to Article 3, Member States shall inform the Commission no later than December 31, 1990 of the measures taken to comply with this Article and shall inform it of any existing regulations or of plans to introduce new licensing procedures or to change existing procedures.

Article 3

As regards packet- or circuit-switched data services, Member States may, until December 31, 1992, under the authorisation procedures referred to in Article 2, prohibit economic operators fro offering leased lines capacity for simple resale to the public.

Member States shall, no later than June 30, 1992, notify to the Commission at the planning stage any licensing or declaration procedure for the provision of packet- or circuit-switched data services for the public which are aimed at compliance with:
— essential requirements, or
— trade regulations relating to conditions of permanence, availability and quality of the service, or
— measures to safeguard the task of general economic interest which they have entrusted to a telecommunications organisation for the provision of switched data services, if the performance of that task is likely to be obstructed by the activities of private service providers.

The whole of these conditions shall form a set of public-service specifications and shall be objective, non-discriminatory and transparent.

Member States shall ensure, no late than December 31, 1992, that such licensing or declaration procedures for the provision of such services are published.

Before they are implemented, the Commission shall verify the compatibility of these projects with the Treaty.

Article 4

Member States which maintain special or exclusive rights for the provision and operation of public telecommunications networks shall take the necessary measures to make the conditions governing access to the networks objective and non-discriminatory and publish them.

In particular, they shall ensure that operators who so request can obtain leased lines within a reasonable period, that there are no restrictions on their use other than those justified in accordance with Article 2.

Member States shall inform the Commission no later than December 31, 1990 of the steps they have taken to comply with this Article.

Each time the charges for leased lines are increased, Member States shall provide information to the Commission on the factors justifying such increases.

Article 5

Without prejudice to the relevant international agreements, Member States shall ensure that the characteristics of the technical interfaces necessary for the use of public networks are published by December 31, 1990 at the latest.

Member States shall communicate to the Commission, in accordance with Directive 83/189/EEC, any draft measure drawn up for this purpose.

Article 6

Member States shall, as regards the provision of telecommunications services, and existing restrictions on the processing of signals before their transmission via the public network or after their reception, unless the necessity of these restrictions for compliance with public policy or essential requirements is demonstrated.

Without prejudice to harmonised Community rules adopted by the Council on the provision of an open network, Member States shall ensure as regards services providers including the telecommunications organisation that there is no discrimination either in the conditions of use or in the charges payable.

Member states shall inform the Commission of the measures taken or draft measures introduced in order to comply with this Article by December 31, 1990 at the latest.

Article 7

Member States shall ensure that from July 1, 1991 the grant of operating licences, the control of type approval and mandatory specifications, the allocation of frequencies and surveillance of usage conditions are carried out by a body independent of the telecommunications organisations.

They shall inform the Commission of the measures taken or draft measures introduced to that end no later than December 31, 1990.

Article 8

Member States shall ensure that as soon as the relevant special or exclusive rights have been withdrawn, telecommunications organisations make it possible for customers bound to them by a contract with more than one year to run for the supply of telecommunications services which was subject to such a right at the time it was concluded to terminate the contract at six months' notice.

Article 9

Member States shall communicate to the Commission the necessary information to allow it to draw up, for a period of three years, at the end of each year, an overall report on the application of this Directive. The Commission shall transmit this report to the Member States, the Council, the European Parliament and the Economic and Social Committee.

Article 10

In 1992, the Commission will carry out an overall assessment of the situation in the telecommunications sector in relation to the aims of this Directive.

In 1994, the Commission shall assess the effects of the measures referred to in Article 3 in order to see whether any amendments need to be made to the provisions of that Article, particularly in the light of technological evolution and the development of trade within the Community.

Article 11

This Directive is addressed to the Member States.

Done at Brussels, June 28, 1990.

4.4 Text of Commission Notice on the application of Community competition rules in the telecommunications sector (reproduced opposite)

Commission Notice of September 6, 1991

Guidelines on the application of EEC competition rules in the telecommunications sector.

([1991] O.J. C233/2)

Preface

These guidelines aim at clarifying the application of Community competition rules to the market participants in the telecommunications sector. They must be viewed in the context of the special conditions of the telecommunications sector, and the overall Community telecommunications policy will be taken into account in their application. In particular, account will have to be taken of the actions the Commission will be in a position to propose for the telecommunications industry as a whole, actions deriving from the assessment of the state of play and issues at stake for this industry, as has already been the case for the European electronics and information technology industry in the communication of the Commission of 3 April 1991.

A major political aim, as emphasised by the Commission, the Council, and the European Parliament, must be the development of efficient Europe-wide networks and services, at the lowest cost and of the highest quality, to provide the European user in the single market of 1992 with a basic infrastructure for efficient operation.

The Commission has made it clear in the past that in this context it is considered that liberalisation and harmonisation in the sector must go hand in hand.

Given the competition context in the telecommunications sector, the telecommunications operators should be allowed, and encouraged, to establish the necessary co-operation mechanisms, in order to create—or ensure—Community-wide full interconnectivity between public networks, and where required between services to enable European users to benefit from a wider range of better and cheaper telecommunications services.

This can and has to be done in compliance with, and respect of, EEC competition rules in order to avoid the diseconomies which otherwise could result. For the same reasons operators and other firms that may be in a dominant market position should be made aware of the prohibition of abuse of such positions.

The guidelines should be read in the light of this objective. They set out to clarify, *inter alia*, which forms of co-operation amount to undesirable collusion, and in this sense they list what is *not* acceptable. They should therefore be seen as one aspect of an overall Community policy towards telecommunications, and notably of policies and actions to encourage and stimulate those forms of co-operation which promote the development and availability of advanced communications for Europe.

The full application of competition rules forms a major part of the Community's overall approach to telecommunications. These guidelines should help market participants to shape their strategies and arrangements for Europe-wide networks and services from the outset in a manner which allows them to be fully in line with these rules. In the event of significant changes in the conditions which prevailed when the guidelines were drawn up, the Commission may find it appropriate to adapt the guidelines to the evolution of the situation in the telecommunications sector.

1. Summary

1. The Commission of the European Communities in its Green Paper on the development of the Common Market for tele-communications services and equipment (COM(87)290) dated 30 June 1987 proposed a number of Community positions. Amongst these, positions (H) and (I) are as follows:

"(H) strict continuous review of operational (commercial) activities of telecommunications administrations according to Articles 85, 86 and 90 EEC. This applies in particular to practices of cross-subsidisation of activities in the competitive services sector and of activities in manufacturing;

(J) strict continuous review of all private providers in the newly opened sectors according to Articles 85 and 86, in order to avoid the abuse of dominant positions;".

2. These positions were restated in the Commission's document of 9 February 1988 'Implementing the Green Paper on the development of the Common Market for telecommunications services and equipment/state of discussions and proposals by the Commission' (COM(88)48). Among the areas where the development of concrete policy actions is now possible, the Commission indicated the following:

"Ensuring fair conditions of competition:

Ensuring an open competitive market makes continuous review of the telecommunications sector necessary.

The Commission intends to issue guidelines regarding the application of competition rules to the telecommunications sector and on the way that the review should be carried out".

This is the objective of this communication.

The telecommunications sector in many cases requires co-operation agreements, *inter alia*, between telecommunications organisations (TOs) in order to ensure network and services interconnectivity, one-stop shopping and one-stop billing which are necessary to provide for Europe-wide services and to offer optimum service to users. These objectives can be achieved, *inter alia*, by TOs co-operating—for example, in those areas where exclusive or special rights for provision may continue in accordance with Community law, including competition law, as well as in areas where optimum service will require certain features of co-operation. On the other hand the overriding objective to develop the conditions for the market to provide European users with a greater variety of telecommunications services, of better quality and at lower cost requires the introduction and safeguardingof a strong competitive structure. Competition plays a central role for the Community, especially in view of the completion of the single market for 1992. This role has already been emphasised in the Green Paper.

The single market will represent a new dimension for telecoms operators and users. Competition will give them the opportunity to make full use of technological development and to accelerate it, and encouraging them to restructure and reach the necessary economies of scale to become competitive not only on the Community market, but world-wide.

With this in mind, these guidelines recall the main principles which the Commission, according to its mandate under the Treaty's competition rules, has applied and will apply in the sector without prejudging the outcome of any specific case which will have to be considered on the facts.

The objective is, *inter alia*, to contribute to more certainty of conditions for investment in the sector and the development of Europe-wide services.

The mechanisms for creating certainty for individual cases (apart from complaints and *ex-officio* investigations) are provided for by the notification and negative clearance procedures provided under Regulation 17, which give a formal procedure for clearing co-operation agreements in this area whenever a formal clearance is requested. This is set out in further detail in this communication.

II. Introduction

3. The fundamental technological development world-wide in the telecommunications sector (telecommunications embraces any transmission, emission or reception of signs, signals, writing, images and sounds or intelligence of any nature by wire, radio, optical and other electromagnetic systems (Article 2 of WATTC Regulation of December 9, 1988)) has caused considerable changes in the competition conditions. The traditional monopolistic administrations cannot alone take up the challenge of the technological revolution. New economic forces have appeared on the telecoms scene which are capable of offering users the numerous enhanced services generated by the new technologies. This has given rise to and stimulated a wide deregulation process propagated in the Community with various degrees of intensity.

This move is progressively changing the face of the European market structure. New private suppliers have penetrated the market with more and more transnational value-added services and equipment. The telecommunications administrations, although keeping a central role as public services providers, have acquired a business-like way of thinking. They have started competing dynamically with private operators in services and equipment. Wide restructuring, through mergers and joint ventures, is taking place in order to compete more effectively on the deregulated market through economies of scale and rationalisation. All these events have a multiplier effect on technological progress.

4. In the light of this, the central role of competition for the Community appears clear, especially in view of the completion of the single market for 1992. This role has already been emphasised in the Green Paper.

5. In the application of competition rules the Commission endeavours to avoid the adopting of State measures or undertakings erecting or maintaining artificial barriers incompatible with the single market. But it also favours all forms of co-operation which foster innovation and economic progress, as contemplated by competition law. Pursuing effective competition in telecoms is not a matter of political choice. The choice of a free market and a competition-oriented economy was already envisaged in the EEC Treaty, and the competition rules of the Treaty are directly applicable within the Community. The abovementioned fundamental changes make necessary the full application of competition law.

6. There is a need for more certainty as to the application of competition rules. The telecommunication administrations together with keeping their duties of public interest, are now confronted with the application of these rules practically without transition from a long tradition of legal protection. Their scope and actual implications are often not easily perceivable. As the technology is fast-moving and huge investments are necessary, in order to benefit from the new possibilities on the market-place, all the operators, public or private, have to take quick decisions, taking into account the competition regulatory framework.

7. This need for more certainty regarding the application of competition rules is already met by assessments made in several individual cases. However, assessments of individual cases so far have enabled a response to only some of the numerous competition questions which arise in telecommunications. Future cases will further develop the Commission's practice in this sector.

Purpose of these guidelines

8. These guidelines are intended to advise public telecommunications operators, other telecommunications service and equipment suppliers and users, the legal profession and the interested members of the public about the general legal and economic principles which have been and are being followed by the Commission in the application of competition rules to undertakings in the telecommunications sector, based on experience gained in individual cases in compliance with the rulings of the Court of Justice of the European Communities.

9. The Commission will apply these principles also to future individual cases in a flexible way, and taking the particular context of each case into account. These guidelines do not cover all the general principles governing the application of competition rules, but only those which are of specific relevance to telecommunication issues. The general principles of competition rules not specifically connected with telecommunications but entirely applicable to these can be found, *inter alia*, in the regulatory acts, the Court judgments and the Commission decisions dealing with the individual cases, the Commission's yearly reports on competition policy, press releases and other public information originating from the Commission.

10. These guidelines do not create enforceable rights. Moreover, they do not prejudice the application of EEC competition rules by the Court of Justice of the European Communities and by national authorities (as these rules may be directly applied in each member-State, by the national authorities, administrative or judicial).

11. A change in the economic and legal situation will not automatically bring about a simultaneous amendment to the guidelines. The Commission, however, reserves the possibility to make such an amendment when it considers that these guidelines no longer satisfy their purpose, because of fundamental and/or repeated changes in legal precedents, methods of

applying competition rules, and the regulatory, economic and technical context.

12. These guidelines essentially concern the direct application of competition rules to undertakings, *i.e.* Articles 85 and 86. They do not concern those applicable to the member-States, in particular Articles 5 and 90(1) and (3). Principles ruling the application of Article 90 in telecommunications are expressed in Commission Directives adopted under Article 90(3) for the implementation of the Green Paper.

Relationship between competition rules applicable to undertakings and those applicable to member-States

13. The Court of Justice of the European Communities has ruled that while it is true that Articles 85 and 86 of the Treaty concern the conduct of undertakings and not the laws or regulations of the member-States, by virtue of Article 5(2) EEC, member-States must not adopt or maintain in force any measure which could deprive those provisions of their effectiveness. The Court has stated that such would be the case, in particular, if a member-State were to require or favour prohibited cartels or reinforce the effects thereof or to encourage abuses by dominant undertakings.

If those measures are adopted or maintained in force *vis-à-vis* public undertakings or undertakings to which a member-State grants special or exclusive rights, Article 90 might also apply.

14. When the conduct of a public undertaking or an undertaking to which a member-State grants special or exclusive rights arises entirely as a result of the exercise of the undertaking's autonomous behaviour, it can only be caught by Articles 85 and 86.

When this behaviour is imposed by a mandatory State measure (regulative or administrative), leaving no discretionary choice to the undertakings concerned, Article 90 may apply to the State involved in association with Articles 85 and 86. In this case Articles 85 and 86 apply to the undertakings' behaviour taking into account the constraints to which the undertakings are submitted by the mandatory State measure.

Ultimately, when the behaviour arises from the free choice of the undertakings involved, but the State has taken a measure which encourages the behaviour or strengthens its effects, Articles 85 and/or 86 apply to the undertakings' behaviour and Article 90 may apply to the State measure. This could be the case, *inter alia*, when the State has approved and/or legally endorsed the result of the undertakings' behaviour (for instance tariffs).

These guidelines and the Article 90 Directives complement each other to a certain extent in that they cover the principles governing the application of the competition rules: Articles 85 and 86 on the one hand, Article 90 on the other.

Application of competition rules and other Community law, including open network provision (ONP) rules

15. Articles 85 and 86 and Regulations implementing those Articles in application of Article 87 EEC Treaty constitute law in force and enforceable throughout the Community. Conflicts should not arise with other Community rules because Community law forms a coherent regulatory framework. Other Community rules, and in particular those specifically governing the telecommunications sector, cannot be considered as provisions implementing Articles 85 and 86 in this sector. However it is obvious that Community acts adopted in the telecommunications sector are to be interpreted in a way consistent with competition rules, so to ensure the best possible implementation of all aspects of the Community telecommunications policy.

16. This applies, *inter alia*, to the relationship between competition rules applicable to undertakings and the ONP rules. According to the Council Resolution of 30 June 1988 on the development of the Common Market for telecommunications services and equipment up to 1992, (O.J. C257/1, 1988) ONP comprises the 'rapid definition, by Council Directives, of technical conditions, usage conditions, and tariff principles for open network provision, starting with harmonised conditions for the use of leased lines'. The details of the ONP procedures have been fixed by Directive 90/387 (O.J. L192/1, 1990) on the establishment of the internal market for telecommunications services through the implementation of open network provision, adopted by Council on 28 June 1990 under Article 100a EEC.

17. ONP has a fundamental role in providing European-wide access to Community-

wide interconnected public networks. When ONP harmonisation is implemented, a network user will be offered harmonised access conditions throughout the EEC, whichever country they address. Harmonised access will be ensured in compliance with the competition rules as mentioned above, as the ONP rules specifically provide.

ONP rules cannot be considered as competition rules which apply to States and/or to undertakings' behaviour. ONP and competition rules therefore constitute two different but coherent sets of rules. Hence, the competition rules have full application, even when all ONP rules have been adopted.

18. Competition rules are and will be applied in a coherent manner with Community trade rules in force. However, competition rules apply in a non-discriminatory manner to EEC undertakings and to non-EEC ones which have access to the EEC market.

III. Common Principles of Application of Articles 85 and 86

Equal application of Articles 85 and 86

19. Articles 85 and 86 apply directly and throughout the Community to all undertakings, whether public or private, on equal terms and to the same extent, apart from the exception provided in Article 90(2).

The Commission and national administrative and judicial authorities are competent to apply these rules under the conditions set out in Council Regulation 17.

20. Therefore, Articles 85 and 86 apply both to private enterprises and public telecommunications operators embracing telecommunications administrations and recognised private operating agencies, hereinafter called "telecommunications organisations" (TOs).

TOs are undertakings within the meaning of Articles 85 and 86 to the extent that they exert an economic activity, for the manufacturing and/or sale of telecommunications equipment and/or for the provision of telecommunications services, regardless of other facts such as, for example, whether their nature is economic or not and whether they are legally distinct entities or form part of the State organisation. Associations of TOs are associations of undertakings within the meaning of Article 85, even though TOs participate as undertakings in organisations in which governmental authorities are also represented.

Articles 85 and 86 apply also to undertakings located outside the EEC when restrictive agreements are implemented or intended to be implemented or abuses are committed by those undertakings within the Common Market to the extent that trade between member-States is affected.

Competition restrictions justified under Article 90(2) or by essential requirements

21. The exception provided in Article 90(2) may apply both to State measures and to practices by undertakings. The Services Directive 90/388, in particular in Article 3, makes provision for a member-State to impose specified restrictions in the licences which it can grant for the provision of certain telecommunications services. These restrictions may be imposed under Article 90(2) or in order to ensure the compliance with State essential requirements specified in the Directive.

22. As far as Article 90(2) is concerned, the benefit of the exception provided by this provision may still be invoked for a TO's behaviour when it brings about competition restrictions which its member-State did not impose in application of the Services Directive. However, the fact should be taken into account that in this case the State whose function is to protect the public and the general economic interest, did not deem it necessary to impose the said restrictions. This makes particularly hard the burden of proving that the Article 90(2) exception still applies to an undertaking's behaviour involving these restrictions.

23. The Commission infers from the case law of the Court of Justice that it has exclusive competence, under the control of the Court, to decide that the exception of Article 90(2) applies. The national authorities including judicial authorities can asses that this exception does not apply, when they find that the competition rules clearly do not obstruct the performance of the task of general economic interest assigned to undertakings. When those authorities cannot make a clear

assessment in this sense they should suspend their decision in order to enable the Commission to find that the conditions for the application of that provision are fulfilled.

24. As to measures aiming at the compliance with 'essential requirements' within the meaning of the Services Directive, under Article 1 of the latter, they can only be taken by member-States and not by undertakings.

The relevant market

25. In order to assess the effects of an agreement on competition for the purposes of Article 85 and whether there is a dominant position on the market for the purposes of Article 86, it is necessary to define the relevant market(s), product or service market(s) and geographic market(s), within the domain of telecommunications. In a context of fast-moving technology the relevant market definition is dynamic and variable.

(a) The product market

26. A product market comprises the totality of the products which, with respect to their characteristics, are particularly suitable for satisfying constant needs and are only to a limited extent interchangeable with other products in terms of price, usage and consumer preference. An examination limited to the objective characteristics only of the relevant products cannot be sufficient: the competitive conditions and the structure of supply and demand on the market must also be taken into consideration.
The Commission can precisely define these markets only within the framework of individual cases.

27. For the guidelines' purpose it can only be indicated that distinct service markets could exist at least for terrestrial network provision, voice communication, data communication and satellites. With regard to the equipment market, the following areas could all be taken into account for the purposes of market definition: public switches, private switches, transmission systems and more particularly, in the field of terminals, telephone sets, modems, telex terminals, data transmission terminals and mobile telephones. The above indications are without prejudice to the definition of further narrower distinct markets. As to other services—such as value-added ones—as well as terminal and network equipment, it cannot be specified here whether there is a market for each of them or for an aggregate of them, or for both, depending upon the interchangeability existing in different geographic markets. This is mainly determined by the supply and the requirements in those markets.

28. Since the various national public networks compete for the installation of the telecommunication hubs of large users, market definition may accordingly vary. Indeed, large tlecommunications users, whether or not they are service providers, locate their premises depending, *inter alia*, upon the features of the telecommunications services supplied by each TO. Therefore, they compare national public networks and other services provided by the TOs in terms of characteristics and prices.

29. As to satellite provision, the question is whether or not it is substantially interchangeable with terrestrial network provision:

(a) communication by satellite can be of various kinds: fixed service (point to point communication), multipoint (point to multipoint and multipoint to multipoint), one-way or two-way;

(b) satellites' main characteristics are: coverage of a wide geographic area not limited by national borders, insensitivity of costs to distance, flexibility and ease of networks deployment, in particular in the very small aperture terminals (VSAT) systems;

(c) satellites' uses can be broken down into the following categories: public switched voice and data transmission, business value-added services and broadcasting;

(d) a satellite provision presents a broad interchangeability with the terrestrial transmission link for the basic voice and data transmission on long distance. Conversely, because of its characteristics it is not substantially interchangeable but rather complementary to terrestrial transmission links for several specific voice and data transmission uses. These uses are: services to peripheral or less-developed regions, links between non-contiguous countries, reconfiguration of capacity and provision of routing for traffic restoration. Moreover, satellites are not currently substantially interchangeable for direct broadcasting and multipoint private networks for value-added business services. Therefore, for all those uses satellites should constitute distinct product markets. Within satellites, there may be distinct markets.

30. In mobile communications distinct services seem to exist such as cellular telephone, paging, telepoint, cordless voice and cordless data communication. Technical development permits providing each of these systems with more and more enhanced features. A consequence of this is that the differences between all these systems are progressively blurring and their interchangeability increasing. Therefore, it cannot be excluded that in future for certain uses several of those systems be embraced by a single product market. By the same token, it is likely that, for certain uses, mobile systems will be comprised in a single market with certain services offered on the public switched network.

(b) The geographic market

31. A geographic market is an area:
    — where undertakings enter into competition with each other, and
    — where the objective conditions of competition applying to the product or service in question are similar for all traders.

32. Without prejudice to the definition of the geographic market in individual cases, each national territory within the EEC seems still to be a distinct geographic market as regards those relevant services or products, where:
    — the customer's needs cannot be satisfied by using a non-domestic service,
    — there are different regulatory conditions of access to services, in particular special or exclusive rights which are apt to isolate national territories,
    — as to equipment and network, there are no Community-common standards, whether mandatory or voluntary, whose absence could also isolate the national markets. The absence of voluntary Community-wide standards shows different national customers' requirements.

However, it is expected that the geographic market will progressively extend to the EEC territory at the pace of the progressive realisation of a single EEC market.

33. It has also to be ascertained whether each national market or a part thereof is a substantial part of the Common Market. This is the case where the services of the product involved represent a substantial percentage of volume within the EEC. This applies to all services and products involved.

34. As to satellite uplinks, for cross-border communication by satellite the uplink could be provided from any of several countries. In this case, the geographic market is wider than the national territory and may cover the whole EEC.

As to space segment capacity, the extension of the geographic market will depend on the power of the satellite and its ability to compete with other satellites for transmission to a given area, in other words on its range. This can be assessed only case by case.

35. As to services in general as well as terminal and network equipment, the Commission assesses the market power of the undertakings concerned and the result for EEC competition of the undertakings' conduct, taking into account their interrelated activities and interaction between the EEC and world markets. This is even more necessary to the extent that the EEC market is progressively being opened. This could have a considerable effect on the structure of the markets in the EEC, on the overall competitivity of the undertakings operating in those markets, and in the long run, on their capacity to remain independent operators.

IV. Application of Article 85

36. The Commission recalls that a major policy target of the Council Resolution of 30 June 1988 on the development of the common market for telecommunications services and equipment up to 1992 was that of:

". . . stimulating European co-operation at all levels, as far as compatible with Community competition rules, and particularly in the field of research and development, in order to secure a strong European presence on the telecommunications markets and to ensure the full participation of all member-States."

In many cases Europe-wide services can be achieved by TOs' co-operation—for example, by ensuring interconnectivity and interoperability

(i) in those areas where exclusive or special rights for provision may continue in accordance with Community law and in particular with the Services Directive 90/388; and

(ii) in areas where optimum service will require certain features of co-operation, such as so-called 'one-stop shopping' arrangements, i.e. the possibility of acquiring Europe-wide services at a single sales point.

The Council is giving guidance, by Directives, Decisions, recommendations and resolutions on those areas where Europe-wide services are most urgently needed: such as by Recommendation 86/659/EEC on the co-ordinated introduction of the integrated services digital network (ISDN) in the European Community (O.J. L382/36, 1986) and by Recommendation 87/371/EEC on the co-ordinated introduction of public pan-European cellular digital land-based mobile communications in the Community (O.J. L196/81, 1987).

The Commission welcomes and fully supports the necessity of co-operation particularly in order to promote the development of trans-European services and strengthen the competitivity of the EEC industry throughout the Community and in the world markets. However, this co-operation can only attain that objective if it complies with Community competition rules. Regulation 17 provides well-defined clearing procedures for such co-operation agreements. The procedures foreseen by Regulation 17 are:

(i) the application for negative clearance, by which the Commission certifies that the agreements are not caught by Article 85, because they do not restrict competition and/or do not affect trade between member-States; and

(ii) the notification of agreements caught by Article 85 in order to obtain an exemption under Article 85(3). Although if a particular agreement is caught by Article 85, an exemption can be granted by the Commission under Article 85(3), this is only so when the agreement brings about economic benefits—assessed on the basis of the criteria in the said paragraph 3—which outweigh its restrictions on competition. In any event competition may not be eliminated for a substantial part of the products in question. Notification is not an obligation; but if, for reasons of legal certainty, the parties decide to request an exemption pursuant to Article 4 of Regulation 17 the agreements may not be exempted until they have been notified to the Commission.

37. Co-operation agreements may be covered by one of the Commission block exemption Regulations or Notices. In the first case the agreement is automatically exempted under Article 85(3). In the latter case, in the Commission's view, the agreement does not appreciably restrict competition and trade between member-States and therefore does not justify a Commission action. In either case, the agreement does not need to be notified; but it may be notified in case of doubt. If the Commission receives a multitude of notifications of similar co-operation agreements in the telecommunications sector, it may consider whether a specific block exemption regulation for such agreements would be appropriate.

38. The categories of agreements (for simplification's sake this term stands also for 'decisions by associations' and 'concerted practices' within the meaning of Article 85) which seem to be typical in telecommunications and may be caught by Article 85 are listed below. This list provides examples only and is, therefore, not exhaustive. The Commission is thereby indicating possible competition restrictions which could be caught by Article 85 and cases where there may be the possibility of an exemption.

39. These agreements may affect trade between member-States for the following reasons:

(i) services other than services reserved to TOs, equipment and spatial segment facilities are traded throughout the EEC; agreements on these services and equipment are therefore likely to affect trade. Although at present cross-frontier trade is limited, there is potentially no reason to suppose that suppliers of such facilities will in future confine themselves to their national market;

(ii) as to reserved network services, one can consider that they also are traded throughout the Community. These services could be provided by an operator located in one member-State to customers located in other member-States, which decide to move their telecommunications hub into the first one because it is economically or qualitatively advantageous. Moreover, agreements on these matters are likely to affect EEC trade at least to the extent they influence the conditions under which the other services and equipment are supplied throughout the EEC.

40. Finally, to the extent that the TOs hold dominant positions in facilities, services and equipment markets, their behaviour leading to—and including the conclusion of—the agreements in question could also give rise to a violation of Article 86, if agreements have or are likely to have as their effect hindering the maintenance of the degree of competition still existing in the market or the growth of that competition, or causing the TOs to reap trading benefits which they would not have reaped if there had been normal and sufficiently effective competition.

A. Horizontal agreements concerning the provision of terrestrial facilities and reserved services

41. Agreements concerning terrestrial facilities (public switched network or leased circuits) or services (e.g. voice telephony for the general public) can currently only be concluded between TOs because of this legal regime providing for exclusive or special rights. The fact that the Services Directive recognises the possibility for a member-State to reserve this provision to certain operators does not exempt those operators from complying with the competition rules in providing these facilities or services. These agreements may restrict competition within a member-State only where such exclusive rights are granted to more than one provider.

42. These agreements may restrict the competition between TOs for retaining or attracting large telecommunications users for their telecommunications centres. Such 'hub competition' is substantially based upon favourable rates and other conditions, as well as the quality of the services. Member-States are not allowed to prevent such competition since the Directive allows only the granting of exclusive and special rights by each member-State in its own territory.

43. Finally, these agreements may restrict competition in non-reserved services from third party undertakings, which are supported by the facilities in question, for example if they impose discriminatory or inequitable trading conditions on certain users.

44. (aa) *Price agreements*: all TOs' agreements on prices, discounting or collection charges for international services, are apt to restrict the hub competition to an appreciable extent. Co-ordination on or prohibition of discounting could cause particularly serious restrictions. In situations of public knowledge such as exists in respect of the tariff level, discounting could remain the only possibility of effective price competition.

45. In several cases the Court of Justice and the Commission have considered price agreements among the most serious infringements of Article 85.

While harmonisation of tariff structures may be a major element for the provision of Community-wide services, this goal should be pursued as far as compatible with Community competition rules and should include definition of efficient pricing principles throughout the Community. Price competition is a crucial, if not the principal, element of customer choice and is apt to stimulate technical progress. Without prejudice to any application for individual exemption that may be made, the justification of any price agreement in terms of Article 85(3) would be the subject of very rigorous examination by the Commission.

46. Conversely, where the agreements concern only the setting up of common tariff structures or principles, the Commission may consider whether this would not constitute one of the economic benefits under Article 85(3) which outweigh the competition restriction. Indeed, this could provide the necessary transparency on tariff calculations and facilitate users' deci-

sions about traffic flow or the location of headquarters or premises. Such agreements could also contribute to achieving one of the Green Paper's economic objectives—more cost-orientated tariffs.

In this connection, following the intervention of the Commission, the CEPT has decided to abolish recommendation PGT/10 on the general principles for the lease of international telecommunications circuits and the establishment of private international networks. This recommendation recommended, *inter alia*, the imposition of a 30 per cent. surcharge or an access charge where third-party traffic was carried on an international telecommunications leased circuit, or if such a circuit was interconnected to the public telecommunications network. It also recommended the application of uniform tariff coefficients in order to determine the relative price level of international telecommunications leased circuits. Thanks to the CEPT's co-operation with the Commission leading to the abolition of the recommendation, competition between telecoms operators for the supply of international leased circuits is re-established, to the benefit of users, especially suppliers of non-reserved services. The Commission had found that the recommendation amounted to a price agreement between undertakings under Article 85 of the Treaty which substantially restricted competition within the European Community. (See Commission press release IP(90) 188 of 6 March 1990).

47. (ab) *Agreements on other conditions for the provision of facilities*

These agreements may limit hub competition between the partners. Moreover, they may limit the access of users to the network, and thus restrict third undertakings' competition as to non-reserved services. This applies especially to the use of leased circuits. The abolished CEPT recommendation PGT/10 on tariffs had also recommended restrictions on conditions of sale which the Commission objected to. These restrictions were mainly:

— making the use of leased circuits between the customer and third parties subject to the condition that the communication concern exclusively the activity for which the circuit has been granted,
— a ban on subleasing,
— authorisation of private networks only for customers tied to each other by economic links and which carry out the same activity,
— prior consultation between the TOs for any approval of a private network and of any modification of the use of the network, and for any interconnection of private networks.

For the purpose of an exemption under Article 85(3), the granting of special conditions for a particular facility in order to promote its development could be taken into account among other elements. This could foster technologies which reduce the costs of services and contribute to increasing competitiveness of European industry structures. Naturally, the other Article 85(3) requirements should also be met.

48. (ac) *Agreements on the choice of telecommunication routes*

These may have the following restrictive effects:

(i) to the extent that they co-ordinate the TOs' choice of the routes to be set up in international services, they may limit competition between TOs as suppliers to users' communications hubs, in terms of investments and production, with a possible effect on tariffs. It should be determined whether this restriction of their business autonomy is sufficiently appreciable to be caught by Article 85. In any event, an argument for an exemption under Article 85(3) could be more easily sustained if common routes designation were necessary to enable interconnections and, therefore, the use of a Europe-wide network;

(ii) to the extent that they reserve the choice of routes already set up to the TOs, and this choice concerns one determined facility, they could limit the use of other facilities and thus services provision possibly to the detriment of technological progress. By contrast, the choice of routes does not seem restrictive in principle to the extent that it constitutes a technical requirement.

49. (ad) *Agreements on the imposition of technical and quality standards on the services provided on the public network*

Standardisation brings substantial economic benefits which can be relevant under Article 85(3). It facilitates *inter alia* the provision of pan-European telecommunications services. As set out in the framework of the Community's approach to standardisation, products and services complying with standards may be used Community-wide. In the context of this approach, European standards institutions have developed in this field (ETSI and CEN-Cenelec). National markets in the EC would be opened up and form a Community market. Service and equipment markets would be enlarged, hence favouring economies of scale. Cheaper products and services are thus available to users. Standardisation may also offer an alternative to specifications controlled by undertakings dominant in the network architecture and in non-reserved services. Standardisation agreements may, therefore, lessen the risk of abuses by these undertakings which could block the access to the markets for non-reserved services and for equipment. However, certain standardisation agreements can have restrictive effects on competition: hindering innovation, freezing a particular stage of technical development, blocking the network access of some users/service providers. This restriction could be appreciable, for example when deciding to what extent intelligence will in future be located in the network or continue to be permitted in customers' equipment. The imposition of specifications other than those provided for by Community law could have restrictive effects on competition. Agreements having these effects are, therefore, caught by Article 85.

The balance between economic benefits and competition restrictions is complex. In principle, an exemption could be granted if an agreement brings more openness and facilitates access to the market, and these benefits outweigh the restrictions caused by it.

50. Standards jointly developed and/or published in accordance with the ONP procedures carry with them the presumption that the co-operating TOs which comply with those standards fulfil the requirement of open and efficient access (see the ONP Directive mentioned in paragraph 16). This presumption can be rebutted, *inter alia*, if the agreement contains restrictions which are not foreseen by Community law and are not indispensable for the standardisation sought.

51. One important Article 85(3) requirement is that users must also be allowed a fair share of the resulting benefit. This is more likely to happen when users are directly involved in the standardisation process in order to contribute to deciding what products or services will meet their needs. Also, the involvement of manufacturers or service providers other than TOs seems a positive element for Article 85(3) purposes. However, this involvement must be open and widely representative in order to avoid competition restrictions to the detriment of excluded manufacturers or service providers. Licensing other manufacturers may be deemed necessary, for the purpose of granting an exemption to these agreements under Article 85(3).

52. (ae) *Agreements foreseeing special treatment for TOs' terminal equipment or other companies' equipment for the interconnection or interoperation of terminal equipment with reserved services and facilities*

53. (af) *Agreements on the exchange of information*

A general exchange of information could indeed be necessary for the good functioning of international telecommunications services, and for co-operation aimed at ensuring interconnectivity or one-stop shopping and billing. It should not be extended to competition-sensitive information, such as certain tariff information which constitutes business secrets, discounting, customers and commercial strategy, including that concerning new products. The exchange of this information would affect the autonomy of each TO's commercial policy and it is not necessary to attain the said objectives.

B. *Agreements concerning the provision of non-reserved services and terminal equipment*

54. Unlike facilities markets, where only the TOs are the providers, in the services markets the actual or potential competitors are numerous and include, besides the TOs, international private companies, computer companies, publishers and others. Agreements on services and terminal equipment could therefore be concluded between TOs, between TOs and private companies, and between private companies.

55. The liberalising process has led mostly to strategic agreements between (i) TOs,

and (ii) TOs and other companies. These agreements usually take the form of joint ventures.

56. (ba) *Agreements between TOs*
The scope of these agreements, in general, is the provision by each partner of a value-added service including the management of the service. Those agreements are mostly based on the 'one-stop shopping' principle, *i.e.* each partner offers to the customer the entire package of services which he needs. These managed services are called managed data network services (MDNS). An MDNS essentially consists of a broad package of services including facilities, value-added services and management. The agreementsmay also concern such basic services as satellite uplink.

57. These agreements could restrict competition in the MDNS market and also in the markets for a service or a group of services included in the MDNS:
 (i) between the participating TOs themselves; and
 (ii) *vis-à-vis* other actual or potential third-party providers.

58. (i) *Restrictions of competition between TOs*
Co-operation between TOs could limit the number of potential individual MDNS offered by each participating TO.
The agreements may affect competition at least in certain aspects which are contemplated as specific examples of prohibited practices under Article 85(1)(*a*) to (*c*), in the event that:
— they fix or recommend, or at least lead (through the exchange of price information) to co-ordination of prices charged by each participant to customers,
— they provide for joint specification of MDNS products, quotas, joint delivery, specification of customers' systems; all this would amount to controlling production, markets, technical development and investments,
— they contemplate joint purchase of MDNS hardware and/or software, which would amount to sharing markets or sources of supply.

59. (ii) *Restrictive effects on third party undertakings*
Third parties' market entry could be precluded or hampered if the participating TOs:

— refuse to provide facilities to third party suppliers of services,
— apply usage restrictions only to third parties and not to themselves (e.g. a private provider is precluded from placing multiple customers on a leased line facility to obtain lower unit costs),
— favour their MDNS offerings over those of private suppliers with respect to access, availability, quality and price of leased circuits, maintenance and other services,
— apply especially low rates to their MDNS offerings, cross-subsidising them with higher rates for monopoly services.

Examples of this could be the restrictions imposed by the TOs on private network operators as to the qualifications of the users, the nature of the messages to be exchanged over the network or the use of international private leased circuits.

60. Finally, as the participating TOs hold, individually or collectively, a dominant position for the creation and the exploitation of the network in each national market, any restrictive behaviour described in paragraph 59 could amount to an abuse of a dominant position under Article 86 (see V below).

61. On the other hand, agreements between TOs may bring economic benefits which could be taken into account for the possible granting of an exemption under Article 85(3). *Inter alia*, the possible benefits could be as follows:
— a European-wide service and 'one-stop shopping' could favour business in Europe. Large multinational undertakings are provided with a European communication service using only a single point of contact,
— the co-operation could lead to a certain amount of European-wide standardisation even before further EEC legislation on this matter is adopted,
— the co-operation could bring a cost reduction and consequently cheaper offerings to the advantage of consumers,
— a general improvement of public infrastructure could arise from a joint service provision.

62. Only by notification of the cases in question, in accordance with the appropri-

ate procedures under Regulation 17, will the Commission be able, where requested, to ascertain, on the merits, whether these benefits outweigh the competition restrictions. But in any event, restrictions on access for third parties seem likely to be considered as not indispensable and to lead to the elimination of competition for a substantial part of the products and services concerned within the meaning of Article 85(3), thus excluding the possibility of an exemption. Moreover, if an MDNS agreement strengthens appreciably a dominant position which a participating TO holds in the market for a service included in the MDNS, this is also likely to lead to a rejection of the exemption.

63. The Commission has outlined the conditions for exempting such forms of co-operation in a case concerning a proposed joint venture between 22 TOs for the provision of a Europe-wide MDNS, later abandoned for commercial reasons. (Commission press release IP(89) 948 of 14.12.1989).
The Commission considered that the MDNS project presented the risks of restriction of competition between the operators themselves and private service suppliers but it accepted that the project also offered economic benefits to telecommunications users such as access to Europe-wide services through a single operator. Such co-operation could also have accelerated European standardisation, reduced costs and increased the quality of the services. The Commission had informed the participants that approval of the project would have to be subject to guarantees designed to prevent undue restriction of competition in the telecommunications services markets, such as discrimination against private services suppliers and cross-subsidisation. Such guarantees would be essential conditions for the granting of an exemption under the competition rules to co-operation agreements involving TOs. The requirement for an appropriate guarantee of non-discrimination and non-cross-subsidisation will be specified in individual cases according to the examples of discrimination indicated in Section V below concerning the application of Article 86.

64. *Agreements between TOs and other service providers*
Co-operation between TOs and other operators is increasing in telecommunications services. It frequently takes the form of a joint venture. The Commission recognises that it may have beneficial effects. However, this co-operation may also adversely affect competition and the opening up of services markets. Beneficial and harmful effects must therefore be carefully weighed.

65. Such agreements may restrict competition for the provision of telecommunications services:
 (i) between the partners; and
 (ii) from third parties.

66. (i) Competition between the partners may be restricted when they are actual or potential competitors for the relevant telecommunications service. This is generally the case, even when only the other partners and not the TOs are already providing the service. Indeed, TOs may have the required financial capacity, technical and commercial skills to enter the market for non-reserved services and could reasonably bear the technical and financial risk of doing it. This is also generally the case as far as private operators are concerned, when they do not yet provide the service in the geographical market covered by the co-operation, but do provide this service elsewhere. They may therefore be potential competitors in this geographic market.

67. (ii) The co-operation may restrict competition from third parties because:
— there is an appreciable risk that the participant TO, *i.e.* the dominant network provider, will give more favourable network access to its co-operation partners than to other service providers in competition with the partners,
— potential competitors may refrain from entering the market because of this objective risk or, in any event, because of the presence on the market-place of a co-operation involving the monopolist for the network provision. This is especially the case when market entry barriers are high: the market structure allows only few suppliers and the size and the market power of the partners are considerable.

68. On the other hand, the co-operation may bring economic benefits which outweigh its harmful effect and therefore justify the granting of an exemption under Article 85(3). The economic benefits can

consist, *inter alia*, of the rationalisation of the production and distribution of telecommunication services, in improvements in existing services or development of new services, or transfer of technology which improves the efficiency and the competitiveness of the European industrial structures.

69. In the absence of such economic benefits a complementarity between partners, *i.e.* between the provision of a reserved activity and that of a service under competition, is not a benefit as such. Considering it as a benefit would be equal to justifying an involvement through restrictive agreements of TOs in any non-reserved service provision. This would be to hinder a competitive structure in this market.

In certain cases, the co-operation could consolidate or extend the dominant position of the TOs concerned to a non-reserved services market, in violation of Article 86.

70. The imposition or the proposal of co-operation with the service provider as a condition for the provision of the network may be deemed abusive (see paragraph 98(vi)).

71. (bc) *Agreements between service providers other than TOs*

The Commission will apply the same principles indicated in (ba) and above also to agreements between private service providers, *inter alia*, agreements providing quotas, price fixing, market and/or customer allocation. In principle, they are unlikely to qualify for an exemption. The Commission will be particularly vigilant in order to avoid co-operation on services leading to a strengthening of dominant positions of the partners or restricting competition from third parties. There is a danger of this occurring for example when an undertaking is dominant with regard to the network architecture and its proprietary standard is adopted to support the service contemplated by the co-operation. This architecture enabling interconnection between computer systems of the partners could attract some partners to the dominant partner. The dominant position for the network architecture will be strengthened and Article 86 may apply.

72. In any exemption of agreements between TOs and other services and/or equipment providers, or between these providers, the Commission will require from the partners appropriate guarantees of non-cross-subsidisation and non-discrimination. The risk of cross-subsidisation and discrimination is higher when the TOs or the other partners provide both services and equipment, whether within or outside the Community.

C. *Agreements on research and development (R&D)*

73. As in other high technology based sectors, R&D in tele- communications is essential for keeping pace with technological progress and being competitive on the market place to the benefit of users. R&D requires more and more important financial, technical and human resources which only few undertakings can generate individually. Co-operation is therefore crucial for attaining the above objectives.

74. The Commission has adopted a Regulation for the block exemption under Article 85(3) of R&D agreements in all sectors, including telecommunications. (Regulation 418/85: [1985] O.J. L53/5).

75. Agreements which are not covered by this Regulation (or the other Commission block exemption Regulations) could still obtain an individual exemption from the Commission if Article 85(3) requirements are met individually. However, not in all cases do the economic benefits of an R&D agreement outweigh its competition restrictions. In telecommunications, one major asset, enabling access to new markets, is the launch of new products or services. Competition is based not only on price, but also on technology. R&D agreements could constitute the means for powerful undertakings with high market shares to avoid or limit competition from more innovative rivals. The risk of excessive restrictions of competition increases when the co-operation is extended from R&D to manufacturing and even more to distribution.

76. The importance which the Commission attaches to R&D and innovation is demonstrated by the fact that it has launched several programmes for this purpose. The joint companies' activities which may result from these programmes are not automatically cleared or exempted as such in all aspects from the application of the competition rules. However, most of those joint activities may be covered by the

Commission's block exemption Regulations. If not, the joint activities in question may be exempted, whererequired, in accordance with the appropriate criteria and procedures.

77. In the Commission's experience joint distribution linked to joint R&D which is not covered by the Regulation on R&D does not play the crucial role in the exploitation of the results of R&D. Nevertheless, in individual cases, provided that a competitive environment is maintained, the Commission is prepared to consider full-range co-operation even between large firms. This should lead to improving the structure of European industry and thus enable it to meet strong competition in the world market place.

V. Application of Article 86

78. Article 86 applies when:
(i) the undertaking concerned holds an individual or a joint dominant position;
(ii) it commits an abuse of that dominant position; and
(iii) the abuse may affect trade between member-States.

Dominant position

79. In each national market the TOs hold individually or collectively a dominant position for the creation and the exploitation of the network, since they are protected by exclusive or special rights granted by the State. Moreover, the TOs hold a dominant position for some telecommunications services, in so far as they hold exclusive or special rights with respect to those services.

80. The TOs may also hold dominant positions on the markets for certain equipment or services, even though they no longer hold any exclusive rights on those markets. After the elimination of these rights, they may have kept very important market shares in this sector. When the market share in itself does not suffice to give the TOs a dominant position, it could do it in combination with the other factors such as the monopoly for the network or other related services and a powerful and wide distribution network. As to the equipment, for example terminal equipment, even if the TOs are not involved in the equipment manufacturing or in the services provision, they may hold a dominant position in the market as distributors.

81. Also, firms other than TOs may hold individual or collective dominant positions in markets where there are no exclusive rights. This may be the case especially for certain non-reserved services because of either the market shares alone of those undertakings, or because of a combination of several factors. Among these factors, in addition to the market shares, two of particular importance are the technological advance and the holding of the information concerning access protocols or interfaces necessary to ensure interoperability of software and hardware. When this information is covered by intellectual property rights this is a further factor of dominance.

82. Finally, the TOs hold, individually or collectively, dominant positions in the demand for some telecommunication equipment, works or software services. Being dominant for the network and other services provisions they may account for a purchaser's share high enough to give them dominance as to the demand, *i.e.* making suppliers dependent on them. Dependence could exist when the supplier cannot sell to other customers a substantial part of its production or change production. In certain national markets, for example in large switching equipment, big purchasers such as the TOs face big suppliers. In this situation, it should be weighed up case by case whether the supplier or the customer position will prevail on the other to such an extent as to be considered dominant under Article 86.

With the liberalisation of services and the expansion of new forces on the services markets, dominant positions of undertakings other than the TOs may arise for the purchasing of equipment.

Abuse

83. Commission's activity may concern mainly the following broad areas of abuses:
A. *TOs' abuses*: in particular, they may take advantage of their monopoly or at least dominant position to acquire a foothold or to extend their power in non-reserved neighbouring markets, to the detriment of competitors and customers.

B. *Abuses by undertaking other than TOs*: these may take advantage of the fundamental information they hold, whether or not covered by intellectual property rights, with the object and/or effect of restricting competition.

C. *Abuses of a dominant purchasing position*: for the time being this concerns mainly the TOs, especially to the extent that they hold a dominant position for reserved activities in the national market. However, it may also increasingly concern other undertakings which have entered the market.

A. *TOs' Abuses*

84. The Commission has recognised in the Green Paper the central role of the TOs, which justifies the maintenance of certain monopolies to enable them to perform their public task. This public task consists in the provision and exploitation of a universal network or, where appropriate, universal service, i.e. one having general coverage and available to all users (including service providers and the TOs themselves) upon request on reasonable and non-discriminatory conditions.

This fundamental obligation could justify the benefit of the exception provided in Article 90(2) under certain circumstances, as laid down in the Services Directive.

85. In most cases, however, the competition rules, far from obstructing the fulfilment of this obligation, contribute to ensuring it. In particular, Article 86 can apply to behaviour of dominant undertakings resulting in a refusal to supply, discrimination, restrictive tying clauses, unfair prices or other inequitable conditions.

If one of these types of behaviour occurs in the provision of one of the monopoly services, the fundamental obligation indicated above is not performed. This could be the case when a TO tries to take advantage of its monopoly for certain services (for instance: network provision) in order to limit the competition they have to face in respect of non-reserved services, which in turn are supported by those monopoly services.

It is not necessary for the purpose of the application of Article 86 that competition be restricted as to a service which is supported by the monopoly provision in question. It would suffice that the behaviour results in an appreciable restriction of competition in whatever way. This means that an abuse may occur when the company affected by the behaviour is not a service provider but an end user who could himself be disadvantaged in competition in the course of his own business.

86. The Court of Justice has set out this fundamental principle of competition in telecommunications in one of its judgments. [*Télémarketing CLT* 124]. An abuse within the meaning of Article 86 is committed where, without any objective necessity, an undertaking holding a dominant position on a particular market reserves to itself or to an undertaking belonging to the same group an ancillary activity which might be carried out by another undertaking as part of its activities on a neighbouring but separate market, with the possibility of eliminating all competition from such undertaking.

The Commission believes that this principle applies, not only when a dominant undertaking monopolises other markets, but also when by anti-competitive means it extends its activity to other markets.

Hampering the provision of non-reserved services could limit production, markets and above all the technical progress which is a key factor of telecommunications. The Commission has already shown these adverse effects of usage restrictions on monopoly provision in its decision in the "British Telecom" case (Cited above).

In this Decision it was found that the restrictions imposed by British Telecom on telex and telephone networks usage, namely on the transmission of international messages on behalf of third parties:

(i) limited the activity of economic operators to the detriment of technological progress;

(ii) discriminated against these operators, thereby placing them at a competitive disadvantage *vis-à-vis* TOs not bound by these restrictions; and

(iii) made the conclusion of the contracts for the supply of telex circuits subject to acceptance by the other parties of supplementary obligations which had no connection with such contracts. These were considered abuses of a dominant position identified respectively in Article 86(b), (c) and (d).

This could be done:

(a) as above, by refusing or restricting the usage of the service provided under monopoly so as to limit the provision of non-reserved services by third parties; or

(b) by predatory behaviour, as a result of cross-subsidisation.

87. The separation of the TOs' regulatory power from their business activity is a crucial matter in the context of the application of Article 86. This separation is provided in the Article 90 Directives on terminals and on services mentioned above.

(a) Usage restrictions

88. Usage restrictions on provisions of reserved services are likely to correspond to the specific examples of abuses indicated in Article 86. In particular:
— they may limit the provision of telecommunications services in free competition, the investments and the technical progress, to the prejudice of telecommunications consumers (Article 86(*b*));
— to the extent that these usage restrictions are not applied to all users, including the TOs themselves as users, they may result in discrimination against certain users, placing them at a competitive disadvantage (Article 86(c));
— they may make the usage of the reserved services subject to the acceptance of obligations which have no connection with this usage (Article 86(d)).

89. The usage restrictions in question mainly concern public networks (public switched telephone network (PSTN) or public switched data networks (PSDN)) and especially leased circuits. They may also concern other provisions such as satellite uplink, and mobile communication networks. The most frequent types of behaviour are as follows:
(i) *Prohibition imposed by TOs on third parties*:
(a) to connect private leased circuits by means of concentrator, multiplexer or other equipment to the public switched network; and/or

(b) to use private leased circuits for providing services, to the extent that these services are not reserved, but under competition.

90. To the extent that the user is granted a licence by State regulatory authorities under national law in compliance with EEC law, these prohibitions limit the user's freedom of access to the leased circuits, the provision of which is a public service. Moreover, it discriminates between users, depending upon the usage (Article 86(c)). This is one of the most serious restrictions and could substantially hinder the development of international telecommunications services (Article 86(b)).

91. When the usage restriction limits the provision of non-reserved service in competition with that provided by the TO itself the abuse is even more serious and the principles of the abovementioned "Telemarketing" judgment apply.

92. In individual cases, the Commission will assess whether the service provided on the leased circuit is reserved or not, on the basis of the Community regulatory acts interpreted in the technical and economic context of each case. Even though a service could be considered reserved according to the law, the fact that a TO actually prohibits the usage of the leased circuit only to some users and not to others could constitute a discrimination under Article 86(c).

93. The Commission has taken action in respect of the Belgian Régie des Télégraphes et Téléphones after receiving a complaint concerning an alleged abuse of dominant position from a private supplier of value-added telecommunications services relating to the conditions under which telecommunications circuits were being leased. Following discussions with the Commission, the RTT authorised the private supplier concerned to use the leased telecommunications circuits subject to no restrictions other than that they should not be used for the simple transport of data.

Moreover, pending the possible adoption of new rules in Belgium, and without prejudice to any such rules, the RTT undertook that all its existing and potential clients for leased telecommunications circuits to which third parties may have access shall be governed by the same conditions as those which were agreed with the private sector supplier mentioned above. (Commission Press release IP(90) 67 of 29 January 1990).

(ii) *Refusal by TOs to provide reserved services (in particular the network and leased circuits) to third parties*

94. Refusal to supply has been considered an abuse by the Commission and the Court of Justice. (Joined Cases 6–7/73 Commercial Solvents v. *E.C. Commission* [1974] E.C.R. 223, [1974] 1 C.M.L.R. 309; United Brands v. *EC Commission,* cited above). This behaviour would make it impossible or at least appreciably difficult for third parties to provide non-reserved services. This, in turn, would lead to a limitation of services and of technical development (Article 86(b)) and, if applied only to some users, result in discrimination (Article 86(c)).

(iii) *Imposition of extra charges or other special conditions for certain usages of reserved services*

95. An example would be the imposition of access charges to leased circuits when they are connected to the public switched network or other special prices and charges for service provision to third parties. Such access charges may discriminate between users of the same service (leased circuits provision) depending upon the usage and result in imposing unfair trading conditions. This will limit the usage of leased circuits and finally non-reserved service provision. Conversely, it does not constitute anabuse provided that it is shown, in each specific case, that the access charges correspond to costs which are entailed directly for the TOs for the access in question. In this case, access charges can be imposed only on an equal basis to all users, including TOs themselves.

96. Apart from these possible additional costs which should be covered by an extra charge, the interconnection of a leased circuit to the public switched network is already remunerated by the price related to the use of this network. Certainly, a leased circuit can represent a subjective value for a user depending on the profitability of the enhanced service to be provided on that leased circuit. However, this cannot be a criterion on which a dominant undertaking, and above all a public service provider, can base the price of this public service.

97. The Commission appreciates that the substantial difference between leased circuits and the public switched network causes a problem of obtaining the necessary revenues to cover the costs of the switched network. However, the remedy chosen must not be contrary to law, *i.e.* the EEC Treaty, as discriminatory pricing between customers would be.

(iv) *Discriminatory price or quality of the service provided*

98. This behaviour may relate, *inter alia,* to tariffs or to restrictions or delays in connection to the public switched network or leased circuits provision, in installation, maintenance and repair, in effecting interconnection of systems or in providing information concerning network planning, signalling protocols, technical standards and all other information necessary for an appropriate interconnection and interoperation with the reserved service and which may affect the interworking of competitive services or terminal equipment offerings.

(v) *Tying the provision of the reserved service to the supply by the TOs or others of terminal equipment to be interconnected or interoperated, in particular through imposition, pressure, offer of special prices or other trading conditions for the reserved service linked to the equipment.*

(vi) *Tying the provisions of the reserved service to the agreement of the user to enter into co-operation with the reserved service provider himself as to the non-reserved service to be carried on the network*

(vii) *Reserving to itself for the purpose of non-reserved service provision or to other service providers information obtained in the exercise of a reserved service in particular information concerning users of a reserved services providers more favourable conditions for the supply of this information*

This latter information could be important for the provision of services under competition to the extent that it permits the targeting of customers of those services and the definition of business strategy. The behaviour indicated above could result in a discrimination against undertakings to which the use of this information is denied in violation of Article 86(c). The information in question can only be disclosed with the agreement of the users concerned and in accordance with relevant data protection legislation (see the proposal for a Council Directive concerning the protection of personal data and privacy in the context of public digital telecommunications networks, in particular the integrated services digital network (ISDN) and public digital mobile networks). (Commission document COM(90) 314 (13 September 1990)).

(viii) *Imposition of unneeded reserved services by supplying reserved and/or non-reserved services when the former reserved services are reasonably separable from the others*

99. The practices under (v) (vi) (vii) and (viii) result in applying conditions which have no connection with the reserved service, contravening Article 86(d).

100. Most of these practices were in fact identified in the Services Directive as restrictions on the provision of services within the meaning of Article 59 and Article 86 of the Treaty brought about by State measures. They are therefore covered by the broader concept of 'restrictions' which under Article 6 of the Directive have to be removed by member-States.

101. The Commission believes that the Directives on terminals and on services also clarify some principles of application of Articles 85 and 86 in the sector.

The Services Directive does not apply to important sectors such as mobile communications and satellites; however, competition rules apply fully to these sectors. Moreover, as to the services covered by the Directive it will depend very much on the degree of precision of the licences given by the regulatory body whether the TOs still have a discretionary margin for imposing conditions which should be scrutinised under competition rules. Not all the conditions can be regulated in licences: consequently, there could be room for discretionary action. The application of competition rules to companies will therefore depend very much on a case-by-case examination of the licences. Nothing more than a class licence can be required for terminals.

(b) Cross-subsidisation

102. Cross-subsidisation means that an undertaking allocates all or part of the costs of its activity in one product or geographic market to its activity in another product or geographic market. Under certain circumstances, cross-subsidisation in telecommunications could distort competition, *i.e.* lead to beating other competitors with offers which are made possible not by efficiency and performance but by artificial means such as subsidies. Avoiding cross-subsidisation leading to unfair competition is crucial for the development of service provision and equipment supply.

103. Cross-subsidisation does not lead to predatory pricing and does not restrict competition when it is the costs of reserved activities which are subsidised by the revenue generated by other reserved activities since there is no competition possible as to these activities. This form of subsidisation is even necessary, as it enables the TOs holders of exclusive rights to perform their obligation to provide a public service universally and on the same conditions to everybody. For instance, telephone provision in unprofitable rural areas is subsidised through revenues from telephone provision in profitable urban areas or long-distance calls. The same could be said of subsidising the provision of reserved services through revenues generated by activities under competition. The application of the general principle of cost-orientation should be the ultimate goal, in order, *inter alia*, to ensure that prices are not inequitable as between users.

104. Subsidising activities under competition, whether concerning services or equipment, by allocating their costs to monopoly activities, however, is likely to distort competition in violation of Article 86. It could amount to an abuse by an undertaking holding a dominant position within the Community. Moreover, users of activities under monopoly have to bear unrelated costs for the provision of these activities. Cross-subsidisation can also exist between monopoly provision and equipment manufacturing and sale. Cross-subsidisation can be carried out through:

— funding the operation of the activities in question with capital remunerated substantially below the market rate;

— providing for those activities premises, equipment, experts and/or services with a remuneration substantially lower than the market price.

105. As to funding through monopoly revenues or making available monopoly material and intellectual means for the

Book One: Part VIII—State Interference

starting up of new activities under competition, this constitutes an investment whose costs should be allocated to the new activity. Offering the new product or service should normally include a reasonable remuneration of such investment in the long run. If it does not, the Commission will assess the case on the basis of the remuneration plans of the undertaking concerned and of the economic context.

106. Transparency in the TOs' accounting should enable the Commission to ascertain whether there is cross-subsidisation in the cases in which this question arises. The ONP Directive provides in this respect for the definition of harmonised tariff principles which should lessen the number of these cases.

This transparency can be provided by an accounting system which ensures the fully proportionate distribution of all costs between reserved and non-reserved activities. Proper allocation of costs is more easily ensured in cases of structural separation, *i.e.* creating distinct entities for running each of these two categories of activities.

An appropriate accounting system approach should permit the identification and allocation of all costs between the activities which they support. In this system all products and services should bear proportionally all the relevant costs, including costs of research and development, facilities and overheads. It should enable the production of recorded figures which can be verified by accountants.

107. As indicated above (paragraph 59), in cases of co-operation agreements involving TOs a guarantee of no cross-subsidisation is one of the conditions required by the Commission for exemption under Article 85(3). In order to monitor properly compliance with that guarantee, the Commission now envisages requesting the parties to ensure an appropriate accounting system as described above, the accounts being regularly submitted to the Commission. Where the accounting method is chosen, the Commission will reserve the possibility of submitting the accounts to independent audit, especially if any doubt arises as to the capability of the system to ensure the necessary transparency or to detect any cross-subsidisation. If the guarantee cannot be properly monitored, the Commission may withdraw the exemption.

108. In all other cases, the Commission does not envisage requiring such transparency of the TOs. However, if in a specific case there are substantial elements converging in indicating the existence of an abusive cross-subsidisation and/or predatory pricing, the Commission could establish a presumption of such cross-subsidisation and predatory pricing. An appropriate separate accounting system could be important in order to counter this presumption.

109. Cross-subsidisation of a reserved activity by a non-reserved one does not in principle restrict competition. However, the application of the exception provided in Article 90(2) to this non-reserved activity could not as a rule be justified by the fact that the financial viability of the TO in question rests on the non-reserved activity. Its financial viability and the performance of its task of general economic interest can only be ensured by the State where appropriate by the granting of an exclusive or special right and by imposing restrictions on activities competing with the reserved ones.

110. Also cross-subsidisation by a public or private operator outside the EEC may be deemed abusive in terms of Article 86 if that operator holds a dominant position for equipment or non-reserved services within the EEC. The existence of this dominant position, which allows the holder to behave to an appreciable extent independently of its competitors and customers and ultimately of consumers, will be assessed in the light of all elements in the EEC and outside.

B. Abuses by undertakings other than the TOs

111. Further to the liberalisation of services, undertakings other than the TOs may increasingly extend their power to acquire dominant positions in non-reserved markets. They may already hold such a position in some services markets which had not been reserved. When they take advantage of their dominant position to restrict competition and to extend their power, Article 86 may also apply to them. The abuses in which they might indulge are broadly similar to most of those previously described in relation to the TOs.

112. Infringements of Article 86 may be committed by the abusive exercise of industrial property rights in relation with

standards, which are of crucial importance for telecommunications. Standards may be either the results of international standardisation, or *de facto* standards and the property of undertakings.

113. Producers of equipment or suppliers of services are dependent on proprietary standards to ensure the interconnectivity of their computer resources. An undertaking which owns a dominant network architecture may abuse its dominant position by refusing to provide the necessary information for the interconnection of other architecture resources to its architecture products. Other possible abuses—similar to those indicated as to the TOs—are, *inter alia*, delays in providing the information, discrimination in the quality of the information, discriminatory pricing or other trading conditions, and making the information provision subject to the acceptance by the producer, supplier or user of unfair trading conditions.

114. On 1 August 1984, the Commission accepted a unilateral undertaking from IBM to provide other manufacturers with the technical interface information needed to permit competitive products to be used with IBM's then most powerful range of computers, the System/370. The Commission thereupon suspended the proceedings under Article 86 which it had initiated against IBM in December 1980. The IBM Undertaking (Reproduced in full in EC Bulletin 10–1984 (para. 3.4.1) [1984] 3 C.M.L.R. 147. As to its continued application, see Commission press release IP(88) 814 of 15 December 1988) also contains a commitment relating to SNA formats and protocols.

115. The question how to reconcile copyrights on standards with the competition requirements is particularly difficult. In any event, copyright cannot be used unduly to restrict competition.

C. Abuses of dominant purchasing position

116. Article 86 also applies to behaviour of undertakings holding a dominant purchasing position. The examples of abuses indicated in that Article may therefore also concern that behaviour.

117. The Council Directive 90/531 (O.J. L297/1, 1990) based on Articles 57(2), 66, 100a and 113 on the procurement procedures of entities operating in *inter alia* the telecommunications sector regulates essentially:

(i) procurement procedures in order to ensure on a reciprocal basis non-discrimination on the basis of nationality; and

(ii) for products or services for use in reserved markets, not in competitive markets. That Directive, which is addressed to States, does not exclude the application of Article 86 to the purchasing of products within the scope of the Directive. The Commission will decide case by case how to ensure that these different sets of rules are applied in a coherent manner.

118. Furthermore, both in reserved and competitive markets, practices other than those covered by the Directive may be established in violation of Article 86. One example is taking advantage of a dominant purchasing position for imposing excessively favourable prices or other trading conditions, in comparison with other purchasers and suppliers (Article 86(*a*)). This could result in discrimination under Article 86(*c*). Also obtaining, whether or not through imposition, an exclusive distributorship for the purchased product by the dominant purchaser may constitute an abusive extension of its economic power to other markets (see "Télémarketing" Court judgment).

119. Another abusive practice could be that of making the purchase subject to licensing by the supplier of standards for the product to be purchased or for other products, to the purchaser itself, or to other suppliers (Article 86(*d*)).

120. Moreover, even in competitive markets, discriminatory procedures on the basis of nationality may exist, because national pressures and traditional links of a non-economic nature do not always disappear quickly after the liberalisation of the markets. In this case, a systematic exclusion or considerably unfavourable treatment of a supplier, without economic necessity, could be examined under Article 86, especially (b) (limitation of outlets) and (c) (discrimination). In assessing the case, the Commission will substantially examine whether the same criteria for awarding the contract have been followed

by the dominant undertaking for all suppliers. The Commission will normally take into account criteria similar to those indicated in Article 27(1) of the Directive. The purchases in question being outside the scope of the Directive, the Commission will not require that transparent purchasing procedures be pursued.

D. Effect on trade between Member States

121. The same principle outlined regarding Article 85 applies here. Moreover, in certain circumstances, such as the case of the elimination of a competitor by an undertaking holding a dominant position, although trade between member-States is not directly affected, for the purposes of Article 86 it is sufficient to show that there will be repercussions on the competitive structure of the common market.

VI. Application of Articles 85 and 86 in the Field of Satellites

122. The development of this sector is addressed globally by the Commission in the 'Green Paper on a common approach in the field of satellite communications in the European Community' of 20 November 1990 (Doc. COM(90) 490 final). Due to the increasing importance of satellites and the particular uncertainty among undertakings as to the application of competition rules to individual cases in this sector, it is appropriate to address the sector in a distinct section in these guidelines.

123. State regulations on satellites are not covered by the Commission Directives under Article 90 EEC respectively on terminals and services mentioned above except in the Directive on terminals which contemplates receive-only satellite stations not connected to a public network. The Commission's position on the regulatory framework compatible with the Treaty competition rules is stated in the Commission Green Paper on satellites mentioned above.

124. In any event the Treaty competition rules fully apply to the satellites domain, *inter alia*, Articles 85 and 86 to undertakings. Below is indicated how the principles set out above, in particular in Sections IV and V, apply to satellites.

125. Agreements between European TOs in particular within international conventions may play an important role in providing European satellites systems and a harmonious development of satellite services throughout the Community. These benefits are taken into consideration under competition rules, provided that the agreements do not contain restrictions which are not indispensable for the attainment of these objectives.

126. Agreements between TOs concerning the operation of satellite systems in the broadest sense may be caught by Article 85. As to space segment capacity, the TOs are each other's competitors, whether actual or potential. In pooling together totally or partially their supplies of space segment capacity they may restrict competition between themselves. Moreover, they are likely to restrict competition *vis-à-vis* third parties to the extent that their agreements contain provisions with this object or effect: for instance provisions limiting their supplies in quality and/or quantity, or restricting their business autonomy by imposing directly or indirectly a co-ordination between these third parties and the parties to the agreements. It should be examined whether such agreements could qualify for an exemption under Article 85(3) provided that they are notified. However, restrictions on third parties' ability to compete are likely to preclude such an exemption. It should also be examined whether such agreements strengthen any individual or collective dominant position of the parties, which also would exclude the granting of an exemption. This could be the case in particular if the agreement provides that the parties are exclusive distributors of the space segment capacity provided by the agreement.

127. Such agreements between TOs could also restrict competition as to the uplink with respect to which TOs are competitors. In certain cases the customer for satellite communication has the choice between providers in several countries, and his choice will be substantially determined by the quality, price and other sales conditions of each provider. This choice will be even ampler since uplink is being progressively liberalised and to the extent that the application of EEC rules to State legislations will open up the uplink markets. Community-wide agreements providing directly or indirectly for co-ordination as to the parties' uplink provision are therefore caught by Article 85.

128. Agreements between TOs and private operators on space segment capacity may be also caught by Article 85, as that provision applies, *inter alia*, to co-operation, and in particular joint venture agreements. These agreements could be exempted if they bring specific benefits such as technology transfer, improvement of the quality of the service or enabling better marketing, especially for a new capacity, outweighing the restrictions. In any event, imposing on customers the bundled uplink and space segment capacity provision is likely to exclude an exemption since it limits competition in uplink provision to the detriment of the customer's choice, and in the current market situation will almost certainly strengthen the TOs' dominant position in violation of Article 86. An exemption is unlikely to be granted also when the agreement has the effect of reducing substantially the supply in an oligopolistic market, and even more clearly when an effect of the agreement is to prevent the only potential competitor of a dominant provider in a given market from offering its services independently. This could amount to a violation of Article 86. Direct or indirect imposition of any kind of agreement by a TO, for instance by making the uplnk subject to the conclusion of an agreement with a third party, would constitute an infringement of Article 86.

VII. Restructuring in Telecommunications

129. Deregulation, the objective of a single market for 1992 and the fundamental changes in the telecommunications technology have caused wide strategic restructuring in Europe and throughout the world as well. They have mostly taken the form of mergers and joint ventures.

(a) Mergers

130. In assessing telecom mergers in the framework of Council Regulation 4064/89 on the control of concentrations between undertakings ([1989] O.J. L395/1, [1990] 4 C.M.L.R. 286; corrigendum: [1990] O.J. L257/13, [1990] 4 C.M.L.R. 859) the Commission will take into account, *inter alia*, the following elements.

131. Restructuring moves are in general beneficial to the European telecommunications industry. They may enable the companies to rationalise and to reach the critical mass necessary to obtain the economies of scale needed to make the important investments in research and development. These are necessary to develop new technologies and to remain competitive in the world market.

However, in certain cases they may also lead to the anti-competitive creation or strengthening of dominant positions.

132. The economic benefits resulting from critical mass must be demonstrated. The concentration operation could result in a mere aggregation of market shares, unaccompanied by restructuring measures or plans. This operation may create or strengthen Community or national dominant positions in a way which impedes competition.

133. When concentration operations have this sole effect, they can hardly be justified by the objective of increasing the competitivity of Community industry in the world market. This objective, strongly pursued by the Commission, rather requires competition in EEC domestic markets in order that the EEC undertakings acquire the competitive structure and attitude needed to operate in the world market.

134. In assessing concentration cases in telecommunications, the Commission will be particularly vigilant to avoid the strengthening of dominant positions through integration. If dominant service providers are allowed to integrate into the equipment market by way of mergers, access to this market by other equipment suppliers may be seriously hindered. A dominant service provider is likely to give preferential treatment to its own equipment subsidiary.

Moreover, the possibility of disclosure by the service provider to its subsidiary of sensitive information obtained from competing equipment manufacturers can put the latter at a competitive disadvantage.

The Commission will examine case by case whether vertical integration has such effects or rather is likely to reinforce the competitive structure in the Community.

135. The Commission has enforced principles on restructuring in a case concerning the GEC and Siemens joint bid for Plessey.

136. Article 85(1) applies to the acquisition by an undertaking of a minority shareholding in a competitor where, *inter alia*, the arrangements involve the creation of a

structure of co-operation between the investor and the other undertakings, which will influence these undertakings' competitive conduct.

(b) Joint ventures

137. A joint venture can be of a co-operative or a concentrative nature. It is of a co-operative nature when it has as its object or effect the co-ordination of the competitive behaviour of undertakings which remain independent. The principles governing co-operative joint ventures are to be set out in Commission guidelines to that effect. Concentrative joint ventures fall under Regulation 4064/89. ([1990] O.J. C203/10, [1990] 4 C.M.L.R. 721).

138. In some of the latest joint venture cases the Commission granted an exemption under Article 85(3) on grounds which are particularly relevant to telecommunications. Precisely in a decision concerning telecommunications, the *"Optical Fibres"* case 249 the Commission considered that the joint venture enabled European companies to produce a high technology product, promoted technical progress, and facilitated technology transfer. Therefore, the joint venture permits European companies to withstand competition from non-Community producers, especially in the USA and Japan, in an area of fast-moving technology characterised by international markets. The Commission confirmed this approach in the *"Canon-Olivetti"* case. [Olivetti/Canon 280].

VIII. Impact of the International Conventions on the Application of EEC Competition Rules to Telecommunications

139. International conventions (such as the Convention of International Telecommunication Union (ITU) or Conventions on Satellites) play a fundamental role in ensuring world-wide co-operation for the provision of international services. However, application of such international conventions on telecommunications by EEC member-States must not affect compliance with the EEC law, in particular with competition rules.

140. Article 234 EEC regulates this matter.
The relevant obligations provided in the various conventions or related Acts do not pre-date the entry into force of the Treaty. As to the ITU and World Administrative Telegraph and Telephone Conference (WATTC), whenever a revision or a new adoption of the ITU Convention or of the WATTC Regulations occurs, the ITU or WATTC members recover their freedom of action. The Satellites Conventions were adopted much later.

Moreover, as to all conventions, the application of EEC rules does not seem to affect the fulfilment of obligations of member-States *vis-à-vis* third countries. Article 234 does not protect obligations between EEC member-States entered into in international treaties. The purpose of Article 234 is to protect the right of third countries only and it is not intended to crystallise the acquired international treaty rights of member-States to the detriment of the EEC Treaty's objectives or of the Community interest. Finally, even if Article 234(1) did apply, the member-States concerned would nevertheless be obliged to take all appropriate steps to eliminate incompatibility between their obligations *vis-à-vis* third countries and the EEC rules. This applies in particular where member-States acting collectively have the statutory possibility to modify the international convention in question as required, e.g. in the case of the Eutelsat Convention.

141. As to the WATTC Regulations, the relevant provisions of the Regulations in force from 9 December 1988 are flexible enough to give the parties the choice whether or not to implement them or how to implement them.

In any event, EEC member-States, by signing the Regulations, have made a joint declaration that they will apply them in accordance with their obligations under the EEC Treaty.

142. As to the International Telegraph and Telephone Consultative Committee (CCITT) recommendations, competition rules apply to them.

143. Members of the CCITT are, pursuant to Article 11(2) of the International Telecommunications Convention, 'administrations' of the Members of the ITU and recognised private operating agencies ('RPOAs') which so request with the approval of the ITU members which have recognised them. Unlike the members of the ITU or the Administrative Conferences which are States, the members of the CCITT are telecommunications administra-

tions and RPOAs. Telecommunications administrations are defined in Annex 2 to the International Telecommunications Conventions as 'tout service ou département gouvernemental responsable des mesures à prendre pour exécuter les obligations de la Convention Internationale des télécommunications et des règlements' (any government service or department responsible for the measures to be taken to fulfil the obligations laid down in the International Convention on Telecommunications and Regulations). The CCITT meetings are in fact attended by TOs. Article 11(2) of the International Telecommunications Convention clearly provides that telecommunications administrations and RPOAs are members of the CCITT by themselves. The fact that, because of the ongoing process of separation of the regulatory functions from the business activity, some national authorities participate in the CCITT is not in contradiction with the nature of undertakings of other members. Moreover, even if the CCITT membership became governmental as a result of the separation of regulatory and operational activities of the telecommunications administrations, Article 90 in association with Article 85 could still apply either against the State measures implementing the CCITT recommendations and the recommendations themselves on the basis of Article 90(1), or if there is no such national implementing measure, directly against the telecommunications organisations which followed the recommendation.

144. In the Commission's view, the CCITT recommendations are adopted, *inter alia*, by undertakings. Such CCITT recommendations, although they are not legally binding, are agreements between undertakings or decisions by an association of undertakings. In any event, according to the case law of the Commission and the European Court of Justice a statutory body entrusted with certain public functions and including some members appointed by the government of a member-State may be an "association of undertakings" if it represents the trading interests of other members and takes decisions or makes agreements in pursuance of those interests.

The Commission draws attention to the fact that the application of certain provisions in the context of international conventions could result in infringements of the EEC competition rules:

— As to the WATTC Regulations, this is the case for the respective provisions for mutual agreement between TOs on the supply of international telecommunications services (Article 1(5)), reserving the choice of telecommunications routes to the TOs (Article 3(3)(3)), recommending practices equivalent to price agreements (Articles 6(6)(1)(2)), and limiting the possibility of special arrangements to activities meeting needs within and/or between the territories of the Members concerned (Article 9) and only where existing arrangements cannot satisfactorily meet the relevant telecommunications needs (Opinion PL A).

— CCITT recommendations D1 and D2 as they stand at the date of the adoption of these guidelines could amount to a collective horizontal agreement on prices and other supply conditions of international leased lines to the extent that they lead to a co-ordination of sales policies between TOs and therefore limit competition between them. This was indicated by the Commission in a CCITT meeting on 23 May 1990. The Commission reserves the right to examine the compatibility of other recommendations with Article 85.

— The agreements between TOs concluded in the context of the Conventions on Satellites are likely to limit competition contrary to Article 85 and/or 86 on the grounds set out in paragraphs 126 to 128 above.

4.5. Cases on telecommunications

British Telecom 188
Eirpage 344
20th Comp. Rep. (paras. 55–58)
Italy v. *Commission* 117
France v. *Commission* 182
RTT v. *GB-Inno* 189

4.6 References to connected legislation

— Commision Directive 80/723 on the transparency of financial relations between Member States and public undertakings, [1980] O.J. L195/35.
— Council Resolution of 30 June 1988, on the development of the common market for telecommunication services and equipment up to 1992, [1989] O.J. C257/1.

Book One: Part VIII—State Interference

— Council Directive 90/377, concerning a Community procedure to improve the transparency of gas and electricity prices charged to industrial end-users, [1990] O.J. L185/16.
— Council Directive 90/387, on the establishment of the internal market for telecommunications services through the implementation of open network provision, [1990] O.J. L192/1.

CHAPTER 2

STATE RESPONSIBILITY

A. STATE RESPONSIBILITY UNDER ARTICLES 3f AND 5 OF THE TREATY FOR FACILITATING OR ENCOURAGING BEHAVIOUR CONTRARY TO ARTICLES 85 & 86

GB-INNO v. *ATAB* 59 (paras. 24–38)
Leclerc 113*
Cullet v. *Leclerc* 114
St. Herblain v. *Syndicat des Libraires* 122
Nouvelles Frontières 131 (grounds 75–77)*
Procureur v. *Cognet* 135
Vlaamse Reisbureaus 144*
BNIC/Aubert 147 (grounds 5, 7–8, 23–24)
Syndicat v. *Leclerc Aigle* 154

Van Eycke v. *Aspa* 155*
Ahmed Saeed v. *Zentrale* 162 (grounds 48–49, 52)
Batista Morais 193
Marchandise 181/a

B. GOVERNMENTAL SILENCE OR APPROVAL IS NO EXCUSE FOR INFRINGING ARTICLES 85 & 86

Franco Japanese Ball Bearings 81
FEDETAB 133 (paras. 83, 88, 107)
SSI 181 (paras. 88–96)
UGAL/BNIC 190
Zinc producer group 217 (paras. 73–74)
Fire Insurance 220 (para. 28)
Aluminium 228 (paras. 10–12)
ENI/Montedison 256 (para. 5)
Welded Steel Mesh 311 (paras. 201, 202, 206)
Ijsselcentrale 335 (paras. 21, 33–38)
Dutch Pharmaceuticals. 8th Comp. Rep. (paras. 81–82)
Van Ameyde v. *UCI* 57
BP v. *Commission* 65 (ground 15)
VBVB & VBBB v. *Commission* 105 (grounds 38–40)*
BNIC v. *Clair* 115 (grounds 17, 20–21)
SSI v. *Commission* 127 (grounds 38–40)*
NSO v. *Commission* 128 (grounds 28–30)

PART IX

SECTORIAL APPLICATION OF EEC COMPETITION RULES

CHAPTER 1

AGRICULTURE

A. TEXT OF REGULATION 26/62
(reproduced below)

Council Regulation 26/62

Applying certain rules of competition to production of and trade in agricultural products

([1959–62] O.J. Spec. Ed. 129)

THE COUNCIL OF THE EUROPEAN ECONOMIC COMMUNITY,

Having regard to the Treaty establishing the European Economic Community, and in particular Articles 42 and 43 thereof;
Having regard to the proposal from the Commission;
Having regard to the Opinion of the European Parliament;

(1) Whereas by virtue of Article 42 of the Treaty one of the matters to be decided under the common agricultural policy is whether the rules on competition laid down in the Treaty are to apply to production of and trade in agricultural products, and accordingly the provisions hereinafter contained will have to be supplemented in the light of developments in that policy;

(2) Whereas the proposals submitted by the Commission for the formulation and implementation of the common agricultural policy show that certain rules on competition must forthwith be made applicable to production of and trade in agricultural products in order to eliminate practices contrary to the principles of the common market and prejudicial to attainment of the objectives set out in Article 39 of the Treaty and in order to provide a basis for the future establishment of a system of competition adapted to the development of the common agricultural policy;

(3) Whereas the rules on competition relating to the agreements, decisions and practices referred to in Article 85 of the Treaty and to the abuse of dominant positions must be applied to production of and trade in agricultural products, in so far as their application does not impede the functioning of national organisations of agricultural markets or jeopardise attainment of the objectives of the common agricultural policy;

(4) Whereas special attention is warranted in the case of farmers' organisations which are particularly concerned with the joint production or marketing of agricultural products or the use of joint facilities, unless such joint action excludes competition or jeopardises attainment of the objectives of Article 39 of the Treaty;

(5) Whereas, in order both to avoid compromising the development of a common agricultural policy and to ensure certainty in the law and non-discriminatory treatment of the undertakings concerned, the Commission must have sole power, subject to review by the Court of Justice, to determine whether the conditions provided for in the two preceding recitals are fulfilled as regards the agreements, decisions and practices referred to in Article 85 of the Treaty;

(6) Whereas, in order to enable the specific provisions of the Treaty regarding agriculture, and in particular those of Article 39 thereof, to be taken into consideration, the Commission must, in questions of dumping, assess all the causes of the practices complained of and in particular the price level at which products from other sources are imported into the market in question; whereas it must, in the light of its assessment, make recommendations and authorise protective measures as provided in Article 91(1) of the Treaty;

(7) Whereas, in order to implement, as part of the development of the common agricultural policy, the rules on aids for production of or trade in agricultural products, the Commission should be in a position to draw up a list of existing, new or proposed aids, to make appropriate observations to the Member States and to propose suitable measures to them;

HAS ADOPTED THIS REGULATION:

Article 1

From the entry into force of this Regulation, Articles 85 to 90 of the Treaty and provisions made in implementation thereof shall, subject to Article 2 below, apply to all agreements, decisions and practices referred to in Articles 85(1) and 86 of the Treaty which relate to production of or trade in the products listed in Annex II to the Treaty.

Article 2

1. Article 85(1) of the Treaty shall not apply to such of the agreements, decisions and practices referred to in the preceding Article as form an integral part of a national market organisation or are necessary for attainment of the objectives set out in Article 39 of the Treaty. In particular, it shall not apply to agreements, decisions and practices of farmers, farmers' associations, or associations of such associations belonging to a single Member State which concern the production or sale of agricultural products or the use of joint facilities for the storage, treatment or processing of agricultural products, and under which there is no obligation to charge identical prices, unless the Commission finds that competition is thereby excluded or that the objectives of Article 39 of the Treaty are jeopardised.

2. After consulting the Member States and hearing the undertakings or associations of undertakings concerned and any other natural or legal person that it considers appropriate, the Commission shall have sole power, subject to review by the Court of Justice, to determine, by decision which shall be published, which agreements, decisions and practices fulfil the conditions specified in paragraph 1.

3. The Commission shall undertake such determination either on its own initiative or at the request of a competent authority of a Member State or of an interested undertaking or association of undertakings.

4. The publication shall state the names of the parties and the main content of the decision; it shall have regard to the legitimate interest of undertakings in the protection of their business secrets.

Article 3

1. Without prejudice to Article 46 of the Treaty, Article 91(1) thereof shall apply to trade in the products listed in Annex II to the Treaty.

2. With due regard for the provisions of the Treaty relating to agriculture, and in particular those of Article 39, the Commission shall assess all the causes of the practices complained of, in particular the price level at which products from other sources are imported into the market in question.

In the light of its assessment, it shall make recommendations and authorise protective measures as provided in Article 91(1) of the Treaty.

Article 4

The provisions of Article 93(1) and of the first sentence of Article 93(3) of the Treaty shall apply to aids granted for production of or trade in the products listed in Annex II to the Treaty.

Article 5

This Regulation shall enter into force on the day following its publication in the *Official Journal of the European Communities*, with the exception of Articles 1 to 3, which shall enter into force on 1 July 1962.

This Regulation shall be binding in its entirety and directly applicable in all Member States.

Done at Brussels, 4 April 1962.

B. CASES REGARDING AGRICULTURE AND COMPETITION

1. General cases

2nd Comp. Rep. (para. 74)
Cerafel v. Le Campion 137
UNILEC v. Larroche 156*

2. Cases in which Regulation 26/62 was applicable

New Potatoes 276

3. Cases in which Regulation 26/62 was not applicable

European Sugar Industry 69
FRUBO 80
Tinned Mushrooms 88
Pabst & Richarz/BNIA 106 (para. II.5)
Cauliflowers 119
Maize Seeds 137
Rennet 149 (paras. 26–27)
Milchförderungsfonds 221 (paras. 18–25)*
Meldoc 253 (paras. 53–55)
VBA 288
Sugar Beet 315 (paras. 87-88)
Frubo v. Commission 44 (grounds 11, 22–29)
Suiker Unie v. Commission 48
Stremsel v. Commission 84 (grounds 19–21)
Nungesser v. Commission 94 (grounds 18–22)*
BNIC v. Clair 115 (ground 15)
BNIC/Aubert 147 (grounds 14–15)

CHAPTER 2

TRANSPORT: GENERAL

A. TEXT OF REGULATION 141/62
(reproduced below)

Council Regulation 141/62

Exempting transport from the application of Council Regulation No. 17

([1959–62] O.J. Spec. Ed. 291)

THE COUNCIL OF THE EUROPEAN ECONOMIC COMMUNITY,

Having regard to the Treaty establishing the European Economic Community, and in particular Article 67 thereof;

Having regard to the first Regulation made in implementation of Articles 85 and 86 of the Treaty (Regulation No. 17) of 6 February 1962, as amended by Regulation No 59 of 3 July 1962;

Having regard to the proposal from the Commission;

Having regard to the Opinion of the Economic and Social Committee;

Having regard to the Opinion of the Assembly;

(1) Whereas, in pursuance of the common transport policy, account being taken of the distinctive features of the transport sector, it may prove necessary to lay down rules governing competition different from those laid down or to be laid down for other sectors of the economy, and whereas Regulation No. 17 should not therefore apply to transport;

(2) Whereas, in the light of work in hand on the formulation of a common transport policy, it is possible, as regards transport by rail, road and inland waterway, to envisage the introduction within a foreseeable period of rules of competition; whereas, on the other hand, as regards sea and air transport it is impossible to foresee whether and at what date the Council will adopt appropriate provisions; whereas accordingly a limit to the period during which Regulation No. 17 shall not apply can be set only for transport by rail, road and inland waterway;

(3) Whereas the distinctive features of transport make it justifiable to exempt from the application of Regulation No. 17 only agreements, decisions and concerted practices directly relating to the provision of transport services;

HAS ADOPTED THIS REGULATION:

Book One: Part IX—Sectorial Application of EEC Competition Rules

Article 1

Regulation No 17 shall not apply to agreements, decisions or concerted practices in the transport sector which have as their object or effect the fixing of transport rates and conditions, the limitation or control of the supply of transport or the sharing of transport markets; not shall it apply to the abuse of a dominant position, within the meaning of Article 86 of the Treaty, within the transport market.

Article 2

The Council, taking account of any measures that may be taken in pursuance of the common transport policy, shall adopt appropriate provisions in order to apply rules of competition to transport by rail, road and inland waterway. To this end, the Commission shall, before 30 June 1964, submit proposals to the Council.

Article 3

Article 1 of this Regulation shall remain in force, as regards transport by rail, road and inland waterway, until 31 December 1965.

Article 4

This Regulation shall enter into force on 13 March 1962. These provisions shall not be invoked against undertakings or associations of undertakings which, before the day following the date of publication of this Regulation in the *Official Journal of the European Communities*, shall have terminated any agreement, decision or concerted practice covered by Article 1.

This Regulation shall be binding in its entirety and directly applicable in all Member States.

Done at Paris, 26 November 1962.

B. CASES ON THE INTERPRETATION OF THE REGULATION

Olympic Airways 229
SABENA 295 (paras. 17–22)
2nd Comp. Rep. (para. 70)

CHAPTER 3

INLAND WATERWAYS, RAIL AND ROAD TRANSPORT

A. LEGISLATION

1. Text of Council Regulation 1017/68 (reproduced below)

Council Regulation 1017/68 of July 19, 1968

Applying rules of competition to transport by rail, road and inland waterway

([1968] O.J. Spec. Ed. 302)

THE COUNCIL OF THE EUROPEAN COMMUNITIES,

Having regard to the Treaty establishing the European Economic Community, and in particular Articles 75 and 87 thereof;

Having regard to the proposal from the Commission;

Having regard to the Opinion of the European Parliament;

Having regard to the Opinion of the Economic and Social Committee;

(1) Whereas Council Regulation No. 141 exempting transport from the application of Regulation No. 17 provides that the said Regulation No. 17 shall not apply to agreements, decisions and concerted practices in the transport sector the effect of which is to fix transport rates and conditions, to limit or control the supply of transport or to share transport markets, nor to dominant positions, within the meaning of Article 86 of the Treaty, on the transport market;

(2) Whereas, for transport by rail, road and inland waterway, Regulation No. 1002/67 provides that such exemption shall not extend beyond 30 June 1968;

(3) Whereas the establishing of rules of competition for transport by rail, road and inland waterway is part of the common transport policy and of general economic policy;

(4) Whereas, when rules of competition for these sectors are being settled, account must be taken of the distinctive features of transport;

(5) Whereas, since the rules of competition for transport derogate from the general rules of competition, it must be made possible for undertakings to ascertain what rules apply in any particular case;

(6) Whereas, with the introduction of a system of rules on competition for transport, it is desirable that such rules should apply equally to the joint financing or acquisition of transport equipment for the joint operation of services by certain groupings of undertakings, and also to certain operations in connection with transport by rail, road or inland waterway of providers of services ancillary to transport;

(7) Whereas, in order to ensure that trade between Member States is not affected or competition within the common market distorted, it is necessary to prohibit in principle for the three modes of transport specified above all agreements between undertakings, decisions of associations of undertakings and concerted practices between undertakings and all instances of abuse of a dominant position within the common market which could have such effects;

(8) Whereas certain types of agreement, decision and concerted practice in the transport sector the object and effect of which is merely to apply technical improvements or to achieve technical co-operation may be exempted from the prohibition on restrictive agreements since they contribute to improving productivity; whereas, in the light of experience following application of this Regulation, the Council may, on a proposal from the Commission, amend the list of such types of agreement;

(9) Whereas, in order that an improvement may be fostered in the sometimes too dispersed structure of the industry in the road and inland waterway sectors, there should also be exempted from the prohibition on restrictive agreements those agreements, decisions and concerted practices providing for the creation and operation of groupings of undertakings in these two transport sectors whose object is the carrying on of transport operations, including the joint financing or acquisition of transport equipment for the joint operation of services; whereas such overall exemption can be granted only on condition that the total carrying capacity of a grouping does not exceed a fixed maximum, and that the individual capacity of undertakings belonging to the grouping does not exceed certain limits so fixed as to ensure that no one undertaking can hold a dominant position within the grouping; whereas the Commission must, however, have power to intervene if, in specific cases, such agreements should have effects incompatible with the conditions under which a restrictive agreement may be recognised as lawful, and should constitute an abuse of the exemption; whereas, nevertheless, the fact that a grouping has a total carrying capacity greater than the fixed maximum, or cannot claim the overall exemption because of the individual capacity of the undertakings belonging to the grouping, does not in itself prevent such a grouping from constituting a lawful agreement, decision or concerted practice if it satisfies the conditions therefor laid down in this Regulation.

(10) Whereas, where an agreement, decision or concerted practice contributes towards improving the quality of transport services, or towards promoting greater continuity and stability in the satisfaction of transport needs on markets where supply and demand may be subject to considerable temporal fluctuation, or towards increasing the productivity of undertakings, or towards furthering technical or economic progress, it must be made possible for the prohibition to be declared not to apply, always provided, however that the agreement, decision or concerted practice takes fair account of the interests of transport users, and neither imposes on the undertakings concerned any restriction not indispensable to the attainment of the above objectives nor makes it possible for such undertakings to eliminate competition in respect of a substantial part of the transport market concerned, having

Book One: Part IX—Sectorial Application of EEC Competition Rules

regard to competition from alternative modes of transport;

(11) Whereas it is desirable until such time as the Council, acting in pursuance of the common transport policy, introduces appropriate measures to ensure a stable transport market, and subject to the condition that the Council shall have found that a state of crisis exists, to authorise, for the market in question, such agreements as are needed in order to reduce disturbance resulting from the structure of the transport market;

(12) Whereas, in respect of transport by rail, road and inland waterway, it is desirable that Member States should neither enact nor maintain in force measures contrary to this Regulation concerning public undertakings or undertakings to which they grant special or exclusive rights; whereas it is also desirable that undertakings entrusted with the operation of services of general economic importance should be subject to the provisions of this Regulation in so far as the application thereof does not obstruct, in law or in fact, the accomplishment of the particular tasks assigned to them, always provided that the development of trade is not thereby affected to such an extent as would be contrary to the interests of the Community; whereas the Commission must have power to see that these principles are applied and to address the appropriate directives or decisions for this purpose to Member States;

(13) Whereas the detailed rules for application of the basic principles of this Regulation must be so drawn that they not only ensure effective supervision while simplifying administration as far as possible but also meet the needs of undertakings for certainty in the law;

(14) Whereas it is for the undertakings themselves, in the first instance, to judge whether the predominant effects of their agreements, decisions or concerted practices are the restriction of competition or the economic benefits acceptable as justification for such restriction and to decide accordingly, on their own responsibility, as to the illegality or legality of such agreements, decisions or concerted practices;

(15) Whereas, therefore, undertakings should be allowed to conclude or operate agreements without declaring them; whereas this exposes such agreements to the risk of being declared void with retroactive effect should they be examined following a complaint or on the Commission's own initiative, but does not prevent their being retroactively declared lawful in the event of such subsequent examination;

(16) Whereas, however, undertakings may, in certain cases, desire the assistance of the competent authorities to ensure that their agreements, decisions or concerted practices are in conformity with the rules applicable; whereas for this purpose there should be made available to undertakings a procedure whereby they may submit applications to the Commission and a summary of each such application is published in the *Official Journal of the European Communities*, enabling any interested third parties to submit their comments on the agreement in question; whereas, in the absence of any complaint from Member States or interested third parties and unless the Commission notifies applicants within a fixed time limit, that there are serious doubts as to the legality of the agreement in question, that agreement should be deemed exempt from the prohibition for the time already elapsed and for a further period of three years;

(17) Whereas, in view of the exceptional nature of agreements needed in order to reduce disturbances resulting from the structure of the transport market, once the Council has found that a state of crisis exists undertakings wishing to obtain authorisation for such an agreement should be required to notify it to the Commission; whereas authorisation by the Commission should have effect only from the date when it is decided to grant it; whereas the period of validity of such authorisation should not exceed three years from the finding of a state of crisis by the Council; whereas renewal of the decision should depend upon renewal of the finding of a state crisis by the Council; whereas, in any event, the authorisation should cease to be valid not later than six months from the bringing into operation by the Council of appropriate measures to ensure the stability of the transport market to which the agreement relates;

(18) Whereas, in order to secure uniform application within the common market of

the rules of competition for transport, rules must be made under which the Commission, acting in close and constant liaison with the competent authorities of the Member States, may take the measures required for the application of such rules of competition;

(19) Whereas for this purpose the Commission must have the co-operation of the competent authorities of the Member States and be empowered throughout the common market to request such information and to carry out such investigations as are necessary to bring to light any agreement, decision or concerted practice prohibited under this Regulation, or any abuse of a dominant position prohibited under this Regulation.

(20) Whereas, if, on the application of the Regulation to a specific case, a Member State is of the opinion that a question of principle concerning the common transport policy is involved, it should be possible for such questions of principle to be examined by the Council; whereas it should be possible for any general questions raised by the implementation of the competition policy in the transport sector to be referred to the Council; whereas a procedure must be provided for which ensures that any decision to apply the Regulation in a specific case will be taken by the Commission only after the questions of principle have been examined by the Council, and in the light of the policy guidelines that emerge from that examination;

(21) Whereas, in order to carry out its duty of ensuring that the provisions of this Regulation are applied, the Commission must be empowered to address to undertakings or associations of undertakings recommendations and decisions for the purpose of bringing to an end infringements of the provisions of this Regulation prohibiting certain agreements, decisions or practices;

(22) Whereas compliance with the prohibition laid down in this Regulation and the fulfilment of obligations imposed on undertakings and associations of undertakings under this Regulation must be enforceable by means of fines and periodic penalty payments;

(23) Whereas undertakings concerned must be accorded the right to be heard by the Commission, third parties whose interests may be affected by a decision must be given the opportunity of submitting their comments beforehand, and it must be ensured that wide publicity is given to decisions taken;

(24) Whereas it is desirable to confer upon the Court of Justice, pursuant to Article 172, unlimited jurisdiction in respect of decisions under which the Commission imposes fines or periodic penalty payments;

(25) Whereas it is expedient to postpone for six months, as regards agreements, decisions and concerted practices in existence at the date of publication of this Regulation in the *Official Journal of the European Communities*, the entry into force of the prohibition laid down in the Regulation, in order to make it easier for undertakings to adjust their operations so as to conform to its provisions;

(26) Whereas, following discussions with the third countries signatories to the Revised Convention for the Navigation of the Rhine, and within an appropriate period of time from the conclusion of those discussions, this Regulation as a whole should be amended as necessary in the light of the obligations arising out of the Revised Convention for Navigation of the Rhine;

(27) Whereas the Regulation should be amended as necessary in the light of the experience gained over a three-year period; whereas it will in particular be desirable to consider whether, in the light of the development of the common transport policy over that period, the scope of the Regulation should be extended to agreements, decisions and concerted practices, and to instances of abuse of a dominant position, not affecting trade between Member States;

HAS ADOPTED THIS REGULATION:

Article 1: Basic provision

The provisions of this Regulation shall, in the field of transport by rail, road and inland waterway, apply both to all agreements, decisions and concerted practices which have as their object or effect the fixing of transport rates and conditions, the limitation or control of the supply of transport, the sharing of transport markets, the application of technical improvements or technical co-operation, or the joint financing or acquisition of transport equipment or supplies where such operations are directly related to the provision of transport services and are necessary for the joint operation of services by a grouping within the meaning of Article 4 of road or inland waterway transport undertakings, and to the abuse of a dominant position on the transport market. These provisions shall apply also to operations of providers of services ancillary to transport which have any of the objects or effects listed above.

Article 2: Prohibition of restrictive practices

Subject to the provisions of Articles 3 to 6, the following shall be prohibited as incompatible with the common market, no prior decision to that effect being required: all agreements between undertakings, decisions by associations of undertakings and concerted practices liable to affect trade between Member States which have as their object or effect the prevention, restriction or distortion of competition within the common market, and in particular those which:
(a) directly or indirectly fix transport rates and conditions or any other trading conditions;
(b) limit or control the supply of transport, markets, technical development or investment;
(c) share transport markets;
(d) apply dissimilar conditions to equivalent transactions with other trading parties, thereby placing them at a competitive disadvantage;
(e) make the conclusion of contracts subject to acceptance by the other parties of additional obligations which, by their nature or according to commercial usage, have no connection with the provision of transport services.

Article 3: Exception for technical agreements

1. The prohibition laid down in Article 2 shall not apply to agreements, decisions or concerted practices the object and effect of which is to apply technical improvements or to achieve technical co-operation by means of:

(a) the standardisation of equipment, transport supplies, vehicles or fixed installations;
(b) the exchange or pooling, for the purpose of operating transport services, of staff, equipment, vehicles or fixed installations;
(c) the organisation and execution of successive, complementary, substitute or combined transport operations, and the fixing and application of inclusive rates and conditions for such operations, including special competitive rates;
(d) the use, for journeys by a single mode of transport, of the routes which are most rational from the operational point of view;
(e) the co-ordination of transport timetables for connecting routes;
(f) the grouping of single consignments;
(g) the establishment of uniform rules as to the structure of tariffs and their conditions of application, provided such rules do not lay down transport rates and conditions.

2. The Commission shall, where appropriate, submit proposals to the Council with a view to extending or reducing the list in paragraph 1.

Article 4: Exemption for groups of small and medium-sized undertakings

1. The agreements, decisions and concerted practices referred to in Article 2 shall be exempt from the prohibition in that Article where their purpose is:
— the constitution and operation of groupings of road or inland waterway transport undertakings with a view to carrying on transport activities;
— the joint financing or acquisition of transport equipment or supplies, where these operations are directly related to the provision of transport services and are necessary for the joint operations of the aforesaid groupings;
always provided that the total carrying capacity of any grouping does not exceed:
— 10 000 metric tons in the case of road transport,
— 500 000 metric tons in the case of transport by inland waterway.
The individual capacity of each undertaking belonging to a grouping shall not exceed 1 000 metric tons in the case of road transport or 50 000 metric tons in the case of transport by inland waterway.

2. If the implementation of any agreement, decision or concerted practice covered by

paragraph 1 has, in a given case, effects which are incompatible with the requirements of Article 5 and which constitute an abuse of the exemption from the provisions of Article 2, undertakings or associations of undertakings may be required to make such effects cease.

Article 5: Non-applicability of the prohibition

The prohibition in Article 2 may be declared inapplicable with retroactive effect to:
— any agreement or category of agreement between undertakings,
— any decision or category of decision of an association of undertakings, or
— any concerted practice or category of concerted practice which contributes towards:
— improving the quality of transport services; or
— promoting greater continuity and stability in the satisfaction of transport needs on markets where supply and demand are subject to considerable temporal fluctuation; or
— increasing the productivity of undertakings; or
— furthering technical or economic progress;

and at the same time takes fair account of the interests of transport users and neither:
(a) imposes on the transport undertakings concerned any restriction not essential to the attainment of the above objectives; nor
(b) makes it possible for such undertakings to eliminate competition in respect of a substantial part of the transport market concerned.

Article 6: Agreements intended to reduce disturbances resulting from the structure of the transport market

1. Until such time as the Council, acting in pursuance of the common transport policy, introduces appropriate measures to ensure a stable transport market, the prohibition laid down in Article 2 may be declared inapplicable to any agreement, decision or concerted practice which tends to reduce disturbances on the market in question.

2. A decision not to apply the prohibition laid down in Article 2, made in accordance with the procedure laid down in Article 14, may not be taken until the Council, either acting by a qualified majority or, where any Member State considers that the conditions set out in Article 75(3) of the Treaty are satisfied, acting unanimously, has found, on the basis of a report by the Commission, that a state of crisis exists in all or part of a transport market.

3. Without prejudice to the provisions of paragraph 2, the prohibition in Article 2 may be declared inapplicable only where:
(a) the agreement, decision or concerted practice in question does not impose upon the undertakings concerned any restriction not indispensable to the reduction of disturbances; and
(b) does not make it possible for such undertakings to eliminate competition in respect of a substantial part of the transport market concerned.

Article 7: Invalidity of agreements and decisions

Any agreement or decision prohibited under the foregoing provisions shall be automatically void.

Article 8: Prohibition of abuse of dominant positions

Any abuse by one or more undertakings of a dominant position within the common market or in a substantial part of it shall be prohibited as incompatible with the common market in so far as trade between Member States may be affected thereby.

Such abuse may, in particular, consist in:
(a) directly or indirectly imposing unfair transport rates or conditions;
(b) limiting the supply of transport, markets or technical development to the prejudice of consumers;
(c) applying dissimilar conditions to equivalent transactions with other trading parties, thereby placing them at a competitive disadvantage;
(d) making the conclusion of contracts subject to acceptance by the other parties of supplementary obligations which, by their nature or according to commercial usage, have no connection with the provision of transport services.

Article 9: Public undertakings

1. In the case of public undertakings and undertakings to which Member States grant special or exclusive rights, Member States shall neither enact nor maintain in force any measure contrary to the provisions of the foregoing Articles.

2. Undertakings entrusted with the operation of services of general economic importance shall be subject to the provisions of the foregoing Articles, in so far as the application thereof does not obstruct, in law or in fact, the accomplishment of the particular tasks assigned to them. The development of trade must not be affected to such an extent as would be contrary to the interests of the Community.

3. The Commission shall see that the provisions of this Article are applied and shall, where necessary, address appropriate directives or decisions to Member States.

Article 10: Procedures on complaint or on the Commission's own initiative

Acting on receipt of a complaint or on its own initiative, the Commission shall initiate procedures to terminate any infringement of the provisions of Article 2 or of Article 8 or to enforce Article 4(2).

Complaints may be submitted by:
(a) Member States;
(b) natural or legal persons who claim a legitimate interest.

Article 11: Result of procedures on complaint or on the Commission's own initiative

1. Where the Commission finds that there has been an infringement of Article 2 or Article 8, it may by decision require the undertakings or associations of undertakings concerned to bring such infringement to an end.

Without prejudice to the other provisions of this Regulation, the Commission may, before taking a decision under the preceding subparagraph, address to the undertakings or associations of undertakings concerned recommendations for termination of the infringement.

2. Paragraph 1 shall apply also to cases falling within Article 4(2).

3. If the Commission, acting on a complaint received, concludes that on the evidence before it there are no grounds for intervention under Article 2, Article 4(2) or Article 8 in respect of any agreement, decision or practice, it shall issue a decision rejecting the complaint as unfounded.

4. If the Commission, whether acting on a complaint received or on its own initiative, concludes that an agreement, decision or concerted practice satisfies the provisions both of Article 2 and of Article 5, it shall issue a decision applying Article 5. Such decision shall indicate the date from which it is to take effect. This date may be prior to that of the decision.

Article 12: Application of Article 5—objections

1. Undertakings and associations of undertakings which seek application of Article 5 in respect of agreements, decisions and concerted practices falling within the provisions of Article 2 to which they are parties may submit applications to the Commission.

2. If the Commission judges an application admissible and is in possession of all the available evidence, and no action under Article 10 has been taken against the agreement, decision or concerted practice in question, then it shall publish as soon as possible in the *Official Journal of the European Communities* a summary of the application and invite all interested third parties to submit their comments to the Commission within thirty days. Such publication shall have regard to the legitimate interest of undertakings in the protection of their business secrets.

3. Unless the Commission notifies applicants, within ninety days from the date of such publication in the *Official Journal of the European Communities*, that there are serious doubts as to the applicability of Article 5, the agreement, decision or concerted practice shall be deemed exempt, in so far as it conforms with the description given in the application, from the prohibition for the time already elapsed and for a maximum of three years from the date of publication in the *Official Journal of the European Communities*.

If the Commission finds, after expiry of the ninety-day time limit, but before expiry of the three-year period, that the conditions for applying Article 5 are not satisfied, it shall issue a decision declaring that the prohibition in Article 2 is applicable. Such decision may be retroactive where the parties concerned have given inaccurate information or where they abuse the exemption from the provisions of Article 2.

4. If, within the ninety-day time limit, the Commission notifies applicants as referred to in the first subparagraph of paragraph 3, it shall examine whether the provisions of Article 2 and of Article 5 are satisfied.

If it finds that the provisions of Article 2 and of Article 5 are satisfied it shall issue a decision applying Article 5. The decision shall indicate the date from which it is to take effect. This date may be prior to that of the application.

Article 13: Duration and revocation of decisions applying Article 5

1. Any decision applying Article 5 taken under Article 11(4) or under the second sub-paragraph of Article 12(4) shall indicate the period for which it is to be valid; normally such period shall not be less than six years. Conditions and obligations may be attached to the decision.

2. The decision may be renewed if the conditions for applying Article 5 continue to be satisfied.

3. The Commission may revoke or amend its decision or prohibit specified acts by the parties:
(a) where there has been a change in any of the facts which were basic to the making of the decision;
(b) where the parties commit a breach of any obligation attached to the decision;
(c) where the decision is based on incorrect information or was induced by deceit;
(d) where the parties abuse the exemption from the provisions of Article 2 granted to them by the decision.
In cases falling within (b), (c) or (d), the decision may be revoked with retroactive effect.

Article 14: Decisions applying Article 6

1. Any agreement, decision or concerted practice covered by Article 2 in respect of which the parties seek application of Article 6 shall be notified to the Commission.

2. Any decision by the Commission to apply Article 6 shall have effect only from the date of its adoption. It shall state the period for which it is to be valid. Such period shall not exceed three years from the finding of a state of crisis by the Council provided for in Article 6(2).

3. Such decision may be renewed by the Commission if the Council again finds, acting under the procedure provided for in Article 6(2), that there is a state of crisis and if the other conditions laid down in Article 6 continue to be satisfied.

4. Conditions and obligations may be attached to the decision.

5. The decision of the Commission shall cease to have effect not later than six months from the coming into operation of the measures referred to in Article 6(1).

6. The provisions of Article 13(3) shall apply.

Article 15: Powers

Subject to review of its decision by the Court of Justice, the Commission shall have sole power:
— to impose obligations pursuant to Article 4(2);
— to issue decisions pursuant to Articles 5 and 6.

The authorities of the Member States shall retain the power to decide whether any case falls within the provisions of Article 2 or Article 8, until such as the Commission has initiated a procedure with a view to formulating a decision in the case in question or has sent notification as provided for in the first subparagraph of Article 12(3).

Article 16: Liaison with the authorities of the Member States

1. The Commission shall carry out the procedures provided for in this Regulation in close and constant liaison with the competent authorities of the Member States; these authorities shall have the right to express their views on such procedures.

2. The Commission shall immediately forward to the competent authorities of the Member States copies of the complaints and applications and of the most important documents sent to it or which it sends out in the course of such procedures.

3. An Advisory Committee on Restrictive Practices and Monopolies in the Transport Industry shall be consulted prior to the taking of any decision following upon a procedure under Article 10 or of any decision under the second subparagraph of Article 12(3), or under the second subpara-

graph of paragraph 4 of the same Article, or under paragraph 2 or paragraph 3 of Article 14. The Advisory Committee shall also be consulted prior to adoption of the implementing provisions provided for in Article 29.

4. The Advisory Committee shall be composed of officials competent in the matter of restrictive practices and monopolies in transport. Each Member State shall appoint two officials to represent it, each of whom, if prevented from attending, may be replaced by some other official.

5. Consultation shall take place at a joint meeting convened by the Commission; such meeting shall be held not earlier than fourteen days after dispatch of the notice convening it. This notice shall, in respect of each case to be examined, be accompanied by a summary of the case together with an indication of the most important documents, and a preliminary draft decision.

6. The Advisory Committee may deliver an opinion notwithstanding that some of its members or their alternates are not present. A report of the outcome of the consultative proceedings shall be annexed to the draft decision. It shall not be made public.

Article 17: Consideration by the Council of questions of principle concerning the common transport policy raised in connection with specific cases

1. The Commission shall not give a decision in respect of which consultation as laid down in Article 16 is compulsory until after the expiry of twenty days from the date on which the Advisory Committee has delivered its Opinion.

2. Before the expiry of the period specified in paragraph 1, any Member State may request that the Council be convened to examine with the Commission any question of principle concerning the common transport policy which such Member State considers to be involved in the particular case for decision.

The Council shall meet within thirty days from the request by the Member State concerned for the sole purpose of considering such questions of principle.

The Commission shall not give its decision until after the Council meeting.

3. Further, the Council may at any time, at the request of a Member State or of the Commission, consider general questions raised by the implementation of the competition policy in the transport sector.

4. In all cases where the Council is asked to meet to consider under paragraph 2 questions of principle or under paragraph 3 general questions, the Commission shall, for the purposes of this Regulation, take into account the policy guidelines which emerge from that meeting.

Article 18: Inquiries into transport sectors

1. If trends in transport, fluctuations in or inflexibility of transport rates, or other circumstances, suggest that competition in transport is being restricted or distorted within the common market in a specific geographical area, or over one or more transport links, or in respect of the carriage of passengers or goods belonging to one or more specific categories, the Commission may decide to conduct a general inquiry into the sector concerned, in the course of which it may request transport undertakings in that sector to supply the information and documentation necessary for giving effect to the principles formulated in Articles 2 to 8.

2. When making inquiries pursuant to paragraph 1, the Commission shall also request undertakings or groups of undertakings whose size suggests that they occupy a dominant position within the common market or a substantial part thereof to supply such particulars of the structure of the undertakings and of their behaviour as are requisite to an appraisal of their position in the light of the provisions of Article 8.

3. Article 16(2) to (6) and Articles 17, 19, 20 and 21 shall apply.

Article 19: Requests for information

1. In carrying out the duties assigned to it by this Regulation, the Commission may obtain all necessary information from the Governments and competent authorities of the Member States and from undertakings and associations of undertakings.

2. When sending a request for information to an undertaking or association of undertakings, the Commission shall at the same time forward a copy of the request to the competent authority of the Member State in whose territory the seat of the undertakings is situated.

3. In its request, the Commission shall state the legal basis and the purpose of the request, and also the penalties provided for in Article 22(1)(*b*) for supplying incorrect information.

4. The owners of the undertakings or their representatives and, in the case of legal persons, companies or firms, or of associations having no legal personality, the person authorised to represent them by law or by their constitution, shall be bound to supply the information requested.

5. Where an undertaking or association of undertakings does not supply the information requested within the time limit fixed by the Commission, or supplies incomplete information, the Commission shall by decision require the information to be supplied. The decision shall specify what information is required, fix an appropriate time limit within which it is to be supplied and indicate the penalties provided for in Article 22(1)(*b*) and Article 23(1)(*c*), and the right to have the decision reviewed by the Court of Justice.

6. The Commission shall at the same time forward a copy of its decision to the competent authority of the Member State in whose territory the seat of the undertaking or association of undertakings is situated.

Article 20: Investigations by the authorities of the Member States

1. At the request of the Commission, the competent authorities of the Member States shall undertake the investigations which the Commission considers to be necessary under Article 21(1), or which it has ordered by decision pursuant to Article 21(3). The officials of the competent authorities of the Member States responsible for conducting these investigations shall exercise their powers upon production of an authorisation in writing issued by the competent authority of the Member State in whose territory the investigation is to be made. Such authorisation shall specify the subject-matter and purpose of the investigation.

2. If so requested by the Commission or by the competent authority of the Member State in whose territory the investigation is to be made, the officials of the Commission may assist the officials of such authority in carrying out their duties.

Article 21: Investigating powers of the Commission

1. In carrying out the duties assigned to it by this Regulation, the Commission may undertake all necessary investigations into undertakings and associations of undertakings. To this end the officials authorised by the Commission are empowered:
(*a*) to examine the books and other business records;
(*b*) to take copies of or extracts from the books and business records;
(*c*) to ask for oral explanations on the spot;
(*d*) to enter any premises, land and vehicles of undertakings.

2. The officials of the Commission authorised for the purpose of these investigations shall exercise their powers upon production of an authorisation in writing specifying the subject-matter and purpose of the investigation and the penalties provided for in Article 22(1)(*c*) in cases where production of the required books or other business records is incomplete.

In good time for the investigation, the Commission shall inform the competent authority of the Member State in whose territory the same is to be made of the investigation and of the identity of the authorised officials.

3. Undertakings and associations of undertakings shall submit to investigations ordered by decision of the Commission. The decision shall specify the subject-matter and purpose of the investigation, appoint the date on which it is to begin and indicate the penalties provided for in Article 22(1)(*c*) and Article 23(1)(*d*) and the right to have the decision reviewed by the Court of Justice.

4. The Commission shall take decisions referred to in paragraph 3 after consultation with the competent authority of the Member State in whose territory the investigation is to be made.

5. Officials of the competent authority of the Member State in whose territory the investigation is to be made, may at the request of such authority or of the Commission, assist the officials of the Commission in carrying out their duties.

6. Where an undertaking opposes an investigation ordered pursuant to this Article, the Member State concerned shall afford the necessary assistance of the officials authorised by the Commission to

enable them to make their investigation. Member States shall, after consultation with the Commission, take the necessary measures to this end before 1 January 1970.

Article 22: Fines

1. The Commission may by decision impose on undertakings or associations of undertakings fines of from one hundred to five thousand units of account where, intentionally or negligently:
(a) they supply incorrect or misleading information in an application pursuant to Article 12 or in a notification pursuant to Article 14; or
(b) they supply incorrect information in response to a request made pursuant to Article 18 or to Article 19(3) or (5), or do not supply information within the time limit fixed by a decision taken under Article 19(5); or
(c) they produce the required books or other business records in incomplete form during investigations under Article 20 or Article 21, or refuse to submit to an investigation ordered by decision issued in implementation of Article 21(3).

2. The Commission may by decision impose on undertakings or associations of undertakings fines of from one thousand to one million units of account, or a sum in excess thereof but not exceeding 10 per cent. of the turnover in the preceding business year of each of the undertakings participating in the infringement, where either intentionally or negligently:
(a) they infringe Article 2 or Article 8; or
(b) they commit a breach of any obligation imposed pursuant to Article 13(1) or Article 14(4).
In fixing the amount of the fine, regard shall be had both to the gravity and to the duration of the infringement.

3. Article 16(3) to (6) and Article 17 shall apply.

4. Decisions taken pursuant to paragraphs 1 and 2 shall not be of a criminal law nature.

Article 23: Periodic penalty payments

1. The Commission may by decision impose on undertakings or associations of undertakings periodic penalty payments of from fifty to one thousand units of account per day, calculated from the date appointed by the decision, in order to compel them:
(a) to put an end to an infringement of Article 2 or Article 8 of this Regulation the termination of which it has ordered pursuant to Article 11 or to comply with an obligation imposed pursuant to Article 4(2);
(b) to refrain from any act prohibited under Article 13(3);
(c) to supply complete and correct information which it has requested by decision taken pursuant to Article 19(5);
(d) to submit to an investigation which it has ordered by decision taken pursuant to Article 21(3).

2. Where the undertakings or associations of undertakings have satisfied the obligation which it was the purpose of the periodic penalty payment to enforce, the Commission may fix the total amount of the periodic penalty payment at a lower figure than that which would arise under the original decision.

3. Article 16(3) to (6) and Article 17 shall apply.

Article 24: Review by the Court of Justice

The Court of Justice shall have unlimited jurisdiction within the meaning of Article 172 of the Treaty to review decisions whereby the Commission has fixed a fine or periodic penalty payment; it may cancel, reduce or increase the fine or periodic penalty payment imposed.

Article 25: Unit of account

For the purpose of applying Articles 23 to 24 the unit of account shall be that adopted in drawing up the budget of the Community in accordance with Articles 207 and 209 of the Treaty.

Article 26: Hearing of the parties and of third persons

1. Before taking decisions as provided for in Articles 11, 12(3), second subparagraph, and 12(4), 13(3), 14(2) and (3), 22 and 23, the Commission shall give the undertakings or associations of undertakings concerned the opportunity of being heard on the matters to which the Commission has taken objection.

2. If the Commission or the competent authorities of the Member States consider

it necessary, they may also hear other natural or legal persons. Applications to be heard on the part of such persons where they show a sufficient interest shall be granted.

3. Where the Commission intends to give negative clearance pursuant to Article 5 or Article 6, it shall publish a summary of the relevant agreement, decision or concerted practice and invite all interested third parties to submit their observations within a time limit which it shall fix being not less than one month. Publication shall have regard to the legitimate interest of undertakings in the protection of their business secrets.

Article 27: Professional secrecy

1. Information acquired as a result of the application of Articles 18, 19, 20 and 21 shall be used only for the purpose of the relevant request or investigation.

2. Without prejudice to the provisions of Articles 26 and 28, the Commission and the competent authorities of the Member States, their officials and other servants shall not disclose information acquired by them as a result of the application of this Regulation and of the kind covered by the obligation of professional secrecy.

3. The provisions of paragraphs 1 and 2 shall not prevent publication of general information or surveys which do not contain information relating to particular undertakings or associations of undertakings.

Article 28: Publication of decisions

1. The Commission shall publish the decisions which it takes pursuant to Articles 11, 12(3), second subparagraph, 12(4), 13(3) and 14(2) and (3).

2. The publication shall state the names of the parties and the main content of the decision; it shall have regard to the legitimate interest of undertakings in the protection of their business secrets.

Article 29: Implementing provisions

The Commission shall have power to adopt implementing provisions concerning the form, content and other details of complaints pursuant to Article 10, applications pursuant to Article 12, notifications pursuant to Article 14(1) and the hearings provided for in Article 26(1) and (2).

Article 30: Entry into force, existing agreements

1. This Regulation shall enter into force on 1 July 1968.

2. Notwithstanding the provisions of paragraph 1, Article 8 shall enter into force on the day following the publication of this Regulation in the *Official Journal of the European Communities*.

3. The prohibition in Article 2 shall apply from 1 January 1969 to all agreements, decisions and concerted practices falling within Article 2 which were in existence at the date of entry into force of this Regulation or which came into being between that date and the date of publication of this Regulation in the *Official Journal of the European Communities*.

4. Paragraph 3 shall not be invoked against undertakings or associations of undertakings which, before the day following publication of this Regulation in the *Official Journal of the European Communities*, shall have terminated any agreements, decisions or concerted practices to which they are party.

Article 31: Review of the Regulation

1. Within six months of the conclusion of discussions with the third countries signatories to the Revised Convention for the Navigation of the Rhine, the Council, on a proposal from the Commission, shall make any amendments to this Regulation which may prove necessary in the light of the obligations arising out of the Revised Convention for the Navigation of the Rhine.

2. The Commission shall submit to the Council, before 1 January 1971, a general report on the operation of this Regulation and, before 1 July 1971, a proposal for a Regulation to make the necessary amendments to this Regulation.

This Regulation shall be binding in its entirety and directly applicable in all Member States.

Done at Brussels, 19 July 1968.

2. Text of Commission Regulation 1629/69 (reproduced below)

Commission Regulation 1629/69 of August 8, 1969

On the form, content and other details of complaints pursuant to Article 10, applications pursuant to Article 12 and notifications pursuant to Article 14(1) of Council Regulation (EEC) No. 1017/68 of July 19, 1968

([1969] O.J. Spec. Ed. II 371)

THE COMMISSION OF THE EUROPEAN COMMUNITIES,

Having regard to the Treaty establishing the European Economic Community, and in particular Articles 75, 87 and 155 thereof;

Having regard to Article 29 of Regulation No. 1017/68 of 19 July 1968 applying rules of competition to transport by rail, road and inland waterway;

Having regard to the Opinion of the Advisory Committee on Restrictive Practices and Monopolies in the field of transport;

1. Whereas, pursuant to Article 29 of Regulation No. 1017/68, the Commission is authorised to adopt implementing provisions concerning the form, content and other details of complaints pursuant to Article 10, applications pursuant to Article 12 and notifications pursuant to Article 14(1) of that Regulation;

2. Whereas the complaints may make it easier for the Commission to take action for infringement of the provisions of Regulation No. 1017/68; whereas it would consequently seem appropriate to make the procedure for submitting complaints as simple as possible; whereas it is appropriate, therefore, to provide for complaints to be submitted in one written copy, the use of forms being left to the discretion of the complainants;

3. Whereas the submission of the applications and notifications may have important legal consequences for each undertaking which is a party to an agreement, decision or concerted practice; whereas each undertaking should, therefore, have the right to submit such applications or notifications to the Commission; whereas, on the other hand, if an undertaking makes use of that right, it must so inform the other undertakings which are parties to the agreement, decision or concerted practice, in order that they may protect their interests;

4. Whereas it is for the undertakings and associations of undertakings to inform the Commission of the facts and circumstances in support of the applications submitted in accordance with Article 12 and the notifications provided for in Article 14(1);

5. Whereas it is desirable to prescribe that forms be used for applications and notifications in order, in the interest of all concerned, to simplify and speed up examination thereof by the competent departments;

HAS ADOPTED THIS REGULATION:

Article 1: Complaints

1. Complaints pursuant to Article 10 of Regulation No. 1017/68 shall be submitted in writing in one of the official languages of the Community; they may be submitted on Form I shown in the Annex.

2. When representatives of undertakings, of associations of undertakings, or of natural or legal persons sign such complaints, they shall produce written proof that they are authorised to act.

Article 2: Persons entitled to submit applications and notifications

1. Any undertaking which is party to agreements, decisions or practices of the kind described in Article 2 of Regulation No. 1017/68 may submit an application under Article 12 or a notification under Article 14(1) of Regulation No. 1017/68. Where the application or notification is submitted by some, but not all, of the undertakings concerned, they shall give notice to the others.

2. Where applications or notifications under Articles 12 and 14(1) of Regulation No. 1017/68 are signed by representatives of undertakings, of associations of undertakings, or of natural or legal persons,

such representatives shall produce written proof that they are authorised to act.

3. Where a joint application or notification is submitted, a joint representative shall be appointed.

Article 3: Submission of applications and notifications

1. Applications pursuant to Article 12 of Regulation No. 1017/68 shall be submitted on Form II shown in the Annex.

2. Notifications pursuant to Article 14(1) of Regulation No. 1017/68 shall be submitted on Form II shown in the Annex.

3. Several participating undertakings may submit an application or notification on a single form.

4. Applications and notifications shall contain the information requested in the forms.

5. Eight copies of each application or notification and of the supporting documents shall be submitted to the Commission.

6. The supporting documents shall be either originals or copies. Copies must be certified as true copies of the original.

7. Applications and notifications shall be in one of the official languages of the Community. Supporting documents shall be submitted in their original language. Where the original language is not one of the official languages, a translation in one of the official languages shall be attached.

Article 4: Entry into force

This Regulation shall enter into force on the day following its publication in the *Official Journal of the European Communities.*

This Regulation shall be binding in its entirety and directly applicable in all Member States.

Done at Brussels, 8 August 1969.

3. **Annex to Commission Regulation 1629/69** (reproduced below)

Annex to Commission Regulation 1629/69

ANNEX

FORM I

This form and the supporting documents should be forwarded in eight copies together with proof in a single copy of the representative's authority to act.

If the space opposite each question is insufficient, please use extra pages, specifying to which item on the form they relate.

To the Commission of the European Communities
Directorate General for Competition
200 rue de la Loi, Brussels 1049

Complaint submitted by natural or legal persons pursuant to Article 10 of Council Regulation 1017/68 of 19 July 1968 and having as its object the opening of proceedings for the verification of infringements of Article 2 or Article 8, or the application of Article 4(2), of that Regulation

I. *Information regarding parties*

1. Name, forenames and address of person submitting the complaint. If such person is acting as representative, state also the name and address of his principal; for undertakings, and associations of undertakings or persons, state the name, forenames and address of the proprietors or partners or, in the case of legal persons, of their legal representatives. Proof of representative's authority to act must be supplied.
If the complaint is submitted by a number of persons or on behalf of a number of persons, the information must be given in respect of each complainant and each principal.
2. Name and address of persons about whom the complaint is made.

II. Object of the complaint

A. Description of the alleged infringement of Article 2 or Article 8

Attach a detailed statement of the facts which, in your opinion, constitute an infringement of Article 2 or Article 8:

State in particular:
1. which practices by undertakings or associations of undertakings, referred to in the complaint, have the object or effect of preventing, restricting or distorting competition or constitute an improper exploitation of a dominant position in the common market, and
2. to what extent trade between Member States may be affected thereby.

B. Description of the alleged abuse of exemption for groups of small or medium-sized undertakings (Article 4(2))

Attach a detailed statement of the facts which, in your opinion, justify the application of Article 4(2):

State in particular:
1. against which of the agreements, decisions or concerted practices referred to in Article 4(1) the complaint is made;
2. to what extent implementation of the agreement, decision or concerted practice leads to results incompatible with the conditions laid down in Article 5;
3. to what extent this fact constitutes an abuse of exemption from the prohibition under Article 2.

III. Existence of legitimate interest

Describe—if necessary in an annex—the reasons for which you consider that you have a legitimate interest in the Commission's initiating the procedure laid down in Article 10.

IV. Evidence

1. State the name, forenames and address of persons in a position to give evidence as to the facts disclosed, in particular of the persons affected by the alleged infringement or abuse.
2. Submit all documents concerning the facts disclosed or directly connected with them (for example, the texts of agreements, minutes of negotiations or meetings, conditions of transport or dealing, documents relating to costs of transport, business letters, circulars).
3. Submit statistics or other data relating to the facts disclosed (concerning, for example, price trends, price determination, alterations in supply or demand with regard to transport services, conditions of transport or dealing, boycotting or discrimination).
4. Specify, where appropriate, any special technical features or name experts who can do so.
5. Indicate any other evidence available to establish that there has been an infringement or abuse as alleged.

V. State all the steps taken and measures adopted, before the complaint, by you or by any other person to whom the disclosed practice is prejudicial, with the object of putting a stop to the alleged infringement or abuse (proceedings before national courts or public authorities specifying in particular the reference number of the case and the results of such proceedings).

Part IX—3 Inland Waterways, Rail and Road Transport

The undersigned declare that the information in this form and in its annexes has been given in all good faith.

.... dated ....

Signatures: ....

....

....

Book One: Part IX—Sectorial Application of EEC Competition Rules

THE EUROPEAN COMMUNITIES
COMMISSION
Directorate General for Competition

Brussels, (date) ....
200 rue de la Loi

To ....

Acknowledgment of receipt

(This form will be returned to the address inserted above if completed in a single copy by the complainant)

Your complaint dated ....

with regard to the opening of proceedings for

—verification of an infringement of Article 2 or Article 8
—application of Article 4(2)

of Regulation 1017/68

(a) Complainant: ....

....

(b) Author of the infringement or abuse: ....

....

was received on ....

and registered under No IV/TR ....

Please quote the above number in all correspondence

Part IX—3 Inland Waterways, Rail and Road Transport

FORM II

This form and the supporting documents should be forwarded in eight copies together with proof in a single copy of the representative's authority to act.

If the space opposite each question is insufficient, please use extra pages, specifying to which item on the form they relate.

To the Commission of the European Communities
Directorate General for Competition
200 rue de la Loi, Brussels 1049

Application pursuant to Article 12 of Council Regulation 1017/68 of 19 July 1968 with a view to obtaining a declaration of non-applicability of the prohibition in Article 2 to agreements, decisions and concerted practices, in accordance with Article 5 of that Regulation

I. *Information regarding parties*

1. Name, forenames and address of person submitting the application. If such person is acting as representative, state also the name and address of the undertaking or association of undertakings represented and the name, forenames and address of the proprietors or partners or, in the case of legal persons, of their legal representatives.

Proof of representative's authority to act must be supplied.

If the application is submitted by a number of persons or on behalf of a number of undertakings, the information must be given in respect of each person or undertaking.

2. Name and address of the undertakings which are parties to the agreement, decision or concerted practice and name, forenames and address of the proprietors or partners or, in the case of legal persons, of their legal representatives (unless this information has been given under I(1)).

If the undertakings which are parties are not all associated in submitting the application, state what steps have been taken to inform the other undertakings.

This information is not necessary in respect of standard contracts (see Section II(2)(*b*) below).

3. If a firm or joint agency has been formed in pursuance of the agreement, decision or concerted practice, state the name and address of such firm or agency and the names, forenames and addresses of its legal or other representatives.

4. If a firm or joint agency is responsible for operating the agreement, decision or concerted practice state the name and address of such firm or agency and the names, forenames and addresses of its legal or other representatives.

Attach a copy of the statutes.

5. In the case of a decision of an association of undertakings, state the name and address of the association and the names, forenames and addresses of its legal representatives.

Attach a copy of the statutes.

6. If the undertakings are established or have their seat outside the territory of the Community (Article 227(1) and (2) of the Treaty), state the name and address of a representative or branch established in the territory of the Community.

II. *Information regarding contents of agreement, decision or concerted practice*

1. Does the agreement, decision or concerted practice concern transport:
   —by rail
   —by road
   —by inland waterway
or operations of providers of services ancillary to transport?

2. If the contents were reduced to writing, attach a copy of the full text unless (*a*) or (*b*) below provides otherwise.

(*a*) Is there only an outline agreement or outline decision? If so, attach also copy of the full text of the individual agreements and implementing provisions.

(*b*) Is there a standard contract, *i.e.* a contract which the undertaking submitting the application regularly concludes with particular persons or groups of persons?

If so, only the text of the standard contract need be attached.

3. If the contents were not, or were only partially, reduced to writing, state the contents in the space opposite.

4. In all cases give the following additional information:
(a) Date of agreement, decision or concerted practice.
(b) Date when it came into force and, where applicable, proposed period of validity.
(c) Subject: exact description of the transport service or services involved, or of any other subject to which the agreement, decision or concerted practice relates.
(d) Aims of the agreement, decision or concerted practice.
(e) Terms of adherence, termination or withdrawal.
(f) Sanctions which may be taken against participating undertakings (penalty clause, exclusion, etc.).

III. *Means of achieving the aims of the agreement, decision or concerted practice*

1. State whether and how far the agreement, decision or concerted practice relates to:
—adherence to certain rates and conditions of transport or other operating conditions
—restriction or control of the supply of transport, technical development or investment
—sharing of transport markets
—restrictions on freedom to conclude transport contracts with third parties (exclusive contracts)
—application of different terms for supply of equivalent services.

2. Is the agreement, decision or concerted practice concerned with transport services:
(a) within one Member State only?
(b) between Member States?
(c) between a Member State and third countries?
(d) between third countries in transit through one or more Member States?

IV. *Description of the conditions to be fulfilled by the agreement, decision or concerted practice so as to be exempt from the prohibition in Article 2*

Describe to what extent:
1. The agreement, decision or concerted practice contributes towards:
—improving the quality of transport services; or
—promoting, in markets subject to considerable temporal fluctuations of supply and demand, greater continuity and stability in the satisfaction of transport needs; or
—increasing the productivity of undertakings; or
—promoting technical or economic progress;

2. takes fair account of the interests of transport users;

3. the agreement, decision or concerted practice is essential for realising the aims set out under 1 above; and

4. the agreement, decision or concerted practice does not eliminate competition in respect of a substantial part of the transport market concerned.

V. State whether you intend to produce further supporting arguments and, if so, on which points.

Part IX—3 Inland Waterways, Rail and Road Transport

The undersigned declare that the information given above and in the annexes attached hereto is correct. They are aware of the provisions of Article 22(1)(*a*) of Council Regulation 1017/68.

.... (date) ....

Signatures:

....

....

Book One: Part IX—Sectorial Application of EEC Competition Rules

EUROPEAN COMMUNITIES
COMMISSION
Directorate General for Competition

                                  Brussels, (date) ....
                                  200 rue de la Loi

To

Acknowledgment of receipt

(This form will be returned to the address inserted above if completed in a single copy by the person lodging it)

Your application dated ....

(a) Parties:

1. ....

2. .... and others

(There is no need to name the other undertakings party to the arrangement)

(b) Subject: ....

....

....

(brief description of the restriction on competition)

was received on ....

and registered under No IV/TR ....

Please quote the above number in all correspondence

Part IX—3 Inland Waterways, Rail and Road Transport

FORM III

This form and the supporting documents should be forwarded in eight copies together with proof in a single copy of the representative's authority to act.

If the space opposite each question is insufficient, please use extra pages, specifying to which item on the form they relate.

To the Commission of the European Communities
Directorate General for Competition
2000, rue de la Loi, Brussels 1049

Notification of an agreement, decision or concerted practice under Article 14(1) of Council Regulation 1017/68 of 19 July 1968 with a view to obtaining a declaration of non-applicability of the prohibition in Article 2, available in states of crisis, under Article 6 of that Regulation

I. *Information regarding parties*

1. Name, forenames and address of person submitting the notification. If such person is acting as representative, state also the name and address of the undertaking or association of undertakings represented and the name, forenames and address of the proprietors or partners or, in the case of legal persons, of their legal representatives.

Proof of representative's authority to act must be supplied.

If the notification is submitted by a number of persons or on behalf of a number of undertakings, the information must be given in respect of each person or undertaking.

2. Name and address of the undertakings which are parties to the agreement, decision or concerted practice and name, forenames and address of the proprietors or partners or, in the case of legal persons, name, forenames and address of their legal representatives (unless this information has been given under I(1)).

If the undertakings which are parties are not all associated in submitting the notification, state what steps have been taken to inform the other undertakings.

This information is not necessary in respect of standard contracts (see Section II(2)(*b*) below).

3. If a firm or joint agency has been formed in pursuance of the agreement, decision or concerted practice, state the name and address of such firm or agency and the names, forenames and addresses of its legal or other representatives.

4. If a firm or joint agency is responsible for operating the agreement, decision or concerted practice, state the name and address of such firm or agency and the names, forenames and addresses of its legal or other representatives.

Attach a copy of the statutes.

5. In the case of a decision of an association of undertakings, state the name and address of the association and the names, forenames and addresses of its legal representatives.

Attach a copy of the statutes.

6. If the undertakings are established or have their seat outside the territory of the Community (Article 227(1) and (2) of the Treaty), state the name and address of a representative or branch established in the territory of the Community.

II. *Information regarding contents of agreement, decision or concerted practice*

1. Does the agreement, decision or concerted practice concern transport:
—by rail
  —by road
  —by inland waterway
or operations of providers of services ancillary to transport?

2. If the contents were reduced to writing, attach a copy of the full text unless (*a*) or (*b*) below provides otherwise.

(*a*) Is there only an outline agreement or outline decision? If so, attach also copy of the full text of the individual agreements and implementing provisions.

(*b*) Is there a standard contract, *i.e.* a contract which the undertaking submitting the notification regularly concludes with particular persons or groups of persons?

If so, only the text of the standard contract need be attached.

3. If the contents were not, or were only partially, reduced to writing, state the contents in the space opposite.

4. In all cases give the following additional information:
(a) Date of agreement, decision or concerted practice.
(b) Date when it came into force and, where applicable, proposed period of validity.
(c) Subject: exact description of the transport service or services involved, or of any other subject to which the agreement, decision or concerted practice relates.
(d) Aims of the agreement, decision or concerted practice.
(e) Terms of adherence, termination or withdrawal.
(f) Sanctions which may be taken against participating undertakings (penalty clause, expulsion, etc.).

III. *Means of achieving the aims of the agreement, decision or concerted practice*

1. State whether and how far the agreement, decision or concerted practice relates to:
—adherence to certain rates and conditions of transport or other operating conditions
  —restriction or control of the supply of transport, technical development or investment
  —sharing of transport markets
  —restrictions on freedom to conclude transport contracts with third parties (exclusive contracts)
  —application of different terms for supply of equivalent services.

2. Is the agreement, decision or concerted practice concerned with transport services:
(a) within one Member State only?
(b) between Member States?
(c) between a Member State and third countries?
(d) between third countries in transit through one or more Member States?

IV. *Description of the conditions to be fulfilled by the agreement, decision or concerted practice so as to be exempt from the prohibition in Article 2*

Describe to what extent:
1. the transport market is disturbed,

2. the agreement, decision or concerted practice is essential for reducing that disturbance,

3. the agreement, decision or concerted practice does not eliminate competition in respect of a substantial part of the transport market concerned.

V. State whether you intend to produce further supporting arguments and, if so, on which points.

Part IX—3   Inland Waterways, Rail and Road Transport

The undersigned declare that the information given above and in the annexes attached hereto is correct. They are aware of the provisions of Article 22(1)(*a*) of Council Regulation 1017/68.

.... (date) ....

Signatures:

....

....

....

EUROPEAN COMMUNITIES　　　　　Brussels, (date) ....
COMMISSION　　　　　　　　　　　　200, rue de la Loi
Directorate General for Competition

To

Acknowledgment of receipt

(This form will be returned to the address inserted above if completed in a single copy by the person lodging it)

Your application dated ....

(*a*) Parties:

1. ....

2. .... and others

(There is no need to name the other undertakings party to the arrangement)

(*b*) Subject: ....

....

....

(brief description of the restriction on competition)

was received on ....

and registered under No IV/TR ....

Please quote the above number in all correspondence

Part IX—3 Inland Waterways, Rail and Road Transport

4. Text of Commission Regulation 1630/69 (reproduced below)

Commission Regulation 1630/69 of August 8, 1969

On the hearings provided for in Article 26(1) and (2) of Council Regulation 1017/68 of July 19, 1968

([1969] O.J. Spec. Ed. II 381)

THE COMMISSION OF THE EUROPEAN COMMUNITIES,
Having regard to the Treaty establishing the European Economic Community, and in particular Articles 75, 87 and 155 thereof;
Having regard to Article 29 of Council Regulation No. 1017/68 of 19 July 1968 applying rules of competition to transport by rail, road and inland waterways;
Having regard to the Opinion of the Advisory Committee on Restrictive Practices and Monopolies in the field of transport;
(1) Whereas, pursuant to Article 29 of Regulation No. 1017/68, the Commission is empowered to adopt implementing provisions concerning the hearings provided for in Article 26(1) and (2) of that Regulation;
(2) Whereas in most cases the Commission will in the course of the procedure already be in close touch with the participating undertakings or associations of undertakings and they will accordingly have the opportunity of making known their views regarding the objections raised against them;
(3) Whereas, however, in accordance with Article 26(1) of Regulation No. 1017/68 and with the rights of defence, the undertakings and associations of undertakings concerned must have the right on conclusion of the procedure to submit their comments on the whole of the objections raised against them which the Commission proposes to deal with in its decisions;
(4) Whereas persons other than the undertakings or associations of undertakings which are involved in the procedure may have an interest in being heard; whereas by the second sentence of Article 26(2) of Regulation No. 1017/68, such persons must have the opportunity of being heard if they apply and show that they have a sufficient interest;

(5) Whereas it is desirable to enable persons who pursuant to Article 10(2) of Regulation No. 1017/68 have lodged a complaint to submit their comments where the Commission considers that on the basis of the information in its possession there are insufficient grounds for action;
(6) Whereas the various persons entitled to submit comments must do so in writing, both in their own interest and in the interests of good administration, without prejudice to oral procedure where appropriate to supplement the written procedure;
(7) Whereas it is necessary to define the rights of persons who are to be heard, and in particular the conditions upon which they may be represented or assisted and the setting and calculation of time limits;
(8) Whereas the Advisory Committee on Restrictive Practices and Monopolies delivers its Opinion on the basis of a preliminary draft decision; whereas it must therefore be consulted concerning a case after the inquiry in respect thereof has been completed; whereas such consultation does not prevent the Commission from re-opening an inquiry if need be;

HAS ADOPTED THIS REGULATION:

Article 1

Before consulting the Advisory Committee on Restrictive Practices and Monopolies, the Commission shall hold a hearing pursuant to Article 26(1) of Regulation No. 1017/68.

Article 2

1. The Commission shall inform undertak-

ings and associations of undertakings in writing of the objections raised against them. The communication shall be addressed to each of them or to a joint agent appointed by them.

2. The Commission may inform the parties by giving notice in the *Official Journal of the European Communities*, if from the circumstances of the case this appears appropriate, in particular where notice is to be given to a number of undertakings but no joint agent has been appointed. The notice shall have regard to the legitimate interest of the undertakings in the protection of their business secrets.

3. A fine or a periodic penalty payment may be imposed on an undertaking or association of undertakings only if the obligations were notified in the manner provided for in paragraph 1.

4. The Commission shall when giving notice of objections fix a time limit up to which the undertakings and associations of undertakings may inform the Commission of their views.

Article 3

1. Undertakings and associations of undertakings shall, within the appointed time limit, make known in writing their views concerning the objections raised against them.

2. They may in their written comments set out all matters relevant to their defence.

3. They may attach any relevant documents in proof of the facts set out. They may also propose that the Commission hear persons who may corroborate those facts.

Article 4

The Commission shall in its decision deal only with those objections raised against undertakings and associations of undertakings in respect of which they have been afforded the opportunity of making known their views.

Article 5

If natural or legal persons showing a sufficient interest apply to be heard pursuant to Article 26(2) of Regulation No 1017/68, the Commission shall afford them the opportunity of making known their views in writing within such time limits as it shall fix.

Article 6

Where the Commission, having received an application pursuant to Article 10(2) of Regulation No 1017/68, considers that on the basis of the information in its possession there are insufficient grounds for granting the application, it shall inform the applicants of its reasons and fix a time limit for them to submit any further comments in writing.

Article 7

1. The Commission shall afford to persons who have so requested in their written comments the opportunity to put forward their arguments orally, if those persons show a sufficient interest or if the Commission proposes to impose on them a fine or periodic penalty payment.

2. The Commission may likewise afford to any other person the opportunity of orally expressing his views.

Article 8

1. The Commission shall summon the persons to be heard to attend on such date as it shall appoint.

2. It shall forthwith transmit a copy of the summons to the competent authorities of the Member States, who may appoint an official to take part in the hearing.

Article 9

1. Hearings shall be conducted by the persons appointed by the Commission for that purpose.

2. Persons summoned to attend shall appear either in person or be represented by legal representatives or by representatives authorised by their constitution. Undertakings and associations of undertakings may moreover be represented by a duly authorised agent appointed from among their permanent staff.

Persons heard by the Commission may be assisted by lawyers or university teachers who are entitled to plead before the Court of Justice of the European Communities in accordance with Article 17 of the Protocol on the Statute of the Court, or by other qualified persons.

3. Hearings shall not be public. Persons shall be heard separately or in the presence of other persons summoned to attend. In the latter case, regard shall be had to the legitimate interest of the undertakings in the protection of their business secrets.

4. The essential content of the statements made by each person heard shall be recorded in minutes which shall be read and approved by him.

Article 10

Without prejudice to Article 2(2), information and summonses from the Commission shall be sent to the addressees by registered letter with acknowledgement of receipt, or shall be delivered by hand against receipt.

Article 11

1. In fixing the time limits provided for in Articles 2, 5 and 6, the Commission shall have regard both to the time required for preparation of comments and to the urgency of the case. The time limit shall be not less than two weeks; it may be extended.

2. Time limits shall run from the day following receipt of a communication or delivery thereof by hand.

3. Written comments must reach the Commission or be dispatched by registered letter before expiry of the time limit. Where the time limit would expire on a Sunday or public holiday, it shall be extended up to the end of the next following working day. For the purpose of calculating the extension, public holidays shall, in cases where the relevant date is the date of receipt of written comments, be those set out in the Annex to this Regulation, and in cases where the relevant date is the date of dispatch, those appointed by law in the country of dispatch.

This Regulation shall enter into force on the day following its publication in the *Official Journal of the European Communities*.

This Regulation shall be binding in its entirety and directly applicable in all Member States.

Done at Brussels, 8 August 1969.

ANNEX

referred to in the third sentence of Article 11(3) (List of public holidays)

New Year	1 Jan
Good Friday	
Easter Saturday	
Easter Monday	
Labour Day	1 May
Schuman Plan Day	9 May
Ascension Day	
Whit Monday	
Belgian National Day	21 July
Assumption	15 Aug
All Saints	1 Nov
All Souls	2 Nov
Christmas Eve	24 Dec
Christmas Day	25 Dec
The day following Christmas Day	26 Dec
New Year's Eve	31 Dec

B. CASES ON THE INTERPRETATION AND APPLICATION OF THE REGULATIONS

EATE Levy 231
Eurotunnel II 19th Comp. Rep. (para. 57)
Railway Companies 20th Comp. Rep. (para. 115)
Antib v. *Commission* 142

CHAPTER 4

MARITIME TRANSPORT

A. LEGISLATION

1. Text of Council Regulation 4056/86 (reproduced over)

Book One: Part IX—Sectorial Application of EEC Competition Rules

Council Regulation 4056/86 of December 22, 1986

Laying down detailed rules for the application of Articles 85 and 86 of the Treaty to maritime transport

([1986] O.J. L378/4)

THE COUNCIL OF THE EUROPEAN COMMUNITIES,

Having regard to the Treaty establishing the European Economic Community, and in particular Articles 84(2) and 87 thereof,

Having regard to the proposal from the Commission,

Having regard to the opinion of the European Parliament,

Having regard to the opinion of the Economic and Social Committee,

(1) Whereas the rules on competition form part of the Treaty's general provisions which also apply to maritime transport; whereas detailed rules for applying those provisions are set out in the Chapter of the Treaty dealing with the rules on competition or are to be determined by procedures laid down therein;

(2) Whereas according to Council Regulation No. 141, Council Regulation 17 does not apply to transport; whereas Council Regulation No. 1017/68 applies to inland transport only; whereas, consequently, the Commission has no means at present of investigating directly cases of suspected infringement of Articles 85 and 86 in maritime transport; whereas, moreover, the Commission lacks such powers of its own to take decisions or impose penalties as are necessary for it to bring to an end infringement established by it;

(3) Whereas this situation necessitates the adoption of a Regulation applying the rules of competition to maritime transport, whereas Council Regulation No. 954/79 of 15 May 1979 concerning the ratification by Member States of, or their accession to, the United Nations Convention on a Code of Conduct for Liner Conference will result in the application of the Code of Conduct to a considerable number of conferences serving the Community; whereas the Regulation applying the rules of competition to maritime transport foreseen in the last recital of Regulation No. 954/79 should take account of the adoption of the Code; whereas, as far as conferences subject to the Code of Conduct are concerned, the Regulation should supplement the code or make it more precise;

(4) Whereas it appears preferable to exclude tramp vessel services from the scope of this Regulation, rates for these services being freely negotiated on a case-by-case basis in accordance with supply and demand conditions;

(5) Whereas this Regulation should take account of the necessity, on the one hand to provide for implementing rules that enable the Commission to ensure that competition is not unduly distorted within the common market, and on the other hand to avoid excessive regulation of the sector;

(6) Whereas this Regulation should define the scope of the provisions of Articles 85 and 86 of the Treaty, taking into account the distinctive characteristics of maritime transport; whereas trade between Member States may be affected where restrictive practices or abuses concern international maritime transport, including intra-Community transport, from or to Community ports; whereas such restrictive practices or abuses may influence competition, firstly, between ports in different Member States by altering their respective catchment areas, and secondly, between activities in those catchment areas, and disturb trade patterns within the common market;

(7) Whereas certain types of technical agreements, decisions and concerted practices may be excluded from the prohibition on restrictive practices on the ground that they do not, as a general rule, restrict competition;

(8) Whereas provision should be made for block exemption of liner conferences; whereas liner conferences have a stabilizing effect, assuring shippers of reliable services; whereas they contribute generally to providing adequate efficient scheduled maritime transport services and give fair consideration to the interests of users; whereas such results cannot be obtained without the cooperation that shipping companies promote within conferences in relation to rates and, where appropriate, availability of capacity or allocation of

292

cargo for shipment, and income; whereas in most cases conferences continue to be subject to effective competition from both non-conference scheduled services and, in certain circumstances, from tramp services and from other modes of transport; whereas the mobility of fleets, which is a characteristic feature of the structure of availability in the shipping field, subjects conferences to constant competition which they are unable as a rule to eliminate as far as a substantial proportion of the shipping services in question is concerned;

(9) Whereas, however, in order to prevent conferences from engaging in practices which are incompatible with Article 85(3) of the Treaty, certain conditions and obligations should be attached to the exemption;

(10) Whereas the aim of the conditions should be to prevent conferences from imposing restrictions on competition which are not indispensable to the attainment of the objectives on the basis of which exemption is granted; whereas, to this end, conferences should not, in respect of a given route, apply rates and conditions of carriage which are differentiated solely by reference to the country of origin or destination of the goods carried and thus cause within the Community deflections of trade that are harmful to certain ports, shippers, carriers or providers of services ancillary to transport; whereas, furthermore, loyalty arrangements should be permitted only in accordance with rules which do not restrict unilaterally the freedom of users and consequently competition in the shipping industry, without prejudice, however, to the right of a conference to impose penalties on users who seek by improper means to evade the obligation of loyalty required in exchange for the rebates, reduced freight rates or commission is granted to them by the conference; whereas users must be free to determine the undertakings to which they have recourse in respect of inland transport or quayside services not covered by the freight charge or by other charges agreed with the shipping line;

(11) Whereas certain obligations should also attach to the exemption; whereas in this respect users must at all times be in a position to acquaint themselves with the rates and conditions of carriage applied by members of the conference, since in the case of inland transport organized by shippers, the latter continue to be subject to Regulation No. 1017/68; whereas provision should be made that awards given at arbitration and recommendations made by conciliators and accepted by the parties be notified forthwith to the Commission in order to enable it to verify that conferences are not thereby exempted from the conditions provided for in the Regulation and thus do not infringe the provisions of Articles 85 and 86;

(12) Whereas consultations between users or associations of users and conferences are liable to secure a more efficient operation of maritime transport services which takes better account of users' requirements; whereas, consequently, certain restrictive practices which could ensue from such consultations should be exempted;

(13) Whereas there can be no exemption if the conditions set out in Article 85(3) are not satisfied; whereas the Commission must therefore have power to take the appropriate measures where an agreement or concerted practice owing to special circumstances proves to have certain effects incompatible with Article 85(3); whereas, in view of the specific role fulfilled by the conferences in the sector of the liner services, the reaction of the Commission should be progressive and proportionate; whereas the Commission should consequently have the power first to address recommendations, then to take decisions;

(14) Whereas the automatic nullity provided for in Article 85(3) in respect of agreements or decisions which have not been granted exemption pursuant to Article 85(3) owing to their discriminatory or other features applies only to the elements of the agreement covered by the prohibition of Article 85(1) and applies to the agreement in its entirety only if those elements do not appear to be severable from the whole of the agreement whereas the Commission should therefore, if it finds an infringement of the block exemption, either specify what elements of the agreement are by the prohibition and consequently automatically void, or indicate the reasons why those elements are not severable from the rest of the agreement and why the agreement is therefore void in its entirety;

(15) Whereas, in view of the characteristics of international maritime transport, account should be taken of the fact that the application of this Regulation to certain restrictive practices or abuses may result in conflicts with the laws and rules of certain third countries and prove harmful to important Community trading and shipping interests; whereas consultations and, where appropriate, negotiations authorized by the Council should be undertaken by the Commission with those countries in pursuance of the maritime transport policy of the Community;

(16) Whereas this Regulation should make provision for the procedures, decision-making powers and penalties that are necessary to ensure compliance with the prohibitions laid down in Article 85(1) and Article 86, as well as the conditions governing the application of Article 85(3);

(17) Whereas account should be taken in this respect of the procedural provisions of Regulation No. 1017/68 applicable to inland transport operations which takes account of certain distinctive features of transport operations viewed as a whole;

(18) Whereas, in particular, in view of the special characteristics of maritime transport, it is primarily the responsibility of undertakings to see to it that their agreements, decisions and concerted practices conform to the rules on competition, and consequently their notification to the Commission need not be made compulsory;

(19) Whereas in certain circumstances undertakings may, however, wish to apply to the Commission for confirmation that their agreements, decisions and concerted practices are in conformity with the provisions in force; whereas a simplified procedure should be laid down for such cases,

HAS ADOPTED THIS REGULATION:

SECTION 1

Article 1: Subject-matter and scope of the Regulation

1. This Regulation lays down detailed rules for the application of Articles 85 and 86 of the Treaty to maritime transport services.

2. It shall apply only to international maritime transport services from or to one or more Community ports, other than tramp vessel services.

3. For the purposes of this Regulation:

(a) "tramp vessel services" means the transport of goods in bulk or in break-bulk in a vessel chartered wholly or partly to one or more shippers on the basis of a voyage or time charter or any other form of contract for non-regularly scheduled or non-advertised sailings where the freight rates are freely negotiated case by case in accordance with the conditions of supply and demand;

(b) "liner conference" means a group of two or more vessel-operating carriers which provides international liner services for the carriage of cargo on a particular route or routes within specified geographical limits and which has an agreement or arrangement, whatever its nature, within the framework of which they operate under uniform or common freight rates and any other agreed conditions with respect to the provision of liner services;

(c) "transport user" means an undertaking (e.g. shippers, consignees, forwarders, etc.) provided it has entered into, or demonstrates an intention to enter into, a contractual or other agreement with a conference or shipping line for the shipment of goods, or any association of shippers.

Article 2: Technical agreements

1. The prohibition laid down in Article 85(1) of the Treaty shall not apply to agreements, decisions and concerted practices whose sole object and effect is to achieve technical improvements or cooperation by means of:

(a) the introduction of uniform application of standards or types in respect of vessels and other means of transport, equipment, supplies or fixed installations;

(b) the exchange or pooling for the purpose of operating transport services, of vessels, space on vessels or slots and other means of transport, staff, equipment or fixed installations;

(c) the organization and execution of successive or supplementary maritime transport operations and the establishment or application of inclusive rates and conditions for such operations;

(d) the coordination of transport timetables for connecting routes;

(e) the consolidation of individual consignments;

(f) the establishment or application of uniform rules concerning the structure and the conditions governing the application of transport tariffs.

2. The Commission shall, if necessary, submit to the Council proposals for the amendment of the list contained in paragraph 1.

Article 3: Exemption for agreements between carriers concerning the operation of scheduled maritime transport services

Agreements, decisions and concerted practices of all or part of the members of one or more liner conferences are hereby exempted from the prohibition in Article 85(1) of the Treaty, subject to the condition imposed by Article 4 of this Regulation, when they have as their objective the fixing of rates and conditions of carriage, and, as the case may be, one or more of the following objectives:
(a) the coordination of shipping timetables, sailing dates or dates of calls;
(b) the determination of the frequency of sailings or calls;
(c) the coordination or allocation of sailings or calls among members of the conference;
(d) the regulation of the carrying capacity offered by each member;
(e) the allocation of cargo or revenue among members.

Article 4: Condition attaching to exemption

The exemption provided for in Articles 3 and 6 shall be granted subject to the condition that the agreement, decision or concerted practice shall not, within the common market, cause detriment to certain ports, transport users or carriers by applying for the carriage of the same goods and in the area covered by the agreement, decision or concerted practice, rates and conditions of carriage which differ according to the country of origin or destination or port of loading or discharge, unless such rates or conditions can be economically justified.

Any agreement or decision or, if it is severable, any part of such an agreement or decision not complying with the preceding paragraph shall automatically be void pursuant to Article 85(2) of the Treaty.

Article 5: Obligations attaching to exemption

The following obligations shall be attached to the exemption provided for in Article 3:

1. *Consultations*

There shall be consultations for the purpose of seeking solutions on general issues of principle between transport users on the one hand and conferences on the other concerning the rates, conditions and quality of scheduled maritime transport services.

These consultations shall take place whenever requested by any of the above-mentioned parties.

2. *Loyalty arrangements*

The shipping lines' members of a conference shall be entitled to institute and maintain loyalty arrangements with transport users, the form and terms of which shall be matters for consultation between the conference and transport users' organizations. These loyalty arrangements shall provide safeguards making explicit the rights of transport users and conference members. These arrangements shall be based on the contract system or any other system which is also lawful.

Loyalty arrangements must comply with the following conditions:
(a) Each conference shall offer transport users a system of immediate rebates or the choice between such a system and a system of deferred rebates:
— under the system of immediate rebates each of the parties shall be entitled to terminate the loyalty arrangement at any time without penalty and subject to a period of notice of not more than six months; this period shall be reduced to three months when the conference rate is the subject of a dispute;
— under the system of deferred rebates neither the loyalty period on the basis of which the rebate is calculated nor the subsequent loyalty period required before payment of the rebate may exceed six months; this period shall be reduced to three months where the conference rate is the subject of a dispute.
(b) The conference shall, after consulting the transport users concerned, set out:
  (i) a list of cargo and any portion of cargo agreed with transport users which is specifically excluded from the scope of the loyalty arrange-

ment; 100 per cent. loyalty arrangements may be offered but may not be unilaterally imposed;
(ii) a list of circumstances in which transport users are released from their obligation of loyalty; these shall include:
— circumstances in which consignments are dispatched from or to a port in the area covered by the conference but not advertised and where the request for a waiver can be justified, and
— those in which waiting time at a port exceeds a period to be determined for each port and for each commodity or class of commodities following consultation of the transport users directly concerned with the proper servicing of the port.

The conference must, however, be informed in advance by the transport user, within a specified period, of his intention to dispatch the consignment from a port not advertised by the conference or to make use of a non-conference vessel at a port served by the conference as soon as he has been able to establish from the published schedule of sailings that the maximum waiting period will be exceeded.

3. *Services not covered by the freight charges*

Transport users shall be entitled to approach the undertakings of their choice in respect of inland transport operations and quayside services not covered by the freight charge and charges on which the shipping line and the transport user have agreed.

4. *Availability of tariffs*

Tariffs, related conditions, regulations and any amendments thereto shall be made available on request to transport users at reasonable cost, or they shall be available for examination at offices of shipping lines and their agents. They shall set out all the conditions concerning loading and discharge, and exact extent of the services covered by the freight charge in proportion to the sea transport and the land transport or by any other charge levied by the shipping line and customary practice in such matters.

5. *Notification to the Commission of awards at arbitration and recommendations*

Awards given at arbitration and recommendations made by conciliators that are accepted by the parties shall be notified forthwith to the Commission when they resolve disputes relating to the practices of conferences referred to in Article 4 and in points 2 and 3 above.

Article 6: Exemption for agreements between transport users and conferences concerning the use of scheduled maritime transport services

Agreements, decisions and concerned practices between transport users, on the one hand, and conferences, on the other hand, and agreements between transport users which may be necessary to that end, concerning the rates, conditions and quality of liner services, as long as they are provided for in Article 5(1) and (2) are hereby exempted from the prohibition laid down in Article 85(1) of the Treaty.

Article 7: Monitoring of exempted agreements

1. *Breach of an obligation*

Where the persons concerned are in breach of an obligation which, pursuant to Article 5, attaches to the exemption provided for in Article 3, the Commission may, in order to put an end to such breach and under the conditions laid down in Section II:
— address recommendations to the persons concerned;
— in the event of failure by such persons to observe those recommendations and depending upon the gravity of the breach concerned, adopt a decision that either prohibits them from carrying out or requires them to perform specific acts or, while withdrawing the benefit of the block exemption which they enjoyed, grants them an individual exemption according to Article 11(4) or withdraws the benefit of the block exemption which they enjoyed.

2. *Effects incompatible with Article 85(3)*

(a) Where, owing to special circumstances as described below, agreements, decisions and concerted practices which qualify for the exemption provided for in Article 3 and 6 have nevertheless effects which are incompatible with the conditions laid down in Article 85(3) of the Treaty, the Commission, on receipt of a complaint or on its own initiative, under the conditions laid down in Section II, shall take the measures described in (c) below. The severity of these measures must be in proportion to the gravity of the situation.

(b) Special circumstances are, *inter alia*, created by:
  (i) acts of conferences or a change of market conditions in a given trade resulting in the absence or elimination of actual or potential competition such as restrictive practices whereby the trade is not available to competition; or
  (ii) acts of conference which may prevent technical or economic progress or user participation in the benefits;
  (iii) acts of third countries which:
  — prevent the operation of outsiders in a trade,
  — impose unfair tariffs on conference members,
  — impose arrangements which otherwise impede technical or economic progress (cargo-sharing, limitations on types of vessels).

(c)(i) If actual or potential competition is absent or may be eliminated as a result of action by a third country, the Commission shall enter into consultations with the competent authorities of the third country concerned, followed if necessary by negotiations under directives to be given by the Council, in order to remedy the situation.

If the special circumstances result in the absence or elimination of actual or potential competition contrary to Article 85(3)(b) of the Treaty the Commission shall withdraw the benefit of the block exemption. At the same time it shall rule on whether and, if so, under what additional conditions and obligations an individual exemption should be granted to the relevant conference agreement with a view, *inter alia*, to obtaining access to the market for non-conference lines;

  (ii) If, as a result of special circumstances as set out in (b), there are effects other than those referred to in (i) hereof, the Commission shall take one or more of the measures described in paragraph 1.

Article 8: Effects incompatible with Article 86 of the Treaty

1. The abuse of a dominant position within the meaning of Article 86 of the Treaty shall be prohibited, no prior decision to that effect being required.

2. Where the Commission, either on its own initiative or at the request of a Member State or of natural or legal persons claiming a legitimate interest, finds that in any particular case the conduct of conferences benefiting from the exemption laid down in Article 3 nevertheless has effects which are incompatible with Article 86 of the Treaty, it may withdraw the benefit of the block exemption and take, pursuant to Article 10, all appropriate measures for the purpose of bringing to an end infringements of Article 86 of the Treaty.

3. Before taking a decision under paragraph 2, the Commission may address to the conference concerned recommendations for termination of the infringement.

Article 9: Conflicts of international law

1. Where the application of this Regulation to certain restrictive practices or clauses is liable to enter into conflict with the provisions laid down by law, regulation or administrative action of certain third countries which would compromise important Community trading and shipping interests, the Commission shall, at the earliest opportunity, undertake with the competent authorities of the third countries concerned, consultations aimed at reconciling as far as possible the abovementioned interest with the respect of Community law. The Commission shall inform the Advisory Committee referred to in Article 15 of the outcome of these consultations.

2. Where agreements with third countries need not be negotiated, the Commission shall make recommendations to the Council, which shall authorise the Commission to open the necessary negotiations.

The Commission shall conduct these negotiations in consultation with an Advisory Committee as referred to in Article 15 and within the framework of such directives as the Council may issue to it.

3. In exercising the powers conferred on it by this Article, the Council shall act in accordance with the decision-making procedure laid down in Article 84(2) of the Treaty.

Book One: Part IX—Sectorial Application of EEC Competition Rules

SECTION II: RULES OF PROCEDURE

Article 10: Procedures on complaint or on the Commission's own initiative

Acting on receipt of a complaint or on its own initiative, the Commission shall initiate procedures to terminate any infringement of the provisions of Articles 85(1) or 86 of the Treaty or to enforce Article 7 of this Regulation.
Complaints may be submitted by:
(a) Member States;
(b) natural or legal persons who claim a legitimate interest.

Article II: Result of procedures on complaint or on the Commission's own initiative

1. Where the Commission finds that there has been an infringement of Articles 85(1) or 86 of the Treaty, it may by decision require the undertakings or associations of undertakings concerned to bring such infringement to an end.
Without prejudice to the other provisions of this Regulation, the Commission may, before taking a decision under the preceding subparagraph, address to the undertakings or associations of undertakings concerned recommendations for termination of the infringement.
2. Paragraph 1 shall apply also to cases falling within Article 7 of this Regulation.
3. If the Commission, acting on a complaint received, concludes that on the evidence before it there are no grounds for intervention under Articles 85(1) or 86 of the Treaty or Article 7 of this Regulation, in respect of any agreement, decision or practice, it shall issue a decision rejecting the complaint as unfounded.
4. If the Commission, whether acting on a complaint received or on its own initiative, concludes that an agreement, decision or concerted practice satisfied the provisions both of Article 85(1) and of Article 85(3) of the Treaty, it shall issue a decision applying Article 85(3). Such decision shall indicate the date from which it is to take effect. This date may be prior to that of the decision.

Article 12: Applications of Article 85(3)—objections

1. Undertakings and associations of undertakings which seek application of Article 85(3) of the Treaty in respect of agreements, decisions and concerted practices falling within the provisions of Article 85(1) to which they are parties shall submit applications to the Commission.
2. If the Commission judges an application admissible and is in possession of all available evidence, and no action under Article 10 has been taken against the agreement, decision or concerted practice in question, then it shall publish as soon as possible in the *Official Journal of the European Communities* a summary of the application and invite all interested third parties and the Member States to submit their comments to the Commission within 30 days. Such publications shall have regard to the legitimate interest of undertakings in the protection of their business secrets.
3. Unless the Commission notifies applicants, within 90 days from the date of such publication in the *Official Journal of the European Communities*, that there are serious doubts as to the applicability of Article 85(3), the agreement, decision or concerted practice shall be deemed exempt, insofar as it conforms with the description given in the application, from the prohibition for the time already elapsed and for a maximum of six years from the date of publication in the *Official Journal of the European Communities*.
If the Commission finds, after expiry of the 90-day time limit, but before expiry of the six-year period, that the conditions for applying Article 85(3) are not satisfied, it shall issue a decision declaring that the prohibition in Article 85(1) is applicable. Such decision may be retroactive where the parties concerned have given inaccurate information or where they abuse the exemption from the provisions of Article 85(1).
4. The Commission may notify applicants as referred to in the first subparagraph of paragraph 3 and shall do so if requested by a Member State within 45 days of the forwarding to the Member State of the application in accordance with Article 15(2). This request must be justified on the basis of considerations relating to the competition rules of the Treaty.
If it finds that the conditions of Article 85(1) and of Article 85(3) are satisfied, the Commission shall issue a decision applying Article 85(3). The decision shall indicate the date from which it is to take effect. This date may be prior to that of the application.

Article 13: Duration and revocation of decisions applying Article 85(3)

1. Any decisions applying Article 85(3) taken under Article 11(4) or under the second subparagraph of Article 12(4) shall indicate the period for which it is to be valid; normally such period shall not be less than six years. Conditions and obligations may be attached to the decision.

2. The decision may be renewed if the conditions for applying Article 85(3) continue to be satisfied.

3. The Commission may revoke or amend its decision or prohibit specified acts by the parties:
(a) where there has been a change in any of the facts which were basic to the making of the decision;
(b) where the parties commit a breach of any obligation attached to the decision;
(c) where the decision is based on incorrect information or was induced by deceit, or
(d) where the parties abuse the exemption from the provisions of Article 85(1) granted to them by the decision.
In cases falling within (b), (c) or (d), the decision may be revoked with retroactive effect.

Article 14: Powers

Subject to review of its decision by the Court of Justice, the Commission shall have sole power:
— to impose obligations pursuant to Article 7;
— to issue decisions pursuant to Article 85(3).

The authorities of the Member States shall retain the power to decide whether any case falls within the provisions of Article 85(1) or Article 86, until such time as the Commission has initiated a procedure with a view to formulating a decision in the case in question or has sent notification as provided for in the first subparagraph of Article 12(3).

Article 15: Liaison with the authorities of the Member States

1. The Commission shall carry out the procedures provided for in this Regulation in close and constant liaison with the competent authorities of the Member States; these authorities shall have the right to express their views on such procedures.

2. The Commission shall immediately forward to the competent authorities of the Member States copies of the complaints and applications, and of the most important documents sent to it or which it sends out in the course of such procedures.

3. An Advisory Committee on agreement and dominant positions in maritime transport shall be consulted prior to the taking of any decision following upon a procedure under Article 10 or of any decision issued under the second subparagraph of Article 12(3), or under the second subparagraph of paragraph 4 of the same Article. The Advisory Committee shall also be consulted prior to the adoption of the implementing provisions provided for in Article 26.

4. The Advisory Committee shall be composed of officials competent in the sphere of maritime transport and agreements and dominant positions. Each Member State shall nominate two officals to represent it, each of whom may be replaced, in the event of his being prevented from attending, by another official.

5. Consultation shall take place at a joint meeting convened by the Commission; such meeting shall be held not earlier than fourteen days after dispatch of the notice convening it. This notice shall, in respect of each case to be examined, be accompanied by a summary of the case together with an indication of the most important documents, and a preliminary draft decision.

6. The Advisory Committee may deliver an opinion notwithstanding that some of its members or their alternates are not present. A report of the outcome of the consultative proceedings shall be annexed to the draft decision. It shall not be made public.

Article 16: Requests for information

1. In carrying out the duties assigned to it by this Regulation, the Commission may obtain all necessary information from the Governments and competent authorities of the Member States and from undertakings and associations of undertakings.

2. When sending a request for information to an undertaking or association of undertakings, the Commission shall at the same time forward a copy of the request to the competent authority of the Member State

in whose territory the seat of the undertaking or association of undertakings is situated.

3. In its request, the Commission shall state the legal basis and the purpose of the request, and also the penalties provided for in Article 19(1)(b) for supplying incorrect information.

4. The owners of the undertakings or their representatives and, in the case of legal persons, companies or firms, of the association having no legal personality, the person authorised to represent them by law or by their constitution, shall be bound to supply the information requested.

5. Where an undertaking or association of undertakings does not supply the information requested within the time limit fixed by the Commission, or supplies incomplete information, the Commission shall by decision require the information to be supplied. The decision shall specify what information is required, fix an appropriate time limit within which it is to be supplied and indicate the penalties provided for in Article 19(1)(b) and Article 20(1)(c) and the right to have the decision reviewed by the Court of Justice.

6. The Commission shall at the same time forward a copy of its decision to the competent authority of the Member State in whose territory the seat of the undertaking or association of undertakings is situated.

Article 17: Investigations by the authorities of the Member States

1. At the request of the Commission, the competent authorities of the Member States shall undertake the investigations which the Commission considers to be necessary under Article 18(1), or which it has ordered by decision pursuant to Article 18(3). The officials of the competent authorities of the Member States responsible for conducting these investigations shall exercise their power upon production of an authorisation in writing issued by the competent authority of the Member State in whose territory the investigation is to be made. Such authorization shall specify the subject matter and purpose of the investigation.

2. If so requested by the Commission or by the competent authority of the Member State in whose territory the investigation is to be made, Commission officials may assist the officials of such authority in carrying out their duties.

Article 18: Investigating powers of the Commission

1. In carrying out the duties assigned to it by this Regulation, the Commission may undertake all necessary investigations into undertakings and associations of undertakings.

To this end the officials authorized by the Commission are empowered:
(a) to examine the books and other business records;
(b) to take copies of or extracts from the books and business records;
(c) to ask for oral explanations on the spot;
(d) to enter any premises, land and vehicles of undertakings.

2. The officials of the Commission authorized for the purpose of these investigations shall exercise their powers upon production of an authorization in writing specifying the subject matter and purpose of the investigation and the penalties provided for in Article 19(1)(c) in cases where production of the required books or other business records is incomplete. In good time before the investigation, the Commission shall inform the competent authority of the Member State in whose territory the same is to be made of the investigation and of the identity of the authorized officials.

3. Undertakings and associations of undertakings shall submit to investigations ordered by decision of the Commission. The decision shall specify the subject matter and purpose of the investigation, appoint the date on which it is to begin and indicate the penalties provided for in Article 19(1)(c) and Article 20(1)(d) and the right to have the decision reviewed by the Court of Justice.

4. The Commission shall take decisions referred to in paragraph 3 after consultation with the competent authority of the Member State in whose territory the investigation is to be made.

5. Officials of the competent authority of the Member State in whose territory the investigation is to be made, may at the request of such authority or of the Commission, assist the officials of the Commission in carrying out their duties.

6. Where an undertaking opposes an investigation ordered pursuant to this Article, the Member State concerned shall afford the necessary assistance to the officials authorized by the Commission to enable them to make their investigation. To this end, Member States shall take the necessary measures, after consulting the Commission, before 1 January 1989.

Article 19: Fines

1. The Commission may by decision impose on undertakings or associations of undertakings fines of from 100 to 5 000 ECU where, intentionally or negligently:
(a) they supply incorrect or misleading information, either in a communication pursuant to Article 5(5) or in an application pursuant to Article 12; or
(b) they supply incorrect information in response to a request made pursuant to Article 16(3) or (5), or do not supply information within the time limit fixed by a decision taken under Article 16(5); or
(c) they produce the required books or other business records in incomplete form during investigations under Article 17 or Article 18, or refuse to submit to an investigation ordered by decision issued in implementation of Article 18(3).

2. The Commission may by decision impose on undertakings or associations of undertakings fines of from 1 000 to one million ECU, or a sum in excess thereof but not exceeding 10 per cent. of the turnover in the preceding business year of each of the undertakings participating in the infringement, where either intentionally or negligently:
(a) they infringe Article 85(1) or Article 86 of the Treaty, or do not comply with an obligation imposed under Article 7 of this Regulation;
(b) they commit a breach of any obligation imposed pursuant to Article 5 or to Article 13(1).
In fixing the amount of the fine, regard shall be had both to the gravity and to the duration of the infringement.

3. Article 15(3) and (4) shall apply.

4. Decisions taken pursuant to paragraphs 1 and 2 shall not be of criminal law nature.
The fines provided for in paragraph 2(a) shall not be imposed in respect of acts taking place after notification to the Commission and before its Decision in application of Article 85(3) off the Treaty, provided they fall within the limits of the activity described in the notification.

However, this provision shall not have effect where the Commission has informed the undertakings concerned that after preliminary examination it is of the opinion that Article 85(1) of the Treaty applies and that application of Article 85(3) is not justified.

Article 20: Periodic penalty payments

1. The Commission may by decision impose on undertakings or associations of undertakings periodic penalty payments of from 50 to 1000 ECU per day, calculated from the date appointed by the decision, in order to compel them:
(a) to put an end to an infringement of Article 85(1) or Article 86 of the Treaty the termination of which it has ordered pursuant to Article 11, or to comply with an obligation imposed pursuant to Article 7;
(b) to refrain from any act prohibited under Article 13(3);
(c) to supply complete and correct information which it has requested by decision taken pursuant to Article 16(5);
(d) to submit to an investigation which it has ordered by decision taken pursuant to Article 18(3).

2. Where the undertakings or associations of undertakings have satisfied the obligation which it was the purpose of the periodic penalty payment to enforce, the Commission may fix the total amount of the periodic penalty payment at a lower figure than that which would arise under the original decision.

3. Article 15(3) and (4) shall apply.

Article 21: Review by the Court of Justice

The Court of Justice shall have unlimited jurisdiction within the meaning of Article 172 of the Treaty to review decisions whereby the Commission has fixed a fine or periodic penalty payment; it may cancel, reduce or increase the fine or periodic penalty imposed.

Article 22: Unit of account

For the purpose of applying Articles 19 to 21 the ECU shall be that adopted in drawing up the budget of the Community in accordance with Articles 207 and 209 of the Treaty.

Article 23: Hearing of the parties and of third persons

1. Before taking decisions as provided for in Articles 11, 12(3) second subparagraph, and 12(4), 13(3), 19 and 20 the Commission shall give the undertakings concerned the opportunity of being heard on the matters to which the Commission has taken objection.

2. If the Commission or the competent authorities of the Member States consider it necessary, they may also hear other natural or legal persons. Applications to be heard on the part of such persons where they show a sufficient interest shall be granted.

3. Where the Commission intends to give negative clearance pursuant to Article 85(3) of the Treaty, it shall publish a summary of the relevant agreement, decision or concerted practice and invite all interested third parties to submit their observations within a time limit which it shall fix being not less than one month. Publication shall have regard to the legitimate interest of undertakings in the protection of their business secrets.

Article 24: Professional secrecy

1. Information acquired as a result of the application of Articles 17 and 18 shall be used only for the purpose of the relevant request or investigation.

2. Without prejudice to the provisions of Articles 23 and 25, the Commission and the competent authorities of the Member States, their officials and other servants shall not disclose information acquired by them as a result of the application of this Regulation and of the kind covered by the obligation of professional secrecy.

3. The provisions of paragraphs 1 and 2 shall not prevent publication of general information or surveys which do not contain information relating to particular undertakings or associations of undertakings.

Article 25: Publication of decisions

1. The Commission shall publish the decision which it takes pursuant to Articles 11, 12(3), second paragraph, 12(4) and 13(3).

2. The publication shall state the names of the parties and the main content of the decision; it shall have regard to the legitimate interest of undertakings in the protection of their business secrets.

Article 26: Implementing provisions

The Commission shall have power to adopt implementing provisions concerning the scope of the obligation of communication pursuant to Article 5(5), the form, content and other details of complaints pursuant to Article 10, application pursuant to Article 12 and the hearings provided for in Article 23(1) and (2).

Article 27: Entry into force

This Regulation shall enter into force on 1 July 1987.

This Regulation shall be binding in its entirety and directly applicable to all Member States.

Done at Brussels, 22 December 1986.

2. Text of Commission Regulation 4260/88 (reproduced opposite)

Part IX—4 Maritime Transport

Commission Regulation 4260/88 of December 16, 1988

On the communications, complaints and applications and the hearings provided for in Council Regulation 4056/86 laying down detailed rules for the application of Articles 85 and 86 of the Treaty to maritime transport

([1988] O.J. L376/1)

THE COMMISSION OF THE EUROPEAN COMMUNITIES,

Having regard to the Treaty establishing the European Economic Community,

Having regard to Council Regulation No. 4056/86 of 22 December 1986 laying down detailed rules for the application of Articles 85 and 86 of the Treaty to maritime transport ([1986] O.J. L378), and in particular Article 26 thereof,

Having regard to the opinion of the Advisory Committee on Agreements and Dominant Positions in the field of Maritime Transport.

(1) Whereas, pursuant to Article 26 of Regulation No. 4056/86, the Commission is empowered to adopt implementing provisions concerning the scope of the obligation of communication pursuant to Article 5(5), the form, content and other details of complaints pursuant to Article 10 and of applications pursuant to Article 12 and the hearings provided for in Article 23(1) and (2) of that Regulation;

(2) Whereas the obligation of communication to the Commission of awards at arbitration and recommendations by conciliators provided for in Article 5(5) of Regulation No. 4056/86 concerns the settlement of disputes relating to the practices of conferences referred to in Articles 4 and 5(2) and (3) of that Regulation; whereas it seems appropriate to make the procedure for this notification as simple as possible; whereas it is appropriate, therefore, to provide for notifications to be made in writing, attaching the documents containing the text of the awards and recommendations concerned;

(3) Whereas complaints pursuant to Article 10 of Regulation No. 4056/86 may make it easier for the Commission to take action for infringement of Articles 85 and 86 of the EEC Treaty in the field of maritime transport; whereas it would consequently seem appropriate to make the procedure for submitting complaints as simple as possible; whereas it is appropriate, therefore, to provide for complaints to be submitted in one written copy, the form, content and details being left to the discretion of the complainants;

(4) Whereas the submission of the applications pursuant to Article 12 of Regulation No. 4056/86 may have important legal consequences for each undertaking which is a party to an agreement, decision or concerted practice; whereas each undertaking should, therefore, have the right to submit such applications to the Commission; whereas, on the other hand, if an undertaking makes use of that right, it must so inform the other undertakings which are parties to the agreement, decision or concerted practice, in order that they may protect their interests;

(5) Whereas it is for the undertakings and associations of undertakings to inform the Commission of the facts and circumstances in support of the applications submitted in accordance with Article 12 of Regulation No. 4056/86;

(6) Whereas it is desirable to prescribe that forms be used for applications in order, in the interest of all concerned, to simplify and expedite examination thereof by the competent departments;

(7) Whereas in most cases the Commission will in the course of the procedure of the hearings provided for in Article 23(1) and (2) of Regulation No. 4056/86 already be in close touch with the participating undertakings or associations of undertakings and they will accordingly have the opportunity of making known their views regarding the objections raised against them;

(8) Whereas in accordance with Article 23(1) and (2) of Regulation No. 4056/86 and with the rights of the defence, the undertakings and associations of undertakings concerned must have the right on conclusion of the procedure to submit

their comments on the whole of the objections raised against them which the Commission proposes to deal with in its decisions;

(9) Whereas persons other than the undertakings or associations of undertakings which are involved in the procedure may have an interest in being heard; whereas, pursuant to the second sentence of Article 23(2) of Regulation No. 4056/86, such persons should have the opportunity of being heard if they apply and show that they have a sufficient interest;

(10) Whereas it is desirable to enable persons who pursuant to Article 10 of Regulation No. 4056/86 have lodged a complaint to submit their comments where the Commission considers that on the basis of the information in its possession there are insufficient grounds for action;

(11) Whereas the various persons entitled to submit comments must do so in writing, both in their own interest and in the interests of good administration, without prejudice to an oral procedure where appropriate to supplement the written procedure;

(12) Whereas it is necessary to define the rights of persons who are to be heard, and in particular the conditions upon which they may be represented or assisted and the setting and calculation of time limits;

(13) Whereas the Advisory Committee on Restrictive Practices and Dominant Positions in Maritime Transport delivers its opinion on the basis of a preliminary draft Decision; whereas it must therefore be consulted concerning a case after the inquiry in that case has been completed; whereas such consultation does not prevent the Commission from re-opening an inquiry if need be,

HAS ADOPTED THIS REGULATION:

SECTION I: NOTIFICATIONS, COMPLAINTS AND APPLICATIONS

Article 1: Notifications

1. Awards at arbitration and recommendations by conciliators accepted by the parties shall be notified to the Commission when they concern the settlement of disputes relating to the practices of conferences referred to in Articles 4 and 5(2) and (3) of Regulation No. 4056/86.

2. The obligation of notification applies to any party to the dispute resolved by the award or recommendation.

3. Notifications shall be submitted forthwith by registered letter with an acknowledgement of receipt or shall be delivered by hand against receipt. They shall be written in one of the official languages of the Community.

Supporting documents shall be either originals or copies. Copies must be certified as true copies of the original. They shall be submitted in their original language. Where the original language is not one of the official languages of the Community, a translation in one of the official languages shall be attached.

4. When representatives of undertakings, of associations of undertakings, or of natural or legal persons sign such notifications, they shall produce written proof that they are authorized to act.

Article 2: Complaints

1. Complaints pursuant to Article 10 of Regulation No. 4056/86 shall be submitted in writing in one of the official languages of the Community, their form, content and other details being left to the discretion of complainants.

2. Complaints may be submitted by:
(a) Member States
(b) natural or legal persons who claim a legitimate interest.

3. When representatives of undertakings, of associations of undertakings, or of natural or legal persons sign such complaints, they shall produce written proof that they are authorized to act.

Article 3: Persons entitled to submit applications

1. Any undertaking which is party to agreements, decisions or practices of the kind described in Article 85(1) of the Treaty may submit an application under Article 12 of Regulation No. 4056/86. Where the application is submitted by some but not all of the undertakings concerned, they shall give notice to the others.

2. Where applications under Article 12 of Regulation No. 4056/86 are signed by representatives of undertakings, of associations of undertakings, or of natural or legal persons, such representatives shall produce written proof that they are authorized to act.

3. Where a joint application is submitted, a joint representative shall be appointed.

Article 4: Submission of applications

1. Applications pursuant to Article 12 of Regulation No. 4056/86 shall be submitted on Form MAR shown in Annex I.

2. Several participating undertakings may submit an application on a single form.

3. Applications shall contain the information requested in the form.

4. Fourteen copies of each application and of the supporting documents shall be submitted to the Commission.

5. The supporting documents shall be either originals or copies. Copies must be certified as true copies of the original.

6. Applications shall be in one of the official languages of the Community. Supporting documents shall be submitted in their original language. Where the original language is not one of the official languages, a translation in one of the official languages shall be attached.

7. The date of submission of an application shall be the date on which it is received by the Commission. Where, however, the application is sent by registered post, it shall be deemed to have been received on the date shown on the postmark of the place of posting.

8. Where an application submitted pursuant to Article 12 of Regulation No. 4056/86 falls outside the scope of that Regulation, the Commission shall without delay inform the applicant that it intends to examine the application under the provisions of such other Regulation as is applicable to the case; however, the date of submission of the application shall be the date resulting from paragraph 7. The Commission shall inform the applicant of its reasons and fix a period for him to submit any comments in writing before it conducts its appraisal pursuant to the provisions of that other Regulation.

SECTION II: HEARINGS

Article 5

Before consulting the Advisory Committee on Agreements and Dominant Positions in the field of Maritime Transport, the Commission shall hold a hearing pursuant to Article 23(1) of Regulation No. 4056/86.

Article 6

1. The Commission shall inform undertakings and associations of undertakings in writing of the objections raised against them. The communication shall be addressed to each of them or to a joint agent appointed by them.

2. The Commission may inform the parties by giving notice in the *Official Journal of the European Communities*, if from the circumstances of the case this appears appropriate, in particular where notice is to be given to a number of undertakings but no joint agent has been appointed. The notice shall have regard to the legitimate interest of the undertakings in the protection of their business secrets.

3. A fine or a periodic penalty payment may be imposed on an undertaking or association of undertakings only if the objections were notified in the manner provided for in paragraph 1.

4. The Commission shall, when giving notice of objections, fix a period within which the undertakings and associations of undertakings may inform the Commission of their views.

Article 7

1. Undertakings and associations of undertakings shall, within the appointed period, make known in writing their views concerning the objections raised against them.

2. They may in their written comments set out all matters relevant to their defence.

3. They may attach any relevant documents in proof of the facts set out. They may also propose that the Commission hear persons who may corroborate those facts.

Article 8

The Commission shall in its Decision deal

only with those objections raised against undertakings and associations of undertakings in respect of which they have been afforded the opportunity of making known their views.

Article 9

If natural or legal persons showing a sufficient interest apply to be heard pursuant to Article 23(2) of Regulation No. 4056/86 the Commission shall afford them the opportunity of making known their views in writing within such period as it shall fix.

Article 10

Where the Commission, having received a complaint pursuant to Article 10 of Regulation No. 4056/86, considers that on the basis of the information in its possession there are insufficient grounds for acting on the complaint, it shall inform the persons who submitted the complaint of its reasons and fix a period for them to submit any further comments in writing.

Article 11

1. The Commission shall afford to persons who have so requested in their written comments the opportunity to put forward their arguments orally, if those persons show a sufficient interest or if the Commission proposes to impose on them a fine or periodic penalty payment.

2. The Commission may likewise afford to any other person the opportunity of orally expressing his views.

Article 12

1. The Commission shall summon the persons to be heard to attend on such date as it shall appoint.

2. It shall forthwith transmit a copy of the summons to the competent authorities of the Member States, who may appoint an official to take part in the hearing.

Article 13

1. Hearings shall be conducted by the persons appointed by the Commission for that purpose.

2. Persons summoned to attend shall either appear in person or be represented by legal representatives or by representatives authorized by their constitution. Undertakings and associations of undertakings may moreover be represented by a duly authorized agent appointed from among their permanent staff.

Persons heard by the Commission may be assisted by lawyers or university teachers who are entitled to plead before the Court of Justice of the European Communities in accordance with Article 17 of the Protocol on the Statute of the Court, or by other qualified persons.

3. Hearings shall not be public. Persons shall be heard separately or in the presence of other persons summoned to attend. In the latter case, regard shall be had to the legitimate interest of the undertakings in the protection of their business secrets.

4. The essential content of the statements made by each person heard shall be recorded in minutes which shall be read and approved by him.

Article 14

Without prejudice to Article 6(2), information and summonses from the Commission shall be sent to the addressees by registered letter with acknowledgement of receipt, or shall be delivered by hand against receipt.

Article 15

1. In fixing the periods provided for in Articles 4(8), 6, 9 and 10, the Commission shall have regard both to the time required for preparation of comments and to the urgency of the case. A period shall not be less than two weeks; it may be extended.

2. Periods shall run from the day following receipt of a communication or delivery thereof by hand.

3. Written comments must reach the Commission or be dispatched by registered letter before expiry of the period. Where the period would expire on a Sunday or a public holiday, it shall be extended up to the end of the next following working day. For the purpose of calculating the extension, public holidays shall, in cases where the relevant date is the date of receipt of

written comments, be those set out in Annex II to this Regulation, and in cases where the relevant date is the date of dispatch, those appointed by law in the country of dispatch.

Article 16

This Regulation shall enter into force on the day following its publication in the *Official Journal of the European Communities*.

This Regulation shall be binding in its entirety and directly applicable in all Member States.

Done at Brussels, 16 December 1988.

3. Annexes to Commission Regulation 4260/88 (reproduced over)

Book One: Part IX—Sectorial Application of EEC Competition Rules

Annexes to Commission Regulation 4260/88

ANNEX I

Note. This form must be accompanied by an Annex containing the information specified in the attached Complementary Note (see page 19 of this Official Journal.

The form and Annex must be supplied in fourteen copies (two for each Member State). Supply three copies of any relevant agreement and one copy of other supporting documents.

Please do not forget to complete the Acknowledgement of Receipt annexed.

If space is insufficient, please use extra pages, specifying to which item on the form they relate.

FORM MAR

TO THE COMMISSION OF THE EUROPEAN COMMUNITIES

Directorate-General for Competition,
200, Rue de la Loi,
B-1049 Brussels.

A. Application under Article 12 of Council Regulation 4056/86 of 22 December 1986 with a view to obtaining a decision under Article 85(3) of the Treaty establishing the European Economic Community.

Identity of the parties

1. *Identity of applicant*

    Full name and address, telephone, telex and facsimile numbers, and brief description of the undertaking(s) or association(s) of undertakings submitting the application.

    For partnerships, sole traders or any other unincorporated body trading under a business name, give, also, the name, forename(s) and address of the proprietor(s) or partner(s).

    Where an application is submitted on behalf of some other person (or is submitted by more than one person) the name, address and position of the representative (or joint representative) must be given, together with proof of his authority to act. Where an aplication or notification is submitted by or on behalf of more than one person they should appoint a joint representative (Article 3(2) and (3) of Commission Regulation No 4260).

Part IX—4 Maritime Transport

2. *Identity of any other parties*

Full name and address and brief description of any other parties to the agreement, decision or concerted practice (hereinafter referred to as 'the arrangements').

State what steps have been taken to inform these other parties of this application.

(This information is not necessary in respect of standard contracts which an undertaking submitting the application or notification has concluded or intends to conclude with a number of parties.)

Purpose of this application (see Complementary Note)

(Please answer yes or no to the questions)

Would you be satisfied with a comfort letter? (See the end of Section VII of the Complementary Note).

The undersigned declare that the information given above and in the ... pages annexed hereto is correct to the best of their knowledge and belief, that all estimates are identified as such and are their best estimates of the underlying facts and that all the opinions expressed are sincere. They are aware of the provisions of Article 19(1)(a) of Regulation 4056/86 (see attached Complementary Note).

Place and date: ....

Signatures: ....

                ....

                ....

                ....

Book One: Part IX—Sectorial Application of EEC Competition Rules

COMMISSION
OF THE
EUROPEAN COMMUNITIES

Brussels ....

Directorate-General for Competition

> To

ACKNOWLEDGEMENT OF RECEIPT

(This form will be returned to the address inserted above if the top half is completed in a single copy by the person lodging it)

Your application ....

....

concerning: ....

Your reference: ....

Parties:

1. ....

2. ....and others

(There is no need to name the other undertakings party to the arrangement)

(To be completed by the Commission.)

was received on: ....

and registered under No IV/MAR/ ....

Please quote the above number in all correspondence

ANNEX II

(List of public holidays)

New Year	1 Jan
Good Friday	
Easter Saturday	
Easter Monday	
Labour Day	1 May
Schuman Plan Day	9 May
Ascension Day	
Whit Monday	
Belgian National Day	21 July
Assumption	15 Aug
All Saints	1 Nov
All Souls	2 Nov
Christmas Eve	24 Dec
Christmas Day	25 Dec
The day following Christmas Day	26 Dec
New Year's Eve	31 Dec

Book One: Part IX—Sectorial Application of EEC Competition Rules

4. Text of Council Regulation 479/92.
(reproduced below)

Council Regulation No. 479/92 of February 25, 1992

On the application of Article 85(3) of the Treaty to certain categories of agreements, decisions and concerted practices between liner shipping companies (consortia)

([1992] O.J. L55/3)

THE COUNCIL OF THE EUROPEAN COMMUNITIES,
Having regard to the Treaty establishing the European Economic Community, and in particular Article 87 thereof,
Having regard to the proposal from the Commission ([1990] O.J. C167/9).
Having regard to the opinion of the European Parliament ([1991] O.J. C305/39).
Having regard to the opinion of the Economic and Social Committee ([1991] O.J. C69/16).

(1) Whereas Article 85(1) of the Treaty may in accordance with Article 85(3) thereof be declared inapplicable to categories of agreements, decisions and concerted practices which fulfil the conditions contained in Article 85(3);

(2) Whereas, pursuant to Article 87 of the Treaty, the provisions for the application of Article 85(3) of the Treaty should be adopted by way of Regulation; whereas, according to Article 87(2)(*b*), such a Regulation must lay down detailed rules for the application of Article 85(3), taking into account the need to ensure effective supervision, on the one hand, and to simplify administration to the greatest possible extent on the other; whereas according to Article 87(2)(*d*), such a Regulation is required to define the respective functions of the Commission and of the Court of Justice;

(3) Whereas liner shipping is a capital intensive industry; whereas containerisation has increased pressures for co-operation and rationalisation; whereas the Community shipping industry needs to attain the necessary economies of scale in order to compete successfully on the world liner shipping market;

(4) Whereas joint-service agreements between liner shipping companies with the aim of rationalising their operations by means of technical, operation and/or commercial arrangements (described in shipping circles as consortia) can help to provide the necessary means for improving the productivity of liner shipping services and promoting technical and economic progress;

Having regard to the importance of maritime transport for the development of the Community's trade and the role which consortia agreements can fulfil in this respect, taking account of the special features of international liner shipping;

(5) Whereas the legalisation of these agreements is a measure which can make a positive contribution to improving the competitiveness of shipping in the Community;

(6) Whereas users of the shipping services offered by consortia can obtain a share of the benefits resulting from the improvements in productivity and service, by means of, *inter alia,* regularity, cost reductions derived from higher levels of capacity utilisation, and better service quality stemming from improved vessels and equipment;

(7) Whereas the Commission should be enabled to declare by way of Regulation that the provisions of Article 85(1) of the Treaty do not apply to certain categories of consortia agreements, decisions and concerted practices, in order to make it easier for undertakings to co-operate in ways which are economically desirable and without adverse effect from the point of view of competition policy;

(8) Whereas the Commission, in close and constant liaison with the competent

authorities of the Member States, should be able to define precisely the scope of these exemptions and the conditions attached to them;

(9) Whereas consortia in liner shipping are a specialised and complex type of joint venture; whereas there is a great variety of different consortia agreements operating in different circumstances; whereas the scope, parties, activities or terms of consortia are frequently altered whereas the Commission should therefore be given the responsibility of defining from time to time the consortia to which a group exemption should apply;

(10) Whereas, in order to ensure that all the conditions of Article 85(3) of the Treaty are met, conditions should be attached to group exemptions to ensure in particular that a fair share of the benefits will be passed on to shippers and that competition is not eliminated;

(11) Whereas pursuant to Article 11(4) of Council Regulation (EEC) No. 4056/86 of December 22, 1986 laying down detailed rules for the application of Articles 85 and 86 of the Treaty to maritime transport ([1986] O.J. L378/4) the Commission may provide that a decision taken in accordance with Article 85(3) of the Treaty shall apply with retroactive effect; whereas it is desirable that the Commission be empowered to adopt, be Regulation, provisions to that effect;

(12) Whereas notification of agreements, decisions and concerted practices falling within the scope of this Regulation must not be made compulsory, it being primarily the responsibility of undertakings to see to it that they conform to the rules on competition, and in particular to the conditions laid down by the subsequent Commission Regulation implementing this Regulation;

(13) Whereas there can be no exemption if the conditions set out in Article 85(3) of the Treaty are not satisfied; whereas the Commission should therefore have power to take the appropriate measures where an agreement proves to have effects incompatible with Article 85(3) of the Treaty; whereas the Commission should be able first to address recommendations to the parties and then to take decisions,

HAS ADOPTED THIS REGULATION:

Article 1

1. Without prejudice to the application of Regulation (EEC) No. 4056/86, the Commission may by regulation and in accordance with Article 85(3) of the Treaty, declare that Article 85(1) of the Treaty shall not apply to certain categories of agreements between undertakings, decisions of associations of undertakings and concerted practices that have as an object to promote or establish co-operation in the joint operation of maritime transport services between liner shipping companies, for the purpose of rationalising their operations by means of technical, operational and/or commercial arrangements — with the exception of price fixing (consortia).

2. Such regulation adopted pursuant to paragrah 1 shall define the categories of agreements, decisions and concerted practices to which it applies and shall specify the conditions and obligations under which, pursuant to Article 85(3) of the Treaty, they shall be considered exempted from the application of Article 85(1) of the Treaty.

Article 2

1. The regulation adopted pursuant to Article 1 shall apply for a period of five years, calculated as from the date of its entry into force.

2. It may be repealed or amended where circumstances have changed with respect to any of the facts which were basic to its adoption.

Article 3

The regulation adopted pursuant to Article 1 may include a provision stating that it applies with retroactive effect to agreements, decisions and concerted practices which were in existence at the date of entry into force of such regulation, provided they comply with the conditions established in that regulation.

Article 4

Before adopting its regulation, the Commission shall publish a draft thereof to enable all the persons and organisations concerned to submit their comments within such reasonable time limit as the Commission shall fix, but in no case less than one month.

Article 5

1. Before publishing the draft regulation

and before adopting the regulation, the Commission shall consult the Advisory Committee on Agreements and Dominant Positions in Maritime Transport established by Article 15(3) of Regulation (EEC) No. 4056/86.

2. Paragraphs 5 and 6 of Article 15 of Regulation (EEC) No. 4056/86 relating to consultation with the Advisory Committee, shall apply, it being understood that joint meetings with the Commission shall take place not earlier than one month after dispatch of the notice convening them.

Article 6

1. Where the persons concerned are in breach of a condition or obligation attaching to an exemption granted by the Regulation adopted pursuant to Article 1, the Commission may, in order to put an end to such a breach:
— address recommendations to the persons concerned, and
— in the event of failure by such persons to observe those recommendations, and depending on the gravity of the breach concerned, adopt a decision that either prohibits them from carrying out, or requires them to perform specific acts or, while withdrawing the benefit of the group exemption which they enjoyed, grants them an individual exemption in accordance with Article 11(4) of Regulation (EEC) No. 4056/86, or withdraws the benefit of the group exemption which they enjoyed.

2. Where the Commission, either on its own initiative or at request of a Member State or of natural or legal persons claiming a legitimate interest, finds that in a particular case an agreement, decision or concerted practice to which the group exemption granted by the Regulation adopted pursuant to Article 1 applies, nevertheless has effects which are incompatible with Article 85(3) of the Treaty or with the prohibition laid down in Article 86 of the Treaty, it may withdraw the benfit of the group exemption from those agreements, decisions or concerted practices and take all appropriate measures for the purpose of bringing these infringements to an end, pursuant to Article 13 of Regulation (EEC) No. 4056/86.

3. Before taking a decision under paragraph 2, the Commission may address recommendations for termination of the infringement to the persons concerned.

Article 7

This Regulation shall enter into force on the day following its publication in the *Official Journal of the European Communities.*

This Regulation shall be binding in its entirety and directly applicable in all Member States.

Done at Brussels, February 25, 1992.

B. CASES

Secrétama 329a

CHAPTER 5

AIR TRANSPORT

A. LEGISLATION

1. Text of Council Regulation 3975/87 (reproduced below)

Council Regulation 3975/87 of December 14, 1987

Laying down the procedure for the application of the rules on competition to undertakings in the air transport sector

([1987] O.J. L374/1)

(as amended by Regulation 1284/91, [1991] O.J. L122/2)

THE COUNCIL OF THE EUROPEAN COMMUNITIES,

Having regard to the Treaty establishing the European Economic Community, and in particular Article 87 thereof,
Having regard to the proposal from the Commission,
Having regard to the opinions of the European Parliament,
Having regard to the opinion of the Economic and Social Committee,

(1) Whereas the rules on competition form part of the Treaty's general provisions which also apply to air transport; whereas the rules for applying these provisions are either specified in the Chapter on competition or fall to be determined by the procedures laid down therein;

(2) Whereas, according to Council Regulation No. 141 ([1962] O.J. 124/62), Council Regulation No. 17 ([1962] O.J. 13/62) does not apply to transport services; whereas Council Regulation No. 1017/68 ([1968] O.J. L175/1) applies only to inland transport; whereas Council Regulation No. 4056/86 ([1986] O.J. L378/4) applies only to maritime transport; whereas consequently the Commission has no means at present of investigating directly cases of suspected infringement of Articles 85 and 86 of the Treaty in air transport; whereas moreover the Commission lacks such powers of its own to take decisions or impose penalties as are necessary for it to bring to an end infringements established by it;

(3) Whereas air transport is characterised by features which are specific to this sector; whereas, furthermore, international air transport is regulated by a network of bilateral agreements between States which define the conditions under which air carriers designated by the parties to the agreements may operate routes between their territories;

(4) Whereas practices which affect competition relating to air transport between Member States may have a substantial effect on trade between Member States; whereas it is therefore desirable that rules should be laid down under which the Commission, acting in close and constant liaison with the competent authorities of the Member States may take the requisite measures for the application of Articles 85 and 86 of the Treaty to international air transport between Community airports.

(5) Whereas such regulations should provide for appropriate procedures, decision-making powers and penalties to ensure compliance with the prohibitions laid down in Articles 85(1) and 86 of the Treaty; whereas account should be taken in this respect of the procedural provisions of Regulation No. 1017/68 applicable to inland transport operations, which takes

account of certain distinctive features of transport operations viewed as a whole;

(6) Whereas undertakings concerned must be accorded the right to be heard by the Commission, third parties whose interests may be affected by a decision must be given the opportunity of submitting their comments beforehand and it must be ensured that wide publicity is given to decisions taken;

(7) Whereas all decisions taken by the Commission under this Regulation are subject to review by the Court of Justice under the conditions specified in the Treaty; whereas it is moreover desirable, pursuant to Article 172 of the Treaty, to confer upon the Court of Justice unlimited jurisdiction in respect of decisions under which the Commission imposes fines or periodic penalty payments;

(8) Whereas it is appropriate to except certain agreements, decisions and concerted practices from the prohibitions laid down in Article 85(1) of the Treaty, insofar as their sole object and effect is to achieve technical improvements or cooperation;

(9) Whereas, given the specific features of air transport, it will in the first instance be for undertakings themselves to see that their agreements, decisions and concerted practices conform to the competition rules, and notification to the Commission need not be compulsory;

(10) Whereas undertakings may wish to apply to the Commission in certain cases for confirmation that their agreements, decisions and concerted practices conform to the law, and a simplified procedure should be laid down for such cases;

(11) Whereas this Regulation does not prejudge the application of Article 90 of the Treaty,

HAS ADOPTED THIS REGULATION:

Article 1: Scope

1. This Regulation lays down detailed rules for the application of Articles 85 and 86 of the Treaty to air transport services.

2. This Regulation shall apply only to international air transport between Community airports.

Article 2: Exceptions for certain technical agreements

1. The prohibition laid down in Article 85(1) of the Treaty shall not apply to the agreements, decisions and concerted practices listed in the Annex, in so far as their sole object and effect is to achieve technical improvements or cooperation. This list is not exhaustive.

2. If necessary, the Commission shall submit proposals to the Council for the amendment of the list in the Annex.

Article 3: Procedures on complaint or on the Commission's own initiative

1. Acting on receipt of a complaint or on its own initiative, the Commission shall initiate procedures to terminate any infringement of the provisions of Article 85(1) or 86 of the Treaty.
Complaints may be submitted by:
(a) Member States;
(b) natural or legal persons who claim a legitimate interest.

2. Upon application by the undertakings or associations of undertakings concerned, the Commission may certify that, on the basis of the facts in its possession, there are no grounds under Article 85(1) or Article 86 of the Treaty for action on its part in respect of an agreement, decision or concerted practice.

Article 4: Result of procedures on complaint or on the Commission's own initiative

1. Where the Commission finds that there has been an infringement of Articles 85(1) or 86 of the Treaty, it may by decision require the undertakings or associations of undertakings concerned to bring such an infringement to an end.

Without prejudice to the other provisions of this Regulation, the Commission may address recommendations for termination of the infringement to the undertakings or associations of undertakings concerned before taking a decision under the preceding subparagraph.

2. If the Commission, acting on a complaint received, concludes that, on the evidence before it, there are no grounds for intervention under Articles 85(1) or 86 of the Treaty in respect of any agreement, decision or concerted practice, it shall take a decision rejecting the complaint as unfounded.

3. If the Commission, whether acting on a complaint received or on its own initiative, concludes that an agreement, decision or concerted practice satisfies the provisions of both Article 85(1) and 85(3) of the Treaty, it shall take a decision applying paragraph 3 of the said Article. Such a decision shall indicate the date from which it is to take effect. This date may be prior to that of the decision.

Article 4a: Interim measures against anti-competitive practices

1. Without prejudice to the application of Article 4(1), where the commission has clear *prima facie* evidence that certain practices are contrary to Article 85 or 86 of the Treaty and have the object or effect of directly jeopardizing the existence of an air service, and where recourse to normal procedures may not be sufficient to protect the air service or the airline company concerned, it may by decision take interim measures to ensure that these practices are not implemented or cease to be implemented and give such instructions as are necessary to prevent the occurrence of these practices until a decision under Article 4(1) is taken.

2. A decision taken pursuant to paragraph 1 shall apply for a period not exceeding six months. Article 8(5) shall not apply.

The Commission may renew the initial decision, with or without modification, for a period not exceeding three months. In such case, Article 8(5) shall apply.

Article 5: Application of Article 85(3) of the Treaty: Objections

1. Undertakings and associations of undertakings which wish to seek application of Article 85(3) of the Treaty in respect of agreements, decisions and concerted practices falling within the provisions of paragraph 1 of the said Article to which they are parties shall submit applications to the Commission.

2. If the Commission judges an application admissible and is in possession of all the available evidence and no action under Article 3 has been taken against the agreement decision or concerted practice in question, then it shall publish as soon as possible in the *Official Journal of the European Communities* a summary of the application and invite all interested third parties and the Member States to submit their comments to the Commission within 30 days. Such publications shall have regard to the legitimate interest of undertakings in the protection of their business secrets.

3. Unless the Commission notifies applicants, within 90 days of the date of such publication in the *Official Journal of the European Communities*, that there are serious doubts as to the applicability of Article 85(3) of the Treaty, the agreement, decision or concerted practice shall be deemed exempt, in so far as it conforms with the description given in the application, from the prohibition for the time already elapsed and for a maximum of six years from the date of publication of the *Official Journal of the European Communities*.

If the Commission finds, after expiry of the 90-day time limit, but before expiry of the six-year period, that the conditions for applying Article 85(3) of the Treaty are not satisfied, it shall issue a decision declaring that the prohibition in Article 85(1) applies. Such decision may be retroactive where the parties concerned have given inaccurate information or where they abuse an exemption from the provisions of Article 85(1) or have contravened Article 86.

4. The Commission may notify applicants as referred to in the first subparagraph of paragraph 3; it shall do so if requested by a Member State within 45 days of the forwarding to the Member State of the application in accordance with Article 8(2). This request must be justified on the basis of considerations relating to the competition rules of the Treaty.

If it finds that the conditions of Article 85(1) and (3) of the Treaty are satisfied, the Commission shall issue a decision applying Article 85(3). The decision shall indicate the date from which it is to take effect. This date may be prior to that of the application.

Article 6: Duration and revocation of decisions applying Article 85(3)

1. Any decision applying Article 85(3) of the Treaty adopted under Article 4 or 5 of this Regulation shall indicate the period for which it is to be valid; normally such period shall not be less than six years. Conditions and obligations may be attached to the decision.

2. The decision may be renewed if the conditions for applying Article 85(3) of the Treaty continue to be satisfied.

3. The Commission may revoke or amend its decision or prohibit specific acts by the parties:
(a) where there has been a change in any of the facts which were basic to the making of the decision; or
(b) where the parties commit a breach of any obligation attached to the decision; or
(c) where the decision is based on incorrect information or was induced by deceit; or
(d) where the parties abuse the exemption from the provisions of Article 85(1) of the Treaty granted to them by the decision.

In cases falling under subparagraph (b), (c), or (d), the decision may be revoked with retroactive effect.

Article 7: Powers

Subject to review of its decision by the Court of Justice, the Commission shall have sole power to issue decisions pursuant to Article 85(3) of the Treaty.

The authorities of the Member States shall retain the power to decide whether any case falls under the provisions of Article 85(1) or Article 86 of the Treaty, until such time as the Commission has initiated a procedure with a view to formulating a decision on the case in question or has sent notification as provided by the first subparagraph of Article 5(3) of this Regulation.

Article 8: Liaison with the authorities of the Member States

1. The Commission shall carry out the procedures provided for in this Regulation in close and constant liaison with the competent authorities of the Member States; these authorities shall have the right to express their views on such procedures.

2. The Commission shall immediately forward to the competent authorities of the Member States copies of the complaints and applications and of the most important documents sent to it or which it sends out in the course of such procedures.

3. An Advisory Committee on Agreements and Dominant Positions in Air Transport shall be consulted prior to the taking of any decision following upon a procedure under Article 3 or of any decision under the second subparagraph 5(3), or under the second subparagraph of paragraph 4 of the same Article or under Article 6. The Advisory Committee shall also be consulted prior to adoption of the implementing provisions provided for in Article 19.

4. The Advisory Committee shall be composed of officials competent in the sphere of air transport and agreements and dominant positions. Each Member State shall nominate two officials to represent it, each of whom may be replaced, in the event of his being prevented from attending, by another official.

5. Consultation shall take place at a joint meeting convened by the Commission; such a meeting shall be held not earlier than 14 days after dispatch of the notice convening it. In respect of each case to be examined, this notice shall be accompanied by a summary of the case, together with an indication of the most important documents, and a preliminary draft decision.

6. The Advisory Committee may deliver an opinion notwithstanding that some of its members of their alternates are not present. A report of the outcome of the consultative proceedings shall be annexed to the draft decision. It shall not be made public.

Article 9: Requests for information

1. In carrying out the duties assigned to it by this Regulation, the Commission may obtain all necessary information from the governments and competent authorities of the Member States and from undertakings and associations of undertakings.

2. When sending a request for information to an undertaking or association of undertakings, the Commission shall forward a copy of the request at the same time to the competent authority of the Member State in whose territory the head office of the undertaking or association of undertakings is situated.

3. In its request, the Commission shall state the legal basis and purpose of the request and also the penalties for supplying incorrect information provided for in Article 12(1)(b).

4. The owners of the undertakings or their representatives and, in the case of legal persons or of companies, firms or associa-

tions having no legal personality, the person authorized to represent them by law or by their rules shall be bound to supply the information requested.

5. When an undertaking or association of undertakings does not supply the information requested within the time limit fixed by the Commission, or supplies incomplete information, the Commission shall by decision require the information to be supplied. The decision shall specify what information is required, fix an appropriate time limit within which it is to be supplied and indicate the penalties provided for in Article 12(1)(b) and Article 13(1)(c), as well as the right to have the decision reviewed by the Court of Justice.

6. At the same time the Commission shall send a copy of its decision to the competent authority of the Member State in whose territory the head office of the undertaking or association of undertakings is situated.

Article 10: Investigations by the authorities of the Member States

1. At the request of the Commission, the competent authorities of the Member States shall undertake the investigations which the Commission considers to be necessary under Article 11(1) or which it has ordered by decision adopted pursuant to Article 11(3). The officials of the competent authorities of the Member States responsible for conducting these investigations shall exercise their powers upon production of an authorization in writing issued by the competent authority of the Member States in whose territory the investigation is to be made. Such an authorization shall specify the subject matter and purpose of the investigation.

2. If so requested by the Commission or by the competent authority of the Member State in whose territory the investigation is to be made, Commission officials may assist the officials of the competent authority in carrying out their duties.

Article 11: Investigation powers of the Commission

1. In carrying out the duties assigned to it by this Regulation, the Commission may undertake all necessary investigations into undertakings and associations of undertakings. To this end the officials authorized by the Commission shall be empowered:

(a) to examine the books and other business records;
(b) to take copies of, or extracts from, the books and business records;
(c) to ask for oral explanations on the spot;
(d) to enter any premises, land and vehicles used by undertakings or associations of undertakings.

2. The authorized officials of the Commission shall exercise their powers upon production of an authorization in writing specifying the subject matter and purpose of the investigation and the penalties provided for in Article 12(1)(c) in cases where production of the required books or other business records is incomplete. In good time, before the investigation, the Commission shall inform the competent authority of the Member State, in whose territory the same is to be made, of the investigation and the identity of the authorized officials.

3. Undertakings and associations of undertakings shall submit to investigations ordered by decision of the Commission. The decision shall specify the subject matter and purpose of the investigation, appoint the date on which it is to begin and indicate the penalties provided for in Articles 12(1)(c) and 13(1)(d) and the right to have the decision reviewed by the Court of Justice.

4. The Commission shall take the decisions mentioned in paragraph 3 after consultation with the competent authority of the Member State in whose territory the investigation is to be made.

5. Officials of the competent authority of the Member State in whose territory the investigation is to be made may assist the Commission officials in carrying out their duties, at the request of such authorities or of the Commission.

6. Where an undertaking opposes an investigation ordered pursuant to this Article, the Member State concerned shall afford the necessary assistance to the officials authorized by the Commission to enable them to make their investigation. To this end, Member States shall take the necessary measures after consultation of the Commission by 31 July 1989.

Article 12: Fines

1. The Commission may, by decision,

impose fines on undertakings or associations of undertakings of from 100 to 5,000 ECU where, intentionally or negligently:
(a) they supply incorrect or misleading information in connection with an application pursuant to Article 3(2) or Article 5; or
(b) they supply incorrect information in response to a request made pursuant to Article 9(3) or (5), or do not supply information within the time limit fixed by decision adopted under Article 9(5); or
(c) they produce the required books or other business records in complete form during investigations under Article 10 or Article 11, or refuse to submit to an investigation ordered by decision taken pursuant to Article 11(3).

2. The Commission may, by decision, impose fines on undertakings or associations of undertakings of from 1,000 to 1,000,000 ECU, or a sum in excess thereof but not exceeding 10 per cent. of the turnover in the preceding business year of the undertakings participating in the infringement, where either intentionally or negligently they:
(a) infringe Article 85(1) or Article 86 of the Treaty; or
(b) commit a breach of any obligation imposed pursuant to Article 6(1) of this Regulation.
In fixing the amount of the fine, regard shall be had both to the gravity and to the duration of the infringement.

3. Article 8 shall apply.

4. Decisions taken pursuant to paragraphs 1 and 2 shall not be of a penal nature.

5. The fines provided for in paragraph 2(a) shall not be imposed in respect of acts taking place after notification to the Commission and before its decision in application of Article 85(3) of the Treaty, provided they fall within the limits of the activity described in the notification.

However, this provision shall not have effect where the Commission has informed the undertakings or associations of undertakings concerned that, after preliminary examination, it is of the opinion that Article 85(1) of the Treaty applies and that application of Article 85(3) is not justified.

Article 13: Periodic penalty payments

1. By decision, the Commission may impose periodic penalty payments on undertakings or associations of undertakings of from 50 ECU to 1,000 ECU per day, calculated from the date appointed by the decision, in order to compel them:
(a) to put an end to an infringement of Article 85(1) or Article 86 of the Treaty, the termination of which has been ordered pursuant to Article 4 of this Regulation;
(b) to refrain from any act prohibited under Article 6(3);
(c) to supply complete and correct information which has been requested by decision, taken pursuant to Article 9(5);
(d) to submit to an investigation which has been ordered by decision taken pursuant to Article 11(3);
(e) to comply with any measure imposed by decision taken under Article 4a.

2. When the undertakings or association of undertakings have satisfied the obligation which it was the purpose of the periodic penalty payment to enforce, the Commission may fix the total amount of the periodic penalty payment at a lower figure than that which would result from the original decision.

3. Article 8 shall apply.

Article 14: Review by the Court of Justice

The Court of Justice shall have unlimited jurisdiction within the meaning of Article 172 of the Treaty to review decisions whereby the Commission has fixed a fine or periodic penalty payment; it may cancel, reduce or increase the fine or periodic penalty payment imposed.

Article 15: Unit of account

For the purpose of applying Articles 12 to 14, the ECU shall be adopted in drawing up the budget of the Community in accordance with Articles 207 and 209 of the Treaty.

Article 16: Hearing of the parties and of third persons

1. Before refusing the certificate mentioned in Article 3(2), or taking decision as provided for in Articles 4, 4a, 5(3) second subparagraph and 5(4), 6(3), 12 and 13, the Commission shall give the undertakings or associations of undertakings concerned the opportunity of being heard on the matters to which the Commission takes, or has taken, objection.

2. If the Commission or the competent authorities of the Member States consider it necessary, they may also hear other natural or legal persons. Applications by such persons to be heard shall be granted when they show a sufficient interest.

3. When the Commission intends to take a decision pursuant to Article 85(3) of the Treaty, it shall publish a summary of the relevant agreement, decision or concerted practice in the *Official Journal of the European Communities* and invite all interested third parties to submit their observations within a period, not being less than one month, which it shall fix. Publication shall have regard to the legitimate interest of undertakings in the protection of their business secrets.

Article 17: Professional secrecy

1. Information acquired as a result of the application of Articles 9 to 11 shall be used only for the purpose of the relevant request or investigation.

2. Without prejudice to the provisions of Articles 16 and 18, the Commission and the competent authorities of the Member States, their officials and other servants shall not disclose information of a kind covered by the obligation of professional secrecy and which has been acquired by them as a result of the application of this Regulation.

3. The provisions of paragraphs 1 and 2 shall not prevent publication of general information or of surveys which do not contain information relating to particular undertakings or associations of undertakings.

Article 18: Publication of decisions

1. The Commission shall publish the decisions which it adopts pursuant to Articles 3(2), 4, 5(3) second subparagraph, 5(4) and 6(3).

2. The publication shall state the names of the parties and the main contents of the decision; it shall have regard to the legitimate interest of undertakings in the protection of their business secrets.

Article 19: Implementing provisions

The Commission shall have the power to adopt implementing provisions concerning the form, content and other details of complaints pursuant to Article 3, applications pursuant to Articles 3(2) and 5 and the hearings provided for in Article 16(1) and (2).

Article 20: Entry into force

This Regulation shall enter into force on 1 January 1988.

This Regulation shall be binding in its entirety and directly applicable in all Member States.

Done at Brussels, 14 December 1987.

ANNEX

List referred to in Article 2

(a) The introduction or uniform application of mandatory or recommended technical standards for aircraft, aircraft parts, equipment and aircraft supplies, where such standards are set by an organisation normally accorded international recognition, or by an aircraft or equipment manufacturer;

(b) the introduction or uniform application of technical standards for fixed installations for aircraft, where such standards are set by an organisation normally accorded international recognition;

(c) the exchange, leasing, pooling, or maintenance of aircraft, aircraft parts, equipment or fixed installations for the purpose of operating air services and the joint purchase of aircraft parts, provided that such arrangements are made on a non-discriminatory basis;

(d) the introduction, operation and maintenance of technical communication networks, provided that such arrangements are made on a non-discriminatory basis;

(e) the exchange, pooling or training of personnel for technical or operational purposes;

(f) the organisation and execution of substitute transport operations for passengers, mail and baggage, in the event of breakdown/delay of aircraft, either under charter or by provision of substitute aircraft under contractual arrangements;

(g) the organisation and execution of successive supplementary air transport operations, and the fixing and application of inclusive rates and conditions for such operations;

(h) the consolidation of individual consignments;

(i) the establishment or application of uniform rules concerning the structure and the conditions governing the application of transport tariffs, provided that such rules do not directly or indirectly fix transport fares and conditions;
(j) arrangements as to the sale, endorsement and acceptance of tickets between air carriers (interlining) as well as the refund, pro-rating and accounting schemes established for such purposes;
(k) the clearing and settling of accounts between air carriers by means of a clearing house, including such services as may be necessary or incidental thereto; the clearing and settling of accounts between air carriers and their appointed agents by means of a centralised and automated settlement plan or systems, including such services as may be necessary or incidental thereto.

2. Text of Council Regulation 3976/87 (reproduced below)

Council Regulation 3976/87 of December 14, 1987

On the application of Article 85(3) of the Treaty to certain categories of agreements and concerted practices in the air transport sector

([1987] O.J. L374/9)

(As amended by [1990] O.J. L217/15)

THE COUNCIL OF THE EUROPEAN COMMUNITIES,
Having regard to the Treaty establishing the European Economic Community and in particular Article 87 thereof,
Having regard to the proposal from the Commission,
Having regard to the opinions of the European Parliament,
Having regard to the opinions of the Economic and Social Committee,

(1) Whereas Council Regulation No. 3975/87 ([1987] O.J. L374/1) lays down the procedure for the application of the rules on competition to undertakings in the air transport sector; whereas Regulation No. 17 of the Council ([1962] O.J. 13/62) lays down the procedure for the application of these rules to agreements, decisions and concerted practices other than those directly relating to the provision of air transport services;

(2) Whereas Article 85(1) of the Treaty may be declared inapplicable to certain categories of agreements, decisions and concerted practices which fulfil the conditions contained in Article 85(3);

(3) Whereas common provisions for the application of Article 85(3) should be adopted by way of Regulation pursuant to Article 87; whereas, according to Article 87(2)(b), such a Regulation must lay down detailed rules for the application of Article 85(3), taking into account the need to ensure effective supervision, on the one hand, and to simplify administration to the greatest possible extent, on the other; whereas, according to Article 87(2)(d), such a Regulation is required to define the respective functions of the Commission and of the Court of Justice;

(4) Whereas the air transport sector has to date been governed by a network of international agreements, bilateral agreement between States and bilateral and mutilateral agreements between air carriers; whereas the changes required to this international regulatory system to ensure increased competition should be effected gradually so as to provide time for the air-transport sector to adapt;

(5) Whereas the Commission should be enabled for this reason to declare by way of Regulation that the provisions of Article 85(1) do not apply to certain categories of agreements between undertakings, decisions by associations of undertakings and concerted practices;

(6) Whereas it should be laid down under what specific conditions and in what circumstances the Commission may exercise such powers in close and constant liaison with the competent authorities of the Member States;

(7) Whereas it is desirable, in particular, that block exemptions be granted for certain categories of agreements, decisions and concerted practices; whereas these exemptions should be granted for a limited period during which air carriers can adapt to a more competitive environment; whereas the Commission, in close liaison with the Member States, should be able to define precisely the scope of these exemptions and the conditions attached to them;

(8) Whereas there can be no exemption if the conditions set out in Article 85(3) are not satisfied; whereas the Commission should therefore have power to take the appropriate measures where an agreement proves to have effects incompatible with Article 85(3); whereas the Commission should consequently be able first to address recommendations to the parties and then to take decisions;

(9) Whereas this Regulation does not prejudge the application of Article 90 of the Treaty;

(10) Whereas the Heads of State and Government, at their meeting in June 1986, agreed that the internal market in air transport should be completed by 1992 in pursuance of Community actions leading to the strengthening of its economic and social cohesion; whereas the provisions of this Regulation, together with those of Council Directive 87/601 of 14 December 1987 on fares for scheduled air services between Member States ([1987] O.J. L374/1) and those of Council Decision 87/602 of 14 December 1987 on the sharing of passenger capacity between air carriers on scheduled air services between Member States and on access for air carriers to scheduled air service routes between Member States ([1987] O.J. L374/19), are a first step in this direction and the Council will therefore, in order to meet the objective set by the Heads of State and Government, adopt further measures of liberalization at the end of a three year intial period,

HAS ADOPTED THIS REGULATION:

Article 1

This regulation shall apply to international air transport between Community airports.

Article 2

1. Without prejudice to the application of Regulation No. 3975/87 and in accordance with Article 85(3) of the Treaty, the Commission may by regulation declare that Article 85(1) shall not apply to certain categories of agreements between undertakings, decisions of associations of undertakings and concerted practices.

2. The Commission may, in particular adopt such regulations in respect of agreements, decisions or concerted practices which have as their object any of the following:
— joint planning and coordination of the capacity to be provided on scheduled air services, in so far as it helps to ensure a spread of services at the less busy times of the day or during less busy periods or on less busy routes, so long as any partner may withdraw without penalty from such agreements, decisions or concerted practices, and is not required to give more than three months' notice of its intention not to participate in such joint planning and coordination for future seasons,
— sharing of revenue from scheduled air services, so long as the transfer does not exceed 1 per cent. of the poolable revenue earned on a particular route by the transferring partner, no costs are shared or accepted by the transferring partner and the transfer is made in compensation for the loss incurred by the receiving partner in scheduling flights at less busy times of the day or during less busy periods,
— consultations for common preparation of proposals on tariffs, fares and conditions for the carriage of passengers and baggage on scheduled services, on condition that consultations on this matter are voluntary, that air carriers will not be bound by their results and that the Commission and the Member States whose air carriers are concerned may participate as observers in any such consultations,
— slot allocation at airports and airport scheduling, on condition that the air carriers concerned shall be entitled to participate in such arrangements, that the national and mutilateral procedures for such arrangements are transparent and that they take into account any constraints and distribution rules defined by national or international authorities and any rights which air carriers may have historically acquired,
— common purchase, development and operation of computer reservation systems relating to timetabling, reserva-

Book One: Part IX—Sectorial Application of EEC Competition Rules

tions and ticketing by air transport undertakings, on condition that air carriers of Member States have access to such systems on equal terms, that participating carriers have their services listed on a non-discriminatory basis and also that any participant may withdraw from the system on giving reasonable notice,
— technical and operational ground handling at airports, such as aircraft push back, refuelling, cleaning and security,
— handling of passengers, mail, freight and baggage at airports,
— services for the provision of in-flight catering,
[— consultations on cargo rates].

3. Without prejudice to paragraph 2, such Commission regulations shall define the categories of agreements, decisions or concerted practices to which they apply and shall specify in particular:
(a) the restrictions or clauses which may, or may not appear in the agreements, decisions and concerted practices;
(b) the clauses which must be contained in the agreements, decisions and concerted practices, or any other conditions which must be satisfied.

Article 3

Any regulation adopted by the Commission pursuant to Article 2 shall expire on [December 31, 1992].

Article 4

Regulations adopted pursuant to Article 2 shall include a provision that they apply with retroactive effect to agreements, decisions and concerted practices which were in existence at the date of the entry into force of such Regulations.

Article 5

Before adopting a regulation, the Commission shall publish a draft thereof and invite all persons and organizations concerned to submit their comments within such reasonable time limit, being not less than one month, as the Commission shall fix.

Article 6

The Commission shall consult the Advisory Committee on Agreements and Dominant Positions in Air Transport established by Article 8(3) of Regulation No. 3975/87 before publishing a draft Regulation and before adopting a Regulation.

Article 7

1. Where the persons concerned are in breach of a condition or obligation which attaches to an exemption granted by a Regulation as adopted pursuant to Article 2, the Commission may, in order to put an end to such a breach:
— address recommendations to the person concerned, and
— in the event of failure by such persons to observe those recommendations, and depending on the gravity of the breach concerned, adopt a decision that either prohibits them from carrying out, or requires them to perform, specific act or, while withdrawing the benefit of the block exemption which they enjoyed, grants them an individual exemption in accordance with Article 4(2) of Regulation No. 3975/87 or withdraws the benefit of the block exemption which they enjoyed.

2. Where the Commission, either on its own initiative or at the request of a Member State or of natural or legal persons claiming a legitimate interest, finds that in any particular case an agreement, decision or concerted practice to which a block exemption granted by a regulation adopted pursuant to Article 2(2) applies, nevertheless has effects which are incompatible with Article 85(3) or are prohibited by Article 86, it may withdraw the benefit of the block exemption from those agreements, decisions or concerted practices and take, pursuant to Article 13 of Regulation No 3975/87, all appropriate measures for the purposes of bringing these infringements to an end.

3. Before taking a decision under paragraph 2, the Commission may address recommendations for termination of the infringement to the persons concerned.

Article 8

The Council shall decide on the revision of this Regulation by [December 31], 1992 on the basis of a Commission proposal to be submitted by [July 1, 1992].

Article 9

This Regulation shall enter into force on 1 January 1988.
This Regulation shall be binding in its entirety and directly applicable in all Member States.

Done at Brussels, 14 December 1987.

3. Text of Commission Regulation 82/91 (reproduced below)

Commission Regulation 82/91 of December 5, 1990

On the application of Article 85(3) of the Treaty to certain categories of agreements, decisions and concerted practices concerning ground handling services

([1991] O.J. L10/7)

THE COMMISSION OF THE EUROPEAN COMMUNITIES,
Having regard to the Treaty establishing the European Economic Community,
Having regard to Council Regulation (EEC) No. 3976/87 of December 14, 1987 on the application of Article 85(3) of the Treaty to certain categories of agreements and concerted practices in the air transport sector ([1987] O.J. L374/9), as amended by Regulation (EEC) No. 2344/90 ([1990] O.J. L217/15), and in particular Article 2 thereof,
Having published a draft of this Regulation ([1990] O.J. C211/12),
Having consulted the Advisory Committee on Agreements and Dominant Positions in Air Transport,

Whereas:
(1) Regulation (EEC) No. 3976/87 empowers the Commission to apply Article 85(3) of the Treaty by regulation to certain categories of agreements, decisions and concerted practices relating directly or indirectly to the provision of air transport services.

(2) Agreements, decisions or concerted practices concerning ground handling services provided either by aircarriers or specialised enterprises, such as technical and operational ground handling, handling of passengers, mail, freight and baggage, and services for the provision of in-flight catering, are liable in certain circumstances to restrict competition and affect trade between Member States. It is appropriate, in the interests of legal certainty for the undertakings concerned, to define a category of agreements which, although not generally restrictive of competition, may benefit from an exemption in the event that, because of particular economic or legal circumstances, they could fall within the scope of Article 85(1).

(3) Such agreements, decisions or concerted practices may produce economic benefits, in so far as they help to ensure services of a high standard provided with continuity and at reasonable cost, and both the air carriers and air transport users share in those benefits.

(4) However, it is necessary to attach conditions to the exemption of such agreements, decisions and concerted practices to ensure that they do not contain restrictions that are not indispensable for the optimal provision of the services, and that they do not lead to the elimination of competition to provide the services.

(5) The exemption granted by the Regulation must therefore be subject to the condition that the agreements do not oblige air carriers to obtain the services exclusively from a particular supplier, that the supply of the services is not tied to the conclusion of contracts for other goods or services, that each airline is free to choose from the range of services offered by a particular supplier those which best meet its needs, that the rates charged are

reasonable for the services actually provided and that air carriers are free to withdraw from the agreements without penalty upon simple notice of not more than three months to that effect.

(6) In accordance with Article 4 of Regulation (EEC) No. 3976/87, this Regulation should apply with retroactive effect to agreements, decisions and concerted practices in existence on the date of entry into force of this Regulation provided that they meet the conditions for exemption set out in this Regulation.

(7) Under Article 7 of Regulation (EEC) No. 3976/87, this Regulation should also specify the circumstances in which the Commission may withdraw the block exemption in individual cases.

(8) Agreements, decisions and concerted practices that are exempted automatically by this Regulation need not be notified under Council Regulation No. 17. However, when real doubt exists, undertakings may request the Commission to declare whether their agreements comply with this Regulation.

(9) This Regulation is without prejudice to the application of Articles 86 and 90, in particular in situations where there is no competition for the provision of certain ground handling services at an airport,

HAS ADOPTED THIS DECISION:

Article 1

Pursuant to Article 85(3) of the Treaty and subject to Article 3 of this Regulation, it is hereby declared that Article 85(1) of the Treaty shall not apply to agreements, decisions or concerted practices to which only two undertakings are party and which deal only with the supply by one party of services referred to in Article 2 to the other, an air carrier, at an airport in the Community open to international air traffic.

Article 2

The exemption granted under Article 1 shall apply to the following services:

1. all technical and operational services generally provided on the ground at airports, such as the provision of the necessary flight documents and information to crews, apron services, including loading and unloading, safety, aircraft servicing and refuelling, and operations before take-off;

2. all services connected with the handling of passengers, mail, freight and baggage, such as information to passengers and visitors, the handling of passengers and their baggage before departure and after arrival, and the handling and storage of freight and mail in conjunction with the postal services;

3. all services for the provision of in-flight catering, including the preparation, storage and delivery of meals and supplies to aircraft and the maintenance of catering equipment.

Article 3

The exemption shall apply only if:

1. the agreements, decisions or concerted practices do not oblige the air carrier to obtain any or all of the ground handling services referred to in Article 2 exclusively from a particular supplier;

2. the supply of the ground handling services referred to in Article 2 is not tied to the conclusion of contracts for or acceptance of other goods or services which, by their nature or according to commercial usage, have no connection with the services referred to in Article 2 or to the conclusion of a similar contract for supply of services at another airport;

3. the agreements, decisions or concerted practices do not prevent an air carrier from choosing from the range of ground handling services offered by a particular supplier those it wants to take from that supplier and do not deny it the right to procure similar or other services from another supplier or to provide them itself;

4. the supplier of the ground handling services does not impose, directly or indirectly, prices or other conditions which are unreasonable and which, in particular, bear no reasonable rela-

tion to the cost of the services provided;

5. the supplier of the ground handling services does not apply dissimilar conditions to equivalent transactions with different customers;

6. the air carrier is able to withdraw from the agreement with the supplier of the ground handling services without penalty, on giving notice of not more than three months to that effect.

Article 4

The Commission may withdraw the benefit of this Regulation, pursuant to Article 7 of Council Regulation (EEC) No. 3976/87, where it finds in a particular case that an agreement, decision or concerted practice exempted by this Regulation nevertheless has certain effects which are incompatible with the conditions laid down by Article 85(3) or are prohibited by Article 86 of the Treaty.

Article 5

This Regulation shall enter into force on February 1, 1991 and expire on December 31, 1992.

It shall apply with retroactive effect to agreements, decisions and concerted practices in existence when it enters into force, from the time when the conditions of application of this Regulation were fulfilled.

This Regulation shall be binding in its entirety and directly applicable in all Member States.

Done at Brussels, December 5, 1990.

---

4. Text of Commission Regulation 83/91 (reproduced below)

Commission Regulation 83/91 of December 5, 1990

on the application of Article 85(3) of the Treaty to certain categories of agreements between undertakings relating to computer reservation systems for air transport services

([1991] O.J. L10/9)

THE COMMISSION OF THE EUROPEAN COMMUNITIES,

Having regard to the Treaty establishing the European Economic Community.

Having regard to Council Regulation (EEC) No. 3976/87 of December 14, 1987 on the application of Article 85(3) of the Treaty to certain categories of agreements and concerted practices in the air transport sector ([1987] O.J. L374/9), as amended by Regulation (EEC) No. 2344/90, and in particular Article 2 thereof,

Having published a draft of this Regulation ([1990] O.J. C211/7).

Having consulted the Advisory Committee on Agreements and Dominant Positions in Air Transport.

Whereas:

(1) Council Regulation (EEC) No. 3976/87 empowers the Commission to apply Article 85(3) of the Treaty by regulation to certain categories of agreements, decisions and concerted practices relating directly or indirectly to the provision of air transport services.

(2) Agreements for the common purchase, development and operation of computer reservation systems relating to timetable, reservations and Ticketing are liable to restrict competition and affect trade between Member States.

(3) Computer reservation systems (CRS) can render useful services to air carriers, travel agents and air travellers alike by giving ready access to up-to-date and detailed information in particular about flight possibilities, fare options and seat availability. They can also be used to make reservations and in some cases to print tickets and issue boarding passes. They thus help the air traveller to exercise choice on the basis of fuller information in order to meet his travel needs in the optimal manner. However, in order for these

Book One: Part IX—Sectorial Application of EEC Competition Rules

benefits to be obtained, flight schedules and fares displays must be as complete and unbiased as possible.

(4) The CRS market is such that few individual European undertakings could on their own make the investment and achieve the economies of scale required to compete with the more advanced existing systems. Cooperation in this field should therefore be permitted. A block exemption should therefore be granted for such cooperation.

(5) In accordance with Council Regulation (EEC) No. 2299/89 ([1989] O.J. L220/1) concerning the code of conduct for computer reservation systems the cooperation should not allow the parent carriers to create undue advantages for themselves and thereby distort competition. It is therefore necessary to ensure that no discrimination exists between parent carriers and participating carriers with regard in particular to access and neutrality of display. The block exemption should be subject to conditions which will ensure that all air carriers can participate in the systems on a non-discriminatory basis as regards access, display, information loading and fees. Moreover, in order to maintain competition in an oligopolistic market subscribers must be able to switch from one system to another at short notice and without penalty, and system vendors and air carriers must not act in ways which would restrict competition between systems.

(6) In accordance with Article 4 of Regulation (EEC) No. 3976/87 this Regulation should apply with retroactive effect to agreements in existence on the date of entry into force of this Regulation provided that they meet the conditions for exemption set out in this Regulations.

(7) Under Article 7 of Regulation (EEC) No. 3976/87, this Regulation should also specify the circumstances in which the Commission may withdraw the block exemption in individual cases.

(8) The agreements which are exempted automatically by this Regulation need not be notified under Council Regulation No. 17 (J.O. 13/62). However when real doubt exists, undertakings may request the Commission to declare whether their agreements comply with this Regulation.

(9) This Regulation is without prejudice to the application of Article 86 of the Treaty.

HAS ADOPTED THIS REGULATION:

Article 1—Exemptions

Pursuant to Article 85(3) of the Treaty and subject to the conditions set out in Articles 3 to 11 of this Regulation, it is hereby declared that Article 85(1) of the Treaty shall not apply to agreements between undertakings the purpose of which is one or more of the following:

(*a*) to purchase or develop a CRS in common; or

(*b*) to create a system vendor to market and operate the CRS; or

(*c*) to regulate the provisions of distribution facilities by the system vendor or by distributors.

The exemption shall apply only to the following obligations:

(i) an obligation not to engage directly or indirectly in the development, marketing or operation of another CRS;

(ii) an obligation on the system vendor to appoint parent carriers or participating carriers as distributors in respect of all or certain subscribers in a defined area of the common market;

(iii) an obligation on the system vendor to grant a distributor exclusive rights to solicit all or certain subscribers in a defined area of the common market; or

(iv) an obligation on the system vendor not to allow distributors to sell distribution facilities provided by other system vendors.

Article 2—Definitions

For the purposes of this Regulation:
"computer reservation system" (CRS) means a computerised system containing information about, *inter alia,* air carriers schedules, fares, seat availability and related services, and through which reservations can be made or tickets issued or both, to the extent that all or some of these services are made available to subscribers,

"distribution facilities" means facilities provided by a system vendor for the display of information to subscribers about air carrier schedules, fares, seat availability, for making reservations or issuing tickets or both, and for providing any other related services,

"distributor" means an undertaking which is authorised by the system vendor to provide distribution facilities to subscribers, "parent carrier" means an air carrier which is a system vendor or which directly or indirectly, alone or jointly with others, owns or controls a system vendor,

"participating carrier" means an air carrier which has an agreement with a system vendor for the distribution of its services through a CRS. To the extent that a parent carrier uses the distribution facilities of its own CRS, it is considered a participating carrier,

"subscribers" means an undertaking other than a participating carrier, using a CRS within the Community under contract or other arrangement with a system vendor or a distributor for the sale of air transport services to members of the public,

"System vendor" means any entity and its affiliates which is responsible for the operation of a CRS.

Article 3—Access

1. A system vendor offering distribution facilities shall allow any air carrier the opportunity to participate, on an equal and non-discriminatory basis, in these facilities within the available capacity of the system concerned, subject to any technical constraints outside the control of the system vendor.

2. (a) A system vendor shall not
— attach unreasonable conditions to any contract with a participating carrier,
— require the acceptance of supplementary conditions which, by their nature or according to commercial usage, have no connection with participation in its CRS and shall apply the same conditions for the same level of service.
(b) A system vendor shall not make it a condition of participation in its CRS that a participating carrier may not at the same time be a participant in another system.
(c) A participating carrier shall have the right to terminate his contract with a system vendor without penalty on giving notice which need not exceed six months, to expire no earlier than the end of the first year.

3. Loading and processing facilities provided by the system vendor shall be offered to all participating carriers without discrimination.

4. If the system vendor adds any improvement to the distribution facilities provided or the equipment used in the provision of the facilities, it shall offer these improvements to all participating carriers on the same terms and conditions, subject to current technical limitations.

Article 4—Display

1. A system vendor shall provide a principal display and shall include therein data provided by participating carriers on schedules, fares and seats available for individual purchase in a clear and comprehensive manner and without discrimination or bias, in particular as regards the order in which information is presented.

2. A system vendor shall not intentionally or negligently display inaccurate or misleading information and, subject to Article 9(5), in particular:
— the criteria to be used for ranking information shall not be based on any factor directly or indirectly relating to carrier identity and shall be applied on a non-discriminatory basis to all participating carriers,
— no discrimination on the basis of different airports serving the same city shall be exercised in constructing and selecting city-pairs.

Article 5—Information loading

1. Participating carriers and others providing material for inclusion in a CRS shall ensure that the data submitted are comprehensive, accurate, non-misleading and transparent.

2. A system vendor shall not manipulate the material referred to in paragraph 1 in a manner that would lead to inaccurate, misleading or discriminatory information being provided.

3. A system vendor shall load and process data provided by participating carriers with equal care and timeliness subject to the constraints of the loading method selected by individual participating carriers and to the standard formats used by the said vendor.

Article 6—Fees

1. Any fee charged by a system vendor shall be non-discriminatory and reasonably related to the cost of the service provided and used, and shall, in particular, be the same for the same level of service.

2. A system vendor shall, on request, provide to interested parties details of current procedures, fees, systems facilities, editing and display criteria used. However, this provision shall not oblige a system vendor to disclose proprietary information such as software programmes.

3. Any charges to fee levels, conditions or facilities offered and the basis therefore shall be communicated to all participating carriers and subscribers on a non-discriminatory basis.

Article 7—Provision of information

A system vendor shall provide information, statistical or otherwise, generated by its CRS, other than that offered as an integral part of the distribution facilities, only as follows:
(a) information concerning individual bookings shall be made available on an equal basis to the air carrier or air carriers participating in the service covered by the booking;
(b) information in aggregate or anonymous form when made available on request to any carrier shall be offered to all participating air carriers on a non-discriminatory basis;
(c) other information generated by the CRS shall be made available with the consent of the air carrier concerned and subject to any agreement between a system vendor and participating carriers;
(d) personal information concerning a consumer and generated by a travel agent shall be made available to others not involved in the transaction only with the consent of the consumer.

Article 8—Reciprocity

1. The obligations of a system vendor under Articles 3 to 7 shall not apply in respect of a parent carrier of a third country to the extent that its CRS does not conform with this Regulation or does not offer Community air carriers equivalent treatment to that provided under this Regulation.

2. The obligation of parent and participating carriers under Article 10 shall not apply in respect of a CRS controlled by air carriers of a third country to the extent that that parent or participating carrier is not accorded equivalent treatment in that country to that provided under this Regulation.

3. A system vendor or an air carrier proposing to avail itself of the provisions of paragraphs 1 or 2 must notify the Commission of its intentions and the reasons therefore at least 14 days in advance of such action. In exceptional circumstances, the Commission may, at the request of the vendor or the air carrier concerned, grant a waiver from the 14-day rule.

4. Upon receipt of a notification, the Commission shall without delay determine whether discrimination within the meaning of paragraph 1 or 2 exists. If this is found to be the case, the Commission shall so inform all system vendors or the air carriers concerned in the Community as well as Member States. If discrimination within the meaning of paragraph 1 or 2 does not exist, the Commission shall so inform the system vendor or air carriers concerned.

Article 9—Contracts with subscribers

1. A system vendor shall make any of the distribution facilities of a CRS available to any subscriber on a non-discriminatory basis.

2. A system vendor shall not require a subscriber to sign an exclusive contract, nor directly or indirectly prevent a subscriber from subscribing to, or using, any other system or systems.

3. A service enhancement offered to any other subscriber shall be offered by the system vendor to all subscribers on a non-discriminatory basis.

4. A system vendor shall not attach unreasonable conditions to any contract with a subscriber and, in particular, a subscriber may terminate his contract with a system vendor, without penalty, on giving notice which need not exceed three months to expire no earlier than the end of the first year.

5. A system vendor shall ensure, either through technical means or through the contract with the subscriber, that the principal display is provided for each individual transaction and that the subscriber does not manipulate material supplied by CRSs in a manner that would lead to inaccurate, misleading or discriminatory presentation of information to consumers. However, for any one transaction a subscriber may re-order data or use alternative displays to meet a preference expressed by a consumer.

6. A system vendor shall not impose any obligation on a subscriber to accept an offer

Article 10—Relations with subscribers

1. A carrier shall not link the use of CRS of which it is parent or participating carrier by a subscriber with the receipt of any commission or other incentive for the sale of or issue of tickets for any of its air transport products.

2. A carrier shall not require use of CRS of which it is parent or participating carrier by a subscriber for any sale or issue of tickets for any air transport products provided either directly or indirectly by itself.

3. Paragraph 1 and 2 shall be without prejudice to any conditions which an air carrier may require of a travel agent when authorising it to sell and issue tickets for its air transport products.

Article 11—Competition between system vendors

The system vendor shall not enter into any agreement or engage in a concerted practice with other system vendors with the object or effect of partitioning the market.

Article 12

The Commission may withdraw the benefit of this Regulation, pursuant to Article 7 of Regulation (EEC) No. 3976/87, where it finds in a particular case that an agreement exempted by this Regulation nevertheless has certain effects which are incompatible with the conditions laid down by Article 85(3) or which are prohibited by Article 86 of the Treaty, and in particular where:

(i) the agreement hinders the maintenance of effective competition in the market for computer reservation systems;
(ii) the agreement has the effect of restricting competition in the air transport or travel related markets;
(iii) the system vendor directly or indirectly imposes unfair prices, fees or charges on subscribers or on participating carriers;
(iv) the system vendor or distributor refuses to enter into a contract with a subscriber for the use of a CRS without an objective and non-discriminatory reason of a technical or commercial nature;
(v) a parent carrier who holds a dominant position within the common market or in a substantial part of it, refuses to participate in the distribution facilities provided by a competing CRS without an objective and non-discriminatory reason of a technical or commercial nature;
(vi) the system vendor denies participating carriers access to any facilities other than distribution facilities without an objective and non-discriminatory reason of a technical or commercial nature.

Article 13

This Regulation shall enter into force on February 1, 1991 and expire on December 31, 1992.

It shall apply with retroactive effect to agreements which were in existence at the date of its entry into force, from the time when the conditions of application of this Regulation were fulfilled.

This Regulation shall be binding in its entirety and directly applicable in all Member States.

Done at Brussels, December 5, 1990.

---

5. Text of Commission Regulation 84/91 (reproduced overleaf)

Commission Regulation (EEC) No. 84/91 of December 5, 1990

on the application of Article 85(3) of the Treaty to certain categories of agreements, decisions and concerted practices concerning joint planning and coordination of capacity, consultations on passenger and cargo tariffs rates on scheduled air services and slot allocation at airports

([1991] O.J. L10/14)

THE COMMISSION OF THE EUROPEAN COMMUNITIES

Having regard to the Treaty establishing the European Economic Community,

Having regard to Council Regulation (EEC) No. 3976/87 of December 14, 1987 on the application of Article 85(3) to certain categories of agreements, decisions and concerted practices in the air transport sector ([1987] O.J. L374/9), as amended by Regulation (EEC) No. 2344/90 ([1990] O.J. L217/15), and in particular Article 2 thereof,

Having published a draft of this Regulation ([1990] O.J. C211/2).

Having consulted the Advisory Committee on Agreements and Dominant Positions in Air Transport,

Whereas:

(1) Regulation (EEC) No. 3976/87 empowers the Commission to apply Article 85(3) of the Treaty by regulation to certain categories of agreements, decisions or concerted practices relating directly or indirectly to the provision of air transport services.

(2) Agreements, decisions or concerted practices concerning joint planning and coordination of capacity, consultations on tariffs and slot allocation at airports are liable to restrict competition and affect trade between Member States.

(3) Joint planning and coordination of capacity can help ensure the maintenance of services at less busy times of the day, during less busy periods or on less busy routes, and the development of onwards connections thus benefitting air transport users. However, no air carrier should be bound by the results of such planning and coordination but must be free to change its planned services unilaterally. Nor must the planning and coordination prevent carriers deploying extra capacity. Any clauses concerning extra flights must not require the approval of the other parties or involve financial penalties. These arrangements must also allow parties to withdraw from them at reasonably short notice.

(4) Consultations on passenger and cargo tariffs may contribute to the generalised acceptance of interlinable fares and rates to the benefit of aircarriers as well as air transport users. However, consultations must not exceed the lawful purpose of facilitating interlining. Council Regulation (EEC) No. 2342/90 of July 24, 1990 on fares for scheduled air services between Member States ([1990] O.J. L217/1), and the proposed Council Regulation on the operation of scheduled air cargo services between Member States ([1990] O.J. C88/7) are a step towards the increase of price competition in air transport and restrict the possibility of innovative and competitive passenger fares and cargo rates being blocked. Hence, competition may not be eliminated under these arrangements. Consultations on passenger and cargo tariffs between air carriers may therefore be permitted for the present time, provided that the participation in such consultations is optional, that they do not lead to an agreement in respect of fares, rates or related conditions, that in the interests of transparency the Commission and the Member States concerned can send observers to them, and that air carriers participating in the consultation mechanism are obliged to interline with all other carriers concerned, at their own tariffs for the tariff category being discussed;

Where the air carrier wishing to benefit from the obligation to interline applies different tariffs from the airline which effects carriage, it may for that purpose file matching tariffs under Article 3(5) of Regulation (EEC) No. 2342/90.

(5) Arrangements on slot allocation at airports and airport scheduling can improve the utilisation of airport capacity and airspace, facilitate air traffic control and help spread out the supply of air transport services from the airport. However, for competition not to be eliminated, entry to congested airports must remain possible. In order to provide a satisfactory degree of security and transparency, such arrange-

ments can only be accepted if all the air carriers concerned can participate in the negotiations, and if the allocation is made on a non-discriminatory and transparent basis.

(6) In accordance with Article 4 of Regulation (EEC) No. 3976/87, this Regulation should apply with retroactive effect to agreements, decisions and concerted practices in existence on the date of entry into force of this Regulation provided that they meet the conditions for exemption set out in this Regulation.

(7) Under Article 7 of Regulation (EEC) No. 3976/87, this Regulation should also specify the circumstances in which the Commission may withdraw the block exemption in individual cases.

(8) No application under Articles 3 or 5 of Council Regulation (EEC) No. 3975/87 ([1987] O.J. L374/1) need be made in respect of agreements automatically exempted by this Regulation. However, when real doubt exists, undertakings may request the Commission to declare whether their agreements comply with this Regulation.

(9) This regulation is without prejudice to the application of Article 86 of the Treaty,

HAS ADOPTED THIS REGULATION:

TITLE I: EXEMPTIONS

Article 1

Pursuant to Article 85(3) of the Treaty and subject to the provisions of this Regulation, it is hereby declared that Article 85(1) of the treaty shall not apply to agreements between undertakings in the air transport sector, decisions by associations of such undertakings and concerted practices between such undertakings which have as their purpose one or more of the following:
— joint planning and coordination of the capacity to be provided on scheduled international air services between Community airports,
— the holding of consultations on tariffs for the carriage of passengers, with their baggage, and of freight on scheduled international air services between Community airports; or
— slot allocation and airport scheduling in so far as they concern international air services between airports in the Community.

TITLE II: SPECIAL PROVISIONS

Article 2—Special provisions for joint planning and coordination of capacity

The exemption concerning joint planning and coordination of the capacity to be provided on scheduled air services shall apply only if:

(*a*) the agreements, decisions and concerted practices do not bind air carriers to the results of the planning and coordination;

(*b*) the planning and coordination are intended to ensure a satisfactory supply of services at less busy times of the day, during less busy periods or on less busy routes, or to establish schedules which will facilitate connections for passengers or freight between services operated by the participants;

(*c*) the agreements, decisions and concerted practices do not include arrangements such as to limit, directly or indirectly, the capacity to be provided by the participants or to share capacity;

(*d*) the agreements, decisions and concerted practices do not prevent carriers taking part in the planning and coordination from changing their planned services, both with respect to capacity and schedules, without incurring penalties and without being required to obtain the approval of the other participants;

(*e*) the agreements, decisions and concerted practices do not prevent carriers from withdrawing from the planning and coordination for future seasons without penalty, on giving notice of not more than three months to that effect;

(*f*) the agreements, decisions and concerted practices do not seek to influence the capacity provided or schedules adopted by carriers not participating in them.

Article 3—Special provisions for consultations on passenger and cargo tariffs

1. The exemption concerning the holding of consultations on passenger and cargo tariffs shall apply only if:

(a) the participants only discuss passenger or cargo tariffs to be paid by air transport users directly to a participating air carrier or to its authorised agents, for carriage as passengers or for the airport-to-airport transport of freight on a scheduled service. The consultations shall not extend to the capacity for which such tariffs are to be available;

(b) the consultations are intended to arrange interlining, i.e. any air carrier participating in the consultations, in respect of the types of tariffs or rates and of the seasons which were the subject of the consultations, grants other air carriers which in accordance with paragraph (d) are entitled to participate in the consultations, the authority:

  (i) to issue or complete transportation documents for carriage over its routes within the Community in accordance with its own tariffs and with other applicable provisions, and
  (ii) to effect changes to its transportation documents for carriage over its routes within the Community in accordance with generally applicable procedures,

provided that an air carrier may refuse to grant this authority for objective and non-discriminatory reasons of a technical or commercial nature, in particular concerned with the creditworthiness of the air carrier to whom this authority is refused of which that carrier must be notified in writing;

(c) the passenger or cargo tariffs which are the subject of the consultations are applied by participating air carriers without discrimination on grounds of passengers' nationality or place of residence or on grounds of origin of the freight within the Community;

(d) participation in the consultations is voluntary and open to any air carrier who operates or has applied to operate direct or indirect services on the route concerned, including air carriers entitled to exercise fifth-freedom traffic rights in accordance with Article 8 of Council Regulation (EEC) No. 2343/90 ([1990] O.J. L217/8);

(e) the consultations are not binding on participants, that is to say, following the consultations the participants retain the right to act independently in respect of passenger and cargo tariffs;

(f) the consultations do not entail agreement on agents' remuneration or other elements of the tariffs discussed;

(g) in respect of each passenger tariff which was the subject of the consultation, each participant informs the Commission without delay of its submission to the aeronautical authorities of the Member States concerned.

2. (a) The Commission and the Member States concerned shall be entitled to send observers to tariff consultations, whether bilateral or multilateral. For this purpose, air carriers shall give the Member States concerned and the Commission the same notice as is given to participants, but not less than 10 days' notice, of the date, venue and subject-matter of the consultations.
(b) Such notice shall be given:
  (i) to the Member States concerned according to procedures to be established by the competent authorities of those Member States;
  (ii) to the Commission according to procedures to be published from time to time in the *Official Journal of the European Communities.*
(c) A full report on these consultations shall be submitted to the Commission by or on behalf of the air carriers involved at the same time as it is submitted to participants, but not later than six weeks after these consultations were held.

Article 4—Special provisions for slot allocation and airport scheduling

Article 4 will be reconsidered by the Commission in the light of progress in the consideration by the Council of common rules on slot allocation.

1. The exemption concerning slot allocation and airport scheduling shall apply only if:
(a) the consultations on slot allocation and airport scheduling are open to all air carriers having expressed an interest in the slots which are the subject of the consultations;

(b) rules of priority are established which neither directly nor indirectly relate to carrier identity or nationality or category of service, take into account constraints or air traffic distribution rules laid down by competent national or international authorities and give due consideration to the needs of the travelling public and of the airport concerned. Such rules of priority may take account of rights acquired by air carriers through the use of particular slots in the previous corresponding season;

(c) the rules of priority established are made available on request to any interested party;

(d) the rules are applied without discrimination, that is to say that, subject to the rules, each carrier shall have an equal right to slots for its services;

(e) new entrants have priority in the allocation of at least 50 per cent. of newly created or unused slots; this priority may be limited to a maximum of at least four slots per carrier on any day.

For the purpose of this point, 'new entrant' means an air carrier
  (i) not holding more than three slots on a day at an airport and requesting further slots at that airport for services on intra-Community routes during that day, or
  (ii) not holding more than 30 per cent. of slots held by all carriers on a day at an airport or at other airports in the same airport system, and requesting further slots at that airport during that day to commence a service falling within the sphere of application of Regulation (EEC) No. 2343/90 on an intra-Community route on which at most two other air carriers ar exercising third-or fourth-freedom traffic rights between the airports concerned during that day.

and hich does not obtain these slots within three hours of the time requested through the normal allocation process;

(f) air carriers participating in the consultations have access, at the latest at the time of the consultations, to information relating to:
— historical slots by air carrier and chronologically for all air carriers,
— requested slots (initial submissions) by air carriers and chronologically for all air carriers,
— allocated slots, and outstanding slot requests if different, by air carrier and chronologically for all air carriers,
— remaining slots available,
— comparisons between requested slots and allocated slots by time interval and by carrier,
— full details on the constraints being used in allocation.

If a request for slots is not accepted, the air carrier concerned shall be entitled to a statement of the reasons therefore.

2. (a) The Commission and the Member States concerned shall be entitled to send observers to consultations on slot allocation and airport scheduling held in the context of a multilateral meeting in advance of each season. For this purpose, air carriers shall give the Member States concerned and the Commission the same notice as is given to participants, but not less than 10 days' notice, of the date, venue and subject-matter of consultations.

(b) Such notice shall be given
  (i) to the Member States concerned according to procedures to be established by the competent authorities of those Member States;
  (ii) to the Commission according to procedures to be published from time to time in the *Official Journal of the European Communities*.

TITLE III: MISCELLANEOUS PROVISIONS

Article 5

The Commission may withdraw the benefit of this Regulation, pursuant to Article 7 of Regulation (EEC) No. 3976/87, where it finds in a particular case that an agreement, decision or concerted practice exempted by this Regulation nevertheless has certain effects which are incompatible with the conditions laid down by Article 85(3) or are prohibited by Article 86 of the Treaty, and in particular where:
  (i) tariff consultations lead to the absence of price competition on any route or group of routes;
  (ii) the operation of Article 4 has not enabled new entrants to obtain such slots as may be required at a congested airport in order to establish schedules which enable these carriers to compete effectively with incumbent carriers on any route to and from that airport and competition on those routes is thereby substantially impaired. In such cases the withdrawal of the benefit of this

Book One: Part IX—Sectorial Application of EEC Competition Rules

Regulation shall be in respect of the slot allocation at the airport in question.

Article 6

This Regulation shall enter into force on February 1, 1991 and expire on December 31, 1992.

It shall apply with retroactive effect to agreements, decisions and concerted practices in existence when it enters into force, from the time when the conditions of application of this Regulation were fulfilled.

This Regulation shall be binding in its entirety and directly applicable in all Member States.

Done at Brussels, December 5, 1990.

6. Text of Commission Regulation 4261/88 (reproduced below)

Commission Regulation 4261/88 of December 16, 1988

On the complaints, applications and hearings provided for in Council Regulation 3975/87 laying down the procedure for the application of the rules on competition to undertakings in the air transport sector

([1988] O.J. L376/10)

THE COMMISSION OF THE EUROPEAN COMMUNITIES,

Having regard to the Treaty establishing the European Economic Community,

Having regard to Council Regulation No. 3975/87 of 14 December 1987 laying down the procedure for the application of the rules on competition to undertakings in the air transport sector ([1987] O.J. L374/1), and in particular Article 19 thereof,

Having regard to the opinion of the Advisory Committee on Agreements and Dominant Positions in Air Transport,

(1) Whereas, pursuant to Article 19 of Regulation No. 3975/87, the Commission is empowered to adopt implementing provisions concerning the form, content and other details of complaints pursuant to Article 3(1) and of applications pursuant to Articles 3(2) and 5 and the hearings provided for in Article 16(1) and (2) of that Regulation;

(2) Whereas complaints pursuant to Article 3(1) of Regulation No 3975/87 may make it easier for the Commission to take action for infringement of Articles 85 and 86 of the EEC Treaty in the field of air transport; whereas it would consequently seem appropriate to make the procedure for submitting complaints as simple as possible; whereas it is appropriate, therefore, to provide for complaints to be submitted in one written copy, the form, content and details being left to the discretion of the complainants;

(3) Whereas the submission of the applications pursuant to Articles 3(2) and 5 of Regulation No. 3975/87 may have important legal consequences for each undertaking which is a party to an agreement, decision or concerted practice; whereas each undertaking should, therefore, have the right to submit such applications to the Commission; whereas, on the other hand, if an undertaking makes use of that right, it must so inform the other undertakings which are parties to the agreement,

decision or concerted practice, in order that they may protect their interests;

(4) Whereas it is for the undertakings and associations of undertakings to inform the Commission of the facts and circumstances in support of the applications submitted in accordance with Articles 3(2) and 5 of Regulation No. 3975/87;

(5) Whereas it is desirable to prescribe that forms be used for applications in order, in the interest of all concerned, to simplify and expedite examination thereof by the competent departments;

(6) Whereas in most cases the Commission will in the course of the procedure for the hearings provided for in Article 16(1) and (2) of Council Regulation No. 3975/87 already be in close touch with the participating undertakings or associations of undertakings and they will accordingly have the opportunity of making known their views regarding the objections raised against them;

(7) Whereas in accordance with Article 16(1) and (2) of Regulation No. 3975/87 and with the rights of the defence, the undertakings and associations of undertakings concerned must have the right on conclusion of the procedure to submit their comments on the whole of the objections raised against them which the Commission proposes to deal with in its decisions;

(8) Whereas persons other than the undertakings or associations of undertakings which are involved in the procedure may have an interest in being heard; whereas, by the second sentence of Article 16(2) of Regulation No. 3975/87, such persons must have the opportunity of being heard if they apply and show that they have a sufficient interest;

(9) Whereas it is desirable to enable persons who pursuant to Article 3(1) of Regulation No. 3975/87 have lodged a complaint to submit their comments where the Commission considers that on the basis of the information in its possession there are insufficient grounds for action;

(10) Whereas the various persons entitled to submit comments must do so in writing, both in their own interest and in the interests of good administration, without prejudice to an oral procedure where appropriate to supplement the written procedure;

(11) Whereas it is necessary to define the rights of persons who are to be heard, and in particular the conditions upon which they may be represented or assisted and the setting and calculation of time limits;

(12) Whereas the Advisory Committee on Restrictive Practices and Dominant Positions in Air Transport delivers its opinion on the basis of a preliminary draft decision; whereas it must therefore be consulted concerning a case after the inquiry in that case has been completed; whereas such consultation does not prevent the Commission from re-opening an inquiry if need be,

HAS ADOPTED THIS REGULATION:

SECTION I: COMPLAINTS AND APPLICATIONS

Article 1: Complaints

1. Complaints pursuant to Article 3(1) of Regulation No. 3975/87 shall be submitted in writing in one of the official languages of the Community, their form, content and other details being left to the discretion of complainants.

2. Complaints may be submitted by:
(*a*) Member States
(*b*) natural or legal persons who claim a legitimate interest.

3. When representatives of undertakings, of associations of undertakings, or of natural or legal persons sign such complaints, they shall produce written proof that they are authorised to act.

Article 2: Persons entitled to submit applications

1. Any undertakings which is party to agreements, decisions or practices of the kind described in Articles 85(1) and 86 of the Treaty may submit an application under Articles 3(2) and 5 of Regulation No. 3975/87. Where the application is submitted by some but not all of the undertakings concerned, they shall give notice to the others.

Book One: Part IX—Sectorial Application of EEC Competition Rules

2. Where applications under Articles 3(2) and 5 of Regulation No. 3975/87 are signed by representatives of undertakings, of associations of undertakings, or of natural or legal persons, such representatives shall produce written proof that they are authorised to act.

3. Where a joint application is submitted, a joint representative shall be appointed.

Article 3: Submission of applications

1. Applications pursuant to Articles 3(2) and 5 of Regulation No. 3975/87 shall be submitted on Form AER shown in Annex 1.

2. Several participating undertakings may submit an application on a single form.

3. Applications shall contain the information requested in the form.

4. Fourteen copies of each application and of the supporting documents shall be submitted to the Commission.

5. The supporting documents shall be either originals or copies. Copies must be certified as true copies of the original.

6. Applications shall be in one of the official languages of the Community. Supporting documents shall be submitted in their original language. Where the original language is not one of the official languages, a translation in one of the official languages shall be attached.

7. The date of submission of an application shall be the date on which it is received by the Commission. Where, however, the application is sent by registered post, it shall be deemed to have been received on the date shown on the postmark of the place of posting.

8. Where an application submitted pursuant to Articles 3(2) and 5 of Regulation No. 3975/87 falls outside the scope of that Regulation, the Commission shall without delay inform the applicant that it intends to examine the application under the provisions of such other Regulation as is applicable to the case; however, the date of submission of the application shall be the date resulting from paragraph 7. The Commission shall inform the applicant of its reasons and fix a period for him to submit any comments in writing before it conducts its appraisal pursuant to the provisions of that other Regulation.

SECTION II: HEARINGS

Article 4

Before consulting the Advisory Committee on Agreements and Dominant Positions in Air Transport, the Commission shall hold a hearing pursuant to Article 16(1) of Regulation No. 3975/87.

Article 5

1. The Commission shall inform undertakings and associations of undertakings in writing of the objections raised against them. The communication shall be addressed to each of them or to a joint agent appointed by them.

2. The Commission may inform the parties by giving notice in the *Official Journal of the European Communities*, if from the circumstances of the case this appears appropriate, in particular where notice is to be given to a number of undertakings but no joint agent has been appointed. The notice shall have regard to the legitimate interest of the undertakings in the protection of their business secrets.

3. A fine or a periodic penalty payment may be imposed on an undertaking or association of undertakings only if the objections were notified in the manner provided for in paragraph 1.

4. The Commission shall, when giving notice of objections, fix a period within which the undertakings and associations of undertakings may inform the Commission of their views.

Article 6

1. Undertakings and associations of undertakings shall, within the appointed period, make known in writing their views concerning the objections raised against them.

2. They may in their written comments set out all matters relevant to their defence.

3. They may attach any relevant documents in proof of the facts set out. They may also propose that the Commission hear persons who may corroborate those facts.

Article 7

The Commission shall in its decision deal

only with those objections raised against undertakings and associations of undertakings in respect of which they have been afforded the opportunity of making known their views.

Article 8

If natural or legal persons showing a sufficient interest apply to be heard pursuant to Article 16(2) of Regulation No. 3975/87 the Commission shall afford them the opportunity of making known their views in writing within such period as it shall fix.

Article 9

Where the Commission, having received a complaint pursuant to Article 3(1) of Regulation No. 3975/87 considers that on the basis of the information in its possession there are insufficient grounds for acting on the complaint, it shall inform the persons who submitted the complaint of its reasons and fix a period for them to submit any further comments in writing.

Article 10

1. The Commission shall afford to persons who have so requested in their written comments the opportunity to put forward their arguments orally, if those persons show a sufficient interest or if the Commission proposes to impose on them a fine or periodic penalty payment.

2. The Commission may likewise afford to any other person the opportunity of orally expressing his views.

Article 11

1. The Commission shall summon the persons to be heard to attend on such date as it shall appoint.

2. It shall forthwith transmit a copy of the summons to the competent authorities of the Member States, who may appoint an official to take part in the hearing.

Article 12

1. Hearings shall be conducted by the persons appointed by the Commission for that purpose.

2. Persons summoned to attend shall either appear in person or be represented by legal representatives or by representatives authorised by their constitution. Undertakings and associations of undertakings may moreover be represented by a duly authorized agent appointed from among their permanent staff.

Persons heard by the Commission may be assisted by lawyers or university teachers who are entitled to plead before the Court of Justice of the European Communities in accordance with Article 17 of the Protocol on the Statute of the Court, or by other qualified persons.

3. Hearings shall not be public. Persons shall be heard separately or in the presence of other persons summoned to attend. In the latter case, regard shall be had to the legitimate interest of the undertakings in the protection of their business secrets.

4. The essential content of the statements made by each person heard shall be recorded in minutes which shall be read and approved by him.

Article 13

Without prejudice to Article 5(2), information and summonses from the Commission shall be sent to the addressees by registered letter with acknowledgement of receipt, or shall be delivered by hand against receipt.

Article 14

1. In fixing the periods provided for in Articles 3(8), 5, 8 and 9, the Commission shall have regard both to the time required for preparation of comments and to the urgency of the case. A period shall not be less than two weeks; it may be extended.

2. Periods shall run from the day following receipt of a communication or delivery thereof by hand.

3. Written comments must reach the Commission or be dispatched by registered letter before expiry of the period. Where

Book One: Part IX—Sectorial Application of EEC Competition Rules

the period would expire on a Sunday or a public holiday, it shall be extended up to the end of the next following working day. For the purpose of calculating the extension, public holidays shall, in cases where the relevant date is the date of receipt of written comments, be those set out in Annex II to this Regulation, and in cases where the relevant date is the date of dispatch, those appointed by law in the country of dispatch.

Article 15

This Regulation shall enter into force on the day following its publication in the *Official Journal of the European Communities*.

This Regulation shall be binding in its entirety and directly applicable in all Member States.

Done at Brussels, 16 December 1988.

7. Annexes I and II to Commission Regulation 4261/88 (reproduced opposite)

Part IX—5 Air Transport

Annexes to Commission Regulation 4261/88

ANNEX I

This form must be accompanied by an Annex containing the information specified in the attached Complementary Note.

The form and Annex must be supplied in fourteen copies (two for the Commission and one for each Member State). Supply three copies of any relevant agreement and one copy of other supporting documents.

Please do not forget to complete the Acknowledgement of Receipt annexed.

If space is insufficient, please use extra pages, specifying to which item on the form they relate.

FORM AER

TO THE COMMISSION OF THE EUROPEAN COMMUNITIES

Directorate-General for Competition,
200 Rue de la Loi,
B-1049 Brussels.

A. Application for negative clearance pursuant to Article 3(2) of Council Regulation 3975/87 of 14 December 1987 relating to implementation of Article 85(1) or of Article 86 of the Treaty establishing the European Economic Community.

B. Application under Article 5 of Council Regulation 3975/87 of 14 December 1987 with a view to obtaining a decision under Article 85(3) of the Treaty establishing the European Economic Community.

Identity of the parties

1. *Identity of applicant*

    Full name and address, telephone, telex and facsimile numbers, and brief description of the undertaking(s) or association(s) of undertakings submitting the application.

    For partnerships, sole traders or any other unincorporated body trading under a business name, give, also, the name, forename(s) and address of the proprietor(s) or partner(s).

    Where an application is submitted on behalf of some other person (or is submitted by more than one person) the name, address and position of the representative (or joint representative) must be given, together with proof of his authority to act. Where an aplication or notification is submitted by or on behalf of more than one person they should appoint a joint representative (Article 2(2) and (3) of Commission Regulation No. 4261/88).

2. *Identity of any other parties*

Full name and address and brief description of any other parties to the agreement, decision or concerted practice (hereinafter referred to as 'the arrangements').

State what steps have been taken to inform these other parties of this application.

(This information is not necessary in respect of standard contracts which an undertaking submitting the application has concluded or intends to conclude with a number of parties.

Purpose of this application *(Please answer yes or*
(see Complementary Note) *no to the questions)*

Are you asking for negative clearance alone? (See Complementary Note—Section IV, end of first paragraph—for the consequence of such a request.)

Are you applying for negative clearance, and also applying for a decision under Article 85(3) in case the Commission does not grant negative clearance?

Are you only applying for a decision under Article 85(3)?

Would you be satisfied with a comfort letter? (See the end of Section VII of the Complementary Note).

The undersigned declare that the information given above and in the ... pages annexed hereto is correct to the best of their knowledge and belief, that all estimates are identified as such and are their best estimates of the underlying facts and that all the opinions expressed are sincere. They are aware of the provisions of Article 12(1)(a) of Regulation 3975/87 (see attached Complementary Note).

Place and date: ....

Signatures: ....

....

....

Part IX—5 Air Transport

COMMISSION Brussels ....
OF THE
EUROPEAN COMMUNITIES

Directorate-General for Competition

To

ACKNOWLEDGEMENT OF RECEIPT

(This form will be returned to the address inserted above if the top half is completed in a single copy by the person lodging it)

Your application dated: ....

concerning: ....

Your reference: ....

Parties:

1. ....

2. ....and others
(There is no need to name the other undertakings party to the arrangement)

(To be completed by the Commission.)

was received on: ....

and registered under No IV/AER/ ....

Please quote the above number in all correspondence

Book One: Part IX—Sectorial Application of EEC Competition Rules

COMPLEMENTARY NOTE

Contents

I   Purpose of Community rules on competition
II Negative Clearance
III Decisions applying Article 85(3)
IV Purpose of the forms
V   Nature of the forms
VI The need for complete and accurate information
VII Subsequent procedure
VIII Secrecy
IX Further information and headings to be used in Annex to forms

Annex 1: Text of Articles 85 and 86 of the EEC Treaty
Annex 2: List of relevant Acts
Annex 3: List of Member States and Commission Press and Information Offices within the Community

Additions or alterations to the information given in these Annexes will be published by the Commission from time to time.
NB: Any undertaking uncertain about how to complete an application or wishing further explanation may contact the Director-General for Competition (DG IV) in Brussels. Alternatively, any Commission Information Office (those in the Community are listed in Annex 3) will be able to obtain guidance or indicate an official in Brussels who speaks the preferred official Community language.

I. Purpose of Community rules on competition

The purpose of these rules is to prevent the distortion of competition in the common market by monopolies or restrictive practices; they apply to any enterprise trading directly or indirectly in the common market wherever established. Article 85(1) of the Treaty establishing the European Economic Community (the text of Articles 85 and 86 is reproduced in Annex I to this note) prohibits restrictive agreements or concerted practices which may affect trade between Member States, and Article 85(2) declares contracts or otherwise legally binding arrangements containing such restrictions void (although the European Court of Justice has held that if restrictive terms of contracts are severable, only those terms are void); Article 85(3), however, gives the Commission power to exempt practices with beneficial effects. Article 86 prohibits the abuse of a dominant position. The original procedures for implementing these Articles, which provide for "negative clearance" and a declaration applying Article 85(3), were laid down for the maritime transport sector in Regulation No. 4056/86 and for the air transport sector in Regulation No. 3975/87 (the references to these and all other acts mentioned in this note or relevant to applications made on the Forms are listed in Annex 2 to this note).

II. Negative Clearance

The negative clearance procedure has been provided only for the air transport sector. Its purpose is to allow businesses ("undertakings") to ascertain whether or not the Commission considers that any of their arrangements or behaviour are prohibited under Articles 85(1) or 86 of the Treaty. (It is governed by Article 3 of Regulation No. 3975/87.) Clearance takes the form of a decision by the Commission certifying that, *on the basis of the facts in its possession*, there are no grounds under Articles 85(1) or 86 of the Treaty for action on its part in respect of the arrangements or behaviour.

Any party may apply for negative clearance, even without the consent (but not without the knowledge) of other parties to arrangements. There would be little point in applying, however, where arrangements or behaviour clearly do not fall within the scope of Article

85(1) or Article 86. Nor is the Commission obliged to give negative clearance—Article 3(2) of Regulation (EEC) No. 3975/87 states that " ... the Commission may certify. ... " The Commission does not usually issue negative clearance decisions in cases which, in its opinion, so clearly do not fall within the scope of the prohibition of Article 85(1) that there is no reasonable doubt for it to resolve by such a decision.

III. Decision applying Article 85(3)

The application for a decision applying Article 85(3) allows undertakings to enter into arrangements which, in fact, offer economic advantages even though they restrict competition. (It is governed by Articles 12 and 13 of Regulation No. 4056/86 and 4, 5 and 6 of Regulation No. 3975/87.) Upon such application the Commission may take a decision declaring Article 85(1) to be inapplicable to the arrangements described in the decision. The Commission is required to specify the period of validity of any such decision, it can attach conditions and obligations and it can amend or revoke decisions or prohibit specified acts by the parties in certain circumstances notably if the decisions were based on incorrect information or if there is any material change in the facts.

Any party may submit an application even without the consent (but not without the knowledge) of other parties.

Regulation No. 4056/86 and No. 3975/87 provide for an "opposition procedure" under which applications can be handled expeditiously. If an application is admissible under the relevant Regulation, if it is complete and if the arrangement which is the subject of the application has not given rise to a complaint or to an own-initiation proceeding, the Commission publishes a summary of the request in the *Official Journal of the European Communities* and invites comments from interested third parties and from Member States. Unless the Commission notifies applicants within 90 days of the date of such publication that there are serious doubts as to the applicability of Article 85(3) the arrangement will be deemed exempt from the time already elapsed and for a maximum of six years from the date of publication. Where the Commission does notify applicants that there are serious doubts, the applicable procedure is outlined in point VII of this Complementary Note.

In the air transport sector, the Commission intends to adopt a number of Regulations declaring that Article 85(1) does not apply to categories of agreements.

A decision applying Article 85(3) may have retroactive effect. Should the Commission find that arrangements in respect of which the application was submitted are indeed prohibited by Article 85(1) and cannot benefit from the application of Article 85(3) and, therefore, take a decision condemning them, the parties are nevertheless protected, from the date of application, against fines for any infringement described in the application (Articles 19(4) of Regulation No. 4056/86 and 12(5) of Regulation No. 3975/87).

IV. Purpose of the forms

The purpose of Form AER is to allow undertakings, or associations of undertakings, wherever situated, to apply to the Commission for negative clearance for arrangements or behaviour, or to apply to have them exempted from the prohibition of Article 85(1) of the Treaty by virtue of Article 85(3). The form allows undertakings applying for negative clearance to apply, at the same time, in order to obtain a decision applying Article 85(3). It should be noted that only an application in order to obtain a decision applying Article 85(3) affords immunity from fines. Form MAR only provides for an application for a decision under Article 85(3).

To be valid, applications in respect of maritime transport must be made on Form MAR (by virtue of Article 4 of Regulation No. 4260/88 and in respect of air transport on Form AER (by virtue of Article 3 of Regulation No. 4261/88).

V. Nature of the Forms

The forms consist of a single sheet calling for the identity of the applicant(s) and of any other parties. This must be supplemented by further information given under the headings and references detailed below (see IX). For preference the paper used should be A5 (21 ×

29.7 cm—the same size as the form) but must not be bigger. Leave a margin of at least 25 mm or one inch on the left hand side of the page and, if you use both sides, on the right hand side of the reverse.

VI. The need for complete and accurate information

It is important that applicants give all the relevant facts. Although the Commission has the right to seek further information from applicants or third parties, and is obliged to publish a summary of the application before granting negative clearance or a decision applying Article 85(3), it will usually base its decision on the information provided by the applicant. Any decision taken on the basis of incomplete information could be without effect in the case of a negative clearance, or voidable in that of a declaration applying Article 85(3). For the same reason it is also important to inform the Commission of any material changes to your arrangements made after your application.

Complete information is of particular importance in order to benefit from the application of Article 85(3) by means of the opposition procedure. This procedure can only apply where the Commission "is in possession of all the available evidence."

Moreover, you should be aware that Article 19(1)(a) of Regulation No. 4056/86 and 12(1)(a) of Regulation No. 3975/87 enable the Commission to impose fines of from Ecu 100 to Ecu 5 000 [The value of the European Currency Unit (Ecu) is published daily in the C series of the *Official Journal of the European Communities*] on undertakings or associations of undertakings where, intentionally or negligently, they supply incorrect or misleading information in connection with an application.

The key words here are "incorrect or misleading information." However, it often remains a matter of judgement how much detail is relevant; the Commission accepts estimates where accurate information is not readily available in order to facilitate applications; and the Commission calls for opinions as well as facts.

You should therefore note that the Commission will use these powers only where applicants have, intentionally or negligently, provided false information or grossly inaccurate estimates or suppressed readily available information or estimates, or have deliberately expressed false opinions in order to obtain negative clearance or a declaration applying Article 85(3).

VII. Subsequent procedure

The application is registered in the Registry of the Directorate-General for Competition (DG IV). The date of receipt by the Commission (or the date of posting if sent by registered post) is the effective date of the submission. The application might be considered invalid if obviously incomplete or not on the obligatory form.

Further information might be sought from the applicants or from third parties, and suggestions might be made as to amendments to the arrangements that might make them acceptable.

An application for a decision under Article 85(3) may be opposed by the Commission either because the Commission does not agree that the arrangements should benefit from Article 85(3) or to allow for more information to be sought.

If, after examination, the Commission intends to issue a decision applying Article 85(3), it is obliged to publish a summary of the application in the *Official Journal of the European Communities* and invite comments from third parties. Subsequently, a preliminary draft Decision has to be submitted to and discussed with the Advisory Committee on Restrictive Practices and Dominant Positions in Air Transport or in Maritime Transport—they will already have received a copy of the application. Only then, and providing nothing has happened to change the Commission's intention, can it adopt a decision.

Sometimes files are closed without any formal decision being taken, for example because it is found that the arrangements are already covered by a block exemption, or because the applicants are satisfied by a less formal letter from the Commission's departments (sometimes called a "comfort letter") indicating that the arrangements do not call for any action by the Commission, at least in present circumstances. Although not a Commission decision, a comfort letter indicates how the Commission's departments view the case on the facts currently in their possession which means that the Commission could if necessary—if, for example, it were to be asserted that a contract was void under Article 85(2)—take an appropriate decision.

VIII. Secrecy

The Commission and Member States are under a duty to disclose information of the kind covered by the obligation of professional secrecy. On the other hand the Commission has to publish a summary of your application, should it intend to grant it, before the relevant decision. In this publication, the Commission " . . . shall have regard to the legitimate interest of undertakings in the protection of their business secrets." In this connection, if you believe that your interests would be harmed if any of the information you are asked to supply were to be published or otherwise divulged to other parties, please put all such information in a second annex, with each page clearly marked "Business Secrets"; in the principal annex, under any affected heading state "see second annex" or "also see second annex"; in the second annex repeat the affected heading(s) and reference(s) and give the information you do not wish to have published, together with your reasons for this. Do not overlook the fact that the Commssion may have to publish a summary of your application.

Before publishing a summary of your application, the Commission will show the undertakings concerned a copy of the proposed text.

IX. Further information and headings to be used in the Annex to the forms

The further information is to be given under the following headings and reference numbers. Wherever possible, give exact information. If this is not readily available, give your best estimate, and identify what you give as an estimate. If you believe any detail asked for to be unavailable or irrelevant, please explain why. This may, in particular, be the case if one party is notifying arrangements alone without the cooperation of other parties. Do not overlook the fact that Commission officials are ready to discuss what detail is relevant (see the *nota bene* at the beginning of this complementary note).

1. *Brief description*

Give a brief description of the arrangements or behaviour (nature, purpose, date(s) and duration)—(full details are requested below).

2. *Market*

The nature of the transport services affected by the arrangements or behaviour. A brief description of the structure of the market (or markets) for these services, *e.g.* who sells in it, who buys in it, its geographical extent, the turnover in it, how competitive it is, whether it is easy for new suppliers to enter the market, whether there are substitute services. If you are submitting a standard contract, say how many you expect to conclude. If you know of any studies of the market, it would be helpful to refer to them.

3. *Fuller details of the party or parties*

3.1. Do any of the parties form part of a group of companies? A group relationship is deemed to exist where a firm:
 —owns more than half the capital or business assets, or
 —has the power to exercise more than half the voting rights, or
 —has the power to appoint more than half the members of the supervisory board, board of directors or bodies legally representing the undertaking, or
 —has the right to manage the affairs of another.
If the answer is yes, give:
 —the name and address of the ultimate parent company;
 —a brief description of the business of the group (and, if possible, one copy of the last set of group accounts);
 —the name and address of any other company in the group competing in a market affected by the arrangements or in any related market, that is to say any other company competing directly or indirectly with the parties ("relevant associated company").

3.2. The most recently available total turnover of each of the parties, and, as the case may be, of the group of which it forms part (it could be helpful also if you could provide one copy of the last set of accounts).

3.3. The sales or turnover of each party in the services affected by the arrangements in the Community and worldwide. If the turnover in the Community is material (say more than a 5 per cent. market share), please also give figures for each Member State [See list in Annex 3], and for previous years (in order to show any significant trends), and give each party's sales targets for the future. Provide the same figures for any relevant associated company. (Under this heading, in particular, your best estimate might be all that you can readily supply.)

3.4. In relation to the market (or markets) for the services described at 2 above, give, for each of the sales or turnover figures in 3.3, your estimate of the market share it represents.

3.5. If you have a substantial interest falling short of control (more than 25 per cent. but less than 50 per cent.) in some other company competing in a market affected by the arrangements, or if some other such company has a substantial interest in yours, give its name and address and brief details.

4. *Full details of the arrangements*

4.1. If the contents are reduced to writing give a brief description of the purpose of the arrangements and attach three copies of the text (except that purely technical descriptions may be omitted; in such cases, however, indicate parts omitted).

If the contents are not, or are only partially, reduced to writing, give a full description.

4.2. Detail any provisions contained in the arrangements which may restrict the parties in their freedom to take independent commercial decisions, for example regarding:
—buying or selling prices, discounts or other trading conditions
—the nature, frequency of capacity of services to be offered
—technical development or investment
—the choice of markets or sources of supply
—purchases from or sales to third parties
—whether to apply similar terms for the supply of equivalent services
—whether to offer different services separately or together.

4.3. State between which Member States [See list in Annex 3] trade may be affected by the arrangements, and whether trade between the Community and any third countries is affected.

5. *Reasons for negative clearance*

If you are applying for negative clearance state, under the reference:
5.1. why, *i.e.* state which provision or effects of the arrangements or behaviour might, in your view, raise questions of compatibility with the Community's rules of competition. The object of this subheading is to give the Commission the clearest possible idea of the doubts you have about your arrangements or behaviour that you wish to have resolved by a negative clearance decision.

Then, under the following two references, give a statement of the relevant facts and reasons as to why you consider Articles 85(1) or 86 to be inapplicable, *i.e.*

5.2. why the arrangements do not have the object or effect of preventing, restricting or distorting competition within the common market to any appreciable extent, or why your undertaking does not have or its behaviour does not abuse a dominant position; and/or

5.3. why the arrangements or behaviour are not such as may affect trade between Member States to any appreciable extent.

6. *Reasons for a decision applying Article 85(3)*

If you are requesting a decision applying Article 85(3), even if only as a precaution, explain how:

Part IX—5 Air Transport

6.1. the arrangements contribute to improving production or distribution, and/or promoting technical or economic progress;

6.2. a proper share of the benefits arising from such improvement or progress accrues to consumers;

6.3. all restrictive provisions of the arrangements are indispensable to the attainment of the aims set out under 6.1 above;

6.4. the arrangements do not eliminate competition in respect of a substantial part of the services concerned.

7. Other information

7.1. Mention any earlier proceedings or informal contacts, of which you are aware, with the Commission and any earlier proceedings with any national authorities or courts even indirectly concerning these arrangements or this behaviour.

7.2. Give any other information presently available that you think might be helpful in allowing the Commission to appreciate whether there are any restrictions contained in the agreement, or any benefits that might justify them.

7.3. State whether you intend to produce further supporting facts or arguments not yet available and, if so, on which points.

7.4. State, with reasons, the urgency of your application.

Annex 1

TEXT OF ARTICLES 85 AND 86 OF THE EEC TREATY

Article 85

1. The following shall be prohibited as incompatible with the common market: all agreements between undertakings, decisions by associations of undertakings and concerted practices which may affect trade between Member States and which have as their object or effect the prevention, restriction or distortion of competition within the common market, and in particular those which:

(a) directly or indirectly fix purchase or selling prices or any other trading conditions;
(b) limit or control production, markets, technical development, or investment;
(c) share markets or sources of supply;
(d) apply dissimilar conditions to equivalent transactions with other trading parties, thereby placing them at a competitive disadvantage;
(e) make the conclusion of contracts subject to acceptance by the other parties of supplementary obligations which, by their nature or according to commercial usage, have no connection with the subject of such contracts.

2. Any agreements or decisions prohibited pursuant to this Article shall be automatically void.

3. The provisions of paragraph 1 may, however, be declared inapplicable in the case of:
   —any agreement or category of agreements between undertakings,
   —any decision or category of decisions by associations of undertakings,
   —any concerted practice or category of concerted practices,
which contributes to improving production or distribution of goods or to promoting technical or economic progress, while allowing consumers a fair share of the resulting benefit, and which does not:
(a) impose on the undertakings concerned restrictions which are not indispensable to the attainment of these objectives;
(b) afford such undertakings the possibility of eliminating competition in respect of a substantial part of the products in question.

Article 86

Any abuse by one or more undertakings of a dominant position within the common market or in a substantial part of it shall be prohibited as incompatible with the common market in so far as it may affect trade between Member States.

Such abuse may, in particular, consist in:
(a) directly or indirectly imposing unfair purchase or selling prices or other unfair trading conditions;
(b) limiting production, markets or technical development to the prejudice of consumers;
(c) applying dissimilar conditions to equivalent transactions with other trading parties, thereby placing them at a competitive disadvantage;
(d) making the conclusion of contracts subject to acceptance by the other parties of supplementary obligations which, by their nature or according to commercial usage, have no connection with the subject of such contracts.

Annex 2

LIST OF RELEVANT ACTS

(AS OF 1 SEPTEMBER 1988)

(If you think it possible that your arrangements do not need to be notified by virtue of any of these Regulations or notices it may be worth your while to obtain a copy.)

IMPLEMENTING REGULATIONS

Council Regulation No. 4056/86 of 22 December 1986 laying down detailed rules for the application of Articles 85 and 86 of the Treaty to maritime transport ([1986] O.J. L378/4).

Commission Regulation No. 4260/88 of 26 July 1988 on the scope of the obligation of communication; the form, content and other details of complaints and of applications, and the hearings provided for in Council Regulation No. 4056/86 of 22 December 1986 laying down detailed rules for the application of Articles 85 and 86 of the Treaty to maritime transport ([1988] O.J. L376/1).

Council Regulation No. 3975/87 of 14 December 1987 laying down the procedure for the application of the rules on competition to undertakings in the air transport sector ([1987] O.J. 374/1).

Commission Regulation No. 4261/88 of 16 December 1988 on the form, content and other details of complaints and of applications, and the hearings provided for in Council Regulation No. 3975/87 laying down the procedure for the application of the rules of competition to undertakings in the air transport sector ([1988] O.J. L376/10).

REGULATIONS GRANTING BLOCK EXEMPTION IN RESPECT OF A WIDE RANGE OF AGREEMENTS

Commission Regulation No. 2671/88 of 26 July 1988 on the application of Article 85(3) of the Treaty to certain categories of agreements between undertakings, decisions of associations of undertakings and concerted practices concerning joint planning and coordination of capacity, sharing of revenue and consultations on tariffs on scheduled air services and slot allocation at airports ([1988] O.J. L239/9).

Part IX—5 Air Transport

Commission Regulation No. 2672/88 of 26 July 1988 on the application of Article 85(3) of the Treaty to certain categories of agreements between undertakings relating to computer reservation systems for air transport services ([1988] O.J. L239/13).

Commmission Regulation No. 2673/88 of 26 July 1988 on the application of Article 85(3) of the Treaty to certain categories of agreements between undertakings, decisions of associations of undertakings and concerted practices concerning ground handling services ([1988] O.J. L239/17).

COMMISSION NOTICES OF A GENERAL NATURE

Commission notice on agreements, decisions and concerted practices of minor importance which do not fall under Article 85(1) of the Treaty ([1986] O.J. C231/2)—in the main, those where the parties have less than 5 per cent. of the market between them, and a combined annual turnover of less than ECU 200 million.

Annex 3

LIST OF MEMBER STATES AND COMMISSION PRESS AND INFORMATION OFFICES WITHIN THE COMMUNITY

(AS OF 1 JANUARY 1986)

The Member States as at the date of this Annex are: Belgium, Denmark, France, Germany, Greece, Ireland, Italy, Luxembourg, the Netherlands, Portugal, Spain and the United Kingdom.

The addresses of the Commission's Press and Information Offices in the Community are:

BELGIUM
Rue Archimède 73,
B-1040 Bruxelles
Tel. 235 11 11

DENMARK
Højbrohus
Østergade 61
Postbox 144
DK-1004 København K
Tel. 14 41 40

FRANCE
61, rue des Belles-Feuilles
F-75782 Paris, Cedex 16
Tel. (1) 45 01 58 85
CMCI/Bureau 320
2, rue Henri Barbusse
F-13241 Marseille, Cedex 01
Tel. 91 08 62 02

FEDERAL REPUBLIC OF GERMANY
Zitelmannstraße 22
D-5300 Bonn
Tel. 23 80 41
Kurfürstendamm 102
D-1000 Berlin 31
Tel. 8 92 40 28
Erhardstraße 27
D-8000 München
Tel. 23 99 29 00

GREECE
2 Vassilissis Sofias
TK 1602
GR-Athina 134
Tel. 724 39 82/724 39 83/724 39 84

IRELAND
39 Molesworth Street
IRL-Dublin 2
Tel. 71 22 44

Book One: Part IX—Sectorial Application of EEC Competition Rules

ITALY
Via Poli 29
I-00187 Roma
Tel. 678 97 22
Corso Magenta 61
I-20123 Milano
Tel. 80 15 05/6/7/8

LUXEMBOURG
Bâtiment Jean Monnet
Rue Alcide de Gasperi
L-2920 Luxembourg
Tel. 430 11

NETHERLANDS
Korte Vijverberg 5
NL-2513 AB Den Haag
Tel. 46 93 26

PORTUGAL
Rue do Sacramento à Lapa 35
P-1200 Lisboa
Tel. 60 21 99

SPAIN
Calle de Serrano 41
5a Planta
E-1 Madrid
Tel. 435 17 00

UNITED KINGDOM
8 Storey's Gate
UK-London SW1P 3AT
Tel. 222 81 22

Windsor House
9/15 Bedford Street
UK-Belfast BT2 7EG
Tel. 407 08

4 Cathedral Road
UK-Cardiff CF1 9SG
Tel. 37 16 31

7 Alva Street
UK-Edinburgh EH2 4PH
Tel. 225 20 58

ANNEX II

(List of public holidays)

New Year	1 Jan
Good Friday	
Easter Saturday	
Easter Monday	
Labour Day	1 May
Schuman Plan Day	9 May
Ascension Day	
Whit Monday	
Belgian National Day	21 July
Assumption	15 Aug
All Saints	1 Nov
All Souls	2 Nov
Christmas Eve	24 Dec
Christmas Day	25 Dec
The day following Christmas Day	26 Dec
New Year's Eve	31 Dec

Book One: Part IX—Sectorial Application of EEC Competition Rules

8. References to connected legislation

8.1. Computer reservation systems

8.1.1. Regulation 2299/89, [1989] O.J. L220/1

Concerning rules of conduct for computer reservation systems

8.1.2. Explanatory note, [1990] O.J. C184/2

On the EEC Code of conduct for computer reservation systems

8.2. Air fares

8.2.1. Regulation 2342/90, [1990] O.J. L124/1

On fares for scheduled air services

8.2.2. Commission Decision of November 27, [1991] O.J. L5/26

On the compliance of certain air fares with the requirements of Article 3(1) of Council Regulation 2342/90

8.3. Regulation 2343/90, [1990] O.J. L217/8

On access for air carriers to scheduled intra-Community air service routes and on sharing of passenger capacity between air carriers on scheduled air services between Member States.

9. Notices

9.1. Notice on Article 4 and 5 of Regulation 2671/88 (reproduced below)

Notice concerning procedures for communications to the Commission pursuant to Articles 4 and 5 of Commission Regulation (EEC) No. 2671/88 of July 26, 1988 on the application of Article 85(3) of the Treaty to certain categories of agreements between undertakings, decisions of associations of undertakings and concerted practices concerning joint planning and co-ordination of capacity, sharing of revenue and consultations on tariffs on scheduled air services and slot allocation at airports

([1988] O.J. C257/4)

The Commission hereby informs undertakings in the air transport sector that the procedures to be observed by them for communications to the Commission are as follows:
— Air carriers interested in holding consultations on tariffs, on slot allocation or on airport scheduling are requested to address all communications to the Commission in one of the following manners:
— by telex to 21877 COMEU B,
— or
— by telefax to 32 2 235 01 28. Mark all messages 'for the attention of DG IV/D-2'. Indicate the name and telephone number of a contact person with the air carrier.
— Communications on the submission of tariffs and reports on tariff consultations should be sent by ordinary mail to:
Commission of the European Communities,
DG IV/D-2,
200, rue de la Loi,
B-1049 Brussels.

9.2. Notice on Article 4(1)(a) of Regulation 2671/88 (reproduced opposite)

Notice concerning the application of Article 4(1)(a) of Commission Regulation (EEC) No. 2671/88 of July 26, 1988 on the application of Article 85(3) of the Treaty to certain categories of agreements between undertakings, decisions of associations of undertakings and concerted practices concerning joint planning and coordination of capacity, sharing of revenue and consultations on tariffs on scheduled air services and slot allocation at airports

([1989] O.J. C119/4)

At the TC2-Europe Conference of IATA in Geneva which started on September 7, 1990 the Commission's observer made a statement explaining the terms and conditions of the block exemption granted by the Commission for agreements on consultations on tariffs. Following that statement a question arose as to whether Article 4(1)(a) of the block exemption applies to inclusive tour (IT) and group inclusive tour (GIT) fares.

As a result of the explanation given on this point, the IATA secretariat developed a proposal under which consultations on IT and GIT fares within IATA would respect the following rules:

(i) fares will only be discussed where the inventory risk is with the carrier (i.e. there will be no discussion of part-charter fares);

(ii) there will be no discussion of minimum tour prices or any aspects of tour arrangements;

(iii) IATA resolutions on IT and GIT fares would be modified to provide that:

— the fare is to appear on the ticket, or (where no ticket is issued) is to be available to the passenger on request,
— the fare is interlinable,
— the fare is available for sale to the public with inclusive tour arrangements to be approved by the sponsoring carrier.

These arrangements would, in the Commission's view be sufficient to bring consultations on IT and GIT fares within the scope of the block exemption, provided that the conditions set out in Article 4(1)(b) to 4(2) are respected and subject to the proviso that carriers participating in the consultations must, after the consultations, observe all the requirements listed. In particular a carrier may not, even on a unilateral basis, introduce a minimum tour price condition or refuse to interline if so requested by the tour operator or travel agent or by the passenger where the latter is dealing directly with the airline. In applying Article 4 of Regulation No. 2671/88 to consultations on IT and GIT fares the Commission will, accordingly, base any action on the above guidelines.

This statement is based on the information currently available to the Commission and cannot be binding on national courts. It may be reviewed if new information comes to the Commission's attention.

While the Commission has at this stage taken no view on the terms of any block exemptions to be proposed in the context of the next stage in the liberalisation of air transport within the Community, it would appear unlikely in any event that such an exemption would be granted for consultations on IT and GIT fares.

B. CASES

Olympic Airways 229
SABENA 295
IATA Passengers 342
IATA Cargo 343
5th Comp. Rep. (para. 14)
9th Comp. Rep. (para. 12–15)
Sterling Airways 10th Comp. Rep. (para. 136–138)
11th Comp. Rep. (para. 5)
15th Comp. Rep. (paras. 27–33)
17th Comp. Rep. (paras. 43–46)
IATA 19th Comp. Rep. (para. 58)
19th Comp. Rep. (para. 44)
20th Comp. Rep. (paras. 73–76, 106–109)
Lord Bethel v. *Commission* 93
Nouvelles Frontieres 131
Ahmed Saeed v. *Zentrale* 162

CHAPTER 6.

FINANCIAL SERVICES

A. LEGISLATION

1. Text of Regulation 1534/91 (reproduced below)

Council Regulation (EEC) No. 1534/91 of 31 May 1991

On the application of Article 85(3) of the Treaty to certain categories of agreements, decisions and concerted practices in the insurance sector

([1991] O.J. L143/1)

THE COUNCIL OF THE EUROPEAN COMMUNITIES,

Having regard to the treaty establishing the European Economic Community, and in particular Article 87 thereof,

Having regard to the proposal from the Commission. ([1990] O.J. C16/13),

Having regard to the opinion of the European Parliament, ([1990] O.J C260/57),

Having regard to the opinion of the Economic and Social Committee, [1990] O.J. C182/27),

(1) Whereas Article 85(1) of the Treaty may, in accordance with Article 85(3), be declared inapplicable to categories of agreements, decisions and concerted practices when satisfy the conditions contained in Article 85(3);

(2) Whereas the detailed rules for the application of Article 85(3) of the Treaty must be adopted by way of a Regulation based on Article 87 of the Treaty;

(3) Whereas co-operation between undertakings in the insurance sector is, to a certain extent, desirable to ensure the proper functioning of this sector and may at the same time promote consumers' interests;

(4) Whereas the application of Council Regulation (EEC) No. 4064/89 of December 21, 1989 on the control of concentrations between undertakings ([1990] O.J. L395/1), enables the Commission to exercise close supervision on issues arising from concentrations in all sectors, including the insurance sector;

(5) Whereas exemptions granted under Article 85(3) of the Treaty cannot themselves affect Community and national provisions safeguarding consumers' interests in this sector;

(6) Whereas agreements, decisions and concerted practices serving such aims may, in so far as they fall within the prohibition contained in Article 85(1) of the Treaty, be exempted therefrom under certain conditions; whereas this applies particularly to agreements, decisions and concerted practices relating to the establishment of common risk premium tariffs based on collectively ascertained statistics or the number of claims, the establishment of standard policy conditions, common coverage of certain types of risks, the settlement of claims, the testing and acceptance of security devices, and registers of and information on aggravated risks;

(7) Whereas in view of the large number of notifications submitted pursuant to Council Regulation No. 17 of February 6 ,1962: First Regulation implementing Articles 85 and 86 of the Treaty [1962] O.J. 13/62), as last amended by the Act of Accession of Spain and Portugal, it is desirable that in order to facilitate the Commissions task it should
be enabled to declare by way of regulation that the provisions of Article 85(1) of the Treaty are inapplicable to certain categories of agreements, decisions and concerted practices;

(8) Whereas it should be laid down under which conditions the Commission, in close

and constant liaison with the competent authorities of the Member States, may exercise such powers;

(9) Whereas, in the exercise of such powers, the Commission will take account not only of the risk of competition being eliminated in a substantial part of the relevant market and of any benefit that might be conferred on policyholders resulting from the agreements, but also of the risk which the proliferation of restrictive clauses and the operation of accomodation companies would entail for policyholders;

(10) Whereas the keeping of registers and the handling of information on aggravated risks should be carried out subject to the proper protection of confidentiality;

(11) Whereas, under Article 6 of Regulation No. 17, the Commission may provide that a decision taken in accordance with Article 85(3) of the Treaty shall apply with retroactive effect; whereas the Commission should also be able to adopt provisions to such effect in a Regulation;

(12) Whereas, under Article 7 of Regulation No. 17, agreements, decisions and concerted practices may, by decision of the Commission, be exempted from prohibition, in particular if they are modified in such manner that they satisfy the requirements of Article 85(3) of the Treaty; whereas it is desirable that the Commission be enabled to grant by regulation like exemption to such agreements, decisions and concerted practices if they are modified in such manner as to fall within a category defined in an exempting regulation;

(13) Whereas it cannot be ruled out that, in specific cases, the conditions set out in Article 85(3) of the Treaty may not be fulfilled; whereas the Commission must have the power to regulate such cases pursuant to Regulation No. 17 by way of a decision having effect for the future,

HAS ADOPTED THIS REGULATION:

Article 1

1. Without prejudice to the application of Regulation No. 17 the Commission may, by means of a Regulation and in accordance with Article 85(3) of the Treaty, declare that Article 85(1) shall not apply to categories of agreements between undertakings, decisions of associations of undertakings and concerted practices in the insurance sector which have as their object cooperation with respect to:
(a) the establishment of common risk premium tariffs based on collectively ascertained statistics or the number of claims;
(b) the establishment of common standard policy conditions;
(c) the common coverage of certain types of risks;
(d) the settlement of claims;
(e) the testing and acceptance of security devices;
(f) registers of and information on aggravated risks, provided that the keeping of these registers and the handling of this information is carried out subject to the proper protection of confidentiality.

2. The Commission Regulation referred to in paragraph 1, shall define the categories of agreements, decisions and concerted practices to which it applies and shall specify in particular:
(a) the restrictions or clauses which may, or may not, appear in the agreements, decisions and concerted practices;
(b) the clauses which must be contained in the agreements, decisions and concerted practices or the other conditions which must be satisfied.

Article 2

Any Regulation adopted pursuant to Article 1 shall be of limited duration.

It may be repealed or amended where circumstances have changed with respect to any of the facts which were essential to it being adopted; in such case, a period shall be fixed for modification of the agreements, decisions and concerted practices to which the earlier regulation applies.

Article 3

A Regulation adopted pursuant to Article 1 may provide that it shall apply with retroactive effect to agreements, decisions and concerted practices to which, at the date of entry into force of the said regulation, a Decision taken with retroactive effect pursuant to Article 6 of Regulation No. 17 would have applied.

Article 4

1. A Regulation adopted pursuant to Arti-

cle 1 may provide that the prohibition contained in Article 85(1) of the Treaty shall not apply, for such period as shall be fixed in that Regulation, to agreements, decisions and concerted practices already in existence on March 13, 1962 which do not satisfy the conditions of Article 85(3), where:
— within six months from the entry into force of the said Regulation, they are so modified as to satisfy the said conditions in accordance with the provisions of the said Regulation, and
— the modifications are brought to the notice of the Commission within the time limit fixed by the said Regulation.

The provisions of the first subparagraph shall apply in the same way to those agreements, decisions and concerted practices existing at the date of accession of new Member States to which Article 85(1) of the Treaty applies by virtue of accession and which do not satisfy the conditions of Article 85(3).

2. Paragraph 1 shall apply to agreements, decisions and concerted practices which had to be notified before February 1, 1963, in accordance with Article 5 of Regulation No. 17, only where they have been so notified before that date.

Paragraph 1 shall not apply to agreements, decisions and concerted practices existing at the date of accession of new Member States to which Article 85(1) of the Treaty applies by virtue of accession and which had to be notified within six months from the date of accession in accordance with Articles 5 and 25 of Regulation No. 17, unless they have been so notified within the said period.

3. The benefit of the provisions adopted pursuant to paragraph 1 may not be invoked in actions pending at the date of entry into force of a regulation adopted pursuant to Article 1; neither may it be invoked as grounds for claims for damages against third parties.

Article 5

Where the Commission proposes to adopt a Regulation, it shall publish a draft thereof to enable all persons and organisations concerned to submit their comments within such time limit, being not less than one month, as it shall fix.

Article 6

1. The Commission shall consult the Advisory Committee on Restrictive Practices and Monopolies:

(a) before publishing a draft Regulation;
(b) before adopting a Regulation.

2. Articles 10(5) and (6) of Regulation No. 17, relating to consultation with the Advisory Committee, shall apply; However, joint meetings with the Commission shall take place not earlier than one month after dispatch of the notice convening them.

Article 7

Where the Commission, either on its own initiative or at the request of a Member State or of natural or legal persons claiming a legitimate interest, finds that in any particular case agreements, decisions and concerted practices to which a regulation pursuant to Article 1 of this Regulation applies have nevertheless certain effects which are incompatible with the conditions laid down in Article 85(3) of the Treaty, it may withdraw the benefit of application of the said regulation and take a decision in accordance with Articles 6 and 8 of Regulation No. 17, without any notification under Article 4(1) of Regulation No. 17 being required.

Article 8

Not later than six years after the entry into force of the Commission Regulation provided for in Article 1, the Commission shall submit to the European Parliament and the Council a report on the functioning of this Regulation, accompanied by such proposals for amendments to this Regulation as may appear necessary in the light of experience.

This Regulation shall be binding in its entirety and directly applicable in all Member States.

Done at Brussels, 31 May 1991.

B. CASES

1. Banking

Uniform Eurochèques 224
Irish Bank Standing Committee 252
Belgian Banking Association 261
ABI 262*

Dutch Banking Association 310*
2nd Comp. Rep. (paras. 52–53)
8th Comp. Rep. (paras. 32–37)
13th Comp. Rep. (paras. 67–69)
Züchner v. *Bayerische Vereinbank* 86
Van Eycke v. *Aspa* 155

2. Insurance

Nuovo—CEGAM 209
Fire Insurance 220

Greek Insurance 230
P&I Clubs 243
Concordato 316
TEKO 317
Assurpol 346
2nd Comp. Rep. (paras. 52–53)
8th Comp. Rep. (paras. 32–37)
Luxemburg Car Insurance 15th Comp. Rep. (para. 71)
Van Ameyde v. *UCI* 51
Fire Insurance v. *Commission* 139

PART X

PROCEDURE AND REMEDIES

CHAPTER 1

PROCEDURAL LEGISLATION

A. RELEVANT PROVISIONS OF THE TREATY

1. Article 87

Article 87

1. Within three years of the entry into force of this Treaty the Council shall, acting unanimously on a proposal from the Commission and after consulting the Assembly, adopt any appropriate regulations or directives to give effect to the principles set out in Articles 85 and 86.

If such provisions have not been adopted within the period mentioned, they shall be laid down by the Council, acting by a qualified majority on a proposal from the Commission and after consulting the Assembly.

2. The regulations or directives referred to in paragraph 1 shall be designed, in particular:

(*a*) to ensure compliance with the prohibitions laid down in Article 85(1) and in Article 86 by making provision for fines and periodic penalty payments;
(*b*) to lay down detailed rules for the application of Article 85(3), taking into account the need to ensure effective supervision on the one hand, and to simplify administration to the greatest possible extent on the other;
(*c*) to define, if need be, in the various branches of the economy, the scope of the provisions of Articles 85 and 86;
(*d*) to define the respective functions of the Commission and of the Court of Justice in applying the provisions laid down in this paragraph;
(*e*) to determine the relationship between national laws and the provisions contained in this Section or adopted pursuant to this Article.

2. Cases on the interpretation of Article 87

Bosch v. *de Geus* 1*
Italy v. *Council and Commission* 5
Walt Wilhelm 9 (paras. 4–5, 9)

ACF Chemiefarma v. *Commission* 14
Nouvelles Frontières 131
Ahmed Saeed v. *Zentrale* 162

3. Article 88–89

Article 88

Until the entry into force of the provisions adopted in pursuance of Article 87, the authorities in Member States shall rule on the admissibility of agreements, decisions and concerted practices and on abuse of a dominant position in the common market in accordance with the law of their country and with the provisions of Article 85, in particular paragraph 3, and of Article 86.

Article 89

1. Without prejudice to Article 88, the Commission shall, as soon as it takes up its duties, ensure the application of the principles laid down in Articles 85 and 86. On application by a Member State or on its own initiative, and in cooperation with the competent authorities in the Member States, who shall give it their assistance, the Commission shall investigate cases of suspected infringement of these principles. If it finds that there has been an infringement, it shall propose appropriate measures to bring it to an end.

2. If the infringement is not brought to an end, the Commission shall record such infringement of the principles in a reasoned decision. The Commission may publish its decision and authorise Member States to take the measures, the conditions and details of which it shall determine, needed to remedy the situation.

4. Cases on the interpretation of Articles 88–89

Bosch v. *de Geus* 1
Nouvelles Frontières 131*
Ahmed Saeed v. *Zentrale* 162

B. RELEVANT LEGISLATIVE PROVISIONS

1. Text of Council Regulation 17/62 (reproduced over)

Council Regulation 17 of February 6, 1962

First Regulation implementing Articles 85 and 86 of the Treaty

(J.O. 204/62; [1959–1962] O.J. Spec.Ed. 87)

THE COUNCIL OF THE EUROPEAN ECONOMIC COMMUNITY,

Having regard to the Treaty establishing the European Economic Community, and in particular Article 87 thereof;

Having regard to the proposal from the Commission;

Having regard to the Opinion of the Economic and Social Committee;

Having regard to the Opinion of the European Parliament;

(1) Whereas in order to establish a system ensuring that competition shall not be distorted in the common market, it is necessary to provide for balanced application of Articles 85 and 86 in a uniform manner in the Member States;

(2) Whereas in establishing the rules for applying Article 85(3) account must be taken of the need to ensure effective supervision and to simplify administration to the greatest possible extent;

(3) Whereas it is accordingly necessary to make it obligatory, as a general principle, for undertakings which seek application of Article 85(3) to notify to the Commission their agreements, decisions and concerted practices;

(4) Whereas, on the one hand, such agreements, decisions and concerted practices are probably very numerous and cannot therefore all be examined at the same time and, on the other hand, some of them have special features which may make them less prejudicial to the development of the common market;

(5) Whereas there is consequently a need to make more flexible arrangements for the time being in respect of certain categories of agreements, decisions and concerted practices without prejudging their validity under Article 85;

(6) Whereas it may be in the interest of undertakings to know whether any agreements, decisions or practices to which they are party, or propose to become party, may lead to action on the part of the Commission pursuant to Article 85(1) or Article 86;

(7) Whereas, in order to secure uniform application of Articles 85 and 86 in the common market, rules must be made under which the Commission, acting in close and constant liaison with the competent authorities of the Member States, may take the requisite measures for applying those Articles;

(8) Whereas for this purpose the Commission must have the co-operation of the competent authorities of the Member States and be empowered, throughout the common market, to require such information to be supplied and to undertake such investigations as are necessary to bring to light any agreement, decision or concerted practice prohibited by Article 85(1) or any abuse of a dominant position prohibited by Article 86;

(9) Whereas in order to carry out its duty of ensuring that the provisions of the Treaty are applied, the Commission must be empowered to address to undertakings or associations of undertakings recommendations and decisions for the purpose of bringing to an end infringements of Articles 85 and 86;

(10) Whereas compliance with Articles 85 and 86 and the fulfilment of obligations imposed on undertakings and associations of undertakings under this regulation must be enforceable by means of fines and periodic penalty payments;

(11) Whereas undertakings concerned must be accorded the right to be heard by the Commission, third parties whose interests may be affected by a decision must be given the opportunity of submitting their comments beforehand, and it must be ensured that wide publicity is given to decisions taken;

(12) Whereas all decisions taken by the Commission under this regulation are subject to review by the Court of Justice under the conditions specified in the

Treaty; whereas it is moreover desirable to confer upon the Court of Justice, pursuant to Article 172, unlimited jurisdiction in respect of decisions under which the Commission imposes fines or periodic penalty payments;

(13) Whereas this regulation may enter into force without prejudice to any other provisions that may hereafter be adopted pursuant to Article 87;

HAS ADOPTED THIS REGULATION:

Article 1: Basic Provision

Without prejudice to Articles 6, 7 and 23 of this regulation, agreements, decisions and concerted practices of the kind described in Article 85(1) of the Treaty and the abuse of a dominant position in the market, within the meaning of Article 86 of the Treaty, shall be prohibited, no prior decision to that effect being required.

Article 2: Negative Clearance

Upon application by the undertakings or associations of undertakings concerned, the Commission may certify that, on the basis of the facts in its possession, there are no grounds under Article 85(1) or Article 86 of the Treaty for action on its part in respect of an agreement, decision or practice.

Article 3: Termination of Infringements

1. Where the Commission, upon application or upon its own intitiative, finds that there is infringement of Article 85 or Article 86 of the Treaty, it may by decision require the undertakings or associations of undertakings concerned to bring such infringement to an end.

2. Those entitled to make application are:
(a) Member States;
(b) natural or legal persons who claim a legitimate interest.

3. Without prejudice to the other provisions of this regulation, the Commission may, before taking a decision under paragraph (1), address to the undertakings or associations of undertakings concerned recommendations for termination of the infringement.

Article 4: Notification of New Agreements, Decisions and Practices

1. Agreements, decisions and concerted practices of the kind described in Article 85(1) of the Treaty which come into existence after the entry into force of this regulation and in respect of which the parties seek application of Article 85(3) must be notified to the Commission. Until they have been notified, no decision in application of Article 85(3) may be taken.

2. Paragraph (1) shall not apply to agreements, decisions or concerted practices where:
(i) the only parties thereto are undertakings from one Member State and the agreements, decisions or practices do not relate either to imports or to exports between Member States;
(ii) not more than two undertakings are party thereto, and the agreements only:
  (a) restrict the freedom of one party to the contract in determining the prices for or conditions of business on which the goods which he has obtained from the other party to the contract may be resold; or
  (b) impose restrictions on the exercise of the rights of the assignee or user of industrial property rights—in particular patents, utility models, designs or trade marks—or of the person entitled under a contract to the assignment, or grant, of the right to use a method of manufacture or knowledge relating to the use and to the application of industrial processes;
(iii) they have as their sole object;
  (a) the development or uniform application of standards or types;
  (b) joint research and development;
  (c) specialisation in the manufacture of products, including agreements necessary for the achieving this;
— where the products which are the object of specialisation do not, in a substantial part of the common market, represent more than 15 per cent. of the volume of business done in identical products or those considered by the consumers to be similar by reason of their characteristics, price and use, and

— where the total annual turnover of the participating undertakings does not exceed 200 million units of accounts.

These agreements, decisions and concerted practices may be notified to the Commission.

Article 5: Notification of Existing Agreements, Decisions and Practices

1. Agreements, decisions and concerted practices of the kind described in Article 85(1) of the Treaty which are in existence at the date of entry into force of this regulation and in respect of which the parties seek application of Article 85(3) shall be notified to the Commission before 1 November 1962. However, notwithstanding the foregoing provisions, any agreements, decisions and concerted practices to which not more than two undertakings are party shall be notified before 1 February 1963.

2. Paragraph (1) shall not apply to agreements, decisions or concerted practices falling within Article 4(2); these may be notified to the Commission.

Article 6: Decisions Pursuant to Article 85(3)

1. Whenever the Commission takes a decision pursuant to Article 85(3) of the Treaty, it shall specify therein the date from which the decision shall take effect. Such date shall not be earlier than the date of notification.

2. The second sentence of paragraph (1) shall not apply to agreements, decisions or concerted practices falling within Article 4(2) and Article 5(2), nor to those falling within Article 5(1) which have been notified within the time limit specified in Article 5(1).

Article 7: Special Provisions for Existing Agreements, Decisions and Practices

1. Where agreements, decisions and concerted practices in existence at the date of entry into force of this regulation and notified within the limits specified in Article 5(1) do not satisfy the requirements of Article 85(3) of the Treaty and the undertakings or associations of undertakings concerned cease to give effect to them or modify them in such manner that they no longer fall within the prohibition contained in Article 85(1) or that they satisfy the requirements of Article 85(3), the prohibition contained in Article 85(1) shall apply only for a period fixed by the Commission. A decision by the Commission pursuant to the foregoing sentence shall not apply as against undertakings and associations of undertakings which do not expressly consent to the notification.

2. Paragraph (1) shall apply to agreements, decisions and concerted practices falling within Article 4(2) which are in existence at the date of entry into force of this regulation if they are notified before 1 January 1967.

Article 8: Duration and Revocation of Decisions under Article 85(3)

1. A decision in application of Article 85(3) of the Treaty shall be issued for a specified period and conditions and obligations may be attached thereto.

2. A decision may on application be renewed if the requirements of Article 85(3) of the Treaty continue to be satisfied.

3. The Commission may revoke or amend its decision or prohibit specified acts by the parties:
(a) where there has been a change in any of the facts which were fundamental in the making of the decision;
(b) where the parties commit a breach of any obligation attached to the decision;
(c) where the decision is based on incorrect information or was induced by deceit;
(d) where the parties abuse the exemption from the provisions of Article 85(1) of the Treaty granted to them by the decision.

In cases to which sub-paragraphs (b), (c) or (d) apply, the decision may be revoked with retroactive effect.

Article 9: Powers

1. Subject to review of its decision by the Court of Justice, the Commission shall

have sole power to declare Article 85(1) inapplicable pursuant to Article 85(3) of the Treaty.

2. The Commission shall have power to apply Article 85(1) and Article 86 of the Treaty; this power may be exercised notwithstanding that the time limits specified in Article 5(1) and in Article 7(2) relating to notification have not expired.

3. As long as the Commission has not initiated any procedure under Articles 2, 3 or 6, the authorities of the Member States shall remain competent to apply Article 85(1) and Article 86, in accordance with Article 88 of the Treaty; they shall remain competent in this respect notwithstanding that the time limits specified in Article 5(1) and in Article 7(2) relating to notification have not expired.

Article 10: Liaison with the Authorities of the Member States

1. The Commission shall forthwith transmit to the competent authorities of the Member States a copy of the applications and notifications together with copies of the most important documents lodged with the Commission for the purpose of establishing the existence of infringements of Articles 85 or 86 of the Treaty or of obtaining negative clearance or a decision in application of Article 85(3).

2. The Commission shall carry out the procedure set out in paragraph (1) in close and constant liaison with the competent authorities of the Member States; such authorities shall have the right to express their views on that procedure.

3. An Advisory Committee on Restrictive Practices and Monopolies shall be consulted prior to the taking of any decision following upon a procedure under paragraph (1), and of any decision concerning the renewal, amendment or revocation of a decision pursuant to Article 85(3) of the Treaty.

4. The Advisory Committee shall be composed of officials competent in the matter of restrictive practices and monopolies. Each Member State shall appoint an official to represent it who, if prevented from attending, may be replaced by another official.

5. The consultation shall take place at a joint meeting convened by the Commission; such meeting shall be held not earlier than fourteen days after dispatch of the notice convening it. The notice shall, in respect of each case to be examined, be accompanied by a summary of the case together with an indication of the most important documents, and a preliminary draft decision.

6. The Advisory Committee may deliver an opinion notwithstanding that some of its members or their alternates are not present. A report of the outcome of the consultative proceedings shall be annexed to the draft decision. It shall not be made public.

Article 11: Requests for Information

1. In carrying out the duties assigned to it by Article 89 and by provisions adopted under Article 87 of the Treaty, the Commission may obtain all necessary information from the Governments and competent authorities of the Member States and from undertakings and associations of undertakings.

2. When sending a request for information to an undertaking or association of undertakings, the Commission shall at the same time forward a copy of the request to the competent authority of the Member State in whose territory the seat of the undertaking or association of undertakings is situated.

3. In its request the Commission shall state the legal basis and the purpose of the request and also the penalties provided for in Article 15(1)(*b*) for supplying incorrect information.

4. The owners of the undertakings or their representatives and, in the case of legal persons, companies or firms, or of associations having no legal personality, the persons authorised to represent them by law or by their constitution, shall supply the information requested.

5. Where an undertaking or association of undertakings does not supply the information requested within the time limit fixed by the Commission, or supplies incomplete information, the Commission shall by decision require the information to be supplied. The decision shall specify what information is required, fix an appropriate time limit within which it is to be supplied and indicate the penalties provided for by Article 15(1)(*b*) and Article 16(1)(*c*) and the right to have the decision reviewed by the Court of Justice.

6. The Commission shall at the same time forward a copy of its decision to the competent authority of the Member State in whose territory the seat of the undertaking or association of undertakings is situated.

Article 12: Inquiry into Sectors of the Economy

1. If in any sector of the economy the trend of trade between Member States, price movements, inflexibility of prices or other circumstances suggest that in the economic sector concerned competition is being restricted or distorted within the common market, the Commission may decide to conduct a general inquiry into that economic sector and in the course thereof may request undertakings in the sector concerned to supply the information necessary for giving effect to the principles formulated in Articles 85 and 86 of the Treaty and for carrying out the duties entrusted to the Commission.

2. The Commission may in particular request every undertaking or association of undertakings in the economic sector concerned to communicate to it all agreements, decisions and concerted practices which are exempt from notification by virtue of Article 4(2) and Article 5(2).

3. When making inquiries pursuant to paragraph (2), the Commission shall also request undertakings or groups of undertakings whose size suggests that they occupy a dominant position within the common market or a substantial part thereof to supply to the Commission such particulars of the structure of the undertakings and of their behaviour as are requisite to an appraisal of their position in the light of Article 86 of the Treaty.

4. Article 10(3) to (6) and Articles 11, 13 and 14 shall apply correspondingly.

Article 13: Investigations by the Authorities of the Member States

1. At the request of the Commission, the competent authorities of the Member States shall undertake the investigations which the Commission considers to be necessary under Article 14(1), or which it has ordered by decision pursuant to Article 14(3). The officials of the competent authorities of the Member States responsible for conducting these investigations shall exercise their powers upon reproduction of an authorisation in writing issued by the competent authority of the Member State in whose territory the investigation is to be made. Such authorisation shall specify the subject-matter and purpose of the investigation.

2. If so requested by the Commission or by the competent authority of the Member State in whose territory the investigation is to be made, the officials of the Commission may assist the officials of such authority in carrying out their duties.

Article 14: Investigating Powers of the Commission

1. In carrying out the duties assigned to it by Article 89 and by provisions adopted under Article 87 of the Treaty, the Commission may undertake all necessary investigations into undertakings and associations of undertakings. To this end the officials authorised by the Commission are empowered:
(*a*) to examine the books and other business records;
(*b*) to take copies of or extracts from the books and business records;
(*c*) to ask for oral explanations on the spot;
(*d*) to enter any premises, land and means of transport of undertakings.

2. The officials of the Commission authorised for the purpose of these investigations shall exercise their powers upon production of an authorisation in writing specifying the subject-matter and purpose

of the investigation and the penalties provided for in Article 15(1)(c) in cases where production of the required books or other business records is incomplete. In good time before the investigation, the Commission shall inform the competent authority of the Member State in whose territory the same is to be made, of the investigation and of the identity of the authorised officials.

3. Undertakings and associations of undertakings shall submit to investigations ordered by decision of the Commission. The decision shall specify the subject-matter and purpose of the investigation, appoint the date on which it is to begin and indicate the penalties provided for in Article 15(1)(c) and Article 16(1)(d) and the right to have the decision reviewed by the Court of Justice.

4. The Commission shall take the decisions referred to in paragraph 3 after consultation with the competent authority of the Member State in whose territory the investigation is to be made.

5. Officials of the competent authority of the Member State in whose territory the investigation is to be made may, at the request of such authority or of the Commission, assist the officials of the Commission in carrying out their duties.

6. Where an undertaking opposes an investigation ordered pursuant to this Article, the Member State concerned shall afford the necessary assistance to the officials authorised by the Commission to enable them to make their investigation. Member States shall, after consultation with the Commission, take the necessary measures to this end before 1 October 1962.

Article 15: Fines

1. The Commission may by decision impose on undertakings or associations of undertakings fines of from one hundred to five thousand units of account where, intentionally or negligently:
(a) they supply incorrect or misleading information in an application pursuant to Article 2 or in a notification pursuant to Articles 4 or 5; or
(b) they supply incorrect information in response to a request made pursuant to Article 11(3) or (5) or to Article 12, or do not supply information within the time limit fixed by a decision taken under Article 11(5); or
(c) they produce the required books or other business records in incomplete form during investigations under Article 13 or 14, or refuse to submit to an investigation ordered by decision issued in implementation of Article 14(3).

2. The Commission may by decision impose on undertakings or associations of undertakings fines of from one thousand to one million units of account, or a sum in excess thereof but not exceeding 10 per cent. of the turnover in the preceding business year of each of the undertakings participating in the infringement where, either intentionally or negligently:
(a) they infringe Article 85(1) or Article 86 of the Treaty; or
(b) they commit a breach of any obligation imposed pursuant to Article 8(1).
In fixing the amount of the fine, regard shall be had both to the gravity and to the duration of the infringement.

3. Article 10(3) to (6) shall apply.

4. Decisions taken pursuant to paragraphs (1) and (2) shall not be of a criminal law nature.

5. The fines provided for in paragraph (2)(a) shall not be imposed in respect of acts taking place:
(a) after notification to the Commission and before its decision in application of Article 85(3) of the Treaty, provided they fall within the limits of the activity described in the notification;
(b) before notification and in the course of agreements, decisions or concerted practices in existence at the date of entry into force of this regulation, provided that notification was effected within the time limits specified in Article 5(1) and Article 7(2).

6. Paragraph (5) shall not have effect where the Commission has informed the undertakings concerned that after preliminary examination it is of opinion that Article 85(1) of the Treaty applies and that application of Article 85(3) is not justified.

Article 16: Periodic Penalty Payments

1. The Commission may by decision impose on undertakings or associations of undertakings periodic penalty payments of from fifty to one thousand units of account per day, calculated from the date appointed by the decision, in order to compel them:
(*a*) to put an end to an infringement of Article 85 or 86 of the Treaty, in accordance with a decision taken pursuant to Article 3 of this regulation;
(*b*) to refrain from any act prohibited under Article 8(3);
(*c*) to supply complete and correct information which it has requested by decision taken pursuant to Article 11(5);
(*d*) to submit to an investigation which it has ordered by decision taken pursuant to Article 14(3).

2. Where the undertakings or associations of undertakings have satisfied the obligation which it was the purpose of the periodic penalty payment to enforce, the Commission may fix the total amount of the periodic payment at a lower figure than that which would arise under the original decision.

3. Article 10(3) to (6) shall apply.

Article 17: Review by the Court of Justice

The Court of Justice shall have unlimited jurisdiction within the meaning of Article 172 of the Treaty to review decisions whereby the Commission has fixed a fine or periodic penalty; it may cancel, reduce or increase the fine or periodic penalty payment imposed.

Article 18: Unit of Account

For the purposes of applying Articles 15 to 17 the unit of account shall be that adopted in drawing up the budget of the Community in accordance with Articles 207 and 209 of the Treaty.

Article 19: Hearing of the Parties and of Third Persons

1. Before taking decisions as provided for in Articles 2, 3, 6, 7, 8, 15 and 16, the Commission shall give the undertakings or associations of undertakings concerned the opportunity of being heard on the matters to which the Commission has taken objection.

2. If the Commission or the competent authorities of the Member States consider it necessary, they may also hear other natural or legal persons. Applications to be heard on the part of such persons shall, where they show a sufficient interest, be granted.

3. Where the Commission intends to give negative clearance pursuant to Article 2 or take a decision in application of Article 85(3) of the Treaty, it shall publish a summary of the relevant application or notification and invite all interested third parties to submit their observations within a time limit which it shall fix being not less than one month. Publication shall have regard to the legitimate interest of undertakings in the protection of their business secrets.

Article 20: Professional Secrecy

1. Information acquired as a result of the application of Articles 11, 12, 13 and 14 shall be used only for the purpose of the relevant request for investigation.

2. Without prejudice to the provisions of Articles 19 and 21, the Commission and the competent authorities of the Member States, their officials and other servants shall not disclose information acquired by them as a result of the application of this regulation and of the kind covered by the obligation of professional secrecy.

3. The provisions of paragraphs (1) and (2) shall not prevent publication of general information or surveys which do not contain information relating to particular undertakings or associations of undertakings.

Article 21: Publication of Decisions

1. The Commission shall publish the decisions which it takes pursuant to Articles 2, 3, 6, 7 and 8.

2. The publication shall state the names of the parties and the main content of the decision; it shall have regard to the legitimate interest of undertakings in the protection of their business secrets.

Article 22: Special Provisions

1. The Commission shall submit to the Council proposals for making certain categories of agreement, decision and concerted practice falling within Article 4(2) or Article 5(2) compulsorily notifiable under Article 4 or 5.

2. Within one year from the date of entry into force of this regulation, the Council shall examine, on a proposal from the Commission, what special provisions might be made for exempting from the provisions of this regulation agreements, decisions and concerted practices falling within Article 4(2) or Article 5(2).

Article 23: Transitional Provisions Applicable to Decisions of Authorities of the Member States

1. Agreements, decisions and concerted practices of the kind described in Article 85(1) of the Treaty to which, before entry into force of this regulation, the competent authority of a Member State has declared Article 85(1) to be inapplicable pursuant to Article 85(3) shall not be subject to compulsory notification under Article 5. The decision of the competent authority of the Member State shall be deemed to be a decision within the meaning of Article 6; it shall cease to be valid upon expiration of the period fixed by such authority but in any event not more than three years after the entry into force of this regulation. Article 8(3) shall apply.

2. Applications for renewal of decisions of the kind described in paragraph (1) shall be decided upon by the Commission in accordance with Article 8(2).

Article 24: Implementing Provisions

The Commission shall have the power to adopt implementing provisions concerning the form, content and other details of applications pursuant to Articles 2 and 3, and of notifications pursuant to Articles 4 and 5, and concerning hearings pursuant to Article 19(1) and (2).

Article 25

1. As regards agreements, decisions and concerted practices to which Article 85 of the Treaty applies by virtue of accession, the date of accession shall be substituted for the date of entry into force of this regulation in every place where reference is made in this regulation to this latter date.

2. Agreements, decisions and concerted practices existing at the date of accession to which Article 85 of the Treaty applies by virtue of accession shall be notified pursuant to Article 5(1) or Article 7(1) and (2) within six months from the date of accession.

3. Fines under Article 15(2)(a) shall not be imposed in respect of any act prior to notification of the agreements, decisions and practices to which paragraph (2) applies and which have been notified within the period therein specified.

4. New Member States shall take the measures referred to in Article 14(6) within six months from the date of accession after consulting the Commission.

5. The provisions of paragraphs (1) to (4) above still apply in the same way in the case of accession of the Hellenic Republic, the Kingdom of Spain and of the Portuguese Republic.

This regulation shall be binding in its entirety and directly applicable in all Member States.

Done at Brussels, 6 February 1962.

---

2. Text of Regulation 27/62 (reproduced below)

Book One: Part X—Procedure and Remedies

Commission Regulation 27 of May 3, 1962

First Regulation implementing Council Regulation 17 of February 6, 1962

(J.O. 1118/62 AMENDED BY [1968] O.J. 189/1; [1975] O.J. L172/7; [1985] O.J. L240/1)

THE COMMISSION OF THE EUROPEAN ECONOMIC COMMUNITY,

Having regard to the provisions of the Treaty establishing the European Economic Community, and in particular Articles 87 and 155 thereof,

Having regard to Article 24 of Council Regulation 17 of 6 February 1962 (First Regulation implementing Articles 85 and 86 of the Treaty),

(1) Whereas under Article 24 of Council Regulation 17 the Commission is authorised to adopt implementing provisions concerning the form, content and other details of applications under Articles 2 and 3 and of notifications under Articles 4 and 5 of that Regulation;

(2) Whereas the submission of such applications and notifications may have important legal consequences for each of the undertakings which is party to an agreement, decision or concerted practice; whereas every undertaking should accordingly have the right to submit an application or a notification to the Commission; whereas, furthermore, an undertaking exercising this right must inform the other undertakings which are parties to the agreement, decision or concerted practice, in order to enable them to protect their interests;

(3) Whereas it is for the undertakings and associations of undertakings to transmit to the Commission information as to facts and circumstances in support of applications under Article 2 and of notifications under Articles 4 and 5;

(4) Whereas it is desirable to prescribe forms for use in applications for negative clearance relating to implementation of Article 85(1) and for notifications relating to implementation of Article 85(3) of the Treaty in order to simplify and accelerate consideration by the competent departments, in the interests of all concerned,

HAS ADOPTED THIS REGULATION:

Article 1: Persons entitled to submit applications and notifications

1. Any undertakings which is party to agreements, decisions or practices of the kind described in Articles 85 and 86 of the Treaty may submit an application under Article 2 or a notification under Articles 4 and 5 of Regulation 17. Where the application or notification is submitted by some, but not all, of the undertakings concerned, they shall give notice to the others.

2. Where applications and notifications under Articles 2, 3(1), 3(2)(*b*), 4 and 5 of Regulation 17 are signed by representatives of undertakings, or associations of undertakings, or natural or legal persons such representatives shall produce written proof that they are authorised to act.

3. Where a joint application or notification is submitted a joint representative should be appointed.

Article 2: Submission of applications and notifications

1. Thirteen copies of each application and notification shall be submitted to the Commission.

2. The supporting documents shall be either original or copies; copies must be certified as true copies of the original.

3. Applications and notifications shall be in one of the official languages of the Community. Supporting documents shall be submitted in their original language. Where the original language is not one of the official languages, a translation in one of the official languages shall be attached.

Article 3: Effective date of submission of applications and registrations

The date of submission of an application or notification shall be the date on which it is received by the Commission. Where, however, the application or notification is sent by registered post, it shall be deemed to have been received on the date shown on the postmark of the place of posting.

Article 4: Content of applications and notifications

1. Applications under Article 2 of Regulation 17 relating to the applicability of Article 85(1) of the Treaty and notifications under Article 4 or Article 5(2) of Regulation 17 shall be submitted on Form A/B, in the manner prescribed in the Form and in the Complementary Note thereto, as shown in the Annex to this Regulation.

2. Applications and notifications shall contain the information asked for in Form A/B and the Complementary Note.

3. Several participating undertakings may submit an application or notification on a single form.

4. Applications under Article 2 of Regulation 17 relating to the applicability of Article 86 of the Treaty shall contain a full statement of the facts, specifying, in particular, the practice concerned and the position of the undertaking or undertakings within the common market or a substantial part thereof in regard to products or services to which the practice relates. Form A/B may be used.

Article 5: Transitional Provisions

1. Applications and notifications submitted prior to the date of entry into force of this Regulation otherwise than on the prescribed forms shall be deemed to comply with Article 4 of this Regulation.

2. The Commission may require a duly completed form to be submitted to it within such time as it shall appoint. In that event, applications and notifications shall be treated as properly made only if the forms are submitted within the prescribed period and in accordance with the provisions of this Regulation.

Article 6

This Regulation shall enter into force on the day following its publication in the *Official Journal of the European Communities*.

This Regulation shall be binding in its entirety and directly applicable in all Member States.

ANNEX

3. Annex to Commission Regulation 27/62 (reproduced over)

Annex to Commission Regulation 27

Note. This form must be accompanied by an Annex containing the information specified in the attached Complementary Note.

The form and Annex must be supplied in 13 copies (one for the Commission and one for each Member State). Supply three copies of any relevant agreement and one copy of other supporting documents.

Please do not forget to complete the Acknowledgement of Receipt annexed.

If space is insufficient, please use extra pages, specifying to which item on the form they relate.

FORM A/B

TO THE COMMISSION OF THE EUROPEAN COMMUNITIES

Directorate-General for Competition,
Rue de la Loi, 200,
B-1049 Brussels.

A. Application for negative clearance pursuant to Article 2 of Council Regulation 17 of 6 February 1962 relating to implementation of Article 85(1) or of Article 86 of the Treaty establishing the European Economic Community.

B. Notification of an agreement, decision or concerted practice under Article 4 (or 5) of Council Regulation 17 of 6 February 1962 with a view to obtaining a exemption under Article 85(3) of the Treaty establishing the European Economic Community, including notifications claiming benefit of an opposition procedure.

Identity of the parties

1. *Identity of applicant/notifier*

    Full name and address, telephone, telex and facsimile numbers, and brief description of the undertaking(s) or association(s) of undertakings submitting the application.

    For partnerships, sole traders or any other unincorporated body trading under a business name, give, also, the name, forename(s) and address of the proprietor(s) or partner(s).

    Where an application is submitted on behalf of some other person (or is submitted by more than one person) the name, address and position of the representative (or joint representative) must be given, together with proof of his authority to act. Where an aplication or notification is submitted by or on behalf of more than one person they should appoint a joint representative (Article 1(2) and (3) of Commission Regulation No 27).

Part X—1 Procedural Legislation

2. Identity of any other parties

Full name and address and brief description of any other parties to the agreement, decision or concerted practice (hereinafter referred to as 'the arrangements').

State what steps have been taken to inform these other parties of this application or notification.

(This information is not necessary in respect of standard contracts which an undertaking submitting the application or notification has concluded or intends to conclude with a number of parties (e.g. a contract appointing dealers).)

Purpose of this application/notification *(Please answer yes or*
(see Complementary Note)   *no to the questions)*

Are you asking for negative clearance alone? (See Complementary Note—Section IV, end of first paragraph—for the consequence of such a request.)

Are you applying for negative clearance, and also notifying the arrangements to obtain an exemption in case the Commission does not grant negative clearance?

Are you only notifying the arrangements in order to obtain an exemption?

Do you claim that this application may benefit from an opposition procedure? (See Complementary Note—Sections III, VI and VII and Annex 2). If you answer 'yes', please specify the Regulation and Article number on which you are relying.

Would you be satisfied with a comfort letter? (See the end of Section VII of the Complementary Note).

The undersigned declare that the information given above and in the . . . pages annexed hereto is correct to the best of their knowledge and belief, that all estimates are identified as such and are their best estimates of the underlying facts and that all the opinions expressed are sincere.

They are aware of the provisions of Article 15(1)(a) of Regulation No 17 (see attached Complementary Note).

Place and date: ....

        Signatures: ....

                               ....

                               ....

                    Brussels ....

COMMISSION　　　　　　Brussels ....
OF THE
EUROPEAN COMMUNITIES

Directorate-General for Competition

> To

ACKNOWLEDGEMENT OF RECEIPT

(This form will be returned to the address inserted above if the top half is completed in a single copy by the person lodging it)

Your application for negative clearance dated: ....

Your notification dated: ....

concerning: ....

Your reference: ....

Parties:

1. ....

2. ....

and others

(There is no need to name the other undertakings party to the arrangement)

(To be completed by the Commission.)

was received on: ....

and registered under No IV/: ....

Please quote the above number in all correspondence

Part X—1 Procedural Legislation

COMPLEMENTARY NOTE

Contents

I   Purpose of Community rules on competition
II   Negative clearance
III Exemption under Article 85(3)
IV   Purpose of the form
V   Nature of the form
VI   The need for complete and accurate information
VII Subsequent procedure
VIII Secrecy
IX   Further information and headings to be used in Annex to Form A/B

Annex 1: Text of Articles 85 and 86 of the EEC Treaty
Annex 2: List of relevant Acts
Annex 3: List of Member States and Commission Press and Information Offices within the Community

Additions or alterations to the information given in these Annexes will be published by the Commission from time to time.
Nota bene: Any undertaking uncertain about how to complete a notification or wishing further explanation may contact the Directorate-General for Competition (DG IV) in Brussels. Alternatively, any Commission Information Office (those in the Community are listed in Annex 3) will be able to obtain guidance or indicate an official in Brussels who speaks the preferred official Community language.

I. Purpose of Community rules on competition

The purpose of these rules is to prevent the distortion of competition in the common market by monopolies or restrictive practices; they apply to any enterprise trading directly or indirectly in the common market, wherever established. Article 85(1) of the Treaty establishing the European Economic Community (the text of Articles 85 and 86 is reproduced in Annex 1 to this note) prohibits restrictive agreements or concerted practices which may affect trade between Member States, and Article 85(2) declares contracts or other otherwise legally binding arrangements containing such restrictions void (although the European Court of Justice has held that if restrictive terms of contracts are severable, only those terms are void); Article 85(3), however, gives the Commission power to exempt practices with beneficial effects. Article 86 prohibits the abuse of a dominant position. The original procedures for implementing these Articles, which provide for "negative clearance" and exemption under Article 85(3), were laid down in Council Regulation No 17 (the references to this and all other acts mentioned in this note or relevant applications made on Form A/B are listed in Annex 2 to this note).

II. Negative clearance

The purpose of the negative clearance procedure is to allow businesses ("undertakings") to ascertain whether or not the Commission considers that any of their arrangements or behaviour are prohibited under Articles 85(1) or 86 of the Treaty. (It is governed by Article 2 of Regulation No. 17.) Clearance takes the form of a decision by the Commission certifying that, on the basis of the facts in its possession, there are no grounds under Article 85(1) or 86 of the Treaty for action on its part in respect of the arrangements or behaviour.

Any party may apply for negative clearance, even without the consent (but not without the knowledge) of other parties to arrangements. There would be little point in applying, however, where arrangements or behaviour clearly do not fall within the scope of Article 85(1) or Article 86. (In this connection, your attention is drawn to the last paragraph of IV below and to Annex 2). Nor is the Commission obliged to give negative clearance—Article 2 of Regulation No. 17 states that ' ... the Commission *may* certify ... ' The Commission does not usually issue negative clearance decisions in cases which, in its opinion, so clearly do not fall within the scope of the prohibition of Article 85(1) that there is no reasonable doubt for it to resolve by such a decision.

III. Exemption under Article 85(3)

The purpose of the procedure for exemption under Article 85(3) is to allow undertakings to enter into arrangements which, in fact, offer economic advantages but which, without an exemption, would be prohibited under Article 85(1). (It is governed by Articles 4, 6 and 8 of Regulation No. 17 and, for new Member States, by Articles 5, 7 and 25.) It takes the form of a decision by the Commission declaring Article 85(1) to be inapplicable to the arrangements described in the decision. Article 8 requires the Commission to specify the period of validity of any such decision, allows the Commission to attach conditions and obligations and provides for decisions to be amended or revoked or specified acts by the parties to be prohibited in certain circumstances, notably if the decisions were based on incorrect information or if there is any material change in the facts.

Any party may notify arrangements, even without the consent (but not without the knowledge) of other parties.

The Commission has adopted a number of Regulations granting exemptions to categories of agreements. Some of these Regulations (see Annex 2 for the latest list) provide that some agreements may benefit by such an exemption only if they are notified to the Commission under Article 4 (or 5) of Regulation No. 17 with a view to obtaining exemption under Article 85(3) of the Treaty and the benefit of an opposition procedure is claimed in the notification.

A decision granting exemption under Article 85(3) may have retroactive effect but, with certain exceptions, cannot be made effective earlier than the date of notification (Article 6 of Regulation No. 17). Should the Commission find that notified arrangements are indeed prohibited by Article 85(1) and cannot be exempted under Article 85(3) and, therefore, take a decision condemning them, the parties are nevertheless protected, from the date of notification, against fines for any infringement described in the notification (Articles 3 and 15(5) and (6)).

IV. Purpose of the form

The purpose of Form A/B is to allow undertakings, or associations of undertakings, wherever situated, to apply to the Commission for negative clearance for arrangements or behaviour, or to notify such arrangements and apply to have them exempted from the prohibition of Article 85(1) of the Treaty by virtue of Article 85(3). The form allows undertakings applying for negative clearance to notify, at the same time, in order to obtain an exemption. It should be noted that only a notification in order to obtain exemption affords immunity from fines (Article 15(5)).

To be valid, applications for negative clearance in respect of Article 85, notifications to obtain an exemption and notifications claiming the benefit of an opposition procedure must be made on Form A/B (by virtue of Article 4 of Commission Regulation No. 27). (Undertakings applying for negative clearance for their behaviour in relation to a possible dominant position—Article 86—need not use Form A/B (see Article 4(4) of Regulation No. 27), but they are strongly recommended to give all the information requested at IX below in order to ensure that their application gives a full statement of the facts.)

Before completing a form, your attention is particularly drawn to the Regulations granting block exemption and the notices listed in Annex 2—these were published to allow undertakings to judge for themselves, in many cases, whether there was any doubt about their arrangements. This would allow them to avoid the considerable bother and expense, both for themselves and for the Commission, of submitting and examining an application or notification where there is clearly no doubt.

V. Nature of the form

The form consists of a single sheet calling for the identity of the applicant(s) or notifier(s) and of any other parties. This must be supplemented by further information given under the headings and references detailed below (see IX). For preference the paper used should be A4 (21×29.7 cm—the same size as the form) but must not be bigger. Leave a margin of at least 25 mm or one inch on the left-hand side of the page and, if you use both sides, on the right-hand side of the reverse.

VI. The need for complete and accurate information

It is important that applicants give all the relevant facts. Although the Commission has the right to seek further information from applicants or third parties, and is obliged to publish a summary of the application before granting negative clearance or exemption under Article 85(3), it will usually base its decision on the information provided by the applicant. Any decision taken on the basis of incomplete information could be without effect in the case of a negative clearance, or voidable in that of an exemption. For the same reason, it is also important to inform the Commission of any material changes to your arrangements made after your application or notification.

Complete information is of particular importance if you are claiming the benefit of a block exemption through an opposition procedure. Such exemption is dependent on the information supplied being ' . . . complete and in accordance with the facts.' If the Commission does not oppose a claim to benefit under this procedure on the basis of the facts in a notification and, subsequently, additional or different facts come to light that could and should have been in the notification, then the benefit of the exemption will be lost, and with retroactive effect. Similarly, there would be little point in claiming the benefit of an opposition procedure with clearly incomplete information; the Commission would be bound either to reject such a notification or oppose exemption in order to allow time for further information to be provided.

Moreover, you should be aware of the provisions of Article 15(1)(a) of Regulation No. 17 which reads:

"The Commission may by decision impose on undertakings or associations of undertakings fines of from 100 to 5,000 units of account where, intentionally or negligently, they supply incorrect or misleading information in an application pursuant to Article 2 or in a notification pursuant to Articles 4 or 5."

The key words here are 'incorrect or misleading information.' However, it often remains a matter of judgment how much detail is relevant; the Commission accepts estimates where accurate information is not readily available in order to facilitate notifications; and the Commission calls for opinions as well as facts.

You should therefore note that the Commission will use these powers only where applicants or notifiers have, intentionally or negligently, provided false information or grossly inaccurate estimates of suppressed readily available information or estimates, or have deliberately expressed false opinions in order to obtain negative clearance or exemption.

VII. Subsequent procedure

The application or notification is registered in the Registry of the Directorate-General for Competition (DG IV). The date of receipt by the Commission (or the date of posting if sent by registered post) is the effective date of the submission. The application or notification might be considered invalid if obviously incomplete or not on the obligatory form.

Further information might be sought from the applicants or from third parties (Article 11 or 14 of Regulation No. 17) and suggestions might be made as to amendments to the arrangements that might make them acceptable.

A notification claiming the benefit of an opposition procedure may be opposed by the Commission either because the Commission does not agree that the arrangements should benefit from a block exemption or to allow for more information to be sought. If the Commission opposes a claim, and unless the Commission subsequently withdraws its opposition, that notification will then be treated as an application for an individual exemption decision.

If, after examination, the Commission intends to grant the application, it is obliged (by Article 19(3) of Regulation No. 17) to publish a summary and invite comments from third parties. Subsequently, a preliminary draft decision has to be submitted to and discussed with the Advisory Committee on Restrictive Practices and Dominant Positions composed of officials to the Member State competent in the matter of restrictive practices and monopolies (Article 10 of Regulation No. 17)—they will already have received a copy of the application or notification. Only then, and providing nothing has happened to change the Commission's intention, can it adopt a decision.

Sometimes files are closed without any formal decision being taken, for example, because it is found that the arrangements are already covered by a block exemption, or because the applicants are satisfied by a less formal letter than the Commission's departments (sometimes called a 'comfort letter') indicating that the arrangements do not call for any action by the Commission, at least in present circumstances. Although not a Commission decision, a comfort letter indicates how the Commission's departments view the case on the facts currently in their possession which means that the Commission could if necessary—if, for example, it were to be asserted that a contract was void under Article 85(2)—take an appropriate decision.

VIII. Secrecy

Article 214 of the Treaty and Articles 20 and 21 of Regulation No. 17 require the Commission and Member States not to disclose information of the kind covered by the obligation of professional secrecy. On the other hand, Article 19 of the Regulation requires the Commission to publish a summary of your application, should it intend to grant it, before taking the relevant decision. In this publication, the Commission ' . . . shall have regard to the legitimate interest of undertakings in the protection of their business secrets (Article 19(3)). In this connection, if you believe that your interests would be harmed if any of the information you are asked to supply were to be published or otherwise divulged to other parties, please put all such information in a second annex, with each page clearly marked 'Business Secrets'; in the principal annex, under any affected heading state 'see second annex' or 'also see second annex'; in the second annex repeat the affected heading(s) and reference(s) and give the information you do not wish to have published, together with your reasons for this. Do not overlook the fact that the Commission may have to publish a summary of your application.

Before publishing an Article 19(3) notice, the Commission will show the undertakings concerned a copy of the proposed text.

IX. Further information and headings to be used in the Annex to Form A/B

The further information is to be given under the following headings and reference numbers. Wherever possible, give exact information. If this is not readily available, give your best estimate, and identify what you give as an estimate. If you believe any detail asked for to be unavailable or irrelevant, please explain why. This may, in particular, be the case if one party is notifying arrangements alone without the co-operation of other parties. Do not overlook the fact that the Commission officials are ready to discuss what detail is relevant (see the *nota bene* at the beginning of this Complementary Note). An example that might help you is available on request.

1. *Brief description*

Give a brief description of the arrangements or behaviour (nature, purpose, date(s) and duration)—(full details are requested below).

2. *Market*

The nature of the goods or services affected by the arrangements or behaviour (include the customs tariff heading number according to the CCC Nomenclature or the Community's Common Customs Tariff or the Nimexe code if you know it—specify which). A brief description of the structure of the market (or market) for these goods or services—*e.g.* who sells in it, who buys in it, its geographical extent, the turnover in it, how competitive it is, whether it is easy for new suppliers to enter the market, whether there are substitute products. If you are notifying a standard contract (*e.g.* a contract appointing dealers), say how many you expect to conclude. If you know of any studies of the market, it would be helpful to refer to them.

3. *Further details of the party or parties*

3.1. Do any of the parties form part of a group of companies? A group relationship is deemed to exist where a firm:
 —owns more than half the capital or business assets, or
 —has the power to exercise more than half the voting rights, or
 —has the power to appoint more than half the members of the supervisory board, board of directors or bodies legally representing the undertaking, or
 —has the right to manage the affairs of another.
If the answer is yes, give:
 —the name and address of the ultimate parent company;
 —a brief description of the business of the group (and, if possible, one copy of the last set of group accounts);
 —the name and address of any other company in the group competing in a market affected by the arrangements or in any related market, that is to say any other company competing directly or indirectly with the parties ("relevant associated company").

3.2. The most recently available total turnover of each of the parties and, as the case may be, of the group of which it forms part (it could be helpful also if you could provide one copy of the last set of accounts).

3.3. The sales or turnover of each party in the goods or services affected by the arrangements in the Community and worldwide. If the turnover in the Community is material (say more than 5 per cent. market share), please also give figures for each Member State, and for previous years (in order to show any significant trends), and give each party's sales targets for the future. Provide the same figures for any relevant associated company. (Under this heading, in particular, your best estimate might be all that you can readily supply.)

3.4. In relation to the market (or markets) for the services described at 2 above, give, for each of the sales or turnover figures in 3.3, your estimate of the market share it represents.

3.5. If you have a substantial interest falling short of control (more than 25 per cent. but less than 50 per cent.) in some other company competing in a market affected by the arrangements, or if some other such company has a substantial interest in yours, give its name and address and brief details.

4. *Full details of the arrangements*

4.1. If the contents are reduced to writing give a brief description of the purpose of the arrangements and attach three copies of the text (except that the technical description often contained in know-how agreements may be omitted; in such cases, however, indicate parts omitted).
 If the contents are not, or are only partially, reduced to writing, give a full description.

4.2. Detail any provisions contained in the arrangements which may restrict the parties in their freedom to take independent commercial decisions, for example regarding:
 —buying or selling prices, discounts or other trading conditions;
 —the quantities of goods to be manufactured or distributed or services to be offered;
 —technical development or investment;
 —the choice of markets or sources of supply;
 —purchases from or sales to third parties;
 —whether to apply similar terms for the supply of equivalent goods or services;
 —whether to offer different services separately or together.
(If you are claiming the benefit of an opposition procedure, identify particularly in this list the restrictions that exceed those automatically exempted by the relevant Regulation.)

4.3. State between which Member States trade may be affected by the arrangements, and whether trade between the Community and any third countries is affected.

5. *Reasons for negative clearance*

 If you are applying for negative clearance state, under the reference:

5.1. why, *i.e.* state which provision or effects of the arrangements or behaviour might, in your view, raise questions of compatibility with the Community's rules of competition. The object of this subheading is to give the Commission the clearest possible idea of the doubts you have about your arrangements or behaviour that you wish to have resolved by a negative clearance decision.

Then, under the following two references, give a statement of the relevant facts and reasons as to why you consider Articles 85(1) or 86 to be inapplicable, *i.e.*

5.2. why the arrangements do not have the object or effect of preventing, restricting or distorting competition within the common market to any appreciable extent, or why your undertaking does not have or its behaviour does not abuse a dominant position; and/or

5.3. why the arrangements or behaviour are not such as may affect trade between Member States to any appreciable extent.

6. *Reasons for exemption under Article 85(3)*

If you are notifying the arrangements, even if only as a precaution, in order to obtain an exemption under Article 85(3), explain how:

6.1. the arrangements contribute to improving production or distribution, and/or promoting technical or economic progress;

6.2. a proper share of the benefits arising from such improvement or progress accrues to consumers;

6.3. all restrictive provisions of the arrangements are indispensable to the attainment of the aims set out under 6.1 above (if you are claiming the benefit of an opposition procedure, it is particularly important that you should identify and justify restrictions that exceed those automatically exempted by the relevant Regulation); and

6.4. the arrangements do not eliminate competition in respect of a substantial part of the goods or services concerned.

7. *Other information*

7.1. Mention any earlier proceedings or informal contacts, of which you are aware, with the Commission and any earlier proceedings with any national authorities or courts concerning these or any related arrangements.

7.2. Give any other information presently available that you think might be helpful in allowing the Commission to appreciate whether there are any restrictions contained in the agreement, or any benefits that might justify them.

7.3. State whether you intend to produce further supporting facts or arguments not yet available and, if so, on which points.

7.4. State, with reasons, the urgency of your application or notification.

Annex 1

Text of Articles 85 and 86 of the EEC Treaty

Article 85

1. The following shall be prohibited as incompatible with the common market: all agreements between undertakings, decisions by associations of undertakings and concerted practices which may affect trade between Member States and which have as their object or effect the prevention, restriction or distortion or competition within the common market, and in particular those which:
    (a) directly or indirectly fix purchase or selling prices or any other trading conditions;
    (b) limit or control production, markets, technical development, or investment;
    (c) share markets or sources of supply;
    (d) apply dissimilar conditions to equivalent transactions withother trading parties, thereby placing them at a competitive disadvantage;
    (e) make the conclusions of contracts subject to acceptance by other parties of supplementary obligations which, by their nature or according to commerical usage, have no connection with the subject of such contracts.
2. Any agreements or decisions prohibited pursuant to this Article shall be automatically void.
3. The provisions of paragraph 1 may, however, be declared inapplicable in the case of:
    — any agreement or category of agreements between undertakings,
    — any decision or category of decisions by associations of undertakings,
    — any concerted practice or category of concerted practices,
which contributes to improving the production or distribution of goods or to promoting technical or economic progress, while allowing consumers a fair share of the resulting benefit, and which does not:
    (a) impose on the undertakings concerned restrictions which are not indispenable to the attainment of these objectives;
    (b) afford such undertakings the possibility of eliminating competition in respect of a substantial part of the products in question.

Article 86

Any abuse by one or more undertakings of a dominant position within the common market or in a substantial part of it shall be prohibited as incompatible with the common market in so far as it may affect between Member States.
Such abuse may, in particular, consist in:
(a) directly or indirectly imposing unfair purchase or selling prices or other unfair trading conditions;
(b) limiting production, markets or technical development to the prejudice of consumers;
(c) applying dissimilar conditions to equivalent transactions with other trading parties, thereby placing them at a competitive disadvantage;
(d) making the conclusion of contracts subject to acceptance by the other parties of supplementary obligations which, by their nature or according to commercial usage, have no connection with the subject of such contracts.

Annex 2

List of Relevant Acts

(As of August 5, 1985)

(If you think it possible that your arrangements do not need to be notified by virtue of any of these Regulations or notices it may be worth your while to obtain a copy.)

Implementing Regulations

Council Regulation 17 of February 6, 1962 implementing Article 85 and 86 of the Treaty (J.O. 204/62; [1959–62] O.J. 87) as amended (J.O. 1655/62; [1959–62] O.J. Spec.Ed. 249; J.O. 2696/63; [1963–64] O.J. Spec.Ed. 55; [1971] O.J. L285/49).

Commission Regulation 27 of May 3, 1962 implementing Council Regulation 17 (J.O. 35/62) English Special Edition 1959–62, November 1972, p. 87) as amended ([1968] O.J. L189/1; [1975] O.J. L172/7; [1985] O.J. L240/11).

Regulations granting block exemption in respect of a wide range of agreements

Commission Regulation 1983/83 of June 22, 1983 on the application of Article 85(3) of the Treaty to categories of exclusive distribution agreements ([1983] O.J. L173/1) as corrected in ([1983] O.J. L281/24).

Commission Regulation 1984/83 of June 22, 1983, on the application of Article 85(3) of the Treaty to categories of exclusive purchasing agreements ([1983] O.J. L173/3) as corrected in ([1983] O.J. L281/24).

See also the Commission notice concerning Commission Regulations 1983/83 and 1984/83 of June 22, 1983 on the application of Article 85(3) of the Treaty of categories of exclusive distribution and exclusive purchasing agreements.

Commission Regulation 2349/84 of July 23, 1984 on the application of Article 85(3) of the Treaty to certain categories of patent licensing agreements ([1984] O.J. L219/15), as corected in ([1985] O.J. L113/34). Article 4 of this Regulation provides for an opposition procedure.

Commission Regulation 123/85 of December 12, 1984 on the application of Article 85(3) of the Treaty to certain categories of motor vehicles distribution and servicing agreements ([1985] O.J. L15/16). See also the Commission notice concerning this Regulation.

Commission Regulation 417/85 of December 19, 1984 on the application of Article 85(3) of the Treaty to categories of specialization agreements ([1985] O.J. L53/1). Article 4 of this Regulation provides for an opposition procedure.

Commission Regulation 418/85 of December 19, 1984 on the application of Article 85(3) of the Treaty to categories of research and development cooperation agreements ([1985] O.J. L53/5). Article 7 of this Regulation provides for an opposition procedure.

Commission Notices of a General Nature

Commission notice on exclusive dealing contracts with commercial agents (J.O. 2921/62). This states that the Commission does not consider most such agreements to fall under the prohibition of Article 85(1).

Commission notice concerning agreements, decisions and concerted practices in the field of cooperation between enterprises. This defines the sorts of cooperation on market studies, accounting, R & D, joint use of production, storage or transport, *ad hoc* consortia, selling or after-sales service, advertising or quality labelling that the Commission considers not to fall under the prohibition of Article 85(1).

Commission notice on agreements, decisions and concerted practices of minor importance which does not fall under Article 85(1) of the Treaty—in the main, those where the parties have less than 5% of the market between them, and a combined annual turnover of less than 50 million ECU.

Commission notice concerning its assessment of certain subcontracting agreements in relation to Article 85(1) of the Treaty.

A collection of these texts (as at June 30, 1981) was published by the Office of Official Publications of the European Communities (Refs. ISBN 92-825-2389-6, Catalogue No CB 30-80-576-EN-C). This is now in short supply in some languages and out of stock in other. An updated collection is in preparation.

Part X—1   Procedural Legislation

Annex 3

List of member states and commission press and information offices within the Community

(as of January 1, 1986)

The Member States as at the date of this Annex are: Belgium, Denmark, France, Germany, Greece, Ireland, Italy, Luxembourg, the Netherlands, Portugal, Spain and the United Kingdom.

The addresses of the Commission's Press and Information Offices in the Community are:

BELGIUM

Rue Archimède 73,
B-1040 Bruxelles
Tel. 235 11 11

DENMARK

Højbrohus
Østergade 61
Postbox 144
DK-1004 København K
Tel. 14 41 40

FRANCE

61, rue des Belles-Feuilles
F-75782 Paris, Cedex 16
Tel. 501 58 85

CMCI/Bureau 320
2, rue Henri Barbusse
F-13241 Marseille, Cedex 01
Tel. 08 62 00

FEDERAL REPUBLIC OF GERMANY

Zitelmannstraße 22
D-5300 Bonn
Tel. 23 80 41

Kurfürstendamm 102
D-1000 Berlin 31
Tel. 892 40 28

Erhardstraße 27
D-8000 München
Tel. 23 99 29 00

GREECE

2 Vassilissis Sofias
TK 1602
GR-Athina 134
Tel. 724 39 82/724 39 83/724 39 84

IRELAND

39 Molesworth Street
IRL-Dublin 2
Tel. 71 22 44

ITALY

Via Poli 29
I-00187 Roma
Tel. 678 97 22

Corso Magenta 61
I-20123 Milano
Tel. 80 15 05/6/7/8

LUXEMBOURG

Bâtiment Jean Monnet
Rue Alcide de Gasperi
L-2920 Luxembourg
Tel. 430 11

NETHERLANDS

Lange Voorhout 29
NL-Den Haag
Tel. 46 93 26

PORTUGAL

Rua do Sacramento à Lapa 35
P-1200 Lisboa
Tel. 60 21 99

SPAIN

Calle de Serrano 41
5a Planta
E-1 Madrid
Tel. 435 17 00

UNITED KINGDOM

8 Storey's Gate
UK-London SW1P 3AT
Tel. 222 81 22

Windsor House
9/15 Bedford Street
UK-Belfast BT2 7EG
Tel. 407 08

4 Cathedral Road
UK-Cardiff CF1 9SG
Tel. 37 16 31

7 Alva Street
UK-Edinburgh EH2 4PH
Tel. 225 20 58

4. Text of Regulation 99/63 (reproduced below)

Commission Regulation 99/63 of July 25, 1963

On the hearings provided for in Article 19(1) and (2) of Regulation 17

(J.O. 2268/63; [1963–64] O.J. Spec.Ed. 47)

THE COMMISSION OF THE EUROPEAN ECONOMIC COMMUNITY,

Having regard to the Treaty establishing the European Economic Community, and in particular Articles 87 and 155 thereof;

Having regard to Article 24 of Regulation 17 of 6 February 1962 (First Regulation implementing Articles 85 and 86 of the Treaty);

(1) Whereas the Commission has power under Article 24 of Regulation 17 to lay down implementing provisions concerning the hearings provided for in Article 19(1) and (2) of that Regulation.

(2) Whereas in most cases the Commission will in the course of its inquiries already be in close touch with the undertakings or associations of undertakings which are the subject thereof and they will accordingly have the opportunity of making known their views regarding the objections raised against them;

(3) Whereas, however, in accordance with Article 19(1) of Regulation 17 and with the rights of defence, the undertakings and associations of undertakings concerned must have the right on conclusion of the inquiry to submit their comments on the whole of the objections raised against them which the Commission proposes to deal with in its decisions;

(4) Whereas persons other than the undertakings or associations of undertakings which are the subject of the inquiry may have an interest in being heard; whereas, by the second sentence of Article 19(2) of Regulation 17, such persons must have the opportunity of being heard if they apply and show that they have a sufficient interest;

(5) Whereas it is desirable to enable persons who pursuant to Article 3(2) of Regulation 17 have applied for an infringement to be terminated to submit their comments where the Commission considers that on the basis of the information in its possession there are insufficient grounds for granting the application;

(6) Whereas the various persons entitled to submit comments must do so in writing, both in their own interest and in the interests of good administration, without prejudice to oral procedure where appropriate to supplement the written evidence;

(7) Whereas it is necessary to define the rights of persons who are to be heard, and in particular the conditions upon which they may be represented or assisted and the setting and calculation of time limits;

(8) Whereas the Advisory Committee on Restrictive Practices and Monopolies delivers its Opinion on the basis of a preliminary draft decision; whereas it must therefore be consulted concerning a case after the inquiry in respect thereof has been completed; whereas such consultation does not prevent the Commission from reopening an inquiry if need be;

HAS ADOPTED THIS REGULATION:

Article 1

Before consulting the Advisory Committee on Restrictive Practices and Monopolies, the Commission shall hold a hearing pursuant to Article 19(1) of Regulation 17.

Article 2

1. The Commission shall inform undertakings and associations of undertakings in writing of the objections raised against them. The communication shall be addressed to each of them or to a joint agent appointed by them.

2. The Commission may inform the parties by giving notice in the *Official Journal of the European Communities*, if from the circumstances of the case this appears appropriate, in particular where notice is to be given to a number of undertakings but no joint agent has been appointed.

The notice shall have regard to the legitimate interest of the undertakings in the protection of their business secrets.

3. A fine or a periodic penalty payment may be imposed on an undertaking or association of undertakings only if the objections were notified in the manner provided for in paragraph (1).

4. The Commission shall when giving notice of objections fix a time limit up to which the undertakings and associations of undertakings may inform the Commission of their views.

Article 3

1. Undertakings and associations of undertakings shall, within the appointed time limit, make known in writing their views concerning the objections raised against them.

2. They may in their written comments set out all matters relevant to their defence.

3. They may attach any relevant documents in proof of the facts set out. They may also propose that the Commission hear persons who may corroborate those facts.

Article 4

The Commission shall in its decisions deal only with those objections raised against undertakings and associations of undertakings in respect of which they have been afforded the opportunity of making known their views.

Article 5

If natural or legal persons showing a sufficient interest apply to be heard pursuant to Article 19(2) of Regulation 17, the Commission shall afford them the opportunity of making known their views in writing within such time limit as it shall fix.

Article 6

Where the Commission, having received an application pursuant to Article 3(2) of Regulation 17, considers that on the basis of the information in its possession there are insufficient grounds for granting the application, it shall inform the applicants of its reasons and fix a time limit for them to submit any further comments in writing.

Article 7

1. The Commission shall afford to persons who have so requested in their written comments the opportunity to put forward their arguments orally, if those persons show a sufficient interest or if the Commission proposes to impose on them a fine or periodic penalty payment.

2. The Commission may likewise afford to any other person the opportunity of orally expressing his views.

Article 8

1. The Commission shall summon the persons to be heard to attend on such date as it shall appoint.

2. It shall forthwith transmit a copy of the summons to the competent authorities of the Member States, who may appoint an official to take part in the hearing.

Article 9

1. Hearings shall be conducted by the persons appointed by the Commission for that purpose.

2. Persons summoned to attend shall appear either in person or be represented by legal representatives or by representatives authorised by their constitution. Undertakings and associations of undertakings may moreover be represented by a duly authorised agent appointed from among their permanent staff.

Persons heard by the Commission may be assisted by lawyers or university teachers who are entitled to plead before the Court of Justice of the European Communities in accordance with Article 17 of the Protocol of the Statute of the Court, or by other qualified persons.

3. Hearings shall not be public. Persons shall be heard separately or in the presence of other persons summoned to attend. In the latter case, regard shall be had to the legitimate interest of the undertakings in the protection of their business secrets.

Book One: Part X—Procedure and Remedies

4. The essential content of the statements made by each person heard shall be recorded in minutes which shall be read and approved by him.

Article 10

Without prejudice to Article 2(2), information and summonses from the Commission shall be sent to the addressees by registered letter with acknowledgement of receipt, or shall be delivered by hand against receipt.

Article 11

1. In fixing the time limits provided for in Articles 2, 5 and 6, the Commission shall have regard both to the time required for preparation of comments and to the urgency of the case. The time limit shall be not less than two weeks; it may be extended.

2. Time limits shall run from the day following receipt of a communication or delivery thereof by hand.

3. Written comments must reach the Commission or be dispatched by registered letter before expiry of the time limit. Where the time limit would expire on a Sunday or public holiday, it shall be extended up to the end of the next following working day. For the purpose of calculating this extension, public holidays shall, in cases where the relevant date is the date of receipt of written comments, be those set out in the Annex to this regulation, and in cases where the relevant date is the date of dispatch, those appointed by law in the country of dispatch.

This regulation shall be binding in its entirety and directly applicable in all Member States.

Done at Brussels, 25 July 1963.

ANNEX

Referred to in the third sentence of Article 11(3)

(List of public holidays)

New Year	1 Jan
Good Friday	
Easter Saturday	
Easter Monday	
Labour Day	1 May
Schuman Plan Day	9 May
Ascension Day	
Whit Monday	
Belgian National Day	21 July
Assumption	15 Aug
All Saints	1 Nov
All Souls	2 Nov
Christmas Eve	24 Dec
Christmas Day	25 Dec
Boxing Day	26 Dec
New Year's Eve	31 Dec

5. Text of Regulation 2988/74 (reproduced below)

Council Regulation 2988/74 of November 26, 1974

Concerning limitation periods in proceedings and the enforcement of sanctions under the Rules of the European Economic Community relating to transport and competition

([1974] O.J. L319/1)

THE COUNCIL OF THE EUROPEAN COMMUNITIES,

Having regard to the Treaty establishing the European Economic Community, and in particular Articles 75, 79 and 87 thereof;

Having regard to the proposal from the Commission;

Having regard to the Opinion of the European Parliament;

Having regard to the Opinion of the Economic and Social Committee;

(1) Whereas under the rules of the European Economic Community relating to transport and competition the Commission has the power to impose fines, penalties and periodic penalty payments on undertakings or associations of undertak-

ings which infringe Community law relating to information or investigation, or to the prohibition on discrimination, restrictive practices and abuse of dominant position; whereas those rules make no provision for any limitation period;

(2) Whereas it is necessary in the interest of legal certainty that the principle of limitation be introduced and that implementing rules be laid down; whereas, for the matter to be covered fully, it is necessary that provision for limitation be made not only as regards the power to impose fines or penalties, but also as regards the power to enforce decisions, imposing fines, penalties or periodic penalty payments; whereas such provisions should specify the length of limitation periods, the date on which time starts to run and the events which have the effect of interrupting or suspending the limitation period; whereas in this respect the interests of undertakings and associations of undertakings on the one hand, and the requirements imposed by administrative practice, on the other hand, should be taken into account;

(3) Whereas this Regulation must apply to the relevant provisions of Regulation 11 concerning the abolition of discrimination in transport rates and conditions, in implementation of Article 79(3) of the Treaty establishing the European Economic Community, of Regulation 17: first Regulation implementing Articles 85 and 86 of the Treaty, and of Council Regulation 1017/68 of 19 July 1968, applying rules of competition to transport by rail, road and inland waterway; whereas it must also apply to the relevant provisions of future regulations in the fields of European Economic Community law relating to transport and competition.

HAS ADOPTED THIS REGULATION:

Article 1: Limitation periods in proceedings

1. The power of the Commission to impose fines or penalties for infringements of the rules of the European Economic Community relating to transport or competition shall be subject to the following limitation periods:
(a) three years in the case of infringements of provisions concerning applications or notifications of undertakings or associations of undertakings, requests for information, or the carrying out of investigations;
(b) five years in the case of all other infringements.

2. Time shall begin to run upon the day on which the infringement is committed. However, in the case of continuing or repeated infringements, time shall begin to run on the day on which the infringement ceases.

Article 2: Interruption of the limitation period in proceedings

1. Any action taken by the Commission, or by any Member State, acting at the request of the Commission, for the purpose of the preliminary investigation or proceedings in respect of an infringement shall interrupt the limitation period in proceedings. The limitation period shall be interrupted with effect from the date on which the action is notified to at least one undertaking or association of undertakings which have participated in the infringement.

Actions which interrupt the running of the period shall include in particular the following:
(a) written requests for information by the Commission, or by the competent authority of a Member State acting at the request of the Commission; or a Commission decision requiring the requested information;
(b) written authorisations issued to their officials by the Commission or by the competent authority of any Member State at the request of the Commission; or a Commission decision ordering an investigation;
(c) the commencement of proceedings by the Commission;
(d) notification of the Commission's statement of objections.

2. The interruption of the limitation period shall apply for all the undertakings or associations of undertakings which have participated in the infringement.

3. Each interruption shall start time running afresh. However, the limitation period shall expire at the latest on the day on which a period equal to twice the limitation period has elapsed without the Commission having imposed a fine or a penalty; that period shall be extended by the time during which limitation is suspended pursuant to Article 3.

Article 3: Suspension of the limitation period in proceedings

Book One: Part X—Procedure and Remedies

The limitation period in proceedings shall be suspended for as long as the decision of the Commission is the subject of proceedings pending before the Court of Justice of the European Communities.

Article 4: Limitation period for the enforcement of sanctions

1. The power of the Commission to enforce decisions imposing fines, penalties or periodic payments for infringements of the rules of the European Economic Community relating to transport or competition shall be subject to a limitation period of five years.

2. Time shall begin to run on the day on which the decision becomes final.

Article 5: Interruption of the limitation period for the enforcement of sanctions

1. The limitation period for the enforcement of sanctions shall be interrupted:
(a) by notification of a decision varying the original amount of the fine, penalty or periodic penalty payments or refusing an application for variation;
(b) by any action of the Commission, or of a Member State at the request of the Commission, for the purpose of enforcing payments of a fine, penalty or periodic penalty payment.

2. Each interruption shall start time running afresh.

Article 6: Suspension of the limitation period for the enforcement of sanctions

The limitation period for the enforcement of sanctions shall be suspended for so long as:
(a) time to pay is allowed; or
(b) enforcement of payment is suspended pursuant to a decision of the Court of Justice of the European Communities.

Article 7: Application to transitional cases

This Regulation shall also apply in respect of infringements committed before it enters into force.

Article 8: Entry into force

This Regulation shall enter into force on 1 January 1975.

This Regulation shall be binding in its entirety and directly applicable in all Member States.

Done at Brussels, 26 November 1974.

CHAPTER 2

THE HANDLING OF A CASE

A. THE OPENING OF A FILE

1. Method of notification; what constitutes a valid notification

Articles 4(1), 5(1) Regulation 27/62
Articles 1–4 Regulation 27/62
Grundig/Consten 5
Cobelpa/VNP 115 (paras. 5, 9, 40)
The Distillers Company 123*
BMW Belgium 126 (para. 25)
Hasselblad 173 (para. 72)
AEG/Telefunken 179 (para. 75)
Zinc Producers Group 217
Aluminium 228 (para. 16)
Sperry New Holland 245 (para. 65)
Eco System 344a (para. 29)
U.K. Tractors 347 (para. 59)
15th Comp. Rep. (para. 48)
Parfums Rochas v. *Bitsch* 13 (grounds 4–6, 7, 11)
De Haecht v. *Wilkin* II 34 (grounds 14–23)
Boekhandels v. *Eldi Records* 73 (grounds 8–11)
Distillers v. *Commission* 75 (grounds 19–24)*
FEDETAB v. *Commission* 80 (grounds 48–56)
Pioneer v. *Commission* 98 (ground 93)

1.1. When is notification necessary

Articles 4(2), 5(2) Regulation 17/62
Article 7 Regulation 19/65
Kabelmetal/Luchaire 94
Vaessen/Moris 143 (paras. 21–22)
BP Kemi/DDSF 147 (paras. 98–102)
NAVEWA-ANSEAU 178 (para. 62)
SSI 181 (para. 143)*
Windsurfing International 194
Fire Insurance 220 (para. 38)
Roofing Felt 248 (paras. 96–98)
Meldoc 253 (para. 74)
1st Comp. Rep. (para. 39)
Bilger v. *Jehle* 12 (grounds 4–6)
De Haecht v. *Wilkin* II 34 (grounds 19–23)
Fonderies Roubaix v. *Fonderies Roux* 49 (grounds 5–8)
De Bloos v. *Boyer* 60 (grounds 11–13)
FEDETAB v. *Commission* 80 (grounds 57–63)

Part X—2 The Handling of a Case

NAVEWA v. *Commission* 101 (grounds 30–35)
SSI v. *Commission* 127 (ground 75)*
Windsurfing v. *Commission* 130 (ground 100).
Metro v. *Commission II* 134 (grounds 30–32)

1.2. Effect of notification

1.2.1. Possibility of the grant of an exemption

Article 4 Regulation 17/62
L'Oréal v. *De Nieuwe AMCK* 81 (ground 13)

1.2.2. Immunity from fines

Article 15(5) Regulation 17/62
Chiquita 101
Theal/Watts 110
AEG/Telefunken 179 (para. 75)
John Deere 226 (para. 38)
Sperry New Holland 245 (para. 65)
Tepea v. *Commission* 64 (grounds 67–72)
Hasselblad v. *Commission* 107 (grounds 54–55)
SSI v. *Commission* 127 (ground 75)*

1.2.3. Provisional validity for old agreements

Article 25 Regulation 17/62
Julien/Van Katwijk 32
Velcro/Aplix 233
Bosch v. *Van Rijn* 1
De Haecht v. *Wilkin I* 7
Portelange v. *Smith Corona* 11
Bilger v. *Jehle* 12 (grounds 4–6)
Parfums Rochas v. *Bitsch* 13 (grounds 6–7)
De Haecht v. *Wilkin II* 34
De Bloos v. *Boyer* 60 (grounds 8–15)
Boekhandels v. *Eldi Records* 73 (grounds 8–11)
Lancôme v. *Etos* 78 (grounds 12–18)
Nouvelles Frontières 131 (grounds 61–69)*
Ahmed Saeed v. *Zentrale* 162 (grounds 5, 21, 32–33)

1.3. Opposition procedures

Article 4 Regulation 2349/84
Patent licensing agreements
Article 4 Regulation 417/85
Specialisation agreements
Article 7 Regulation 418/85
R&D agreements
Article 4 Regulation 4087/88
Franchising
Article 4 Regulation 556/89
Know-how licensing

2. Complaints

2.1. Method of lodging a complaint, *locus standi*

Article 3(2) Regulation 17/62
Herbage Seed. 6th Comp. Rep. (para. 119)
BBC. 6th Comp. Rep. (para. 163)
PSA Peugeot-Citroën. 8th Comp. Rep. (para. 149)
BB/TGWU. 16th Comp. Rep. (para. 43)

2.2. Rights and obligations of complainant

Pabst & Richarz/BNIA 106
11th Comp. Rep. (para. 118)
Gema v. *Commission* 70 (grounds 10–23)
CICCE v. *Commission* 118*
BAT v. *Commission & Philip Morris* 146 (grounds 19–20, 23–24)*

3. Ex-officio investigation

Article 3 Regulation 17/62
Bayer/Dental 327 (para. 20)
GAARM v. *Commission* 112 (grounds 21–24)

B. THE INVESTIGATION OF A CASE

1. By letter

1.1. Potential addressees of a letter pursuant to Article 11 Regulation No. 17/62

Article 11(1),(4) Regulation 17/62

1.2. Simple request for information

Article 11(2),(3) Regulation 17/62

1.2.1. Text of a typical example of a letter sent pursuant to Article 11

Text of typical example of a letter

"Notification" (parties to)
"Complaints" (complainants)
Re Case No. IV/(
(Please quote reference in all correspondence).
/Notification dated..........by..........of an /agreement/ /decision/
/concerted practice/
/complaint dated..........against........../

Request for information

Dear Sirs,

1. I refer to the above-mentioned /notification/ /complaint/.

2. This letter is a formal request for information made in accordance with the provisions of Article 11 of Council

Book One: Part X—Procedure and Remedies

Regulation No. 17, of which the relevant extracts are printed on the reverse of this page, together with extracts of Article 15 of that Regulation to which I also draw your attention.

The purpose of this request is to enable the Commission to assess the compatibility of the /agreement/ /decision/ /concerted practice/ referred to above with the EEC rules on competition in particular Article /85/ /86/ of the EEC Treaty in full knowledge of the facts and in their correct economic context. I shall be grateful, therefore, if you will supply the information requested in the annex to this letter which annex forms an integral part thereof.

In formulating the questions use has been made of the abbreviations used in the /notification/ /complaint/.

I have to inform you that it may be necessary to request further and/or supplementary information at a later date.

3. Your reply will be covered by the provisions of Article 20 of Regulation No. 17 concerning professional secrecy. In this connection, may I ask you to indicate in your reply any parts of it which you regard as constituting business secrets, giving your reasons.

I also have to inform you that it is the practice of the Commission in cases where it is envisaged to adopt /an unfavourable decision under Regulation 17/ /a decision rejecting a complaint/ to offer the parties having a legitimate interest therein access to its file. You should, therefore, put any information that you wish to be withheld from inspection by other parties, should the occasion arise, in separate annexes to your reply, marking them clearly as such and, again, giving your reasons.

4. I am writing in the same terms to the other party(ies), with a copy to your legal advisor(s)./

5, 6. In accordance with Article 11(5) of Regulation No. 17 the time limit for reply to this letter is .... weeks from receipt thereof. Should you have any query about this request you may contact .... (235.....).

Yours faithfully,
Director

(On the minute:
instruction about transmission to M.S.)

1.2.2. Cases

Comptoir d'Importation 167
Telos 170
National Panasonic (Belgium) 176
National Panasonic (France) 177
Peugeot 250 (paras. 27–31, 48–53)*
Boekhandels v. Eldi Records 73 (grounds 12–13)
CICCE v. Commission 118 (grounds 5–6)

1.3. Request for information by decision

Article 11(5), (6) Regulation 17/62
CICG 36
ALBRA 39
Union des Brasseries 40
Maes 41
Asphaltoïd/Keller 42
SIAE 44
Rodenstock 61
Misal 62
CSV 105
RAI/UNITEL 131
Fire Insurance 175
Castrol 192
Olympic Airways 229*
SEP v. Commission T8
SEP v. Commission T22 (grounds 25, 30, 51, 52)
Orkem v. Commission 172*

2. By inspection

2.1. Inspectors

2.1.1. National inspectors

Article 13(1) Regulation 17/62

2.1.2. Commission inspectors

Articles 13(2), 14 Regulation 17/62

2.2. Powers of inspectors

Article 14(1) Regulation 17/62
Hoechst v. Commission III (grounds 10–38)*
Dow Benelux v. Commission 170
Dow Iberica v. Commission 171

2.3. Inspection without decision

Article 14(2) Regulation 17/62

2.3.1. Text of typical authorisation to investigate (reproduced opposite)

Part X—2 *The Handling of a Case*

Procedure and Remedies

Text of a typical authorisation to investigate

AUTHORISATION TO INVESTIGATE

Mr. ....

holder of internal service pass No. ....

is hereby authorized to carry out an investigation at ....

....

for the purpose of ....

....

....

....

To this end, he has been invested with the powers set out in Article 14 Paragraph 1 Regulation No. 17/62, of 6 February 1962 (Official Journal of the European Communities No. 13 of 21 February 1962).
The Commission, with reference to Article 14 Paragraph 2 of Council Regulation No. 17/62, hereby draws attention to the provisions of Article 15 Paragraph 1(c) of that Regulation [The Commission may, by decision, impose fines of from 100 to 5000 units of account on undertakings or associations of undertakings which, while submitting to an investigation, intentionally or negligently produce the required books or other business records in incomplete form (Article 15 Paragraph 1 of Regulation No. 17/62 of the Council of the EEC).]

For the Commission,

Book One: Part X—Procedure and Remedies

2.3.2. Text of annex to authorisation to investigate under Article 14(2) (reproduced below)

Explanatory note to authorization to investigate under Article 14(2) of Regulation No. 17/62

This note is for information only and is without prejudice to any formal interpretation of the Commission's powers of enquiry.

1. The officials of the Commission authorized for the purpose of carrying out an investigation under Article 14(2) of Regulation No 17 exercise their powers upon production of an authorization in writing. They prove their identity by means of their staff card.
2. Before starting the investigation the Commission officials shall, at the undertaking's request, provide explanations on the subject matter and purpose of the proposed investigation and also on procedural matters particularly confidentiality. These explanations cannot modify the authorization and may not compromise the purpose of, nor unduly delay the investigation.
3. The authorization, not being in execution of a Commission decision under Article 14(3), does not oblige the undertaking to submit to the investigation. The undertaking may accordingly refuse the investigation. The Commission officials shall minute this refusal, no particular form being required. The undertaking shall receive a copy of the minute if it so wishes.
4. Where the undertaking is prepared to submit to the investigation, the Commission officials are empowered, pursuant to Article 14(1) of Regulation No 17:
    (a) to examine the books and other business records;
    (b) to take copies of or extracts from the books and business records;
    (c) to ask for oral explanations on the spot;
    (d) to enter any premises, land and means of transport of undertakings.
5. Officials of the competent authority of the Member State in whose territory the investigation is made are entitled to be present at the investigation to assist the officials of the Commission in carrying ouyt their duties. They shall prove their identity in accordance with the relevant national rules.
6. The undertaking may consult a legal adviser during the investigation. However, the presence of a lawyer is not a legal condition for the validity of the investigation, nor must it unduly delay or impede it. Any delay pending a lawyer's arrival must be kept to the strict minimum, and shall be allowed only where the management of the undertaking simultaneously undertakes to ensure that the business records will remain in the place and state they were in when the Commission officials arrived. The officials' acceptance of delay is also conditional upon their not being hindered from entering into and remaining in occupation of offices of their choice. If the undertaking has an inhouse legal service, Commission officials are instructed not to delay the investigation by awaiting the arrival of an external legal adviser.
7. Where the undertaking gives oral explanations on the spot on the subject matter of the investigation at the request of the Commission officials, the explanations may be minuted at the request of the undertaking or of the Commission officials. The undertaking shall receive a copy of the minute if it so wishes.
8. The Commission officials are entitled to take copies of or extracts from books and business records. The undertaking may request a signed inventory of the copies and extracts taken by the Commission officials during the investigation.
    Where the undertakings makes available photocopies of documents at the request of the Commission officials, the Commission shall, at the request of the undertaking, reimburse the cost of the photocopies.
9. In addition to the documents requested by the Commission officials, the undertaking is entitled to draw attention to other documents or information where it considers this necessary for the purpose of protecting its legitimate interest in a complete and

2.3.3. Cases on the interpretation of Article 14(2)

AM & S Europe 146
Fabbrica Pisana 153 (paras. 10, 12)
Fabbrica Lastre 154
Fédération Chaussure de France 183 (para. 8)
11th Comp. Rep. (paras. 17–21)
12th Comp. Rep. (para. 32)
13th Comp. Rep. (para. 74)

AM&S v. *Commission* 92*

2.4. Inspection with decision

Article 14(3)–(6) Regulation 17/62
Bayer v. *Commission* T13

2.4.1. Text of explanatory document accompanying Article 14(3) decision (reproduced below)

Text of explanatory document accompanying Article 14(3) decision

Explanatory note to authorization to investigate in execution of a Commission decision under Article 14(3) of Regulation No. 17/62

This note is for information only and is without prejudice to any formal interpretation of the Commission's powers of enquiry.

1. Enterprises are legally obliged to submit to an investigation ordered by decision of the Commission under Article 14(3) of Regulation No. 17. Written authorizations serve to name the officials charged with the execution of the decision. They prove their identity by means of their staff card.

2. Officials cannot be required to enlarge upon the subject matter as set out in the decision or to justify in any way the taking of the decision. They may however explain procedural matters, particularly confidentiality, and the possible consequences of a refusal to submit.

3. A certified copy of the decision is to be handed to the undertaking. The minute of notification of service serves only to certify delivery and its signature by the recipient does not imply submission.

4. The Commission officials are empowered, pursuant to Article 14(1) of Regulation No. 17:
    (a) to examine the books and other business records;
    (b) to take copies of or extracts from the books and business records;
    (c) to ask for oral explanations on the spot;
    (d) to enter any premises, land and means of transport of undertakings.

5. Officials of the competent authority of the Member State in whose territory the investigation is made are entitled to be present at the investigation to assist the officials of the Commission in carrying out their duties. They shall prove their identity in accordance with the relevant national rules.

6. The undertaking may consult a legal adviser during the investigation. However, the presence of a lawyer is not a legal condition for the validity of the investigation, nor must it unduly delay or impede it. Any delay pending a lawyer's arrival must be kept to the strict minimum, and shall be allowed only where the management of the undertaking simultaneously undertakes to ensure that the business records will remain in the place and state they were in when the Commission officials arrived. The officials' acceptance of delay is also conditional upon their not being hindered from entering into and remaining in occupation of offices of their choice. If the undertaking has an inhouse

Book One: Part X—Procedure and Remedies

legal service, Commission officials are instructed not to delay the investigation by awaiting the arrival of an external legal adviser.

7. Where the undertaking gives oral explanations on the spot of the subject matter of the investigation at the request of the Commission officials, the explanations may be minuted at the request of the undertaking or of the Commission officials. The undertaking shall receive a copy of the minute if it so wishes.

8. The Commission officials are entitled to take copies of or extracts from books and business records. The undertaking may request a signed inventory of the copies and extracts taken by the Commission officials during the investigation.

Where the undertaking makes available photocopies of documents at the request of the Commission officials, the Commission shall, at the request of the undertaking, reimburse the cost of the photocopies.

9. In addition to the documents requested by the Commission officials, the undertaking is entitled to draw attention to other documents or information where it considers this necessary for the purpose of protecting its legitimate interest in a complete and objective clarification of the matters raised provided that the investigation is not thereby unduly delayed.

2.4.2. Cases on the interpretation of Article 14(3)

German Blacksmiths 120
Fides 145
AM&S Europe 146
11th Comp. Rep. (paras. 17–20)
12th Comp. Rep. (para. 32)
13th Comp. Rep. (para. 74)
17th Comp. Rep. (para. 57)
National Panasonic v. *Commission* 74
AM&S v. *Commission* 92*
AKZO v. *Commission II* 133*
Hoechst v. *Commission II* 140
Dow v. *Commission* 145
Hoechst v. *Commission II* 169 (grounds 10–38)*
Dow Benelux v. *Commission* 170
Dow Iberica v. *Commission* 171

3. Sectorial investigation

Article 12 Regulation 17/62
ALBRA 39
Union des Brasseries 40
Maes 41

4. Co-operation with national authorities

SEP v. Commission T22 (ground 53)

C. PROCEDURAL STEPS AND SAFEGUARDS

1. In relation to an infringement decision

1.1. Initiation of proceedings

Article 9(3) Regulation 17/62
De Haecht v. *Wilkin II* 34 (ground 16)*
BMW Belgium v. *Commission* 69 (paras. 17–18)
Anne Marty v. *Estée Lauder* 77 (paras. 12–16)
IBM v. *Commission* 87
ACF Chemiefarma v. *Commission* 14
BRT v. *SABAM II* 38
Nouvelles Frontières 131 (grounds 55–56)

1.2. Statement of objections

Article 19(1) Regulation 17/62
Articles 2, 10 Regulation 99/63
Vichy v. *Commission* T29 (ground 121)
Continental Can v. *Commission* 35 (ground 5)
ACF Chemifarma v. *Commission* 14 (ground 27)
ICI v. *Commission* 23 (grounds 17, 24)
BASF v. *Commission* 24
Bayer v. *Commission* 25
Geigy v. *Commission* 26
Sandoz v. *Commission* 27
Francolor v. *Commission* 28
Cassella v. *Commission* 29
Hoechst v. *Commission* 30
ACNA v. *Commission* 31
Boehringer v. *Commission* 16
FEDETAB v. *Commission* 80 (grounds 29–35, 67–78)*
IBM v. *Commission* 87*
Pioneer v. *Commission* 98 (ground 14)

1.3. Grant of access to all documents upon which the commission relies

British Sugar 286 (paras. 67–68)
PVC 305 (para. 27)
LdPE 306 (para. 34)
11th Comp. Rep. (paras. 22–25)*
12th Comp. Rep. (paras. 34–35)*
13th Comp. Rep. (para. 74)*
18th Comp. Rep. (para. 43)
20th Comp. Rep. (para. 89)
Hercules v. *Commission* T25 (grounds 45–56)*

DSM v. *Commission* T26 (ground 37)
BASF v. *Commission* T23 (ground 36)
Hüls v. *Commission* T31 (grounds 46–49)
Hoechst v. *Commission* T32 (grounds 51–54)
Linz v. *Commission* T37 (grounds 51–54)
Cement Industries v. *Commission* T39
Consten & Grundig v. *Commission* 4
ACF Chemiefarma v. *Commission* 14 (grounds 37–43)
Buchler v. *Commission* 15 (grounds 12–15)
Boehringer v. *Commission* 16 (grounds 12–15)
Hoffmann-La Roche v. *Commission* 67
FEDETAB v. *Commission* 80 (grounds 36–40)*
Michelin v. *Commission* 102 (grounds 5, 8–10)
VBVB & VBBB v. *Commission* 105 (ground 25)*
Consten & Grundig v. *Commission* 4
FEDETAB v. *Commission* 80 (grounds 36–40)*
Pioneer v. *Commission* 98
AEG v. *Commission* 100
Michelin v. *Commission* 102 (ground 7)
VBVB & VBBB v. *Commission* 105 (grounds 24–25)
AKZO v. *Commission III* 186 (grounds 15–24)

1.4. Reply to the statement of objections by the parties

1.4.1. In writing

Article 3 Regulation 99/63
18th Comp. Rep. (para. 44)
FEDETAB v. *Commission* 80

1.4.2. Oral hearing

Article 19(2) Regulation 17/62
Articles 5, 7, 8 Regulation 99/63
11th Comp. Rep. (paras. 26–28)
12th Comp. Rep. (paras. 36–37)
13th Comp. Rep. (para. 75)
ACF Chemiefarma v. *Commission* 14 (grounds 44–53)
Buchler v. *Commission* 15 (grounds 16–17, 19–22)
Boehringer v. *Commission* 16 (grounds 16–18)
ICI v. *Commission* 23 (grounds 28–32, 63)
BASF v. *Commission* 24 (grounds 10–12)
Bayer v. *Commission* 25 (grounds 13–15)
Geigy v. *Commission* 26
Sandoz v. *Commission* 27
Cassella v. *Commission* 29
Hoechst v. *Commission I* 30
ACNA v. *Commission* 31

18th Comp. Rep. (para. 44)
FEDETAB v. *Commission* 80 (grounds 16–18, 22–24, 64–66)*
VBVB & VBBB v. *Commission* 105 (grounds 15–18)*
ANCIDES v. *Commission* 143 (paras. 7–8)

1.4.3. Commission Decision of November 23, 1990 on the implementation of hearings in connection with procedures for the application of Articles 85 and 86 of the EEC Treaty and Articles 65 and 66 of the ECSC Treaty (reproduced below)

(20th Comp. Rep. pages 312–314)

Article 1

1. The hearings foreseen in the provisions implementing Articles 85 and 86 EEC Treaty and Articles 65 and 66 ECSC Treaty are decided on by the Member of the Commission responsible for competition and conducted by the Hearing Officer;

2. Implementing provisions in the sense of paragraph (1) are:
   (a) Regulation No. 99/63/EEC of the Commission of July 25, 1963 on the hearings provided for in Article 19(1) and (2) of Council Regulation No. 17; ([1963] O.J. L127/63)
   (b) Regulation (EEC) No. 1630/69 of the Commission of August 8, 1969 on the hearings provided for in Article 26(1) and (2) of Council Regulation (EEC) No. 1017/68 of July 19, 1968; ([1963] O.J. L127/63)
   (c) Commission Regulation (EEC) No. 4260/88 of December 16, 1988 on the communications, complaints and applications and the hearings provided for in Council Regulation (EEC) No. 4056/86 laying down detailed rules for the application of Articles 85 and 86 of the Treaty to maritime transport; ([1969] O.J. L376/11)
   (d) Commission Regulation (EEC) No. 4261/88 of December 16, 1988 on the complaints, applications and hearings provided for in Council Regulation (EEC) No. 3975/87 laying down the procedure for the application of the rules on competition to undertakings in the air transport sector; ([1988] O.J. L376/10)
   (e) Article 36(1) ECSC Treaty.

3. Administratively the Hearing Officer shall belong to the Directorate-General for Competition. To ensure his independence

in the performance of his duties, he shall have the right of direct acces, as defined in Article 6 below, to the Member of the Commission with special responsibilty for competition.

4. Where the Hearing Officer is unable to act, the Director-General, in concert with the Hearing Officer, shall designate another official, who is in the same grade and is not involved in the case in question, to carry out the duties described herein.

Article 2

1. The Hearing Officer shall ensure that the hearing is properly conducted and thus contibute to the objectivity of the hearing itself and of any decision taken subsequently. He shall seek to ensure in particular that in the preparation of draft Commission decisions in competition cases due account is taken of all the relevant facts, whether favourable or unfavourable to the parties concerned.

2. In performing his duties he shall see to it that the rights of the defence are respected, while taking account of the need for effective application of the competition rules in accordance with the regulations in force and the principles laid down by the Court of Justice.

Article 3

1. Where the appropiate in view of the need to ensure that the hearing is properly prepared, and particulary that questions of fact are clarified as far as possible, the Hearing Officier may, after consulting the appropiate director, supply in advance to the firms concerned a list of the questions on which he wishes them to explain their point of view.

2. For this purpose, after consulting the director responsible for investigating the case which is the subject of the hearing, he may hold a meeting with the parties concerned and, where appropriate, the Commission staff, in order to prepare for the hearing itself.

3. For the same purpose he may ask for prior written notification of the essential contents of the intended statement of persons whom the undertakings concerned have proposed for hearing.

Article 4

1. After cinsulting the director responsible, the Hearing Officer shall determine the date, the duration and the place of the hearing, and, where a postponement is requested, he shall decide whether or not to allow it.

2. He shall be fully responsible for the conduct of the hearing.

3. In this regard, he shall decide whether fresh documents should be admitted during the hearing, whether persons should be heard and whether the persons concerned should be heard separately or in the presence of other persons summoned to attend.

4. He shall ensure that the essential content of the statement made by each person heard shall be recorded in minutes which shall be read and approved by that person.

Article 5

The Hearing Officer shall report to the Director-General for Competition on the hearing and the conclusions he draws from it. He may take observations on the further progress of the proceedings. Such observations may relate among other things to the need for further information, the withdrawal of certain objections, or the formulation of further objections.

Article 6

In performing the duties defined in Article 2 above, the Hearing Officer may, if he deems it appropiate, refer his observations direct to the Member of the Commission with special responsibility for competition, at the time when the preliminary draft decision is submitted to the latter for reference to the Advisory Committee on Restrictive Practices and Dominant Positions.

Article 7

Where appropriate, the Member of the Commission with special responsibility for competition may decide, at the Hearing Officer's request, to attach the Hearing Officer's final report to the draft decision submitted to the Commission, in order to ensure that when it reaches a decision on an individual case it is fully apprised of all relevant information.

1.4.4. Role of the Hearing Officer

10th Comp. Rep. (para. 44)
13th Comp. Rep. (paras 273–274)
Petrofina v. *Commission* T19 (grounds 51–55)
BASF v. *Commission* T23 (ground 51)
Enichem v. *Commission* T24 (grounds 53–55)
Hercules v. *Commission* T25 (grounds 30–34)

1.4.5. General considerations on the right to be heard

Articles 4, 9, 11 Regulation 99/63
Hilti v. *Commission* T21 (grounds 36–38)*
ACF Chemiefarma v. *Commission* 14 (grounds 54–58)
Boehringer v. *Commission* 16 (grounds 8–11)
Komponistenverband v. *Commission* 20
Transocean Marine Paint Association 42 (grounds 15–16)
FEDETAB v. *Commission* 80 (grounds 29–35, 64–74, 79–81)
AM&S v. *Commission* 92 (ground 23)*
Pioneer v. *Commission* 98 (grounds 10, 30)
VBVB & VBBB v. *Commission* 105 (grounds 18, 21)*
AKZO v. *Commission III* 186 (grounds 27–33)

1.5. Advisory committee

13th Comp. Rep. (para. 79)
RTE v. *Commission* T14 (grounds 21–28)
Petrofina v.*Commission* T19 (grounds 43–51)
BASF v. *Commission* T23 (grounds 23–45)
Enichem v. *Commission* T24 (grounds 45)
Vichy v. *Commission* T29 (grounds 31–41)
Buchler & Co. v. *Commission* 15 (ground 1*)
Frubo v. *Commission* 44 (ground 11)
Pioneer v. *Commission* 98 (ground 36)

2. Relating to a positive decision

2.1. Publication of Notice

Article 19(3) Regulation 17/62
ANCIDES v. *Commission* 143

2.2. Advisory committee

13th Comp. Rep. (para. 79)

3. Relating to a rejection of a complaint

Article 6 Regulation 99

GEC-Siemens/Plessey 325
11th Comp. Rep. (para. 118)
British Sugar-Berisford. 12th Comp. Rep. (paras. 104–106)
Standardised bottles in Germany. 17th Comp. Rep. (para. 75)*
Automec v. *Commission* T6*

4. General procedural safeguards

4.1. Legal professional privilege

AM&S Europe 146*
11th Comp. Rep. (para. 21)
12th Comp. Rep. (para. 33)
13th Comp. Rep. (para. 78)
AM&S v. *Commission* 92*

4.2. Obligation of the Commission as to confidentiality

4.2.1. General obligation

Article 20 Regulation 17/62
Article 214 EEC
15th Comp. Rep. (50–51)
SEP v. *Commission* T8
SEP v. *Commission* T22 (grounds 52–60)
Cement Industries v. *Commission* T39
Dow Benelux v. *Commission* 170* (grounds 13–21)
Michelin v. *Commission* 102 (ground 8)
Stanley Adams v. *Commission* 125*

4.2.2. Business secrets

CSV 105
ACF Chemiefarma v. *Commission* 14 (grounds 37–43)
Boehringer v. *Commission* 16 (grounds 12–15)
Hoffmann-La Roche v. *Commission* 67 (grounds 14–15)
FEDETAB v. *Commission* 80 (grounds 41–47)
AKZO v. *Commission I* 132*
BAT v. *Commission & Philip Morris* 146 (ground 21)

4.2.3. Result of disclosure of business secrets or confidential information

FEDETAB v. *Commission* 80 (para. 47)*
Stanley Adams v. *Commission* 125
AKZO v. *Commission I* 132*

D. INFORMAL STEPS OFTEN TAKEN BY THE COMMISSION

1. Negotiations and modifications of agreements

Article 7 Regulation 17/62

ACEC/Berliet 14
Cobelaz 15, 16 (para. 8)
CFA 18
VVVF 22
SEIFA 23
Supexie 34
Du Pont de Nemours Germany 71
Transocean Marine Paint Association II 75
SABA I 99
CSV 134 (paras. 81–87)
Zanussi 139
White Lead 142 (para. 19)
Natursteinplatten 159 (paras. 17–24, 46–47)
VBBB/VBVB 169 (paras. 24–31)
National Panasonic 186 (para. 5)
Grundig 232
Velcro/Aplix 233
British Sugar 286 (paras. 9–10, 82)
Tetra Pak I 289 (para. 69)
UIP 309 (paras. 25–33)
APB 314 (paras. 28–33)
Man-made fibres 8th Comp. Rep. (para. 42)
Hachette. 8th Comp. Rep. (paras. 114–115)
Feldmühle-Stora 12th Comp Rep. (paras. 73–74)
13th Comp Rep. (para. 81)
IBM 14th Comp. Rep. (paras. 94–95); 16th Comp. Rep. (para. 75); 17th Comp. Rep. (para. 85); (Bulletin 12/88. Pt. 2.1.116)*
Instituto/IMC & Angus 16th Comp. Rep. (para. 76)
Philip Morris 14th Comp. Rep. (paras. 98–100)

Macron/Angus 17th Comp. Rep. (para. 81)
Irish Distillers 18th Comp. Rep. (para. 80)
De Haecht v. *Wilkin II* 34 (ground 6)
BAT v. *Commission & Philip Morris* 145

2. Informal settlement

2.1. Undertakings

British Sugar 286 (paras. 9–10, 82)*
GEC-Siemens/Plessey 325
Pilkington/BSN. 10th Comp. Rep. (paras. 152–155)
Woollen fabrics. 12th Comp. Rep. (para. 71)
IBM 14th Comp. Rep. (paras. 94–95)
IBM 16th Comp. Rep. (para. 75)
IBM 17th Comp. Rep. (para. 85)
IBM 18th Comp. Rep. (para. 78)
Carnaud/Sofreb 17th Comp. Rep. (para. 70)
Irish Distillers 18th Comp. Rep. (para. 80)
AKZO Coatings 19th Comp. Rep. (para. 45)
Coca-Cola 19th Comp. Rep. (para. 50)
Consolidated Goldfields 19th Comp. Rep. (para. 68)

3. Comfort letter

3.1. Text of Commission Notices

3.1.1. Text of Notice concerning applications for negative clearance pursuant to Article 2 Regulation 17/62 (reproduced opposite)

Notice from the Commission on procedures concerning applications for negative clearance pursuant to Article 2 of council Regulation 17/62

([1982] O.J. C343/4)

In publishing the notice below, it is the intention of the Commission to open the way for a more flexible administrative practice in assessing applications for negative clearance under Article 2 of Regulation 17/62 ([1962] J.O. 13/62) which empowers the Commission to certify that Article 85(1) of the EEC Treaty does not apply to an agreement. Experience has, indeed, shown that in certain cases a 'comfort letter' closing the procedure sent by the Commission's Directorate-General for Competition was an appropriate response to an application for negative clearance. However, in order to enhance the declaratory value of such a letter, and without prejudice to the possibility of terminating the procedure by a formal decision, the Commission is now publishing the essential content of such agreements pursuant to Article 19(3) of Regulations 17/62, so as to give interested third parties an opportunity to make known their views. In appropriate cases, it would be possible to send a comfort letter closing the procedure after publication, so as to simplify and shorten the procedure.

Cases closed by a comfort letter following publication will be brought to the attention of interested third parties by the subsequent publication of a notice in the *Official Journal of the European Communities*.

3.1.2. Text of Notice concerning notification pursuant to Article 4 Regulation 17/62 (reproduced below)

Notice from the Commission on procedures concerning notifications pursuant to Article 4 of council Regulation 17/62

([1983] O.J. C295/6)

In publishing this notice, it is the intention of the Commission to open the way for a more flexible administrative practice in assessing notifications under Article 4 of Regulation 17/62 ([1962] J.O. 13/62) in the light of its past experience in this area. This has shown that in certain cases a provisional letter sent by the Commission's Directorate-General for Competition would be an appropriate response to a notification made for the purposes of obtaining an Article 85(3) Decision. However, in order to enhance the declaratory value of such a letter, and without prejudice to the possibility of terminating the procedure by a formal Decision, the Commission will now publish the essential content of such agreements pursuant to Article 19(3) of Regulation 17/62, so as to give interested third parties an opportunity to make known their views. In the light of the comments received after publication, it would then be possible, in appropriate cases, to send a provisional letter, so as to simplify and shorten the procedure. Such letters will not have the status of Decisions and will therefore not be capable of appeal to the Court of Justice. They will state that the Directorate-General for Competition, in agreement with the undertakings concerned, does not consider it necessary to pursue the formal procedure through to the adoption of a Decision under Article 85(3) in accordance with Article 6 of Regulation 17/62.

A list of the cases dealt with by dispatch of provisional letters following publication will be appended to the Report on Competition Policy.

Book One: Part X—Procedure and Remedies

3.2. Text of a typical comfort letter

Registered with advice of delivery
Re Case No. IV/(........................
    Notification of (......................
    (date), by (..........................
    Agreement between (................

Dear Sirs,
I refer to the notification of the above agreement.
On the basis of the information provided on notification of the agreement (as well as contained in documents subsequently received), the Commission's Directorate General for Competition has now completed a preliminary examination of this case.

This examination has not revealed the existence of any grounds under Article (85(1)) (86) for further action on the part of the Commission in respect of the notified agreement.

(A notice containing a summary of the agreement was published in the Official Journal of the European Communities No. C(... of (... The Directorate-General for Competition has received no observations from interested third parties following publication of that Notice.

As it was indicated in the Notice—and as it has been agreed with you—the notification under consideration might be dealt with by means of an administrative letter closing the file.)

(You have indicated that you can agree to the notification under consideration being dealt with by means of an administrative letter closing the file.)

However, the case could be reconsidered if the factual or legal situation changes as concerns as essential aspect of the agreement which affects its evaluation.

Naturally, any reopening of the file would be without prejudice to the legal consequences of the notification, particularly as regards the immunity from fines provided by Article 15(5) of Council Regulation No. 17/62.

               Yours faithfully,
               Director
cc: All Member States

3.3. Cases on comfort letters

GEC-Siemens/Plessey 325
11th Comp. Rep. (para. 15)
12th Comp. Rep. (para. 30)
13th Comp. Rep. (para. 72)

Frubo v. *Commission* 44 (grounds 18–21)
De Bloos v. *Boyer* 60 (grounds 17–18)
Procureur v. *Guerlain* 76 (grounds 9–13)
Anne Marty v. *Estée Lauder* 77 (grounds 5–10)*
Lancôme v. *Etos* 78 (grounds 6–18)
L'Oréal v. *De Nieuwe AMCK* 81 (grounds 7–12)
AEG v. *Commission* 100 (grounds 3, 4)

E. COMMISSION DECISIONS

1. Administrative decisions

Article 11(5) Regulation 17/62
See above, page 333
Article 14(3) Regulation 17/62
See above, page 334

2. Provisional decisions

2.1. Removal of immunity from fines

Article 15(6) Regulation 17
Sirdar-Phildar 89*
Bronbemaling 95
SNPE/LEL 132
P&I Clubs 243 (para. 2)
Decca 304 (paras. 77–78)
Vichy 334 (para. 32)
Beecham Pharma. 6th Comp. Rep. (para. 133)
Prodifarma v. *Commission II* T12 (grounds 39–49)
Vichy v. *Commission* T29
Cimenteries v. *Commission* 6*
Portelange v. *Smith Corona* 11 (grounds 16–17)
IBM v. *Commission* 87 (ground 19)
Ford v. *Commission* 108 (ground 23)

2.2. Interim measures

Ford Werke–Interim measures 182
ECS/AKZO-Interim measures 197
Boosey & Hawkes 273
Hilti 282 (paras. 27–29)
British Sugar (para. 9)
Cosimex v. *Commission* T1
Peugeot v. *Commission* T17
La Cinq v. *Commission* T27*
Camera Care v. *Commission* 72*
Hasselblad v. *Commission* 107 (ground 19)
Ford v. *Commission* 108 (ground 19)

3. Recommendation

Convention Faïence 2

4. Final decisions

4.1. Negative clearance

Article 2 Regulation 17/62

Gema Statutes 174

4.2. Exemption Article 85(3)

4.2.1. Duration of exemption

Article 8(1) Regulation 17/62
United Reprocessors 102
Grundig 232
Enichem/ICI 279 (para. 52)
KSB 328 (para. 30–32)
Eirpage 344 (para 22)

4.2.2. Conditions or obligations for exemption

Article 8(1) Regulation 17/62
Transocean Marine Paint Association I 10*
United Reprocessors 102

4.2.3. Renewal of exemption

Article 8(2) Regulation 17/62
Transocean Marine Paint Association II 75*
Cematex II 193
Transocean Marine Paint Association 42
Metro v. *Commission II* 134 (grounds 30–32)
ANCIDES v. *Commission* 143

4.2.4. Revocation of exemption

Article 8(3) Regulation 17/62
Tetra Pak I 289
Eco System 344a (paras. 25, 33)

4.2.5 Effect of an exemption

L'Oreal v. *De Nieuwe AMCK* 81 (grounds 22–23)

4.3. Prohibition

Article 3 Regulation 17/62

4.3.1. Order to cease

Gema I 37
Aluminium 228 (para. 18)
Decca 300 (para. 131)
Ijsselcentrale 335 (para. 55)
GVL v. *Commission* 97 (grounds 23–28)*
AKZO v. *Commission III* 186 (grounds 155–157)

4.3.2. Order to act

Zoja C.S.C.-I.C.I.64
ECS/AKZO—Interim measures 197 (paras. 36–38)
ECS/AKZO 242 (para. 99)
Net Book Agreements 301 (para. 89)

Magill 307 (para. 27)
RTE v. *Commission* T14 (grounds 97–99)
BBC v. *Commission* T15 (grounds 71–73)
ITV v. *Commission* T16 (grounds 70–72)
ICI & CSC v. *Commission* 37*

4.3.3. Neutral; obligation of parties to suggest remedy

VBBB/VBVB 169 (paras. 64–65)

4.3.4. Date of commencement of prohibition

Velcro/Aplix 233
VBA 288 (paras. 164–168)*

4.3.5. Effects in time

Article 7 Regulation 17/62
Du Pont Germany 71
Bosch v. *Van Rijn* 1

4.4. Rejection of complaint

Article 6 Regulation 99/63
GEC-Siemens/Plessey 325
11th Comp. Rep. (para. 118)
British Sugar-Berisford. 12th Comp. Rep. (paras. 104–106)
VEB/Shell. 16th Comp. Rep. (para. 55)
Standardised bottles in Germany. 17th Comp. Rep. (para. 75)
Automec v. *Commission* T6 (grounds 46–58)
Gema v. *Commission* 70 (grounds 10–23)
Lord Bethell v. *Commission* 93
Demo Schmidt v. *Commission* 99*
CICCE v. *Commission* 118
BAT v. *Commission & Philip Morris* 146 (grounds 26–27, 70)*

5. Formal requirements regarding the form/content of decisions

5.1. Decisions must be reasoned

Article 190 EEC
PVC 305 (paras. 45–46)
LdPE 306 (paras. 28–29)
DSM v. *Commission* T26 (ground 257)
La Cinq v. *Commission* T27*
Consten & Grundig v. *Commission* 4
Cimenteries v. *Commission* 6
ACF Chemiefarma v. *Commission* 14 (ground 80)
Boehringer v. *Commission* 16
ITV v. *Commission* T16 (grounds 64)
BASF v. *Commission* 24 (grounds 13–15)
Cassella v. *Commission* 29
Hoechst v. *Commission* 30

Kali & Salz v. *Commission* 43 (grounds 8–15)
Papiers Peints v. *Commission* 47 (grounds 28–33)
FEDETAB v. *Commission* 80 (grounds 75–78)*
GVL v. *Commission* 97 (ground 12)
Michelin v. *Commission* 102 (ground 14)
VBVB & VBBB v. *Commission* 105 (ground 22)*
Hasselblad v. *Commission* 107 (ground 17)
Remia v. *Commission* 121 (grounds 26–36, 44)
SSI v. *Commission* 127 (ground 88)
BAT v. *Commission & Philip Morris* 128 (grounds 70–72)
Hoechst v. *Commission III* 169 (grounds 39–43)

5.2. Burden of proof

John Deere 226 (para. 26)
Woodpulp 227 (paras. 101, 107)*
Papiers Peints v. *Commission* 47 (grounds 15–21)*

5.3. Must contain only that which figured in the statement of objections

Article 4 Regulation 99/63
ACF Chemiefarma v. *Commission* 14
FEDETAB v. *Commission* 80 (grounds 67–74)*
Pioneer v. *Commission* 98
AEG v. *Commission* 100 (grounds 27)
Michelin v. *Commission* 102 (ground 19)

5.4. Obligation to take account of the defendant's views in the decision

FEDETAB v. *Commission* 80 (grounds 64–66)
BAT v. *Commission & Philip Morris* 146 (ground 72)*

5.5. Obligation to respect internal procedural rules

PVC T28*
Cimenteries v. *Commission* 6 (grounds 10–14)
ICI v. *Commission* 23 (grounds 11–15)
VBVB & VBBB v. *Commission* 105 (ground 19)
AK20 v. *Commission II* 133

F. FINES AND PERIODIC PENALTY PAYMENTS

1. Periodic penalty payments

Article 16 Regulation 17/62

Baccarat 338*
Hugin/Liptons 121
Hoechst v. *Commission II* 140
Hoechst v. *Commission III* 169 (grounds 49–66)*

2. Fines for infringement of procedural rules

Article 15(1) Regulation 17
Fides 145
Fabbrica Pisana 153
Fabbrica Lastre 154
Comptoir d'Importation 167
Telos 171
National Panasonic (Belgium) 176
National Panasonic (France) 177
Fédération Chaussure de France 183
Peugeot 250 (para. 52)*
Secrétama 329a
1st Comp. Rep. (para. 99)
Tepea v. *Commission* 64 (grounds 67–72)

3. Fines for substantive infringements

Article 15(2) Regulation 17
1st Comp. Rep. (para. 98)
13th Comp. Rep. (paras. 62–66)

3.1. Requirements for the imposition of a fine

3.1.1 Intentional infringement

Quinine Cartel 24 (para. 27)*
Vegetable Parchment 129 (para. 83)
Kawasaki 141 (paras. 51–55, 57)
Fatty Acids 254 (para. 55)
Miller v. *Commission* 61
Belasco v. *Commission* 166 (ground 41)
Tipp-Ex v. *Commission* 175 (grounds 29–30)

3.1.2. Negligence

Deutsche Philips 73*
BMW Belgium 126 (para. 27)
United Brands v. *Commission* 62 (grounds 289–304)*
SSI v. *Commission* 127 (ground 65)
Sandoz v. *Commission* 174 (grounds 6–8)

4. Factors taken into account in assessing the level of the fine for substantive infringements

4.1. Gravity of the infringement

Article 15(2) Regulation 17/62
Quinine Cartel 24 (para. 38)
BMW Belgium 126 (para. 26)

Part X—2 The Handling of a Case

PVC 305 (para. 52)
LdPE 306 (para. 64)
ACF Chemiefarma v. Commission 14 (ground 176)
Boehringer v. Commission 16 (grounds 52–61)
Pioneer v. Commission 98 (grounds 106, 120)*
Michelin v. Commission 102 (ground 11)
Windsurfing v. Commission 130 (grounds 112–114)

4.2. Length of the infringement

Article 15(2) Regulation 17/62
PVC 305 (paras. 48–49)
LdPE 306 (paras. 60–61)
SSI v. Commission 127 (ground 95)*

4.3. Effect of the infringement

Quinine Cartel 24 (para. 38)
Tinned Mushrooms 88
Theal/Watts 110
Vegetable Parchment 129 (para. 82)
White Lead 142 (paras. 41–42)*
Floral 148
Zinc Producer Group 217
Woodpulp 227 (para. 148)
Polypropylene 247 (para. 108)
Meldoc 253 (para. 76)
Fatty Acids 254 (para. 56)
Hudson Bay 294 (para. 13)
British Plasterboard 299 (para. 169)*

4.4. Extent of culpability

Quinine Cartel 24 (para. 40)
Dyestuffs 27
European Sugar Industry 69
BMW Belgium 126 (para. 26)
AEG/Telefunken 179 (para. 74)
AROW/BNIC 190 (para. 77)
Windsurfing International 194
Polypropylene 247 (para. 109)
Roofing Felt 248 (paras. 75, 114–115)
Meldoc 253 (paras. 80, 81)
Tipp-Ex 269 (paras. 76–79)
Sandoz 272 (para. 33)
Fisher-Price 275 (para. 26)*
Konica 277
PVC 305 (paras. 53–54)
LDPE 306 (paras. 65–67)
BAT v. Commission & Philip Morris 146 (ground 43)
Tipp-Ex v. Commission 175 (grounds 40–41)

4.5. Non-enforcement of infringement

British Telecommunications 188 (para. 45)

4.6. Difficult market conditions

Quinine Cartel 24 (para. 38)
ABG/Oil Companies 113
Cast-Iron & Steel Rolls 198 (paras. 72–73)
Flat Glass (Benelux) 216
Zinc Producer Group 217 (para. 104)*
Polypropylene 247 (para. 108)
Roofing felt 248
Meldoc 253 (para. 79)
Flat Glass 300 (para. 84)
LdPE 306 (para. 64)
Welded Steel Mesh 311 (para. 200)
Hercules v. Commission T25 (grounds 331–335)
Rhône Poulenc v. Commission T18 (grounds 159–167)

4.7. Size and profitability of the undertaking

Deutsche Philips 73
BMW Belgium 126 (para. 26)
Cast-Iron & Steel Rolls 198 (paras. 72–73)
Fatty Acids 254 (para. 56)*
Tipp-Ex 269 (para. 75)
Sandoz 272 (para. 39)
Hudson Bay 294 (para. 14)
PVC 305 (para. 52)
LdPE 306 (para. 64)
ACF Chiemefarma v. Commission 14 (ground 186)
Boehringer v. Commission 16 (grounds 52–61)
United Brands v. Commission 62 (grounds 125–128)*
Hoffmann-La Roche v. Commission 67
Belasco v. Commission 166 (ground 60)
Tipp-Ex v. Commission 175 (grounds 37–39)

4.8. Co-operative attitude of the undertaking

4.8.1. Undertakings and modification of agreements at Commission's request

General Motors Continental 84
Chiquita 101 (para. II.B)
Miller 108 (para. 7)
Kawasaki 141 (para. 61)
Floral 148
John Deere 226 (para. 41)
Hilti 282 (para. 103)
Hudson Bay 294 (para. 14)*
ICI v. Commission T35 (grounds 391–394)*
Sandoz v. Commission 174 (paras. 21–22)*

4.8.2. Introduction of a compliance programme

National Panasonic 186 (paras. 5, 43–47)

403

Sperry New Holland 245 (para. 68)
Tipp-Ex 269 (para. 75)
Fisher-Price 275 (para. 27)
British Sugar 286 (paras. 10, 82, 85)*
Viho/Toshiba 341 (paras. 28–30)*
ICI v. *Commission* T35 (ground 395)
British Leyland v. *Commission* 136 (ground 44)

4.9. State of the law

4.9.1. State of legal development

Chiquita 101 (para. II.B)
Vitamins 104
Vegetable Parchment 129 (para. 83)
Italian Cast Glass 163
Windsurfing International 194
Woodpulp 227 (para. 146)
Roofing Felt 248
Fatty Acids 254 (para. 58)
British Sugar 286 (paras. 87–88)*
SABENA 295 (para. 40)
Flat Glass 300 (para. 84)
Decca 304 (para. 133)
Eco System 344a (para. 34)
Shell v. *Commission* T33 (ground 369)
Solvay v. *Commission* T34 (ground 309)
Montedips v. *Commission* T36 (ground 346)
Hoffmann-La Roche v. *Commission* 67 (grounds 128–137)
Michelin v. *Commission* 102 (ground 107)*

4.9.2. Well-documented infringement

WEA/Filipacchi Music S.A. 68
Miller 108 (para. 21)
BMW Belgium 126 (para. 26)
Kawasaki 141 (para. 56)
Pioneer 152 (para. 93)*
Michelin 165 (para. 55)
Moët et Chandon (London) Ltd. 172 (para. 21)
AEG–Telefunken 179 (para. 78)
AROW/BNIC 190 (paras. 73–73)
Windsurfing International 194
Polistil/Arbois 211
British Leyland 212
Flat Glass (Benelux) 216
Pernoxide Products 218
Joh Deere 226 (para. 42)
Sandoz 272 (para. 39)
Konica 277
BMW Belgium v. *Commission* 69 (grounds 52–55)

4.9.3. Ignorance of the law, obtaining wrong legal opinion

Kawasaki 141 (paras. 30, 36–37)

Johnson & Johnson 160 (para. 41)*
Roofing Felt 248 (para. 109)*
Miller v. *Commission* 61 (ground 18)*
BMW Belgium v. *Commission* 69 (grounds 39–44)

4.9.4. Repeated infringement

Floral 148
Moët et Chandon (London) Ltd. 172 (para. 20)
Hasselblad 173 (para. 72)
Flat Glass (Benelux) 216
Polypropylene 247 (para. 107)
Flat Glass 300 (para. 84)*
PVC 305 (para. 52)
Solvay/ICI 330 (para. 64)*
Hercules v. *Commission* T25 (ground 348)
Enichem v. *Commission* T24 (ground 295)

4.9.5. Continuation of infringement following clarification of the law

ECS/AKZO 242 (para. 97)

4.10. Governmental pressure

AROW/BNIC 190 (para. 77)
Hüls v. *Commission* T31 (grounds 365–366)
Hoechst v. *Commission* T32 (grounds 358–359)
SSI v. *Commission* 127 (ground 94)*

4.11. Additional profit from infringement

Kawasaki 141 (paras. 58–59)

4.12. *Non bis in idem:* (double jeopardy)

Boehringer 45
Cast-iron & Steel Rolls 198 (para. 71)
Flat Glass 300 (para. 84)
Welded Steel Mesh 311 (para. 205)
1st Comp. Rep. (para. 130)
2nd Comp. Rep. (para. 26)
Walt Wilhelm 9 (grounds 10–11)
Boehringer v. *Commission* 16*
Boehringer v. *Commission* 33

4.13. Unco-operative attitude

Bayonox 313 (para. 69)

5. Limitation periods

Quinine Cartel 24 (para. 36)
Vegetable parchment 129 (para. 54)
Toltecs/Dorcet 191
Cast-iron & Steel Rolls 198 (paras. 67–68)
Aluminium 228*
Polypropylene 247 (para. 103)

PVC 305 (para. 47)
LDPE 306 (paras. 58–59)
Welded Steel Mesh 311 (para. 196)
2nd Comp. Rep. (paras. 13–14)
4th Comp. Rep. (paras. 48–50)
Hercules v. *Commission* T25 (grounds 309–310)
ACF Chemiefarma v. *Commission* 14 (grounds 17–20)
Boehringer v. *Commission* 16 (grounds 5–7)
ICI v. *Commission* 23 (grounds 45–50)
BASF v. *Commission* 24
Bayer v. *Commission* 25
Geigy v. *Commission* 26
Sandoz v. *Commission* 27
Francolor v. *Commission* 28
Cassella v. *Commission* 29
Hoechst v. *Commission* 30
ACNA v. *Commission* 31

CHAPTER 3

JUDICIAL REVIEW

A. JURISDICTION

1. Text of Article 164 (reproduced below)

Article 164

The Court of Justice shall ensure that in the interpretation and application of this Treaty the law is observed.

2. Text of Article 172 (reproduced below)

Article 172

Regulations made by the Council pursuant to the provisions of this Treaty may give the Court of Justice unlimited jurisdiction in regard to the penalties provided for in such regulations.

3. Article 17 Regulation 17/62

See page 367

4. Competence of the Court of First Instance

PTT v. *Commission* T136
Sofacar v. *Commission* T38
PTT v. *Commission* 184a

B. TYPES OF PROCEDURE

1. Article 169

1.1. Text of Article 169 (reproduced below)

Article 169

If the Commission considers that a Member State has failed to fulfil an obligation under this Treaty, it shall deliver a reasoned opinion on the matter after giving the State concerned the opportunity to submit its observations.

If the State concerned does not comply with the opinion within the period laid down by the Commission, the latter may bring the matter before the Court of Justice.

1.2. Cases on the interpretation of Article 169

Commission v. *Greece* 153

2. Article 173

2.1. Text of Article 173 (reproduced below)

Article 173

The Court of Justice shall review the legality of acts of the Council and the Commission other than recommendations or opinions. It shall for this purpose have jurisdiction in actions brought by a Member State, the Council or the Commission on grounds of lack of competence, infringement of an essential procedural requirement, infringement of this Treaty or of any rule of law relating to its application, or misuse of powers.

Any natural or legal person may, under the same conditions, institute proceedings against a decision addressed to that person or against a decision which, although in the form of a regulation or a decision addressed to another person, is of direct and individual concern to the former.

The proceedings provided for in this Article shall be instituted within two months of the publication of the measure, or of its notification to the plaintiff, or, in the absence thereof, of the day on which it came to the knowledge of the latter, as the case may be.

2.2. Direct and individual concern

Metro v. *Commission I* 58 (grounds 5–13)*

Book One: Part X—Procedure and Remedies

Metro v. Commission II 134
Ancides v. Commission 143

2.3. Challengeable acts

2.3.1. Procedural steps

IBM v. Commission 87*
Automec v. Commission T6
Nefarma v. Commission T9
VNZ v. Commission T10
Prodifarma v. Commission T11
Cement Industries v. Commission T39

2.3.2. Interim decisions

Cimenteries v. Commission 6
Ford v. Commission 108*

2.3.3. Disclosure of confidential information

AKZO v. Commission I 132 (grounds 17–22)

2.3.4. Rejection of a complaint

Automec v. Commission T6
Lord Bethell v. Commission 93
Demo Schmidt v. Commission 99*
CICCE v. Commission 118
BAT v. Commission & Philip Morris 146 (ground 12)

2.3.5. Absence of legal effect

Bosman v. Commission 187

2.4. Limitation periods

Norsk Hydro v. Commission T4
Filtrona v. Commission T5
Bayer v. Commission T13*

2.5. Estoppel

Hilti v. Commission T21 (grounds 25, 34–39)

2.6. Scope of Judicial Review

Flat Glass T30 (grounds 315–320)

3. Article 175

3.1. Text of Article 175 (reproduced below)

Article 175

Should the Council or the Commission, in infringement of this Treaty, fail to act, the Member States and the other institutions of the Community may bring an action before the Court of Justice to have the infringement established.

The action shall be admissible only if the institution concerned has first been called upon to act. If, within two months of being so called upon, the institution concerned has not defined its position, the action may be brought within a further period of two months.

Any natural or legal person may, under the conditions laid down in the preceding paragraphs, complain to the Court of Justice that an institution of the Community has failed to address to that person any act other than a recommendation or an opinion.

3.2. Cases on the interpretation of Article 175

Solomon v. Commission T2
Prodifarma v. Commission II T12 (grounds 35–37)
Komponistenverband v. Commission 20*
Gema v. Commission 70*
Lord Bethell v. Commission 93

4. Article 177

4.1. Text of Article 177 (reproduced below)

Article 177

The Court of Justice shall have jurisdiction to give preliminary rulings concerning:
(a) the interpretation of this Treaty;
(b) the validity and interpretation of acts of the institutions of the Community;
(c) the interpretation of the statutes of bodies established by an act of the Council, where those statutes so provide.
Where such a question is raised before any court or tribunal of a Member State, that court or tribunal may, if it considers that a decision on the question is necessary to enable it to give judgment, request the Court of Justice to give a ruling thereon.

Where any such question is raised in a case pending before a court or tribunal of a Member State, against whose decisions there is no judicial remedy under national law, that court or tribunal shall bring the matter before the Court of Justice.

4.2. Cases on the interpretation of Article 177

Bosch v. De Geus 1
Hoffmann-La Roche v. Centrafarm 56*

Van Eycke v. *Aspa* 155
BRT v. *SABAM* I 36
De Haecht v. *Wilkin* II 34
Ministère Public v. *Tournier* 167 (ground 25)
Lucazeau v. *SACEM* 168 (ground 1a)

5. Articles 178, 215

5.1. Text of Articles 178, 215 (reproduced below)

Article 178

The Court of Justice shall have jurisdiction in disputes relating to compensation for damage provided for in the second paragraph of Article 215.

Article 215

The contractual liability of the Community shall be governed by the law applicable to the contract in question.

In the case of non-contractual liability, the Community shall, in accordance with the general principles common to the laws of the Member States, make good any damage caused by its institutions or by its servants in the performance of their duties.

The personal liability of its servants towards the Community shall be governed by the provisions laid down in their Staff Regulations or in the Conditions of Employment applicable to them.

5.2. Cases on the interpretation of Articles 178, 215

GAARM v. *Commission* 112
Stanley Adams v. *Commission* 125*
Bosman v. *Commission* 187

6. Interim measures

6.1. Text of Articles 185 and 186 (reproduced below)

Article 185

Actions brought before the Court of Justice shall not have suspensory effect. The Court of Justice may, however, if it considers that circumstances so require, order that application of the contested act be suspended.

Article 186

The Court of Justice may in any cases before it prescribe any necessary interim measures.

6.2. Cases on the interpretation of Articles 185 and 186

Cosimex v. *Commission* T1
Peugeot v. *Commission* T3
SEP v. *Commission* T8
Vichy v. *Commission* T13a
Cement Industries v. *Commission* T39
Camera Care v. *Commission* 72
Hoechst v. *Commission* II 140
Dow v. *Commission* 145
RTE & BBC v. *Commission* 163
Publisher's Association v. *Commission* 165

7. Request of interpretation of court judgment

Générale Sucrière 55

CHAPTER 4

NATIONAL JURISDICTIONS AND AUTHORITIES

A. NATIONAL AUTHORITIES

1. What is a national authority?

BRT v. *SABAM* I 36 (ground 19)
Nouvelles Frontières 131 (grounds 55–56)

2. Competence

Article 88 EEC
Article 9(3) Regulation 17/62
Anne Marty v. *Estée Lauder* 77 (grounds 12–16)

3. Co-operation between the national authorities and the commission

Articles 10, 11(2), 11(6), 13, 14(2), 14(5), 14(6) Regulation 17/62
6th Comp. Rep. (paras. 114–116)
16th Comp. Rep. (paras. 41–42)
SEP v. *Commission* T8

B. NATIONAL JURISDICTIONS

1. Direct effect of Articles 85 and 86

Bosch v. *de Geus* 1
BRT v. *SABAM* I 36 (ground 16)
Ahmed Zaeed v. *Zentrale* 162
Tetra Pak v. *Commission* T7 (paras. 40–42)
Application des Gaz SA v. *Falks Veritas Ltd.* [1974] C.M.L.R. 75 at 84

Garden Cottage Foods Ltd. v. Milk Marketing Board ([1982] A.C. 130; [1983] 2 All E.R. 770)

2. Conflict rules

2.1. General

Chaufourniers 20
Fireplaces 90
Bronbemaling 95
AOIP/Beyrard 98
VBBB/VBVB 169 (para. 33)
VBA 288 (para. 168)
13th Comp. Rep. (paras. 217–218)
De Haecht v. Wilkin II 34 (grounds 10–13)
BRT v. SABAM I 36 (ground 20–23)*
Procureur v. Gueralin 76 (ground 13)
Anne Marty v. Estée Lauder 77 (grounds 5–10, 14)
Lancôme v. Etos 78 (grounds 6–11)
L'Oréal v. De Nieuwe AMCK 81 (grounds 7–12)
VBVB & VBBB v. Commission 105 (ground 5)
Delimitis v. Henninger Bräu 181 (grounds 43–55)*

2.2. Provisional validity for old agreements

Julien/Van Katwijk 32
Velcro v. Aplix 233
Bosch-Van Rijn 1
Portelange v. Smith Corona 11
Bilger v. Jehle 12 (grounds 4–6)
Parfums Rochas v. Bitsch 13 (grounds 6–7)
De Haecht v. Wilkin II 34 (ground 9)*
De Bloos v. Boyer 60 (paras. 8–15)
Boekhandels v. Eldi Records 73 (paras. 8–11)
Lancôme v. Etos 78 (paras. 12–18)
Nouvelles Frontières 131 (grounds 61–69)*
Ahmed Saeed v. Zentrale 162 (grounds 5, 21, 32–33)
Delimitis v. Henninger Bräu 181 (grounds 48–49)

3. Commission desire to encourage national enforcement of Articles 85/86

ECS/AKZO–Interim Measures 197 (paras. 6, 35)
Clutch-type disc brakes. 8th Comp. Rep. (para. 121)*
13th Comp. Rep. (paras. 217 & 218)
15th Comp. Rep. (paras 38–43)
Delimitis v. Henninger Bräu 181 (grounds 53)*

4. Suspension of Commission decision by national court

VBVB & VBBB v. Commission 105 (ground 5)

5. Damages for breach of competition rules

Garden Cottage Foods Ltd. v. Milk Marketing Board ([1982] A.C. 130; [1983] 2 All E.R. 770)

CHAPTER 5

CONFLICT RULES

A. NATIONAL LAW

1. Supremacy of EEC competition law over national law in general

Grundig/Consten 5
1st Comp. Rep. (para. 129)
4th Comp. Rep. (paras. 43–47)
Costa v. ENEL 2
Walt Wilhelm 9*
Fire Insurance v. Commission 139 (grounds 22–24)

2. Supremacy of EEC law over national competition rules

Dyestuffs 27
Centraal Bureau voor de Rijwielhandel 118
SSI 181 (para. 101)
Fire Insurance 220 (para. 28)
Net Book Agreements 301 (para. 43)
Welded Steel Mesh 311 (para 206)
2nd Comp. Rep. (para. 27)
4th Comp. Rep. (paras. 43–47)
Pilkington v. BSN 10th Comp. Rep. (paras. 152–154)
Walt Wilhelm 9*
Procureur v. Guerlain 76 (grounds 14–19)
CICCE v. Commission 118 (grounds 26–27)

3. National property law

Article 222
VBA 288
Consten & Grundig v. Commission 4*
Italy v. Commission 5 (ground 22)

4. National defence interests

Articles 223(b), 224
SNPE/LEL 132
WANO 138

B. INTERNATIONAL LAW, INCLUDING EUROPEAN CONVENTION ON HUMAN RIGHTS

1. General

British Telecommunications 188 (para. 43)
Woodpulp 227 (paras. 78–80)

2nd Comp. Rep. (paras. 4–6)
Consten & Grundig v. *Commission* 4
RTE v. *Commission* T14 (grounds 102–104)
BBC v. *Commission* T15 (grounds 76–79)
ITV v. *Commission* T16 (grounds 75–77)
National Panasonic v. *Commission* 74 (grounds 17–23)
FEDETAB v. *Commission* 80 (ground 81)
AM & S v. *Commission* 92
VBVB & VBBB v. *Commission* 105 (grounds 34–37)
Woodpulp 157
Italy v. *Commission* 117 (ground 40)
Orkem v. *Commission* 172 (ground 30)

2. European Convention on Human Rights

2.1. Selected Articles

Article 6: Right to a Fair and Public Hearing

1. In the determination of his civil rigts and obligations or of any criminal charge against him, everyone is entitled to a fair and public hearing within a reasonable time by an independent and impartial tribunal established by law. Judgement shall be pronounced publicly but the press and public may be excluded from all or part of the trial in the interest of morals, public order or national security in a democratic society, where the interests of juveniles or the protection of the private life of the parties so require, or to the extent strictly necessary in the opinion of the court in special circumstances where publicity would prejudice the interests of justice.

2. Everyone charged with a criminal offence shall be presumed innocent until proved guilty according to law.

3. Everyone charged with a criminal offence has the following minimum rights:
   (a) to be informed promptly, in a language which he understands and in detail, of the nature and cause of the accusation against him
   (b) to have adequate time and facilities for the preparation of his defence;
   (c) to defend himself in person or through legal assistance of his own choosing or, if he has not sufficient means to pay for legal assistance, to be given it free when the interests of justice so require;
   (d) to examine or have examined witnesses on his behalf under the same conditions as witnesses against him;
   (e) to have the free assistance of an interpreter if he cannot understand or speak the language used in court.

Article 7: Freedom From Retrospective Effect of Penal Legislation

1. No one shall be held guilty of any criminal offence on account of any act or omission which did not constitute a criminal offence under national or international law at the time when it was committed. Nor shall a heavier penalty be imposed than the one that was applicable at the time the criminal offence was committed.

2. This Article shall not prejudice the trial and punishment of any person for any act or omission which, at the time when it was committed, was criminal according to the general principles of law recognised by civilised nations.

Article 8: Right to Respect for Privacy

1. Everyone has the right to respect for his private and family life, his home and his correspondence.
2. There shall be no interference by a public authority with the exercise of this right except such as in accordance with the law and is necessary in a democratic society in the interests of national security, public safety or the economic well-being of the country, for the prevention of disorder or crime, for the protection of health or morals, or for the protection of the rights and freedoms of others.

Article 10: Freedom of Expression

1. Everyone has the right to freedom of expression. This right shall include freedom to hold opinions and to receive and impart information and ideas without interference by public authority and regardless of frontiers. This Article shall not prevent States from requiring the licensing of broadcasting, televsion or cinema enterprises.
2. The exercise of these freedoms, since it carries with it duties and responsibilities, may be subject to such formalities, conditions, restrictions or penalties as are prescribed by law and are necessary in a democratic society, in the interests of national security, territorial integrity or public safety, for the prevention of disorder or crime, for the protection of health or morals, for the protection of the reputation or rights of others, for preventing the disclosure of information received in confidence, or for maintaining the authority and impartiality of the judiciary.

Article 11: Freedom of Association and Assembly

1. Everyone has the right to freedom of peaceful assembly and to freedom of association with others, including the right to form and to join trade-unions for the protection of his interests.
2. No restrictions shall be placed on the exercise of these rights other than such as prescribed by law and are necessary in a democratic society in the interests of national security or public safety, for the prevention of disorder or crime, for the protection of health or morals or for the protection of the rights and freedoms of others. This Article shall not prevent the imposition of lawful restrictions on the exercise of the administration of the State.

2.2 Cases

2.2.1. Community cases

Montedipe v. *Commission* T36 (para. 319)
National Panasonic v. *Commission* 74 (ground 17)
Fedetab v. *Commission* 80 (grounds 79–81)
Pioneer v. *Commission* 98 (grounds 6–7)
VBVB & VBBB v. *Commission* 105 (grounds 21, 32, 33)
Cinéthèque 122a (ground 25)
Stanley Adams v. *Commission* 125 (ground 19, 45)
AKZO v. *Commission II* 133 (ground 25, 27)
Bond van Adverteerders 149a (grounds 2, 40)
Hoechst v. *Commission III* 169 (ground 13 & 18)
Dow Iberica v. *Commission* 171 (grounds 10, 15)
Dow Benelux v. *Commission* 170 (grounds 24 & 29)
Orkem v. *Commission* 172 (grounds 18 & 30)
ERT v. *DEP* 185 (grounds 42 – 45)

2.2.2. Strasbourg cases

SA Stenuit v. *France* Decision of Commission No. 11598/85, 11.7.89.
CM & Co v. *Germany* Decision of Commission No. 1258/87, 9.2.90

3. Agreements concluded by the Community

3.1. Text of Competition Laws Co-operation Agreement 1991 (EEC-USA) (reproduced opposite)

Competition Laws Co-operation Agreement 1991 (EEC-USA)

Adopted by the Commission of the European Communities and the Government of the United States of America

(Signed by Sir Leon Brittan for the EC Commission, William P. Barr for the U.S. Government and Janet L. Steiger for the Federal Trade Commission)

THE AGREEMENT

Recognising that the world's economies are becoming increasingly interrelated, and inm particular that this is true of the economies the European Communities and the United States of America;
Noting that the Commission of the European Communities and the Government of the United States of America share the view that the sound and effective enforcement of competition law is a matter of importance to the efficient operation of their respective markets and to trade between them;
the sound and effective enforcement of the Parties' competition laws would be enhanced by co-operation and, in appropiate cases, co-ordination between them in the application of those laws;
Noting further that from time to time differences may arise between the Parties concerning the application of their competition laws to conduct or transactions that implicate significant interests of both Parties;
Having regard to the Recommendation of the Council of the Organisation for Economic Co-operation and Development Concerning Co-operation Between Member Countries on Restrictive Business Practices Affecting International Trade, adopted on 5 June, 1986;
and
to the Declaration on US-EC Relations adopted on November 23, 1990;

The EC COMMISSION and the GOVERNMENT OF THE UNITED STATES OF AMERICA

HAVE AGREED AS FOLLOWS:

Article I: Purpose and Definitions

1. The purpose of this Agreement is to promote co-operation and co-ordination and lessen the possibility or impact of differences between the Parties in the application of their competition laws.

2. For the purposes of this Agreement, the following terms shall have the following definitions:
   (a) 'Competition law(s)' shall mean
      (i) for the European Communities, Articles 85, 86, 89 and 90 EEC, Regulation 4064/89 on the control of concentrations between undertakings, Article 65 and 66 ECSC and their Implementing Regulations including High Authority Decision 24–54, and
      (ii) for the United States of America, the Sherman Act (15 U.S.C. §§ 1–7), the Clayton Act (15 U.S.C. §§ 12–27), the Wilson Tariff Act (15 U.S.C. §§ 8–11, and the Federal Trade Commission Act (15 U.S.C. §§ 41–68, except as these sections relate to consumer protection functions). as well as such other laws or regulations as the Parties shall jointly agree in writing to be a 'competition law' for purposes of this Agreement;
   (b) 'Competition authorities' shall mean
      (i) for the European Communities the Commission of the European Communities, as to its responsibilities pursuant to the competition laws of the European Communities, and
      (ii) for the United States, the Antitrust Division of the United States Department of Justice and the Federal Trade Commission;
   (c) 'Enforcement activities' shall mean any application of competition law by way of investigation or proceeding conducted by the competition authorities of a Party; and
   (d) 'Anticompetitive activities' shall mean any conduct or transaction that is impermissible under the competition laws of a Party.

Article II: Notification

1. Each Party shall notify the other whenever its competition authorities become

aware that their enforcement activities may affect important interests of the other Party.

2. Enforcement activities as to which notification ordinarily will be appropiate include those that:
   (a) Are relevant to enforcement activities of the other Party;
   (b) Involve anticompetitive activities (other than a merger or acquisition) carried out in significant part in the other Party's territory;
   (c) Involve a merger or acquisition in which one or more of the parties to the transaction, or a company controlling one or more of the parties to the transaction, is a company incorporated or organised under the laws of the other Party or one of its states or member-states;
   (d) Involve conduct believed to have been required, encouraged or approved by the other Party; or
   (e) Involve remedies that would, in significant respects, require or prohibit conduct in the other Party's territory.

3. With respect to mergers or acquisitions required by law to be reported to the competition authorities, notification under this Article shall be made:
   (a) In the case of the Government of the United States of America,
      (i) not later than the time its competition authorities request, pursuant to 15 U.S.C. § 18a(e), additional information or documentary material concerning the proposed transaction,
      (ii) when its competition authorities decide to file a complaint challenging the transaction, and
      (iii) where this is possible, far enough in advance of the entry of a consent decree to enable the other Party's views to be taken into account; and
   (b) In the case of the Commission of the European Communities,
      (i) when notice of the transaction is published in the Official Journal, pursuant to Article 4(3) of Council Regulation 4064/89, or when notice of the transaction is received under Article 66 ECSC and a prior authorisation from the Commission is required under that provision
      (ii) when its competition authorities decide to initiate proceedings with respect to Article 6(1)(c) of Council Regulation 4064/89, and
      (iii) far enough in advance of the adoption of a decision in the case to enable the other Party's views to be taken into account.

4. With respect to other matters, notification shall ordinarily be provided at the stage in an investigation when it becomes evident that notifiable circumstances are present, and in any event far enough in advance of
   (a) the issuance of a statement of objections in the case of the Commission of the European Communities, or a complaint or indictment in the case of the Government of the United States of America, and
   (b) the adoption of a decision or settlement in the case of the Commission of the European Communities, or the entry of a consent decree in the case of the Goverment of the United States of America,
to enable the other Party's views to be taken into account.

5. Each Party shall also notify the other whenever its competition authorities intervene or otherwise participate in a regulatory or judicial proceeding that does not arise from its enforcement activities, if the issues addressed in the intervention or participation may affect the other Party's important interests. Notification under this paragraph shall apply only to
   (a) regulatory or judicial proceedings that are public,
   (b) intervention or participation that is public and pursuant to formal procedures, and
   (c) in the case of regulatory proceedings in the United States, only proceedings before federal agencies.

Notification shall be made at the time of the intervention or participation or as soon thereafter as possible.

6. Notifications under this Article shall include sufficient information to permit an initial evaluation by the recipient Party of any effects on its interests.

Article III: Exchange of Information

1. The Parties agree that it is in their common interest to share information that will (a) facilitate effective application of their respective competition laws, or (b) promote better understanding by them of economic conditions and theories relevant to their competition authorities' enforcement activities and interventions or participation of the kind described in Article II(5).

2. In furtherance of this common interest, appropriate officials from the competition authorities of each Party shall meet at least twice each year, unless otherwise agreed, to (a) exchange information on their current enforcement activities and priorities, (b) exchange information on economic sectors of common interest, (c) discuss policy changes which they are considering, and (d) discuss other matters of mutual interest relating to the application of competition laws.

3. Each Party will provide the other Party with any significant information that comes to the attention of its competition authorities about anti-competitive activities that its competition authorities believe is relevant to, or may warrant, enforcement activity by the other party's competition authorities.

4. Upon receiving a request from the other Party, and within the limits of Articles VIII and IX, a Party will provide to the requesting Party such information within its possession as the requesting Party may describe that is relevant to an enforcement activity being considered or conducted by the requesting party's competition authorities.

Article IV: Co-operation and co-ordination in enforcement activities

1. The competition authorities of each Party will render assistance to the competition authorities of the other party in their enforcement activities, to the extent compatible with the assisting Party's laws and important interests, and within its reasonably available resources.

2. In cases where both Parties have an interest in pursuing enforcement activities with regard to related situations, they may agree that is in their mutual interest to co-ordinate their enforcement activities. In considering whether particular enforcement activities should be co-ordinated, the Parties shall take account of the following factors, among others:
 (a) the opportunity to make more efficient use of their resources devoted to the enforcement activities;
 (b) the relative abilities of the Parties' competition authorities to obtain information necessary to conduct the enforcement activities;
 (c) the effect of such co-ordination on the ability of both Parties to achieve the objectives of their enforcement activities; and
 (d) the possibility of reducing costs incurred by persons subject to the enforcement activities.

3. In any co-ordination arrangement, each Party shall conduct its enforcement activities expeditiously and, in so far as possible, consistently with the enforcement objectives of the other Party.

4. Subject to appropriate notice to the other Party, the competition authorities of either party may limit or terminate their participation in a co-ordination arrangement and pursue their enforcement activities independently.

Article V: Co-operation regarding Anti-competitive Activities in the Territory of one Party that Adversely Affect the Interest of the Other Party

1. The Parties note that anti-competitive activities may occur within the territory of one Party that, in addition to violating that party's competition laws, adversely affect important interests of the other Party. The Parties agree that it is in both their interests to address anti-competitive activities of this nature.

2. If a Party believes that anti-competitive activities carried out on the territory of the other Party are adversely affecting its important interests, the first Party may notify the other Party and may request that the other Party's competition authorities initiate appropriate enforcement activities. The notification shall be as specific as possible about the nature of the anti-competitive activities and their effects on the interests of the notifying Party, and shall include an offer of such further information and other co-operation as the notifying Party is able to provide.

3. Upon receipt of a notification under paragraph 2, and after such other discussion between the Parties as may be appropriate and useful in the circumstances, the competition authorities of the notified Party will consider whether or not to initiate enforcement activities, or to expand ongoing enforcement activities, with respect to the anti-competitive activities identified in the notification. The notified Party will advise the notifying Party of its decision. If enforcement activities are initiated, the notified Party will advise the notifying Party of their outcome and, to the extent possible, of significant interim developments.

4. Nothing in this Article limits the discretion of the notified Party under its competition laws and enforcement policies as to whether or not to undertake enforcement activities with respect to the notified anti-competitive activities, or precludes the

notifying Party from undertaking enforcement activities with respect to such anti-competitive activities.

Article VI: Avoidance of Conflicts over Enforcement Activities

Within the framework of its own laws and to the extent compatible with its important interests, each Party will seek, at all stages in its enforcement activities, to take into account the important interests of the other Party. Each Party shall consider important interests of the other Party in decisions as to whether or not to intitiate an investigation or proceeding, the scope of an investigation or proceeding, the nature of the remedies or penalties sought, and in other ways, as appropriate. In considering one another's important interests in the course of their enforcement activities, the Parties will take account of, but will not be limited to, the following principles:

1. While an important interest of a Party may exist in the absence of official involvement by the Party with the activity in question, it is recognised that such interests would normally be reflected in antecedent laws, decisions or statements of policy by its competent authorities.

2. A Party's important interests may be affected at any stage of enforcement activity by the other Party. The Parties recognise, however, that as a general matter the potential for adverse impact on one Party's important interests arising from enforcement activity by the other Party is less at the investigative stage and greater at the stage at which conduct is prohibited or penalised, or at which other forms of remedial orders are imposed.

3. Where it appears that one Party's enforcement activities may adversely affect important interests of the other Party, the Parties will consider the following factors. In addition to any other factors that appear relevant in the circumstances, in seeking an appropriate accommodation of the competing interests:

(a) the relative significance to the anti-competitive activities involved of conduct within the enforcing Party's territory as compared to conduct within the other Party's territory;
(b) the presence or absence of a purpose on the part of those engaged in the anti-competitive activities to affect consumers, suppliers, or competitors within the enforcing Party's territory;
(c) the relative significance of the effects of the anti-competitive activities on the enforcing Party's interests as compared to the effects on the other Party's interests;
(d) the existence or absence of reasonable expectations that would be furthered or defeated by the enforcement activities;
(e) the degree of conflict or consistency between the enforcement activities and the other Party's laws or articulated economic policies; and
(f) the extent to which enforcement activities of the other party with respect to the same persons, including judgments or undertakings resulting from such activities, may be affected.

Article VII: Consultation

1. Each Party agrees to consult promptly with the other Party in response to a request by the other Party for consultations regarding any matter related to this Agreement and to attempt to conclude consultations expeditiously with a view to reaching mutually satisfactory conclusions. Any request for consultations shall include the reasons therefor and shall state whether procedural time limits or other considerations require the consultations to be expedited.

These consultations shall take place at the appropriate level, which may include consultations between the heads of the competition authorities concerned.

2. In each consultation under paragraph 1, each Party shall take into account the principles of co-operation set forth in this Agreement and shall be prepared to explain to the other Party the specific results of its application of those principles to the issue that is the subject of consultation.

Article VIII: Confidentiality of Information

1. Notwithstanding any other provision of this Agreement, neither Party is required to provide information to the other Party if disclosure of that information to the requesting Party (a) is prohibited by the law of the Party possessing the information, or (b) would be incompatible with important interests of the Party possessing the information.

2. Each Party agrees to maintain, to the fullest extent possible, the confidentiality of any information provided to it in confidence by the other Party under this Agreement and to oppose, to the fullest extent possible, any application for disclosure of

such information by a third party that is not authorised by the Party that supplied the information.

Article IX: Existing Law

Nothing in this Agreement shall be interpreted in a manner inconsistent with the existing laws, or as requiring any change in the laws, of the United States of America or the European Communities or of their respective states or Member States.

Article X: Communications under this Agreement

Communications under this Agreement, including notifications under Articles II and V, may be carried out by direct oral, telephonic written or facsimile communication from one Party's competition authority to the other Party's authority. Notifications under Articles II, V and XI, and requests under Article VII, shall be confirmed promptly in writing through diplomatic channels.

Article XI: Entry into Force, Termination and Review

1. This Agreement shall enter into force upon signature.
2. This Agreement shall remain in force until 60 days after the date on which either party notifies the other Party in writing that it wishes to terminate the Agreement.
3. The parties shall review the operation of this Agreement not more than 24 months from the date of its entry into force, with a view to assessing their co-operative activities, identifying additional areas in which they could usefully co-operate and identifying any other ways in which the Agreement could be improved.

The Parties agree that this review will include, among other things, an analysis of actual or potential cases to determine whether their interests could be better served through closer co-operation.

BOOK TWO

MERGERS AND ACQUISITIONS

BOOK TWO—CONTENTS

Lists and Tables

Table 1:	Chronological List of Merger Decisions (EEC)—References..	421
Table 2:	Chronological List of Merger Decisions (EEC)—Contents....	424
Table 3:	Chronological List of Relevant Commission Decisions (Articles 85 and 86) (EEC)—References.........................	427
Table 4:	Chronological List of Relevant Court of First Instance Judgments (Articles 85 and 86) (EEC)—References..............	429
Table 5:	Chronological List of Relevant European Court Judgments (Articles 85 and 86) (EEC)—References.....................	430
Table 6:	Alphabetical List of Merger Decisions......................	431

TABLE 1
CHRONOLOGICAL LIST OF MERGER DECISIONS (EEC)—REFERENCES

No.	NAME	DATE	O.J.	C.M.L.R.	C.C.H.
M1	Renault/Volvo	7.11.90	[1990] C281/2	4 [1991] 297	—
M2	AG/AMEV	21.11.90	[1990] C304/27	4 [1991] 847	—
M3	ICI/Tioxide	28.11.90	[1990] C304/27	4 [1991] 792	—
M4	Arjomari/Wiggins Teape	10.12.90	[1990] C321/16	4 [1991] 854	—
M5	Promodes/Dirsa	17.12.90	[1990] C321/16	4 [1991] 8	—
M6	Cargill/Unilever	20.12.90	[1990] C327/14	4 [1992] M55	—
M7	Mitsubishi/UCAR	4.1.91	[1991] C5/7	4 [1992] M50	—
M8	Matsushita/MCA	10.1.91	[1991] C12/15	4 [1992] M36	—
M9	AT&T/NCR	18.1.91	[1991] C16/20	4 [1992] M41	—
M10	BNP/Dresdner Bank	4.2.91	[1991] C34/20	—	—
M11	Baxter/Nestlé/Salvia	6.2.91	[1991] C37/11	4 [1991] 245	—
M12	Fiat/Ford New Holland	8.2.91	[1991] C118/14	4 [1991] 330	—
M13	Asko/Omni	21.2.91	[1991] C51/12	4 [1991] 330	—
M14	Digital/Kienzle	25.2.91	[1991] C56/16	4 [1991] 330	—
M15	MBB/Aerospatiale	25.2.91	[1991] C59/13	4 [1992] M70	—
M16	Kyowa/Saitama	7.3.91	[1991] C66/13	4 [1991] 331	—
M17	Otto/Grattan	21.3.91	[1991] C93/6	—	1 [1991] 2112
M18	Alcatel/Telettra	12.4.91	[1991] L122/48	4 [1991] 778	—
M19	Redoute/Empire Stores	25.4.91	[1991] C156/10	4 [1991] 739	—
M20	Usinor/ASD	29.4.91	[1991] C193/34	4 [1991] 663	—
M21	Elf/Ertoil	29.4.91	[1991] C124/13	4 [1991] 493	—
M22	Asko/Jacobs/ADIA	16.5.91	[1991] C132/13	4 [1991] 493	2 [1991] 2146
M23	Magneti-Marelli/CEAC	29.5.91	[1991] L222/38	4 [1992] M61	—
M24	CONAGRA/IDEA	30.5.91	[1991] C175/18	4 [1991] 580	—

421

Book Two—Table 1

No.	NAME	DATE	O.J.	C.M.L.R.	C.C.H.
M25	RVI/VBC/HEULIEZ	3.6.91	[1991] C149/15	4 [1991] 493	—
M26	VIAG/Continental Can	6.6.91	[1991] C156/10	4 [1991] 739	—
M27	Sanofi/Sterling Drugs	10.6.91	[1991] C156/10	4 [1991] 739	—
M28	ELF/Occidental	13.6.91	[1991] C160/20	—	—
M29	ELF/BC/CEPSA	18.6.91	[1991] C172/8	—	—
M30	Apollinaris/Schweppes	24.6.91	[1991] C203/14	4 [1991] 580	—
M31	Pechiney-Usinor/Sacilor	24.6.91	[1991] C175/18	4 [1991] 580	—
M32	Nissan/Richard Nissan	28.6.91	[1991] C181/21	4 [1991] 581	—
M33	Draeger/IBM/HMP	28.6.91	[1991] C236/6	4 [1991] 817	—
M34	Lyonnaise des Eaux/Brochier	11.7.91	[1991] C188/20	4 [1991] 663	—
M35	ICL/Nokia Data	17.7.91	[1991] C236/6	4 [1991] 817	—
M36	EDS/SD-Scicon	17.7.91	[1991] C237/44	4 [1991] 740	—
M37	Tetra Pak/Alfa-Laval	22.7.91	[1991] C290/35	—	2 [1991] 2203
M38	ELF/Enterprise	24.7.91	[1991] C203/14	—	—
M39	BP/Petromed	29.7.91	[1991] C208/24	4 [1991] 817	—
M40	Eridania/ISI	30.7.91	[1991] C204/12	4 [1991] 663	—
M41	Varta/Bosch	31.7.91	[1991] L320/26	—	1 [1992] 2022
M42	Kelt/American Express	20.8.91	[1991] C223/38	4 [1991] 740	—
M43	BNP/Dresdner (Czechoslovakia)	26.8.91	[1991] C266/28	4 [1991] 818	—
M44	Digital/Philips	2.9.91	[1991] C235/13	4 [1991] 740	—
M45	ABC/Générale des Eaux/Canal & W.H. Smith	10.9.91	[1991] C244/5	4 [1991] 818	—
M46	Delta Airlines/Pan Am	13.9.91	[1991] C289/14	4 [1991] 898	—
M47	Mannesmann/Boge	23.9.91	[1991] C265/8	4 [1991] 818	—
M48	Aérospatiale-Alenia/de Havilland	2.10.91	[1991] C334/42	4 [1992] M2	1 [1992] 2034
M49	Metallgesellschaft/Dynamit Nobel	14.10.91	[1991] C276/4	4 [1991] 898	—
M50	Paribas/MTH	17.10.91	[1991] C277/18	4 [1991] 897	—
M51	Thomson/Pilkington	23.10.91	[1991] C279/19	4 [1991] 898	—
M52	Bank America/Security Pacific	24.10.91	[1991] C289/14	4 [1992] 13	—
M53	Metallgesellschaft/Safic Alcan	8.11.91	[1991] C300/22	4 [1992] 13	—
M54	UAP/Transatlantic/Sunlife	11.11.91	[1991] C296/12	4 [1992] 13	—
M55	Cereol/Continentale Italiana	27.11.91	[1992] C7/7	4 [1992] 346	—
M56	TNT/Canada Post	2.12.91	[1991] C322/19	4 [1992] 12	—
M57	Lucas/Eaton	9.12.91	[1991] C328/15	—	—
M58	Mannesman/VDO	13.12.91	[1992] C88/13	—	—
M59	Ingersoll Rand/Dresser	18.12.91	[1992] C86/15	4 [1992] 349	—

Chronological List of Merger Decisions (EEC)—References

No.	NAME	DATE	O.J.	C.M.L.R.	C.C.H.
M60	Eurocom/RSCG	18.12.91	[1991] C332/16	4 [1992] 80	—
M61	Alcatel/AEG Kabel	18.12.91	[1992] C6/23	4 [1992] 80	—
M62	Courtaulds/SNIA	19.12.91	[1991] C333/16	4 [1992] 349	—
M63	CAMPSA	19.12.91	[1991] C334/23	4 [1992] 80	—
M64	VIAG/Brühl	19.12.91	[1991] C333/16	4 [1992] 342	—
M65	Mediobanca/Generali	19.12.91	[1991] C334/23	4 [1992] 81	—
M66	Gambogi/Cogei	19.12.91	[1991] C334/23	4 [1992] 81	—
M67	Sunrise	13.1.92	[1992] C18/15	4 [1992] 344	—
M68	Saab/Ericsson Space	13.1.92	[1992] C17/10	4 [1992] 345	—
M69	Volvo/Atlas	14.1.92	[1992] C17/10	4 [1992] 345	—
M70	Schweizer Rück/ELVIA	14.1.92	[1992] C27/14	4 [1992] 81	—
M71	Inchcape/IEP	21.1.92	[1992] C21/27	4 [1992] 81	—
M72	Ericsson/Kolbe	22.1.92	[1992] C27/14	4 [1992] 81	—
M73	Spar/Dansk Supermarket	3.2.92	[1992] C29/18	4 [1992] 81	—
M74	Grand Met./Cinzano	7.2.92	[1992] C47/23	4 [1992] 349	—
M75	Tarmac/Steetley	12.2.92	[1992] C50/25	4 [1992] 343	—
M76	James River/Rayne	13.2.92	[1992] C43/19	4 [1992] 342	—
M77	BSN/Nestlé/Cokoladovni	17.2.92	[1992] C47/23	—	—
M78	Torras/Sarrio	24.2.92	[1992] C58/20	4 [1992] 341	—
M79	INFINT/EXOR	2.3.92	[1992] C88/13	—	—

423

TABLE 2

CHRONOLOGICAL LIST OF MERGER DECISIONS (EEC)—CONTENTS

No.	NAME	TYPE OF DECISION	TYPE OF CONCENTRATION	PRODUCT SECTOR
M1	Renault/Volvo	Clearance Art. 6(1)(b)	Merger	Vehicles
M2	AG/AMEV	Clearance Art. 6(1)(b)	Merger	Insurance
M3	ICI/Tioxide	Clearance Art. 6(1)(a)	Acquisition	Chemicals
M4	Arjomari/Wiggins Teape	Clearance Art. 6(1)(b)	Acquisition	Paper & Pulp
M5	Promodes/Dirsa	Clearance Art. 6(1)(b)	Acquisition	Retailing
M6	Cargill/Unilever	Clearance Art. 6(1)(b)	Acquisition	Agricultural Merchanting
M7	Mitsubishi/UCAR	Clearance Art. 6(1)(b)	Joint Venture	Graphite & Carbon Electrodes
M8	Matsushita/MCA	Clearance Art. 6(1)(b)	Acquisition	Films, Consumer Electronics
M9	AT&T/NCR	Clearance Art. 6(1)(b)	Contested Takeover	Computers
M10	BNP/Dresdner Bank	Clearance Art. 6(1)(b)	Joint Venture	Banking
M11	Baxter/Nestlé/Salvia	Clearance Art. 6(1)(a)	Joint Venture	Clinical nutrition
M12	Fiat/Ford New Holland	Clearance Art. 6(1)(b)	Acquisition	Agicultural machinery
M13	Asko/Omni	Clearance Art. 6(1)(b)	Acquisition	Personal & other services
M14	Digital/Kienzle	Clearance Art. 6(1)(b)	Merger	Computers
M15	MBB/Aeorspatiale	Clearance Art. 6(1)(b)	Merger	Helicopters
M16	Kyowa/Saitama	Clearance Art. 6(1)(b)	Merger	Banking
M17	Otto/Grattan	Clearance Art. 6(1)(b)	Acquisition	Mail order
M18	Alcatel/Telettra	Clearance Art. 8(2)	Acquisition	Batteries
M19	Redoute/Empire Stores	Clearance Art. 6(1)(b)	Contested takeover	Retail/Mail order
M20	Usinor/ASD	Clearance Art. 6(1)(b)	Acquisition	Coal & Steel
M21	Elf/Ertoil	Clearance Art. 6(1)(b)	Acquisition	Petrol, lubricants
M22	Asko/Jacobs/ADIA	Clearance Art. 6(1)(b)	Joint venture: concentrative	Personnel Services
M23	Magneti-Marcelli/CEAC	Clearance with conditions and obligations Art. 8(2)	—	Batteries

Chronological List of Merger Decisions (EEC)—Contents

No.	NAME	TYPE OF DECISION	TYPE OF CONCENTRATION	PRODUCT SECTOR
M24	CONAGRA/IDEA	Clearance Art. 6(1)(b)	Joint venture: concentrative	Slaughter of animals/meat products
M25	RVI/VBC/HEULIEZ	Clearance Art. 6(1)(b)	Joint venture: concentrative	Buses and coaches
M26	VIAG/Continental Can	Clearance Art. 6(1)(b)	Acquisition majority	Packaging
M27	Sanofi/Sterling Drugs	Clearance Art. 6(1)(b)	Joint venture:concentrative	Pharmaceuticals
M28	ELF/Occidental	Clearance Art. 6(1)(b)	Acquisition 100%	Petroleum products
M29	ELF/BC/CEPSA	Clearance Art. 6(1)(b)	Joint venture: concentrative	Petroleum products
M30	Apollinaris/Schweppes	Clearance Art. 6(1)(b)	Joint venture: cooperative	Soft-drinks
M31	Pechiney-Usinor/Secilor	Clearance Art. 6(1)(b)	Joint venture: concentrative	Mechanical parts
M32	Nissan/Richard Nissan	Clearance Art. 6(1)(b)	Acquisition 81.6%	Automobile distribution
M33	Draeger/IBM/HMP	Clearance Art. 6(1)(b)	Joint venture: concentrative	Hospital data management systems
M34	Lyonnaise des Eaux/Brochier	Clearance Art. 6(1)(b)	Joint venture: concentrative	—
M35	ICL/Nokia Data	Clearance Art. 6(1)(b)	Acquisition 100%	Computers
M36	EDS/SD-Scicon	Clearance Art. 6(1)(b)	Contested take-over bid	High-Tech Services
M37	Tetra Pak/Alfa-Laval	Without conditions and obligations Art. 8(2)	Non-contested take-over bid	Packaging machines — Food processing machines
M38	ELF/Enterprise	Clearance Art. 6(1)(a)	Joint venture: co-operative	Petroleum products
M39	BP/Petromed	Clearance Art. 6(1)(b)	Acquisition 100%	Petroleum products
M40	Eridania/ISI	Clearance Art. 6(1)(b)	Acquisition 65%	Sugar
M41	Varta/Bosch	With conditions and obligations Art. 8(2)	Joint venture: concentrative	Batteries
M42	Kelt/American Express	Clearance Art. 6(1)(b)	Joint venture: concentrative	Petroleum products
M43	BHP/Dresdner (Czechoslovakia)	Clearance Art. 6(1)(b)	Acquisition 100%	Banking
M44	Digital/Philips	Clearance Art. 6(1)(b)	Acquisition 100%	Computers
M45	ABC/Générale des Eaux/Canal & W.H. Smith	Clearance Art. 6(1)(b)	Joint venture: concentrative	Television
M46	Delta Airlines/Pan Am	Clearance Art. 6(1)(b)	Acquisition 100%	Air transport
M47	Mannesman/Boge	Clearance Art. 6(1)(b) Art. 8(3)	Acquisition 50.01%	Shock absorbers
M48	Aérospatiale-Alenia/de Havilland		Non-contested public bid	Turboprop aircraft
M49	Metallgesellschaft/Dynamit Nobel	Clearance Art. 6(1)(b)	Acquisition 90%	Mining metal ores
M50	Paribas/MTH	Clearance Art. 6(1)(b)	Joint venture: concentrative	Machinery wholesaling
M51	Thomson/Pilkington	Clearance Art. 6(1)(b)	Joint venture: concentrative	Optronics
M52	Bank America/Security Pacific	Clearance Art. 6(1)(b)	Merger	Banking
M53	Metallgesellschaft/Safic Alcan	Clearance Art. 6(1)(b)	Joint venture: concentrative	Rubber and latex
M54	UAP/Transatlantic/Sunlife	Clearance Art. 6(1)(b)	Joint venture: concentrative	Insurance

Book Two—Table 2

No.	NAME	TYPE OF DECISION	TYPE OF CONCENTRATION	PRODUCT SECTOR
M55	Cereal/Continentale Italiana	Clearance Art. 6(1)(a)	Acquisition 100%	Oils and fats
M56	TNT/Canada Post	Clearance Art. 6(1)(b)	Joint venture: concentrative	Express mail services
M57	Lucas/Eaton	Clearance Art. 6(1)(b)	Joint venture: concentrative	Heavy duty braking systems
M58	Mannesmann/VDO	Clearance Art. 6(1)(b)	Acquisition	Car parts
M59	Ingersoll Rand/Dresser	Clearance Art. 6(1)(b)	Joint venture: concentrative	Industrial pumps
M60	Eurocom/RSCG	Clearance Art. 6(1)(b)	Merger	Advertising
M61	Alcatel/AEG Kabel	Clearance Art. 6(1)(b)	Acquisition 96.8%	Cables and Wires
M62	Courtaulds/SNIA	Clearance Art. 6(1)(b)	Joint venture: concentrative	Acetate yarn
M63	CAMPSA	Clearance Art. 6(1)(b)	De-concentration	Petroleum distribution
M64	VIAG/Brühl	Clearance Art. 6(1)(b)	Acquisition	Metal Casting
M65	Mediobanca/Generali	Clearance Art. 6(1)(b)	Acquisition 12.84%	Banking
M66	Gambogi/Cogei	Clearance Art. 6(1)(a)	Joint venture: co-operative	Construction
M67	Sunrise	Clearance Art. 6(1)(b)	Joint venture: concentrative	Television
M68	Saab/Ericsson Space	Clearance Art. 6(1)(b)	Joint venture: concentrative	Space equipment
M69	Volvo/Atlas	Clearance Art. 6(1)(b)	Joint venture: concentrative	Hydraulic pumps
M70	Schweizer Rück/ELVIA	Clearance Art. 6(1)(b)	Acquisition majority	Insurance
M71	Inchcape/IEP	Clearance Art. 6(1)(b)	Acquisition 100%	Vehicle distribution
M72	Ericsson/Kolbe	Clearance Art. 6(1)(b)	Joint venture: concentrative	Telecommunications equipment
M73	Spar/Dansk Supermarket	Clearance Art. 6(1)(b)	Joint venture: concentrative	Retailing
M74	Grand Met./Cinzano	Clearance Art. 6(1)(b)	Acquisition 100%	Alcoholic beverages
M75	Tarmac/Steetley	Clearance Art. 6(1)(b)	Joint venture: concentrative	Building materials
M76	James River/Rayne	Clearance Art. 6(1)(b)	Acquisition 50%	Tissue paper
M77	BSN/Nestlé/Cokoladovni	Clearance Art. 6(1)(a)	Joint venture: co-operative	Confectionery products
M78	Torras/Sarrio	Clearance Art. 6(1)(b)	Acquisition of assets	Printing papers
M79	INFINT/EXOR	Clearance Art. 6(1)(b)	Public bid	Mineral water

TABLE 3

CHRONOLOGICAL LIST OF RELEVANT COMMISSION DECISIONS
(ARTICLES 85 AND 86) (EEC)—REFERENCES[1]

No.	NAME	DATE	O.J.[2]	C.M.L.R.[3]		C.C.H.[4]
4.	Nicholas Frères Vitapro	30.7.64	J.O. 2287/64	(1964)	505	—
46.	Continental Can	9.12.71	[1972] L7/25	(1972)	D11	9481
64.	Zoja/CSC-ICI	14.12.72	[1972] L299/51	[1973]	D50	9543
69.	European Sugar Industry	2.1.73	[1973] L140/17	[1973]	D65	9570
84.	General Motors	19.12.74	[1975] L29/14	1 [1975]	D20	9705
87.	SHV/Chevron	20.12.74	[1975] L38/14	1 [1975]	D68	9709
101.	Chiquita	17.12.75	[1976] L95/1	1 [1976]	D28	9800
104.	Vitamins	9.6.76	[1976] L223/27	2 [1976]	D25	9853
107.	Reuter/BASF	26.7.76	[1976] L254/40	2 [1976]	D44	9862
113.	ABG/Oil Companies	19.4.77	[1977] L117/1	2 [1977]	D1	9944
114.	DeLaval/Stork I	25.7.77	[1977] L215/11	2 [1977]	D69	9972
121.	Hugin/Liptons	8.12.77	[1978] L22/23	1 [1978]	D19	10,007
165.	Michelin	7.10.81	[1981] L353/33	1 [1982]	643	10,340
166.	GVL	29.10.81	[1981] L370/49	1 [1982]	223	10,345
197.	ECS/AKZO-Interim Measures	29.7.83	[1983] L252/13	3 [1983]	694	10,517
206.	Nutricia	12.12.83	[1983] L376/22	2 [1984]	165	10,567
212.	British Leyland	2.7.84	[1984] L207/11	3 [1984]	92	10,601
215.	BPCL/ICI	19.7.84	[1984] L212/1	1 [1985]	330	10,611
225.	Mecaniver/PPG	12.12.84	[1985] L35/54	3 [1985]	359	10,650
242.	ECS/AKZO	14.12.85	[1985] L374/1	3 [1986]	273	10,748
256.	ENI/Montedison	4.12.86	[1987] L5/13	4 [1989]	444	10,860
273.	Boosey & Hawkes	29.7.87	[1987] L286/36	4 [1988]	67	10,920

[1] Details of the contents of these decisions are listed in Table 2 of Book One.
[2] Official Journal of the European Communities.
[3] Common Market Law Reports.
[4] Commerce Clearing House.

No.	NAME	DATE	O.J.	C.M.L.R.		C.C.H.	
286.	British Sugar	18.7.88	[1988] L284/41	4	[1990] 196		11,012
295.	SABENA	4.11.88	[1988] L317/47	4	[1989] 662		11,043
299.	British Plasterboard	5.12.88	[1989] L10/50	4	[1990] 464	1 [1989]	2,008
300.	Flat Glass	7.12.88	[1989] L33/44	4	[1990] 535	1 [1989]	2,077
304.	Decca	21.12.88	[1989] L43/24	4	[1990] 627	1 [1989]	2,137
307.	Magill	21.12.88	[1989] L78/43	4	[1989] 749	1 [1989]	2,223
321.	Metaleurop	12.7.90	[1990] L179/41	4	[1991] 222	2 [1990]	2,033
325.	GEC-Siemens/Plessey	1.9.90	[1990] C239/2		—		—
332.	Solvay	19.12.90	[1991] L152/21		—	2 [1991]	2,029
333.	ICI	19.12.90	[1991] L152/40		—	2 [1991]	2,053

TABLE 4

CHRONOLOGICAL LIST OF RELEVANT COURT OF FIRST INSTANCE JUDGMENTS (ARTICLES 85 AND 86) (EEC)—REFERENCES[1]

No.	NAME	CASE No.	DATE	ECR-T	C.M.L.R.	C.C.H.	APPEAL
T14	RTE v. Commission	T–69/89	10.7.91	—	4 [1991] 586	2 [1991] 114	*
T15	BBC v. Commission	T–70/89	10.7.91	—	4 [1991] 669	2 [1991] 147	*
T16	ITV v. Commission	T–76/89	10.7.91	—	4 [1991] 745	2 [1991] 174	*

[1] Details of the contents of these judgments are listed in Table 4 of Book One.
* Appeal pending.

TABLE 5

CHRONOLOGICAL LIST OF RELEVANT EUROPEAN COURT JUDGMENTS (ARTICLES 85 AND 86) (EEC)—REFERENCES[1]

No.	NAME	CASE No.	DATE	E.C.R.[2]	C.M.L.R.[3]	C.C.H.[4]
35.	Continental Can v. Commission	6/72	21.2.73	[1973] 215	[1973] 199	8171
46.	General Motors v. Commission	26/75	13.11.75	[1975] 1367	1[1976] 95	8320
62.	United Brands v. Commission	27/76	14.2.78	[1978] 207	1[1978] 429	8429
65.	Benzine & Petroleum BV v. Commission	77/77	29.6.78	[1978] 1513	3[1978] 174	8465
67.	Hoffmann-La Roche v. Commission	85/76	13.2.79	[1979] 461	3[1979] 211	8527
68.	Hugin v. Commission	22/78	31.5.79	[1979] 869	3[1979] 345	8524
97.	GVL v. Commission	7/82	2.3.83	[1983] 483	3[1983] 645	8636
121.	Remia v. Commission	42/84	11.7.85	[1985] 2545	1[1987] 1	14,217
124.	Télémarketing v. CLT	311/84	3.10.85	[1985] 3261	2[1986] 558	14,246
136.	British Leyland	226/84	11.11.86	[1986] 3263	1[1987] 184	14,336
146.	BAT v. Commission & Philip Morris	142 & 156/84	17.11.87	[1987] 4487	2[1987] 551	14,405
150.	Bodson v. Pompes Funebres	30/87	4.5.88	[1988] 2479	4[1989] 984	1 [1990] 3
159.	Volvo v. Veng	238/87	5.10.88	[1988] 6232	4[1989] 122	14,498
160.	Alsatel v. Novosam	247/86	5.10.88	[1988] 5987	4[1990] 434	1 [1990] 248
161.	Maxicar v. Renault	53/87	5.10.88	[1988] 6039	4[1990] 265	1 [1990] 59
168.	Lucazeau v. SACEM	110,241,242/88	13.7.89	[1989] 2811	4[1991] 248	2 [1990] 856
186.	AKZO v. Commission III	C-62/86	3.7.91	—	—	—

[1] Details of the contents of these judgments are listed in Table 6 of Book One.
[2] European Court Reports.
[3] Common Market Law Reports.
[4] Commerce Clearing House.

TABLE 6
ALPHABETICAL LIST OF MERGER DECISIONS

ABC/Générale des Eaux/Canal & W.H. Smith	M45
AG/AMEV	M2
AT&T/NCR	M9
Aérospatiale-Alenia/de Havilland	M48
Alcatel/AEG Kabel	M61
Alcatel/Telettra	M18
Apollinaris/Schweppes	M30
Arjomari/Wiggins Teape	M4
Asko/Jacobs/ADIA	M22
Asko/Omni	M13
BNP/Dresdner Bank	M10
BNP/Dresdner (Czechoslovakia)	M43
BSN/Nestlé/Cokoladovni	M77
BP/Petromed	M39
Bank America/Security Pacific	M52
Baxter/Nestlé/Salvia	M11
CAMPSA	M63
CONAGRA/IDEA	M24
Cargill/Unilever	M6
Cereol/Continentale Italiana	M55
Courtaulds/SNIA	M62
Delta Airlines/Pan Am	M46
Digital/Kienzle	M14
Digital/Philips	M44
Draeger/IBM/HMP	M33
EDS/SD-Scicon	M36
ELF/BC/CEPSA	M29
ELF/Enterprise	M38
ELF/Ertoil	M21
ELF/Occidental	M28
Ericsson/Kolbe	M72
Eridania/ISI	M40
Eurocom/RSCG	M60
Fiat/Ford New Holland	M12
Gambogi/Cogel	M66
Grand Met./Cinzano	M74
ICI/Tioxide	M3
ICL/Nokia Data	M35
INFINT/EXOR	M79
Inchapel/IEP	M71
Ingersoll Rand/Dresser	M59
James River/Rayne	M76
Kelt/American Express	M45
Kyowa/Saitama	M16
Lucas/Eaton	M57
Lyonnaise des Eaux/Brochier	M34
MBB/Aerospatiale	M15
Magneti-Marelli/CEAC	M23
Mannesmann/Boge	M47
Mannesmann/VDO	M58
Matsushita/MCA	M8
Mediobanca/Generali	M65
Metallgesellachft/Dynamit Nobel	M49
Metallgesellachft/Safic Alcan	M53
Mitsubishi/UCAR	M7
Nissan/Richard Nissan	M32
Otto/Grattan	M17
Paribas/MTH	M50
Pechiney-Usinor/Sacilor	M31
Promodes/Dirsa	M5
RVI/VBC/HEULIEZ	M25
Redoute/Empire Stores	M19
Renault/Volvo	M1
Saab/Ericsson Space	M68
Sanofi/Sterling Drugs	M27
Schweizer Rück/ELVIA	M70
Spar/Dansk Supermarket	M73
Sunrise	M67
TNT/Canada Post	M56
Tarmac/Steetley	M75
Tetra Pak/Alfa-Laval	M37
Thomson/Pilkington	M51
Torras/Sarrio	M78
UAP/Transatlantic/Sunlife	M54
Usinor/ASD	M20
VIAG/Brühl	M64
VIAG/Continental Can	M26
Varta/Bosch	M41
Volvo/Atlas	M69

BOOK TWO

MERGERS AND ACQUISITIONS

CHAPTER ONE

LEGISLATION

1. Text of Council Regulation 4064/89 of December 21, 1989, on the control of concentrations between undertakings (reproduced below)

Council Regulation 4064/89 of September 21, 1990

This is a revised text of the Regulation. As a corrigendum to the original text ([1989] O.J. L395/1) it incorporates numerous minor amendments throughout on the control of concentrations between undertakings

([1990] O.J. L257/14)

THE COUNCIL OF THE EUROPEAN COMMUNITIES,

Having regard to the Treaty establishing the European Economic Community, and in particular Articles 87 and 235 thereof,

Having regard to the proposal from the Commission ([1988] O.J. C130/4),

Having regard to the opinion of the European Parliament ([1988] O.J. C309/55),

Having regard to the opinion of the Economic and Social Committee ([1988] O.J. C208/11),

(1) Whereas, for the achievement of the aims of the Treaty establishing the European Economic Community, Article 3(f) gives the Community the objective of instituting "a system ensuring that competition in the common market is not distorted";

(2) Whereas this system is essential for the achievement of the internal market by 1992 and its further development;

(3) Whereas the dismantling of internal frontiers is resulting and will continue to result in major corporate reorganizations in the Community, particularly in the form of concentrations;

(4) Whereas such a development must be welcomed as being in line with the requirements of dynamic competition and capable of increasing the competitiveness of European industry, improving the conditions of growth and raising the standard of living in the Community;

(5) Whereas, however, it must be ensured that the process of reorganization does not result in lasting damage to competition; whereas Community law must therefore include provisions governing those concentrations which may significantly impede effective competition in the common market or in a substantial part of it;

(6) Whereas Articles 85 and 86, while applicable, according to the case-law of the Court of Justice, to certain concentrations, are not, however, sufficient to control all operations which may prove to be incompatible with the system of undistorted competition envisaged in the Treaty;

(7) Whereas a new legal instrument should therefore be created in the form of a Regulation to permit effective control of all concentrations from the point of view of their effect on the structure of competition in the Community and to be the only instrument applicable to such concentrations;

(8) Whereas this Regulation should therefore be based not only on Article 87 but, principally, on Article 235 of the Treaty,

under which the Community may give itself the additional powers of action necessary for the attainment of its objectives, including with regard to concentrations on the markets for agricultural products listed in Annex II to the Treaty;

(9) Whereas the provisions to be adopted in this Regulation should apply to significant structural changes the impact of which on the market goes beyond the national borders of any one Member State;

(10) Whereas the scope of application of this Regulation should therefore be defined according to the geographical area of activity of the undertakings concerned and be limited by quantitative thresholds in order to cover those concentrations which have a Community dimension; whereas, at the end of an initial phase of the application of this Regulation, these thresholds should be reviewed in the light of the experience gained;

(11) Whereas a concentration with a Community dimension exists where the combined aggregate turnover of the undertakings concerned exceeds given levels worldwide and within the Community and where at least two of the undertakings concerned have their sole or main fields of activities in different Member States or where, although the undertakings in question act mainly in one and the same Member State, at least one of them has substantial operations in at least one other Member State; whereas that is also the case where the concentrations are effected by undertakings which do not have their principal fields of activities in the Community but which have substantial operations there;

(12) Whereas the arrangements to be introduced for the control of concentrations should, without prejudice to Article 90(2) of the Treaty, respect the principle of non-discrimination between the public and the private sectors; whereas, in the public sector, calculation of the turnover of an undertaking concerned in a concentration needs, therefore, to take account of undertakings making up an economic unit with an independent power of decision, irrespective of the way in which their capital is held or of the rules of administrative supervision applicable to them;

(13) Whereas it is necessary to establish whether concentrations with a Community dimension are compatible or not with the common market from the point of view of the need to maintain and develop effective competition in the common market; whereas, in so doing, the Commission must place its appraisal within the general framework of the achievement of the fundamental objectives referred to in Article 2 of the Treaty, including that of strengthening the Community's economic and social cohesion, referred to in Article 130a;

(14) Whereas this Regulation should establish the principle that a concentration with a Community dimension which creates or strengthens a position as a result of which effective competition in the common market or in a substantial part of it is significantly impeded is to be declared incompatible with the common market;

(15) Whereas concentrations which, by reason of the limited market share of the undertakings concerned, are not liable to impede effective competition may be presumed to be compatible with the common market; whereas, without prejudice to Articles 85 and 86 of the Treaty, an indication to this effect exists, in particular, where the market share of the undertakings concerned does not exceed 25% either in the common market or in a substantial part of it;

(16) Whereas the Commission should have the task of taking all the decisions necessary to establish whether or not concentrations with a Community dimension are compatible with the common market, as well as decisions designed to restore effective competition;

(17) Whereas to ensure effective control undertakings should be obliged to give prior notification of concentrations with a Community dimension and provision should be made for the suspension of concentrations for a limited period, and for the possibility of extending or waiving a suspension where necessary; whereas in the interests of legal certainty the validity of transactions must nevertheless be protected as much as necessary;

(18) Whereas a period within which the Commission must initiate proceedings in respect of a notified concentration and periods within which it must give a final decision on the compatibility or incompatibility with the common market of a notified concentration should be laid down;

(19) Whereas the undertakings concerned must be afforded the right to be heard by the Commission when proceedings have been initiated; whereas the members of the management and supervisory bodies and the recognized representatives of the employees of the undertakings concerned,

and third parties showing a legitimate interest, must also be given the opportunity to be heard;

(20) Whereas the Commission should act in close and constant liaison with the competent authorities of the Member States from which it obtains comments and information;

(21) Whereas, for the purposes of this Regulation, and in accordance with the case-law of the Court of Justice, the Commission must be afforded the assistance of the Member States and must also be empowered to require information to be given and to carry out the necessary investigations in order to appraise concentrations;

(22) Whereas compliance with this Regulation must be enforceable by means of fines and periodic penalty payments; whereas the Court of Justice should be given unlimited jurisdiction in that regard pursuant to Article 172 of the Treaty;

(23) Whereas it is appropriate to define the concept of concentration in such a manner as to cover only operations bringing about a lasting change in the structure of the undertakings concerned; whereas it is therefore necessary to exclude from the scope of this Regulation those operations which have as their object or effect the coordination of the competitive behaviour of undertakings which remain independent, since such operations fall to be examined under the appropriate provisions of the Regulations implementing Articles 85 and 86 of the Treaty; whereas it is appropriate to make this distinction specifically in the case of the creation of joint ventures;

(24) Whereas there is no coordination of competitive behaviour within the meaning of this Regulation where two or more undertakings agree to acquire jointly control of one or more other undertakings with the object and effect of sharing amongst themselves such undertakings or their assets;

(25) Whereas this Regulation should still apply where the undertakings concerned accept restrictions directly related and necessary to the implementation of the concentration;

(26) Whereas the Commission should be given exclusive competence to apply this Regulation, subject to review by the Court of Justice;

(27) Whereas the Member States may not apply their national legislation on competition to concentrations with a Community dimension, unless this Regulation makes provision therefor; whereas the relevant powers of national authorities should be limited to cases where, failing intervention by the Commission, effective competition is likely to be significantly impeded within the territory of a Member State and where the competition interests of that Member State cannot be sufficiently protected otherwise by this Regulation; whereas the Member States concerned must act promptly in such cases; whereas this Regulation cannot, because of the diversity of national law, fix a single deadline for the adoption of remedies;

(28) Whereas, furthermore, the exclusive application of this Regulation to concentrations with a Community dimension is without prejudice to Article 223 of the Treaty, and does not prevent the Member States from taking appropriate measures to protect legitimate interests other than those pursued by this Regulation, provided that such measures are compatible with the general principles and other provisions of Community law;

(29) Whereas concentrations not covered by this Regulation come, in principle, within the jurisdiction of the Member States; whereas, however, the Commission should have the power to act, at the request of a Member State concerned, in cases where effective competition could be significantly impeded within that Member State's territory;

(30) Whereas the conditions in which concentrations involving Community undertakings are carried out in non-member countries should be observed, and provision should be made for the possibility of the Council giving the Commission an appropriate mandate for negotiation with a view to obtaining non-discriminatory treatment for Community undertakings;

(31) Whereas this Regulation in no way detracts from the collective rights of employees as recognized in the undertakings concerned,

HAS ADOPTED THIS REGULATION

Article 1: Scope

1. Without prejudice to Article 22 this Regulation shall apply to all concentrations with a Community dimension as defined in paragraph 2.

2. For the purposes of this Regulation, a concentration has a Community dimension where:

(a) the combined aggregate worldwide turnover of all the undertakings concerned is more than ECU 5,000 million; and

(b) the aggregate Community-wide turnover of each of at least two of the undertakings concerned is more than ECU 250 million, unless each of the undertakings concerned achieves more than two-thirds of its aggregate Community-wide turnover within one and the same Member State.

3. The thresholds laid down in paragraph 2 will be reviewed before the end of the fourth year following that of the adoption of this Regulation by the Council acting by a qualified majority on a proposal from the Commission.

Article 2: Appraisal of concentrations

1. Concentrations within the scope of this Regulation shall be appraised in accordance with the following provisions with a view to establishing whether or not they are compatible with the common market.

In making this appraisal, the Commission shall take into account:
(a) the need to maintain and develop effective competition within the common market in view of, among other things, the structure of all the markets concerned and the actual or potential competition from undertakings located either within or outwith the Community;
(b) the market position of the undertakings concerned and their economic and financial power, the alternatives available to suppliers and users, their access to supplies or markets, any legal or other barriers to entry, supply and demand trends for the relevant goods and services, the interests of the intermediate and ultimate consumers, and the development of technical and economic progress provided that it is to consumers' advantage and does not form an obstacle to competition.

2. A concentration which does not create or strengthen a dominant position as a result of which effective competition would be significantly impeded in the common market or in a substantial part of it shall be declared compatible with the common market.

3. A concentration which creates or strengthens a dominant position as a result of which effective competition would be significantly impeded in the common market or in a substantial part of it shall be declared incompatible with the common market.

Article 3: Definition of concentration

1. A concentration shall be deemed to arise where:
(a) two or more previously independent undertakings merge, or
(b)— one or more persons already controlling at least one undertaking, or
— one or more undertakings
acquire, whether by purchase of securities or assets, by contract or by any other means, direct or indirect control of the whole or parts of one or more other undertakings.

2. An operation, including the creation of a joint venture, which has as its object or effect the coordination of the competitive behaviour of undertakings which remain independent shall not constitute a concentration within the meaning of paragraph 1(b).

The creation of a joint venture performing on a lasting basis all the functions of an autonomous economic entity, which does not give rise to coordination of the competitive behaviour of the parties amongst themselves or between them and the joint venture, shall constitute a concentration within the meaning of paragraph 1(b).

3. For the purposes of this Regulation, control shall be constituted by rights, contracts or any other means which, either separately or in combination and having regard to the considerations of fact or law involved, confer the possibility of exercising decisive influence on an undertaking, in particular by:
(a) ownership or the right to use all or part of the assets of an undertaking;
(b) rights or contracts which confer decisive influence on the composition, voting or decisions of the organs of an undertaking.

4. Control is acquired by persons or undertakings which:
(a) are holders of the rights or entitled to rights under the contracts concerned; or
(b) while not being holders of such rights or entitled to rights under such contracts, have the power to exercise the rights deriving therefrom.

5. A concentration shall not be deemed to arise where:
(a) credit institutions or other financial institutions or insurance companies, the normal activities of which include transactions and dealing in securities for their own account or for the account of others, hold on a temporary basis securities which they have acquired in an undertaking with a view to reselling them, provided

that they do not exercise voting rights in respect of those securities with a view to determining the competitive behaviour of that undertaking or provided that they exercise such voting rights only with a view to preparing the disposal of all or part of that undertaking or of its assets or the disposal of those securities and that any such disposal takes place within one year of the date of acquisition; that period may be extended by the Commission on request where such institutions or companies can show that the disposal was not reasonably possible within the period set;
(b) control is acquired by an office-holder according to the law of a Member State relating to liquidation, winding up, insolvency, cessation of payments, compositions or analogous proceedings;
(c) the operations referred to in paragraph 1(b) are carried out by the financial holding companies referred to in Article 5(3) of the Fourth Council Directive 78/660/EEC of 25 July 1978 on the annual accounts of certain types of companies ([1978] O.J. L222/11), as last amended by Directive 84/569/EEC ([1984] O.J. L314/28), provided however that the voting rights in respect of the holding are exercised, in particular in relation to the appointment of members of the management and supervisory bodies of the undertakings in which they have holdings, only to maintain the full value of those investments and not to determine directly or indirectly the competitive conduct of those undertakings.

Article 4: Prior notification of concentrations

1. Concentrations with a Community dimension defined in this Regulation shall be notified to the Commission not more than one week after the conclusion of the agreement, or the announcement of the public bid, or the acquisition of a controlling interest. That week shall begin when the first of those events occurs.

2. A concentration which consists of a merger within the meaning of Article 3(1)(a) or in the acquisition of joint control within the meaning of Article 3(1)(b) shall be notified jointly by the parties to the merger or by those acquiring joint control as the case may be. In all other cases, the notification shall be effected by the person or undertaking acquiring control of the whole or parts of one or more undertakings.

3. Where the Commission finds that a notified concentration falls within the scope of this Regulation, it shall publish the fact of the notification, at the same time indicating the names of the parties, the nature of the concentration and the economic sectors involved. The Commission shall take account of the legitimate interest of undertakings in the protection of their business secrets.

Article 5: Calculation of turnover

1. Aggregate turnover within the meaning of Article 1(2) shall comprise the amounts derived by the undertakings concerned in the preceding financial year from the sale of products and the provision of services falling within the undertakings' ordinary activities after deduction of sales rebates and of value added tax and other taxes directly related to turnover. The aggregate turnover of an undertaking concerned shall not include the sale of products or the provision of services between any of the undertakings referred to in paragraph 4.

Turnover, in the Community or in a Member State, shall comprise products sold and services provided to undertakings or consumers, in the Community or in that Member State as the case may be.

2. By way of derogation from paragraph 1, where the concentration consists in the acquisition of parts, whether or not constituted as legal entities, of one or more undertakings, only the turnover relating to the parts which are the subject of the transaction shall be taken into account with regard to the seller or sellers.

However, two or more transactions within the meaning of the first subparagraph which take place within a two-year period between the same persons or undertakings shall be treated as one and the same concentration arising on the date of the last transaction.

3. In place of turnover the following shall be used:
(a) for credit institutions and other financial institutions, as regards Article 1(2)(a), one-tenth of their total assets.

As regards Article 1(2)(b) and the final part of Article 1(2), total Community-wide turnover shall be replaced by one-tenth of total assets multiplied by the ratio between loans and advances to credit institutions and customers in transactions with Community residents and the total sum of those loans and advances.

As regards the final part of Article 1(2), total turnover within one Member State shall be replaced by one-tenth of total assets multiplied by the ratio between loans and advances to credit institutions and customers in transactions with residents of that Member State and the total sum of those loans and advances;

(b) for insurance undertakings, the value of gross premiums written which shall comprise all amounts received and receivable in respect of insurance contracts issued by or on behalf of the insurance undertakings, including also outgoing reinsurance premiums, and after deduction of taxes and parafiscal contributions or levies charged by reference to the amounts of individual premiums or the total volume of premiums; as regards Article 1(2)(b) and the final part of Article 1(2), gross premiums received from Community residents and from residents of one Member State respectively shall be taken into account.

4. Without prejudice to paragraph 2, the aggregate turnover of an undertaking concerned within the meaning of Article 1(2) shall be calculated by adding together the respective turnovers of the following:
(a) the undertaking concerned;
(b) those undertakings in which the undertaking concerned, directly or indirectly:
— owns more than half the capital or business assets, or
— has the power to exercise more than half the voting rights, or
— has the power to appoint more than half the members of the supervisory board, the administrative board or bodies legally representing the undertakings, or
— has the right to manage the undertakings' affairs;
(c) those undertakings which have in the undertaking concerned the rights or powers listed in (b);
(d) those undertakings in which an undertaking as referred to in (c) has the rights or powers listed in (b);
(e) those undertakings in which two or more undertakings as referred to in (a) to (d) jointly have the rights or powers listed in (b).

5. Where undertakings concerned by the concentration jointly have the rights or powers listed in paragraph 4(b), in calculating the aggregate turnover of the undertakings concerned for the purposes of Article 1(2):
(a) no account shall be taken of the turnover resulting from the sale of products or the provision of services between the joint undertaking and each of the undertakings concerned or any other undertaking connected with any one of them, as set out in paragraph 4(b) to (e);
(b) account shall be taken of the turnover resulting from the sale of products and the provision of services between the joint undertaking and any third undertakings. This turnover shall be apportioned equally amongst the undertakings concerned.

Article 6: Examination of the notification and initiation of proceedings

1. The Commission shall examine the notification as soon as it is received.
(a) Where it concludes that the concentration notified does not fall within the scope of this Regulation, it shall record that finding by means of a decision.
(b) Where it finds that the concentration notified, although falling within the scope of this Regulation, does not raise serious doubts as to its compatibility with the common market, it shall decide not to oppose it and shall declare that it is compatible with the common market.
(c) If, on the other hand, it finds that the concentration notified falls within the scope of this Regulation and raises serious doubts as to its compatibility with the common market, it shall decide to initiate proceedings.

2. The Commission shall notify its decision to the undertakings concerned and the competent authorities of the Member States without delay.

Article 7: Suspension of concentrations

1. For the purposes of paragraph 2 a concentration as defined in Article 1 shall not be put into effect either before its notification or within the first three weeks following its notification.

2. Where the Commission, following a preliminary examination of the notification within the period provided for in paragraph 1, finds it necessary in order to ensure the full effectiveness of any decision taken later pursuant to Article 8(3) and (4), it may decide on its own initiative to continue the suspension of a concentration in whole or in part until it takes a final decision, or to take other interim measures to that effect.

3. Paragraphs 1 and 2 shall not prevent the implementation of a public bid which has

been notified to the Commission in accordance with Article 4(1), provided that the acquirer does not exercise the voting rights attached to the securities in question or does so only to maintain the full value of those investments and on the basis of a derogation granted by the Commission under paragraph 4.

4. The Commission may, on request, grant a derogation from the obligations imposed in paragraphs 1, 2 or 3 in order to prevent serious damage to one or more undertakings concerned by a concentration or to a third party. That derogation may be made subject to conditions and obligations in order to ensure conditions of effective competition. A derogation may be applied for and granted at any time, even before notification or after the transaction.

5. The validity of any transaction carried out in contravention of paragraph 1 or 2 shall be dependent on a decision pursuant to Article 6(1)(b) or Article 8(2) or (3) or on a presumption pursuant to Article 10(6).

This Article shall, however, have no effect on the validity of transactions in securities including those convertible into other securities admitted to trading on a market which is regulated and supervised by authorities recognized by public bodies, operates regularly and is accessible directly or indirectly to the public, unless the buyer and seller knew or ought to have known that the transaction was carried out in contravention of paragraph 1 or 2.

Article 8: Powers of decision of the Commission

1. Without prejudice to Article 9, all proceedings initiated pursuant to Article 6(1)(c) shall be closed by means of a decision as provided for in paragraphs 2 to 5.

2. Where the Commission finds that, following modification by the undertakings concerned if necessary, a notified concentration fulfils the criterion laid down in Article 2(2), it shall issue a decision declaring the concentration compatible with the common market.

It may attach to its decision conditions and obligations intended to ensure that the undertakings concerned comply with the commitments they have entered into *vis-à-vis* the Commission with a view to modifying the original concentration plan.

The decision declaring the concentration compatible shall also cover restrictions directly related and necessary to the implementation of the concentration.

3. Where the Commission finds that a concentration fulfils the criterion laid down in Article 2(3), it shall issue a decision declaring that the concentration is incompatible with the common market.

4. Where a concentration has already been implemented, the Commission may, in a decision pursuant to paragraph 3 or by separate decision, require the undertakings or assets brought together to be separated or the cessation of joint control or any other action that may be appropriate in order to restore conditions of effective competition.

5. The Commission may revoke the decision it has taken pursuant to paragraph 2 where:
(a) the declaration of compatibility is based on incorrect information for which one of the undertakings is responsible or where it has been obtained by deceit; or
(b) the undertakings concerned commit a breach of an obligation attached to the decision.

6. In the cases referred to in paragraph 5, the Commission may take a decision under paragraph 3, without being bound by the deadline referred to in Article 10(3).

Article 9: Referral to the competent authorities of the Member States

1. The Commission may, by means of a decision notified without delay to the undertakings concerned and the competent authorities of the other Member States, refer a notified concentration to the competent authorities of the Member State concerned in the following circumstances.

2. Within three weeks of the date of receipt of the copy of the notification a Member State may inform the Commission, which shall inform the undertakings concerned, that a concentration threatens to create or to strengthen a dominant position as a result of which effective competition would be significantly impeded on a market, within that Member State, which presents all the characteristics of a distinct market, be it a substantial part of the common market or not.

3. If the Commission considers that, having regard to the market for the products

or services in question and the geographical reference market within the meaning of paragraph 7, there is such a distinct market and that such a threat exists, either:

(a) it shall itself deal with the case in order to maintain or restore effective competition on the market concerned; or

(b) it shall refer the case to the competent authorities of the Member State concerned with a view to the application of that State's national competition law.

If, however, the Commission considers that such a distinct market or threat does not exist it shall adopt a decision to that effect which it shall address to the Member State concerned.

4. A decision to refer or not to refer pursuant to paragraph 3 shall be taken:

(a) as a general rule within the six-week period provided for in Article 10(1), second subparagraph, where the Commission, pursuant to Article 6(1)(b), has not initiated proceedings; or

(b) within three months at most of the notification of the concentration concerned where the Commission has initiated proceedings under Article 6(1)(c), without taking the preparatory steps in order to adopt the necessary measures under Article 8(2), second subparagraph, (3) or (4) to maintain or restore effective competition on the market concerned.

5. If within the three months referred to in paragraph 4(b) the Commission, despite a reminder from the Member State concerned, has not taken a decision on referral in accordance with paragraph 3 nor has taken the preparatory steps referred to in paragraph 4(b), it shall be deemed to have taken a decision to refer the case to the Member State concerned in accordance with paragraph 3(b).

6. The publication of any report or the announcement of the findings of the examination of the concentration by the competent authority of the Member State concerned shall be effected not more than four months after the Commission's referral.

7. The geographical reference market shall consist of the area in which the undertakings concerned are involved in the supply and demand of products or services, in which the conditions of competition are sufficiently homogeneous and which can be distinguished from neighbouring areas because, in particular, conditions of competition are appreciably different in those areas. This assessment should take account in particular of the nature and characteristics of the products or services concerned, of the existence of entry barriers or of consumer preferences, of appreciable differences of the undertakings' market shares between the area concerned and neighbouring areas or of substantial price differences.

8. In applying the provisions of this Article, the Member State concerned may take only the measures strictly necessary to safeguard or restore effective competition on the market concerned.

9. In accordance with the relevant provisions of the Treaty, any Member State may appeal to the Court of Justice, and in particular request the application of Article 186, for the purpose of applying its national competition law.

10. This Article will be reviewed before the end of the fourth year following that of the adoption of this Regulation.

Article 10: Time limits for initiating proceedings and for decisions

1. The decisions referred to in Article 6(1) must be taken within one month at most. That period shall begin on the day following that of the receipt of a notification or, if the information to be supplied with the notification is incomplete, on the day following that of the receipt of the complete information.

That period shall be increased to six weeks if the Commission receives a request from a Member State in accordance with Article 9(2).

2. Decisions taken pursuant to Article 8(2) concerning notified concentrations must be taken as soon as it appears that the serious doubts referred to in Article 6(1)(c) have been removed, particularly as a result of modifications made by the undertakings concerned, and at the latest by the deadline laid down in paragraph 3.

3. Without prejudice to Article 8(6), decisions taken pursuant to Article 8(3) concerning notified concentrations must be taken within not more than four months of the date on which proceedings are initiated.

4. The period set by paragraph 3 shall exceptionally be suspended where, owing to circumstances for which one of the undertakings involved in the concentration

1 Legislation

is responsible, the Commission has had to request information by decision pursuant to Article 11 or to order an investigation by decision pursuant to Article 13.

5. Where the Court of Justice gives a Judgment which annuls the whole or part of a Commission decision taken under this Regulation, the periods laid down in this Regulation shall start again from the date of the Judgment.

6. Where the Commission has not taken a decision in accordance with Article 6(1)(b) or (c) or Article 8(2) or (3) within the deadlines set in paragraphs 1 and 3 respectively, the concentration shall be deemed to have been declared compatible with the common market, without prejudice to Article 9.

Article 11: Requests for information

1. In carrying out the duties assigned to it by this Regulation, the Commission may obtain all necessary information from the Governments and competent authorities of the Member States, from the persons referred to in Article 3(1)(b), and from undertakings and associations of undertakings.

2. When sending a request for information to a person, an undertaking or an association of undertakings, the Commission shall at the same time send a copy of the request to the competent authority of the Member State within the territory of which the residence of the person or the seat of the undertaking or association of undertakings is situated.

3. In its request the Commission shall state the legal basis and the purpose of the request and also the penalties provided for in Article 14(1)(c) for supplying incorrect information.

4. The information requested shall be provided, in the case of undertakings, by their owners or their representatives and, in the case of legal persons, companies or firms, or of associations having no legal personality, by the persons authorized to represent them by law or by their statutes.

5. Where a person, an undertaking or an association of undertakings does not provide the information requested within the period fixed by the Commission or provides incomplete information, the Commission shall by decision require the information to be provided. The decision shall specify what information is required, fix an appropriate period within which it is to be supplied and state the penalties provided for in Articles 14(1)(c) and 15(1)(a) and the right to have the decision reviewed by the Court of Justice.

6. The Commission shall at the same time send a copy of its decision to the competent authority of the Member State within the territory of which the residence of the person or the seat of the undertaking or association of undertakings is situated.

Article 12: Investigations by the authorities of the Member States

1. At the request of the Commission, the competent authorities of the Member States shall undertake the investigations which the Commission considers to be necessary under Article 13(1), or which it has ordered by decision pursuant to Article 13(3). The officials of the competent authorities of the Member States responsible for conducting those investigations shall exercise their powers upon production of an authorization in writing issued by the competent authority of the Member State within the territory of which the investigation is to be carried out. Such authorization shall specify the subject matter and purpose of the investigation.

2. If so requested by the Commission or by the competent authority of the Member State within the territory of which the investigation is to be carried out, officials of the Commission may assist the officials of that authority in carrying out their duties.

Article 13: Investigative powers of the Commission

1. In carrying out the duties assigned to it by this Regulation, the Commission may undertake all necessary investigations into undertakings and associations of undertakings.

To that end the officials authorized by the Commission shall be empowered:
(a) to examine the books and other business records;
(b) to take or demand copies of or extracts from the books and business records;
(c) to ask for oral explanations on the spot;
(d) to enter any premises, land and means of transport of undertakings.

2. The officials of the Commission authorized to carry out the investigations shall

exercise their powers on production of an autorization in writing specifying the subject matter and purpose of the investigation and the penalties provided for in Article 14(1)(d) in cases where production of the required books or other business records is incomplete. In good time before the investigation, the Commission shall inform, in writing, the competent authority of the Member State within the territory of which the investigation is to be carried out of the investigation and of the identities of the authorized officials.

3. Undertakings and associations of undertakings shall submit to investigations ordered by decision of the Commission. The decision shall specify the subject matter and purpose of the investigation, appoint the date on which it shall begin and state the penalties provided for in Articles 14(1)(d) and 15(1)(b) and the right to have the decision reviewed by the Court of Justice.

4. The Commission shall in good time and in writing inform the competent authority of the Member State within the territory of which the investigation is to be carried out of its intention of taking a decision pursuant to paragraph 3. It shall hear the competent authority before taking its decision.

5. Officials of the competent authority of the Member State within the territory of which the investigation is to be carried out may, at the request of that authority or of the Commission, assist the officials of the Commission in carrying out their duties.

6. Where an undertaking or association of undertakings opposes an investigation ordered pursuant to this Article, the Member State concerned shall afford the necessary assistance to the officials authorized by the Commission to enable them to carry out their investigation. To this end the Member States shall, after consulting the Commission, take the necessary measures within one year of the entry into force of this Regulation.

Article 14: Fines

1. The Commission may by decision impose on the persons referred to in Article 3(1)(b), undertakings or associations of undertakings fines of from ECU 1,000 to 50,000 where intentionally or negligently:
(a) they fail to notify a concentration in accordance with Article 4;
(b) they supply incorrect or misleading information in a notification pursuant to Article 4;
(c) they supply incorrect information in response to a request made pursuant to Article 11 or fail to supply information within the period fixed by a decision taken pursuant to Article 11;
(d) they produce the required books or other business records in incomplete form during investigations under Article 12 or 13, or refuse to submit to an investigation ordered by decision taken pursuant to Article 13.

2. The Commission may by decision impose fines not exceeding 10% of the aggregate turnover of the undertakings concerned within the meaning of Article 5 on the persons or undertakings concerned where, either intentionally or negligently, they:
(a) fail to comply with an obligation imposed by decision pursuant to Article 7(4) or 8(2), second subparagraph;
(b) put into effect a concentration in breach of Article 7(1) or disregard a decision taken pursuant to Article 7(2);
(c) put into effect a concentration declared incompatible with the common market by decision pursuant to Article 8(3) or do not take the measures ordered by decision pursuant to Article 8(4).

3. In setting the amount of a fine, regard shall be had to the nature and gravity of the infringement.

4. Decisions taken pursuant to paragraphs 1 and 2 shall not be of criminal law nature.

Article 15: Periodic penalty payments

1. The Commission may by decision impose on the persons referred to in Article 3(1)(b), undertakings or associations of undertakings concerned periodic penalty payments of up to ECU 25,000 for each day of delay calculated from the date set in the decision, in order to compel them:
(a) to supply complete and correct information which it has requested by decision pursuant to Article 11;
(b) to submit to an investigation which it has ordered by decision pursuant to Article 13.

2. The Commission may by decision impose on the persons referred to in Article 3(1)(b) or on undertakings periodic penalty payments of up to ECU 100,000 for each day of delay calculated from the date

set in the decision, in order to compel them:
(a) to comply with an obligation imposed by decision pursuant to Article 7(4) or Article 8(2), second subparagraph, or
(b) to apply the measures ordered by decision pursuant to Article 8(4).

3. Where the persons referred to in Article 3(1)(b), undertakings or associations of undertakings have satisfied the obligation which it was the purpose of the periodic penalty payment to enforce, the Commission may set the total amount of the periodic penalty payments at a lower figure than that which would arise under the original decision.

Article 16: Review by the Court of Justice

The Court of Justice shall have unlimited jurisdiction within the meaning of Article 172 of the Treaty to review decisions whereby the Commission has fixed a fine or periodic penalty payments; it may cancel, reduce or increase the fine or periodic penalty payments imposed.

Article 17: Professional secrecy

1. Information acquired as a result of the application of Article 11, 12, 13 and 18 shall be used only for the purposes of the relevant request, investigation or hearing.

2. Without prejudice to Articles 4(3), 18 and 20, the Commission and the competent authorities of the Member States, their officials and other servants shall not disclose information they have acquired through the application of this Regulation of the kind covered by the obligation of professional secrecy.

3. Paragraphs 1 and 2 shall not prevent publication of general information or of surveys which do not contain information relating to particular undertakings or associations of undertakings.

Article 18: Hearing of the parties and of third persons

1. Before taking any decision provided for in Articles 7(2) and (4), Article 8(2), second subparagraph, and (3) to (5) and Articles 14 and 15, the Commission shall give the persons, undertakings and associations of undertakings concerned the opportunity, at every stage of the procedure up to the consultation of the Advisory Committee, of making known their views on the objections against them.

2. By way of derogation from paragraph 1, a decision to continue the suspension of a concentration or to grant a derogation from suspension as referred to in Article 7(2) or (4) may be taken provisionally, without the persons, undertakings or associations of undertakings concerned being given the opportunity to make known their views beforehand, provided that the Commission gives them that opportunity as soon as possible after having taken its decision.

3. The Commission shall base its decision only on objections on which the parties have been able to submit their observations. The rights of the defence shall be fully respected in the proceedings. Access to the file shall be open at least to the parties directly involved, subject to the legitimate interest of undertakings in the protection of their business secrets.

4. In so far as the Commission or the competent authorities of the Member States deem it necessary, they may also hear other natural or legal persons. Natural or legal persons showing a sufficient interest and especially members of the administrative or management bodies of the undertakings concerned or the recognized representatives of their employees shall be entitled, upon application, to be heard.

Article 19: Liaison with the authorities of the Member States

1. The Commission shall transmit to the competent authorities of the Member States copies of notifications within three working days and, as soon as possible, copies of the most important documents lodged with or issued by the Commission pursuant to this Regulation.

2. The Commission shall carry out the procedures set out in this Regulation in close and constant liaison with the competent authorities of the Member States, which may express their views upon those procedures. For the purposes of Article 9 it shall obtain information from the competent authority of the Member State as referred to in paragraph 2 of that Article and give it the opportunity to make known its views at every stage of the procedure up to the adoption of a decision pursuant to paragraph 3 of that Article; to that end it shall give it access to the file.

3. An Advisory Committee on concentrations shall be consulted before any deci-

sion is taken pursuant to Article 8(2) to (5), 14 or 15, or any provisions are adopted pursuant to Article 23.

4. The Advisory Committee shall consist of representatives of the authorities of the Member States. Each Member State shall appoint one or two representatives; if unable to attend, they may be replaced by other representatives. At least one of the representatives of a Member State shall be competent in matters of restrictive practices and dominant positions.

5. Consultation shall take place at a joint meeting convened at the invitation of and chaired by the Commission. A summary of the case, together with an indication of the most important documents and a preliminary draft of the decision to be taken for each case considered, shall be sent with the invitation. The meeting shall take place not less than 14 days after the invitation has been sent. The Commission may in exceptional cases shorten that period as appropriate in order to avoid serious harm to one or more of the undertakings concerned by a concentration.

6. The Advisory Committee shall deliver an opinion on the Commission's draft decision, if necessary by taking a vote. The Advisory Committee may deliver an opinion even if some members are absent and unrepresented. The opinion shall be delivered in writing and appended to the draft decision. The Commission shall take the utmost account of the opinion delivered by the Committee. It shall inform the Committee of the manner in which its opinion has been taken into account.

7. The Advisory Committee may recommend publication of the opinion. The Commission may carry out such publication. The decision to publish shall take due account of the legitimate interest of undertakings in the protection of their business secrets and of the interest of the undertakings concerned in such publication's taking place.

Article 20: Publication of decisions

1. The Commission shall publish the decisions which it takes pursuant to Article 8(2) to (5) in the *Official Journal of the European Communities*.

2. The publication shall state the names of the parties and the main content of the decision; it shall have regard to the legitimate interest of undertakings in the protection of their business secrets.

Article 21: Jurisdiction

1. Subject to review by the Court of Justice, the Commission shall have sole jurisdiction to take the decisions provided for in this Regulation.

2. No Member State shall apply its national legislation on competition to any consideration that has a Community dimension.

The first subparagraph shall be without prejudice to any Member State's power to carry out any enquiries necessary for the application of Article 9(2) or after referral, pursuant to Article 9(3), first subparagraph, indent (b), or (5), to take the measures strictly necessary for the application of Article 9(8).

3. Notwithstanding paragraphs 1 and 2, Member States may take appropriate measures to protect legitimate interests other than those taken into consideration by this Regulation and compatible with the general principles and other provisions of Community law.

Public security, plurality of the media and prudential rules shall be regarded as legitimate interests within the meaning of the first subparagraph.

Any other public interest must be communicated to the Commission by the Member State concerned and shall be recognized by the Commission after an assessment of its compatibility with the general principles and other provisions of Community law before the measures referred to above may be taken. The Commission shall inform the Member State concerned of its decision within one month of that communication.

Article 22: Application of the Regulation

1. This Regulation alone shall apply to concentrations as defined in Article 3.

2. Regulations No. 17 (J.O. 204/62), (EEC) No. 1017/68 ([1968] O.J. L175/1), (EEC) No. 4056/86 ([1986] O.J. L378/4) and (EEC) No. 3975/87 ([1987] O.J. L374/1) shall not apply to concentrations as defined in Article 3.

3. If the Commission finds, at the request of a Member State, that a concentration as defined in Article 3 that has no Community dimension within the meaning of

Article 1 creates or strengthens a dominant position as a result of which effective competition would be significantly impeded within the territory of the Member State concerned it may, in so far as the concentration affects trade between Member States, adopt the decisions provided for in Article 8(2), second subparagraph, (3) and (4).

4. Articles 2(1)(a) and (b), 5, 6, 8 and 10 to 20 shall apply. The period within which proceedings may be initiated pursuant to Article 10(1) shall begin on the date of the receipt of the request from the Member State. The request must be made within one month at most of the date on which the concentration was made known to the Member State or effected. This period shall begin on the date of the first of those events.

5. Pursuant to paragraph 3 the Commission shall take only the measures strictly necessary to maintain or store effective competition within the territory of the Member State at the request of which it intervenes.

6. Paragraphs 3 to 5 shall continue to apply until the thresholds referred to in Article 1(2) have been reviewed.

Article 23: Implementing provisions

The Commission shall have the power to adopt implementing provisions concerning the form, content and other details of notifications pursuant to Article 4, time limits pursuant to Article 10, and hearings pursuant to Article 18.

Article 24: Relations with non-member countries

1. The Member States shall inform the Commission of any general difficulties encountered by their undertakings with concentrations as defined in Article 3 in a non-member country.

2. Initially not more than one year after the entry into force of this Regulation and thereafter periodically the Commission shall draw up a report examining the treatment accorded to Community undertakings, in the terms referred to in paragraphs 3 and 4, as regards concentrations in non-member countries. The Commission shall submit those reports to the Council, together with any recommendations.

3. Whenever it appears to the Commission, either on the basis of the reports referred to in paragraph 2 or on the basis of other information, that a non-member country does not grant Community undertakings treatment comparable to that granted by the Community to undertakings from that non-member country, the Commission may submit proposals to the Council for an appropriate mandate for negotiation with a view to obtaining comparable treatment for Community undertakings.

4. Measures taken under this Article shall comply with the obligations of the Community or of the Member States, without prejudice to Article 234 of the Treaty, under international agreements, whether bilateral or multilateral.

Article 25: Entry into force

1. This Regulation shall enter into force on 21 September 1990.

2. This Regulation shall not apply to any concentration which was the subject of an agreement or announcement or where control was acquired within the meaning of Article 4(1) before the date of this Regulation's entry into force and it shall not in any circumstances apply to any concentration in respect of which proceedings were initiated before that date by a Member State's authority with responsibility for competition.

This regulation shall be binding in its entirety and directly applicable in all Member States.

2. **Text of Commission Regulation 2367/90 of July 25, 1990 on notifications, time limits and hearings (reproduced below).**

Commission Regulation 2367/90 of July 25, 1990

On the notifications, time limits and hearings provided for in Council Regulation (EEC) No. 4064/89 on the control of concentrations between undertakings

([1990] O.J. L219/5)

THE COMMISSION OF THE EUROPEAN COMMUNITIES,

Having regard to the Treaty establishing the European Economic Community,

Having regard to Council Regulation (EEC) No. 4064/89 of 21 December 1989 on the control of concentrations between undertakings (O.J. No. L395, 30.12.89, p. 1), and in particular Article 23 thereof,

Having regard to Council Regulation No. 17 of 6 February 1962, First Regulation implementing Articles 85 and 86 of the Treaty (O.J. No. 13, 21.2.62, p. 204/62), as last amended by the Act of Accession of Spain and Portugal, and in particular Article 24 thereof,

Having regard to Council Regulation (EEC) No. 1017/68 of 19 July 1968 applying rules of competition to transport by rail, road and inland waterway (O.J. No. L175, 23.7.68, p. 1), as last amended by the Act of Accession of Spain and Portugal, and in particular Article 29 thereof,

Having regard to Council Regulation (EEC) No. 4056/86 of 22 December 1986 laying down detailed rules for the application of Articles 85 and 86 of the Treaty to maritime transport (O.J. No. L378, 31.12.86, p. 4), and in particular Article 26 thereof,

Having regard to Council Regulation (EEC) No. 3975/87 of 14 December 1987 laying down detailed rules for the application of the competition rules to undertakings in air transport (O.J. No. L374, 31.12.87, p. 1), and in particular Article 19 thereof,

Having consulted the Advisory Committee on Concentrations, as well as the Advisory Committees on Restrictive Practices and Monopolies in the Transport Industry, in Maritime Transport and in Air Transport.

(1) Whereas Article 23 of Regulation (EEC) No 4064/89 empowers the Commission to adopt implementing provisions concerning the form, content and other details of notifications pursuant to Article 4, time limits pursuant to Article 10, and hearings pursuant to Article 18;

(2) Whereas Regulation (EEC) No. 4064/89 is based on the principle of compulsory notification of concentrations before they are put into effect; whereas, on the one hand, a notification has important legal consequences which are favourable to the parties, while, on the other hand, failure to comply with the obligation to notify renders the parties liable to a fine and may also entail civil law disadvantages for them; whereas it is therefore necessary in the interests of legal certainty to define precisely the subject matter and content of the information to be provided in the notification;

(3) Whereas it is for the parties concerned to make full and honest disclosure to the Commission of the facts and circumstances which are relevant for taking a decision on the notified concentration;

(4) Whereas in order to simplify and expedite examination of the notification it is desirable to prescribe that a form be used;

(5) Whereas since notification sets in motion legal time limits for initiating proceedings and for decisions, the conditions governing such time limits and the time when they become effective must also be determined;

(6) Whereas rules must be laid down in the interests of legal certainty for calculating the time limits provided for in Regulation (EEC) No. 4064/89; whereas in particular the beginning and end of the period and the circumstances suspending the running of the period must be determined; whereas the provisions should be based on the principles of Regulation (EEC, Euratom) No. 1182/71 of 3 June 1971 determining the rules applicable to periods, dates and time

limits ([1971] O.J. L124/1), subject to certain adaptations made necessary by the exceptionally short legal time limits referred to above;

(7) Whereas the provisions relating to the Commission's procedure must be framed in such way as to safeguard fully the right to be heard and the rights of defence;

(8) Whereas the Commission will give the parties concerned, if they so request, an opportunity before notification to discuss the intended concentration informally and in strict confidence; whereas in addition it will, after notification, maintain close contact with the parties concerned to the extent necessary to discuss with them any practical or legal problems which it discovers on a first examination of the case and if possible to remove such problems by mutual agreement;

(9) Whereas in accordance with the principle of the right to be heard, the parties concerned must be given the opportunity to submit their comments on all the objections which the Commission proposes to take into account in its decisions;

(10) Whereas third parties having sufficient interest must also be given the opportunity of expressing their views where they make a written application;

(11) Whereas the various persons entitled to submit comments should do so in writing, both in their own interest and in the interest of good administration, without prejudice to their right to request an oral hearing where appropriate to supplement the written procedure; whereas in urgent cases, however, the Commission must be able to proceed immediately to oral hearings of the parties concerned or third parties; whereas in such cases the persons to be heard must have the right to confirm their oral statements in writing;

(12) Whereas it is necessary to define the rights of persons who are to be heard, to what extent they should be granted access to the Commission's file and on what conditions they may be represented or assisted;

(13) Whereas it is also necessary to define the rules for fixing and calculating the time limits for reply fixed by the Commission;

(14) Whereas the Advisory Committee on Concentrations shall deliver its opinion on the basis of a preliminary draft decision; whereas it must therefore be consulted on a case after the inquiry into that case has been completed; whereas such consultation does not, however, prevent the Commission from re-opening an inquiry if need be,

HAS ADOPTED THIS REGULATION

SECTION I: NOTIFICATIONS

Article 1: Persons entitled to submit notifications

1. Notifications shall be submitted by the persons or undertakings referred to in Article 4(2) of Regulation (EEC) No. 4064/89.

2. Where notifications are signed by representatives of persons or of undertakings, such representatives shall produce written proof that they are authorized to act.

3. Joint notifications should be submitted by a joint representative who is authorized to transmit and to receive documents on behalf of all notifying parties.

Article 2: Submission of notifications

1. Notifications shall be submitted in the manner prescribed by form CO as shown in Annex I. Joint notifications shall be submitted on a single form.

2. Twenty copies of each notification and fifteen copies of the supporting documents shall be submitted to the Commission at the address indicated in form CO.

3. The supporting documents shall be either originals or copies of the originals; in the latter case the notifying parties shall confirm that they are true and complete.

4. Notifications shall be in one of the official languages of the Community. This language shall also be the language of the proceeding for the notifying parties. Supporting documents shall be submitted in their original language. Where the original language is not one of the official languages, a translation into the language of the proceeding shall be attached.

Article 3: Information to be provided

1. Notifications shall contain the information requested by form CO. The information must be correct and complete.

2. Material changes in the facts specified in the notification which the notifying parties know or ought to have known must be communicated to the Commission voluntarily and without delay.

3. Incorrect or misleading information shall be deemed to be incomplete information.

Book Two: Mergers and Acquisitions

Article 4: Effective date of notifications

1. Subject to paragraph 2 notifications shall become effective on the date on which they are received by the Commission.

2. Subject to paragraph 3, where the information contained in the notification is incomplete in a material respect, the Commission shall without delay inform the notifying parties or the joint representative in writing and shall fix an appropriate time limit for the completion of the information; in such cases, the notification shall become effective on the date on which the complete information is received by the Commission.

3. The Commission may dispense with the obligation to provide any particular information requested by form CO where the Commission considers that such information is not necessary for the examination of the case.

4. The Commission shall without delay acknowledge in writing to the notifying parties or the joint representatives receipt of the notification and of any reply to a letter sent by the Commission pursuant to paragraph 2 above.

Article 5: Conversion of notifications

1. Where the Commission finds that the operation notified does not constitute a concentration within the meaning of Article 3 of Regulation (EEC) No. 4064/89 it shall inform the notifying parties or the joint representative in writing. In such a case, the Commission may, if requested by the notifying parties, as appropriate and subject to paragraph 2 below, treat the notification as an application within the meaning of Article 2 or a notification within the meaning of Article 4 of Regulation No. 17, as an application within the meaning of Article 12 or a notification within the meaning of Article 14 of Regulation (EEC) No. 1017/68, as an application within the meaning of Article 12 of Regulation (EEC) No. 4056/86 or as an application with the meaning of Article 3(2) or of Article 5 of Regulation (EEC) No. 3975/87.

2. In cases referred to in paragraph 1, second sentence, the Commission may require that the information given in the notification be supplemented within an appropriate time limit fixed by it in so far as this is necessary for assessing the operation on the basis of the abovementioned Regulations. The application or notification shall be deemed to fulfil the requirements of such Regulations from the date of the original notification where the additional information is received by the Commission within the time limit fixed.

SECTION II: TIME LIMITS FOR INITIATING PROCEEDINGS AND FOR DECISIONS

Article 6: Beginning of the time limit

1. The periods referred to in Article 10(1) of Regulation (EEC) No. 4064/89 shall start at the beginning of the day following the effective date of the notification, within the meaning of Article 4(1) and (2) of this Regulation.

2. The period referred to in Article 10(3) of Regulation (EEC) No. 4064/89 shall start at the beginning of the day following the day on which proceedings were initiated.

3. Where the first day of a period is not a working day within the meaning of Article 19, the period shall start at the beginning of the following working day.

Article 7: End of the time limit

1. The period referred to in the first sub-paragraph of Article 10(1) of Regulation (EEC) No. 4064/89 shall end with the expiry of the day which in the month following that in which the period began falls on the same date as the day from which the period runs. Where such a day does not occur in that month, the period shall end with the expiry of the last day of that month.

2. The period referred to in the second sub-paragraph of Article 10(1) of Regulation (EEC) No. 4064/89 shall end with the expiry of the day which in the sixth week following that in which the period began is the same day of the week as the day from which the period runs.

3. The period referred to in Article 10(3) of Regulation (EEC) No. 4064/89 shall end with the expiry of the day which in the fourth month following that in which the period began falls on the same date as the day from which the period runs. Where such a day does not occur in that month, the period shall end with the expiry of the last day of that month.

4. Where the last day of the period is not a working day within the meaning of Article

19, the period shall end with the expiry of the following working day.

5. Paragraphs 2 to 4 above shall be subject to the provisions of Article 8.

Article 8: Addition of holidays

Where public holidays or other holidays of the Commission as defined in Article 19 fall within the periods referred to in Article 10(1) and in Article 10(3) of Regulation (EEC) No. 4064/89, these periods shall be extended by a corresponding number of days.

Article 9: Suspension of the time limit

1. The period referred to in Article 10(3) of Regulation (EEC) No. 4064/89 shall be suspended where the Commission, pursuant to Articles 11(5) or 13(3) of the same Regulation, has to take a decision because:
(a) Information which the Commission has requested pursuant to Article 11(2) of Regulation (EEC) No. 4064/89 from an undertaking involved in a concentration is not provided or not provided in full within the time limit fixed by the Commission;
(b) an undertaking involved in the concentration has refused to submit to an investigation deemed necessary by the Commission on the basis of Article 13(1) of Regulation (EEC) No. 4064/89 or to cooperate in the carrying out of such an investigation in accordance with the abovementioned provision;
(c) the notifying parties have failed to inform the Commission of material changes in the facts specified in the notification.

2. The period referred to in Article 10(3) of Regulation (EEC) No. 4064/89 shall be suspended:
(a) in the cases referred to in subparagraph 1(a) above, for the period between the end of the time fixed in the request for information and the receipt of the complete and correct information required by decision;
(b) in the cases referred to in subparagraph 1(b) above, for the period between the unsuccessful attempt to carry out the investigation and the completion of the investigation ordered by decision;
(c) in the cases referred to in subparagraph 1(c) above, for the period between the occurrence of the change in the facts referred to therein and the receipt of the complete and correct information requested by decision or the completion of the investigation ordered by decision.

3. The suspension of the time limit shall begin on the day following that on which the event causing the suspension occurred. It shall end with the expiry of the day on which the reason for suspension is removed. Where such day is not a working day within the meaning of Article 19, the suspension of the time limit shall end with the expiry of the following working day.

Article 10: Compliance with the time limit

The time limits referred to in Article 10(1) and (3) of Regulation (EEC) No. 4064/89 shall be met where the Commission has taken the relevant decision before the end of the period. Notification of the decision to the undertakings concerned must follow without delay.

SECTION III: HEARING OF THE PARTIES AND OF THIRD PARTIES

Article 11: Decisions on the suspension of concentrations

1. Where the Commission intends to take a decision under Article 7(2) of Regulation (EEC) No. 4064/89 or a decision under Article 7(4) of that Regulation which adversely affects the parties, it shall, pursuant to Article 18(1) of that Regulation, inform the parties concerned in writing of its objections and shall fix a time limit within which they may make known their views.

2. Where the Commission pursuant to Article 18(2) of Regulation (EEC) No. 4064/89 has taken a decision referred to in paragraph 1 provisionally without having given the parties concerned the opportunity to make known their views, it shall without delay and in any event before the expiry of the suspension send them the text of the provisional decision and shall fix a time limit within which they may make known their views.

Once the parties concerned have made known their views, the Commission shall take a final decision annulling, amending or confirming the provisional decision. Where the parties concerned have not made known their view within the time limit fixed, the Commission's provisional decision shall become final with the expiry of that period.

3. The parties concerned shall make known their views in writing or orally within the time limit fixed. They may confirm their oral statements in writing.

Article 12: Decisions on the substance of the case

1. Where the Commission intends to take a decision pursuant to Article 8(2), second subparagraph, Article 8(3)(4) and (5), Article 14 or Article 15 of Regulation (EEC) No. 4064/89, it shall, before consulting the Advisory Committee on Concentrations, hold a hearing of the parties concerned pursuant to Article 18 of that Regulation.

2. The Commission shall inform the parties concerned in writing of its objections. The communication shall be addressed to the notifying parties or to the joint representative. The Commission shall, when giving notice of objections, fix a time limit within which the parties concerned may inform the Commission of their views.

3. Having informed the parties of its objections, the Commission shall upon request give the parties concerned access to the file for the purposes of preparing their observations. Documents shall not be accessible in so far as they contain business secrets of other parties concerned or of third parties, or other confidential information including sensitive commercial information the disclosure of which would have a significant adverse effect on the supplier of such information or where they are internal documents of the authorities.

4. The parties concerned shall, within the time limit fixed, make known in writing their views on the Commission's objections. They may in their written comments set out all matters relevant to the case and may attach any relevant documents in proof of the facts set out. They may also propose that the Commission hear persons who may corroborate those facts.

Article 13: Oral hearings

1. The Commission shall afford parties concerned who have so requested in their written comments the opportunity to put forward their arguments orally, if those persons show a sufficient interest or if the Commission proposes to impose a fine or periodic penalty payment on them. It may also in other cases afford the parties concerned the opportunity of expressing their views orally.

2. The Commission shall summon the persons to be heard to attend on such date as it shall appoint.

3. It shall forthwith transmit a copy of the summons to the competent authorities of the Member States, who may appoint an official to take part in the hearing.

Article 14: Hearings

1. Hearings shall be conducted by persons appointed by the Commission for that purpose.

2. Persons summoned to attend shall either appear in person or be represented by legal representatives or representatives authorized by their constitution. Undertakings and associations of undertakings may be represented by a duly authorized agent appointed from among their permanent staff.

3. Persons heard by the Commission may be assisted by lawyers or university teachers who are entitled to plead before the Court of Justice of the European Communities in accordance with Article 17 of the Protocol on the Statute (EEC) of the Court of Justice, or by other qualified persons.

4. Hearings shall not be public. Persons shall be heard separately or in the presence of other persons summoned to attend. In the latter case, regard shall be had to the legitimate interest of the undertakings in the protection of their business secrets.

5. The statements made by each person heard shall be recorded.

Article 15: Hearing of third parties

1. If natural or legal persons showing a sufficient interest, and especially members of the administrative or management organs of the undertakings concerned or recognized workers' representatives of those undertakings, apply in writing to be heard pursuant to the second sentence of Article 18(4) of Regulation (EEC) No. 4064/89, the Commission shall inform them in writing of the nature and subject matter of the procedure and shall fix a time limit within which they may make known their views.

2. The third parties referred to in paragraph 1 above shall make known their views in writing or orally within the time limit fixed. They may confirm their oral statements in writing.

3. The Commission may likewise afford to any other third parties the opportunity of expressing their views.

SECTION IV: MISCELLANEOUS PROVISIONS

Article 16: Transmission of documents

1. Transmission of documents and summonses from the Commission to the addressees may be effected in any of the following ways:
(a) delivery by hand against receipt;
(b) registered letter with acknowledgement of receipt;
(c) telefax with a request for acknowledgement of receipt;
(d) telex.

2. Subject to Article 18(1), paragraph 1 above also applies to the transmission of documents from the parties concerned or from third parties to the Commission.

3. Where a document is sent by telex or by telefax, it shall be presumed that it has been received by the addressee on the day on which it was sent.

Article 17: Setting of time limits

1. In fixing the time limits provided for in Articles 4(2), 5(2), 11(1) and (2), 12(2) and 15(1), the Commission shall have regard to the time required for preparation of statements and to the urgency of the case. It shall also take account of public holidays in the country of receipt of the Commission's communication.

2. The day on which the addressee received a communication shall not be taken into account for the purpose of fixing time limits.

Article 18: Receipt of documents by the Commission

1. Subject to Article 4(1), notifications must be delivered to the Commission at the address indicated in form CO or have been dispatched by registered letter before expiry of the period referred to in Article 4(1) of Regulation (EEC) No. 4064/89. Additional information requested to complete notifications pursuant to Article 4(2) or to supplement notifications pursuant to Article 5(2) of this Regulation must reach the Commission at the aforesaid or have been dispatched by registered letter before the expiry of the time limit fixed in each case. Written comments on Commission communications pursuant to Articles 11(1) and (2), 12(2) and 15(1) must be delivered to the Commission at the aforesaid address before the time limit fixed in each case.

2. Where the last day of a period referred to in paragraph 1 is a day by which documents must be received and that day is not a working day within the meaning of Article 19, the period shall end with the expiry of the following working day.

3. Where the last day of a period referred to in paragraph 1 is a day by which documents must be dispatched and that day is a Saturday, Sunday or public holiday in the country of dispatch, the period shall end with the expiry of the following working day in that country.

Article 19: Definition of Commission working days

The term "working days" in Articles 6(3), 7(4), 9(3) and 18(2) means all days other than Saturdays, Sundays, public holidays set out in Annex II and other holidays as determined by the Commission and published in the *Official Journal of the European Communities* before the beginning of each year.

Article 20: Entry into force

This Regulation shall enter into force on 21 September 1990.
This Regulation shall be binding in its entirety and directly applicable in all Member States.

ANNEX

3. Form CO (reproduced over).

Book Two: Mergers and Acquisitions

Form CO Annex to Commission Regulation No. 2367/90.

Form CO Relating to the Notification of a Concentration Pursuant to Council Regulation No. 4064/89

A. Introduction

This form specifies the information to be provided by an undertaking or undertakings when notifying the Commission of a concentration with a Community dimension. A "concentration" is defined in Article 3 and "Community dimension" by Article 1 of Regulation (EEC) No. 4064/89.

Your attention is particularly drawn to Regulation (EEC) No. 4064/89 and to Commission Regulation (EEC) No. 2367/90. In particular you should note that:
(a) all information requested by this form must be provided. However if, in good faith, you are unable to provide a response to a question or can only respond to a limited extent on the basis of available information, indicate this and give reasons. If you consider that any particular information requested by this form may not be necessary for the Commission's examination of the case, you may ask the Commission to dispense with the obligation to provide that information, under Article 4(3) of Regulation (EEC) No. 2367/90;
(b) unless all sections are completed in full or good reasons are given explaining why it has not been possible to complete unanswered questions (for example, because of the unavailability of information on a target company during a contested bid) the notification will be incomplete and will only become effective on the date on which all the information is received. The notification will be deemed to be incomplete if information is incorrect or misleading;
(c) incorrect or misleading information where supplied intentionally or negligently could make you liable to a fine.

B. Who must notify

In the case of a merger (within the meaning of Article 3(1)(a) of Regulation (EEC) No. 4064/89 or the acquisition of joint control in a undertaking within the meaning of Article 3(1)(b) of Regulation (EEC) No. 4064/89, the notification shall be completed jointly by the parties to the merger or by those acquiring joint control as the case may be.

In the case of the acquisition of a controlling interest in an undertaking by another, the acquirer must complete the notification.

In the case of a public bid to acquire an undertaking, the bidder must complete the notification.

Each party completing the notification is responsible for the accuracy of the information which it provides.

For the purposes of this form "the parties to the concentration" ("the parties") includes the undertaking in which a controlling interest is being acquired or which is the subject of a public bid.

C. Supporting documentation

The completed notification must be accompanied by the following:
(a) copies of the final or most recent versions of all documents bringing about the concentration, whether by agreement between the parties concerned, acquisition of a controlling interest or a public bid;
(b) in a public bid, a copy of the offer document. If unavailable on notification it should be submitted as soon as possible and not later than when it is posted to shareholders;

(c) copies of the most recent annual reports and accounts of all the parties to the concentration;
(d) copies of reports or analyses which have been prepared for the purposes of the concentration and from which information has been taken in order to provide the information requested in sections 5 and 6;
(e) a list and short description of the contents of all other analyses, reports, studies and surveys prepared by or for any of the notifying parties for the purpose of assessing or analysing the proposed concentration with respect to competitive conditions, competitors (actual and potential), and market conditions. Each item in the list must include the name and position held of the author.

D. How to notify

The notification must be completed in one of the official languages of the European Community. This language shall thereafter be the language of the proceeding for all notifying parties.

The information requested by this form is to be set out using the sections and paragraph numbers of the form.

Supporting documents shall be submitted in their original language; where this is not an official language of the Community they shall be translated, into the language of the proceeding (Article 2(4) of Regulation (EEC) No. 2367/90).

The supporting documents may be originals or copies of the originals. In the latter case the notifying party shall confirm that they are true and complete.

The financial data requested in Section 2.4 below must be provided in Ecus at the average conversion rates prevailing for the years or other period in question.

Twenty copies of each notification and fifteen copies of all supporting documents must be provided.

The notification should be sent to:

Commission of the European Communities,
Directorate General for Competition (DG IV),
Merger Task Force (Cort. 150),
200, rue de la Loi,
B-1049 Brussels;

or be delivered by hand during normal Commission working hours at the following address:

Commission of the European Communities,
Directorate General for Competition (DG IV),
Merger Task Force,
150, avenue de Cortenberg,
B-1040 Brussels.

E. Secrecy

Article 214 of the Treaty and Article 17(2) of Regulation (EEC) No. 4064/89 require the Commission and the Member States, their officials and other servants not to disclose information they have acquired through the application of the Regulation of the kind covered by the obligation of professional secrecy. The same principle must also apply to protect confidentiality as between notifying parties.

If you believe that your interests would be harmed if any of the information you are asked to supply was to be published or otherwise divulged to other parties, submit this information separately with each page clearly marked "Business secrets." You should also give reasons why this information should not be divulged or published.

In the case of mergers or joint acquisitions, or in other cases where the notification is completed by more than one of the parties, business secrets may be submitted under separate cover, and referred to in the notification as an annex. In such cases the notification will be considered complete on receipt of all the annexes.

F. References

All references contained in this form are to the relevant articles and paragraphs of Council Regulation (EEC) No. 4064/89.

SECTION 1

1.1. *Information on notifying party (or parties)*

Give details of:

1.1.1. name and address of undertaking,

1.1.2. nature of the undertaking's business,

1.1.3. name, address, telephone, fax and/or telex of, and position held by, the person to be contacted.

1.2. *Information on other parties to the concentration*[1]/[2]

For each party to the concentration (except the notifying party) give details of:

1.2.1. name and address of undertaking,

1.2.2. nature of the undertaking's business,

1.2.3. name, address, telephone, fax and/or telex of, and position held by, the person to be contacted.

1.3. *Address for service*

Give an address in Brussels if available to which all communications may be made and documents delivered in accordance with Article 1(4) of Commission Regulations (EEC) No. 2367/90.

1.4. *Appointment of representatives*

Article 1(2) of Commission Regulation (EEC) No. 2367/90 states that where notifications are signed by representatives of undertakings, such representatives shall produce written proof that they are authorized to act. Such written authorization must accompany the notification and the following details of the representatives of the notifying party or parties and other parties to the concentration are to be given below.

1.4.1. is this a joint notification?

1.4.2. if "yes," has a joint representative been appointed?

    if "yes," please give the details requested in 1.4.3 to 1.4.6 below;

    if "no," please give details of the representatives who have been authorized to act for each of the parties to the concentration indicating who they represent;

---

[1] A concentration is defined in Art. 3.
[2] This includes the target company in the case of a contested bid, in which case the details should be completed as far as is possible.

1 Legislation

1.4.3. name of representative;

1.4.4. address of representative;

1.4.5. name of person to be contacted (and address if different from 1.4.4);

1.4.6. telephone, telefax and/or telex.

SECTION 2: DETAILS OF THE CONCENTRATION

2.1 Briefly describe the nature of the concentration being notified. In doing so state:
— whether the proposed concentration is a full legal merger, an acquisition, a concentrative joint venture or a contrast or other means conferring direct or indirect control within the meaning of Article 3(3);
— whether the whole or parts of parties are subject to the concentration;
— whether any public offer for the securities of one party by another has the support of the former's supervisory boards of management or other bodies legally representing the party concerned.

2.2. List the economic sectors involved in the concentration.

2.3. Give a brief explanation of the economic and financial details of the concentration. In doing so provide, where relevant, information about the following:
— any financial or other support received from whatever source (including public authorities) by any of the parties and the nature and amount of this support,
— the proposed or expected date of any major events designed to bring about the completion of the concentration,
— the proposed structure of ownership and control after the completion of the concentration.

2.4. For each of the parties, the notifying party shall provide the following data for the last three financial years:

2.4.1. worldwide turnover,[3]

2.4.2. Community-wide turnover,[3/4]

2.4.3. turnover in each Member State,[3/4]

2.4.4. the Member State, if any, in which more than two-thirds of Community-wide turnover is achieved,[3/4]

2.4.5. profits before tax worldwide,[5]

2.4.6. number of employees worldwide.[6]

---

[3] See Art. 5 for the definition of turnover and note the special provisions for credit, insurance, other financial institutions and joint undertakings.
or insurance undertakings, credit and other financial institutions, Community-residents and residents of a Member State are defined as natural or legal persons having their residence in a Member State, thereby following the respective national legislation. The corporate customer is to be treated as resident in the country in which it is legally incorporated.
For the calculation of turnover, the notifying party should also refer to the examples: guidance note I for credit and other financial institutions; guidance note II for insurance undertakings; guidance note III for joint undertakings.

[4] See guidance note IV for the calculation of turnover in one Member State with respect to Community-wide turnover.

[5] "Profits before tax" shall comprise profit on ordinary activities before tax on profit.

[6] Employees shall comprise all persons employed in the enterprise who have a contract of employment and receive remuneration.

Book Two: Mergers and Acquisitions

SECTION 3: OWNERSHIP AND CONTROL[7]

For each of the parties provide a list of all undertakings belonging to the same group. This list must include:

3.1. all undertakings controlled by the parties, directly or indirectly, within the meaning of Article 3(3);

3.2. all undertakings or persons controlling the parties directly or indirectly within the meaning of Article 3(3);

3.3. for each undertaking or person identified in 3.2 above, a complete list of all undertakings controlled by them directly or indirectly, within the meaning of Article 3(3).

For each entry to the list the nature and means of control shall be specified;

3.4. provide details of acquisitions made during the last three years by the groups identified above, of undertakings active in affected markets as defined in section 5 below.

The information sought in this section may be illustrated by the use of charts or diagrams where this helps to give a better understanding of the pre-concentration structure of ownership and control of the undertakings.

SECTION 4: PERSONAL AND FINANCIAL LINKS

With respect to each undertaking or person disclosed in response to Section 3 provide:

4.1. a list of all other undertakings which are active on affected markets (affected markets are defined in section 5) in which the undertakings of the group hold individually or collectively 10% or more of the voting rights or issued share capital. In each case state the percentage held;

4.2. a list of all other undertakings which are active on affected markets in which the persons disclosed in response to Section 3 hold 10% or more of the voting rights or issued share capital. In each case state the percentage held;

4.3. a list for each undertaking of the members of their boards of management who are also members of the boards of management or of the supervisory boards of any other undertaking, which is active on affected markets; and (where applicable) for each undertaking a list of the members of their supervisory boards who are also members of the boards of management of any other undertaking which is active on affected markets;

in each case stating the name of the other undertaking and the position held.

Information provided here may be illustrated by the use of charts or diagrams where this helps to give a better understanding.

---

[7] See Arts. 3(3) to (6).

1 Legislation

SECTION 5: INFORMATION ON AFFECTED MARKETS

The notifying party shall provide the data requested having regard to the following definitions:

Product Markets

A relevant product market comprises all those products and/or services which are regarded as interchangeable or substitutable by the consumer, by reason of the products' characteristics, their prices and their intended use.

A relevant product market may in some cases be composed of a number of individual product groups. An individual product group is a product or small group of products which present largely identical physical or technical characteristics and are fully interchangeable. The difference between products within the group will be small and usually only a matter of brand and/or image. The product market will usually be the classification used by the undertaking in its marketing operations.

Relevant Geographic Market

The relevant geographic market comprises the area in which the undertakings concerned are involved in the supply of products or services, in which the conditions of competition are sufficiently homogeneous and which can be distinguished from neighbouring areas because, in particular, conditions of competition are appreciably different in those areas.

Factors relevant to the assessment of the relevant geographic market include the nature and characteristics of the products or services concerned, the existence of entry barriers or consumer preferences, appreciable differences of the undertakings' market shares between neighbouring areas or substantial price differences.

Affected Markets

Affected markets consist of relevant product markets or individual product groups, in the Common Market or a Member State or, where different, in any relevant geographic market where:
(a) two or more of the parties (including undertakings belonging to the same group as defined in Section 3) are engaged in business activities in the same product market or individual product group and where the concentration will lead to a combined market share of 10% or more. These are horizontal relationships; or
(b) any of the parties (including undertakings belonging to the same group as defined in Section 3) is engaged in business activities in a product market which is upstream or downstream of product market or individual product group in which any other party is engaged and any of their market shares is 10% or more, regardless of whether there is or is not any existing supplier/customer relationship between the parties concerned. These are vertical relationships.

I. *Explanation of the affected relevant product markets*

5.1 Describe each affected relevant product market and explain why the products and/or services in these markets are included (and why others are excluded) by reason of their characteristics, their prices and their intended use.

5.2. List the individual product groups defined internally by your undertaking for marketing purposes which are covered by each relevant product market described under 5.1 above.

II. *Market data on affected markets*

For each affected relevant product market and, where different, individual product group, for each of the last three financial years:
(a) for the Community as a whole;
(b) individually for each Member State where the parties (including undertakings belonging to the same group as defined in Section 3) do business;
(c) and where different, for any relevant geographic market,
provide the following:

5.3. an estimate of the value of the market and, where appropriate, of the volume (for example in units shipped or delivered) of the market.[8] If available, include statistics prepared by other sources to illustrate your answers. Also provide a forecast of the evolution of demand on the affected markets;

5.4. the turnover of each of the groups to which the parties belong (as defined in Section 3);

5.5. an estimate of the market share of each of the groups to which the parties belong;

5.6. an estimate of the market share (in value and where appropriate volume) of all competitors having at least 10% of the geographic market under consideration. Provide the name, address and telephone number of these undertakings;

5.7. a comparison of prices charged by the groups to which the parties belong in each of the Member States and a similar comparison of such price levels between the Community and its major trading partners (eg the United States, Japan and EFTA);

5.8. an estimate of the value (and where appropriate volume) and source of imports to the relevant geographic market;

5.9. the proportion of such imports that are derived from the groups to which the parties belong;

5.10. an estimate of the extent to which any of these imports are affected by any tariff or non-tariff barriers to trade.

III. *Market data on conglomerate aspects*

In the absence of horizontal or vertical relationships, where any of the parties (including undertakings belonging to the same group as defined in Section 3) holds a market share of 25% or more for any product market or individual product group, provide the following information:

5.11. a description of each relevant product market and explain why the products and/or services in these markets are included (and why others are excluded) by reason of their characteristics, their prices and their intended use;

5.12. a list of the individual product groups defined internally by your undertaking for marketing purposes which are covered by each relevant product market described;

5.13. an estimate of the value of the market and the market shares of each of the groups to which the parties belong for each affected relevant product market and, where different, individual product group, for the last financial year:
(a) for the Community as a whole;
(b) individually for each Member State where the groups to which the parties belong do business;
(c) and where different, for any relevant geographic market.
In each response in Section 5 the notifying party shall explain the basis of the estimates used or assumptions made.

---

[8] The value and volume of a market should reflect output less exports plus imports for the geographic market under consideration.

1 Legislation

SECTION 6: GENERAL CONDITIONS IN AFFECTED MARKETS

The following information shall be provided in relation to the affected relevant product markets and, where different, affected individual product groups:

Record of Market Entry

6.1 Over the last five years (or a longer period if this is more appropriate) has there been any significant entry to these markets in the Community? If the answer is "yes," provide information on these entrants, estimating their current market shares.

6.2 In the opinion of the notifying party are there undertakings (including those at present operating only in extra-Community markets) that could enter the Community's markets? If the answer is "yes," provide information on these potential entrants.

6.3 In the opinion of the notifying party what is the likelihood of significant market entry over the next five years?

Factors Influencing Market Entry

6.4 Describe the various factors influencing entry into affected markets that exist in the present case, examining entry from both a geographical and product viewpoint. In so doing take account of the following where appropriate:
— the total costs of entry (capital, promotion, advertising, necessary distribution systems, servicing etc.) on a scale equivalent to a significant viable competitor, indicating the market share of such a competitor;
— to what extent is entry to the markets influenced by the requirement of government authorization or standard setting in any form? Are there any legal or regulatory controls on entry to these markets?
— to what extent is entry to the markets influenced by the availability of raw materials?
— to what extent is entry to the markets influenced by the length of contracts between an undertaking and its suppliers and/or customers?
— describe the importance of licensing patents, know-how and other rights in these markets.

Vertical Integration

6.5. Describe the nature and extent of vertical integration of each of the parties.

Research and Development

6.6. Give an account of the importance of research and development in the ability of a firm operating on the relevant market to compete in the long term. Explain the nature of the research and development in affected markets carried out by the undertakings to the connection.
In so doing take account of the following where appropriate:
— the research and development intensities[9] for these markets and the relevant research and development intensities for the parties concerned;
— the course of technological development for these markets over an appropriate time period (including developments in products and/or services, production processes, distribution systems etc.);
— the major innovations that have been made in these markets over this time period and the undertakings responsible for these innovations;
— the cycle of innovation in these markets and where the parties are in this cycle of innovation;
— describe the extent to which the parties concerned are licensees or licensors of patents, know-how and other rights in affected markets.

---

[9] Research and development intensity is defined as research and development expenditure as a proportion of turnover.

Distribution and Service Systems

6.7. Explain the distribution channels and service networks that exist on the affected markets. In so doing take account of the following where appropriate:
— the distribution systems prevailing on the market and their importance. To what extent is distribution performed by third parties and/or undertakings belonging to the same group as the parties as disclosed in Section 3?
— the service networks (for example maintenance and repair) prevailing and their importance in these markets. To what extent are such services performed by third parties and/or undertakings belonging to the same group as the parties as disclosed in Section 3?

Competitive Environment

6.8. Give details (names, addresses and contacts) of the five largest supliers to the notifying parties and their individual share of the purchases of the notifying parties.

6.9. Give details (names, addresses and contacts) of the five largest customers of the notifying parties and their individual share of the sales of the notifying parties.

6.10. Explain the structure of supply and demand in affected markets. This explanation should allow the Commission further to appreciate the competitive environment in which the parties carry out their business. In so doing take account of the following where appropriate:
— the phases of the markets in terms of, for example, take-off, expansion, maturity and decline. In the opinion of the notifying party, where are the affected products in these phases?
— the structure of supply. Give details of the various identifiable categories that comprise the supply side and describe the "typical supplier" of each category;
— the structure of demand. Give details of the various identifiable groups that comprise the demand side and describe the "typical customer" of each group;
— whether public authorities, government agencies or state enterprises or similar bodies are important participants as sources of supply or demand. In any instance where this is so give details of this participation;
— the total Community-wide capacity for the last three years. Over the period what proportion of this capacity is accounted for by the parties and what have been their rates of capacity utilization?

Co-operative Agreements

6.11. To what extent do co-operative agreements (horizontal and/or vertical) exist in the affected markets?

6.12. Give details of the most important co-operative agreements engaged in by the parties in the affected markets, such as licensing agreements, research and development, specialization, distribution, long-term supply and exchange of information agreements.

Trade Associations

6.13. List the names and addresses of the principal trade associations in the affected markets.

Worldwide Context

6.14 Describe the worldwide context of the proposed concentration indicating the position of the parties in this market.

1 Legislation

SECTION 7: GENERAL MATTERS

7.1. Describe how the proposed concentration is likely to affect the interests of intermediate and ultimate consumers, and the development of technical progress.

7.2. In the event that the Commission finds that the operation notified does not constitute a concentration within the meaning of Article 3 of Regulation (EEC) No. 4064/89, do you request that it be treated as an application within the meaning of Article 2 or a notification within the meaning of Article 4 of Regulation No. 17, as an application within the meaning of Article 12 or a notification within the meaning of Article 14 of Regulation (EEC) No. 1017/68, as an application within the meaning of Article 12 of Regulation (EEC) No. 4056/86 or as an application within the meaning of Article 3(2) or Article 5 of Regulation (EEC) No. 3975/87?

SECTION 8: DECLARATION

The notification must conclude with the following declaration which is to be signed by or on behalf of all the notifying parties.

The undersigned declare that the information given in this notification is correct to the best of their knowledge and belief, that all estimates are identified as such and are their best estimates of the underlying facts and that all the opinions expressed are sincere.

They are aware of the provisions of Article 14(1)(b) of Regulation (EEC) No. 4064/89.

Place and date:

Signatures:

Book Two: Mergers and Acquisitions

GUIDANCE NOTE I*

CALCULATION OF TURNOVER FOR CREDIT AND OTHER FINANCIAL INSTITUTIONS

(Article 5(3)(a))

For the calculation of turnover for credit institutions and other financial institutions, we give the following example (proposed merger between bank A and bank B)

I. Consolidated balance sheets

(in million ecu)

Assets	Bank A		Bank B	
Loans and advances to credit institutions	20 000		1 000	
— to credit institutions within the community:		(10 000)		(500)
— to credit institutions within one (and the same) Member State X:		(5 000)		(500)
Loans and advances to customers	60 000		4 000	
— to Community residents:		(30 000)		(2 000)
— to residents of one (and the same) Member State X:		(15 000)		(500)
Other assets:	20 000		1 000	
Total assets:	100 000		6 000	

II. Calculation of turnover

In place of turnover, the following figures shall be used:

	Bank A	Bank B
1. *Aggregate worldwide turnover* is replaced by one-tenth of total assets:	10 000	600

the total sum of which is more than ECU 5 000 million.

2. *Community-wide turnover*

is replaced by, for each bank, one-tenth of total assets multiplied by the ration between loans and advances to credit institutions and customers within the community; to the total sum of loans and advances to credit institutions and customers.

	Bank A	Bank B
This is calculated as follows: one-tenth of total assets:	10 000	600
which is multiplied for each bank by the ration between:		
loans and advances to credit institutions and customers	10 000	500
within the Community	30 000	2 000
	40 000	2 500

---

* In the following guidance notes, the terms "institution" or "undertaking" are used subject to the exact delimitation in each case.

1 Legislation

and the total sum of loans and advances to credit institutions and customers	20 000	1 000
	60 000	4 000
	80 000	5 000

For
Bank A: 10 000 multiplied by (40 000:80 000) = 5 000
Bank B: 600 multiplied by (2 500: 5 000) =   300

which exceeds ECU 250 million for each of the banks.

3. *Total turnover within one (and the same) Member State X*

	Bank A	Bank B
is replaced by one-tenth of total assets:	10 000	600

which is multiplied for each bank by the ration between loans and advances to credit institutions and customers within one and the same Member State X; to the total sum of loans and advances to credit institutions and customers.

	Bank A	Bank B
This is calculated as follows:		
loans and advances to credit institutions and customers within one (and and same) Member State X	5 000 15 000	500 500
	20 000	5 000
and the total sum of loans and advances to credit institutions and customers	80 000	5 000

For
Bank A: 10 000 multiplied by (20 000:80 000) = 2 500
Bank B: 600 multiplied by (1 000: 5 000) =   120

Result:
50% of bank A's and 40% of bank B's Community-wide turnover are achieved in one (and the same) Member State X.

III. Conclusion:

Since
(a) the aggregate worldwide turnover of bank A plus bank B is more than ECU 5,000 million;
(b) the Community-wide turnover of each of the banks is more than ECU 250 million; and
(c) each of the banks achieves less than two-thirds of its Community-wide turnover in one (and the same) Member State,
the proposed merger would fall under the scope of the Regulation.

GUIDANCE NOTE II

CALCULATION OF TURNOVER FOR INSURANCE UNDERTAKINGS

(Article 5(3)(a))

For the calculation of turnover for insurance undertakings, we give the following example (proposed concentration between insurances A and B):

I. Consolidated profit and loss account

(in million ecu)

Income	Insurance A		Insurance B	
Gross premiums written	5 000		300	
— gross premiums received from Community residents:		(4 500)		(300)
— gross premiums received from residents of one (and the same) Member State X:		(3 600)		(270)
Other income:	500		50	
Total income:	5 500		350	

II. Calculation of Turnover

1. Aggregate worldwide turnover

is replaced by the value of gross premiums written worldwide, the sum of which is ECU 5,300 million.

2. Community-wide turnover

is replaced, for each insurance undertaking, by the value of gross premiums written with Community residents. For each of the insurance undertakings, this amount is more than ECU 250 million.

3. Turnover within one (and the same) Member State X

is replaced, for insurance undertakings, by the value of gross premiums written with residents of one (and the same) Member State X.
For insurance A, it achieves 80% of its gross premiums written with Community residents within Member State X, whereas for insurance B, it achieves 90% of its gross premiums written with Community residents in that Member State X.

III. Conclusion

Since
- (a) the aggregate worldwide turnover of insurances A and B, as replaced by the value of gross premiums written worldwide, is more than ECU 5,000 million;
- (b) for each of the insurance undertakings, the value of gross premiums written with Community residents is more than ECU 250 million; but
- (c) each of the insurance undertakings achieves more than two-thirds of its gross premiums written with Community residents in one (and the same) Member State X,

the proposed concentration would not fall under the scope of the Regulation.

GUIDANCE NOTE III

CALCULATION OF TURNOVER FOR JOINT UNDERTAKINGS

A. *Creation of a Joint Undertaking* (Article 3(2))

In a case where two (or more) undertakings create a joint undertaking that constitutes a concentration, turnover is calculated for the undertakings concerned.

B. *Existence of a Joint Undertaking* (Article 5(5))

For the calculation of turnover in case of the existence of a joint undertaking C between two undertakings A and B concerned in a concentration, we give the following example:

I. Profit and loss accounts

(in million ecu)

Turnover	Undertaking A	Undertaking B
Sales revenues worldwide	10 000	2 000
— Community	(8 000)	(1 500)
— Member State Y	(4 000)	(900)

(in million ecu)

Turnover	Joint undertaking C
Sales revenues worldwide	100
— with undertaking A	(20)
— with undertaking B	(10)
Turnover with third undertakings	70
— Community-wide	(60)
— in Member State Y	(50)

II. Consideration of the Joint Undertaking

(a) The undertakinc C is jointly controlled (in the meaning of Article 3(3) and (4)) by the undertakings A and B concerned by the concentration, irrespective of any third undertaking participating in that undertaking C.
(b) The undertaking C is not consolidated by A and B in their profit and loss accounts.
(c) The turnover of C resulting from operations with A and B shall not be taken into account.
(d) The turnover of C resulting from operations with any third undertaking shall be apportioned equally amongst the undertakings A and B, irrespective of their individual shareholdings in C.
(e) Any joint undertaking existing between one of the undertakings concerned and any third undertaking shall (unless already consolidated) not be taken into account.

III. Calculation of Turnover

(a) Undertaking A's aggregate worldwide turnover shall be calculated as follows: ECU 10,000 million and 50% of C's worldwide turnover with third undertakings (i.e. ECU 35 million), the sum of which is ECU 10,035 million.
Undertaking B's aggregate worldwide turnover shall be calculated as follows: ECU 2,000 million and 50% of C's worldwide turnover with third undertakings (i.e. ECU 35 million), the sum of which is ECU 2,035 million.
(b) The aggregate worldwide turnover of the undertakings concerned is ECU 12,070 million.
(c) Undertaking A achieves ECU 4,025 million within Member State Y (50% of C's turnover in this Member State taken into account), and a Community-wide turnover of ECU 8,030 million (including 50% of C's Community-wide turnover);
and undertaking B achieves ECU 925 million within Member State Y (50% of C's turnover in this Member State taken into account), and a Community-wide turnover of ECU 1,530 million (including 50% of C's Community-wide turnover.

IV. Conclusion

Since
(a) the aggregate worldwide turnover of undertakings A and B is more than ECU 5,000 million,
(b) each of the undertakings concerned by the concentration achieves more than ECU 250 million within the Community,
(c) each of the undertakings concerned (undertaking A 50.1% and undertaking B 60.5%) achieves less than two-thirds of its Community-wide turnover in one (and the same) Member State Y,
the proposed concentration would fall under the scope of the Regulation.

1 Legislation

GUIDANCE NOTE IV

APPLICATION OF THE TWO-THIRDS RULE

(Article 1)

For the application of the two-thirds rule for undertakings, we give the following examples (proposed concentration between undertakings A and B):

I. Consolidatd profit and loss accounts

EXAMPLE 1

(in million ecu)

Turnover	Undertaking A	Undertaking B
Sales revenues worldwide	10 000	500
— within the Community	(8 000)	(400)
— in Member State X:	(6 000)	(200)

EXAMPLE 2(a)

(in million ecu)

Turnover	Undertaking A	Undertaking B
Sales revenues worldwide	4 800	500
— within the Community:	(2 400)	(400)
— in Member State X:	(2 100)	(300)

EXAMPLE 2(b)
same figures as in example 2(a), BUT undertaking B achieves ECU 300 million in Member State Y.

II. Application of the Two-Thirds Rule

EXAMPLE 1

1. *Community-wide turnover*

is, for undertaking A, ECU 8,000 million and for undertaking B ECU 400 million.

2. *Turnover in one (and the same) Member State X*

is, for undertaking A (ECU 6,000 million), 75% of its Community-wide turnover and is, for undertaking B (ECU 200 million), 50% of its Community-wide turnover.

3. *Conclusion*

In this case, although undertaking A achieves more than two-thirds of its Community-wide turnover in Member State X, the proposed concentration would fall under the scope of the

Regulation due to the fact that undertaking B achieves less than two-thirds of its Community-wide turnover in Member State X.

EXAMPLE 2(a)

1. *Community-wide turnover*

of undertaking A is ECU 2,400 million and of undertaking B, ECU 400 million.

2. *Turnover in one (and the same) Member State X*

is, for undertaking A, ECU 2,100 million (i.e. 87.5% of its Community-wide turnover); and, for undertaking B, ECU 300 million (i.e. 75% of its Community-wide turnover).

3. *Conclusion*

In this case, each of the undertakings concerned achieves more than two-thirds of its Community-wide turnover in one (and the same) Member State X; the proposed concentration would not fall under the scope of the Regulation.

EXAMPLE 2(b)

Conclusion

In this case, the two-thirds rule would not apply due to the fact that undertakings A and B achieve more than two-thirds of their Community-wide turnover in different Member States X and Y. Therefore, the proposed concentration would fall under the scope of the Regulation.

1 Legislation

4. Text of Commission Notice regarding concentrative and co-operative operations (reproduced below).

Commission Notice regarding the concentrative and co-operative operations under Council Regulation 4064/89 of December 21, 1989 on the control of concentrations between undertakings

([1989] O.J. C203/10)

I. Introduction

1. Article 3(1) of Council Regulation (EEC) No. 4064/89 ("the Regulation") contains an exhaustive list of the factual circumstances which fall to be considered as concentrations. In accordance with the 23rd recital, this term refers only to operations that lead to a lasting change in the structures of the participating undertakings.

By contrast, the Regulation does not deal with operations whose object or effect is the co-ordination of the competitive activities of undertakings that remain independent of each other. Situations of this kind are co-operative in character. Accordingly, they fall to be assessed under the provisions of Regulations (EEC) No. 17 (J.O. 204/62), (EEC) No. 1017/68 ([1968] O.J. L175/1), No. 4056/86 ([1986] O.J. L378/4) or No. 3975/87 ([1987] O.J. L374/1). The same applies to an operation which includes both a lasting structural change and the co-ordination of competitive behaviour, where the two are inseparable.

If the structural change can be separated from the co-ordination of competitive behaviour, the former will be assessed under the Regulation and the latter, to the extent that it does not amount to an ancillary restriction within the meaning of Article 8(2), second subparagraph of the Regulation, falls to be assessed under the other Regulations implementing Articles 85 and 86 of the EEC Treaty.

2. The purpose of this notice is to define as clearly as possible, in the interests of legal certainty, concentrative and co-operative situations. This is particularly important in the case of joint ventures. The same issue is raised in other forms of association between undertakings such as unilateral or reciprocal shareholdings and common directorships, and of certain operations involving more than one undertaking, such as unilateral or reciprocal transfers of undertakings or parts of undertakings, or joint acquisition of an undertaking with a view to its division. In all these cases, operations may not fall within the scope of the Regulation, where their object or effect is the co-ordination of the competitive behaviour of the undertakings concerned.

3. This notice sets out the main considerations which will determine the Commission's view to what extent the aforesaid operations are or are not caught by the Regulation. It is not concerned with the assessment of these operations, whether under the Regulation or any other applicable provisions, in particular Articles 85 and 86 of the EEC Treaty.

4. The principles set out in this notice will be followed and further developed by the Commission's practice in individual cases. As the operations considered are generally of a complex nature, this notice cannot provide a definitive answer to all conceivable situations.

5. This notice is without prejudice to the interpretation which may be given by the Court of Justice or the Court of First Instance of the European Communities.

II. Joint Ventures within Article 3 of the Regulation

6. The Regulation in Article 3(2) refers to two types of joint venture: those which have as their object or effect the co-ordination of the competitive behaviour of undertakings which remain independent (referred to as "co-operative joint ventures") and those which perform on a lasting basis all the functions of an autonomous economic entity and which do not

give rise to co-ordination amongst themselves or between them and the joint venture (referred to as "concentrative joint ventures"). The latter are concentrations and as such are caught by the Regulation. Cooperative joint ventures fall to be considered under other regulations implementing Articles 85 and 86 (see O.J. references cited above).

A. Concept of Joint Venture

7. To define the term "joint venture" within the meaning of Article 3(2), it is necessary to refer to the provision of Article 3(1)(b) of the Regulation. According to the latter, JVs are undertakings that are jointly controlled by several other undertakings, the parent companies. In the context of the Regulation the term JV thus implies several characteristics:

1. *Undertaking*

8. A JV must be an undertaking. That is to be understood as an organized assembly of human and material resources, intended to pursue a defined economic purpose on a long-term basis.

2. *Control by other undertakings*

9. In the context of the Regulation, a JV is controlled by other undertakings. Pursuant to Article 3(3) of the Regulation, control means the possibility of exercising, directly or indirectly, a decisive influence on the activities of the JV; whether this condition is fulfilled can only be decided by reference to all the legal and factual circumstances of the individual case.

10. Control of a JV can be based on legal, contractual or other means, within which the following elements are especially important:
— ownership or rights to the use of all or some of the JV's assets,
— influence over the composition, voting or decisions of the managing or supervisory bodies of the JV,
— voting rights in the managing or supervisory bodies of the JV,
— contracts concerning the running of the JV's business.

3. *Joint control*

11. A JV under the Regulation is jointly controlled. Joint control exists where the parent companies must agree on decisions concerning the JV's activities, either because of the rights acquired in the JV or because of contracts or other means establishing the joint control. Joint control may be provided for in the JV's constitution (memorandum or articles of association). However, it need not be present from the beginning, but may also be established later, in particular by taking a share in an existing undertaking.

12. There is no joint control where one of the parent companies can decide alone on the JV's commercial activities. This is generally the case where one company owns more than half the capital or assets of the undertaking, has the right to appoint more than half of the managing or supervisory bodies, controls more than half of the votes in one of those bodies, or has the sole right to manage the undertaking's business. Where the other parent companies either have completely passive minority holdings or, while able to have a certain influence on the undertaking, cannot, individually or together, determine its behaviour, a relative minority of the capital or of the votes or seats on the decision-making bodies will suffice to control the undertaking.

13. In many cases, the joint control of the JV is based on agreements or concertation between the parent companies. Thus, a majority shareholder in a JV often extends to one or more minority shareholders a contractual right to take part in the control of the JV. If two undertakings each hold half of a JV, even if there is no agreement between them, both parent companies will be obliged permanently to co-operate so as to avoid reciprocal blocking votes on decisions affecting the JV's activity. The same applies to JV's with three or more parents, where each of them has a right of veto. A JV can even be controlled by a considerable number of undertakings that can together muster a majority of the capital or the seats or votes on the JV's decision-making bodies. However, in such cases, joint control can be presumed only if the factual and legal circumstances—especially a convergence of economic interests—support the notion of a deliberate common policy of the parent companies in relation to the JV.

14. If one undertaking's holding in another is, by its nature or its extent, insufficient to establish sole control, and if there is no

joint control together with third parties, then there is no concentration within the meaning of Article 3(1)(b) of the Regulation. Articles 85 or 86 of the EEC Treaty may however be applicable on the basis of Regulation (EEC) No. 17 or other implementing Regulations (see III.1).

B. Concentrative Joint Ventures

15. For a joint venture to be regarded as concentrative it must fulfil all the conditions of Article 3(2), subparagraph 2, which lays down a positive condition and a negative condition.

1. *Positive condition: joint venture performing on a lasting basis all the functions of an autonomous economic entity*

16. To fulfil this condition, a JV must first of all act as an independent supplier and buyer on the market. JVs that take over from their parents only specific partial responsibilities are not to be considered as concentrations where they are merely auxiliaries to the commercial activities of the parent companies. This is the case where the JV supplies its products or services exclusively to its parent companies, or when it meets its own needs wholly from them. The independent market presence can even be insufficient if the JV achieves the majority of its supplies or sales with third parties, but remains substantially dependent on its parents for the maintenance and development of its business.

17. A JV exists on a lasting basis if it is intended and able to carry on its activity for an unlimited, or at least for a long, time. If this is not the case there is generally no long-term change in the structures of the parent companies. More important than the agreed duration are the human and material resources of the JV. They must be of such nature and quantity as to ensure the JV's existence and independence in the long term. This is generally the case where the parent companies invest substantial financial resources in the JV, transfer an existing undertaking or business to it, or give it substantial technical or commercial know-how, so that after an initial starting-up period it can support itself by its own means.

18. A decisive question for assessing the autonomous character of the JV is whether it is in a position to exercise its own commercial policy. This requires, within the limits of its company objects, that it plans, decides and acts independently. In particular, it must be free to determine its competitive behaviour autonomously and according to its own economic interests. If the JV depends for its business on facilities that remain economically integrated with the parent companies' businesses, that weakens the case for the autonomous nature of the JV.

19. The JV's economic independence will not be contested merely because the parent companies reserve to themselves the right to take certain decisions that are important for the development of the JV, namely those concerning alterations of the objects of the company, increases or reductions of capital, or the application of profits. However, if the commercial policy of the JV remains in the hands of the parent undertakings, the JV may take on the aspect of an instrument of the parent undertakings' market interests. Such a situation will usually exist where the JV operates in the market of the parent undertakings. It may also exist where the JV operates in markets neighbouring, or upstream or downstream of, those of the parent undertakings.

2. *Negative condition: absence of co-ordination of competitive behaviour*

20. Subject to what is said in the first paragraph of this notice a JV can only be considered to be concentrative within the meaning of Article 3(2), subparagraph 2 of the Regulation, if it does not have as its object or effect the co-ordination of the competitive behaviour of undertakings that remain independent of each other. There must not be such co-ordination either between the parent companies themselves or between any or all of them on the one hand and the JV on the other hand. Such co-ordination must not be an object of the establishment or operation of the JV, nor may it be the consequence thereof. The JV is not to be regarded as concentrative if as a result of the agreement to set up the JV or as a result of its existence or activities it is reasonably foreseeable that the competitive behaviour of a parent or of the JV on the relevant market will be influenced. Conversely, there will normally be no foreseeable co-ordination when all the parent companies withdraw entirely and permanently from

the JV's market and do not operate on markets neighbouring those of the JV's.

21. Not every co-operation between parent companies with regard to the JV prevents a JV from being considered concentrative. Even concentrative JV's generally represent a means for parent companies to pursue common or mutually complementary interests. The establishment and joint control of a JV is, therefore, inconceivable without an understanding between the parent companies as concerns the pursuit of those interests. Irrespective of its legal form, such a concordance of interests is an essential feature of a JV.

22. As regards the relations of the parent undertakings, or any one of them, with the JV, the risk of co-ordination within the meaning of Article 3(2) will not normally arise where the parent undertakings are not active in the markets of the JV or in neighbouring or upstream or downstream markets. In other cases, the risk of co-ordination will be relatively small where the parents limit the influence they exercise to the JV's strategic decisions, such as those concerning the future direction of investment, and when they express their financial, rather than their market-oriented, interests. The membership of the JV's managing and supervisory bodies is also important. Common membership of the JV's and the parent companies' decision-making bodies may be an obstacle to the development of the JV's autonomous commercial policy.

23. The dividing line between the concordance of interests in a JV and a co-ordination of competitive behaviour that is incompatible with the notion of concentration cannot be laid down for all conceivable kinds of case. The decisive factor is not the legal form of the relationship between the parent companies and between them and the JV. The direct or indirect, actual or potential effects of the establishment and operation of the JV on market relationships, have determinant importance.

24. In assessing the likelihood of co-ordination of competitive behaviour, it is useful to consider some of the different situations which often occur:

(a) JVs that take over pre-existing activities of the parent companies;

(b) JVs that undertake new activities on behalf of the parent companies;

(c) JVs that enter the parent companies' markets;

(d) JVs that enter upstream, downstream or neighbouring markets.

(a) *JVs that take over pre-existing activities of the parent companies*

25. There is normally no risk of co-ordination where the parent companies transfer the whole of certain business activities to the JV and withdraw permanently from the JV's market so that they remain neither actual nor potential competitors—of each other nor of the JV. In this context, the notion of potential competition is to be interpreted realistically, according to the Commission's established practice (See the Thirteenth Report (1983) on Competition Policy, point 55). A presumption of a competitive relationship requires not only that one or more of the parent companies could re-enter the JV's market at any time: this must be a realistic option and represent a commercially reasonable course in the light of all objective circumstances.

26. Where the parent companies transfer their entire business activities to the JV, and thereafter act only as holding companies, this amounts to complete merger from the economic viewpoint.

27. Where the JV takes on only some of the activities that the parent companies formerly carried on independently, this can also amount to a concentration. In this case, the establishment and operation of the JV must not lead to a co-ordination of the parent companies' competitive behaviour in relation to other activities which they retain. Coordination of competitive behaviour between any or all of the parent companies and the JV must also be excluded. Such co-ordination is likely where there are close economic links between the areas of activity of the JV on one side and of the parent companies on the other. This applies to upstream, downstream and neighbouring product markets.

28. The withdrawal of the parent companies need not be simultaneous with the establishment of the JV. It is possible—so far as necessary—to allow the parent companies a short transitional period to overcome any starting-up problems of the JV, especially bottlenecks in production or supplies. This period should not normally exceed one year.

29. It is even possible for the establishment of a JV to represent a concentration situation where the parent companies remain permanently active on the JV's product or service market. In this case, however, the parent companies' geographic market must be different from that of the JV. Moreover, the markets in question must be so widely separated, or must present structures so different, that, taking account of the nature of the goods or services concerned and of the cost of (first or renewed) entry by either into the other's market, competitive interaction may be excluded.

30. If the parent companies' markets and the JV's are in different parts of the Community or neighbouring third countries, there is a degree of probability that either, if it has the necessary human and material resources, could extend its activities from the one market to the other. Where the territories are adjacent or very close to each other, this may even be assumed to be the case. At least in this last case, the actual allocation of markets gives reason to suppose that it follows from a co-ordination of competitive behaviour between parent companies and the JV.

(b) *JVs that undertake new activities on behalf of the parent companies*

31. There is normally no risk of co-ordination in the sense described above where the JV operates on a product or service market which the parent companies individually have not entered and will not enter in the foreseeable future, because they lack the organizational, technical or financial means or because, in the light of all the objective circumstances, such a move would not represent a commercially reasonable course. An individual market entry will also be unlikely where, after establishing the JV, the parent companies no longer have the means to make new investments in the same field, or where an additional individual operation on the JV's market would not make commercial sense. In both cases there is no competitive relationship between the parent companies and the JV. Consequently, there is no possibility of co-ordination of their competitive behaviour. However, this assessment is only true if the JV's market is neither upstream nor downstream of, nor neighbouring, that of the parent companies.

32. The establishment of a JV to operate in the same product or service market as the parent companies but in another geographic market involves the risk of co-ordination if there is competitive interaction between the parent companies' geographic market and that of the JV.

(c) *JVs that enter the parent companies' market*

33. Where the parent companies, or one of them, remain active on the JV's market or remain potential competitors of the JV, a co-ordination of competitive behaviour between the parent companies or between them and the JV must be presumed. So long as this presumption is not rebutted, the Commission will take it that the establishment of the JV does not fall under Article 3(2), subparagraph 2 of the Regulation.

(d) *JVs that operate in upstream, downstream or neighbouring markets*

34. If the JV is operating in a market that is upstream or downstream of that of the parent companies, then, in general, co-ordination of purchasing or, as the case may be, sales policy between the parent companies is likely where they are competitors on the upstream or downstream market.

35. If the parent companies are not competitors, it remains to be examined whether there is a real risk of co-ordination of competitive behaviour between the JV and any of the parents. This will normally be the case where the JV's sales or purchases are made in substantial measure with the parent companies.

36. It is not possible to lay down general principles regarding the likelihood of co-ordination of competitive behaviour in cases where the parent companies and the JV are active in neighbouring markets. The outcome will depend in particular on whether the JV's and the parent companies' products are technically or economically linked, whether they are both components of another product or are otherwise mutually complementary, and whether the parent companies could realistically enter the JV's market. If there are no concrete opportunities for competitive interaction of this kind, the Commission will treat the JV as concentrative.

III. Other Links between Undertakings

1. *Minority shareholdings*

37. The taking of a minority shareholding in an undertaking can be considered a concentration within the meaning of Article 3(1)(*b*) of the Regulation if the new shareholder acquires the possibility of exercising a decisive influence on the undertaking's activity. If the acquisition of a minority shareholding brings about a situation in which there is an undertaking jointly controlled by two or more others, the principles described above in relation to JVs apply.

38. As long as the threshold of individual or joint decisive influence has not been reached, the Regulation is not in any event applicable. Accordingly, the assessment under competition law will be made only in relation to the criteria laid down in Articles 85 and 86 of the EEC Treaty and on the basis of the usual procedural rules for restrictive practices and abuses of dominant position.[1]

39. There may likewise be a risk of co-ordination where an undertaking acquires a majority or minority interest in another in which a competitor already has a minority interest. If so, this acquisition will be assessed under Articles 85 and 86 of the EEC Treaty.

2. *Cross-shareholding*

40. In order to bring their autonomous and hitherto separate undertakings or groups closer together, company owners often cause them to exchange shareholdings in each other. Such reciprocal influences can serve to establish or to secure industrial or commercial co-operation between the undertakings or groups. But they may also result in establishing a "single economic entity." In the first case, the co-ordination of competitive behaviour between independent undertakings is predominant; in the second, the result may be a concentration. Consequently, reciprocal directorships and cross-shareholdings can only be evaluated in relation to their foreseeable effects in each case.

41. The Commission considers that two or more undertakings can also combine without setting up a parent-subsidiary relationship and without either losing its legal personality. Article 3(1) of the Regulation refers not only to legal, but also to economic concentrations. The condition for the recognition of a concentration in the form of a combined group is, however, that the undertakings or groups concerned are not only subject to a permanent, single economic management, but are also amalgamated into a genuine economic unit, characterised internally by profit and loss compensation between the various undertakings within the groups and externally by joint liability.

3. *Representation on controlling bodies of other undertakings*

42. Common membership of managing or supervisory boards of various undertakings is to be assessed in accordance with the same principles as cross-shareholdings.

43. The representation of one undertaking on the decision-making bodies of another is usually the consequence of an existing shareholding. It reinforces the influence of the investing undertaking over the activities of the undertaking in which it holds a share, because it affords it the opportunity of obtaining information on the activities of a competitor or of taking an active part in its commercial decisions.

44. Thus, common membership of the respective boards may be the vehicle for the co-ordination of the competitive behaviour of the undertakings concerned, or for a concentration of undertakings within the meaning of the Regulation. This will depend on the circumstances of the individual case, among which the economic link between the shareholding and the personal connection must always be examined. This is equally true of unilateral and reciprocal relationships between undertakings.

45. Personal connections not accompanied by shareholdings are to be judged according to the same criteria as shareholding relationships between undertakings. A majority of seats on the managing or supervisory board of an undertaking will normally imply control of the latter; a minority of seats at least a degree of influence over its commercial policy, which may further entail a co-ordination of behaviour. Reciprocal connections justify a presumption that the undertakings concerned are co-ordinating their business conduct. A very wide communality of

membership of the respective decision-making bodies—that is, up to half of the members or more—may be an indication of a concentration.

4. Transfers of undertakings or parts of undertakings

46. A transfer of assets or shares falls within the definition of a concentration, according to Article 3(1)(b) of the Regulation, if it results in the acquirer gaining control of all or of part of one or more undertakings. However, the situation is different where the transfer conferring control over part of an undertaking is linked with an agreement to co-ordinate the competitive behaviour of the undertakings concerned, or where it necessarily leads to or is accompanied by co-ordination of the business conduct of undertakings which remain independent. Cases of this kind are not covered by the Regulation: they must be examined according to Articles 85 and 86 of the EEC Treaty and under the appropriate implementing Regulations.

47. The practical application of this rule requires a distinction between unilateral and reciprocal arrangements. A unilateral acquisition of assets or shares strongly suggests that the Regulation is applicable. The contrary needs to be demonstrated by clear evidence of the likelihood of co-ordination of the parties' competitive behaviour. A reciprocal acquisition of assets or shares, by contrast, will usually follow from an agreement between the undertakings concerned as to their investments, production or sales, and thus serves to co-ordinate their competitive behaviour. A concentration situation does not exist where a reciprocal transfer of assets or shares forms part of a specialization or restructuring agreement or other type of co-ordination. Coordination presupposes in any event that the parties remain at least potential competitors after the exchange has taken place.

5. Joint acquisition of an undertaking with a view to its division

48. Where several undertakings jointly acquire another, the principles for the assessment of a joint venture are applicable, provided that within the acquisition operation, the period of joint control goes beyond the very short term. In this case the Regulation may or may not be applicable, depending on the concentrative or co-operative nature of the JV. If, by contrast, the sole object of the agreement is to divide up the assets of the undertaking and this agreement is put into effect immediately after the acquisition, then, in accordance with the 24th recital, the Regulation applies.

---

5. Text of Commission Notice regarding restrictions ancillary to concentration. (reproduced below).

Commission Notice regarding restrictions ancillary to concentrations

([1990] O.J. C203/5)

I. Introduction

1. Council Regulation (EEC) No. 4064/89 of December 21, 1989 on the control of concentrations between undertakings ("the Regulation") ([1989] O.J. L395/1) states in its 25th recital that its application is not excluded where the undertakings concerned accept restrictions which are directly related and necessary to the implementation of the concentration, hereinafter referred to as "ancillary restrictions." In the scheme of the Regulation, such restrictions are to be assessed together with the concentration itself. It follows, as confirmed by Article 8(2), second subparagraph, last sentence of the Regulation, that a decision declaring the concentration compatible also covers these restrictions. In this situation, under the provisions of Article 22, paragraphs 1 and 2, the Regulation is solely applicable, to the exclusion of Regulation No. 17 (J.O. 204/62), (EEC) No. 4056/86 ([1986] O.J.

L378/4) and (EEC) No. 3975/87 ([1987] O.J. L374/1). This avoids parallel Commission proceedings, one concerned with the assessment of the concentration under the Regulation, and the other aimed at the application of Articles 85 and 86 to the restrictions which are ancillary to the concentration.

2. In this notice, the Commission sets out to indicate the interpretation it gives to the notion of "restrictions directly related and necessary to the implementation of the concentration." Under the Regulation such restrictions must be assessed in relation to the concentration, whatever their treatment might be under Articles 85 and 86 if they were to be considered in isolation or in a different economic context. The Commission endeavours, within the limits set by the Regulation, to take the greatest account of business practice and of the conditions necessary for the implementation of concentrations.

This notice is without prejudice to the interpretation which may be given by the Court of Justice of the European Communities.

II. Principles of Evaluation

3. The "restrictions" meant are those agreed on between the parties to the concentration which limit their own freedom of action in the market. They do not include restrictions to the detriment of third parties. If such restrictions are the inevitable consequence of the concentration itself, they must be assessed together with it under the provisions of Article 2 of the Regulation. If, on the contrary, such restrictive effects on third parties are separable from the concentration they may, if appropriate, be the subject of an assessment of compatibility with Articles 85 and 86 of the EEC Treaty.

4. For restrictions to be considered "directly related" they must be ancillary to the implementation of the concentration, that is to say subordinate in importance to the main object of the concentration. They cannot be substantial restrictions wholly different in nature from those which result from the concentration itself. Neither are they contractual arrangements which are among the elements constituting the concentration, such as those establishing economic unity between previously independent parties, or organizing joint control by two undertakings of another undertaking. As integral parts of the concentration, the latter arrangements constitute the very subject matter of the evaluation to be carried out under the Regulation.

Also excluded, for concentrations which are carried out in stages, are the contractual arrangements relating to the stages before the establishment of control within the meaning of Article 3, paragraphs 1 and 3 of the Regulation. For these, Articles 85 and 86 remain applicable as long as the conditions set out in Article 3 are not fulfilled.

The notion of directly related restrictions likewise excludes from the application of the Regulation additional restrictions agreed at the same time which have no direct link with the concentration. It is not enough that the additional restrictions exist in the same context as the concentration.

5. The restrictions must likewise be "necessary to the implementation of the concentration," which means that in their absence the concentration could not be implemented or could only be implemented under more uncertain conditions, at substantially higher cost, over an appreciably longer period or with considerably less probability of success. This must be judged on an objective basis.

6. The question of whether a restriction meets these conditions cannot be answered in general terms. In particular as concerns the necessity of the restriction, it is proper not only to take account of its nature, but equally to ensure, in applying the rule of proportionality, that its duration and subject matter, and geographic field of application, do not exceed what the implementation of the concentration reasonably requires. If alternatives are available for the attainment of the legitimate aim pursued, the undertakings must choose the one which is objectively the least restrictive of competition.

These principles will be followed and further developed by the Commission's practice in individual cases. However, it is already possible, on the basis of past experience, to indicate the attitude the Commission will take to those restrictions most commonly encountered in relation to

III. Evaluation of Common Ancillary Restrictions in Cases of the Transfer of an Undertaking

A. *Non-competition clauses*

1. Among the ancillary restrictions which meet the criteria set out in the Regulation are contractual prohibitions on competition which are imposed on the vendor in the context of a concentration achieved by the transfer of an undertaking or part of an undertaking. Such prohibitions guarantee the transfer to the acquirer of the full value of the assets transferred, which in general include both physical assets and intangible assets such as the goodwill which the vendor has accumulated or the know-how he has developed. These are not only directly related to the concentration, but are also necessary for its implementation because, in their absence, there would be reasonable grounds to expect that the sale of the undertaking or part of an undertaking could not be accomplished satisfactorily. In order to take over fully the value of the assets transferred, the acquirer must be able to benefit from some protection against competitive acts of the vendor in order to gain the loyalty of customers and to assimilate and exploit the know-how. Such protection cannot generally be considered necessary when *de facto* the transfer is limited to physical assets (such as land, buildings or machinery) or to exclusive industrial and commercial property rights (the holders of which could immediately take action against infringements by the transferor of such rights).

However, such a prohibition on competition is justified by the legitimate objective sought of implementing the concentration only when its duration, its geographical field of application, its subject matter and the persons subject to it do not exceed what is reasonably necessary to that end.

2. With regard to the acceptable duration of a prohibition on competition, a period of five years has been recognized as appropriate when the transfer of the undertaking includes the goodwill and know-how, and a period of two years when it includes only the goodwill. However, these are not absolute rules; they do not preclude a prohibition of longer duration in particular circumstances, where for example the parties can demonstrate that customer loyalty will persist for a period longer than two years or that the economic life cycle of the products concerned is longer than five years and should be taken into account.

3. The geographic scope of the non-competition clause must be limited to the area where the vendor had established the products or services before the transfer. It does not appear objectively necessary that the acquirer be protected from competition by the vendor in territories which the vendor had not previously penetrated.

4. In the same manner, the non-competition clause must be limited to products and services which form the economic activity of the undertaking transferred. In particular, in the case of a partial transfer of assets, it does not appear that the acquirer needs to be protected from the competition of the vendor in the products or services which constitute the activities which the vendor retains after the transfer.

5. The vendor may bind himself, his subsidiaries and commercial agents. However, an obligation to impose similar restrictions on others would not qualify as an ancillary restriction. This applies in particular to clauses which would restrict the scope for resellers or users to import or export.

6. Any protection of the vendor is not normally an ancillary restriction and is therefore to be examined under Articles 85 and 86 of the EEC Treaty.

B. *Licences of industrial and commercial property rights and of know-how*

1. The implementation of a transfer of an undertaking or part of an undertaking generally includes the transfer to the acquirer, with a view to the full exploitation of the assets transferred, of rights to industrial or commercial property or know-how. However, the vendor may remain the owner of the rights in order to exploit them for activities other than those transferred. In these cases, the usual means for ensuring that the acquirer will have the full use of the assets transferred is to conclude licensing agreements in his favour.

2. Simple or exclusive licences of patents, similar rights or existing know-how can be accepted as necessary for the completion of the transaction, and likewise agreements to grant such licences. They may be limited to certain fields of use, to the extent that they correspond to the activities of the undertaking transferred. Normally it will not be necessary for such licences to include territorial limitations on manufacture which reflect the territory of the activity transferred. Licences may be granted for the whole duration of the patent or similar rights or the duration of the normal economic life of the know-how. As such licences are economically equivalent to a partial transfer of rights, they need not be limited in time.

3. Restrictions in licence agreements, going beyond what is provided above, fall outside the scope of the Regulation. They must be assessed on their merits according to Article 85(1) and (3). Accordingly, where they fulfil the conditions required, they may benefit from the block exemptions provided for by Regulation (EEC) No. 2349/84 on patent licences ([1984] O.J. L219/15) or Regulation (EEC) No. 559/89 on know-how licences ([1989] O.J. L61/1).

4. The same principles are to be applied by analogy in the case of licences of trademarks, business names or similar rights. There may be situations where the vendor wishes to remain the owner of such rights in relation to activities retained, but the acquirer needs the rights to use them to market the products constituting the object of the activity of the undertaking or part of an undertaking transferred.

In such circumstances, the conclusion of agreements for the purpose of avoiding confusion between trademarks may be necessary.

C. Purchase and supply agreements

1. In many cases, the transfer of an undertaking or part of an undertaking can entail the disruption of traditional lines of internal procurement and supply resulting from the previous integration of activities within the economic entity of the vendor. To make possible the break up of the economic unity of the vendor and the partial transfer of the assets to the acquirer under reasonable conditions, it is often necessary to maintain, at least for a transitional period, similar links between the vendor and the acquirer. This objective is normally attained by the conclusion of purchase and supply agreements between the vendor and the acquirer of the undertaking or part of an undertaking. Taking account of the particular situation resulting from the break up of the economic unity of the vendor such obligations, which may lead to restrictions of competition, can be recognized as ancillary. They may be in favour of the vendor as well as the acquirer.

2. The legitimate aim of such obligations may be to ensure the continuity of supply to one or other of the parties of products necessary to the activities retained (for the vendor) or taken over (for the acquirer). Thus, there are grounds for recognizing, for a transitional period, the need for supply obligations aimed at guaranteeing the quantities previously supplied within the vendor's integrated business or enabling their adjustment in accordance with the development of the market.

Their aim may also be to provide continuity of outlets for one or the other of the parties, as they were previously assured within the single economic entity. For the same reason, obligations providing for fixed quantities, possibly with a variation clause, may be recognized as necessary.

3. However, there does not appear to be a general justification for exclusive purchase or supply obligations. Save in exceptional circumstances, for example resulting from the absence of a market or the specificity of products, such exclusivity is not objectively necessary to permit the implementation of a concentration in the form of a transfer of an undertaking or part of an undertaking.

In any event, in accordance with the principle of proportionality, the undertakings concerned are bound to consider whether there are no alternative means to the ends pursued, such as agreements for fixed quantities, which are less restrictive than exclusivity.

4. As for the duration of procurement and supply obligations, this must be limited to a period necessary for the replacement of the relationship of dependency by autonomy in market. The duration of such a period must be objectively justified.

IV. Evaluation of Ancillary Restrictions in the Case of a Joint Acquisition

1. As set out in the 24th recital, the Regulation is applicable when two or more undertakings agree to acquire jointly the control of one or more other undertakings, in particular by means of a public tender offer, where the object or effect is the division among themselves of the undertakings or their assets. This is a concentration implemented in two successive stages; the common strategy is limited to the acquisition of control. For the transaction to be concentrative, the joint acquisition must be followed by a clear separation of the undertakings or assets concerned.

2. For this purpose, an agreement by the joint acquirers of an undertaking to abstain from making separate competing offers for the same undertaking, or otherwise acquiring control, may be considered an ancillary restriction.

3. Restrictions limited to putting the division into effect are to be considered directly related and necessary to the implementation of the concentration. This will apply to arrangements made between the parties for the joint acquisition of control in order to divide among themselves the production facilities or the distribution networks together with the existing trademarks of the undertaking acquired in common. The implementation of this division may not in any circumstances lead to the coordination of the future behaviour of the acquiring undertakings.

4. To the extent that such a division involves the break up of a pre-existing economic entity, arrangements that make the break up possible under reasonable conditions must be considered ancillary. In this regard, the principles explained above in relation to purchase and supply arrangements over a transitional period in cases of transfer of undertakings should be applied by analogy.

V. Evaluation of Ancillary Restrictions in Cases of Concentrative Joint Ventures within the meaning of Article 3(2) subparagraph 2 of the Regulation

This evaluation must take account of the characteristics peculiar to concentrative joint ventures, the constituent elements of which are the creation of an autonomous economic entity exercising on a long-term basis all the functions of an undertaking, and the absence of coordination of competitive behaviour between the parent undertakings and between them and the joint venture. This condition implies in principle the withdrawal of the parent undertakings from the market assigned to the joint venture and, therefore, their disappearance as actual or potential competitors of the new entity.

A. *Non-competition obligations*

To the extent that a prohibition on the parent undertakings competing with the joint venture aims at expressing the reality of the lasting withdrawal of the parents from the market assigned to the joint venture, it will be recognized as an integral part of the concentration.

B. *Licences for industrial and commercial property rights and know-how*

The creation of a new autonomous economic entity usually involves the transfer of the technology necessary for carrying on the activities assigned to it, in the form of a transfer of rights and related know-how. Where the parent undertakings intend nonetheless to retain the property rights, particularly with the aim of exploitation in other fields of use, the transfer of technology to the joint venture may be accomplished by means of licences. Such licences may be exclusive, without having to be limited in duration or territory, for they serve only as a substitute for the transfer of property rights. They must therefore be considered necessary to the implementation of the concentration.

C. *Purchase and supply obligations*

If the parent undertakings remain present in a market upstream or downstream of that of the joint venture, any purchase and supply agreements are to be examined in accordance with the principles applicable in the case of the transfer of an undertaking.

6. **Text of Notes of the Council and Commissin on Council Regulation (EEC) No. 4064/89 (reproduced over).**

Notes on Council Regulation (EEC) 4064/89

For all appropriate purposes and in particular with a view to clarifying the scope of certain articles of the regulation, the following texts are drawn to the notice of interested parties:

re Article 1

The Commission considers that the threshold for world turnover as set in Article 1(2)(a) of this regulation for the initial stage of implementation must be lowered to ECU 2,000 million at the end of that period. The *de minimis* threshold as set out in (b) should also be revised in the light of experience and the trend of the main threshold. It therefore undertakes to submit a proposal to that effect to the Council in due course.

The Council and the Commission state their readiness to consider taking other factors into account in addition to turnover when the thresholds are revised.

The Council and the Commission consider that the review of the thresholds as provided for in Article 1(3) will have to be combined with a special re-examination of the method of calculation of the turnover of joint undertakings as referred to in Article 5(5).

re Article 2

The Commission states that among the factors to be taken into consideration for the purpose of establishing the compatibility or incompatibility of a concentration—factors as referred to in Article 2(1) and explained in Recital 13—account should be taken in particular of the competitiveness of undertakings located in regions which are greatly in need of restructuring owing *inter alia* to slow development.

Under the first subparagraph of Article 2(1), the Commission has to establish in respect of each concentration covered by the regulation whether that concentration is compatible or incompatible with the common market.

The appraisal necessary for this purpose will have to be made on the basis of the same factors as defined in Article 2(1)(a) and (b) and within the context of a single appraisal procedure.

If, at the end of the first stage of appraisal (within one month of notification), the Commission reaches the conclusion that the concentration is not likely to create or reinforce a dominant position within the meaning of Article 2(3), it will decide against initiating proceedings. Such a decision will then establish the concentration's compatibility with the common market. It will be presented in the form of a letter and will be notified to the undertakings concerned and to the competent authorities of the Member States.

If the Commission has decided to initiate proceedings because it concludes that there is prima facie a real risk of creating or reinforcing a dominant position, and if further investigation (within a maximum period of four months of the initiation of proceedings) confirms this suspicion it will declare the concentration incompatible with the common market. If, on the contrary, the initial assumption is proved to be unfounded in the light of the further investigation, possibly in view of the changes made by the undertakings concerned to their initial project, the Commission will adopt a final decision noting that the operation is compatible with operation of the common market.

The decision on compatibility is therefore only the counterpart to a decision on incompatibility or prohibition.

The Commission considers that the concept of "the structure of all the markets concerned" refers both to markets within the Community and to those outside it.

The Commission considers that the concept of technical and economic progress must be understood in the light of the principles enshrined in Article 85(3) of the Treaty, as interpreted by the case law of the Court of Justice.

re Article 3(2), first indent

The Commission considers that this rule also applies to consortia in the liner trades sector.

re Article 5(3)(a)

The Council and the Commission consider

that the criterion defined as a proportion of assets should be replaced by a concept of banking income as referred to in Directive 86/635 on the annual accounts and consolidated accounts of banks and other financial institutions, either at the actual time of entry into force of the relevant provisions of that directive or at the time of the review of thresholds referred to in Article 1 of this regulation and in the light of experience acquired.

re Article 9

The Council and the Commission consider that, when a specific market represents a substantial part of the common market, the referral procedure provided for in Article 9 should only be applied in exceptional cases. There are indeed grounds for taking as a basis the principle that a concentration which creates or reinforces a dominant position in a substantial part of the common market must be declared incompatible with the common market. The Council and the Commission consider that such an application of Article 9 should be confined to cases in which the interests in respect of competition of the Member State concerned could not be adequately protected in any other way.

They consider that the review of Article 9 referred to in paragraph 10 thereof should be carried out in the light of the experience gained in its application (which it is envisaged will be exceptional), having regard to the importance of the principle of exclusivity and the need to provide clarity and certainty for firms, with a view to considering whether it remains appropriate to include it in the regulation.

The Commission states that the preparatory steps within the meaning of Article 9(4)(b) which must be taken during the period of three months are preliminary measures which should lead to a final decision within the remaining period of two-and-a-half months and normally take the form of the notification of objections within the meaning of Article 18(1).

re Articles 9(5) and 10(5)

The Commission states that it intends, in all cases of concentrations which are duly notified, to take the decision provided for in Article 6(1), Article 8(2) and (3) and Article 9(3). Any Member State or undertaking concerned may ask the Commission to give written confirmation of its position with regard to the concentration.

re Articles 12 and 13

The Commission states that, pursuant to the principle of proportionality, it will carry out investigations within the meaning of Articles 12 and 13 only where particular circumstances so require.

re Article 19

The Council and the Commission agree that the arrangements for publication referred to in Article 19(7) will be reviewed after four years in the light of the experience acquired.

re Article 21(3)

1. Application of the general clause on "legitimate interests" must be subject to the following principles:

It shall create no new rights for Member States and shall be restricted to sanctioning the recognition in Community law of their present reserved powers to intervene in certain aspects of concentrations affecting the territory coming within their jurisdiction on grounds other than those covered by this regulation. The application of this clause therefore reaffirms Member States' ability on those grounds either to prohibit a concentration or to make it subject to additional conditions and requirements. It does not imply the attribution to them of any power to authorize concentrations which the Commission may have prohibited under this regulation.

Nor, by invoking the protection of the legitimate interests referred to, may a Member State justify itself on the basis of considerations which the Commission must take into account in assessing concentrations on a European scale. While mindful of the need to conserve and develop effective competition in the common market as required by the Treaty, the Commission must—in line with consistent decisions of the Court of Justice concerning the application of the rules of competition contained in the Treaty—place its assessment of the compatibility of a concentration in the overall context of the achievement of the fundamental objectives of the Treaty mentioned in Article 2, as well as that of strengthening the Community's economic and social cohesion referred to in Article 130a.

In order that the Commission may recognize the compatibility of the public interest claimed by a Member State with the general principles and other provisions of Community law, it is essential that prohibitions or restrictions placed on the forming of concentrations should constitute neither a form of arbitrary discrimination nor a disguised restriction in trade between Member States.

In application of the principle of necessity or efficacy and of the rule of proportionality, measures which may be taken by Member States must satisfy the criterion of appropriateness for the objective and must be limited to the minimum of action necessary to ensure protection of the legitimate interest in question. The Member States must therefore choose, where alternatives exist, the measure which is objectively the least restrictive to achieve the end pursued.

2. The Commission considers that the three specific categories of legitimate interests which any Member State may freely cite under this provision are to be interpreted as follows:

The reference to "public security" is made without prejudice to the provisions of Article 223 on national defence, which allow a Member State to intervene in respect of a concentration which would be contrary to the essential interests of its security and is connected with the production of or trade in arms, munitions and war material. The restriction set by that article concerning products not intended for specifically military purposes should be complied with.

There may be wider considerations of public security, both in the sense of Article 224 and in that of Article 36, in addition to defence interests in the strict sense. Thus the requirement for public security, as interpreted by the Court of Justice, could cover security of supplies to the country in question of a product or service considered of vital or essential interest for the protection of the population's health.

The Member States' right to plead the "plurality of the media" recognizes the legitimate concern to maintain diversified sources of information for the sake of plurality of opinion and multiplicity of views.

Legitimate invocation may also be made of the prudential rules in Member States, which relate in particular to financial services; the application of these rules is normally confined to national bodies for the surveillance of banks, stockbroking firms and insurance companies. They concern, for example, the good repute of individuals, the honesty of transactions and the rules of solvency. These specific prudential criteria are also the subject of efforts aimed at a minimum degree of harmonization being made in order to ensure uniform "rules of play" in the Community as a whole.

re Article 22

The Commission states that it does not normally intend to apply Articles 85 and 86 of the Treaty establishing the European Economic Community to concentrations as defined in Article 3 other than by means of this regulation.

However, it reserves the right to take action in accordance with the procedures laid down in Article 89 of the Treaty, for concentrations as defined in Article 3, but which do not have a Community dimension within the meaning of Article 1, in cases not provided for by Article 22.

In any event, it does not intend to take action in respect of concentrations with a world-wide turnover of less than ECU 2,000 million or below a minimum Community turnover level of ECU 100 million or which are not covered by the threshold of two-thirds provided for in the last part of the sentence in Article 1(2), on the grounds that below such levels a concentration would not normally significantly affect trade between Member States.

The Council and the Commission note that the Treaty establishing the European Economic Community contains no provisions making specific reference to the prior control of concentrations.

Acting on a proposal from the Commission, the Council has therefore decided, in accordance with Article 235 of the Treaty, to set up a new mechanism for the control of concentrations.

The Council and the Commission consider, for pressing reasons of legal security, that this new regulation will apply solely and exclusively to concentrations as defined in Article 3.

The Council and the Commission state that the provisions of Article 22(3) to (5) in no way prejudice the power of Member States other than that at whose request the Commission intervenes to apply their national laws within their respective territories.

CHAPTER 2

JURISDICTION: CASES AND REFERENCES

A. CONCENTRATION

1. Definition of the term "concentration" (control)

Article 3, Regulation 4064/89
Volvo/Renault M1 (para. 2)
Arjomari/Wiggins Teape M4 (para. 4)*
MBB/Aérospatiale M15 (para. 1)
CONAGRA/IDEA M24 (para. 5–14)*
Pechiney/Usinor M31 (paras. 3–8)
ELF/Enterprise M38 (paras. 3–4)
Eridania/ISI M40 (paras. 3–5)*
Lucas/Eaton M57 (paras. 6–9)
Ingersoll Rand/Dresser M59 (para. 8)*
Mediobanca/Generali M65 (paras. 6–11)
Sunrise M67 (paras. 15–17)

2. Specific types of concentrations

2.1. Acquisitions of sole control

Arjomari/Wiggins Teape M4 (para. 4)*
Usinor/ASD M21 (paras. 3–4)
Eridania/ISI M40 (paras. 3–5)

2.2. Acquisition/creation of joint control

Volvo/Renault M1 (paras. 5–7)
AG/Amev M2 (paras. 1–2)
ICI/Tioxide M3 (paras. 3–4)
MBB/Aérospatiale M15 (para. 1)
CONAGRA/IDEA M24 (paras. 5–14)*
Pechiney-Usinor/Sacilor M31 (paras. 3–8)
ELF/Enterprise M38 (paras. 3–8)*
Eridania/ISI M40 (paras. 3–5)*
ABC/Générale des Eaux M45 (paras. 6–7)
Thompson/Pilkington M51 (para. 6)
Metallgesellschaft/Safic Alcan M53 (para. 6)
UAP/Transatlantic/Sunlife M54 (paras. 7–10)*
TNT/GD Net M56 (para. 12)
Lucas/Eaton M57 (paras. 6–9)
Ingersoll Rand/Dresser M59 (para. 8)*
Eurocom/RSCG M60 (paras. 3–4)
Mediobanca/Generali M65 (paras. 6–11)
Sunrise M67 (paras. 15–17)

2.3. Purchase of option

2.4. Passage from joint to sole control

ICI/Tioxide M3 (paras. 2–4)

2.5. Break-up of a company

CAMPSA M63 (paras. 8–9)

B. COMMUNITY DIMENSION

1. Calculation of turnover

Article 5, Regulation 4064/89
Cereol/Continentale Italiana M55

2. Companies taken into account in calculation: definition of "control" for purposes of turnover calculation

Article 5(4)–(5), Regulation 4064/89
Arjomari/Wiggins Teape M4 (paras. 5–7)
Erocom/RSCG M60 (paras. 5–6)

3. Specific cases

3.1. Joint ventures

Article 5(4)–(5), Regulation 4064/89
TNT/GD M56 (paras. 9–11)
Sunrise M67 (paras. 14)

3.2. Acquisition of part of an undertaking

Article 5(2), Regulation 4064/89

3.3. Banks and other financial institutions

Article 3(5), 5(3), Regulation 4064/89
Notes on Council Regulation 4064/89 see page 480

3.4. Insurance companies

Article 5(3), Regulation 4064/89
AG/Amev M2 (paras. 3–6)

3.5. Airlines

Delta Airlines/Pan Am M46 (para. 9)

C. CONCENTRATIONS v. CO-OPERATION: PARTIAL MERGERS

1. List of relevant cases

Article 3(2), Regulation 4064/89
SHV/Chevron 87 (para. 5)
De Laval/Stork 114 (para. 5)
BPCL/ICI (para. 31)
ENI/Montedison 256
Zip Fasteners 7th Comp. Rep. (paras. 29–32)
Kaiser/Estel 9th Comp. Rep. (para. 131)
TWIL/Bridon 19th Comp. Rep. (para. 64)
Ibercoer/Utokumpu 19th Comp. Rep.
Volvo/Renault M1

Mitsubishi/UCAR M7 (paras. 4–8)
BNP/Dresdner Bank M10
Baxter/Nestlé/Salvia M11
CONAGRA/IDEA M24
Sanofi/Sterling Drug M27
Apollinaris/Schweppes M30
Draeger/IBM/HMP M33
ELF/Enterprise M38
ABC/Générale des Eaux M45
Thompson/Pilkington M51
Metallgesellschaft/Safic Alcan M53
UAP/Transatlantic/Sunlife M54
Lucas/Eaton M57
Ingersoll Rand/Dresser M59
Courtaulds/SNIA M62
Sunrise M67
Saab/Encsson Space M68
Volvo Atlas M69
Ericsson/Kolbe M72
Spar/Dansk Supermarket M73
Tarmac/Steetley M75

2. Autonomous economic entity

2.1. Full function JV

Baxter/Nestlé/Salvia M11 (paras. 6–8)
Sanofi/Sterling Drug M27 (para. 7)
Draeger/IBM/HMP M33 (para. 5)*
ABC/Générale des Eaux M45 (para. 8)
Thompson/Pilkington M51 (para. 8)
UAP/Transatlantic/Sunlife M54 (para. 11)
TNT/GD Net M56 (paras. 13–15)
Lucas/Eaton M57 (paras. 11–12)*
Courtaulds/SNIA M62 (paras. 7–9)*

2.2 Own commercial policy

Sanofi/Sterling Drug M27 (para. 7)
Courtaulds/SNIA M62 (paras. 7–8)

2.3. Permanent structural change

Baxter/Nestlé/Salvia M11 (para. 6)*
Sanofi/Sterling Drug M27 (paras. 7–8)
Draeger/IBM/HMP M33 (paras. 6–12)
Lucas/Eaton M57 (paras. 11–12)*

3. No co-ordination of competitive behaviour

3.1. Actual competition between parents

Baxter/Netlé/Salvia M11 (para. 8)
Apollinaris/Schweppes M30 (paras. 5–8)
ELF/Enterprise M38 (paras. 6–7)
ABC/Générale des Eaux M45 (para. 9)
Thompson/Pilkington M51 (paras. 9–10)*
UAP/Transatlantic/Sunlife M54 (para. 12)
TNT/GD Net, M56 (paras. 14–17)
Sunrise M67 (paras. 30–42)*

3.2. Potential competition between parents

Mitsubishi/UCAR M7 (paras. 7–8)
Baxter/Nestlé/Salvia M11 (para. 6)
Sanofi/Sterling Drug M27 (para. 9)
Apollinaris/Schweppes M30 (para. 8)
Draeger/IBM/HMP M33 (paras. 6–12)
ABC/Générale des Eaux M45 (para. 9)
Thompson/Pilkington M51 (para. 11)*
UAP/Transatlantic/Sunlife M54 (para. 15)

3.3. Neighbouring market spill-over

Baxter/Nestlé/Salvia M11 (para. 10)
Apollinaris/Schweppes M30 (para. 8)*
ABC/Générale des Eaux M45 (para. 9)
UAP/Transatlantic/Sunlife M54 (para. 14–15)
Lucas/Eaton M57 (paras. 14–19)*
Ingersoll Rand/Dresser, M59 (paras. 9–10)
Courtaulds/SNIA M62 (para. 6)

3.4. Upstream/downstream market spill-over

Draeger/IBM/HMP M33 (para. 11)
ABC/Générale des Eaux M45 (para. 9)
Courtaulds/SNIA M62 (para. 7)

3.5. Competition between parents and the JV

Thompson/Pilkington M51 (para. 12)*
UAP/Transatlantic/Sunlife M54 (paras. 16–17)
Sunrise M67 (paras. 30–42)

D. RESIDUAL APPLICABILITY OF ARTICLES 85 AND 86

1. Do Articles 85 and 86 still apply to concentrations?

Article 22(2), Regulation 4064/89

2. List of cases relevant to Article 85(1)

Nicholas Frères Vitapro 4
SHV/Chevron 87
Reuter/BASF 107
Nutricia 206
BPCL/ICI 215
Mecaniver/PPG 225
ENI/Montedison 256
1st Comp. Rep. (para. 81)
2nd Comp. Rep. (paras. 19–20)
3rd Comp. Rep. (paras. 22–38)
4th Comp. Rep. (paras. 17–18)
Philip Morris, 14th Comp. Rep. (paras. 98–100)*
Carnaud/Sofreb. 17th Comp. Rep. (para. 70)*

2 Jurisdiction: Cases and References

British Airways/British Caledonian, 18th Comp. Rep. (para. 81)
Irish Distillers Group 18th Comp. Rep. (para. 80)*
Carnaud/Metal Box 19th Comp. Rep. (para. 69)
Stena-Holder 19th Comp. Rep. (para. 70)
GEC-Siemens/Plessey 325
Remia v. *Commission* 121
BAT v. *Commission & Philip Morris* 146*

3. List of cases relevant to Article 86

Continental Can 46*
Tetra Pak I 289*
Metaleurop 321
Michelin 165 8th Comp. Rep. (para. 146)
Avebe/ KSH 8th Comp. Rep. (paras. 147–148)
PSA Peugeot-Citroën 8th Comp. Rep. (para. 149)
BP-Ruhrgas 9th Comp. Rep. (paras. 94–95)
ITA-Tubi 9th Comp. Rep. (paras. 126, 127)
Vallourec 9th Comp. Rep. (paras. 128, 129)
Kaiser/Estel 9th Comp. Rep. (para. 131)
Coats Patons 9th Comp. Rep. (para. 132)
Fichtel 9th Comp. Rep. (para. 133)
10th Comp. Rep. (paras. 150-151)
Pilkington/BSN 10th Comp. Rep. (paras. 152–155)
Michelin/Kleber-Colombes 10th Comp. Rep. (para. 156)
Baxter Tavenol Labs 10th Comp. Rep. (para. 157)
Amicon/Fortia & Wright 11th Comp. rep. (para. 112)
Eagle Star 12th Comp. Rep. (para. 103)
British Sugar-Berisford 12th Comp. Rep. (paras. 104–106)
British Bright Bar 13th Comp. Rep. (para. 160)
Dillingen 13th Comp. Rep. (para. 162)
British Steel 13th Comp. Rep. (para. 163)
Fagersta 13th Comp. Rep. (para. 164)
Berisford-Napier Brown 13th Comp. Rep. (paras. 165–166)
Ashland Oil Inc 14th Comp. Rep. (para. 109)
Stanton & Stavely 14th Comp. Rep. (para. 110)
Rhone Poulenc/Monsanto 19th Comp. Rep. (para. 67)
Consolidated Goldfields 19th Comp. Rep. (para. 68)
Continental Can v. *Commission* 35*
BAT v. *Commission & Philip Morris* 146*

E. ARTICLE 9: REFERRAL TO A MEMBER STATE

1. Concept

Article 9, Regulation 4064/89

2. Accepted requests

Tarmac/Steetley M75

3. Rejected requests

Alcatel/AEG Kabel M61

4. Cases in which request received and proceedings opened

Magneti-Marelli/CEAC M23
Varta/Bosch M41

F. ARTICLE 22(3): REFERRAL TO THE COMMISSION

G. LEGITIMATE INTERESTS

Article 21(3), Regulation 4064/89
Article 223(*b*) EEC

CHAPTER 3

SUBSTANTIVE ISSUES: ISSUES AND REFERENCES

A. RELEVANT MARKET

1. Relevant product market

1.1. Definition of the term "relevant product market"

Aérospatiale-Alenia/de Havilland M48 (paras. 8–19)
(see also position under Article 86 page 215)

1.2. Relevant factors

1.2.1. Physical characteristics/end use

Renault/Volvo M1
Aérospatiale/MBB M15 (para. 9)
VIAG/Continental Can M26 (para. 12)
Tetra Pak/Alfa-Laval M37 (IV.B.2.1)*
Eridania/ISI M40 (para. 14)
Aérospatiale-Alénia/de Havilland M48 (paras. 8–19)*
Metallgesellschaft/Safic Alcan M53 (para. 14)
TNT/GD Net M56 (paras. 20–29)
Eurocom/RSCG M60 (paras. 8–11)
Courtaulds/SNIA M62 (para. 9–14)

1.2.2. Price

Digital/Kienzle M14 (para. 10)
VIAG/Continental Can M26 (para. 12)
Mannesmann/Boge M47 (para. 11)
Aérospatiale-Alenia/de Havilland M48*

Book Two: Mergers and Acquisitions

Metallgesellschaft/Safic Alcan M53 (para. 15)
Courtaulds/SNIA M62 (para. 13)

1.2.3. Consumer preference

VIAG/Continental Can M26 (para. 12)
Courtaulds/SNIA M62 (para. (c)

1.2.4. Supply-side substitutability/potential competition

VIAG/Continental Can M26 (para. 13)
Aérospatiale-Alenia/de Havilland M48 (para. 14)*
Metallgesellschaft/Safic Alcan M53 (para. 14)
Lucas/Eaton M57 (paras. 21–22)*

1.2.5. industry product classifications

Sanofi/Sterling Drug M27 (paras. 21–24)

1.2.6. Relevant evidence

1.2.6.1. Consumer surveys

Tetra Pak/Alfa-Laval M37 (para. IV.B.2)*
Aérospatiale-Alenia/de Havilland M48 (para. 13)

1.2.6.2. "Conditions of competition"

Magneti-Marelli/CEAC M23 (para. 10)*
Varta/Bosch M41 (paras. 13–16, 37)*
Mannesmann/Boge M47 (paras. 10–13)
Metallgesellschaft/Safic Alcan M53 (para. 14)

1.2.6.3. Historical evidence on cross-elasticity

Chiquita, 101

2. Relevant geographic market

2.1. Definition of the term "relevant geographic market"

Eridania/ISI M40
(See also position under Article 86 p.215)

2.2. Relevant factors

2.2.1. Regulatory trade barriers

ELF/ERTOIL M20
Sanofi/Sterling Drug M27 (paras. 17–20)*
UAP/Transatlantic/Sunlife M54 (para. 21)*
Alcatel/AEG Kabel M61 (paras. 14–17)
Courtaulds/SNIA M62 (paras. 15–16)

2.2.2. Local specification requirements

Renault/Volvo M1 (para. 17)*
Magneti-Marelli/CEAC M23 (para. 16)
Varta/Bosch M41 (paras. 21–22)
Alcatel/AEG Kabel M61 (paras. 14–17)

2.2.3. National procurement policies

MBB/Aérospatiale M15 (paras. 10–12)*
Alcatel/Telettra M18 (paras. 33–34)
Thompson/Pilkington M51 (paras. 21-24)
Alcatel/AEG Kabel M61 (paras. 14–17)*

2.2.4. Adequate distribution facilities

Fiat Genotech/Ford New Holland M12 (paras. 26–30)*
Magneti-Marelli/CEAC M23 (para. 16)
Eridania/ISI M40 (para. 22)
Varta/Bosch M41 (paras. 28–30, 40)

2.2.5. Transport costs

VIAG/Continental Can M26 (para. 15)*
Eridania/ISI M40 (para. 22)

2.2.6. Language

Otto/Grattan M17 (para. 10)
La Redoute/Empire M19 (para. 12)

2.2.7. Consumer preferences

Renault/Volvo M1 (para. 17)
Magneti-Marelli/CEAC M23*
Varta/Bosch M41 (paras. 25–27, 40)*

2.3. Relevant evidence

2.3.1. Price differences between neighbouring areas

ICI/Tioxide M3 (para. 12)
Mitsubishi/UCAR M7 (para. 10)
Magneti-Marelli/CEAC M23 (para. 16)*
Varta/Bosch M41 (para. 18)*
Mannesmann/Boge M47 (para. 11)

2.3.2. Market share differences between neighbouring areas

Magneti-Marelli/CEAC M23 (para. 16)*
Varta/Bosch M41 (para. 18)*

2.3.3. Homogeneous conditions of competition

Magneti-Marelli/CEAC M23 (para. 16)*
Varta/Bosch M41 (para. 29)*
Mannesmann/Boge M47 (para. 15)

3 Substantive Issues: Issues and References

2.4. Examples of local markets

Promodes/Dirsa M5 (para. 8)

2.5. Examples of regional markets

VIAG/Continental Can M26 (paras. 16–17)
Eridania/ISI M40 (paras. 22–25)

2.6. Examples of national markets

AG/Amev M2 (para. 12)
Fiat/Ford New Holland M12 (paras. 16–18, 24–26, 30)
Otto/Grattan M17 (para. 10)
Alcatel/Telettra M18 (paras. 33–34)
La Redoute/Empire M19 (para. 12)
Usinor/ASD M21 (para. 8)
Sanofi/Sterling Drug M27 (para. 17)
Thompson/Pilkington M51 (paras. 21–24)
UAP/Transatlantic/Sunlife M54 (para. 21)
TNT/GD Net M56 (paras. 31–33)
Alcatel/AEG Kabel M61 (paras. 13–17)

2.7. Examples of Community markets

Fiat/Ford New Holland M12 (paras. 16–18, 21–22)
Tetra Pak/Alfa-Laval M37 (paras. IV.B.2.3)
Mannesmann/Boge M47 (paras. 14–16)
Metallgesellschaft/Safic Alcan M53 (paras. 20–21)
Lucas/Eaton M57 (para. 35)
Alcatel/AEG Kabel M61 (paras. 13–17)
Courtaulds/SNIA M62 (paras. 15–16)

2.8. Examples of world markets

Aérospatiale/MBB M17 (para. 18)
Aérospatiale-Alenia/de Havilland M30 (para. 20)
Metallgesellschaft/Safic Alcan M53 (paras. 17–19)

B. DOMINANCE

1. Definition of the term "dominance"

Continental Can (para. 3)*
United Brands v. *Commission* 62 (grounds 63–65)
Hoffman-La Roche v. *Commission* 67 (grounds 38–41, 70–71)*
Michelin v. *Commission* 102 (grounds 57–59)
Renault/Volvo M1

2. Relevant factors

2.1. Market share

Hoffman-La Roche v. *Commission* 67, (grounds 38–41, 51, 57–58, 61–63)*
Akzo v. *Commission III* 186 (grounds 60)
Alcatel/Telettra M18 (para. 37)
Magneti-Marelli/CEAC M23 (para. 16)
Tetra Pak/Alfa-Laval M37 (para. IV.B.3.2)*
Varta/Bosch M41 (paras. 32–33)
Digital/Philips M44 (para. 18)
Mannesmann/Boge M47 (paras. 18–19, 27)
Aérospatiale-Alenia/de Havilland, M48 (paras. 28–31)*
Lucas/Eaton M57 (paras. 36–37)

2.2. Size and importance of competitors

Michelin 165 (paras. 15, 17, 35)
United Brands v. *Commission* 62 (grounds 109–121)
Hoffman-La Roche v. *Commission* 67 (grounds 48, 51, 58)*
Volvo/Renault M1 (para. 14)
Tetra Pak/Alfa-Laval M37 (paras. IV.B.3.3, B.3.4, C.3.2)*
Varta/Bosch M41 (paras. 33–34, 45–50, 58–63)
Mannesmann/Boge M47 (paras. 20–28, 34–36)
Aérospatiale-Alenia/de Havilland M48 (paras. 34–42)*
Metallgesellschaft/Safic Alcan M53 (paras. 22, 24)
Courtaulds/SNIA M62 (paras. 20–29)*

2.3. Commercial advantages over competitors (product range)

Vitamins, 104, (paras. 4, 6, 8, 21)
British Plaster Board 299, (paras, 43, 120)
Michelin 165 (paras. 13, 36)
United Brands v. *Commission* 62 (grounds 69–96)
AT&T/NCR M9 (paras. 28–30)
Aérospatiale-Alenia/de Havilland M48 (paras. 32–33)

2.4. Technical advantages over competitors

Tetra Pak I 289 (para. 44)
United Brands v. *Commission* 62 (grounds 82–83)*
Michelin 165 (para. 13)

2.5. Statutory dominance or monopoly

General Motors 84*
British Telecommunications 188 (paras. 25–27)*
General Motors v. *Commission* 46 (ground 4–10)*
Télémarketing v. *CLT* 124 (ground 17)
British Leyland v. *Commission* 136

2.6. Supply-side substitutability: entry barriers

2.6.1. Basic concept

Alcatel/Telettra M18 (paras. 38–40)
Tetra Pak/Alfa-Laval M37 (paras. IV.B.3.4)*
Varta/Bosch M41 (paras. 31–40)
Aérospatiale-Alenia/de Havilland M48 (paras. 53–63)*
Lucas/Eaton M57 (para. 371)
Courtaulds/SNIA M62 (paras. 22–29)*

2.6.2. Regulatory barriers

Eridania/ISI M40 (para. 14)
Courtaulds/SNIA M62 (paras. 22–29)*

2.6.3. Risk

Draeger/IBM/HMP M33 (para. 10)
Tetra Pak/Alfa-Laval M37 (paras. IV.3.4, IV.4)
Aérospatiale-Alenia/de Havilland M48 (paras. 54–63)

2.6.4. Commercial/technical/marketing entry barriers

Metallgesellschaft/Safic Alcan M53 (para. 22)
Tetra Pak/Alfa-Laval M37 (para. IV.B.3.4)*

2.7 Imperfect substitutes

Sanofi/Sterling Drug M27 (paras. 12, 24–25)
Courtauld/SNIA M62 (para. 26)

2.8. Buying power

Alcatel/Telettra M18
VIAG/Continental Can M26 (para. 21)
Pechiney/Usinor-Sacilor M31 (para. 30)
Mannesmann/Boge M47 (paras. 29–31)
Aérospatiale-Alenia/de Havilland M48 (paras. 43–50)
Metallgesellschaft/Safic Alcan M53 (para. 22)
Lucas/Eaton M57 (para. 37(d)

2.9. Stage of market development

Tetra Pak/Alfa-Laval M37 (para. IV.B.3.4.)
Aérospatiale-Alenia/de Havilland M48 (paras. 54–63)*
TNT/GD Net M56 (para. 43)

2.10. Capital requirements

3. Vertical mergers

Chiquita 101 (para. 11.A.2)
United Brands v. *Commission* 62 (grounds 69–96)
ICI/Tioxide M3 (paras. 15–18)

Cargill/Unilever M6 (para. 5)
VIAG/Continental Can M26 (paras. 41–51)*

4. Conglomerate mergers

Matsushita/MCA M8
AT&T/NCR M9 (para. 23–31)
Tetra Pak/Alfa-Laval M37*
INFINT/EXOR M79

C. SIGNIFICANT IMPEDIMENT OF COMPETITION

Aérospatiale/Alenia/de Havilland M48

D. EFFICIENCY DEFENCE

Article 2(1)(b) and preamble 13, Regulation 4064/89
AT&T/NCR M9 (paras. 28–30)
Aérospatiale-Alenia/de Havilland M48 (paras. 65–71)*

E. FAILING-FIRM DEFENCE

Kelt/American Express M42

F. OLIGOPOLISTIC OR JOINT DOMINANCE

European Sugar Industry 69
Flat Glass 300 (paras. 78–79)
Alsatel v. *Novosam* 160 (ground 21)
Varta/Bosch M41 (para. 32)
Alcatel/AEG Kabel M61 (paras. 19–27)

G. ANCILLARY RESTRAINTS

1. Trademark Licences

Article 8(2), Regulation 4064/89
Fiat/Ford New Holland M12 (paras. 7–9)

2. Patent/know-how licences

Article 8(2), Regulation 4064/89
Thompson/Pilkington M51 (para. 14)

3. Product/service supply agreement

Article 8(2), Regulation 4064/89
SHV/Chevron 87
Reuter/BASF 107
BPCL/ICI 215
ENI-Montedison 256
Fiat/Ford New Holland M12 (paras. 7–9)
Otto/Grattan M17 (paras. 5–6)
Digital/Philips M44 (para. 26)
Courtaulds/SNIA M62 (paras. 30–31)

4. Non-competition clause

Article 8(2), Regulation 4064/89

3 Substantive Issues: Issues and References

Nicholas Frères Vitapro 4
SHV/Chevron 87
Reuter/BASF 107
Nutricia 206*
Mechaniver/PPG 225
ENI-Montedison 256
6th Comp. Rep. (paras. 60–63)
Sedame/Precilec. 11th Comp. Rep. (para. 95)
Tyler/Linde.11th Comp. Rep. (para. 96)
Allied/VIL 19th Comp. Rep. (para. 41)
Fiat/Ford New Holland M12 (paras. 8–9)
VIAG/Continental Can M26 (para. 52)
Sanofi/Sterling Drug M27 (point V)
Draeger/IBM/HMP M33 (paras. 12–20)
ELF/Enterprise M38 (para. 7)
Digital/Philips M44 (para. 25)
ABC/Générale des Eaux M45 (para. 14)
Thompson/Pilkington M51 (para. 14)
TNT/GD Net M56 (paras. 58–61)*
Ingersoll Rand/Dresser M59 (para. 18)
Courtaulds/SNIA M62 (para. 32)

CHAPTER 4

PROCEDURAL ASPECTS

1. Pre-notification guidance

Preamble 8 regulation 2367/90

2. Notification

Article 4 Regulation 4064/89
Articles 1–5 Regulation 2367/90

3. Suspension

Article 7 Regulation 4064/89
Article 11 Regulation 2367/90

4. Fact finding

Articles 11–13 Regulation 4064/89
See also position under Articles 85 and 86, page 389 *et seq.*

5. Opening of proceedings

Article 6 Regulation 4064/89

6. Rights of defense and complainants

Article 18 Regulation 4064/89
Articles 11–15 Regulation 2367/90
See also position under Articles 85 and 86, pages 389, 394 *et seq.*

7. Role of the Member States

Article 19 Regulation 4064/89

8. Time limits

Article 10 Regulation 4064/89
Articles 6–10, 17, 19 Regulation 2367/90

9. Types of decisions available to the Commission

Articles 7, 8, 14–15 Regulation 4064/89

10. Amendments to concentration to get clearance/undertakings

10.1. 1st stage

Fiat/Ford New Holland M12, (para. 30)
TNT/GD Net, M56, (paras. 46–47)
Grand Met./Cinzano M74

10.2. 2nd stage

Alcatel/Telettra M18 (paras. 44–46)
Magnetti-Marelli/CEAC M23 (para. 19)
Varta/Bosch M41 (para. 51-56)

BOOK THREE

COAL AND STEEL

BOOK THREE—CONTENTS

Lists and Tables

Table 1:	Chronological List of ECSC Legislation.....................	495
Table 2:	Chronological List of Commission Decisions (ECSC)—References...	496
Table 3:	Chronological List of Commission Decision (ECSC)—Contents..	500
Table 4:	Chronological List of European Court Judgments (ECSC)—References..	504
Table 5:	Chronological List of European Judgments (ECSC)—Contents..	505
Table 6:	Alphabetical List of Commission Decisions (ECSC)	506
Table 7:	Alphabetical List of European Court Judgments (ECSC).....	507

TABLE 1

CHRONOLOGICAL LIST OF ECSC LEGISLATION

1. **High Authority Decision No. 24–54** of May 6, 1954 laying down in implementation of Article 66(1) of the Treaty a regulation on what constitutes control of an undertaking. ([1954] J.O. 345; [1952–58] O.J. Spec. Ed. 16)

2. **High Authority Decision No. 26–54** of May 6, 1954 laying down in implementation of Article 66(4) of the Treaty a regulation concerning information to be furnished ([1954] J.O. 350; [1952–58] O.J. Spec. Ed. 17)

3. **High Authority Decision No. 14–64** of July 8, 1964 on business books and accounting documents which undertakings must produce for inspection by officials or agents of the High Authority carrying out checks or verifications as regards prices. ([1964] O.J. 120/1967)

4. **High Authority Decision No. 1–65** of February 3, 1965 concerning notification of decisions on information to be obtained from checks to be made on associations of undertakings for the purposes of application of Article 65 of the Treaty. ([1965] O.J. 27/438).

5. **High Authority Decision No. 25–67** of June 22, 1967 laying down in implementation of Article 66(3) of the Treaty a Regulation concerning exemption from prior authorisation, ([1967] O.J. 154/11; [1967] O.J. Spec. Ed. 186).

    as amended by Commission decision No. 2495/78/ECSC ([1978] O.J. L300/21). Text of Decision No. 25–67 as amended: ([1978] O.J. C255/2).

    and by Commission Decision No. 3654/91/ECSC ([1991] O.J. L348/12).

6. **Commission Decision No. 715/78/ECSC** of April 6, 1978 concerning limitation periods in proceedings and the enforcement of sanctions under the Treaty establishing the European Coal and Steel Community ([1978] O.J. L94/22).

7. **Commission Decision No. 379/84/ECSC** of February 15, 1984 defining the powers of officials and agents of the Commission instructed to carry out the checks provided for in the ECSC Treaty and the decisions taken in application thereof. ([1984] O.J. L46/23).

8. **Communication on co-operation ([1968] O.J. C75/3; as modified by [1968] O.J. C84/17).**

Book 3—Table 2

TABLE 2

CHRONOLOGICAL LIST OF COMMISSION DECISIONS (ECSC)—REFERENCES

No.	NAME	DATE	O.J.[1]	C.M.L.R.[2]	C.C.H.[3]
CS1	Scrap Fund I	26.3.55	55/685	—	—
CS2	COBECHAR I	3.10.56	56/295	—	—
CS3	Scrap Fund II	26.1.57	57/61	—	—
CS4	OKB I	26.7.57	57/352	—	—
CS5	Union Charbonnière	4.11.59	59/1147	—	—
CS6	OKB II	28.3.62	62/873	—	—
CS7	COBECHAR II	16.1.63	63/162	—	—
CS8	Präsident I	20.3.63	63/1191	—	—
CS9	Geitling I	20.3.63	63/1173	—	—
CS10	Geitling II	27.6.63	63/1838	—	—
CS11	SOREMA	15.7.64	64/1969	—	—
CS12	Geitling III	15.12.65	65/3249	—	—
CS13	Präsident II	15.12.65	65/3255	—	—
CS14	COBECHAR III	27.1.66	66/309	—	—
CS15	OKB III	23.11.66	66/3796	—	—
CS16	Walzstahlkontor I	15.3.67	67/1373	—	—
CS17	Stahlring I	14.6.67	67/2517	—	—
CS18	Geitling IV	22.6.67	67/1	—	—

[1] Official Journal of the European Communities
[2] Common Market Law Reports
[3] Commerce Clearing House

Chronological List of Commission Decisions (ECSC)—References

No.	NAME	DATE	O.J.		C.M.L.R.		C.C.H.
CS19	Präsident III	22.6.67	67/4		—		—
CS20	Kempense	19.12.67	67/10		—		—
CS21	Falck/Redaelli I	21.12.67	[1968]	L24/16	[1968]	91	—
CS22	Walzstahlkontor II	19.6.68	[1968]	L218/6			—
CS23	Creusot/Loire	9.7.68	[1968]	L164/17			—
CS24	Saarlor I	19.12.68	[1969]	L7/1			—
CS25	Geitling V	27.11.69	[1969]	L69/11			—
CS26	Präsident IV	27.11.69	[1969]	L304/12			—
CS27	COBECHAR IV	22.12.69	[1970]	L10/16			—
CS28	German scrap cartel	21.1.70	[1970]	L29/30	[1970]	503	—
CS29	Thyssen/Krupp/Wuppermann	27.7.71	[1971]	L201/1			—
CS30	Hoesch/Rheinstahl	27.7.71	[1971]	L201/12			—
CS31	Maxhütte/Klöckner I	27.7.71	[1971]	L201/19			—
CS32	Dillinger/Arbed I	27.7.71	[1971]	L201/27			—
CS33	Stahlring II	22.3.72	[1972]	L85/17			—
CS34	OKB IV	21.4.72	[1972]	L112/22	[1972]	D110	—
CS35	Hoesch/Benteler	9.11.72	[1972]	L283/17	[1973]	D121	—
CS36	COBECHAR V	20.3.73	[1973]	L102/19	[1973]	D197	—
CS37	Ruhrkohle	21.12.72	[1973]	L120/14	[1973]	D199	—
CS38	Thyssen/Rheinstahl	20.12.73	[1974]	L84/36	2 [1974]	D1	—
CS39	Danish Steel Distributors	21.12.73	[1974]	L30/29	2 [1974]	D43	—
CS40	Steelmaking Supplies	22.1.74	[1974]	L52/22	2 [1974]	D37	—
CS41	GKN/Miles Druce	14.3.74	[1974]	L132/28	2 [1974]	D17	—
CS42	Saarlor II	4.4.74	[1974]	L113/18	2 [1974]	D48	—
CS43	BSC/Lye Trading	14.10.74	[1975]	L13/45	[1975]	D38	—
CS44	Thyssen/SOLMER	20.11.74	[1975]	L49/13			—
CS45	Gelsenberg	16.12.74	[1975]	L65/16			—
CS46	Ruhrkohle	19.12.74	[1975]	L21/19			—
CS47	Marcoke	24.1.75	[1975]	L65/19			—
CS48	CLIF/Marine-Firminy	5.3.75	[1975]	L196/27	1 [1975]	D42	—
CS49	Krupp/Stahlwerke	2.4.75	[1975]	L130/13			—
CS50	IVECO	7.4.75	[1975]	L196/41			—
CS51	Minerais Préréduits	3.7.75	[1975]	L249/22	2 [1975]	D64	—
CS52	EGAM/Vetrocoke	11.7.75	[1976]	L7/13			—
CS53	Maxhütte/Klöckner II	13.2.76	[1976]	L95/21	1 [1976]	D90	—
CS54	Dillinger/Arbed II	13.2.76	[1976]	L95/23			—
CS55	COBECHAR VI	18.2.76	[1976]	L95/25			—

497

Book 3—Table 2

No.	NAME	DATE	O.J.		C.M.L.R.		C.C.H.
CS56	Saarlor III	12.3.76	[1976]	L78/18	1 [1976]	D96	—
CS57	BSC/Walter Blume	30.3.76	[1976]	L94/44	—		—
CS58	Walker/Champion	20.5.76	[1976]	L198/6	—		—
CS59	Maxhütte/Klockner III	28.7.76	[1976]	L270/31	1 [1977]	D4	—
CS60	Dillinger/Arbed III	28.7.76	[1976]	L270/33	—		—
CS61	Rötzel/Krupp	20.12.76	[1976]	L45/25	—		—
CS62	Arbed	20.12.76	[1976]	L45/32	1 [1977]	D97	—
CS63	Klöckner/Maxhütte IV	22.12.76	[1977]	L43/32	1 [1977]	D108	—
CS64	Saarlor IV	4.3.77	[1977]	L78/20	—		—
CS65	Stahlring III	5.4.77	[1977]	L97/33	—		—
CS66	British steel producers	17.6.77	[1977]	L173/19	2 [1977]	D58	—
CS67	Maier/Röchling	12.7.77	[1977]	L217/11	[1977]	D63	—
CS68	Röchling-Burbach	27.7.77	[1977]	L243/20	2 [1977]	D25	—
CS69	COIMPRE	14.11.77	[1977]	L309/18	[1978]	D1	—
CS70	Framtek	23.11.77	[1977]	L320/52	1 [1978]	D17	—
CS71	Arbed/Rodange	6.6.78	[1978]	L164/14	2 [1978]	767	—
CS72	Ruhrkohle/Brennstoffhandel	7.6.78	[1978]	L191/38	3 [1978]	40	—
CS73	Creusot-Loire/Vgine	20.7.78	[1978]	L242/10	1 [1979]	349	—
CS74	VCRO	28.7.78	[1978]	L238/28	1 [1979]	527	—
CS75	Falck/Redaelli II	20.10.78	[1978]	L324/26	1 [1979]	357	—
CS76	COBECHAR VII	16.11.78	[1978]	L329/37	1 [1979]	462	—
CS77	Cockerill/Klöckner	12.1.79	[1979]	L19/37	2 [1979]	236	—
CS78	Cockerill/Estel	12.1.79	[1979]	L19/41	2 [1979]	243	—
CS79	Lange/Stinnes	15.1.79	[1979]	L19/44	2 [1979]	207	—
CS80	Irish Steel/Dunkerque	27.3.79	[1979]	L103/27	2 [1979]	527	—
CS81	BSC/Dunlop & Ranken	26.7.79	[1979]	L245/30	3 [1979]	631	—
CS82	Saarlor V	6.11.79	[1979]	L295/24	2 [1980]	161	—
CS83	Manganese	20.12.79	[1980]	L24/43	3 [1980]	762	—
CS84	German rolled steel	8.2.80	[1980]	L62/28	3 [1980]	193	—
CS85	Hoogovens/Ijzerhandel	14.3.80	[1980]	L85/47	2 [1980]	605	—
CS86	Chamber of Coal Traders	19.12.80	[1980]	L374/34	2 [1982]	730	—
CS87	Boël/Claberg	31.3.81	[1981]	L167/1	1 [1983]	226	—
CS88	Rogesa	18.6.81	[1981]	L189/54	3 [1982]	438	—
CS89	Eurocoal	14.9.81	[1981]	L290/21	2 [1982]	659	—
CS90	Zentralkokerei	30.11.81	[1981]	L364/39	3 [1982]	41	—
CS91	Chamber of Coal Traders II	10.12.81	[1981]	L8/21	—		—
CS92	Usinor/Sacilor/Normandie	2.4.82	[1982]	L139/1	2 [1983]	462	—

498

Chronological List of Commission Decisions (ECSC)—References

No.	NAME	DATE	O.J.	C.M.L.R.	C.C.H.
CS93	Stahlring IV	26.7.82	[1982] L237/34	2 [1983] 307	—
CS94	UNICO	24.4.84	[1984] L139/37	—	—
CS96	Arbed/Cockerill-Sambre	28.5.84	[1984] L163/37	2 [1985] 83	—
CS96	Steelmaking Supplies II	21.9.84	[1984] L268/35	1 [1985] 801	—
CS97	Manganese II	24.4.85	[1985] L119/42	—	—
CS98	Röchling-Posserl	5.2.86	[1986] L39/57	4 [1988] 213	—
CS99	NICIA	21.3.86	[1986] L115/19	—	—
CS100	Saarlor VI	12.12.86	[1987] L20/37	—	—
CS101	British Fuel	9.7.87	[1987] L224/16	—	—
CS102	Arbed/Unimetal	14.7.88	[1988] L223/39	—	—
CS103	Eschweiler/Ruhrkohle	19.12.88	[1989] L14/37	—	—
CS104	Ruhrkohle	30.3.89	[1989] L101/35	—	—
CS105	British Steel/Walker	8.5.90	[1990] L131/27	—	—
CS106	Stainless Steel Cartel	18.7.90	[1990] L220/17	—	—
CS107	Arbed/Usinor-Sacilor	9.9.91	[1991] L281/17	—	—

TABLE 3
CHRONOLOGICAL LIST OF COMMISSION DECISIONS (ECSC)—CONTENTS

No.	NAME	TYPE OF DECISION	PRODUCT	SUBJECT	FINE	No. of ECJ Ruling
CS1	Scrap fund I	Authorisation	Scrap	Equalization	—	—
CS2	COBECHAR I	Authorisation	Coal	Joint sales	—	—
CS3	Scrap fund II	Authorisation	Scrap	Equalization	—	CS6 & CS16
CS4	OKB I	Authorisation	Coal	Joint buying	—	CS5 & CS9
CS5	Union Charbonnière	Authorisation	Coal	Joint sales	—	—
CS6	OKB II	Authorisation	Coal	Joint buying	—	—
CS7	COBECHAR II	Authorisation	Coal	Joint sales	—	—
CS8	Präsident I	Authorisation	Coal	Joint sales	—	CS19
CS9	Geitling I	Authorisation	Coal	Joint sales	—	CS19
CS10	Geitling II	Modification	Coal	Joint sales	—	CS19
CS11	SOREMA	Revocation	Coal	Joint sales	—	CS20
CS12	Geitling III	Authorisation	Coal	Joint buying	—	—
CS13	Präsident II	Authorisation	Coal	Joint sales	—	—
CS14	COBECHAR III	Authorisation	Coal	Joint sales	—	—
CS15	OKB III	Authorisation	Coal	Joint buying	—	—
CS16	Walzstahlkontor I	Authorisation	Steel	Joint sales	—	—
CS17	Stahlring I	Authorisation	Steel	Joint buying	—	—
CS18	Geitling IV	Authorisation	Coal	Joint sales	—	—
CS19	Präsident III	Authorisation	Coal	Joint sales	—	—
CS20	Kempense	Authorisation	Coal	Joint sales	—	—
CS21	Falck/Redaelli I	Authorisation	Steel	Specialisation	—	—
CS22	Walzstahlkontor II	Authorisation	Steel	Joint sales	—	—
CS23	Creusot/Loire	Authorisation	Steel	Specialisation	—	—
CS24	Saarlor I	Authorisation	Coal	Joint sales	—	—
CS25	Geitling V	Revocation	Coal	Joint sales	—	—
CS26	Präsident IV	Revocation	Coal	Joint sales	—	—
CS27	COBECHAR IV	Authorisation	Coal	Joint sales	—	—

Chronological List of Commission Decisions (ECSC)—Contents

No.	NAME	TYPE OF DECISION	PRODUCT	SUBJECT	FINE	No. of ECJ Ruling
CS28	German scrap cartel	Prohibition	Scrap	Cartel 1–291	—	—
CS29	Thyssen/Krupp/Wuppermann	Authorisation	Steel	Specialisation	—	—
CS30	Hoesch/Rheinstahl	Authorisation	Steel	Specialisation	—	—
CS31	Maxhütte/Klöckner I	Authorisation	Steel	Specialisation	—	—
CS32	Dillinger/Arbed I	Authorisation	Steel	Specialisation	—	—
CS33	Stahlring II	Authorisation	Steel	Joint buying	—	—
CS34	OKB IV	Authorisation	Coal	Joint buying	—	—
CS35	Hoesch/Benteler	Authorisation	Steel	Specialisation	—	—
CS36	COBECHAR V	Authorisation	Coal	Joint sales	—	—
CS37	Ruhrkohle	Authorisation	Coal	Article 66	—	CS23
CS38	Thyssen/Rheinstahl	Authorisation	Iron	Article 66	—	—
CS39	Danish Steel Distributors	Authorisation	Steel	Joint buying	—	—
CS40	Steelmaking Supplies	Authorisation	Scrap	Joint buying	—	CS21 & CS22
CS41	GKN/Miles Druce	Authorisation	Steel	Article 66	—	—
CS42	Saarlor II	Authorisation	Coal	Joint sales	—	—
CS43	BSC/Lye Trading	Authorisation	Steel	Article 66	—	—
CS44	Thyssen/SOLMER	Authorisation	Iron	Article 66	—	—
CS45	Gelsenberg	Authorisation	Coal	Article 66	—	—
CS46	Ruhrkohle	Authorisation	Coal	Article 66	—	—
CS47	Marcoke	Authorisation	Coke	Article 66	—	—
CS48	CLIF/Marine-Firminy	Authorisation	Steel	Article 66	—	—
CS49	Krupp/Stahlwerke	Authorisation	Steel	Article 66	—	—
CS50	IVECO	Authorisation	Steel	Article 66	—	—
CS51	Minerais Préréduits	Authorisation	Iron	Joint buying	—	—
CS52	EGAM/Vetrocoke	Authorisation	Coke	Article 66	—	—
CS53	Maxhütte/Klöckner II	Authorisation	Steel	Article 66	—	—
CS54	Dillinger/Arbed II	Authorisation	Steel	Article 66	—	—
CS55	COBECHAR VI	Authorisation	Coal	Joint sales	—	—
CS56	Saarlor III	Authorisation	Coal	Joint sales	—	—
CS57	BSC/Walter Blume	Authorisation	Steel	Article 66	—	—
CS58	Walker/Champion	Authorisation	Steel	Joint buying	—	—
CS59	Maxhütte/Klöckner III	Authorisation	Steel	Article 66	—	—
CS60	Dillinger/Arbed III	Authorisation	Steel	Article 66	—	—
CS61	Rötzel/Krupp	Authorisation	Steel	Specialisation	—	—
CS62	Arbed	Authorisation	Steel	Article 66	—	—
CS63	Klöckner/Maxhütte IV	Authorisation	Steel	Article 66	—	—

Book 3—Table 3

No.	NAME	TYPE OF DECISION	PRODUCT	SUBJECT	FINE	No. of ECJ Ruling
CS64	Saarlor IV	Authorisation	Coal	Joint sales	—	—
CS65	Stahlring III	Authorisation	Steel	Joint buying	—	—
CS66	British steel producers	Authorisation	Scrap	Joint buying	—	—
CS67	Maier/Röchling	Authorisation	Coal	Joint buying	—	—
CS68	Röchling-Burbach	Inspection	Steel	Article 47	—	—
CS69	COIMPRE	Authorisation	Iron	Joint buying	—	—
CS70	Framtek	Authorisation	Steel	Article 66	—	—
CS71	Arbed/Rodange	Authorisation	Steel	Article 66	—	—
CS72	Ruhrkohle/Brennstoffhandel	Authorisation	Coal	Article 66	—	—
CS73	Creusot-Loire/Ugine	Authorisation	Steel	Specialisation	—	—
CS74	UCRO	Authorisation	Steel	Joint sales	—	—
CS75	Falck/Redaelli II	Authorisation	Steel	Joint buying	—	—
CS76	COBECHAR VII	Authorisation	Coal	Joint sales	—	—
CS77	Cockerill/Klöckner	Authorisation	Steel	Specialisation	—	—
CS78	Cockerill/Estel	Authorisation	Steel	Specialisation	—	—
CS79	Lange/Stinnes	Authorisation	Coal	Article 66	—	—
CS80	Irish Steel/Dunkerque	Authorisation	Steel	Specialisation	—	—
CS81	BSC/Dunlop & Ranken	Authorisation	Steel	Article 66	—	—
CS82	Saarlor V	Authorisation	Coal	Joint sales	—	—
CS83	Manganese	Authorisation	Manganese	Joint sales	—	—
CS84	German rolled steel	Prohibition	Steel	Trade Assoc.	—	—
CS85	Hoogovens/Ijzerhandel	Authorisation	Scrap	Article 66	—	—
CS86	Chamber of Coal Traders	Authorisation	Coal	Equalization	—	—
CS87	Boël/Clabecq	Authorisation	Steel	Joint sales	—	—
CS88	Rogesa	Authorisation	Iron	Article 66	—	—
CS89	Eurocoal	Authorisation	Coal	Article 66	—	—
CS90	Zentralkokerei	Authorisation	Coke	Article 66	—	—
CS91	Chamber of Coal Traders II	Authorisation	Coal	Equalization	—	—
CS92	Usinor/Sacilor/Normandie	Authorisation	Steel	Article 66	—	—
CS93	Stahlring IV	Authorisation	Steel	Joint buying	—	—
CS94	UNICO	Authorisation	Coal	Article 66	—	—
CS95	Arbed/Cockerill-Sambre	Authorisation	Steel	Specialisation	—	—
CS96	Steelmaking Supplies II	Authorisation	Steel	Joint buying	—	—
CS97	Manganese II	Authorisation	Manganese	Joint sales	—	—
CS98	Röchling-Possehl	Authorisation	Steel	Article 66	—	—
CS99	NICIA	Authorisation	Coal	Joint buying	—	—
CS100	Saarlor VI	Authorisation	Coal	Joint sales	—	—

Chronological List of Commission Decisions (ECSC)—Contents

No.	NAME	TYPE OF DECISION	PRODUCT	SUBJECT	FINE	No. of ECJ Ruling
CS101	British Fuel	Authorisation	Coal	Article 66	—	—
CS102	Arbed/Unimétal	Authorisation	Steel	Specialisation	—	—
CS103	Eschweiler/Ruhrkohle	Authorisation	Coal	Article 66	—	—
CS104	Ruhrkohle	Authorisation	Coal	Joint buying	—	—
CS105	British Steel/Walker	Authorisation	Steel	Article 66	—	—
CS106	Stainless steel cartel	Prohibition	Steel	Cartel	25–100	2
CS107	Arbed/Usinor-Sacilor	Authorisation	Steel	Joint Sales	—	—

TABLE 4

CHRONOLOGICAL LIST OF EUROPEAN COURT JUDGMENTS (ECSC)—REFERENCES

Book 3—Table 4

No.	NAME	CASE No.	DATE	E.C.R.[1]	C.M.L.R.[2]	C.C.H.[3]
CS1	France v. HA	—	21.12.54	1	—	—
CS2	Italy v. HA	—	21.12.54	37	—	—
CS3	Netherlands v. HA	—	21.3.55	103	—	—
CS4	Geitling v. HA	—	20.3.57	3	—	—
CS5	Nold v. HA	—	4.12.57	121	—	—
CS6	Eisen und Stahlindustrie v. HA	—	21.6.58	265	—	—
CS7	Centre-Midi v. HA	—	26.6.58	375	—	—
CS8	Stork v. HA	—	4.2.59	17	—	—
CS9	Nold v. HA	—	20.3.59	41	—	—
CS10	Geitling v. HA	—	12.5.59	[1960] 34	—	—
CS11	Knutange v. HA	—	12.2.60	1	—	—
CS12	Geitling v. HA	—	12.2.60	17	—	—
CS13	Präsident v. HA	—	15.7.60	423	—	—
CS14	Opinion: Amendment to Article 65	—	13.12.61	243	—	—
CS15	Geitling v. HA	—	18.5.62	83	—	—
CS16	Worms v. HA	—	12.7.62	195	(1962) 113	—
CS17	Schlieker v. HA	—	4.7.63	85	(1963) 1	—
CS18	SOREMA v. HA	—	19.3.64	151	(1964) 350	—
CS19	Netherlands v. HA	—	15.7.64	533	(1964) 522	—
CS20	SOREMA v. HA	—	2.6.65	329	(1965) 329	—
CS21	Miles Druce v. Commission I	—	11.10.73	1049	1 (1974) 224	—
CS22	Miles Druce v. Commission II	—	16.3.74	281	2 (1974) D22	—
CS23	Nold v. Commission	—	14.5.74	491	2 (1974) 338	—

[1] European Court Reports   [2] Common Market Law Reports   [3] Commerce Clearing House

TABLE 5

CHRONOLOGICAL LIST OF EUROPEAN JUDGMENTS (ECSC)—CONTENTS

No.	NAME	ARTICLE	SUBJECT	RESULT	PRODUCT
CS1	*France v. H A*	33	Prices	Annulled in part	—
CS2	*Italy v. H A*	33	Prices	Annulled in part	—
CS3	*Netherlands v. H A*	33	Prices	Dismissed	Article 66
CS4	*Geitling v. H A*	33	Joint sales	Dismissed	Coal
CS5	*Nold v. H A*	33	Joint buying	Dismissed	Coal
CS6	*Eisen und Stahlindustrie v. H A*	33	Equalization	Dismissed	Scrap
CS7	*Centre – Midi v. H A*	33	Equalization	Dismissed	Scrap
CS8	*Stork v. H A*	33	Distribution	Dismissed	Coal
CS9	*Nold v. H A*	33	Joint buying	Dismissed	Coal
CS10	*Geitlung v. H A*	39	Joint sales	Dismissed	Coal
CS11	*Knutange v. H A*	33	Joint buying	Dismissed	Scrap
CS12	*Geitling v. H A*	33	Joint sales	Inadmissible	Coal
CS13	*Präsident v. H A*	33	Joint sales	Annulled in part	Coal
CS14	Opinion: Amendment to Article 65	95	—	Incompatibility	—
CS15	*Geitling v. H A*	35	Joint sales	Dismissed	Coal
CS16	*Worms v. H A*	40	Equalization	Dismissed	Scrap
CS17	*Schlieker v., H A*	35	Concentration	Dismissed	Steel
CS18	*SOREMA v. H A*	33	Joint buying	Annulled	Coal
CS19	*Netherlands v. H A*	33	Joint sales	Annulled in part	Coal
CS20	*SOREMA v. H A*	33 & 39	Joint buying	Dismissed	Coal
CS21	*Miles Druce v. Commission I*	39	Concentration	Dismissed	Steel
CS22	*Miles Druce v. Commission II*	—	—	—	—
CS23	*Nold v. Commission*	—	—	—	—

505

TABLE 6

ALPHABETICAL LIST OF COMMISSION DECISIONS (ECSC)

Arbed	CS62
Arbed/Cockerill-Sambre	CS96
Arbed/Rodange	CS71
Arbed/Unimetal	CS102
Arbed/Usinor-Sacilor	CS107
BSC/Dunlop & Ranken	CS81
BSC/Lye Trading	CS43
BSC/Walter Blume	CS57
Boël/Claberg	CS87
British Fuel	CS101
British steel producers	CS66
British Steel/Walker	CS105
CLIF/Marine-Firminy	CS48
COBECHAR I	CS2
COBECHAR II	CS7
COBECHAR III	CS14
COBECHAR IV	CS27
COBECHAR V	CS36
COBECHAR VI	CS55
COBECHAR VII	CS76
COIMPRE	CS69
Chamber of Coal Traders	CS86
Chamber of Coal Traders II	CS91
Cockerill/Estel	CS78
Cockerill/Klöckner	CS77
Creusot/Loire	CS23
Creusot-Loire/Vgine	CS73
Danish Steel Distributors	CS39
Dillinger/Arbed I	CS32
Dillinger/Arbed II	CS54
Dillinger/Arbed III	CS60
EGAM/Vetrocoke	CS52
Eschweiler/Ruhrkohle	CS103
Euro coal	CS89
Falck/Redaelli I	CS21
Falck/Redaelli II	CS75
Framtek	CS70
GKN/Miles Druce	CS41
Geitling I	CS9
Geitling II	CS10
Geitling III	CS12
Geitling IV	CS18
Geitling V	CS25
Gelsenberg	CS45
German rolled steel	CS84
German Scrap Cartel	CS28
Hoesch/Benteler	CS35
Hoesch/Rheinstahl	CS30
Hoogovens/Ijzerhandel	CS85
IVECO	CS50
Irish Steel/Dunkerque	CS80
Kempense	CS20
Klöckner/Maxhütte IV	CS63
Krupp/Stahlwerke	CS49
Lange/Stinnes	CS79
Maier/Röchling	CS67
Manganese	CS83
Manganese II	CS97
Marcoke	CS47
Maxhütte/Klöckner I	CS31
Maxhütte/Klöckner II	CS53
Maxhütte/Klockner III	CS59
Minerais Préréduits	CS51
NICIA	CS99
OKB I	CS4
OKB II	CS6
OKB III	CS15
OKB IV	CS34
Präsident I	CS8
Präsident II	CS13
Präsident III	CS19
Präsident IV	CS26
Röchling-Posser I	CS98
Rogesa	CS88
Rötzel/Krupp	CS61
Ruhrkohle	CS37
Ruhrkohle	CS46
Ruhrkohle	CS104
Ruhrkohle/Brennstoff handel	CS72
Röchling-Biobach	CS68
SOREMA	CS11
Saarlor I	CS24
Saarlor II	CS42
Saarlor III	CS56
Saarlor IV	CS64
Saarlor V	CS82
Saarlor VI	CS100
Scrap Fund I	CS1
Scrap Fund II	CS3
Stahlring I	CS17
Stahlring II	CS33
Stahling III	CS65
Stahlring IV	CS93
Stainless Steel Cartel	CS106
Steelmaking Supplies	CS40
Steelmaking Supplies II	CS96
Thyssen/Krupp/Wuppermann	CS29
Thyssen/Rheinstahl	CS38
Thyssen/Solmer	CS44
UNICO	CS94
Union Charbonnière	CS5
Usinor/Sacilor/Normandie	CS92
VCRO	CS74
Walker/Champion	CS58
Walzatahlkontor I	CS16
Walzstahlkontor II	CS22
Zentralkokerei	CS90

TABLE 7

ALPHABETICAL LIST OF EUROPEAN COURT JUDGMENTS (ECSC)

Centre-Midi v. HA	CS7	Nold v. HA	CS5
Eisen und Stahlindustrie v. HA	CS6	Nold v. HA	CS9
France v. HA	CS1	Nold v. Commission	CS23
Geitling v. HA	CS4	Opinion: Amendment to Article 65	CS14
Geitling v. HA	CS10	Präsident v. HA	CS13
Geitling v. HA	CS15	SOREMA v. HA	CS18
Italy v. HA	CS2	SOREMA v. HA	CS20
Miles Druce v. Commission I	CS21	Schlieker v. HA	CS17
Miles Druce v. Commission II	CS22	Stork v. HA	CS8
Netherlands v. HA	CS3	Worms v. HA	CS16
Netherlands v. HA	CS19		

BOOK THREE

COAL AND STEEL

CHAPTER 1

RESTRICTIVE PRACTICES

A. TEXT OF ARTICLE 65 ECSC

Article 65

1. All agreements between undertakings, decisions by associations of undertakings and concerted practices tending directly or indirectly to prevent, restrict or distort normal competition within the common market shall be prohibited, and in particular those tending:
(a) to fix or determine prices;
(b) to restrict or control production, technical development or investments;
(c) to share markets, products, customers or sources of supply.

2. However, the High Authority shall authorise specialisation agreements or joint-buying or joint-selling agreements in respect of particular products, if it finds that:
(a) such specialisation or such joint-buying or selling will make for a substantial improvement in the production or distribution of those products;
(b) the agreement in question is essential in order to achieve these results and is not more restrictive than is necessary for that purpose; and
(c) the agreement is not liable to give the undertakings concerned the power to determine the prices, or to control or restrict the production or marketing, of a substantial part of the products in question within the common market, or to shield them against effective competition from other undertakings within the common market.

If the High Authority finds that certain agreements are strictly analogous in nature and effect to those referred to above, having particular regard to the fact that that this paragraph applies to distributive undertakings, it shall authorise them also when satisfied that they meet the same requirements.

Authorisations may be granted subject to specified conditions and for limited periods. In such cases the High Authority shall renew an authorisation once or several times if it finds that the requirements of subparagraphs (a) to (c) are still met at the time of renewal.

The High Authority shall revoke or amend an authorisation if it finds that as a result of a change in circumstances the agreement no longer meets these requirements, or that the actual results of the agreement or of the application thereof are contrary to the requirements for its authorisation.

Decisions granting, renewing, amending, refusing or revoking an authorisation shall be published together with the reasons therefor; the restrictions imposed by the second paragraph of Article 47 shall not apply thereto.

3. The High Authority may, as provided in Article 47, obtain any information needed for the application of this Article, either by making a special request to the parties concerned or by means of regulations stating the kinds of agreement decision or practice which must be communicated to it.

4. Any agreement or decision prohibited by paragraph 1 of this Article shall be automatically void and may not be relied upon before any court or tribunal in the Member States.

The High Authority shall have sole jurisdiction, subject to the right to bring actions before the Court, to rule whether any such agreement or decision is compatible with this Article.

5. On any undertaking which has entered into an agreement which is automatically void, or has enforced or attempted to enforce, by arbitration, penalty, boycott or any other means, an agreement or decision which is automatically void or an agreement for which authorisation has been refused or revoked, or has obtained an authorisation by means of information which it knew to be false or misleading, or has engaged in practices prohibited by paragraph 1 of this Article, the High Authority may impose fines or periodic penalty payments not exceeding twice the

Book Three: Coal and Steel

turnover on the products which were subject of the agreement decision or practice, prohibited by this article; if, however, the purpose of the agreement, decision or practice is to restrict production, technical development or investment, this maximum may be raised to 10 per cent. of the annual turnover of the undertakings in question in the case of fines, and 20 per cent. of the daily turnover in the case of periodic penalty payments.

Communication: Outlines of competition policy on the structures of the Iron and Steel Industry, p.15

Opinion: Amendment to Article 65 [1970] O.J. C30, CS14

B. FORM OF PRACTICE WITHIN THE AMBIT OF THE TREATY

1. Binding agreements

German rolled steel CS84
NICIA CS100

2. Recommendations

German rolled steel CS84

3. Concerted practices

OKB I CS4
Präsident I CS8
Geitling I CS9
Geitling II CS10

4. Declarations of intent

Minerals Préréduits CS51

5. Associations of undertakings

German scrap cartel CS28
German rolled steel CS84
Stainless Steel Cartel CS106
NICIA CS100
SOREMA v. H A (pp. 161–162) CS18

C. PROHIBITED PRACTICES

1. Text of Communication on co-operation [1968] O.J. C75/3; modified [1968] O.J. C84/14

(reproduced below in French; there is no special edition translation)

Communication relative aux accords, décisions et pratiques concertées concernant la coopération entre entreprises

([1968] O.J. C75/3)

La Commission des Communautés européennes a été souvent interrogée sur la position qu'elle compte adopter, dans le cadre de l'application des règles de concurrence des traités de Rome et de Paris, à l'égard de la coopération entre entreprises. C'est pourquoi elle s'efforce, par la présente communication, de donner aux entreprises un certain nombre de précisions qui, tout en n'étant pas exhaustives, devraient néanmoins fournir aux entreprises des indications utiles sur l'interprétation à donner aux dispositions notamment de l'article 85 paragraphe 1 C.E.E. et de l'article 65 paragraphe 1 C.E.C.A.

I

La Commission considère avec faveur une coopération entre petites et moyennes entreprises dans la mesure où elle met celles-ci en état de travailler d'une manière plus rationnelle et d'augmenter leur productivité et leur compétitivité sur un marché élargi. Tout en estimant que sa tâche est de faciliter en particulier la coopération entre petites er moyennes entreprises, la Commission reconnaît que la coopération entre grandes entreprises peut, elle aussi, être économiquement souhaitable sans donner lieu à des objections du point de vue de la politique de concurrence.

En vertu de l'article 85 paragraphie 1 du traité instituant la Communauté économique européenne (traité C.E.E.) et de l'article 65 paragraph 1 du traité instituant la Communauté européenne du charbon et de l'acier (traité C.E.C.A.) sont incompatible savec le marché commun et interdits tous accords, toutes décisions et toutes pratiques concertées (ci-après appelés: accords) qui ont pour objet ou pour effet d'empêcher, de restreindre ou de fausser le jeu de la concurrence dans le marché commun (ci-après appelés: restrictions de concurrence) à la condition, toutefois, en ce qui concerne l'article 85 paragraphe 1 du traité C.E.E., que ces accords soient susceptibles d'affecter le commerce entre Etats membres.

La Commission estime qu'il est approprié et en particulier intéressant pour les petites et moyennes entreprises de faire connaître les considérations dont elle s'inspirera dans l'interprétation le l'article 85 paragraphe 1 du traité C.E.E. et de l'article 65 paragraphe 1 du traité C.E.C.A. er de leur application à certaines mesures de coopération entre entreprises et d'indiquer celles qui, à son avis, ne tombent pas sous ces dispositions. La présente communication s'adresse à toutes les entreprises, sans distinction de taille.

Il est possible que d'autres formes de coopération entre entreprises que celles citées ne soient pas interdites par l'article 85 paragraphe 1 du traité C.E.E. ou l'article 65 paragraphe 1 du traité C.E.C.A. C'est en particulier le cas, si la position globale sur le marché des entreprises coopérantes est trop faible pour que leur accord de coopération provoque une restriction sensible de la concurrence dans le marché commun et affecte, quant à l'application de l'article 85 du traité C.E.E., le commerce entre Etats membres.

Il convient, par ailleurs, de souligner que d'autres modes de coopération entre entreprises ou des accords comportant des clauses additionnelles, auxquels s'appliquent les règles de la concurrence des traités, peuvent être exemptés conformément à l'article 85 paragraphe 3 du traité C.E.E. ou autorisés conformément à l'article 65 paragraphe 2 du traité C.E.C.A. La Commission a l'intention de préciser rapidement par des décisions individuelles appropriées ou par des communications générales la situation des différentes formes de coopération par rapport aux règles des traités.

Il n'est pas possible de donner actuellement des indications générales sur l'application de l'article 86 du traité C.E.E. qui concerne l'exploitation abusive d'une position dominante sur le marché commun ou sur une partie de celui-ci. Cela est également valable pour l'article 66 paragraphe 7 du traité C.E.C.A.

La présente communication devrait, en règle générale, faire disparaître l'intérêt à obtenir une attestation négative au sens de l'article 2 du règlement n° 17 (J.O. 62/13) pour les accords visés. Il ne devrait pas, non plus, être nécessaire de vouloir clarifier la situation juridique par une décision individuelle de la Commission; il n'y a donc pas lieu de notifier dans ce but des accords de cette nature. Cependant, lorsqu'il y a un doute dans un cas particulier sur la question de savoir si un accord de coopération restreint la concurrence ou lorsque d'autres modes de coopération entre entreprises qui, de l'avis des entreprises, ne restreignent pas la concurrence ne sont pas mentionnées ici, les entreprises ont, dans le domaine d'application de l'article 85 paragraphe 1 du traité C.E.E., la possibilité de demander une attestation négative ou de présenter, à titre préventif, dans le domaine d'application de l'article 65 paragraphe 1 du traité C.E.C.A., une demande conformément à l'article 65 paragraphe 2 de ce traité.

La présente communication ne préjuge pas l'interprétation de la Cour de justice des Communautés européennes.

II

La Commission considère que les accords suivants ne restreignent pas la concurrence.

1. *Les accords qui ont uniquement pour objet:*
   (a) L'échange d'opinions et d'expériences,
   (b) l'étude en commun des marchés,
   (c) la réalisation en commun d'études comparées sur les entreprises et les secteurs économiques,
   (d) l'établissement en commun de statistiques et de schémas de calcul.

Les accords dont le seul but est de procurer en commun les informations dont les différentes entreprises ont besoin pour déterminer de manière autonome et indépendante leur comportement futur sur le marché ou de recourir individuellement à un organisme consultatif commun n'ont pour objet ou pour effet de restreindre la concurrence. Mais si la liberté d'action des entreprises est limitée ou si le comportement sur le marché est coordonné expressément ou par voie de pratiques concertées, il peut y avoir une restriction de la concurrence. C'est le cas notamment lorsque des recommandations sont faites concrètement ou lorsque des conclusions sont précisées de telle manière qu'elles provoquent de la part d'au moins une partie des entreprises participantes un comportement uniforme sur le marché.

L'échange d'informations peut avoir lieu entre les entreprises elles-mêmes ou par l'intermédiaire d'un organisme tiers. Toutefois, la distinction entre informations neutres du point de vue de la concurrence et un comportement restrictif de la concurrence est particulièrement difficile à faire dans les cas où des organismes sont chargés d'enregistrer les commandes, les chiffres d'affaires, les investissements et les prix, de sorte qu'en règle générale il n'est pas possible d'admettre sans plus que l'article 85 paragraphe 1 du traité C.E.E. ou l'article 65 paragraphe 1 du traité C.E.C.A. ne leur sont pas applicables. Une restriction de la concurrence peut, notamment, se réaliser dans un marché oligopolistique de produits homogènes.

L'étude des marchés en commun et les études comparées sur les entreprises et les secteurs économiques, destinées à recueillir les renseignements et à constater des faits et les conditions du marché, n'affectent pas par elles-mêmes la concurrence sans autre coopération plus ample entre les entreprises participantes. Pour d'autres mesures de cette nature telles que, par exemple, l'établissement en commun d'analyses de conjoncture et de structure, cela est si évident qu'il n'est pas nécessaire de les mentionner spécialement.

Les schémas de calcul qui contiennent des taux déterminés de calcul, doivent être considérés comme des recommandations qui peuvent conduire à une restriction de la concurrence.

2. Les accords qui ont uniquement pour objet:
   (a) La coopération en matière de comptabilité,
   (b) la garantie en commun du crédit,
   (c) les bureaux communs d'encaissement,
   (d) la consultation d'organismes communs en matière d'organisation des entreprises ou en matière fiscale.

Dans ces cas, il s'agit d'une coopération dans les domaines qui ne concernent ni l'offre de produits er de services, ni les décisions économiques des entreprises intéressées, de sorte qu'il n'en résulte aucune restriction de la concurrence.

La coopération en matière comptable est neutre du point de vue de la concurrence car elle ne sert qu'à la réalisation technique de la comptabilité. De même, la création de communautés de garantie pour le crédit, ne tombe pas sous les dispositions réglant la concurrence, puisqu'elle ne modifie pas les relations entre l'offre et la demande.

Les bureaux communs d'encaissement qui ne se limitent pas à l'encaissement des créances conformément à la volonté et aux conditions des participants ou qui fixent les prix ou exercent une influence quelconque sur la formation des prix peuvent restreindre la concurrence. L'application de conditions uniformes pour tous les participants peut constituer une pratique concertée, de même que la réalisation de comparaisons en commun de prix peut y aboutir. Dans ce cadre il n'existe pas d'objection contre l'utilisation d'imprimés uniformes; elle ne doit cependant pas être liée à l'accord ou à une concertation tacite concernant des prix uniformes, des remises ou des conditions de vente.

3. Les accords qui ont uniquement pour objet:
   (a) L'exécution en commun de projets de recherche et de développement,
   (b) l'attribution en commun de mandats de recherche et de mandats concernant de développement,
   (c) la répartition de projets de recherche et de développement entre les participants.

Dans le domaine de la recherche également le simple échange d'expériences et de résultats ne sert qu'à l'information et ne restreint pas la concurrence. Il n'est donc pas nécessaire de le mentionner spécialement.

Les accords passés en vue d'entreprendre une recherche en commun ou de développer en commun les résultats de la recherche jusqu'au stade de l'application industrielle ne touchent pas la situation concurrentielle des parties. Ceci vaut également lorsqu'il y a répartition des secteurs de recherche et des travaux de développement, à condition que les résultats restent accessibles à tous les participants. Mais si les entreprises contractent des obligations restreignant leur propre activité de recherche et de développement ou l'exploitation du résultat des travaux effectués en commun, de sorte que, en dehors du projet commun, elles ne sont pas libres dans leur recherche et leur développement pour compte propre, il peut y avoir violation des règles de concurrence des traités. S'il n'y a pas de recherche commune, toute obligation contractuelle ou toute concertation de renoncer totalement ou partiellement à la recherche propre, peut avoir pour effet de restreindre la concurrence.

Il y a la spécialisation qui peut restreindre la concurrence dans le cas d'une répartition des secteurs de recherche sans accord stipulant l'accès réciproque aux résultats.

La restriction de la concurrence peut également exister, lorsque des accords relatifs à l'exploitation pratique des résultats des travaux de recherche et de développement réalisés en commun sont conclus, ou des pratiques concertées correspondantes appliquées, notamment, lorsque les participants s'engagent ou s'accordent à ne fabriquer que les produits ou les types de produits développés en commun, ou à répatir entre eux la production future.

La recherche en commun veut que les résultats puissent être exploités par tous les participants au prorata de leur participation. Si la participation de certaines entreprises se confine à un secteur déterminé de la recherche en commun ou à la prestation d'une contribution financière limitée, il n'y a pas — dans la mesure où l'on peut parler ici d'une recherche en commun — de restrictions à la concurrence si ces participants n'ont accès aux résultats de la recherche qu'en fonction de leur participation. En revanche, la concurrence peut être restreinte si certains participants sont exclus de l'exploitation en totalité ou dans une mesure inappropriée à leur participation.

Si la concession de licences à des tiers est exclude de manière expresse ou tacite, il peut y avoir restriction de la concurrence; cependant, la mise en commun de la recherche justifie l'obligation de ne concéder des licences à des tiers que d'un commun accord ou par décision majoritaire.

Le statut juridique de l'activité de recherche et de développement en commun est sans importance pour l'appréciation de la compatibilité de l'accord avec les règles de concurrence.

4. *Accords qui ont uniquement pour objet l'utilisation en commun d'installations, de production, de moyens de stockage et de transport.*

Ces formes de coopération ne restreignent pas la concurrence parce qu'elles ne vont pas au-delà des règles de l'organisation et de la technique d'utilisation des installations. Par contre, il peut y avoir une restriction de la concurrence si les entreprises intéressées ne supportent pas elles-mêmes les frais d'utilisation des installations et des équipements, ou bien si des accords concernant une production en commun ou la répartition de la production ou encore la création ou l'exploitation d'une entreprise commune sont conclus ou des pratiques concertées appliquées à ce sujet.

5. *Les accords qui ont uniquement pour objet la constitution d'associations temporaires de travail en vue de l'exécution en commun des commandes lorsque les entreprises participantes ne sont pas en concurrence pur les prestations à fournir ou ne sont pas individuellement en mesure d'exécuter les commandes.*

Du moment que des entreprises ne sont pas en concurrence entre elles, elles ne peuvent pas restreindre la concurrence entre elles en créant des associations temporaires. Cela est vrai, en particulier, pour les entreprises qui appartiennent à des secteurs économiques différents mais aussi pour les entreprises du même secteur, dans la mesure où elles ne participent à l'association temporaire de travail qu'avec des produits ou des prestations qui ne peuvent pas êrre fournis par les autres participants. Il importe peu que les entreprises soient en concurrence dans d'autres secteurs; ce qui importe, c'est de savoir si, étant donné les circonstances concrètes des cas particuliers, une concurrence est possible dans un avenir rapproché pour les produits ou les prestations en cause. Si l'absence de concurrence entre les entreprises et la persistance de cette situation repose sur des accords ou des pratiques concertées, on peut être en présence d'une restriction de la concurrence.

En outre, même des associations temporaires d'entreprises qui se trouvent en concurrence entre elles ne restreignent pas la concurrence lorsque les entreprises participantes ne peuvent pas à elles seules exécuter une commande déterminée. C'est en particulier le cas lorsque, isolément, faute d'une expérience, de connaissances spéciales, de capacité ou de surface financière suffisantes, elles travaillent sans aucune chance de succès ou sans pouvoir terminer dans les délais les travaux ou supporter le risque financier.

Il n'y a pas non plus de restriction de la concurrence si seule la création de l'association temporaire de travail permet aux entreprises de faire une offre intéressante. Il peut toutefois y avoir une restriction de la concurrence si les entreprises s'engageaient à n'agir que dans le cadre d'une association temporaire de travail.

6. Les accords qui ont uniquement pour objet:
   (a) La vente en commun,
   (b) le service après-vente et de réparation en commun,
lorsque les entreprises participantes ne sont pas en concurrence entre elles pour les produits ou les services qui relèvent de l'accord.

Comme il a déjà été exposé en détail sous le point 5, la coopération entre entreprises ne peut pas restreindre la concurrence du moment que les entreprises ne sont pas en concurrence entre elles.

Très souvent, la vente en commun effectuée par de petites ou moyennes entreprises, même lorsqu'elles sont en concurrence entre elles, ne constitue pas une restriction sensible de la concurrence; cependant, il est impossible d'établir des critères généraux ou de déterminer le cercle des petites ou moyennes entreprises dans le cadre de cette communication.

Il n'y a pas de service après-vente et de réparation en commun lorsque plusieurs producteurs, sans se concerter à ce sujet, confient à la même entreprise indépendante par rapport à eux, du service après-vente et du service de réparation de leurs produits. En pareil cas, il n'y a pas non plus de restriction de la concurrence si les fabricants sont en concurrence entre eux.

7. Accords qui ont uniquement pour objet de faire de la publicité en commun.

La publicité en commun doit attirer l'attention des acheteurs sur certains produits d'une branche ou sur une marque commune, en tant que telle, elle ne restreint pas la concurrence des entreprises participantes. Cependant, il peut y avoir restriction de la concurrence lorsque celles-ci sont empêchées, totalement ou partiellement, d'effectuer également leur propre publicité à la suite d'un accord ou d'une politique concertée, ou lorsque d'autres restrictions leur sont imposées.

8. Accords qui ont uniquement pour objet l'utilisation d'un label commun en vue de caractériser des produits d'une certaine qualité et auxquels tout concurrent peut participer aux mêmes conditions.

De telles communautés de label ne restreignent pas la concurrence, si d'autres concurrents, dont les produits satisfont objectivement aux exigences de qualité requises, peuvent utiliser le label dans les mêmes conditions que les membres. De même, l'obligation de se soumettre à un contrôle de qualité des produits munis du label ou d'indiquer un mode d'emploi uniforme ou de munir du label les produits répondant aux normes de qualité ne constitue pas une restriction de la concurrence. Mais une restriction de la concurrence peut exister si le droit d'utiliser le label est lié à des obligations relatives à la production, à la commercialisation à la formation des prix et autres quand, par exemple, les entreprises participantes sont obligées à ne fabriquer ou à ne vendre que des produits de qualité garantie.

RECTIFICATIFS

Rectificatif à la communication de la Commission relative aux accords, décision et pratiques concertés concernant la coopération entre entreprises.

(Journal officiel des Communauté européennes n° C 75 du 29 juillet 1968)

Page 6, colonne de gauche, première et deuxième lignes,
lire: « ... même des associations temporaires *de travail* d'entreprises, ... »

Walker/Champion CS58
Stork v. HA CS8

1.1. Agreements fixing or determining prices

1.2. Uniform pricing method/joint prices

COBECHAR I CS2
COBECHAR II CS7
Präsident I CS8
Geitling I CS9
Geitling II CS10
Walzstahlkontor I CS16
Hoesch/Rheinstahl CS30
Danish Steel Distributors CS39
German rolled steel CS84
Stainless Steel Cartel CS106

1.3. Circulation of price lists

German rolled steel CS84

1 Restrictive Practices

1.4. Uniform discounts

German rolled steel CS84

1.5. Setting maximum prices

German scrap cartel CS28

1.6. Most favoured customer clause

Ruhrkohle CS105
Stainless Steel Cartel CS106

1.7. Mutually co-ordinated prices

Ruhrkohle CS105

1.8. Common point based transport tariff

German scrap cartel CS28

1.9. Purchase quotas

German scrap cartel CS28

1.10. Information on producer prices

German rolled steel CS84

1.11. Price equalisation system

Scrap fund I CS1
Scrap fund II CS3
Präsident I CS8
Geitling I CS9
Geitling II CS10
Walzstahlkontor I CS16
Chamber of Coal Traders CS86
Worms v. *H A* CS16

1.12. Equalisation system in event of market change

Thyssen/Krupp/Wuppermann CS29
Maxhütte/Klöckner I CS31
Dillinger/Arbed I CS32
Rötzel/Krupp CS61

2. Restricting or controlling production, technical development or investment

2.1. Agreement to stop/prohibit production

Walzstahlkontor I CS16
Creusot/Loire CS23**
Thyssen/Krupp/Wuppermann CS29
Hoesch/Rheinstahl CS30
Maxhütte/Klöckner I CS31
Dillinger/Arbed I CS32
Hoesch/Benteler CS35

Rötzel/Krupp CS61
Creusot-Loire/Ugine CS73
Cockerill/Klöckner CS77
Cockerill/Estel CS78
Irish Steel/Dunkerque CS80
Boël/Clabecq CS87
Arbed/Cockerill-Sambre CS95
Arbed/Unimétal CS103
Ruhrkohle CS105
Stainless Steel Cartel CS106

2.2. Co-ordination of production

Falck/Redaelli I CS21
Thyssen/Krupp/Wuppermann CS29
Maxhütte/Klöckner I CS31
Creusot-Loire/Ugine CS73
Falck/Redaelli II CS75
Stainless Steel Cartel CS106

2.3. Co-ordination of investment

Falck/Redaelli I CS21
Creusot/Loire CS23
Thyssen/Krupp/Wuppermann CS29
Hoesch/Rheinstahl CS30
Maxhütte/Klöckner I CS31
Dillinger/Arbed CS32
Minerais Préréduits CS51
Rötzel/Krupp CS61
COIMPRE CS69
Falck/Redaelli II CS75
Cockerill/Klöckner CS77
Cockerill/Estel CS78
Boël/Clabecq CS87
Arbed/Cockerill-Sambre CS95
Arbed/Unimétal CS103

2.4. Purchase of shareholding

Falck/Redaelli I CS21
Falck/Redaelli II CS75
Cockerill/Klöckner CS77
Cockerill/Estel CS78

3. Sharing markets, products, customers or sources of supply

3.1. Joint buying agreements

OKB I CS4
SOREMA CS11
Stahlring I CS17
Falck/Redaelli I CS21
Dillinger/Arbed I CS32
Danish Steel Distributors CS39
Steelmaking Supplies I CS40
Minerais Préréduits CS51
Walker/Champion CS58
Stahlring III CS65
Maier/Röchling CS67

Book Three: Coal and Steel

COIMPRE CS69
Falck/Redaelli II CS75
Boël/Clabecq CS87
Steelmaking Supplies II CS96
NICIA CS100
Ruhrkohle CS105

3.2. Agreements to refrain from buying

Maier/Röchling CS67

3.3. Joint selling agreements

COBECHAR I CS2
Union Charbonnière CS5
COBECHAR II CS7
Präsident I CS8
Geitling I CS9
Geitling II CS10
Walzstahlkontor I CS16
Falck/Redaelli I CS21
Walzstahlkontor II CS22
Creusot/Loire CS23
Thyssen/Krupp/Wuppermann CS29
Hoesch/Rheinstahl CS30
Maxhütte/Klöckner I CS31
UCRO CS74
Falck/Redaelli II CS75
Boël/Clabecq CS87
Röchling/Possehl CS98
Saarlor V CS101
Geitling v. H A CS4
Präsident v. H A CS13
Geitling v. H A CS15
Netherlands v. H A CS19

3.4. Agreements to refrain from selling/market partitioning

Maier/Röchling CS67
Irish Steel/Dunkerque CS80
Röchling-Possehl CS98
Stainless Steel Cartel CS106

3.5. Exclusive purchasing/selling agreements

Walzstahlkontor I CS16
Hoesch/Rheinstahl CS30
Hoesch/Benteler CS35
Danish Steel Distributors CS39
Creusot-Loire/Ugine CS73
Ruhrkohle CS105

3.6. Product/know-how exchange agreements

Walker/Champion CS58
Boël/Clabecq CS87
Arbed/Unimétal CS103

3.7. Direct sales obligation

Präsident I CS8

Geitling I CS9
Geitling II CS10
Walzstahlkontor I CS16
Geitling v. H A CS4
Präsident v. H A CS13

3.8. Joint production

Creusot-Loire/Ugine CS73
Arbed/Cockerill-Sambre CS95

3.9. Allocation system in times of shortage

NICIA CS100

3.10. Co-ordination of transport

NICIA CS100

3.11. New undertaking joining cartel

Kempense CS20

D. VOID AGREEMENTS

Article 65(4)
Stork v. H A CS8

E. AUTHORISATION OF AGREEMENTS

Article 65(2)

1. Specialisation agreements

Walzstahlkontor I CS16
Creusot/Loire* CS23
Thyssen/Krupp/Wuppermann CS29
Hoesch/Rhienstahl CS30
Maxhütte/Klöckner I CS31
Dillinger/Arbed I CS32
Hoesch/Benteler CS35
Rötzel/Krupp CS61
Creusot-Loire/Ugine CS73
Cockerill/Klöckner CS77
Cockerill/Estel CS78
Irish Steel/Dunkerque CS80
Boël/Clabecq CS87
Arbed/Cockerill-Sambre CS95
Arbed/Unimétal CS103

2. Joint buying agreements

OKB I CS4
Stahlring I CS17
Falck/Redaelli I CS21
Dillinger/Arbed I CS32
Danish Steel Distributors CS39
Steelmaking Supplies I CS40
Minerais Préréduits CS51
Walker/Champion CS58
Stahlring III CS65
Maier/Röchling CS67

1 Restrictive Practices

COIMPRE CS69
Falck/Redaelli II CS75
Boël/Clabecq CS87
Steelmaking Supplies II CS96
NICIA CS100
Ruhrkohle CS105

3. Joint selling agreements

COBECHAR I CS2
Union Charbonniére CS5
COBECHAR II CS7
Präsident I CS8
Geitling I CS9
Geitling II CS10
Walzstahlkontor I CS16
Kempense CS20
Falck/Redaelli I CS21
Walzstahlkontor II CS22
Thyssen/Krupp/Wuppermann CS29
Hoesch/Rheinstahl CS30
Maxhütte/Klöckner I CS31
UCRO CS74
Falck/Redaelli II CS75
Chamber of Coal Traders I CS86
Boël/Clabecq CS87
Saarlor V CS101
Arbed/Usinor-Sacilor CS107
Geitling v. *H A* (p. 104) CS15
Netherlands v. *H A (pp.* 548–549) CS19

4. Formation of a jointly held undertaking

Präsident I CS8
Geitling I CS9
Geitling II CS10
Creusot/Loire* CS23
Danish Steel Distributors CS39
Röchling-Possehl CS98

5. Factors considered in assessing these agreements

5.1. Improvement in production or distribution

5.1.1. Efficient allocation of production

Walzstahlkontor I CS16
Falck/Redaelli I CS21
Creusot/Loire* CS23
Thyssen/Krupp/Wuppermann CS29
Hoesch/Rheinstahl CS30
Maxhütte/Klockner I CS31
Dillinger/Arbed I CS32
Hoesch/Benteler CS35
Creusot-Loire/Ugine CS73
Falck/Redaelli II CS75
Cockerill/Klöckner CS77
Cockerill/Estel CS78

Irish Steel/Dunkerque CS80
Boël/Clabecq CS87
Arbed/Cockerill-Sambre CS95
Arbed/Unimétal CS103
Arbed/Usinor-Sacilor CS107

5.1.2 Avoid duplication of investment

Hoesch/Benteler CS35
Rötzel/Krupp CS61

5.1.3. Reduce overcapacity

Arbed/Cockerill-Sambre CS95
Röchling-Possehl CS98
Arbed/Usinor-Sacilor CS107

5.1.4 Adjustment to structural decline

COBECHAR II CS7
Kempense CS20
Maier/Röchling CS67
Irish Steel/Dunkerque CS80
Boël/Clabecq CS87
Nold v. *Commission* CS23

5.1.5. Injection of capital

Cockerill/Klöckner CS77
Cockerill/Estel CS78

5.1.6. Reduce overheads

Union Charbonnière CS5
Präsident I CS8
Geitling I CS9
Geitling II CS10
Walzstahlkontor I CS16
Falck/Redaelli I CS21
Thyssen/Krupp/Wuppermann CS29
Dillinger/Arbed I CS32
Danish Steel Distributors CS39
Minerais Préréduits CS51
COIMPRE CS69
UCRO CS74
Falck/Redaelli II CS75
Arbed/Usinor-Sacilor CS107

5.1.7. Ensure continuity of supply

Scrap fund I CS1
Scrap fund II CS3
Hoesch/Benteler CS35
Steelmaking Supplies I CS40
Walker/Champion CS58
Chamber of Coal Traders CS86
Steelmaking Supplies II CS96
NICIA CS100
Ruhrkohle CS105

5.1.8. Existence of Community crisis measures

UCRO CS74

5.1.9. Non-exclusive agreement
Minerais Préréduits CS51

5.2. Agreements essential and no more restrictive than necessary
COBECHAR I CS2
Präsident I CS8
Geitling I CS9
Geitling II CS10
SOREMA* CS11
Walzstahlkontor I CS16
Thyssen/Krupp/Wuppermann CS29
Hoesch/Rheinstahl CS30
Maxhütte/Klöckner I CS31
Dillinger/Arbed I CS32
Steelmaking Supplies I CS40
Rötzel/Krupp CS61
Boël/Clabecq CS87
Arbed/Cockerill-Sambre CS95
Steelmaking Supplies II CS96
Röchling-Possehl CS98
Arbed/Unimétal CS103
Arbed/Usinor-Sacilor CS107
Geitling v. H A CS4
Eisen und Stahlindustrie v. H A (p. 286) CS6
Centre-Midi v. H A (para. 393) CS7
Knutange v. H A* CS11

5.3. Power to determine prices, or control or restrict production or marketing
Opinion: *Amendment to Article 65* (p. 260) CS14
Geitling v. H A (para. 102) CS15

5.3.1. Relevant market: whole Community
COBECHAR I CS2
Falck/Redaelli I CS21
Walzstahlkontor II CS22
Creusot/Loire* CS23
Thyssen/Krupp/Wuppermann CS29
Hoesch/Rheinstahl CS30
Maxhütte/Klöckner I CS31
Dillinger/Arbed I CS32
Danish Steel Distributors CS39
Rötzel/Krupp CS61
Creusot-Loire/Ugine CS73
Falck/Redaelli II CS75
Cockerill/Klöckner CS77
Cockerill/Estel CS78
Irish Steel/Dunkerque CS80
Boël/Clabecq CS87
Arbed/Unimétal CS103
Stainless Steel Cartel CS106
Arbed/Usinor-Sacilor CS107
Geitling v. H A (p. 115) CS15
Netherlands v. H A (p. 650) CS19

5.3.2. Relevant market: whole or part of Member State
Walker/Champion CS58

NICIA CS100
Ruhrkohle CS105

5.3.3. Competition from outside Community
Walzstahlkontor II CS22
Chamber of Coal Traders CS86
Boël/Clabecq CS87
Arbed/Cockerill-Sambre CS95
Arbed/Unimétal CS103
Geitling v. H A (p. 104) CS15

5.3.4. Competition from alternative products
Minerais Préréduits CS51
COIMPRE CS69
Chamber of Coal Traders I CS86
NICIA CS100
Netherlands v. H A (p. 549) CS19

5.3.5 *De minimis*/small market share
Union Charbonnière CS5
Kempense CS20
Falck/Redaelli I CS21
Thyssen/Krupp/Wuppermann CS29
Hoesch/Rheinstahl CS30
Maxhütte/Klöckner I CS31
Hoesch/Benteler CS35
Danish Steel Distributors CS39
Steelmaking Supplies I CS40
Walker/Champion CS58
Rötzel/Krupp CS61
Maier/Röchling CS67
Creusot-Loire/Ugine CS73
Falck/Redaelli II CS75
Steelmaking Supplies II CS96
Röchling-Possehl CS98
Ruhrkohle CS105

5.3.6 Group effect
Dillinger/Arbed I CS32
Röchling-Possehl CS98

5.3.7. Cumulative effect of agreements with other undertakings
Cockerill/Klöckner CS77
Cockerill/Estel CS78

5.3.8. Independence of the parties maintained
Creusot/Loire* CS23
Thyssen/Krupp/Wuppermann CS29
Hoesch/Rheinstahl CS30
Maxhütte/Klöckner I CS31
Dillinger/Arbed I CS32
Rötzel/Krupp CS61
Arbed/Cockerill-Sambre CS95

Arbed/Unimétal CS103

CHAPTER 2

CONCENTRATIONS

A. TEXT OF ARTICLE 66 ECSC
(reproduced below)

Article 66

1. Any transaction shall require the prior authorisation of the High Authority subject to the provisions of paragraph 3 of this Article, if it has in itself the direct or indirect effect of bringing about within the territories referred to in the first paragraph of Article 79, as a result of action by any person or undertaking or group of persons or undertakings, a concentration between undertakings at least one of which is covered by Article 80, whether the transaction concerns a single product or a number of different products, and whether it is effected by merger, acquisition of shares or parts of the undertaking or assets, loan, contract or any other means of control. For the purpose of applying these provisions, the High Authority shall, by regulations made after consulting the Council, define what constitutes control of an undertaking.

2. The High Authority shall grant the authorisation referred to in the preceding paragraph if it finds that the proposed transaction will not give to the persons or undertakings concerned the power, in respect of the product or products within its jurisdiction:
— to determine prices, to control or restrict production or distribution or to hinder effective competition in a substantial part of the market for those products; or
— to evade the rules of competition instituted under this Treaty, in particular by establishing an artificially privileged position involving a substantial advantage in access to supplies or markets.
In assessing whether this is so, the High Authority shall, in accordance with the principle of non-discrimination laid down in Article 4(b), take account of the size of like undertakings in the Community, to the extent it considers justified in order to avoid or correct disadvantages resulting from unequal competitive conditions.
The High Authority may make its authorisation subject to any conditions which it considers appropriate for the purposes of this paragraph.

Before ruling on a transaction concerning undertakings at least one of which is not subject to Article 80, the High Authority shall obtain the comments of the Governments concerned.

3. The High Authority shall exempt from the requirement of prior authorisation such classes of transactions as it finds should, in view of the size of the assets or undertakings concerned, taken in conjunction with the kind of concentration to be effected, be deemed to meet the requirements of paragraph 2. Regulations made to this effect, with the assent of the Council, shall also lay down the conditions governing such exemption.

4. Without prejudice to the application of Article 47 to undertakings within its jurisdiction, the high Authority may, either by regulations made after consultation with the Council stating the kind of transaction to be communicated to it or by a special request under these regulations to the parties concerned, obtain from the natural or legal persons who have acquired or regrouped or are intending to acquire or regroup the rights or assets in question any information needed for the application of this Article concerning transactions liable to produce the effect referred to in paragraph 1.

5. If a concentration should occur which the High Authority finds has been effected contrary to the provisions of paragraph 1 but which nevertheless meets the requirements of paragraph 2, the High Authority shall make its approval of that concentration subject to payment by the persons who have acquired or regrouped the rights or assets in question of the fine provided for in the second subparagraph of paragraph 6; the amount of the fine shall not be less than half of the maximum determined in that subparagraph should it be clear that authorisation ought to have been applied for. If the fine is not paid, the High Authority shall take the steps hereinafter provided for in respect of concentrations found to be unlawful.
If a concentration should occur which the High Authority finds cannot fulfil the general or specific conditions to which an authorisation under paragraph 2 would be subject, the High Authority shall, by means of a reasoned decision, declare the concentration unlawful and, after giving the parties concerned the opportunity to submit their comments, shall order separation of the undertakings or assets

improperly concentrated or cessation of joint control, and any other measures which it considers appropriate to return the undertakings or assets in question to independent operation and restore normal conditions of competition. Any person directly concerned may institute proceedings against such decisions, as provided in Article 33. By way of derogation from Article 33, the Court shall have unlimited jurisdiction to assess whether the transaction effected is a concentration within the meaning of paragraph 1 and of regulations made in application thereof. The institution of proceedings shall have suspensory effect. Proceedings may not be instituted until the measures provided for above have been ordered, unless the High Authority agrees to the institution of separate proceedings against the decision declaring the transaction unlawful.

The High Authority may at any time, unless the third paragraph of Article 39 is applied, take or cause to be taken such interim measures of protection as it may consider necessary to safeguard the interests of competing undertakings and of third parties, and to forestal any step which might hinder the implementation of its decisions. Unless the Court decides otherwise, proceedings shall not have suspensory effect in respect of such interim measures.

The High Authority shall allow the parties concerned a reasonable period in which to comply with its decisions, on expiration of which it may impose daily penalty payments not exceeding one tenth of one per cent. of the value of the rights or assets in question.

Furthermore, if the parties concerned do not fulfil their obligations, the High Authority shall itself take steps to implement its decision; it may in particular suspend the exercise, in undertakings within its jurisdiction, of the rights attached to the assets acquired irregularly, obtain the appointment by the judicial authorities of a receiver of such assets, organise the forced sale of such assets subject to the protection of the legitimate interests of their owners, and annul with respect to natural or legal persons who have acquired the rights or assets in question through the unlawful transaction, the acts, decisions, resolutions or proceedings of the supervisory and managing bodies or undertakings over which control has been obtained irregularly.

The High Authority is also empowered to make such recommendations to the Member States concerned as may be necessary to ensure that the measures provided for in the preceding subparagraphs are implemented under their own law.

In the exercise of its powers, the High Authority shall take account of the rights of third parties which have been acquired in good faith.

6. The High Authority may impose fines not exceeding:

—3 per cent. of the value of the assets acquired or regrouped or to be acquired or regrouped, on natural or legal persons who have evaded the obligations laid down in paragraph 4;

—10 per cent. of the value of the assets acquired or regrouped, on natural or legal persons who have evaded the obligations laid down in paragraph 1; this maximum shall be increased by one twenty-fourth for each month which elapses after the end of the twelfth month following completion of the transaction until the High Authority establishes that there has been an infringement;

—10 per cent. of the value of the assets acquired or regrouped or to be acquired or regrouped, on natural or legal persons who have obtained or attempted to obtain authorisation under paragraph 2 by means of false or misleading information;

—15 per cent. of the value of the assets acquired or regrouped, on undertakings within its jurisdiction which have engaged in or been party to transactions contrary to the provisions of this Article.

Persons fined under this paragraph may appeal to the Court as provided in Article 36.

7. If the High Authority finds that public or private undertakings which, in law or in fact, hold or acquire in the market for one of the products within its jurisdiction a dominant position shielding them against effective competition in a substantial part of the common market are using that position for purposes contrary to the objectives of this Treaty, it shall make to them such recommendations as may be appropriate to prevent the position from being so used. If these recommendations are not implemented satisfactorily within a reasonable time, the High Authority shall, by decisions taken in consultation with the Government concerned, determine the prices and conditions of sale to be applied by the undertaking in question or draw up

2 Concentrations

production or delivery programmes with which it must comply, subject to liability to the penalties provided for in Articles 58, 59 and 64.

B. CONCENTRATIONS SUBJECT TO PRIOR AUTHORISATION

Article 66 (1)
Decision No. 24–54 of May 6, 1954 laying down in implementation of Article 66(1) of the Treaty a regulation on what constitutes control of an undertaking.

1. Decisions applying Decision No. 24–54

Creusot/Loire* CS23
Thyssen/Rheinstahl CS38
GKN/Miles Druce CS41
BSC/Lye Trading CS43
Thyssen/SOLMER CS44
Gelsenberg CS45
Marcoke CS47
CLIF/Marine-Firminy CS48
Krupp/Stahlwerke CS49
IVECO CS50
EGAM/Vetrocoke CS52
BSC/Walter Blume CS57
Klockner/Maxhütte II CS53
Framtek CS70
Arbed/Rodange CS71
Ruhrkohle/Brennstoffhandel CS72
Lange/Stinnes CS79
BSC/Dunlop & Ranken CS81
Hoogovens/Ijzerhandel CS85
Rogesa CS88
Eurocoal CS89
Zentralkokerei CS90
Usinor/Sacilor/Normandie CS92
UNICO CS94
Röchling-Possehl CS98
British Fuel CS102
Eschweiler/Ruhrkohle CS104
British Steel/Walker CS106

1.1. Acquisitions of under 25 per cent. of share capital

Ruhrkohle/Brennstoffhandel CS72
British Fuel CS102

1.2. Acquisitions of over 25 per cent. but under 50 per cent. of share capital

GKN/Miles Druce CS41
Thyssen/SOLMER CS44
Arbed/Rodange CS71
UNICO CS94
20th Comp. Rep. (para. 120)

1.3. Acquisitions of over 50 per cent. of share capital

Thyssen/Rheinstahl CS38
BSC/Lye Trading CS43
Krupp/Stahlwerke CS49
CLIF/Marine-Firminy* CS48
EGAM/Vetrocoke CS52
BSC/Walter Blume CS57
Klockner/Maxhutte IV CS63
Arbed/Rodange CS71
Lange/Stinnes CS79
BSC/Dunlop & Ranken CS81
Hoogovens/Ijzerhandel CS85
Eschweiler/Ruhrkohle CS104
British Steel/Walker CS106

1.4. Creation of jointly held undertaking

Marcoke CS47
IVECO CS50
Framtek CS70
Rogesa CS88
Eurocoal CS89
Zentralkokerei CS90
Röchling-Possehl CS98
British Fuel CS102

1.5. Contested or hostile bids

CLIF/Marine-Firminy* CS48
4th Comp. Rep. (paras. 141–143)
Miles Druce v. Commission I CS21
Miles Druce v. Commission II CS22

1.6. Acquisition by the State

Gelsenberg CS45
Usinor/Sacilor/Normandie* CS92

C. CONDITIONS FOR AUTHORISATION

Article 66(2)
1st Comp. Rep. (paras. 95–97)
3rd Comp. Rep. (paras. 70–76)
4th Comp. Rep. (paras. 120–143)
6th Comp. Rep. (paras. 180–187)
13th Comp. Rep. (paras. 158–164)
16th Comp. Rep. (paras. 79–87)
17th Comp. Rep. (paras. 87–96)
18th Comp. Rep. (paras. 83–96)
20th Comp. Rep. (paras. 116–144)

1. Power to determine prices

BSC/Lye Trading CS43
Thyssen/SOLMER CS44
Marcoke CS47
CLIF/Marine-Firminy CS48
Krupp/Stahlwerke CS49
IVECO CS50
EGAM/Vetrocoke CS52
BSC/Walter Blume CS57
Framtel CS70
Arbed/Rodange CS71
Ruhrkohle/Brennstoffhandel CS72
Lange/Stinnes CS79

Rogesa CS88
Eurocoal CS89
Usinor/Sacilor/Normandie CS92
UNICO CS94
British Fuel CS102
Eschweiler/Ruhrkohle CS104
British Steel/Walker* CS106

2. Power to control or restrict production or distribution

BSC/Lye Trading CS43
Thyssen/SOLMER CS44
Gelsenberg CS45
Marcoke CS47
IVECO CS50
EGAM/Vetrocoke CS52
BSC/Walter Blume CS57
Framtek CS70
Lange/Stinnes CS79
Rogesa CS88
Eurocoal CS89
Usinor/Sacilor/Normandie CS92
Eschweiler/Ruhrkohle CS104
British Steel Walker CS106

3. Power to hinder effective competition

Thyssen/Rheinstahl CS38
GKN/Miles Druce CS41
BSC/Lye Trading CS43
Thyssen/SOLMER CS44
Gelsenberg CS45
Marcoke CS47
CLIF/Marine-Firminy CS48
Krupp/Stahlwerke CS49
IVECO CS50
EGAM/Vetrocoke CS52
BSC/Walter Blume CS57
Rogesa CS88
Eurocoal CS89
Usinor/Sacilor/Normandie CS92
Röchling-Possehl CS98
British Fuel CS102
British Steel/Walker* CS106

4. Establishing an artificially privileged position

Thyssen/Rheinstahl CS38
GKN/Miles Druce CS41
Thyssen/SOLMER CS44
CLIF/Marine-Firminy CS48
Krupp/Stahlwerke CS49
BSC/Walter Blume CS57
Klöckner/Maxhütte IV CS63
Framtek CS70
Lange/Stinnes CS79
BSC/Dunlop & Ranken CS81
Hoogovens/Ijzerhandel CS85
Zentralkokerei* CS90
UNICO CS94

Röchling-Possehl CS98
British Fuel CS102
Eschweiler/Ruhrkohle CS104

D. ANALYSIS OF THE MARKET

1. Relevant geographical market: whole of Common Market

Thyssen/SOLMER CS44
Krupp/Stahlwerke CS49
Arbed/Rodange CS71
Lange/Stinnes CS79

2. Relevant geographical market: Member State

Thyssen/Rheinstahl CS38
GKN/Miles Druce CS41
BSC/Lye Trading CS43
BSC/Walter Blume CS57
Frantek CS70
BSC/Dunlop & Ranken CS81
Hoogovens/Ijzerhandel CS85
UNICO CS94
British Steel/Walker CS106

3. Competition from third countries

Thyssen/Rheinstahl CS38
Hoogovens/Ijzerhandel CS85
Eschweiler/Ruhrkohle CS104
British Steel/Walker CS106

4. Competition from substitute products

EGAM/Vetrocoke CS52
Ruhrkohle/Brennstoffhandel CS72
British Fuel CS102

5. Small market share

GKN/Miles Druce CS41
Eurocoal CS89
UNICO CS94

6. Compatibility with EEC rules on competition

1st Comp. Rep. (para. 97)
13th Comp. Rep. (paras. 160–164)
16th Comp. Rep. (paras. 81 & 85)

E. EXEMPTION BY CATEGORY

1. Article 66(3)

1.1. Text of Decision No. 25–67 laying down in implementation of Article 66(3) of the Treaty a regulation concerning exemption from prior authorisation. (reproduced opposite)

2 Concentrations

Decision No. 25–67 of June 22, 1967

Laying down in implementation of Article 66(3) of the Treaty a regulation concerning exemption from prior authorisation

([1952–67] O.J. Spec.Ed. 186; amended by [1978] O.J. L300/21 and [1991] O.J. L348/12)

THE HIGH AUTHORITY,
Having regard to Articles 47, 66 and 80 of the Treaty;
Having regard to Decision No. 25–54 of May 6, 1954 on rules for the application of Article 66(3) of the Treaty, relating to exemption from prior authorisation *(Official Journal of the European Coal and Steel Community,* May 11, 1954, pp. 346 *et seq.),* as supplemented by Decision No. 28–54 of May 26, 1954 *(Official Journal of the European Coal and Steel Community,* May 31, 1954, p.381);

(1) Whereas under Article 66(1), and subject to Article 66(3), any transaction which would in itself have the direct or indirect effect of bringing about a concentration between undertakings at least one of which falls within the scope of application of Article 80, requires the prior authorisation of the High Authority; whereas the High Authority grants the authorisation referred to in paragraph (1) if it finds that the proposed transaction will not give to the persons or undertakings concerned the power to influence competition within the common market, within the meaning of Article 66(2);
(2) Whereas by Decision No. 25–54, and with the concurring Opinion of the Council, the High Authority in accordance with Article 66(3) exempted from the requirement of prior authorisation certain classes of transactions which would bring about concentration of undertakings and which, in view of the size of the assets or of the undertakings to which they relate, taken in conjunction with the kind of concentration which they effect, and having regard to the totality of the undertakings grouped under the same control, must be deemed to meet the requirements of Article 66(2);
(3) Whereas experience has shown that Decision No. 25–54 should be adapted to take account of the changes which have occurred since that time in the volume of production, in economic structure, in market and competitive conditions; whereas this applies particularly to quantitative limits and to the ties which exist between Community undertakings and undertakings in other sectors and trading undertakings;
(4) Whereas in concentrations between undertakings engaged in the production of coal and steel, the size of the industrial entity being formed depends on the volume of production of the different types of products; whereas this volume should be limited both in absolute figures and in relation to production within the Community as shown in the official statistics;
(5) Whereas in the case of concentration between undertakings engaged in production and undertakings which are not within the scope of the Treaty, account must be taken of the privileged position which concentration can secure for Community undertakings by ensuring disposal of their products; whereas the relevant consumption of coal and steel in this respect is either the total consumption of the undertakings concerned or that of the different undertakings which are not within the scope of the Treaty but are involved in the concentration;
(6) Whereas any concentration of undertakings in the wholesale trade which are subject to Article 66 should, in accordance with Article 80, be assessed on the basis of the volume of their sales of coal and turnover of steel, the ties which exist between a wholesale undertaking and an undertaking engaged in production not forming an obstacle to exemption for purposes of concentration with another wholesaler; whereas with regard to steel, repeated concentrations and concentrations which relate to several distribution undertakings at the same time should be limited;
(7) Whereas special limits must be fixed for sales of scrap;
(8) Whereas concentrations between producer undertakings and retailers and between distribution undertakings and undertakings which are not within the scope of the Treaty, may, in general, be exempted from the requirement of prior authorisation;
(9) Whereas, as regards concentrations effected by establishing control over

groups, it is impossible to define general criteria for exemption; whereas concentrations of this type should accordingly be excluded from the field of application of this Decision, whether involving joint formation of new undertakings or control over groups of existing undertakings;

(10) Whereas the High Authority should be informed of any concentration effected within the common market for coal and steel, even if exempt from prior authorisation by virtue of this Decision; whereas the undertakings or the persons who obtained control should accordingly be required to declare any such concentration the size of which are not substantially below the limits fixed for exemption;

With the concurring Opinion of the Council of Ministers;

DECIDES:

Concentrations between producers

Article 1

Transactions referred to in Article 66(1) which have the direct or indirect effect of bringing about concentration between undertakings engaged in production in the coal or steel industry shall be exempted from the requirement of prior authorisation where:

1. The annual output of products specified below, achieved by all the undertakings involved in the concentration, does not exceed the following tonnages:

(a) Coal (net production screened and washed) 10 000 000 metric tonnes;
(b) Manufactured fuels made from coal 1 000 000 metric tonnes;
(c) Coke 3 000 000 metric tonnes;
(d) Iron ore (gross production) No limit;
(e) Agglomerated ore 4 000 000 metric tonnes;
(f) Pre-reduced ore 400 000 metric tonnes;
(g) Steelmaking pig iron 4 000 000 tonnes;
(h) Other forms of pig iron, ferro-alloys 250 000 tonnes;
(i) Crude steel (ordinary steel: ingots, semi-finished products and liquid steel) 6 000 000 tonnes;
(j) Alloy and non-alloy special steels (ingots, semi-finished products and liquid steel) 1 000 000 tonnes;
(k) Finished rolled steel products including end products 6 000 000 tonnes.

2. The annual output of undertakings involved in the concentration shall not exceed, for any of the types of steel products listed in the Annex to this Decision, 30% of the overall output of products of this type within the Community. The overall output within the Community shall be determined according to the production statistics published by the Statistical Office of the European Communities.

Concentrations between coal producers and undertakings not falling within the scope of the Treaty

Article 2

Transactions referred to in Article 66(1) shall be exempted from the requirement of prior authorization where they have the direct or indirect effect of bringing about a concentration between:

(a) undertakings engaged in steel production; and
(b) undertakings not falling within the scope of Article 80, if:

— either the annual coal consumption considered as a whole for all the undertakings involved in the concentration does not exceed 5 000 000 tonnes or
— the annual coal consumption of each of the undertakings referred to in (b) is less than 500 000 tonnes.

Concentrations between steel producers and undertakings not falling within the scope of the Treaty

Article 3

1. Transactions referred to in Article 66(1) shall be exempted from the requirement of prior authorisation where they have the direct or indirect effect of bringing about concentration between:

(a) undertakings engaged in steel production; and
(b) undertakings not falling within the scope of Article 80, if

— the annual production of undertakings referred to in (a) does not exceed 20% of the tonnages set out for the groups of products referred to in Article 1(1)(g) to (k), or
— the annual consumption of the products in question by the new group as a whole does not exceed 50% of its production of such products, or
— the undertakings referred to in (b) use no more than 50 000 tonnes of ordinary

steel or 5 000 tonnes of special steels, and the resulting expansion in outlets by the undertakings referred to in (a) is no more than 100 000 tonnes of ordinary steel or 10 000 tonnes of special steels in any three-year period.

2. Tonnages used in the production of steel and in the upkeep and renewal of installations of the undertakings in question shall not be considered as steel consumption.

Concentrations between distributors

COAL

Article 4

1. Transactions referred to in Article 66(1) shall be exempted from the requirement of prior authorisation where they have the direct or indirect effect of bringing about concentration between undertakings engaged in coal distribution, other than sales to domestic consumers or to small craft industries (hereinafter called 'distribution undertakings') if
    (a) either the total volume of business dealt with annually by distribution undertakings involved in the concentration does not exceed 5 000 000 tonnes of coal; or
    (b) the increase in the annual volume of business brought about by the concentration does not exceed 200 000 tonnes of coal. However, transactions of this type which are repeated or involve several distribution undertakings at the same time shall be exempted from the requirement of authorization only if the consequent total increase in the volume of business does not exceed 600 000 tonnes.

2. 'Volume of business' means the quantities sold by the distribution undertakings for their own account and for account of third parties. Sales to domestic consumers and to the small craft industries are not to be taken into account.

STEEL

Article 5

1. Transactions referred to in Article 66(1) shall be exempted from the requirement of prior authorization where they have the direct or indirect effect of bringing about a concentration between undertakings engaged in steel distribution, other than sales to domestic consumers or to small craft industries (hereinafter called "distribution undertakings"), if:
    (a) either the total annual turnover of steel—not including scrap—achieved by the distribution undertakings involved in the concentration does not exceed ECU 500 million; or
    (b) the annual turnover of steel—not including scrap—achieved by the distribution undertaking which represents one of the parties to a concentration involving only two parties does not exceed ECU 100 million. However, transactions of this type which are repeated shall be exempted from the requirement of prior authorization only if the consequent total increase in turnover does not exceed ECU 200 million in any three-year period.

2. Transactions referred to in Article 66(1) shall be exempted from the requirement of prior authorization where they have the direct or indirect effect of bringing about a concentration between undertakings engaged in scrap distribution, if:
    (a) either the total annual volume of business of the distribution undertakings involved in the concentration does not exceed 1 500 000 tonnes of scrap; or
    (b) the annual volume of business of the distribution undertaking which represents one of the parties to a concentration involving only two parties does not exceed 500 000 tonnes of scrap. However, transactions of this type which are repeated shall be exempted from the requirement of prior authorization only if the consequent total increase in the volume of business does not exceed 1 000 000 tonnes of scrap in any three-year period.

3. The turnover shall be ascertained by reference to the amount of products sold and invoiced for own account and for account of third parties. 'Volume of business' means the amounts sold by the distribution undertakings for their own account and for account of third parties.

Other concentrations exempted from authorisation

Article 6

Transactions referred to in Article 66(1) shall be exempted from prior authorisa-

tion to the extent that they have the effect of bringing about concentration:
— between undertakings engaged in production as defined in Article 80, and undertakings which sell coal or steel exclusively to domestic consumers or to small craft industries;
— between distribution undertakings and undertakings not coming within Article 80.

Concentrations effected by providing for group control

Article 7

1. Article 6 shall not apply to transactions referred to in Article 66(1) where a concentration results from the joint formation of a new undertaking or the establishment of joint control of an existing undertaking and where the transaction has the effect of bringing about a concentration between:
   (a) on the one hand, a number of undertakings of which at least one falls within the scope of Article 80 and which are not concentrated among themselves but which, in fact or in law, exercise joint control (group control) over the undertaking or undertakings at (b); and
   (b) on the other hand, one or more undertakings which produce, distribute or process coal or steel as a raw material.
2. Articles 1 to 5 shall not apply to transactions referred to in paragraph 1 where the production, consumption, volume of business or turnover, expressed in terms of tonnes or in terms of ecus respectively, of the undertakings involved in the concentration exceeds 50% of the levels fixed in whichever of Articles 1 to 5 would be applicable to the transaction.
3. This Article shall be without prejudice to the possible application of Article 65 to the formation of joint ventures on a cooperative basis and to restrictions which are not directly related and necessary to the implementation of the concentration.

General provisions

Article 8

1. The figures to be considered in applying Articles 1 to 5 above shall be the average annual figures for production, consumption, turnover and volume of business attained during the last three financial years preceding the date of concentration.

2. In the case of undertakings which have been in existence for less than three years, the figures to be considered shall be the yearly averages calculated on the basis of production, consumption, turnover and volume of business since those undertakings came into existence.

Article 9

1. In applying Articles 1 to 7 regard shall be had to the whole of the undertakings and activities already grouped under one control or which would, as a result of concentration, be under such control.
2. Transactions within the meaning of Article 66(1), to which more than one of Articles 1 to 6 above apply, shall only be exempted from the requirement of prior authorisation if the conditions of each of the relevant Articles are satisfied.

Article 10

1. Transactions referred to in Article 66(1) which in accordance with Articles 1 to 5 are exempted from authorisation, shall be notified to the Commission within two months from the time when the concentration was effected.
The notification shall be made by the undertakings or persons who have acquired control.
The notification shall contain the following information:
— a description of the transaction leading to concentration,
— the description of the undertakings which will be directly or indirectly concentrated,
— an estimate of production, sales or consumption of coal or steel of the concentrated undertakings.

2. Paragraph 1 shall not apply to concentrations which achieve less than 50% of the figures required under Articles 1 to 5 of this Decision for exemption from authorisation.

Article 11

This Decision shall be published in the *Official Journal of the European Communities*. It shall enter into force on July 15, 1967.
On the same date, Decisions Nos. 25–54 and 28–54 shall cease to be in force.
This Decision was considered and adopted by the High Authority at its meeting on 22 June 1967.

ANNEX

(Article 1(2) and Article 3(1))

Permanent railway material

Sheet pilings

Wide-flanged beams
Other angles, shapes and sections, 80mm or more and Omega sections

Tube rounds and squares

Wire rod in coils

Merchant steel

Universal plates

Hoop and strip and hot-rolled tube strip

Hot-rolled plates of 4·76mm or more

Hot-rolled plates of 3 to 4·75mm

Hot-rolled sheets under 3mm

Coils (end products)

Cold-rolled sheets under 3mm
Hoop and strip, cold-rolled, for making tinplate

Tinplate

Blackplate used as such
Galvanised, lead-coated and other clad sheets

Electrical sheet

F. DOMINANT POSITION

Article 66(7)
NICIA CS100
Netherlands v. H A CS3

CHAPTER 3

STATE BEHAVIOUR

1. Article 67

CHAPTER 4

PROCEDURE

A. CONTROL BY COMMISSION

1. Exclusive control of Article 65

Article 65(4) second indent
Geitling v. *H A* CS10

2. Exclusive power in concentrations

Article 66(1)

B. OBTAINING INFORMATION

1. In general

Text of Article 47

Article 47

The High Authority may obtain the information it requires to carry out its tasks. It may have any necessary checks made.

The High Authority must not disclose information of the kind covered by the obligation of professional secrecy, in particular information about undertakings, their business relations or their cost components. Subject to this reservation, it shall publish such data as could be useful to Governments or to any other parties concerned.

The High Authority may impose fines or periodic penalty payments on undertakings which evade their obligations under decisions taken in pursuance of this Article or which knowingly furnish false information. The maximum amount of such fines shall be 1 per cent. of the annual turnover, and the maximum amount of such penalty payments shall be 5 per cent. of the average daily turnover for each day's delay.

Any breach of professional secrecy by the High Authority which has caused damage to an undertaking may be the subject of an action for compensation before the Court, as provided in Article 40.

Text of decision no. 14–64 of July 8, 1964 on business books and accounting documents which undertakings must produce for inspection by officials or agents of the High Authority carrying out checks or verifications as regards prices. (not printed)

Text of Commission decision no. 379/84/ECSC of February 15, 1984 defining the powers of officials and agents of the Commission instructed to carry out the checks provided for in the ECSC Treaty and decisions taken in application thereof. (not printed)

Röchling-Burbach* CS68

2. For the purposes of Article 65

Article 65(3)

Text of decision no. 1–65 of February 3, 1965 concerning notification of decisions on information to be obtained from or checks to be made on associations of undertakings for the purposes of application of Article 65 of the Treaty. (not printed)
Röchling/Burbach* CS68

3. For the purposes of Article 66

Article 66(4)

C. RIGHTS OF THE DEFENCE

Text of Article 36

Article 36

Before imposing a pecuniary sanction or ordering a periodic penalty payment as provided for in this Treaty, the High Authority must give the party concerned the opportunity to submit its comments.

D. SECRECY

Text of Article 47(2)

Article 47(2)

The High Authority must not disclose information of the kind covered by the obligation of professional secrecy, inparticular information about undertakings, their business relations or their cost components. Subject to this reservation, it shall publish such data as could be useful to Governments or to any other parties concerned.

Article 65(2)(5)

E. NOTIFICATION

1. Notification of agreements under Article 65

Article 65(2) & 4(2)

Stainless Steel Cartel CS106

2. Notification of concentrations

2.1. Obligatory notification

Article 66(1)

2.2. Failure to notify

2.2.1. Authorisation withheld

2.2.2. Authorisation with fine for failure to notify

Article 66(5)(1)

2.3. Effects of notification

F. DECISIONS TAKEN BY THE COMMISSION

Article 14(2)
Article 15(1), (2) & (3)

1. Decisions pursuant to Article 65

1.1. Authorisation

Geitling v. H A CS10

1.1.1. Conditional authorisation

Article 65(2)(3)

1.1.2. Conditions aiming to prevent discrimination between trading partners

COBECHAR I CS2
OKB I CS4
Union Charbonnière CS5
COBECHAR II CS7
Walzstahlkontor I CS16
NICIA CS100
SOREMA v. H A CS20

1.1.3. Conditions preventing cross directorships or management

Präsident I CS8
Thyssen/Krupp/Wuppermann CS29
Hoesch/Rheinstahl CS30
Maxhütte/Klöckner I CS31
Dilliner/Arbed I CS32
Rötzel/Krupp CS61
Boël/Clabecq CS87

1.1.4 Other conditions to safeguard competition

OKB I CS4

4 Procedure

Union Charbonnière CS5
Präsident I CS8
Walzstahlkontor I CS16
Thyssen/Krupp/Wuppermann CS29
Maxhütte/Klöckner I CS31
Dillinger/Arbed I CS32
Creusot-Loire/Ugine CS73
UCRO CS74
Cockerill/Klöckner CS77
Cockerill/Estel CS78
Arbed/Cockerill-Sambre CS95

1.1.5. Authorisation conditional upon existence of crisis measures

URCO CS74

1.1.6. Conditions requiring submission of information

Walzstahlkontor I CS16
Stahlring I CS17
Falck/Redaelli I CS21
Creusot/Loire CS23
Danish Steel Distributors CS39
Maier/Röchling CS67
COIMPRE CS69
Falck/Redaelli II CS75
Chamber of Coal Traders I CS86
Arbed/Unimétal CS103

1.1.7 Temporary authorisation

Article 65(2)(3)
Union Charbonniére CS5
Stahlring III CS65

1.1.8 Revocation of authorisation

Article 65(2)(4)
SOREMA CS11
Geitling III CS12
Präsident II CS13
SOREMA v. *H A* (p. 339) CS20

1.2. Prohibition

Article 65(4)(2)
German rolled steel CS84
Stainles Steel Cartel CS106

1.3. Fines

Article 65(5)
German scrap cartel CS28
Stainles Steel Cartel CS106

1.4. Limitation periods

6th Comp. Rep. (paras. 19–21)

2. Decisions pursuant to Article 66

2.1. Authorisation

2.1.1. Conditional authorisation

Article 66(2)(3)
Nold v. *Commission* CS23

2.1.2. Conditions aiming to prevent discrimination between trading partners

Ruhrkohle CS37
British Fuel CS102
Nold v. *Commission* CS23

2.1.3. Conditions preventing cross directorships or management

Thyssen/Rheinstahl CS38
Thyssen/SOLMER CS44
CLIF/Marine-Firminy CS48
Krupp/Stahlwerke CS49
Arbed/Rodange 6.6.78 CS71
Rogesa CS88
Usinor/Sacilor/Normandie CS92
17th Comp. Rep. (para. 92)

2.1.4. Other conditions to safeguard competition

Ruhrkohle CS37
Thyssen/SOLMER CS44
CLIF/Marine-Firminy CS48
Krupp/Stahlwerke CS49
Arbed/Rodange CS71
Usinor/Sacilor/Normandie CS92
British Fuel CS102

2.1.5 Conditions requiring submission of information

British Fuel CS102
British Steel/Walker CS106

2.1.6. Authorisation with fines for failure to notify

Article 66(5)(1)

2. Prohibition

Article 66(5)(2)

2.2.1. Interim order

Article 66(5)(3)
CLIF/Marine-Firminy** CS48
4th Comp. Rep. (paras. 141–143)

2.2.2. Divestiture order

Article 66(5)(2)

2.2.3. Executory measures

Article 66(5)(5)

2.3. Periodic penalty payments

Article 66(5)(4)

2.4. Fines

Article 66(6)
GKN/Miles Druce CS41

G. CHALLENGING DECISIONS BEFORE THE COURT OF JUSTICE

1. Exercise of control by the Court

1.1. In general

Text of Article 33(1) ECSC

Article 33(1)

The Court shall have jurisdiction in actions brought by a Member State or by the Council to have decisions or recommendations of the High Authority declared void on grounds of lack of competence, infringement of an essential procedural requirement, infringement of this Treaty or of any rule of law relating to its application, or misuse of powers. The Court may not, however, examine the evaluation of the situation, resulting from economic facts or circumstances, in the light of which the High Authority took its decisions or made its recommendations, save there the High Authority is alleged to have misused its powers or to have manifestly failed to observe the provisions of this Treaty or any rule of law relating to its application.

Text of Article 33(2) & Article 35(3) ECSC

Article 33(2)

Undertakings or the associations referred to in Article 48 may, under the same conditions, institute proceedings against decisions or recommendations concerning them which are individual in character or against general decisions or recommendations which they consider to involve a misuse of powers affecting them.

Article 35(3)

If at the end of two months the High Authority has not taken any decision or made any recommendation, proceedings may be instituted before the Court within one month against the implied decision of refusal which is to be inferred from the silence of the High Authority on the matter.

Article 65(4) ECSC
Nold v. *H A* CS5
Stork v. *H A* CS8
Nold v. *H A* CS9
Geitling v. *H A* CS12
Schlieker v. *H A* CS17
SOREMA v. *H A* (pp. 161–162) CS18

1.2. In cases of concentrations

Article 66(5)(2) ECSC
Schlieker v. *H A* CS17

2. Time limits

Text of Article 33(3) ECSC

Article 33(3)

The proceedings provided for in the first two paragraphs of this Article shall be instituted within one month of the notification or publication, as the case may be, of the decision or recommendation.

3. Interim measures

Text of Article 39(3) ECSC

Article 39(3)

The Court may prescribe any other necessary interim measures.

Geitling v. *H A* CS10
SOREMA v. *H A* CS20
Miles Druce v. *Commission I* CS21
Miles Druce v. *Commission II* CS22

4. Suspensory effect

4.1. In general

Text of Article 39(1) ECSC

Article 39(1)

Actions brought before the Court shall not have suspensory effect.

4.2. In cases of interim measures

Text of Article 39(2) & (3) and Article 66(5)(3)

4 Procedure

Article 39(2)(3)

The Court may, however, if it considers that the circumstances so require, order that application of the contested decision or recommendation be suspended.

The Court may prescribe any other necessary interim measures.

Article 66(5)(3)

The Court may, however, if it considers that the circumstances so require, order that application of the contested decision or recommendation be suspended.

The Court may prescribe any other necessary interim measures.

The High Authority may at any time, unless the third paragraph of Article 39 is applied, take or cause to be taken such interim measures of protection as it may consider necessary to safeguard the interests of competing undertakings and of third parties, and to forestall any step which might hinder the implementation of its decisions. Unless the Court decides otherwise, proceedings shall not have suspensory effect in respect of such interim measures.

Nold v. *H A* CS5

EEC TREATY ARTICLES

Article 2

The Community shall have as its task, by establishing a common market and progressively approximating the economic policies of Member States, to promote throughout the Community a harmonious development of economic activities, a continuous and balanced expansion, an increase in stability, an accelerated raising of the standard of living and closer relations between the States belonging to it.

Article 3f

For the purposes set out in Article 2, the activities of the Community shall include, as provided in this Treaty and in accordance with the timetable set out therein:

(f) the institution of a system ensuring that competition in the common market is not distorted;

Article 5

Member States shall take all appropriate measures, whether general or particular, to ensure fulfilment of the obligations arising out of this Treaty or resulting from action taken by the institutions of the Community. They shall facilitate the achievement of the Community's tasks.

They shall abstain from any measure which could jeopardise the attainment of the objectives of this Treaty.

Article 30

Quantitative restrictions on imports and all measures having equivalent effect shall, without prejudice to the following provisions, be prohibited between Member States.

Article 36

The provisions of Articles 30 to 34 shall not preclude prohibitions or restrictions on imports, exports or goods in transit justified on grounds of public morality, public policy or public security; the protection of health and life of humans, animals or plants; the protection of national treasures possessing artistic; historic or archaeological value; or the protection of industrial and commercial property. Such prohibitions or restrictions shall not, however, constitute a means of arbitrary discrimination or a disguised restriction on trade between Member States.

Article 59

Within the framework of the provisions set out below, restrictions on freedom to provide services within the Community shall be progressively abolished during the transitional period in respect of nationals of Member States who are established in a State of the Community other than that of the person for whom the services are intended.

The Council may, acting by a qualified majority on a proposal from the Commission, extend the provisions of this Chapter to nationals of a third country who provide services and who are established within the Community.

Article 85

1. The following shall be prohibited as incompatible with the common market: all agreements between undertakings, decisions by associations of undertakings and con-

certed practices which may affect trade between Member States and which have as their object or effect the prevention, restriction or distortion of competition within the common market, and in particular those which:
(a) directly or indirectly fix purchase or selling prices or any other trading conditions;
(b) limit or control production, markets, technical development, or investment;
(c) share markets or sources of supply;
(d) apply dissimilar conditions to equivalent transactions with other trading parties, thereby placing them at a competitive disadvantage;
(e) make the conclusion of contracts subject to acceptance by the other parties of supplementary obligations which, by their nature or according to commercial usage, have no connection with the subject of such contracts.
2. Any agreements or decisions prohibited pursuant to this Article shall be automatically void.
3. The provisions of paragraph 1 may, however, be declared inapplicable in the case of:
— any agreement or category of agreements between undertakings;
— any decision or category of decisions by associations of undertakings;
— any concerted practice or category of concerted practices;
which contributed to improving the production or distribution of goods or to promoting technical or economic progress, while allowing consumers a fair share of the resulting benefit, and which does not:
(a) impose on the undertakings concerned restrictions which are not indispensable to the attainment of these objectives;
(b) afford such undertakings the possibility of eliminating competition in respect of a substantial part of the products in question.

Article 86

Any abuse by one or more undertakings of a dominant position within the common market or in a substantial part of it shall be prohibited as incompatible with the common market in so far as it may affect trade between Member States. Such abuse may, in particular, consist in:
(a) directly or indirectly imposing unfair purchase or selling prices or other unfair trading conditions;
(b) limiting production, markets or technical development to the prejudice of consumers;
(c) applying dissimilar conditions to equivalent transactions with other trading parties, thereby placing them at a competitive disadvantage;
(d) making the conclusion of contracts subject to acceptance by the other parties of supplementary obligations which, by their nature or according to commercial usage, have no connection with the subject of such contracts.

Article 87

1. Within three years of the entry force of this Treaty the Council shall, acting unanimously on a proposal from the Commission and after consulting the Assembly, adopt any appropriate regulations or directives to give effect to the principles set out in Articles 85 and 86.
If such provisions have not been adopted within the period mentioned, they shall be laid down by the Council, acting by a qualified majority on a proposal from the Commission and after consulting the Assembly.
2. The regulations or directives referred to in paragraph 1 shall be designed, in particular:
(a) to ensure compliance with the prohibitions laid down in Article 85(1) and in Article 86 by making provision for fines and periodic penalty payments;
(b) to lay down detailed rules for the application of Article 85(3), taking into account the need to ensure effective supervision on the one hand, and to simplify administration to the greatest possible extent on the other,
(c) to define, if need be, in the various branches of the economy, the scope of the provisions of Article 85 and 86.
(d) to define the respective functions of the Commission and of the Court of Justice in applying the provisions laid down in this paragraph;
(e) to determine the relationship between national laws and the provisions contained in this Section or adopted pursuant to this Article.

EEC Treaty Articles

Article 88

Until the entry into force of the provisions adopted in pursuance of Article 87, the authorities in Member States shall rule on the admissibility of agreements, decisions and concerted practices and on abuse of a dominant position in the common market in accordance with the law of their country and with the provisions of Article 85, in particular paragraph 3, and of Article 86.

Article 89

1. Without prejudice to Article 88, the Commission shall, as soon as it takes up its duties, ensure the application of the principles laid down in Articles 85 and 86. On application by a Member State or on its own initiative, and in co-operation with the competent authorities in the Member States, who shall give it their assistance, the Commission shall investigate cases of suspected infringement of these principles. If it finds that there has been an infringement, it shall propose appropriate measures to being it to an end.
2. If the infringement is not brought to an end, the Commission shall record such infringement of the principles in a reasoned decision. The Commission may publish its decision and authorise Member States to take the measures, the conditions and details of which it shall determine, needed to remedy the situation.

Article 90

1. In the case of public undertakings and undertakings to which Member States grant special or exclusive rights, Member States shall neither enact nor maintain in force any measure contrary to the rules contained in this Treaty, in particular to those rules provided for in Article 7 and Articles 85 to 94.
2. Undertakings entrusted with the operation of services of general economic interest or having the character of a revenue-producing monopoly shall be subject to the rules contained in this Treaty, in particular to the rules on competition, in so far as the application of such rules does not obstruct the performance, in law or in fact, of the particular tasks assigned to them. The development of trade must not be affected to such an extent as would be contrary to the interests of the Community.
3. The Commission shall ensure the application of the provisions of this Article and shall, where necessary, address appropriate directives or decisions to Member States.

Article 164

The Court of Justice shall ensure that in the interpretation and application of this Treaty the law is observed.

Article 169

If the Commission considers that a Member State has failed to fulfil an obligation under this Treaty, it shall deliver a reasoned opinion on the matter after giving the State concerned the opportunity to submit its observations.
If the State concerned does not comply with the opinion within the period laid down by the Commission, the latter may bring the matter before the Court of Justice.

Article 168a

1. At the request of the Court of Justice and after consulting the Commission and the European Parliament, the Council may, acting unanimously, attach to the Court of Justice a court with jurisdiction to hear and determine at first instance, subject to a right of appeal to the Court of Justice on points of law only and in accordance with the conditions laid down by the Statute, certain classes of action or proceedings brought by natural or legal persons. That court shall not be competent to hear and determine actions brought by Member States or by Community Institutions or questions referred for a preliminary ruling under Article 177.
2. The Council, following the procedure laid down in paragraph 1, shall determine the composition of that court and adopt the necessary adjustments and additional provisions to

the Statute of the Court of Justice. Unless the Council decides otherwise, the provisions of this Treaty relating to the Court of Justice, in particular the provisions of the Protocol on the Statute of the Court of Justice, shall apply to that court.

3. The Members of that court shall be chosen from persons whose independence is beyond doubt and who possess the ability required for appointment to judicial office; they shall be appointed by common accord of the Governments of the Member States for a term of six years. The membership shall be partially renewed every three years. Retiring members shall be eligible for reappointment.

4. That court shall establish its rules of procedure in agreement with the Court of Justice. Those rules shall require the unanimous approval of the Council.

Article 172

Regulations made by the Council pursuant to the provisions of this Treaty may give the Court of Justice unlimited jurisdiction in regard to the penalties provided for in such regulations.

Article 173

The Court of Justice shall review the legality of acts of the Council and the Commission other than recommendations or opinions. It shall for this purpose have jurisdiction in actions brought by a Member State, the Council or the Commission on grounds of lack of competence, infringement of an essential procedural requirement, infringement of this Treaty or of any rule of law relating to its application, or misuse of powers.

Any natural or legal person may, under the same conditions, institute proceedings against a decision addressed to that person or against a decision which, although in the form of a regulations or a decision addressed to another person, is of direct and individual concern to the former.

The proceedings provided for in this Article shall be instituted within two months of the publication of the measure, or of its notification to the plaintiff, or, in the absence thereof, of the day on which it came to the knowledge of the latter, as the case may be.

Article 175

Should the Council or the Commission, in infringement of this Treaty, fail to act, the Member States and the other institutions of the Community may bring an action before the Court of Justice to have the infringement established.

Article 177

The Court of Justice shall have jurisdiction to give preliminary rulings concerning:
   (a) the interpretation of this Treaty;
   (b) the validity and interpretation of acts of the institutions of the Community;
   (c) the interpretation of the statutes of bodies established by an act of the Council, where those statutes so provide.

Where such a question is raised before any court or tribunal of a Member State, that court or tribunal may, if it considers that a decision on the question is necessary to enable it to give judgment, request the Court of Justice to give a ruling thereon.

Where any such question is raised in a case pending before a court or tribunal of a Member State, against whose decisions there is no judicial remedy under national law, that court or tribunal shall bring the matter before the Court of Justice.

Article 178

The Court of Justice shall have jurisdiction in disputes relating to compensation for damage provided for in the second paragraph of Article 215.

Article 185

Actions brought before the Court of Justice shall not have suspensory effect. The Court of Justice may, however, if it considers that circumstances so require, order that application of the contested act be suspended.

EEC Treaty Articles

Article 186

The Court of Justice may in any cases before it prescribe any necessary interim measures.

Article 215

The contractual liability of the Community shall be governed by the law applicable to the contract in question.
In the case of non-contractual liability, the Community shall, in accordance with the general principles common to the laws of the Member States, make good any damage caused by its institutions or by its servants in the performance of their duties.
The personal liability of its servants towards the Community shall be governed by the provisions laid down in the Staff Regulations or in the Conditions of Employment applicable to them.

Article 222

This Treaty shall in no way prejudice the rules in Member States governing the system of property ownership.

Article 223

1. The provisions of this Treaty shall not preclude the application of the following rules:
(a) No Member State shall be obliged to supply information the disclosures of which it considers contrary to the essential interests of its security;
(b) Any Member State may take such measures as it considers necessary for the protection of the essential interests of its security which are connected with the production of or trade in arms, munitions and war material; such measures shall not adversely affect the conditions of competition in the common market regarding products which are not intended for specifically military purposes.
2. During the first year after the entry into force of this Treaty, the Council shall, acting unanimously, draw up a list of products to which the provisions of paragraph 1(b) shall apply.
3. The Council may, acting unanimously on a proposal from the Commission, make changes in this list.

Article 224

Member States shall consult each other with a view to taking together the steps needed to prevent the functioning of the common market being affected by measures which a Member State may be called upon to take in the event of serious internal disturbances affecting the maintenance of law and order, in the event of war or serious international tension constituting a threat of war, or in order to carry out obligations it has accepted for the purpose of maintaining peace and international security.

List of Staff at DG IV

Directorate-General IV

Competition

Rue de la Loi 200, 1049 Bruxelles,
Wetstraat 200, 1049 Brussel
Tel. 235 11 11
Telex 21877 COMEU B

Director-General	Claus Dieter EHLERMANN
Deputy Director-General (with special responsibility for Directorates A and D)	Raymond SIMONNET
Principal Adviser	Robert SUNNEN
Hearing Officer	Hartmut JOHANNES
Adviser responsible for confidentiality of information and hearings in Merger cases	Joseph GILCHRIST
Advisers	Georgios ROUNIS Klaus STÖVER
Assistants to Director-General	Irene SOUKA-PAPAYANNIDES Luc GYSELEN
Head of Data Processing (directly responsible to Director General)	—

Merger Task Force	Henry Colin OVERBURY
1. Operation Unit I	—
2. Operations Unit II	Götz DRAUZ
3. Operations Unit III	Roger DAOUT

Administrative Unit	**Head**
Directorate A	
General competition and co-ordination policy	Rafael GARCIA PALENCIA
1. General policy and international aspects: relations with the European Parliament and the Economic and Social Committee	Auke HAAGSMA
Deputy Head of Division (with special responsibility for international questions)	Claude ROUAM
2. Legal and procedural problems, regulations, infringements procedures, and intra-Community dumping	—
3. Economic questions and studies	David DEACON
4. Co-ordination of competition decisions — Horizontal agreements and abuse of dominant positions, joint ventures and mergers	Helmut SCHRÖTER

List of Staff at DG IV

    — Industrial and intellectual property rights, research and development   Sebastiano GUTTUSO

5. Public enterprises and State monopolies, implementation of Articles 101 and 102   Claude RAKOVSKY

6. Documentation, data processing and registry   —

Directorate B
Restrictive practices, abuse of dominant positions and other distortions of competition I   Jean DUBOIS (acting director)

1. Electrical and electronic manufactured products including Telecommunications   Jean DUBOIS

2. Mechanical manufactured products and the textile, clothing, leather and other manufacturing industries   Franco GIUFFRIDA

3. Banking, Insurance and other services   Gisèle VERNIMMEN

4. Media, Leisure Electronics, Music Publications, Trade   Norbert MENGES

Directorate C
Restrictive practices, abuse of dominant positions and other distortions of competition II   Gianfranco ROCCA

1. Non-ferrous metals, non-metallic mineral products, construction, timber, paper, glass and rubber industries   Maurice GUERRIN

2. Energy (other than coal), basic products of the chemicals industry   Kurt RITTER

3. Processed chemical products, agricultural products and foodstuffs   Jürgen MENSCHING

Directorate D
Restrictive practices, abuse of dominant positions and other distortions of competition III   John TEMPLE LANG

1. Steel and coal   Juan Antonio RIVIERE MARTI
2. CECA Inspector
—Studies, co-ordination and Training   Pierre DUPRAT
3. Transport and tourist industries
Deputy Head of Division   —
4. Motor vehicles and other means of transport, and associated mechanical manufactured products   Dieter SCHWARZ

Directorate E
State aids   Asger PETERSEN

Adviser   Ronald FETKAMP

1. General aid schemes   Gerhard THIES
2. Aids to research and development   Serge DURANDE
3. Regional aids
Deputy Head of Division   Luigi CAMPOGRANDE
Alfredo MARQUES
4. Sectoral aids I   Francisco ESTEVE REY
5. Sectoral aids II   —
6. Inventory and analysis   —

GLOSSARY

Active sales

Active promotion of the sales of a product or a service; *e.g.* advertising campaign or establishment of brands or subsidiary.

Agency

Undertaking that does not assume the financial risk of the transactions concluded on behalf of its principal. Normally such an undertaking does not own the stock it sells and is not responsible for unsold stocks.

Agreements intended to control the supply of a product

Schemes intended to limit the availability of a product for non-participating companies by changing the state of the products and/or by prescribing the places where it may be sold.

Appreciability

One of the conditions for the application of both Articles 85 and 86 is that the restriction of competition and the resulting effect on trade should not be of minor importance.

Barriers to entry

Factors which made the access to a market difficult. These factors can roughly be classified into three categories; natural obstacles such as mountains or oceans; obstacles of a legal nature such as patents, quotas and tariffs, and finally obstacles which result from the market structure such as large economies of scale and product differentiation. Sometimes large capital requirements for "start-up" are also considered to be a barrier to entry.

Best-endeavours clause

Clause in a contract which obliges a contracting party to fulfil its contractual obligations to the best possible extent. Such an obligation normally means that this party should concentrate its attention upon the activities covered by the contract.

Breeder's right

Exclusive intellectual and industrial property right granted to a person which develops a new plant variety.

Circular argument

A factor sometimes considered to be relevant to the establishment of dominance; if a company can act sufficiently independently of its competitors to carry out a course of conduct that may be considered to be an abuse, this may in some cases be taken to be evidence of the existence of dominance itself.

Collective exclusive dealing

Agreements or practices by which companies at different levels of the production and distribution chain agree to deal only amongst and with each other.

Collective or aggregated rebates

Discounts which are granted to categories of customers defined in the agreement in question and which are based upon the total bought by each of these customers from all parties to that agreement or from all manufacturers which operate in the same territory as these parties.

Glossary

Collective resale price maintenance

Agreement or practice by which the participating companies agree to fix the prices of their products for resale (see resale price maintenance). This does not imply the uniformity of these prices.

Comfort letter

Letter from a senior official of the Directorate General for Competition of the European Communities informing the parties involved that the services of the Commission do not intend to adopt a final decision upon the case in question. Such an administrative letter normally contains a preliminary assessment of the practice concerned. This assessment does not have a binding effect.

Commercial advantages

Factors of a commercial nature which are indicative of a firm's performance, such as a well developed and established network of salesmen and the reputation of its brands.

Common rebate or discount policy

Practice or agreement according to which the parties concerned determine when, where, to whom and/or to which discounts will be granted.

Compensation scheme

System that enforces the allocation of quotas between the participating companies. According to such a system, the company that exceeds its quota must pay a compensatory amount to the company or companies that did not implement their quota.

Competition

Independent striving for patronage by the various sellers in a market.
Several kinds of competition can be distinguished, such as:
— price competition and non-price competition on items such as quality of the product sold, advertising, brands, after sales-service, speedy delivery, etc.
— Competition between products of different brands, so-called interbrand competition and competition concerning the sale of products with the same brand, so called interbrand competition. The latter is only relevant for the distribution of the branded product.
— competition between the parties to an agreement (internal competition), and external competition between these parties other companies.

Conflict rules

Rules to solve a competence conflict between authorities dealing with the same legal issue and wishing or refusing to apply the same substantive law.

Concerted practice

Collusion or form of collaboration looser than a contract or an agreement.

Co-operation agreement

Agreement offering the possibility for normally small or medium sized companies to rationalise and to increase their performance and competitiveness on a wider market.

Co-ordination centre

Supervising entity without assets, created by competitors to coordinate their production capacity, production, sales and/or prices.

Crisis cartel

Agreement between competitors to reduce excess capacity in a stagnating market.

Glossary

Direct sales

See **Export-ban.**

English clause

Provision in a sales-contract according to which the buyer is free to purchase from another company than his contractor partner if the latter does not match a competing offer.

Exclusivity

Obligation of one contracting party to confer the right which is the object of an agreement only to the other contracting party in a given area, or contract territory. Normally such an obligation is accompanied by two other ancillary obligations, according to which grantor shall not compete with the later in respect of the object of their agreement in the contract territory and recipient of the exclusive right shall not compete with the former in the territory reserved to him.

Exclusive purchase

Obligation imposed on one contracting party to purchase the contract goods or services only from the other contracting party.

Export-ban

Clause prohibiting a contract party to export outside the contract territory. If this prohibition is imposed only in respect of sales by this contract party the clause is called an export ban on direct sales. If the party is obliged to reimpose this prohibition on its resellers, then it is called an export ban on indirect sales.

Field of use

Clause in a license agreement limiting the right to use the licensed technology or know-how only to a defined category of products or services.

Indirect-sales

See **Export-ban.**

Joint venture

Entity created by two or more companies to undertake certain commercial activities. This entity may take any legal form, joint subsidiary, joint committee etc.

Most favoured customer or licensee clause

Obligation of a contracting party to grant the other contracting party, the most advantageous contractual terms which the former offered to any other customer or licensee.

New agreements

Agreements made after the entry into force of Regulation 17/62 and/or after the accession of a new Member State.

No-challenge clause

Provision normally figuring in a license agreement which forbids the licensee to challenge the validity of the licensed intellectual or industrial property right.

No-competition clause

Prohibition of one contracting party to undertake activities competing with the subject matter of the agreement. This prohibition can be specified as an (1) obligation of a contracting party not to sell products which compete with the contract product, (2) obligation of a contracting party not to be interested, directly or indirectly, in commercial activities similar or comparable to those foreseen by the contract, and, finally, (3) an obligation of a contracting party to abstain from exercising a commercial activity similar or

Glossary

comparable to that foreseen by the contract, for a certain period after the termination of that contract.

Objective justification

Factors beyond the control of a company which explain or justify the behaviour of that company.

Opposition procedure

Procedure figuring in certain block-exemption regulations which enables companies to obtain legal security regarding whether their agreements benefit from a block-exemption.

Old agreements

Agreement made before the entry into force of Regulation 17/62 and/or before the accession of a new Member State.

Parallel imports

Imports into a territory outside the official distribution network set up by the producer. These imports occur if there are significant price differences between Member States which allow someone to buy in the low priced area and sell in the high.

Passive sales

Accepting unsolicited offers within a certain territory from customers outside that territory.

Patent pooling

Cross-licensing patents between two or more companies and/or collective decision by these companies whether or not to license third parties or not.

Predatory pricing

Price setting to eliminate competitiots whilst benefitting from advantages which are not directly related to competitiveness.

Profit pass-over clause

Provision making export by one distributor to a territory other than the contract territory conditional upon the payment of a certain amont of money to the official distributor in that other territory.

Provisional validity

A notified old agreement must be considered to be valid until the Commission has pronounced itself on the possibility of exemption of that agreement.

Post termination provisions

Clauses regulating the situation after the term or termination of a contract.

Quotas

Allocation between competititors of quantities fixed in percentages or in real terms for their production or sales, typically related to specific territories or customers.

Resale price maintenance

Policy of a producer or principal to determine the resale price of its resellers.

Relevant market

Market in which the behaviour of one or more companies will be assessed for the purpose of competition policy. It normally corresponds to the geographical area in which companies selling a certain commodity or service and its close substitutes compete for the patronage of the customers.

Glossary

Rule of reason

Making the assessment of the prohibition of a certain restrictive practice dependent on the effects which that practice has or will have in the market. Such an analysis not only requires a balancing between the restriction of intra-brand or internal competition with the possible increase in inter-brand or external competition, but also a comparison of the competitive nature of the relevant market before and after the practice has occurred. The concept of the rule of reason is also related to the assessment of "ancillary restraints". These restraints restrict competition in a formal sense (intra-brand or internal competition), but may be considered as indispensable to the achievement of a result which is pro-competitive in a wider sense (inter-brand or external competition)—See **Competition**.

Selective distribution

A policy according to which the manufacturer or principal ensurer that his product is only sold through competent dealers. This policy is important when the product is of a particular nature (*e.g.* high technology) or when its marketing concentrates on certain specific types of customer.

Spill-over effect

Cooperation between companies in certain areas and/or in respect of certain commercial activities may negatively affect the willingness of these companies to compete in other areas and/or in respect of other activities.

Technical advantages

Factors of a technical nature which are indicative of a firm's performance such as its R&D activities, its patents and know-how.

Tying

Making the conclusion of one business transaction dependent upon the conclusion of another.

BIBLIOGRAPHY

Table of Contents

		page
General		549
Book One: General Competition Rules		551
Part I	**Conditions for the application of both Articles 85 and 86**	551
Part II	**Article 85(1),(2) and (3)**	552
Part III	**Horizontal agreements**	554
	1. Cartels	554
	2. Co-operation agreements	554
	4. Research & development agreements	554
	5. Trade Associations	555
Part IV	**Vertical agreements**	556
	1. Exclusive and non-exclusive distribution agreements	557
	2. Exclusive purchasing agreements	557
	3. Selective distribution agreements	557
	5. Franchising agreements	558
Part V	**Industrial and intellectual property agreements**	559
	1. Articles 30, 36 & 59 EEC; free movement	560
	2. Patent licensing agreements	560
	3. Know-how licensing agreements	561
	4. Trademark licensing and cession agreements	562
	5. Copyright and design right agreements	562
Part VI	**Joint ventures**	563
Part VII	**Article 86**	565
Part VIII	**State interference**	567

Bibliography—Table of Contents

Part IX	**Sectorial application of EEC competition rules**	569
	1. Agriculture	569
	3. Inland waterways, rail and road transport	569
	4. Maritime transport	569
	5. Air Transport	570
	6. Financial Services	571
Part X	**Procedure and remedies**	571
	1. Procedural legislation	573
	2. The handling of a case	574
	3. Judicial Review	575
	4. National jurisdictions and authorities	576

Book Two: Mergers and Acquisitions 576

Book Three: Coal and Steel 579

General

Assant,
"Anti-trust Intracorporate Conspiracies. A comparative study of French, EEC and American Law," *European Competition Law Review* Vol. 2, 1990

Bellamy, Christopher; Child, Graham D.,
Common Market Law of Competition (3rd ed., Sweet & Maxwell, 1987; 3rd supp., 1991)

Bork, R,
The Antitrust Paradox (1978)

Bourgeois, Jacques H.J.,
"Antitrust and Trade Policy: A Peaceful Coexistence? European Community Perspective," *International Business Lawyer,* Vol. 17/1989, No. 2, pp. 58–67 and No. 3, pp.115–122

Compendium of EC Competition Law
(ed. Butterworths European Information Services, 1989)

Gleiss, Alfred; Hirsch, Martin,
Common Market Cartel Law,
(3rd ed., The Bureau of National Affairs, 1981)

Goyder, D.G.,
EEC Competition Law
(Oxford European Community Law Series, Clarendon, 1988)

Goyens, M.(ed)
"E.C. Competition Policy and the Consumer Interest Proceedings of the Third Workshop on Consumer Law",
held in Louvain-la-Neuve, May 10 and 11, 1984
(Collection Droit et Consommation; 9 Cabay, 1985)

Green, Nicholas,
Commercial Agreements and Competition Law: Practice and Procedure in the UK and EEC
(Graham & Trotman, 1986)

Hawk, Barry E.,
"The American (Anti-Trust) Revolution: Lessons for the EEC?"
European Competition Law Review, Vol. 9/1988, No. 1, pp. 53–87

"1992 and EEC/U.S. Competition and Trade Law,"
Annual Proceedings of the Fordham Corporate Law Institue; 1989
(Bender, 1989)

U.S., Common Market—International Antitrust: A Comparative Guide
(Law and Business Inc., 1985)

Johannes, Hartmut,
"Technology Transfer under EEC Law—Europe between the Divergent Opinions of the Past and the New Administration: A Comparative Approach,"
Annual Proceedings of the Fordham Corporate Law Institute: Antitrust, Technology Transfers and Joint Ventures in International Trade
(1982), pp. 65–94

Joliet, R,
The Rule of Reason in Antitrust Law: American, German and Common Market laws in comparative perspective*, (Nijhoff, 1967)

Korah, Valentine,
An Introductory Guide to EEC Competition Law and Practice
(4th ed., ESC/Sweet & Maxwell, 1990)

Kulms, R,
"Competition, Trade Policy and Competition Policy in the EEC: The Example of Antidumping"
Common Market Law Review Vol. 2, 1990, p.285

Merkin, Robert; Williams, Karen,
Competition Law: Antitrust Policy in the U.K. and the EEC
(Sweet & Maxwell, 1984)

Marques Mendes, M,
"Antitrust in a world of Interrelated Economics. The Interplay between Antitrust and Trade Policies in the U.S. and the EEC (Etudes Européennes)" (Université de Bruxelles, 1991)

Pescatore, Pierre,
"Public and Private Aspects of European Community Competition Law,"
Fordham International Law Journal,
Vol. 10/1987, No. 3, pp. 373–419

Posner, R,
Antitrust Law (1976)

Ritter, L., Braun, D., Rawlinson, F.
EEC Competition Law A Practitioner's Guide
(Kluwer, 1991)

Scherer, F.
Industrial Market Structure and Economic Performance
(2nd ed., 1980)

Swann, Dennis,
Competition and Industrial Policy in the European Community
(The Methuen EEC Series, Methuen, 1983)

Temple Lang, John; Sundstrom, Zacharias,
"The Antitrust Law of the European Community and the UNCTAD Code on Restrictive Business Practices'
International Business Lawyer,
1984, 2–7 September, pp. 353–355

Temple Lang, John,
"Reconciling European Community Antitrust and Antidumping, Transport and Trade Safeguard Policies Practical problems"
Annual Proceedings of the Fordham Corporate Law Institute; 1988, Chaps. 7.1–7.90
(Bender, 1989)

Bibliography

B. Hawk (ed.,) (1984)
"EEC Competition Actions in Member States' Courts-Claims for Damages, Declarations and Injunctions for Breach of Community Anti-Trust Law"
Fordham Corporate Law Institute, 1983, p.219

Van Bael, Ivo; Bellis, Jean-François,
Competition Law of the European Economic Community
(Julian O van Kalinowski ed. Bender, 1988) Looseleaf

Van Bael, Ivo; Bellis, Jean-François,
Competition Law of the EEC
(2nd ed., CCH, 1990)

Vandoren, P.,
"The Interface between Anti-Dumping and Competition Law and Policy in the European Community,"
Legal Issues of European Integration,
1986, No. 2, pp. 1–16

Whish, Richard,
Competition Law
(2nd ed., Butterworths, 1989)

Book One

Part I Conditions for both the application of Article 85 and 86 EEC

Adinolfi, Aelina,
"The Legal Notion of the Group Enterprise,"
"The EC Approach,"
"Regulation Corporate Groups in Europe"
(Baden-Baden, Nomos, 1990), pp. 495–514

Assant, Gilles,
"Anti-Trust Intracorporate Conspiracies
A comparative Study of French, EEC and American Laws,"
European Competition Law Review,
Vol. 11/1990, No. 2, pp. 65–79

Barack, Boaz,
The Application of the Competition Rules (Antitrust Law) of the European Economic Community to Enterprises and Arrangements external to the Common Market
(Kluwer, 1981)

Cubbin, John S.; Geroski, Paul A.,
"European Conglomerate Firms, A Report,"
Commission of the European Communities Luxembourg, Office for Official Publications of the European Communities, 1990

Faull, Jonathan,
"Effect on Trade between Member States 1992 and EEC/U.S. Competition and Trade Law,"
Annual Proceedings of the Fordham Corporate Law Institute, 1989, pp. 259-294

Ferry, J.E.,
"Towards Completing the Charm, The Woodpulp Judgment,"
European Competition Law Review,
Vol. 10/1989, No. 1, pp. 58-73

Gleichmann, Karl,
"The Law of Corporate Groups in the European Community Regulating Corporate Groups in Europe,"
(Baden-Baden, Nomos, 1990), pp. 435-456

Kalmansohn, Mark E.,
"Application of EEC Articles 85 and 86 to Foreign Multinationals,"
Legal Issues of European Integration,
1984, No. 2, pp. 1-40

Kuyper, P.J.,
"European Community Law and Extraterritoriality: Some Trends and New Developments,"
International and Comparative Law Quarterly,
Vol. 33/1984, P.4, October, pp. 1013-1021

Lange, Dieter G.F.; Sandage, John Byron,
"The Woodpulp Decision and its Implications for the Scope of EC Competition Law,"
Common Market Law Review,
Vol. 26/1989, No. 2, pp. 137-165

Van Gerven, Walter,
"EC Jurisdiction in Antitrust Matters,"
"The Woodpulp Judgment,"
"1992 and EEC/U.S. Competition and Trade Law,"
Annual Proceedings of the Fordham Corporate Law Institute 1989, (Bender, 1990), pp. 295-359

Part II   Article 85(1),(2) and (3)

Cope Huie, Marsha,
"The Intra-Enterprise Conspiracy Doctrine in the United States and the European Economic Community"
The American journal of Comparative law,
Vol. 36/1988, No. 2, pp. 307-327

Evans, Andrew C.,
"Article 85(3) Exemption, the Notion of 'Allowing the Consumers a fair Share of the Resulting Benefit' E.C. Competition Policy and the Consumer Interest"
(Cabay, 1985), pp. 99-120

Evans, Andrew C.,
"European Competition Law and Consumers, the Article 85(3) Exemption,"
European Competition Law Review,
Vol. 2/1981, No. 4, pp. 425–437

Forrester, Ian; Norrall, Christopher,
"The Laicization of Community Law: Self-help and the Rule of Reason: How Competition Law is and could be applied,"
Common Market Law Review,
Vol. 21/1984, No. 1, pp.11–51

Green, Nicholas,
"Article 85 in Perspective: Stretching jurisdiction, Narrowing the Concept of a Restriction and Plugging a few Gaps,"
European Competition Law Review
Vol. 9/1988, No. 2, pp. 190–206

Korah, Valentine,
"The Rise and Fall of Provisional Validity: The Need for a Rule of Reason in EEC Antitrust Symposium of the European Economic Community"
(Northwestern University School of Law, 1981), pp. 320–357

Kon, Stephen,
"Article 85, para. 3: A Case for Application by National Courts,"
Common Market Law Review,
Vol. 19/1982, No. 4, pp. 541–561

Peeters, Jan,
"The Rule of Reason Revisited Prohibition on Restraints of Competition in the Sherman Act and the EEC Treaty,"
The American Journal of Comparative Law,
Vol. 37/1989, No. 3, pp. 521-570

Schroeter, Helmuth R.B.,
Antitrust and Analysis under Article 85(1) and (3),"
Annual Proceedings of the Fordham Corporate Law Institute
(Bender, 1987), pp. 645–692

Steindorff, Ernst,
"Article 85, para. 3: No Case for Application by National Courts,"
Common Market Law Review,
Vol. 20/1983, No. 1, pp. 125–130

"Article 85 and the Rule of Reason,"
Common Market Law Review,
Vol. 21/1984, No. 4, pp. 639–646

Van Houtte, Ben,
"A Standard of Reason in EEC Antitrust Law: Some Comments on the Application of Parts 1 and 3 of Article 85,"
Northwestern Journal of International Law & Business,
Vol. 4/1982, No. 1, pp. 497–516

Van Rijn, Thomas,
"Intra-Enterprise Conspiracy and Article 85 of the Treaty,"
Essays in European Law and Integration
(Kluwer, 1982), pp. 123–138

Waelbroeck, M.,
"Antitrust and Analysis under Article 85(1) and Article 85(3),"
Annual Proceedings of the Fordham Corporate Law Institute, 1987,
(Bender, 1988), pp. 693–724

Whish, Richard; Sufrin, Brenda,
"Article 85 and the Rule of Reason,"
Yearbook of European Law 1987
(1988), Vol. 7, pp. 1–38

Part III Horizontal agreements

1. Cartels

Pathak, Anand S.,
Articles 85 and 86 and anti-competitive Exclusion in EEC Competition Law,"
European Competition Law Review,
Vol. 10/1989, No. 1, pp.74–104 and No. 2, pp. 256–272

Vogelaar, Floris O.W.,
"The Impact of the Economic Recession on EEC Competition Policy Part Two: Crisis and Export Cartels,"
Swiss Review of International Competition Law,
1985, No. 24, pp. 35–52

2. Co-operation Agreements

Vollmer, Andrew N.,
"Product and Technical Standardisation under Article 85,"
European Competition Law Review,
Vol. 7, 1986, pp. 388–402

4. Research and Development Agreements

Johannes, Hartmut,
"Technology Transfer under EEC Law— Europe between the Divergent Opinions of the Past and the New Administration: A Comparative Approach,"
Annual Proceedings of the Fordham Corporate Law Institute: Antitrust, Technology Transfers and Joint Ventures in International Trade law
(1982), pp. 65–94

Korah, Valentine,
"R & D and the EEC Competition Rules: Regulation 418/85,"
European Competition Law Monographs
(ESC Publishing Limited, 1986), pp. XXI–114 P

Lutz, Helmuth; Broderick, Terry R.,
"A Model EEC Research and Development Cooperation Agreement"
International Business Lawyer
(November, 1985), pp. 456–461

Overbury, Colin,
"EEC Competition Law and High Technology,"
Annual Proceedings of the Fordham Corporate Law Institute and Trade Policy in the US and the EC
(Matthew Bender, 1986), Vol. 1985

Plompen, P.M.A.L.,
"Commission Regulation No. 418/85 of December 19, 1984 on the Application of Article 85(3) of the Treaty to Categories of Research and Development Agreements,"
Legal Issues of European Integration,
1985, No. 2, pp. 46–59

Venit, James S.,
"The Research and Development Block Exemption Regulation,"
European Law Review,
Vol. 10/1985, No. 3, pp. 151–172

Whish, R.P.,
"The Commission's Block Exemption on Research and Development Agreements,"
European Competition Law Review,
Vol. 6/1985, No. 1, pp. 84–100

5. Trade Associations

Corones, S.G.,
"The Application of Article 85 of the Treaty of Rome to the Exchange of Market Information between Members of a Trade Association,"
European Competition Law Review,
Vol. 3/1982, No. 1, pp. 67–85

Evans, David S.,
"Trade Associations and the Exchange 1992 and EEC/U.S. Competition and Trade Law,"
Annual Proceedings of the Fordham Corporate Law Institute, 1989
(Bender, 1990) pp. 221–258

Reynolds, J.,
"Trade Associations and the EEC Competition Rules,"
Swiss Review of International Competition Law,
1985, No. 23, pp. 49–63

Watson, Philippa; Williams, Karen,
"The Application of the EEC Competition Rules to Trade Associations,"
Yearbook of European Law,
Vol. 8/1988, pp. 121–139

Part IV Vertical Agreements

Christou, Richard,
International Agency, Distribution and Licensing Agreements
(Longman Commercial Series, 1986), pp. XI-363

Collins, Wayne D.,
"Efficiency and Equity in Vertical Competition Law: Balancing the Tensions in the EEC and the United States Annual Proceedings of the Fordham Corporate Law,"
Institute: Antitrust and Trade Policies of the European Economic Community, 1983
(Bender, 1983), pp. 501–526

Daout, Roger,
"Distribution under EEC Law—An Official View,"
Annual Proceedings of the Fordham Corporate Law Institute: Antitrust and Trade Policies of the European Economic Community 1983
(Bender, 1983), pp. 441–500

Fine, Frank L.,
"EEC Consumer Warranties: A New Antitrust Hurdle Facing Exporters,"
Harvard International Law Journal,
Vol. 20/1988, No. 2, pp. 367/391

Green, Nicholas,
"New EEC Legislation on Exclusive Dealing and Purchasing
I: General Considerations,
II: Exclusive Dealing,
III: Exclusive Purchasing,"
New Law Journal,
Vol. 133/1983, No. 6113, pp. 663–665, No. 6114, pp. 683–685, No. 6115, pp. 693–696, 701

Gyselen, Luc,
"Vertical Restraints in the Distribution Process: Strength and Weakness of the free Rider Rationale under EEC Competition Law,"
Common Market Law Review,
Vol. 21/1984, No. 4, pp. 647–668

Korah, Valentine,
"Group Exemptions for Exclusive Distribution and Purchasing in the EEC,"
Common Market Law Review,
Vol. 21/1984, No. 1, pp. 53–80

Pathak, Anand S.,
"Vertical Restraints in EEC Competition Law"
"*Legal Issues of European Integration,*"
1988, No. 2, pp. 15–59

Bibliography

Philips, Bernard J.,
"Territorial Restraints and Inter-Brand Competition in the EEC,"
World Competition,
Vol. 12/1989, No. 4, pp. 23–30

Waelbroeck, Michel,
"Vertical Agreements: Is the Commission Right not to Follow the Current U.S. Policy?"
Swiss Review of International Competition Law,
1985, No. 25, pp. 45–52

White, Eric, L.,
"The New Block Exemption Regulations on Exclusive Dealing,"
European Law Review,
Vol. 9/1984, No. 5, pp. 356–365

1. Exclusive and Non-Exclusive Distribution Agreements

Chard, John S.,
"The Economics of Exclusive Distributorship Arrangements with Special Reference to EEC Competition Policy"
The Antitrust Bulletin
Vol. XXV/1980, No. 2, pp. 405–436

Korah, Valentine,
"Exclusive Dealing Agreements in the EEC Regulation 67/67 Replaced"
European Law Centre Limited,
1984, XV, p. 101

Schroeter, Helmuth R.B.,
"The Application of Article 85 of the EEC Treaty to Exclusive Distribution Agreements,"
Fordham International Law Journal,
Vol. 8/1984–85, No. 1, pp. 1–38

2. Exclusive Purchasing Agreements

Morris, A.L.,
"Requirements Contracts and their Treatment under the EEC Treaty,"
European Law Review,
Vol. 6/1981, No. 4, pp. 257–273

Pavesio, Carlo,
"Requirements Contracts under EEC Law in the Light of the BP Kemi Case,"
Common Market Law Review,
Vol. 18/1981, No. 3, pp. 309–333

3. Selective Distribution Agreements

Chard, J.S.,
"The Economics of the Application of Article 85 to Selective Distribution Systems,"
European Law Review,
Vol. 7/1982, No. 2, pp. 83–102

Demaret, Paul,
"Selective Distribution and EEC Law After the Ford, Pronuptia and Metro II Judgments,"
Annual Proceedings of the Fordham Corporate Law Institute,
Vol. 1986: United States and Common Market Antitrust Policies
(Bender, 1987), pp. 149–184

Goebel, Roger J.,
"Metro II's Confirmation of the Selective Distribution Rules: Is this the End of the Road?"
Common Market Law Review,
Vol. 24/1987, No. 4, pp. 605–634

Groves, Peter,
"Motor Vehicle Distribution: The Block Exemption,"
European Competition Law Review,
Vol. 8/1987, No. 1, pp. 77–87

Lebel, Claude; Aicardi, Simone,
"Legal Aspects of Selective Distribution of Luxury Products in France,"
European Intellectual Property Review,
Vol. 12/1990, No. 7, pp. 246–249

Lukoff, F.L.,
"European Competition Law and Distribution in the Motor Vehicle Sector: Commission Regulation 123/85 of December 12, 1984,"
Common Market Law Review,
Vol. 23, 1986, No. 4, pp. 841–866

Temple Lang, John,
"Selective Distribution,"
Fordham International Law Journal,
Vol. 8/1984–85, No. 3, pp. 323–361

5. Franchising Agreements

Clough, Mark,
"Franchising in Europe since the Pronuptia Case,"
European Intellectual Property Review,
Vol. 9/1987, No. 11, pp. 317–329

De Cockborne, Jean-Eric,
"The New EEC Block Exemption Regulation on Franchising,"
Fordham International Law Journal,
Vol. 12/1989, No. 2, pp. 242–310

Dubois, Jean,
"Franchising under EEC Competition Law: Implications of the Pronuptia Judgment and the proposed Block Exemption Annual Proceedings of the Fordham Corporate Law Institute,"
United States and Common Market Antitrust Policies, Vol. 1986: pp. 115–145

Goebel, Roger J.,
"The Uneasy Fate of Franchising under EEC Antitrust Laws"
Common Market Law Review,
Vol. 10/1985, No. 2, pp. 87–118

Goyder, Joanna,
"EEC Block Exemption for Franchising Contracts,"
Business Law Review,
Vol. 10/1989, No. 6, pp. 152–156 and 172

Howe, Martin,
"Franchising and Restrictive Practices Law,"
"The Office of Fair Trading View,"
European Competition Law Review,
Vol. 9/1988, No. 4, pp. 439–445

Korah, Valentine,
"Franchising and the EEC Competition Rules Regulation 4087/88,"
European Competition Law Monographs
(ESC/Sweet & Maxwell, 1989)

Franchising, The Marriage of Reason and the EEC Competition Rules
European Intellectual Property Review Vol. 8/1986 No. 4, p.99 *et seq.*

Mendelsohn, M.; Harris, B.
Franchising and the Block Exemption Regulation (Longman, 1991)

Van Empel, M.,
"Franchising and Strict Liability in the EEC,"
International Business Lawyer,
Vol. 18/1990, No. 4, pp. 169–172

Part V Industrial and Intellectual Property Agreements

Alexander, Willy,
"The Horizontal Effects of Licensing a Technology as Dealt with by EEC Competition Policy,"
Annual Proceedings of the Fordham Corporate Law Institute, 1988
(Bender, 1989), Chap. 11.1–11.16

Cornish, W.R.,
Intellectual Property: Patents, Copyright, Trade Marks & Allied Rights
(2nd ed., Sweet & Maxwell 1989)

Demaret, P.,
"Patents, Territorial Restrictions and EEC Law" *IIC Studies*
Vol. 2 1978

Fox, Eleanor M.,
"Maize Seeds: A Comparative Comment,"
Annual Proceedings of the Fordham Corporate Law Institute: Antitrust, Technology Transfers and Joint Ventures in International Trade
(Bender, 1982), pp. 151–162

Korah, Valentine,
"The Group Exemption for Patent and Knowhow Licences,"
Revue International de la Concurrence,
1985, No. 1, pp. 15–27

Merkin, Robert M.,
"The Interface between Anti-Trust and Intellectual Property,"
European Competition Law Review,
Vol. 6/1985, No. 4, pp. 377–391

Van der Esch, Bastiaan,
"Industrial Property Rights under EEC Law,"
Annual Proceedings of the Fordham Corporate Law Institute: Antitrust and Trade policies of the European Economic Community
(Bender 1983,) pp. 539–561

White, Robin
"Licensing in Europe,"
European Intellectual Property Review,
Vol. 12/1990, No. 3, pp. 88–98

1. Articles 30, 36 & 59 EEC—free movement

Banks, Karen and Marenco, Giuliano,
"Intellectual Property and the Community Rules on Free Movement: Discrimination Unearthed,"
European Law Review,
Vol. 15, No. 3, June 1990, pp. 224–256

Friden, Georges,
"Recent Developments in EEC Intellectual Property Law The Distinction between Existence and Exercise Revisited,"
Common Market Law Review,
Vol. 26/1989, No. 2, pp. 193–217

2. Patent Licensing Agreements

Alexander, Willy,
"Block Exemption for Patent Licensing Agreements: EC Regulation No. 2349/84,"
International Review of industrial Property and Copyright law,
Vol. 17/1986, No. 1, pp. 1–40

Cawthra, B.I.,
Patent Licensing in Europe
(2nd ed., Butterworths, 1986)

Coleman, Michael L.; Schmitz, Dieter A.,
"The EEC Patent Licencing Regulation— Practical Guidelines,"
The Business Lawyer,
Vol. 42, 1986, No. 1, pp. 101–119

Jeanrenaud, Yves,
"Exclusive Licences of Patent Rights and Territorial Restraints in the EEC, Certainty v. Flexibility,"
Swiss Review of International Competition Law,
1986, No. 26, pp. 21–48

Korah, Valentine,
"Patent Licensing and EEC Competition Rules Regulations 2349/84,"
European Competition Law Monographs
(ESC/Sweet & Maxwell, 1985)

Lutz, Helmut; Broderick, Terry R.,
"A Model EEC Patent Licensing Agreement,"
International Business Lawyer,
1985, April, pp. 161–163

Pevtchin and Williams
"Pharmon v. Hoechst—Limits on the Community Principle in Respect of Compulsory Patent Licences" 1986
Fordham Corporate Law Institute p.289
(B. Hawk ed. 1987)

Pickard, Stephen J.,
"The Commission's Patent Licensing Regulation, A Guide,"
European Competition Law Review,
Vol. 5/1984, No. 4, pp. 384–403

Venit, James,
"EEC Patent Licensing Revisited: The Commission's Patent Licence Regulation,"
The Antitrust Bulletin,
Vol. XXX/1985, No. 2, pp. 457–526

"In the Wake of Windsurfing: Patent Licensing in the Common Market,"
International Review of Industrial Property and Copyright Law,
Vol. 18, 1987, No. 1, pp. 1–40

Winn, D.
"Commission Know-how Regulation 556/89: Innovation and Territorial Exclusivity: Improvements and the Quid Pro Quo"
European Competition Law Review Vol 4 (1990)

3. Know-How Licensing Agreements

Cabanellas, G.; Massaguer, J.,
"Know-how Agreements and EEC Competition Law"
IIC Studies—Studies in Industrial Property and Copyright Law Vol. 12, 1991

Guttuso, S.,
Know-how and Patents under EEC Competition Law 1986 Fordham Corporate Law Institute 637 (B. Hawk Ed. 1987)

Hoyng, W.A.; Biesheuvel, M.B.W.,
"The Know-How Group Exemption,"
Common Market Law Review,
Vol. 26/1989, No. 2, pp. 219–234

Korah, Valentine,
"Know-How Licensing Agreements and the EEC Competition Rules, Regulation 556/89,"
European Competition Law Monographs
(ESC/Sweet & Maxwell, 1989)

Moritz, Hans-Werner,
"Assignment of Computer Software for Use on a Data processing System and the Applicability of Know-How Licensing Rules,"
International Review of Industrial Property and Copyright Law,
Vol. 21/1990, No. 6, pp. 799–816

Orr, Anthony; Farr, Sebastian,
"Know-How and the Competition Rules of the EEC-Treaty,"
World Competition,
Vol. 12/1988, No. 2, pp. 5–15

Price, D.R.,
"The Secret of the Know-How Block Exemption,"
European Competition Law Review,
Vol. 10/1989, No. 2, pp. 273–286

Rosen, Norman E.,
"New EEC Regulation on Know-How Licensing,"
Annual Proceedings of the Fordham Corporate Law Institute 1988 (Bender, 1989), Chap. 10.1–10.29

Winn, David B.,
"Commission Know-How Regulation 556/89
Innovation and Territorial Exclusivity, Improvements and the Quid pro Quo,"
European Competition Law Review,
Vol. 11/1990, No. 4, pp. 135–146

4. Trademark Licensing and Cession Agreements

Baden Fuller, C.W.F.,
"Economic Issues Relating to Property Rights in Trademarks: Export Bans, Differential Pricing, Restrictions on Resale and Repackaging,"
European Law Review,
Vol. 6/1981, No. 3, pp. 162–179

Joliet, René,
"Territorial and Exclusive Trademark Licensing under the EEC Law of Competition,"
IIC International Review of Industrial Property and Copyright Law,
Vol. 15/1984, pp. 21–38

Sherliker, Christopher,
"Trademark Delimitation Agreements in the EEC,"
New Law Journal,
Vol. 134/1984, No. 6158, pp. 545–547

Subiotto, Romano,
"Moosehead/Whitbread: Industrial Franchises and no-challenge Clauses relating to Licensed Trade Marks under EEC Competition Law,"
European Competition Law Review,
Vol. 11/1990, No. 5, pp. 226–232

5. Copyright and Design Right Agreements

Desurmont, Thierry,
"LA SACEM et le droit de la Concurrence; the SACEM and Competition Law, La SACEM y el Derecho de la Competencia,"
Revue Internationale de Droit d'Auteur,
1981, No. 140, pp. 116–179

Reischl, Gerhard,
"Industrial Property and Copyright before the European Court of Justice,"
IIC—International Review of Industrial Property and Copyright Law,
Vol. 13/1982, No. 4, pp. 415–430

Rose, Michael,
"Passing Off, Unfair Competition and Community Law,"
European Intellectual Property Review,
Vol. 12/1990, No. 4, pp. 123–128

Rothnie, Warwich A.,
"Commission Re-runs Same Old Bill (Film Purchases by German Television Stations),"
European Intellectual Property Review,
Vol. 12/1990, No. 2, pp. 72–75

Shaw, Josephine,
"Music to their Ears,"
European Law Review,
Vol. 15/1990, No. 1, pp. 68–73

Von Gamm, Otto-Friedrich,
"Copyright License Contracts and Restrictions under the EEC Treaty,"
IIC—International Review of industrial Property and Copyright Law,
Vol. 14/1983, No. 5, pp. 579–595

Part VI Joint Ventures

Brodley
"Joint Ventures and Anti-Trust Policy"
Harvard Law Review, 1982, 95

Caspari, Manfred,
"Joint Ventures under EEC Law and Policy,"
Annual Proceedings of the Fordham Corporate Law Institute, 1987 (Bender, 1988), pp. 353–371

Claydon, Jeanne-Marie,
"Joint Ventures—An Analysis of Commission Decisions,"
European Competition Law Review,
Vol. 7, 1986, No. 2, pp. 151–192

Ellison, J.; Kling E.,
Joint Ventures in Europe, (Butterworths, 1991)

Faull, Jonathan,
"Joint Ventures under the EEC Competition Rules,"
European Competition Law Review,
Vol. 5/1984, No. 4, pp. 358–374

Hawk, Barry E.,
"Antitrust, Technology Transfers and Joint Ventures in International Trade,"
Annual Proceedings of the Fordham Corporate Law Institute, 1982
(Bender, 1983)

"Joint Ventures—The Intersection of Antitrust and Industrial Policy in the EEC,"
Fordham Corporate Law Institute, Antitrust and Trade policy in the U.S. and the E.C., 1985 p.449
(Bender, 1986)

Jacquemin; Spinoir
Economic & Legal Aspects of Cooperative Research: A European View
Fordham Corporate Law Institute, 1985 p.487 (B. Hawk ed. 1986)

Korah, Valentine,
"Critical Comments on the Commission's Recent Decisions Exempting Joint Ventures to Exploit Research that Needs Further Development,"
European Law Review,
Vol. 12, 1987, No. 1, pp. 18–39

Patak, A.,
The EC Commission's Approach to Joint Ventures: A Policy of Contradictions
European Competition Law Review Vol. 5, 1991

Riggs, J.H.; Giustini, A.,
Joint Ventures under EEC Competition Law
Business Lawyer Vol. 46/1991, No. 3, pp. 849–908

Ritter, K.; Overbury, C.,
An Attempt at a Practical Approach to joint Ventures under EEC Rules on Competition
Common Market Law Review Vol. 14, p.601

Strivens, Robert,
"Mitchell Cotts/Sofiltra: Joint Ventures—EEC Competition Policy,"
European Intellectual Property Review,
Vol. 9/1987, No. 12, pp. 369–372

Temple Lang, John,
"European Community Antitrust Law and Joint Ventures Involving Transfer of Technology,"
Fordham Corporate Law Institute: Antitrust, Technology Transfers and Joint Ventures in International Trade, 1982, pp. 203–276 (B. Hawk ed. 1983)

Venit, J.,
"The Evaluation of Concentrations under the merger Control Regulation: The Nature of the Beast"
Fordham International Law Journal
Vol. 14/1990–91, No. 2, pp. 412–454

"The 'Merger' Control Regulation Europe comes of Age . . . or Caliban's Dinner"
Common Market Law Review,
Vol. 27/1990, No. 1, pp. 7–50

The Research & Develoment Block Exemption Regulation
European Law Review Vol. 10, 1985 p.151

Weiser, Gerhard J.,
"Antitrust Aspects of the Joint Venture in the European Economic Community,"
The Journal of Reprints for Antitrust Law and Economics,
Vol. XV/1984, No. 1, pp. 495–525

White, Eric L.,
"Research and Development Joint Ventures under EEC Competition Law,"
International Review of Industrial Property and Copyright Law,
Vol. 16/1985, No. 6, pp. 663–703

Part VII   Article 86

Bishop, William.
"Political Economy in the European Community," *Modern Law Review* 1986.

Fejoe, Jens,
Monopoly Law and Market,
Studies of EC Competition Law with U.S. Antitrust Law as a Frame of Reference and supported by Basic Market Economics
(Deventer, Kluwer, 1990)

Fishwick, Francis,
"Definition of Monopoly Power in the Antitrust Policies of the United Kingdom and the European Community,"
Anti-Trust Bulletin Vol. XXXIV/1989, No. 3, pp. 451–488

"Definition of the Relevant Market in Community Competition Policy, Document—Commission of the European Communities,"
Office for Official Publications of the European Communities, 1986

Fox, Eleanor, M.,
"Abuse of a Dominant Position under the Treaty of Rome—Comparison with U.S. Law,"
Fordham Corporate Law Institute: Antitrust and trade Policies of the European Economic Community
(Bender, 1983), pp. 367–421

Gyselen, Luc,
"Abuse of Monopoly Power within the Meaning of Article 86 of the EEC Treaty: Recent Developments 1992 and EEC/U.S. Competition and Trade Law,"
Fordham Corporate Law Institute: 1989,
(B. Hawk Ed. 1990 Bender, 1990) pp. 360–428

Gyselen, Luc; Kyriazis, Nicholas,
"Article 86 EEC: The Monopoly Power Measurement Issue Revisited,"
European Law Review,
Vol. 11, 1986, No. 2, pp. 134–148

Joliet, R.,
Monopolization and Abuse of Dominant Position (1970):
A Comparative Study of American and European Approaches to the Control of Economic Power
(The Hague, Nijhoff 1970)

Korah, Valentine,
"No Duty to License Independent Repairers to make Spare Parts, The Renault, Volvo and Bayer & Hennecke Cases,"
European Intellectual Property Review,
Vol. 10/1988, No. 12, pp. 381–386

"Concept of a Dominant Position within the meaning of Article 86,"
Common Market Law Review,
Vol. 17/1980, No. 3, pp. 395–414

Price, Diane R.,
"Abuse of a Dominant Position, The Tale of Nails, Milk Cartons and TV Guides,"
European Competition Law Review,
Vol. 11/1990, No. 2, pp. 80–90

Rapp, Richard T.,
"Predatory Pricing and Entry Deterring Strategies: The Economics of AKZO,"
European Competition Law Review,
Vol. 7, 1986, No. 3, pp. 233–240

Schoedermeier, Martin,
"Collective Dominance Revisited
An Analysis of the EC Commission's New Concepts of Oligopoly Control,"
European Competition Law Review,
Vol. 11/1990, No. pp. 28–34

Sharpe, Thomas,
"Predation,"
European Competition Law Review,
Vol. 8/1987, No. 1, pp. 53–76

Shaw, Josephine,
"Music to their Ears,"
European Law Review,
Vol. 15/1990, No. 1, pp. 68–73

Smith, Paul,
"The Wolf in Wolf's Clothing, The Problem with Predatory Pricing,"
European Law Review,
Vol. 14/1989, No. 4, pp. 209–222

Temple Lang, J.,
"Abuse of Dominant Positions in European Community Law, Present & Future: Some Aspects"
Fordham Corporate Law Institute, 1978 p. 25 (B. Hawk ed. 1979)

Turner, Donals; Adelmann, A.; Marshall, Alfred,
"Relevant Markets in Antitrust,"
The Journal of Reprints for Antitrust Law and Economics,
Vol. XIV/1984, No. 2, pp. 1–1194

Vajda, Christopher,
"Article 86 and a Refusal to Supply,"
European Competition Law Review,
Vol. 2/1981, No. 1, pp. 97–115

Van Damme (ed.)
Regulating the Behaviour of Monopolies and Dominant Undertakings in Community Law
(1977)

Zanon Di Valgiurata, Lucio,
"Price Discrimination under article 86 of the EEC Treaty, The United Brands Case,"
The International and Comparative Law Quarterly,
Vol. 31/1982, No. 1, pp. 36–58

Part VIII State Interference

Bazex, M.,
"L'Entreprise publique et le droit européen Public Entreprise and European Law"
Revue de droit des affaires internationales,
1991, pp. 461–485

Bentil, Kodwo J.,
"Common Market Anti-Trust Law and Restrictive Business or Practices prompted by National Regulatory Measures,"
European Competition Law Review,
Vol. 9/1988, No. 3, pp. 354–383

Brothwood, Michael,
"The Court of Justice on Article 90 of the EEC Treaty,"
Common Market Law Review,
Vol. 20/1983, No. 2, pp. 335–346

Coleman, Martijn,
'European Competition Law in the Telecommunications and Broadcasting Sectors,"
European Competition Law Review,
Vol. 11/1990, No. 5, pp. 204–212

Edward, David,
"Constitutional Rules of Community Law in EEC Competition Case, 1992 and EEC/US Competition and Trade Law,"
Annual Proceedings of the Fordham Corporate Law Institute
(Bender, 1989), pp. 198–220

Ehricke, Ulrich,
"State Intervention and EEC Competition Law Opportunities and Limits of the European Court of Justice's Approach, A critical Analysis of four Key-Cases,"
World Competition,
Vol. 14/1990, No. 1, pp. 79–102

Gyselen, Luc,
"State Action and the Effectiveness of the EEC Treaty's Competition Provisions,"
Common Market Law Review,
Vol. 26/1989, No. 1, pp. 33–60

Hancher, Leigh; Slot, Piet Jan,
"Article 90,"
European Competition Law Review,
Vol. 11/1990, No. 1, pp. 35–39

Hoffman, Alan B.,
"Anti-competitive State Legislation Condemned under Articles 5, 85 and 86 of the EEC Treaty.
How far should the Court go after Van Eycke?"
European Competition Law Review,
Vol. 11/1990, No. 1, pp. 11–27

Joliet, René,
"National Anti-competitive Legislation and Community Law,"
Annual Proceedings of the Fordham Corporate Law Institute
(Bender, 1988), Chap. 16.1–16.25

Marenco, Giuliano,
"Public Sector and Community Law,"
Common Market Law Review,
Vol. 20/1983, No. 3, pp. 495–527

"Government Action and Antitrust in the United States: What Lessons for Community Law?"
Legal Issues of European Integration,
1987, No. 1, pp. 1–81

Meal, Douglas H.,
"Governmental Compulsion as a defence under United States and European Community Antitrust Law,"
Columbia Journal of Transnational Law,
Vol. 20/1981, No. 1, pp. 51–131

Page, Alan C.,
"Member States, Public Undertakings and Article 90,"
European Law Review,
Vol. 7/1982, No. 1, pp. 19–35

Pappalardo, A.,
State Measures and Public Undertakings Article 90 of the EEC Treaty Revisited *European Competition Law Review,*
Vol. 12/1991, No. 1, pp. 29–39

Overbury, H. Colin,
"The Application of EEC Law to Telecommunications 1992 and EEC/US Competition and Trade Law,"
Annual Proceedings of the Fordham Corporate Law Institute
(Bender, 1989), pp. 495–521

Schulte-Braucks, Reinhard,
"European Telecommunications Law in the Light of the British Telecom Judgment,"
Common Market Law Review,
Vol. 23, 1986, No. 1, pp. 39–59

Slot, Piet Jan, "The Application of Articles 3(f), 5 and 85 to 94 EEC," *European Law Review,* Vol 12/1987, p. 179

Bibliography

Van der Esch, Bastiaan,
"EC Rules on Undistorted Competition and U.S. Antitrust Laws. The Limits of Comparability,"
Annual Proceedings of the Fordham Corporate Law Institute
(Bender, 1988), Chap. 18.1–18.29

Wainwright, Richard,
"Public Undertakings under Article 90 1992 and EEC/US Competition and Trade Law,"
Annual Proceedings of the Fordham Corporate Law Institute
(Bender, 1989), pp. 602–636

Part IX Sectorial Application of EEC Competition Rules

1. Agriculture

Ottervanger, T. R.,
"Antitrust and Agriculture in the Common Market 1992 and EEC/U.S. Competition and Trade Law"
Fordham Corporate Law Institute, 1989, pp. 203–223

3. Inland waterways, rail and road transport

Kuyper
"Airline Fare-fixing and Competition: An English Lord, Commission Proposals and U.S. Parallel"
20 *Common Market Law Review,* 1983, p. 20

4. Maritime Transport

Clough, M.; Randolph, F.,
Shipping and EC Competition Law (Current and Legal Developments)
(Butterworths, 1991)

Green, Nicolas,
"Competition and Maritime Trade: A Critical View,"
European Transport Law,
Vol. XXIII/1988, No. 5, pp. 612–628

Kreis, Helmut W.R.,
"Maritime Transport and EEC Competition Rules,"
European Transport Law,
Vol. XXIII/1988, No. 5, pp. 562–570

Rabe, Dieter; Schütte, Michael,
"EEC Competition Rules and Maritime Transport,"
Lloyd's Maritime and Commercial Law Quarterly,
1988, Pt. 2, May, pp. 182–210

Ruttley, P.,
International Shipping and EEC Competition Law
European Competition Law Review 1991, p.1.

Rycken, Willem,
"European Antitrust Aspects of Maritime and Air Transport,"
European Transport Law,
Vol. XXII/1987, No. 5, pp. 484-504 and Vol. XXIII/1988, No. 1, pp. 3-25

Slot, P.J.,
Shipping and Competition Exploiting the Internal Market
(Kluwer, 1988), pp. 31-43

5. Air Transport

Argyris, N.,
"The EEC Rules of Competition and the Air transport Sector,"
Common Market Law Review,
Vol. 26/1989, No. 1, pp. 5-32

Basedow, Jürgen,
"National Authorities in European Airline Competition,"
European Competition Law Review,
Vol. 9/1988, No. 3, pp. 342-353

Button, Kenneth; Swan, Dennis,
"European Community Airlines Deregulation and its Problems,"
Journal of Common Market Studies,
Vol. XXVII/1989, No. 4, pp. 259-282

Garland, Gloria Jean,
"The American Deregulation Experience and the Use of Article 90 to Expedite EEC Air Transport Liberalisation,"
European Competition Law Review,
Vol. 7/1986, No. 2, pp. 193-232

Kark, Anderas,
"Prospects for a Liberalisation of the European Air Transport Industry. A Study of Commercial Air Transport Policy for the European Community,"
European Competition Law Review,
Vol. 10/1989, No. 3, pp. 377-406

Van Houtte, Ben,
"Relevant Markets in Air Transport,"
Common Market Law Review,
Vol. 27/1990, No. 3, pp. 521-546

Verstrynge, Jean-François,
"Competition Policy in the Air Transport Sector Towards a Community Air Transport Policy,"
(Kluwer, 1989), pp. 63-113

Van der Esch, Bastiaan; Verstrynge, Jean-François,
"Main Issues of Community Law Governing access to Air Transport and Member States Control of Fares"
F.I.D.E. Reports of the 13th Congress
(*Community Law and Civil Aviation*, Thessaloniki, 1988), Vol. 3, pp. 39-167

6. Financial Services

Child, Graham D.,
"Banking and the Treaty of Rome, Article 85"
International Business Lawyer
Vol. 16/1988, No. 11, pp. 487–491

Pardon, Jean,
"Application du Droit Européen de la Concurrence en Matière Bancaire et Financière.
Revue de Droit des Affaires Internationales"
International Business Law Journal,
1990, No. 1, pp. 115–137

Ratliff, John; Tupper, Stephen; Curschmann, Jan,
"Competition Law and Insurance Recent Developments in the European Community"
International Business Lawyer,
Vol. 18/1990, No. 8, pp. 352–358

Rosell, José,
"Banking Agreements. Are They Anti-Competitive?"
International Financial Law Review,
1987, July, pp. 11–16

Usher, J.A.,
"Financial Services in EEC Law"
International and Comparative Law Quarterly,
Vol. 37/1988, Part 1, pp. 144–154

Part X Procedures and Remedies

1. Procedural Legislation

Burnside, Alec,
"Enforcement of EEC Competition Law by Interim Measures. The Ford Case,"
Journal of World Trade Law,
Vol. 19/1985, No. 1, pp. 34–53

Christoforou, Theofanis,
"Protection of Legal Privilege in EEC Competition Law The Imperfections of a Case,"
Fordham International Law Journal,
Vol. 9/1985–86, No. 1, pp. 1–62

Ferry, John E.,
"Of Cameras, Chemicals, Cars and Salami: A Fresh Look at Interim Relief under the Rome Treaty,"
European Intellectual Property Review,
Vol. 8/1986, No. 11, pp. 337–341

Gijlstra, Douwe J.,
"Legal Protection in Competition Cases,"
Legal Issues of European Integration,
1983, No. 1, pp. 87–98

Graupner, Frances,
"Anti-trust Compliance Policy—Who needs it?"
Business Law Review,
Vol. 9/1988, No. 1, pp. 17–19 and 21

Hughes, Justin,
"Antitrust Law: Commission of the European Communities suspends Proceedings against International Business Machines Corporation,"
Harvard International Law Journal,
Vol. 26/1985, No. 1, pp. 189–201

Johannes, Harmut,
"The Role of the Hearing Officer 1992 and EEC/U.S. Competition and Trade Law,"
Annual Proceedings of the Corporate Law Institute, 1989
(Bender, 1990), pp. 429–447

Joshua, Julian Mathic,
"The Element of Surprise: EEC Competition Investigations under Article 14(3) of Regulation 17,"
European Law Review,
Vol. 8/1983, No. 1, pp. 3–23

"Information in EEC Competition Law Procedures,"
European Law Review,
Vol. 11, 1986, No. 6, pp. 409–429

"Proof in Contested EEC Competition Cases. A Comparison with the Rules of Evidence in Common Law,"
European Law Review,
Vol. 12/1987, No. 5, pp. 315–353

"Requests for Information in EEC Factfinding Procedures,"
European Competition Law Review,
Vol. 3/1982, No. 2, pp. 173–184
"The right to be heard in EEC competition procedure",
Fordham International Law Journal 1991/1992, p. 16

Korah, Valentine,
"Comfort Letters—Reflections on the Perfume Cases,"
European Law Review,
Vol. 6/1981, No. 1, pp. 14–39

Kerse, C.S.,
"EEC Antitrust Procedure,"
European Law Centre at Sweet & Maxwell,
(2nd ed, 1987)

Reynolds, Michael J.,
"Practical Aspects of Notifying Agreements and the New Form A/B,"
Annual Proceedings of the Corporate Law Institute, Antitrust and Trade policy in the U.S. and the E.C.
(Bender, 1986), Vol. 1985

Rodriguez Galindo, Blanca,
"L'application des regles de concurrence: les pouvoir d'enquete de la commission," *Revue du Marché unique Europeen,* Vol. 1/1991 No. 2 pp. 62–86.

Stanbrook, Clive; Ratcliff, John,
"EEC Anti-Trust Audit,"
European Competition Law Review,
Vol. 9/1988, No. 3, pp. 334–341

Temple Lang, John,
"The Powers of the Commission to Order Interim Measures in Competition Cases,"
Common Market Law Review,
Vol. 18/1981, No. 1, pp. 49–61

"Community Antitrust Law—Compliance and Enforcement,"
Common Market Law Review,
Vol. 18/1981, No. 3, pp. 335–362

Van Bael, Ivo,
The Antitrust Settlement Practice of the EEC Commission Annual Proceedings of the Fordham Corporate Law Institute, Antitrust and Trade Policy in the U.S. and the E.C.
(Bender, 1986), Vol. 1985, pp. 759–788

"The Antitrust Settlement Practice of the EC Commission,"
Common Market Law Review,
Vol. 23, 1986, No. 1, pp. 61–90

"Comment on the EEC Commission's Antitrust Settlement Practice: The Shortcircuiting of Regulation 17,"
Swiss Review of International Competition Law
(Werner & Sieber, 1984), No. 22, pp. 67–71

Venit, James S.,
"The Commission's Opposition Procedure—Between the Scylla of Ultra Vires and the Charybdis of Perfume: Legal Consequences and Practical Considerations,"
Common Market Law Review,
Vol. 22/1985, No. 2, pp. 167–202

Waelbroeck, Denis,
"New Forms of Settlement of Anti-Trust Cases and Procedural Safeguards: Is Regulation 17 falling into Abeyance?"
European Law Review,
Vol. 11, 1986, No. 4, pp. 268–280

2. The Handling of a case

Jacobs, Francis G.,
"Court of Justice Review of Competition Cases"
Fordham Corporate Law Institute, 1987
(Bender, 1988), pp. 541–577

Mancini, Frederic,
"Access to Justice. Individual Undertakings and EEC Antitrust Law Problems and Pitfalls"
Fordham International Law Journal,
Vol. 12/1989, No. 2, pp. 189–203

Mertens de Wilmars J.,
"Statement of Reasons and Methods of Interpretation in the Case of the EC Court of Justice Relating to Articles 85 and 86,"
Fordham Corporate Law Institute, 1987
(Bender, 1988), pp. 607–628

Slynn, Gordon,
"EEC Competition Law from the Perspective of the Court of Justice,"
Fordham Corporate Law Institute, Antitrust and Trade policy in the US and the EC
(Bender, 1986), Vol. 1985

Temple Lang, John,
"The Impact of the New Court of First Instance in EEC Antitrust and Trade Cases,"
Fordham Corporate Law Institute
(Bender, 1987), pp. 579–606

Waelbroeck, Michel,
"Judicial Review of Commission Action in Competition Matters"
Fordham Corporate Law Institute: Antitrust and Trade Policies of the European Economic Community
(B. Hawke ed. 1984 Bender, 1983), pp. 179–217

3. Judicial Review

Banks, Karen,
"National Enforcement of Community Rights— A Boost for Damocles,"
Common Market Law Review,
Vol. 21/1984, No. 4, pp. 669–674

Claydon, Jeanne-Marie,
"Civil Actions under Articles 85 and 86 of the EEC Treaty: The Garden Cottage Case,"
European Competition Law Review,
Vol. 4/1983, No. 3, pp. 245–252

Davidson, J.S.,
"Actions for Damages in the English Courts for Breach of EEC Competition Law,"
International and Comparative Law Quarterly,
Vol. 34/1985, No. 1, pp. 178–189

Greaves, Rosa,
"Concurrent Jurisdiction in EEC Competition Law: When should a National Court Stay Proceedings?"
European Competition Law Review,
Vol. 8/1987, No. 3, pp. 256–272

Korah, Valentine,
"The Rise and Fall of Provisional Validity. The Need for a Rule of Reason in EEC Antitrust,"
Northwestern Journal of International Law & Business,
Vol. 3/1981, No. 1, pp. 320–357

Jacobs, Francis G.,
"Civil Enforcement of EEC Antitrust Law,"
Michigan Law Review,
Vol. 82/1984, Nos. 5/6, pp. 1364–1376

Picanol, Enric,
"Remedies in National Law for Breach of Articles 85 et 86 of the EEC Treaty: A Review,"
Legal Issues of European Integration,
1983, No. 2, pp. 1–37

Steindorff, Ernst,
"Common Market Antitrust Law in Civil Proceedings before National Courts and Arbitrators,"
Annual Proceedings of the Fordham Corporate Law Institute, Anti-Trust and Trade policy in the U.S. and the EC
(Bender, 1986), Vol. 1985

Temple Lang, John,
"EEC Competition Actions in Member States' Courts Claims for Damages, Declarations and Injunctions for Breach of Community Anti-Trust Law,"
Fordham International Law Journal,
Vol. 7/1983–84, No. 3, pp. 389–466

"EEC Competition Actions in Member State Courts—Claims for Damages, Declarations and Injunctions for Breach of Community Anti-Trust Law,"
Fordham Corporate Law Institute: Anti-Trust and Trade Policies of The European Economic Community
(Bender, 1983), pp. 219–302

4. National Jurisdiction and Authorities

Eccles, Richard,
"Transposing EEC Competition Law into UK Restrictive Trading Agreements Legislation: The Government Green Paper,"
European Competition Law Review,
Vol. 9/1988, No. 2, pp. 227–252

Grehan, Duncan S.J.,
"EEC and Irish Competition Policy and Law Rabels Zeitschrift für Ausländisches und Internationales Privatrecht"
47. JG/1983, No. 1, pp. 22–63

Grendell, Timothy,
"The Anti-Trust Legislation of the United States, the European Economic Community, Germany and Japan,"
The International and Comparative Law Quarterly,
Vol. 29/1980, No. 1, pp. 64–86

Stockman, Kurt,
"EEC Competition Law and Member State Competition Laws,"
Fordham Corporate Law Institute, 1987
(Bender, 1988), pp. 265–300

Voillemot, Dominique,
"The Influence of EEC Law on the French Legislation and the Practice of French Courts,"
Fordham Corporate Law Institute, 1987, pp. 323–337

Book Two: Mergers and Acquisitions

Axinn, Stephen M.; Glick, Mark,
Dual Enforcement of Merger Law in the EEC, Lessons from the American Experience 1992 and EEC/U.S. Competition and Trade Institute; 1989, pp. 22–58
(Bender, 1990)

Banks, Karen,
"Mergers and Partial Mergers under EEC Law"
Annual Proceedings of the Fordham Corporate Law Institute, 1987, (Bender, 1988), pp. 373–428

Bellamy, Christopher,
"Mergers Outside the Scope of the New Merger Regulation, Implications of the Philip Morris Judgment,"
Annual Proceedings of the Fordham Corporate Law Institute, 1988 (Bender, 1989), Chap. 22.1–22.28

Bentil, J. Kodwo,
"Competition Ban Clauses in Enterprise Transfer Contracts under Common Market Law,"
The Journal of Business Law,
1989, July, pp. 321–338

Bourgeois, J.; Langeheine, B.,
"Jurisdictional Issues: EEC Merger Regulation Member States Laws and Articles 85 & 86, (p.583)
Fordham International Law Journal",
Vol. 1990–1991, No. 387–411

Bright, C.,
"The European Merger Control Regulation: Do Member States still have an Independent Role in Merger Control?"
European Competition Law Review Vols. 4, 5, 1991

Brittan, Leon,
"The Law and Policy of Merger Control in the EEC,"
European Law Review,
Vol. 15/1990, No. 5, pp. 351–357

Control of Concentrations in the EEC,
14ème Congrès F.I.D.E., (Madrid 1990)
Vol. III: Le contrôle des concentrations d'entreprises

Downes, T.A.; Ellison, J.,
The Legal Control of Mergers in the EC
(Blackstone, 1991)

Elland, W.,
The Merger Control Regulation and its effect on National Merger
  Controls and the Residual Application of Articles 85 and 86
European Competition Law Review
Vol. 12/1991, No. 1, pp. 19–28

Fine, Frank L.,
"EC Merger Control, An Analysis of the New Regulation,"
European Competition Law Review,
Vol. 11/1990, No. 2, pp. 47–51

Fox, Eleanor M.,
"Federalism, Standards and Common Market Merger Control,"
Annual Proceedings of the Fordham Corporate Law Institute, 1988
(Bender, 1989) Chap. 23.1–23.9

Goetting, Horst-Peter; Nikowitz, Werner,
"EEC Merger Control, Distinguishing Concentrative Joint Ventures from
  Cooperative Joint Ventures,"
Fordham International Law Review,
Vol. 13/1989–1990, No. 2, pp. 185–204

Hay, Hilke; Nelson,
"Geographic market definition in an International Context"
Fordham Corporate Law Institute (B. Hawk ed. 1991 Bender 1990) p.51

Holley, D.,
Ancillary Restrictions in Mergers and Joint Ventures,
p.423

Hölzer, Heinrich,
"Merger Control, European Competition Policy"
(Pinter, 1990), pp. 9–30

Hornsby, Stephen,
"National and Community Control of Concentrations in a single Market:
  Should Member States be allowed to impose stricter Standards?"
European Law Review,
Vol. 13/1988, No. 5, pp. 295–317

Jones, C.,
"The Scope of Application of the Merger Regulation"
Fordham International Law Journal
Vol. 14, 1990–1991, No. 2, pp. 359–386

Korah, Valentine; Lasok, Paul,
"Philip Morris and it's Aftermath—Merger Control?"
Common Market Law Review,
Vol. 25/1988, No. 2, pp. 333–368

Langeheine, B.,
Substantive Review under the EEC Merger Regulation
p. 483

Le Bolzer, Jean-Marc,
"The New EEC Merger Control Policy after the Adoption of Regulation
  4064/89,"
World Competition,
Vol. 14/1990, No. 1, pp.31–47

Bibliography

Lofthouse, Stephen,
"Competition Policies as Take-over Defences,"
The Journal of Business Law,
1984, July, pp. 320–333

Merger Control in the EEC, A Survey of European Competition Law
(Kluwer, 1988)

"Merger Control with Evidence House of Lords Select Committee on the European Communities"
(Session 1988–89, 6th Report, HMSO, 1989)

Mestmaecker, Ernst-Joachim,
"Merger Control in the Common Market between Competition Policy and Industrial Policy,"
Annual Proceedings of the Fordham Corporate Law Institute, 1988 (Bender, 1989), Chap. 20.1–20.34

Overbury, C.; Jones, C.,
EEC Merger Regulation Procedure: A Practical View, p. 353.

Pathak, Anand S.,
"EEC Concentration Control The Forseeable Uncertaintities,"
European Competition Law Review,
Vol. 11/1990, No. 3, pp. 119–125

Reynolds, Michael J.,
"Extraterritorial Aspects of Mergers and Joint Vergers, The EEC Position,"
International Business Lawyer,
1985, September, pp. 347–356

Reynolds, M.; Weightman, E.,
International Mergers; The Antitrust Process, Ed. J. William Rowley, Q.C. and Donald I. Baker
(Sweet & Maxwell, 1991), pp. 1–126

Scherer, F.M.,
"European Community Merger Policy: Why? Why not?"
Annual Proceedings of the Fordham Corporate Law Institute, 1988 (Bender, 1989) Chap. 24.1–24.16

Siragusa, M.; Subiotto, R.,
"The EEC Merger Control Regulation The Commission's Evolving Case Law" *Common Market Law Review*
Vol. 28/1991, No. 4, pp.877–934

Soames, Trevor,
"The 'Community Dimension' in the EEC Merger Regulation The Calculation of the Turnover Criteria,"
European Competition Law Review,
Vol. 11/1990, No. 5, pp. 213–225

Van Empel, Martijn,
"Merger Control in the EEC,"
World Competition,
Vol. 13/1990, No. 3, pp. 5–22

Venit, J.,
"The Evaluation of Concentrations under the merger Control Regulation: The Nature of the Beast"
Fordham International Law Journal
Vol. 14, 1990–91, No. 2, pp. 412–454.

Book Three: Coal and Steel

Mestmaecker, Ernst-Joachim,
"The applicability of the ECSC—Cartel Prohibition (Article 65) during a 'Manifest Crisis'. The Art of Governance—Festschrift zu Ehren von Eric Stein"
(Baden-Baden, Nomos, 1987)

INDEX

Abuse of a dominant position, 217–219
  circular argument, 219
  concept of, 217
  examples of,
    discount systems, 219
    discrimination,
      between different customers, 218
      on grounds of nationality, 218
    discriminatory,
      allocation of products, 218
      pricing, 218
    exclusive distribution systems, 218
    exclusive purchasing, 218
    industrial property rights, abusive use of, 219
    intellectual property rights, abusive use of, 219
    mergers and acquisitions, 209, 379
    parallel trade, actions preventing, 219
    predatory pricing, 218
    prices,
      excessive, 217
      unfair, 217
    rebate schemes, 219
    refusal,
      to disclose technical details, 219
      to supply, 218
    telecommunications sector, 235–259
    terms, unfair, imposed on clients, 217
    trademark, abusive registration of, 219
    tying, 218

absolute territorial protection *see* **territorial provisions**

acquisitions *see* **mergers**

active sales *see* **territorial provisions**

administrative letter *see* **comfort letter**

advertising
  common, 101
  franchising schemes, in, 165

Advisory Committee on Restrictive Practices and Dominant Positions, 397

agency agreements, 156–158
  Notice on, 157, 158

after sales service *see* **guarantee clauses**

aggregated rebates,
  cartel, 94

agreements,
  agency, 156–158
  amendment of, at Commission request, 397, 398
  assessment of, factors considered in, 517, 518
  authorisation of, 516–518
  banking, 101
  beer supply, 129–132, 139, 140
  bidding, 92
  circulars and, 75
  concerted practice, as, 75
  copyright, 196
  definition, 75
  delimitation,
    patent, 179
    trademark, 195
  design right, 196
  distribution,
    discriminatory pricing in, 134
    exclusive, 119–134
    joint, 93, 101, 105, 200
    non-exclusive, 119–134
    selective, 142–156
  effect of, after formal termination, 76
  emergency supply, 90, 94
  exchange,
    know-how, 516
    product, 516
  exhibition, 116, 117
  form of, irrelevance of, 75
  franchising, 158–166
  horizontal, 89, 95, 105, 106, 115, 116, 199–213
  inter-bank, 101
  joint buying, 93, 199, 515, 516
  joint selling, 516, 517
  licensing,
    know-how, 165, 180–195
    patent, 169–180
    trademark, 101, 106, 165, 179, 194–196, 213, 219
  minor importance, of, 79–80

agreements—*cont.*
  national, effect on trade of, 73
  network of, 72
  price fixing, 91–93, 116, 514
  pricing obligations in, 116, 134, 156, 166, 179, 194, 197, 213
  public authority decision and, 76
  quota, 94
  refusal to sell and, 75
  research and development, 106–115
  sales conditions, 87
  sales, 94
  service station, 131, 133, 140
  specialisation, 105
  standardisation, 101, 516
  supply, 90, 134
  territorial provisions in, 106, 113, 132, 133, 155, 166, 178, 193, 197, 213
  tied-house, 129–132, 139, 140
  tying, 179, 196, 218
  understanding, 75
  unilateral actions by undertaking and, 75

agriculture, 261–263

air transport,
  agreements and concerted practices, 322–325
  competition rules, application of, 315–323, 336–353
  computer reservation systems, 327–331
  ground handling services, 325–327
  joint planning, 332–336, 354, 355

amendment of agreement,
  Commission request, at, 397, 398

ancillary restraints, 81, 488

appeal,
  Commission decision, from, 405–407

appreciability,
  agreements of minor importance, Notice on, 79–81
  restriction of competition, 79–81
  trade, effect on, 73

Article 2 EEC (text), 533

Article 3f EEC (text), 533

Article 5 EEC (text), 533

Article 30 EEC (text), 533

Article 33(1) ECSC (text), 530

Article 33(2) ECSC (text), 530

Article 33(3) ECSC (text), 530

Article 35(3) ECSC (text), 530

Article 36 ECSC (text), 528

Article 36 EEC (text), 533

Article 39(2) ECSC (text), 531

Article 39(3) ECSC (text), 530

Article 47 ECSC (text), 527

Article 47(2) ECSC (text), 528

Article 59 EEC (text), 533

Article 65 ECSC (text), 509

Article 66 ECSC (text), 519

Article 66(5)(3) ECSC (text), 531

Article 85 EEC (text), 533

Article 85(3) EEC (text), 534

Articles 88–89 EEC (text), 361

Article 86 EEC (text), 534

Article 87 EEC (text), 534

Article 88 EEC (text), 361, 534

Article 89 EEC (text), 361, 535

Article 90 EEC (text), 221, 535

Article 164 EEC (text), 405, 535

Article 168a EEC (text), 535

Article 169 EEC (text), 405, 535

Article 172 EEC (text), 405, 536

Article 173 EEC (text), 405, 536

Article 175 EEC (text), 406, 536

Article 177 EEC (text), 406, 536

Article 178 EEC (text), 407, 536

Index

Article 185 EEC (text), 407, 536

Article 186 EEC (text), 407, 537

Article 215 EEC (text), 407, 537

Articles 222–224 EEC (text), 537

assets, sale of, *see* **mergers**

assignment of trademark, 196

associations of undertakings, 71

authorities, *see* **public bodies**

Banking agreements, 101, 358

barriers,
dominance, to, 217
entry, to, 217

beer supply agreements, 129–132, 139, 140

Bibliography, 547

bidding agreements, 92

block exemption,
exclusive distribution, 120
exclusive purchasing, 135
franchising, 158
generally, 84–88
licensing,
know-how, 181
patent, 170
research and development, 106
selective distribution,
vehicles, 143
specialisation, 106

boycotting,
Cartels, 94

breeders' rights, 196
licensed rights, improvements to, 197
no-challenge clause, 197
non-competition clause, 197
purchasing agreements in, 197
purchasing clauses in, 197

brewery ties, 129–132, 139, 140

building consortia, 101

burden of proof, *see* **proof**

business secrets, 397

buying,
agreement to refrain from, 516

buying groups, 93, 199

Cartels,
collective exclusive dealing, 93, 94
compensation schemes, 91
crisis, 90, 94
enforcement practices, 94
exclusionary practices, 93, 94
export, 93
market sharing schemes, 90, 91, 200
national, effect on trade of, 73
price-fixing agreements, 91–93
production related, 90
quota agreements, 94
resale price maintenance, 92
sales agreements, 93, 94
trade association acting as, 116

coal and steel,
agreements,
assessment of, 517, 518
authorisation of, 516–518
concentrations, 519–527
dominant position, 527
market analysis, 522
prior authorisation of, 521
conditions for, 521
exemption, 523–527
exemption by category, 522–527
joint buying agreements, 515, 516
joint selling agreements, 516, 517
jointly held undertaking, formation of, 517
practice, form of,
associations of undertakings, 510
binding agreements, 510
concerted practices, 510
declarations of intent, 510
recommendations, 510
procedure,
Commission, control by, 527
Commission, decisions taken by, 528–530
Court of Justice, challenges before, 530
defence, rights of, 528
notification, 528
obtaining information, 527
secrecy, 528

583

Index

coal and steel—*cont.*
  prohibited practices,
    customer sharing, 515
    market sharing, 515
    price fixing agreements, 514
    product sharing, 515
    restriction of investment, 515
    restriction of production, 515
    restriction of technical
      development, 515
    sharing sources of supply, 515
  restrictive practices, 509–514
  specialisation agreements, 516
  state behaviour, 527
  void agreements, 516

collective dominance, 216

collective exclusive dealing, 94, 95

collective resale price maintenance, 92

comfort letter, 398–400

Commission of the European Communities,
  appeal against decision of, 405–407
  complaint to, 389
  damages against, 405
  decision of, 528–530
    administrative, 400
    appeal against, 405–407
    content of, 397
    exemption, 401
    fines, 402–405
    form of, 400–402
    information, requiring, 389, 390
    infringement, 394
    inspection, authorising, 390
    judicial review of, 405–407
    periodic penalty payments, 402
    prohibition, 401
    provisional, 400
    reasoning in, 401
    terminating infringements, 400
  Directorate-General for Competition,
    staff list, 539
  failure to act,
    remedy for, 406
  file of, access to, 389, 390
  fining policy of, 402–405
  interim measures of, 400
  investigation,
    ex-officio, by, 389
    powers of, 389, 390
  notification to, 388, 389, 528
  obligation of,
    not to disclose business secrets,
      397, 528
    to reason decisions, 401, 402

Commission of the European Communities—*cont.*
  oral hearing before, 395
  proceedings, opening of, 394
  recommendations, 400
  right to be heard by, 397
  sectoral inquiries of, 394
  types of decisions of, 400–402

Common Market,
  substantial part of, 215
  within, 74

common sales conditions, 93, 101

Community law, supremacy of, 408

compensation schemes,
  cartel agreements, in, 90

competent authorities, 407

competition,
  actual, 78
  distortion of, 78
  inter brand, 78
  intra brand, 78
  non-price, 78
  potential, 78
  price, 78
  restriction of,
    appreciability, 81
    concept, 78
    de minimis, 79
    rule of reason, 81
    state interference, 78
    third party, 78

compliance programme, 397, 398, 403, 404

complainant,
  obligations of, 389
  rights of, 389

complaint,
  locus standi, 389
  method of making, 389
  rejection of, 401, 406
    appeal against, 406
    Article 6 letter, 401
    decision for, 401

concentrations, 433, 483, 519–527
  Article 85 and 86, residual application
    of, 484

Index

concerted practices, 76
   concept of, 76
   indication of, 77
   proof of, 77

confidentiality,
   Commission obligation of, 397

conflict rules,
   international law, 408–415
   national law, 408

consumer,
   benefit to, under Article 85(3) EEC, 82

Convention,
   European Convention on Human Rights, 408–410

co-operation agreements,
   cases, 95
   intellectual property rights, licensing of, in, 101
   Notice on, 95–99
   production, 101
   types of, 101

copyright agreements,
   licensed rights, improvements to, 196
   no-challenge clause, 196
   non-competition clause, 196
   royalty provisions in, 196

Court of Justice of the European Communities,
   appeal, Commission decision, from, 405–407

crisis cartel, *see* **cartels**

customer limitation clauses,
   breeders' rights, in, 197
   distribution, in,
      exclusive, 134
      selective, 155
   franchising agreements, in, 166
   licensing agreements, in,
      know-how, 194
      patent, 179
   research and development agreements, in, 114

Damages,
   breach of competition rules, for, 408

dawn raids, 390, 391

dealerships, *see* **exclusive distribution agreements, franchising agreements, selective distribution agreements**

decisions, *see* **Commission**

declaration of inapplicability, 400

defence,
   Member States', interests of, 408

delimitation agreements,
   patent, 179
   trademark, 195

de minimis,
   Commission Notice, 79
   restriction of competition, 81
   trade between Member States, 73

design right agreements,
   licensed rights, improvements to, 196
   no-challenge clause, 196
   non-competition clause, 196
   royalty provisions in, 196

direct effect,
   competition rules, of, 407, 408

Directorate-General for Competition (DG IV),
   staff list, 539

discounts, *see* **rebates**

discrimination,
   Article 86, under, 218
   nationality, on grounds of, 167, 218
   selective distribution in, 154
   trade associations, 115, 116
   trade fairs, 116

discriminatory pricing,
   distribution agreements, in, 134

distortion of competition, 78

distribution,
   cartels, 93
   joint ventures, 213
   preventing trade and, 167
   specialisation agreements, 105

Index

distribution agreements,
exclusive, 119–134
joint, 93, 101, 105, 200
non-exclusive, 119–134
selective, 142, 155

distribution schemes,
industry organised, 73, 116

dominance,
ancillary markets, moving into, 219
definition of, 216
determination of, factors relevant to, list 216, 217
joint, 216
statutory, 217

double jeopardy rule, 404
see also **fines**

EEC Treaty, relevant Articles of, 533

effects doctrine, 73

emergency supply agreements,
crisis cartels, 90, 94
generally, 90, 94
products, distribution of, during supply shortages, 218

enforcement,
national courts, in, 408

English clause, 142
environmental considerations, 82

European Commission, see **Commission**

European Convention on Human Rights, 408–410

European Court of Justice, see **Court of Justice**

excessive pricing, 217

exclusionary practices,
Article 85 and, 93, 94
Article 86 and, 217–219

exclusive distribution, 119–134
joint venture, 213

exclusive distribution agreements,
cases, 119
customer limitation clauses in, 134
exclusive purchasing agreements in, 133
guarantee clauses in, 133
non-competition clause, 133
purchasing clauses in, 133
territorial restrictions, 132, 133

exclusive purchasing,
distribution agreements, in,
exclusive, 133
non-exclusive, 133
selective, 156
patent licensing agreements, in, 179

exclusive purchasing agreements, 134–141, 516
most favoured customer clause in, 142
non-competition clause, 142

exclusive selling agreements, 516

exclusivity, see **territorial provisions**

exemption,
individual,
assessment, relevant elements of, 92
conditions for, 82, 401
duration of, 401
notification requirement, 389
obligations upon, 401
renewal of, 401
requirements for, 82
revocation of, 401
social considerations, 82

exemption by category,
block exemption,
benefit of, withdrawal from, 88
effect of, 88
regulations, list of, 88
opposition procedures, 88
regulations, adoption of by Commission, regulations empowering, 84–88

exhibition agreements, 116, 117

ex-officio **investigation,**
Commission by, 389

export ban, see **territorial provisions**

Index

export cartels, 93

extra-territoriality, 74

Fact-finding, Commission powers of,
inspection by, 390–394
letter, by, 389, 390

failure to act, see **Commission**

fair hearing, right to, 397

fidelity rebates, see **discount systems**

file, access to,
Commission, of, 389, 390
documents relied on by Commission, of, 389, 390

financial services
banking, 358
insurance, 356–359

fines,
breach, for,
procedural rules, of, 402
substantive rules, of, 402
cartel members, on, 94
immunity from, 389
imposition of,
formal requirements for, 402
infringement, non-enforcement, 403
level of, assessment of,
factors taken into account in,
compliance programme, 403
culpability of undertaking, 403
double jeopardy rule, 404
infringement,
effect on market of, 403
gravity of, 402
length of, 403
limitation periods, 404
market situation, 403
modification of agreement, 403
ne bis in idem (double jeopardy), 404
state of the law, 404
undertakings given, 403
negligence and, 402

franchising agreements, 158–166
customer limitation clauses in, 166
guarantee clauses in, 166
intellectual property rights, licensing of, in, 165
licensed rights in,
improvements to, 165
post-term use restrictions on, 165
no-challenge clause, 165
non-competition clause, 165

franchising agreements—*cont.*
purchasing requirements in, 166
quality norms in, 166
royalty provisions in, 165

Glossary, 541

group responsibility, see **infringement**

guarantee clauses,
distribution agreements, in,
exclusive, 133
selective, 156
franchising agreements, in, 166

Hearing Officer, 395

hearing, oral,
right to be heard, 397

horizontal agreements,
cartels, 89
co-operation agreements, 95
joint ventures, 199
research and development agreements, 106
specialisation agreements, 105
trade associations, 115
trade fair and exhibition agreements, 116

human rights, European Convention on, 408–410
see also **Convention**

Immunity,
fines, from, 389

industrial and intellectual property rights,
abuse of dominant position and, 219
breeders' rights agreements, 196
co-operation agreements, in, 101
copyright agreements, in, 196
design right agreements, in, 196
franchising agreements, in, 165
free movement, 169
licensing agreements, in,
know-how, 180–195
patent, 169–180
joint venture agreements, in, 213
licensing of, Article 86 and, 219
research and development agreements, in, 115
specialisation agreements, in, 106
trademark agreements,
assignment, 196
delimitation, 175, 195
licensing, 195

Index

information exchange agreements,
joint venture agreements, in, 213
market sharing agreements, in, 90
price-fixing agreements, in, 93
production-sharing agreements, in, 90
reseach and development agreements, in, 114
specialisation agreements, in, 105

information, request for,
cases, 389, 390
decision, by,
   cases, 390
letter, by,
   Article 11 letter, example of, 389, 390

infringement, group responsibility for, 71

infringement proceedings, rights of parties in, *see* **rights of parties**

initiation of proceedings, 394

injunction,
Commission, interim measure of, 400
Court of Justice, interim decision of, 407

inspection,
authorisation,
   example documents 390–394
decision,
   with, 393
   without, 390
inspectors,
   documents produced by,
      example of, 390–394
   powers of, 390

insurance,
competition rules, application of, 356–359

intellectual property rights, *see* **industrial and intellectual property rights**

intentional infringement,
fines and, 402

inter-bank agreements, 101

interim measures,
Article 85 cases, in, 400
Article 86 cases, in, 400
Court of Justice, of, 400

international agreements,
United States, co-operation agreement with, 411–415

international law, 408

intra-enterprise conspiracy doctrine, 71

invalidity, agreements, of, 81

investigation,
authority, 390–394
inspection, by, 390, 394
letter, by, 389–390
sector, by, 394

investment
restriction of, 515

Japanese products, Notice on imports of, 74

joint buying agreements, 93, 199, 515, 516

joint dominance, 216

joint sales,
agency, 101, 200
conditions, 93, 101
policy, 93, 101

joint venture agreements,
information exchange agreements in, 213
intellectual property rights, licensing of, in, 213
licensed rights in, post term use restrictions on, 213
non-competition clauses, 212
purchasing clauses in, 213

joint ventures, 199–213
draft Notice, 200–212
exclusive distribution, 213
joint buying, 93, 199
joint production, 113, 199
joint research and development, 113, 199
joint sales, 101, 200
non-competition clause, 212
post-termination provisions, 213
price-fixing, 213
purpose of, 200
restriction of competition, 212
technical information, exclusion of, 213
territorial restrictions, 213

Index

judicial review, Commission decisions, of, see **appeal**

Know-how licensing agreements,
  180–195
  customer limitation clauses in, 194
  franchising agreements, in, 165
  intellectual property rights, licensing
    of, in, 180
  licensed rights in,
    improvements to, 194
    post term use restrictions on, 195
  mergers, 488
  no-challenge clause, 194
  non-competition clause, 194
  purchasing clauses in, 194
  quality norms in, 194
  royalty provisions in, 195
  territorial restrictions, 193

Legal professional privilege, 397

licensed rights, improvements to,
  breeders' rights agreements, 197
  copyright agreements, 196
  design right agreements, 196
  franchising agreements, 165
  know-how agreements, 194
  patent licensing agreements, 180

licensing,
  agreements,
    know-how, 180–195
    patent, 169–180
  breeders' rights, of, 196
  copyright, of, 196
  design rights, of, 196
  intellectual property rights, of,
    Article 86 and, 219
  co-operation agreements, in, 101
  franchising agreements, in, 165
  joint venture agreements, in, 213
  research and development
    agreements, in, 114
  specialisation agreements, in, 106

limitation periods, 386–388, 404

locus standi,
  appeal Commission decision, to, 405
  complainant, for, 389

Mandate,
  inspection, for, 391

manufacturing,
  uniform standards, 101

market,
  relevant,
    Article 85 and, 78
    Article 86 and, 215
  structure of,
    effect on trade, 72

market partitioning,
  agreement to refrain from, 516

market share,
  de minimis, 79
  dominant position and, 215

market sharing, see **cartels**

Member States,
  competent authorities of, 407

mergers and acquisitions, 433–489
  ancillary restraints, 488
  dominance, 487, 488
  efficiency defence, 488
  failing firm defence, 488
  joint dominance, 488
  oligopolistic dominance, 488
  partial, 483, 484
  procedural aspects, 489
  referral to Commission, 485
  Regulation, 433
  relevant market, 485–487
  significant impediment of competition,
    488
  vertical, 488

minor importance,
  agreements of, Notice on, 79–81
  competition, restriction of, 78–81
  trade between member states, 73

monopoly, see **abuse,** see **dominance**

most favoured customer clause,
  exclusive purchasing agreements, 142
  licensing agreements, in,
    know-how, 195
    patent, 180
  research and development
    agreements, in, 114
  specialisation agreements, in, 105

Index

motor vehicles,
  selective distribution and, 143–154

mutual supply agreements,
  customers, between, 90, 134

National agreements,
  effect on trade and, 73

national authorities, 407

national competition law, 407, 408

national enforcement,
  Article 85, of, 408
  Article 86, of, 408

national jurisdiction, 407, 408

national remedies,
  generally, 407, 408

nationality,
  discrimination on grounds of, 167, 218

negative clearance, 400
  Notice, 399

negligence,
  fines and, 402

negotiations,
  Commission decision, prior to, 397

network of agreements, 72

no-challenge clause,
  breeders' rights, 197
  copyright, 196
  design rights, 196
  franchising agreements, 165
  licensing agreements,
    know–how, 194
    patent, 179
  research and development
    agreements, 115
  trademark agreements,
    assignment, 196
    licensing, 196

non-competition clauses,
  breeders' rights, 197
  copyright, 196
  design rights, 196
  distribution,
    exclusive, 133
    non-exclusive, 133
    selective, 156
  franchising, 165
  joint ventures, 212
  licensing,
    know–how, 194
    patent, 179
  mergers and acquisitions, 488
  purchasing, exclusive, 142
  research and development, 114

non-exclusive distribution agreements,
  exclusive purchasing in, 133
  non-competition clause, 133
  purchasing clauses in, 133

Notice, publication of, by Commission,
  prior to positive decision, 395

Notices,
  agency agreements, Notice on, 157, 158
  agreements of minor importance, Notice on, 79–81
  co-operation agreements, Notice on, 95–99
  imports of Japanese products, Notice on, 74
  joint venture (draft), 200–212
  list of, 68, 69
  negative clearance, 399
  notifications, Notice on, 399
  Regulation 1983/83 and Regulation 1984/83, Notice on, 124–132
  Regulation 123/85, Notice on, 151–154
  sub-contracting agreements, Notice on, 99–100

notification, 388
  Notice on, 399

nullity, 81–82
  retroactive effect of, 81

Object, effect of, 78

objective justification,
  abuse of a dominant position, of, 219

Index

opposition procedure, 88, 389

oral hearing, 395

Parallel imports, *see* **territorial provisions**

parallel trade,
 agreements preventing, 166, 167
 selective distribution and, 155
 trademark, use of to prevent, 193

partial mergers, 483, 484

passive sales, *see* **territorial provisions**

patent dispute settlements, 180

patent licensing agreements, 169–180
 customer limitation clauses in, 179
 exclusive purchasing in, 179
 intellectual property rights, licensing of, in, 169
 licensed rights in,
  improvements to, 180
  post term use restrictions on, 180
 mergers, 488
 most favoured licensee clause in, 180
 no-challenge clause, 179
 non-competition clause, 179
 purchasing clauses in, 179
 royalty provisions in, 180
 territorial restrictions, 178

patent pooling, 94, 101

penalties, *see* **fines**

periodic penalty payments, 402

***per se* rules,**
 trade, effect on, 72

plant breeders' rights, 196, 197

plea bargaining, 403

post-term use restrictions,
 licensed rights on,
  franchising agreements, in, 165
  joint venture agreements, in, 213
 licensing agreements, in,
  know-how, 195
  patent, 180
 research and development agreements, in, 115

predatory pricing,
 Article 85 and, 94
 Article 86 and, 218

prevention of competition, *see* **competition, restriction of**

price discrimination,
 Article 85 and, 134
 Article 86 and, 218

price-fixing agreements,
 cartels, 91–93
 information exchange agreements in, 93
 joint venture, 213
 trade associations, by, 116

pricing obligations,
 other agreements, in,
  breeders' rights, 197
  distribution,
   exclusive, 134
   non-exclusive, 134
   selective, 156
  franchising, 166
  joint ventures, 213
  licensing,
   know-how, 194
   patent, 179
  purchasing, exclusive, 133
  trade associations, 116

privilege, legal professional, 397

procedures
 Commission decisions, relating to,
  advisory committee, 397
  decision, obligation to reason, 401
  file, access to, 394
  Hearing Officer, 397
  hearing, oral, 395
  hearings, implementation of, 395, 396
  objections, statement of, 394
  proceedings, opening of, 394
 limitation periods, 386–388

proceedings, initiation of, 394

product differentiation, 167

Index

production,
 cartels, 90
 co-operation agreements, 101
 joint ventures, 113, 199
 research and development
  agreements, 113
 restriction of, 515
 specialisation agreements, 105

production sharing agreements,
 information exchange agreements in, 90

prohibited practices,
 coal and steel sector, 514, 515

prohibition decisions,
 commencement, date of, 401
 effects in time of, 401
 order,
  to act, 401
  to cease, 401
 neutral decision, 401

proof, burden of,
 Article 85(1), 402
 Article 85(3), 82
 Article 86

property,
 national law, 408

provisional validity, 389

public bodies,
 decision of, different to agreement, 76
 interference by, 78, 221–260
 silence of, no excuse for Treaty
  infringement, 260
 responsibilities of,
  not to assist infringement, 260
  not to encourage infringement, 260
 restriction of competition by, 78, 221–260
 undertakings, difference from, 76

purchasing agreements,
 breeders' rights agreements, in, 197
 distribution agreements, in,
  exclusive, 133
  non-exclusive, 133
  selective, 156, 157
 exclusive purchasing, 134–141
 franchising agreements, in, 166
 joint purchasing, 93, 199
 joint venture agreements, in, 213

purchasing agreements—*cont.*
 licensing agreements, in,
  know-how, 194
  patent, 179
 research and development
  agreements, in, 114
 specialisation agreements, 105

purchasing clauses, *see* **purchasing agreements**

Quality marks,
 common, 101
 use of, to prevent trade between
  Member States, 167

quality norms,
 franchising agreements, in, 166
 know-how agreements, in, 194
 patent licensing agreements, in, 179

quotas,
 production, 90
 sales, 91
 territory related, 91, 92

Rationalisation, 105, 114

reasons,
 Commission decision, in, obligation to
  give, 401, 402

rebates
 aggregated, 94
 Article 85 and, 92
 Article 86 and, 219
 common policy, 92

reciprocal supply agreements, 90, 134

recommendation, Commission, of, 400

recommended prices,
 agreed, 92
 distribution agreements, in,
  exclusive, 134
  non-exclusive, 134
 franchising agreements, in, 166

refusal to publish,
 technical data, 219

refusal to supply,
 Article 86 and, 94, 218
 distribution systems, context of, in, 154

regulations,
 implementing Articles 85 and 86, 362–385

regulations, exemption by category,
 distribution,
  exclusive, 120, 124
  selective,
   motor vehicles, 143
 franchising, 158
 licensing,
  know-how, 181
  patent, 170
 list of, 64–66
 purchasing, exclusive, 124
 research and development, 106
 specialisation, 102

rejection of complaint, *see* **complainant,** *see* **complaint**

relevant market,
 Article 85 and, 78
 geographic,
  concept of, under Article 86, 215
 product,
  concept of, under Article 86, 215
  definition of, in Article 86, 215

remedies,
 Commission decisions, challenge to, in, *see* **appeal**

request for information
 decision, by,
  cases, 390
 letter, by,
  Article 11 letter, example of, 389, 390
  cases, 389, 390

resale price maintenance,
 cartels, 92
 distribution agreements,
  exclusive, 134
  non-exclusive, 134
  selective, 156
 purchasing agreements, exclusive, 142

research and development agreements, 106–115
 customer limitation clauses in, 114
 information exchange agreements in, 114
 intellectual property rights, licensing of, in, 114

research and development agreements—*cont.*
 licensed rights in, post term use restrictions on, 115
 most favoured customer clause in, 114
 no-challenge clause, 115
 non-competition clause, 114
 production, 113
 purchasing clauses in, 114
 royalty provisions in, 115

restraints, ancillary, 81, 488

restriction of competition, *see* **competition, restriction of**

restructuring,
 cartels and, 105
 joint research and development and, 114
 joint ventures and, 114

retroactive effect,
 Commission decision, of, 82
 nullity, of, 81

rights of parties,
 infringement proceedings, in,
  to appeal, 405–407
  to be heard, 397
  to have access to documents, 390
  to have a reasoned decision, 401, 402

royalty provisions,
 copyright agreements, in, 196
 design right agreements, in, 196
 franchising agreements, in, 165
 licensing agreements, in,
  know-how, 195
  patent, 180
 research and development agreements, in, 115

rule of reason, 81

Sales,
 agency, 101
 conditions of,
  common, 101
  export ban, in, 200

sanctions,
 fines, 402–404
 Regulation 17/62,
  orders pursuant to Article 3 of, 401

sectoral investigation, 394

Index

selective distribution agreements, 142–156
  customer limitation clauses in, 155
  exclusive purchasing in, 179
  guarantee clauses in, 156
  non-competition clause, 156
  purchasing clauses in, 155, 156

selling,
  agreement to refrain from, 516

service station agreements, 131, 133, 140

settlement, 398

severability, infringing clauses, of, 81

social considerations,
  Article 85(3), under, 82

specialisation agreements,
  cases, 101–105
  coal and steel, 516
  distribution, 105
  information exchange agreements in, 105
  intellectual property rights, licensing of, in, 106
  most favoured customer clause in, 105
  most favoured licensee clause in, 105
  production, 105
  purchasing agreements in, 105
  purchasing clauses in, 105

spill-over effects
  agreement, from, 212
  competition, restriction of, from, 212

staff list, Directorate-General IV, of, 537

standard conditions of sale
  cartel, 93
  co-operation agreements, 101

standardisation agreements, 101

state behaviour, 527

state interference, 221
  competition, restriction of, 78, 221–260
  competition rules, infringement of,
    responsibility not to assist, 260
    responsibility not to encourage, 260
    state silence no excuse for, 260

statement of objections, 394

state monopoly, 221

stocking requirements,
  distribution agreements, in,
    exclusive, 119–134
    non-exclusive, 119–134
    selective, 156

sub-contracting agreements
  agency, 156
  joint venture, 114
  licensing,
    know-how, 194
    patent, 180
  Notice on, 99–100
  research and development, 114

substantial part, *see* **Common Market**

supply agreements,
  cartels, 90
  joint venture agreements, 213
  patent licensing agreements, 179
  purchasing agreements, exclusive, 142
  research and development agreements, 114
  specialisation agreements, 105

supply clauses, *see* **supply agreements**

supremacy, Community law, of, 408

Technical development,
  restriction of, 515

technical progress,
  Article 85(3) and, 82

telecommunications,
  Commission Directive on,
    competition rules, application of, 235–259
  market, 227, 234
  terminal equipment, 222–226

territorial provisions,
  breeders' rights agreements, in, 197
  distribution agreements, in,
    exclusive, 132, 133
    non-exclusive, 132, 133
    selective, 155
  franchising agreements, in, 166
  joint venture agreements, in, 213
  licensing agreements, in,
    know-how, 193
    patent, 178

Index

territorial provisions—*cont.*
research and development agreements, in, 113
specialisation agreements, in, 106
trademark agreements, in,
  assignment, 195
  licensing, 195

tied-house agreements, 129–132, 139, 140

trade associations, 115, 116
pricing obligations in, 116

trade, Member States, between,
appreciability, effect of, on, 73
concept of, 71, 72
cumulative effect of, 72
export bans, effect of, on, 72
export boosters, effect of, on, 73
national cartels, effect of, on, 73
trade with Third states, effect of, on, 73

trade fairs, 116

trademark, abusive registration of, 219

trademark agreements,
assignment, 196
  no-challenge clause, 196
joint venture, 213
licensing,
  Article 86 and, 219
  common trademark agreements, 101, 195
  delimitation agreements, 179, 195
  franchising agreements, in, 165
  joint venture agreements, in, 213
  know-how, 194
  mergers, 488
  patent, 179
  specialisation agreements, in, 106
  territorial restrictions, 195

trading conditions, *see* **sales, condition of**

trading terms, *see* **sales, conditions of**

transport,
air, 315–355
general, 263–265
inland waterway, 264–291

transport—*cont.*
liner shipping companies, 312–314
maritime, 291–312
rail, 264–291
road, 264–291

turnover, *de minimis,* **in,** 79–81

tying agreements,
Article 86 and, 218
copyright agreements and, 196
design right agreements and, 196
patent licensing and, 179

Undertakings
association of, decision of, 77
concept of, 71
giving of, to terminate proceedings, 398, 403
jointly held, formation of, 517

unfair pricing, 217

unfair terms, imposition of, on clients, 217

uniform prices,
common prices, 91, 92
common price increase, 92

United States,
co-operation agreement with, 411–415

Vertical agreements,
agency agreements, 156
distribution agreements,
  exclusive, 119–134
  non-exclusive, 119–134
  selective, 142
franchising agreements, 158
licensing agreements,
  know-how, 180
  patent, 169
purchasing agreements,
  exclusive, 119, 134
  non-exclusive, 119
trademark agreements, 196

void agreements,
coal and steel sector, 516

Warranties, 133, 156, 166